ISBN 978-1-330-82679-9
PIBN 10110539

1 MONTH OF
FREE
READING

at

www.ForgottenBooks.com

By purchasing this book you are eligible for one month membership to ForgottenBooks.com, giving you unlimited access to our entire collection of over 700,000 titles via our web site and mobile apps.

To claim your free month visit:

English
Français
Deutsche
Italiano
Español
Português

www.forgottenbooks.com

Mythology Photography **Fiction**
Fishing Christianity **Art** Cooking
Essays Buddhism Freemasonry
Medicine **Biology** Music **Ancient
Egypt** Evolution Carpentry Physics
Dance Geology **Mathematics** Fitness
Shakespeare **Folklore** Yoga Marketing
Confidence Immortality Biographies
Poetry **Psychology** Witchcraft
Electronics Chemistry History **Law**
Accounting **Philosophy** Anthropology
Alchemy Drama Quantum Mechanics
Atheism Sexual Health **Ancient History**
Entrepreneurship Languages Sport
Paleontology Needlework Islam
Metaphysics Investment Archaeology
Parenting Statistics Criminology
Motivational

CASES

RELATING TO THE

LAW OF RAILWAYS,

DECIDED IN THE

SUPREME COURT OF THE UNITED STATES,

AND IN THE

COURTS OF THE SEVERAL STATES.

WITH NOTES, BY

CHAUNCEY SMITH AND SAMUEL W. BATES,

COUNSELLORS AT LAW.

VOL. I.

BOSTON:
LITTLE, BROWN AND COMPANY,
1854.

RIVERSIDE, CAMBRIDGE:
PRINTED BY H. O. HOUGHTON AND COMPANY.

ADVERTISEMENT.

THE introduction of railways has given rise to much litigation upon questions, either peculiar to that species of property, or involving novel applications of the principles of the common law. In England it has been found convenient to publish the railway cases as a separate series of reports, and a conviction that a similar collection of the cases in this country would be of great service to the profession has led to the preparation of these volumes. The extension of railways to all parts of the country, and the intimate relation which each road bears to all the others, makes it important that the decisions of the various courts in the United States, affecting this species of property, should be as uniform and harmonious as possible. A collection of the cases, by bringing all the decisions within the reach of every member of the profession, cannot fail to promote these results. The cases have been taken from the various reports, and a note at the commencement of each case indicates the volume and page from which it is taken. The undersigned wish here to acknowledge their obligations to the reporters and proprietors of the reports from which the cases have been taken, for their kindness in allowing them the use of their works.

CHAUNCEY SMITH.
SAMUEL W. BATES.

BOSTON, *August*, 1854.

TABLE OF CASES.

	PAGE
Aldrich v. The Cheshire Railroad Company	206
Androscoggin and Kennebec Railroad Co. v. Stevens	140
Ashby v. Eastern Railroad Co.	356
Atlantic and St. Lawrence R. Co. v. Cumberland County Commissioners	133
Babcock, The Boston and Maine Railroad v.	561
Babcock, Western Railroad Corporation v.	365
Babcock v. Western Railroad Corporation	399
Baltimore and Ohio Railroad Co., State of Maryland v.	1
Baltimore and Susquehanna Railroad Co. v. Nesbit	39
Bangor and Piscataquis Railroad Co. v. Harris	131
Baxter, Vermont Central Railroad Co. v.	240
Berkshire Railroad Co., Carey v.	442
Boston and Lowell Railroad Corporation, Lowell v.	284
Boston and Maine Railroad v. Babcock	561
Boston and Maine Railroad, Bradley v.	457
Boston and Maine Railroad Co., Cheney v.	601
Boston and Maine Railroad, Commonwealth v.	482
Boston and Maine Railroad, Davidson v.	534
Boston and Maine Railroad, The Fitchburg Railroad Co. v.	508
Boston and Maine Railroad, Morss v.	454
Boston and Maine Railroad, Parker v.	547
Boston and Maine Railroad, Walker v.	462
Boston and Providence Railroad Corporation, Thomas v.	403
Boston Water Power Co. v. Boston and Worcester Railroad Corporation	267
Boston Water Power Co. v. Boston and Worcester Railroad Corporation	298
Boston and Worcester Railroad Corporation, Farwell v.	339
Boston and Worcester Railroad Co., Lyman v.	581
Bradley v. The Boston and Maine Railroad	457
Bristol, County Commissioners of, Carpenter v.	280

PAGE

Boynton v. The Peterborough and Shirley Railroad Co.   595
Buckfield Branch Railroad, Porter v.   185

Calais Railroad Co., Peavey v.   147
Cambridge and Somerville, inhabitants of, v. Charlestown Branch Railroad Co.   377
Carey v. Berkshire Railroad Co.   442
Carpenter v. County Commissioners of Bristol   280
Chandler, Lexington and West Cambridge Railroad Co. v.   422
Charlestown Branch Railroad Co. v. County Commissioners   383
Charlestown Branch Railroad Co., Inhabitants of Cambridge and Somerville v.   377
Cheney v. The Boston and Maine Railroad Co.   601
Cheshire Railroad Co., Aldrich v.   206
Cheshire Railroad Co., Towns v.   210
Cheshire Railroad Co., Tucker v.   196
Clapp, Connecticut River Railroad Co. v.   450
Clayes, Vermont Central Railroad Co. v.   226
Commonwealth v. The Boston and Maine Railroad   482
Commonwealth v. Power   389
Connecticut River Railroad Co. v. Clapp   450
Connecticut River Railroad Co., Inhabitants of Springfield v.   572
Cumberland County Commissioners, Atlantic and St. Lawrence Railroad Co. v.   133
Curtis v. Vermont Central Railroad Co.   258

Davidson v. The Boston and Maine Railroad   534
Dean v. The Sullivan Railroad Co.   214
Deering v. The York and Cumberland Railroad Co.   152
Derby, Philadelphia and Reading Railroad Co. v.   109
Dodge v. County Commissioners of Essex   336
Draper v. The Worcester and Norwich Railroad Co.   607

Eastern Railroad Co., Ashby v.   356
Eastern Railroad Co., Newburyport Turnpike Corporation v.   294
Eastern Railroad Co., Perkins v.   144
Eastern Railroad Co., Webber v.   331
Essex, County Commissioners of, Dodge v.   336

Farwell v. Boston and Worcester Railroad Corporation   339
Fitchburg Railroad Co. v. The Boston and Maine Railroad   508
Fitchburg Railroad Co., Meacham v.   584
Fitchburg Railroad Co., White v.   594
Foster, Pittsfield and North Adams Railroad Co. v.   448
Fowler v. Kennebec and Portland Railroad Co.   157

Gold v. The Vermont Central Railroad Co.   220
Graham, The Portland, Saco, and Portsmouth Railroad Co. v.   598

Hall v. Power   410
Harris, Bangor and Piscataquis Railroad Co. v.   131
Hart v. The Western Railroad Co.   414

PAGE

Haswell v. Vermont Central Railroad Co. . 248
Hayes v. The Western Railroad Co.` . 564
Hills, Vermont Central Railroad Co. v. . . . 262
Howard, Philadelphia, Wilmington, and Baltimore Railroad Co. v. . 70

Kennebec and Portland Railroad Co., Fowler v. 157
Kennebec and Portland Railroad Co., Mason v. . 162

Lewis v. The Western Railroad Corporation . . . 610
Lexington and West Cambridge Railroad Co. v. Chandler . 422
Lexington and West Cambridge Railroad Co., Wyman v. . 426
Louisa Railroad Co., Richmond, &c., Railroad Co. v. ., . 48
Lowell v. Boston and Lowell Railroad Corporation . 284
Lyman v. The Boston and Worcester Railroad Co. . 581

Maryland v. Baltimore and Ohio Railroad Co. . 1
Maryland, Philadelphia and Wilmington Railroad Co. v.` 21
Mason v. Kennebec and Portland Railroad Co. .` 162
McElroy v. The Nashua and Lowell Railroad Co. . 591
Meacham v. Fitchburg Railroad Co. 584
Middlesex, County Commissioners of, Charlestown Branch Railroad Co. v. 383
Morss v. The Boston and Maine Railroad . . . 454

Nashua and Lowell Railroad Co., McElroy v. . 591
Nesbit, Baltimore and Susquehanna Railroad Co. v. . 39
Newburyport Turnpike Corporation v. Eastern Railroad Co. . 294
Norfolk, County Commissioners of, Porter v. . , ` 439

Parker v. The Boston and Maine Railroad 547
Peavey v. The Calais Railroad Co. . .. . ` 147
Perkins v. The Eastern Railroad Co. . . ·144
Peterborough and Shirley Railroad Co., Boynton v. . 595
Philadelphia and Reading Railroad Co. v. Derby . . ·109
Philadelphia, Wilmington, and Baltimore Railroad Co. v. Howard 70
Philadelphia and Wilmington Railroad Co. v. Maryland . 21 ·
Pittsfield and North Adams Railroad Corporation v. Foster . 448
Plymouth, County Commissioners of, Taylor v. ` . 436
Porter v. The Buckfield Branch Railroad . 185
`Porter v. County Commissioners of Norfolk . 439
Portland, Saco, and Portsmouth Railroad Co. v. Graham . . . 598
Portsmouth, S. and P. and E. Railroad Co. Sager v. 171
Power, Commonwealth v. . . . 389
Power, Hall v. . . . ·410

Quimby v. Vermont Central Railroad Co. . . 251

Richmond, &c., Railroad Co. v. The Louisa Railroad Co. . 48

Sager v. Portsmouth, S. and P. and E. Railroad Co. . , 171
Springfield, Inhabitants of, v. The Connecticut River Railroad Co. 572

	PAGE
Stevens, Androscoggin and Kennebec Railroad Co. v.	140
Stiles v. Western Railroad Corporation	397
Stiles v. The Western Railroad Corporation	604
Sullivan Railroad Co., Dean v.	214
Taylor v. County Commissioners of Plymouth	436
Thomas v. Boston and Providence Railroad Corporation	403
Towns v. The Cheshire Railroad Co.	210
Tucker v. The Cheshire Railroad Co.	196
Vermont Central Railroad Co. v. Baxter	240
Vermont Central Railroad Co. v. Clayes	226
Vermont Central Railroad Co., Curtis v.	258
Vermont Central Railroad Co., Gold v.	220
Vermont Central Railroad Co., Haswell v.	248
Vermont Central Railroad Co. v. Hills	262
Vermont Central Railroad Co., Quimby v.	251
Vermont Central Railroad Co., White River Turnpike Co. v.	233
Walker v. The Boston and Maine Railroad	462
Webber v. The Eastern Railroad Co.	331
Western Railroad Corporation v. Babcock	365
Western Railroad Corporation, Babcock v.	399
Western Railroad Corporation, Hart v.	414
Western Railroad Corporation, Hayes v.	564
Western Railroad Corporation, In the matter of.	360
Western Railroad Corporation, Inhabitants of Worcester v.	350
Western Railroad Corporation, Lewis v.	610
Western Railroad Corporation, Stiles v.	397
Western Railroad Corporation, Stiles v.	604
White v. The Fitchburg Railroad Co.	594
White River Turnpike Co. v. Vermont Central Railroad Co.	233
Worcester, Inhabitants of, v. The Western Railroad Corporation	350
Worcester and Norwich Railroad Co., Draper v.	607
Wyman v. Lexington and West Cambridge Railroad Co.	426
York and Cumberland Railroad Co. Deering v.	152

CASES

ARGUED AND DETERMINED

IN THE

SUPREME COURT OF THE UNITED STATES.

THE STATE OF MARYLAND, for the use of Washington County, Plaintiff in Error, v. THE BALTIMORE AND OHIO RAILROAD COMPANY, Defendants.[1]

January Term, 1845.

Conditional Subscription — Penalty for Nonperformance of Condition — Location of Road.

The State of Maryland, in 1836, passed a law directing a subscription of $3,000,000 to be made to the capital stock of the Baltimore and Ohio Railroad Company, with the following proviso, "That if the said company shall not locate the said road in the manner provided for in this act, then, and in that case, they shall forfeit $1,000,000 to the State of Maryland for the use of Washington County.

In March, 1841, the State passed another act repealing so much of the prior act as made it the duty of the company to construct the road by the route therein prescribed, remitting and releasing the penalty, and directing the discontinuance of any suit brought to recover the same.

The proviso was a measure of State policy, which it had a right to change, if the policy was afterwards discovered to be erroneous, and neither the commissioners, nor the county, nor any one of its citizens acquired any separate or private interest under it, which could be maintained in a court of justice.

It was a penalty, inflicted upon the company as a punishment for disobeying the law; and the assent of the company to it, as a supplemental charter, is not sufficient to deprive it of the character of a penalty.

A clause of forfeiture in a law is to be construed differently from a similar clause in an engagement between individuals. A legislature can impose it as a punishment, but individuals can only make it a matter of contract.

The provision in this case being a penalty imposed by law, the legislature had a right to remit it.

THIS case was brought up by writ of error, under the 25th section

---

of the Judiciary Act, from the Court of Appeals for the Western Shore of Maryland.

The facts were these: —

On the 4th of June, 1836, (Laws of Maryland, 1835, chap. 395,) the legislature of Maryland passed an act entitled "An act for the promotion of internal improvement," by which subscriptions were directed to be made, on certain terms, to the capital stock of the Chesapeake and Ohio Canal Company, and Baltimore and Ohio Railroad Company, to the amount of $3,000,000 to each company. The conduct of the canal company having no bearing upon the question involved in the present suit; it is not necessary to notice any further the parts of the law which related to it.

A part of the 5th section of the act was as follows: —

" And the said treasurer shall not make any payment aforesaid for subscription to the stock of the Baltimore and Ohio Railroad Company, until after a majority of the directors appointed therein on behalf of this State shall have certified to the treasurer in writing, supported by the oath or affirmation of a majority of said directors, that they sincerely believe in their certificate and statement, that, with the subscription by this act authorized to be made to said company's stock, and with the subscription which the city of Baltimore may have made by virtue of an act, passed at December session of the year eighteen hundred and thirty-five of this Assembly, or that independently of any subscription by any other public authority than the city of Baltimore, as aforesaid, and of the cities of Pittsburg and Wheeling, and exclusive of any loan secured to it, exclusive of all future profits and debts due by the company on interest, the said Railroad Company in their opinion have funds sufficient to complete the said railroad from the Ohio River, by way of and through Cumberland, Hagerstown, and Boonsborough, to its present track near to Harper's Ferry; and it is hereby declared to be and made the duty of the said company to, and they shall so locate and construct the said road as to pass through each of said places; which certificate of said directors shall be accompanied by an estimate or estimates of one or more skilful and competent engineers, made out after a particular and minute survey of the route of said road by him or them, and verified by his or their affidavit, showing that the whole cost of said work will not be greater than the amount of funds the said directors shall certify to have been received by said company, and applicable to the construction of the said road: Provided, That if the said Baltimore and Ohio Railroad Company shall not locate the said road in the manner provided for in this act, then, and in that case, they shall forfeit one million of dollars to the State of Maryland, for the use of Washington County."

This act was accepted by the Railroad Company, in a general meeting of stockholders, and information thereof communicated to the governor, on the 26th of July, 1836.

On the 24th of September, 1836, the treasurer made his subscription of 3,000,000, to the capital stock of the company.

On the 1st of October, 1838, a majority of directors on behalf of the State gave the certificate and statement required by the act.

The Railroad Company having finally located, and being in the act of constructing their road, without the limits of Washington County, within which Hagerstown and Boonsborough are situated, a suit was brought in Frederick County, Maryland, in February, 1841, in the name of the State of Maryland, for the use of Washington County, against the Railroad Company, in an action of debt to recover $1,000,000.

In March, 1841, the legislature of Maryland passed an act in which they say, "that so much of the 5th section of the Act of 1835, as makes it the duty of the Baltimore and Ohio Railroad Company to construct the said road so as to pass through Hagerstown and Boonsborough, be and the same is hereby repealed; and that the forfeiture of one million of dollars reserved to the State of Maryland as a penalty, in case the said Baltimore and Ohio Railroad Company shall not locate the said road in the manner provided for in that act, be and the same is hereby remitted and released, and any suit instituted to recover the same sum of one million of dollars, or any part thereof, be and the same is hereby declared to be discontinued and of no effect."

In October, 1841, the defendant pleaded the general issue, and set forth the above act.

In February, 1842, the case came on for trial, upon the following agreed statement of facts:

"It is admitted in this case, that the commissioners of Washington County, the parties at whose instance this action was instituted for the use of Washington County, were at the time of institution of this suit, and still are a body corporate, duly elected and organized, under and by virtue of the Act of Assembly of Maryland, of 1829, chap 21, and its supplementary acts. It is also admitted that the defendants are, and were at the institution of this suit, a body corporate, duly existing under and by virtue of the Act of Assembly of Maryland of 1826, chap. 123, and its supplementary acts. It is also admitted that this suit is brought at the instance of said commissioners of Washington County to recover, for the use of said county, the $1,000,000 which they allege to be forfeited to the said State, for use of said county, under the provisions of the 5th section of the

Act of 1835, chap. 395; and it is admitted that the said defendants have not, and had not at the institution of this suit, constructed or located their road from the Ohio River, by way of and through Hagerstown and Boonsborough, to the track of said road to Harper's Ferry, as the same existed at the time of the passage of the said Act of 1835, chap. 395; but, on the contrary, had at the institution of this suit finally located, and are, were then, and are now constructing their said road by a different route, and without the limits of Washington County, within which the said Hagerstown and Boonsborough are situated. It is admitted that the said Baltimore and Ohio Railroad Company, in general meeting of the said corporation, did accept, assent, and agree to the several provisions of the said Act of 1835, chap. 395, and did duly communicate their said approval, assent, and agreement, under their corporate seal and the signature of their president, to the governor of this State, in the manner and within the time prescribed by the said act; which approval, assent, and agreement, together with the report of the engineer of the said Railroad Company, which was required by the said act to accompany the same, were as follows, viz."—

(The statement then set out all these documents *in extenso.* The engineer framed his estimates for a road to Pittsburg which would cost $6,681,468. That part of it passing through Washington County is thus described. " The route departs from the Baltimore and Ohio Railroad at the mouth of the Little Catoctin, ascends that stream to the eastern base of the Blue Ridge, or South Mountain, and thence continues to ascend along its slope to a depression in its crest called ' Crampton's Gap;' thence passing through the mountain by a tunnel of 1500 feet in length, it descends into ' Pleasant Valley,' lying between the South Mountain and the Elk Mountain, and proceeds along the western base of the former, to and through the town of Boonsborough; thence to a point near the village of Funkstown; and thence across the Antietam creek, above the turnpike bridge, to the borough of Hagerstown; thence through the streets of that town, and over the Salesbury bridge, to and across the Conococheague creek, about two miles north of Williamsport; thence," &c., &c.)

" It is also admitted, that after this suit was instituted for the purpose of recovering the said forfeiture of a million of dollars, the legislature of Maryland, on the 10th day of March, 1841, passed the Act of December session, 1840, chap. 260, repealing the said 5th section of the said Act of 1835, chap. 395, as far as relates to the said forfeiture of a million of dollars, and releasing the said defendants from the said forfeiture, and every part thereof, and directing any suit instituted to recover the same to be discontinued, and to have no effect.

It is also admitted, that the said repealing Act of 1840, chap. 260, was passed upon the following memorial of the said defendants to the legislature, and that at the time of passing the same there was then before the legislature a counter memorial upon the said subject from the said commissioners of Washington County, which memorial and counter memorial, it is agreed, were as follows, to wit:"

(These documents are too long to be inserted.) .

" It is further admitted and agreed, that the several Acts of Assembly herein particularly referred to, as well as any other acts or resolutions of the General Assembly of Maryland, that either party may deem applicable in the argument of this case, either in the County Court, or Court of Appeals, or Supreme Court of the United States, should the case be hereafter carried by either party to said courts, or either of them, shall be read from the printed statute-books, and have the same effect and operation in the case, as if duly authenticated copies thereof were made a part of these statements.

" It is further agreed that all errors of pleading and of form in any part of the proceedings of either party in this case are waived; it being the object and understanding of the parties that the matters of right in controversy between them shall be fairly and fully presented to all or either of the said courts, in which the same may be pending, and that either of the said parties shall have his pleading and proceedings considered as being as perfect as they could be made to give him the benefit of the case here stated. It is admitted that this suit was the only suit ever brought by the said commissioners, or at their instance, to recover the said forfeiture of a million of dollars, and was pending when the said Act of 1835, chap. 395, was passed.   Upon this statement it is further agreed that, if the court shall be of opinion that this action could not be maintained if the said repealing Act of 1840, chap. 260, had not been passed, or that the operation and effect of that repealing act is to release the said forfeiture of $1,000,000, and to discontinue and put an end to this suit, then judgment to be entered for the defendants, otherwise such judgment is to be entered for the plaintiffs as the court may think right and proper.   It is further agreed that the County Court shall enter judgment *pro forma* for the defendants.   The plaintiff to have the same right to take up the case, by appeal or writ of error, to the court of appeals, or ultimately to the Supreme Court of the United States, as if the judgment in the County Court had been rendered upon demurrer, or upon a bill of exceptions taken in due and legal form upon the facts herein before agreed upon."

Upon this statement of facts the court of Frederick county gave

1 *

judgment for the defendant, and the case being carried to the Court of Appeals the judgment below was affirmed.

The writ of error was brought to review this judgment.

Jervis, Spencer, and *Sergeant,* for the plaintiff in error.

Nelson, (Attorney-General,) and *Johnson,* for defendants.

Spencer, for the plaintiff in error, made the following points:
1. That the Act of 1835 is a contract.
2. That Washington County is a party to that contract.
3. That the forfeiture is in no sense a penalty.
1st. It is not for any criminal or prohibited act amounting to a public offence.
2d. It is not introduced *in terrorem,* but is a sum to be paid for using the license given by the act as a compensation to the injured party.
4. That, by the use of the license by the company, Washington County acquired a vested right in the sum stipulated to be paid.
5. That to take away this right from Washington County would be inequitable, unjust, and contrary to the first principles of the social compact; and therefore the act ought to be so construed, if possible, as to avoid that result; and it may be so construed by confining its operation to whatever right the State had, if any. The State might release her own power over the matter, leaving in force the right of the county.
6. If otherwise construed, it is repugnant to the State Constitution, and void.
7. In the same view, it is repugnant to the Constitution of the United States, and void.
And then said —
This suit is brought in the name of State of Maryland, to recover $1,000,000, which is claimed by the county, under the provisions of the 5th section of the Act of the Legislature of Maryland, at the session of 1835, chap. 395, which are substantially set forth in the declaration.

It is maintained, to support the claim of the plaintiff, that the whole act constituted a contract between the State and company; and the 5th section a part of said contract, in which the county is a party beneficially interested.

The provisions of the 1st section of the act are in the very terms of contract, and embrace the 5th section as well as the rest of the law: " If the Railroad Company shall approve, assent, and agree to the several provisions of this act so far as they are applicable to said corporation," &c. The approval, assent, and agreement of the company were given as provided for by the act, and that agreement gave vitality to the whole law. The State offered, and the company accepted the offer, on mutual considerations. It was the *congregatio mentium,* which is of the very essence of contract.

The case stated shows that at the time of commencing this suit the road had been located out of the limits of Washington County, and that, under the law, the company was liable to pay the money.

But the defence relies on the Act of 1840, chap. 260, which undertakes to repeal the provision of the Act of 1835, chap. 395, under which the claim is asserted; and the question is, whether that Act of 1840 violates the tenth section of the Constitution of the United States.

The first aspect in which the question is to be examined, is, whether the 5th section is part of a contract at all, or only criminal penalty, which it is maintained to be by the defendant. We maintain that it is not only contract, but that it could have no operation as criminal penalty.

What is a contract? Chitty on Contracts, 1, &c.; Canal Company *v.* Railroad Company, 4 Gill & Johns. 128, &c.

The Court of Appeals say, we must look to concurrent legislation to find the meaning of the 5th section; and refer to the Act of 1840, chap. 260, which uses the term "penalty." But could the Act of 1840, after the suit was brought, alter the character of the thing? If it was contract when the suit was brought, the Act of 1840 could not make it criminal penalty. The legislature could not stretch the shoe or contract it, and make the previous law mean one thing or another, as they might choose to call it, and when they had a manifest motive in endeavoring to alter its character.

Concurrent legislation, prior to the Act of 1840, proves that the legislature understood it as contract, and nothing else. The Act of 1826, chap. 123, sect. 14, which was the original charter, authorized the company to enter upon any lands for a location. Afterwards, by the Act of 1827, chap. 104, sect. 3, the legislature thought proper to restrict the company to a location within Frederick and Washington counties, but did they do it by a criminal enactment? No. They knew they could not do that, and they entered into a distinct contract for the purpose. Stress is laid by the other side on the fact that the terms of contract are used in the same section of the Act of 1827, which makes the restriction; and the inference is deduced that if the 5th section of the Act of 1835 were intended to be contract, the terms of contract would have been used in that section also. But the important fact is entirely overlooked, that the words of contract, in the first section of the Act of 1835, embrace the whole act; whereas, in the Act of 1827, there were no such general words of assent and agreement to the whole act, but they applied only to the respective sections.

The Court of Appeals refer to the 9th section of the Act of 1835 and say that, inasmuch as a special contract was required to be made, by that section, therefore the legislature could not have intended to make the 5th section contract. This construction cannot be justified. It would involve the construction that many of the most essential stipulations of the company are not its contract, because the particular sections in which they occur do not require other special contracts with reference to the same. The 9th section required a distinct contract, in order that if the State should ever have occasion to sue on it, this suit should not be embarrassed by all the various matter embraced by the law. It was an arrangement of convenience. When the company agreed to the law, and accepted the same, it was under contract to fulfil the 9th section by an additional contract. That section was a contract to be performed by entering into another contract; and it was as much a contract as the subsequent contract would be such, after it should be entered into.

There are thousands of instances of this, where contracts are in part, or the whole, to be performed by entering into other contracts.

The right to choose a location was a vested franchise of the company, its property, which the legislature of Maryland had no right to interfere with by a criminal enactment. Canal Company *v.* Railroad Company, 4 Gill & Johns. R. 144. The obligation to go through Frederick and Washington counties, under the Act of 1827, was released by the Act of 1831, chap. 251; and the company stood untrammelled, without any power of control by the legislature. Their contract or agreement was absolutely essential to bind them down to any particular location. The 5th section, in any other sense but contract, is a dead letter.

It has been asked, suppose the act had said that the company should be liable to Washington County in damages, would that be contract? And again, that if the road should leave the prescribed points it should be a misdemeanor, would that be contract? It is submitted, that it would be, in both cases. The courts have said, in the authorities I have read, that the right to choose a location is the property of the company, and it could be liable neither for damages nor a misdemeanor, for using properly its own property. It might contract to use its property in a certain way, and if nothing be said about damages for the breach, a liability for such damages is implied in every contract. To declare, in express terms, what is implied in every contract, certainly would not vitiate it. Private individuals could not contract that the act of one should be a misdemeanor, but a misdemeanor is an offence against the State, and surely a party, who has an absolute right to do a thing, independent of legislative control, may contract with the State that he will not do it, and if he does, it shall be a misdemeanor. A State may do many things in the way of contract, that an individual cannot do, for there is no public policy to restrain her, nothing but the written Constitution.

There is another kind of penalty which is the penalty of a contract. This is not such a case, but it is the actual contract of the party to pay the million, in the event which has happened. 2 Pothier on Obligations, 86, &c., 93, 94, 95, 96; 7 Wheat. 18.

Washington County had a good subsisting interest in the contract. If any consideration were necessary to sustain the use, it amply exists in the moral obligation which the State owes to the people to protect their interest and nourish their prosperity. The Court of Appeals say, that, " as a county, she stands to the State in the relation of a child to a parent;" and this would furnish consideration enough. Green v. Biddle, 8 Wheat. 151; Lloyd v. Spillet, 2 Atk. 149.

But no question of consideration can arise here, as the acceptance and contract of the company are under the solemnities of a seal, which implies a consideration.

No consideration is necessary. Dartmouth College case, 4 Wheat. 698; 3 Story on the Const. 257, 258; Carnigan v. Morrison, 2 Metcalf, 396 ; Willis on Trustees, 216 ; Cooker v. Child, 2 Levinz; 74; 4 Kent's Com. 307, and cases there referred to.

The sovereignty of a State is above the restrictions of the common law and the statutory law. They must all yield to the sovereign will; and what would be necessary to the contract or grant of an individual would by no means be necessary to the same thing of a State.

Even though Washington County had been ignorant of the provision in the law, made for her benefit at the time of its passage, she could have availed herself of it; and she did affirm it when she instituted the suit, if not before. 4 Kent's Com. 307, &c.

The use declared in the Act of 1835 ought to be as sacred as any other right of property. It is property to the county. It is vested under the law of the State. It vests under the same sanction which secures to a citizen his estate. It is an interest in a contract, vested under the sacred sanction of the law, and is inviolate under the Constitution.

The county enjoyed great advantages before the construction of this road. One of the greatest thoroughfares in the country (the great national road) passed for fifty miles through her territory. Twenty four-horse stage-coaches, filled with passengers, daily passed over the road, and it was constantly lined with immense wagon-teams, travelling to and from the great west. All these people and horses had to be fed. It made a most profitable market for our farmers. Houses were built all along the road, to accommodate the custom. It is now all gone. The farmers lose the profits of their provender and marketing; the whole country feels the depression; and the houses which were a few years ago comfortable inns, and profitable to their proprietors, are going to decay, a dead loss. The million we seek to recover can never indemnify the county for the injury she has sustained.

Maryland was about to apply large sums to the construction of this great work, (the Baltimore and Ohio Railroad); the means were to be obtained in part from Washington County; and could any more cruel injustice be conceived than for the State to appropriate the money of the people, and pledge the property of Washington County, for the construction of a work which would take from the county all the benefits it enjoyed? Surely every principle of justice and moral duty required that the State should protect the county; and the stipulations of the 5th section were no doubt intended for that.

The State was a mere trustee after the contract was made, and could not deny to the county the right to use her name in bringing the suit. Paine v. Rogers, 1 Doug. 407; Carter & Moore v. Insurance Company, 1 Johns. Ch. R. 463; Green v. Biddle, 8 Wheat. 89; Kierstead v. The State, 1 Gill & Johns. 246.

It has been argued, by the other side, that the State has entire control over the corporation of Washington County, and can destroy it at her pleasure. We admit that the legislature has absolute control of the political powers of a political corporation, to amend, or modify, or repeal them. But as long as the corporate organization continues, the county is as capable of taking as a natural person, and its contracts are equally protected. The Act of 1829, chap. 21, sect. 3, incorporates the commissioners of Washington County, and enables them to hold all kinds of estate. The Constitution made no distinction in the classes of contracts whose obligation was forbidden to be impaired, but protects those made by corporations equally with those made by individuals. Green v. Biddle, 5 Pet. Cond. Rep. 390.

The right of a legislature over charters does not imply a right to the property held under these charters. 9 Cranch, 335; 16 Mass. Rep. 84, 85, 86; 2 Kent's Com. 275, 3d ed.

Nelson, (Attorney-General,) for defendants in error, referred to and commented on the various laws of Maryland respecting the Railroad Company, and said, that the only question in the case was, whether the Act of 1840 was valid and legitimate. Upon this point three propositions could be stated —

.1. The proviso in the preceding. act, which declares a forfeiture, imposes it as a penalty.

2. If it be a penalty, the legislature had a right to remit it, and did remit it.

3. If the stipulation in the 5th section of the Act of 1835 be a contract in its nature, the legislature was competent to release it, and did so.

1. Is the proviso a contract or mere penalty? This must be answered by a reference to the terms of the act, to the circumstances under which it was passed, and to acts *in pari materia.* Let us examine each. The 5th section prescribes a duty to be performed by the Railroad Company. It says, " It shall be the duty of the company," and the performance of it is sanctioned by a forfeiture. The language is not that they shall pay if they fail to comply, but that they shall forfeit $1,000,000. What is a forfeiture? It is a penalty imposed by a superior power for an omission to perform a duty. The terms of the act, therefore, mean a penalty by denouncing forfeiture as a punishment. The Act of 1837, 4th section, contained an offer to the company, which was not accepted; but its language is, that it shall "not be construed to repeal the forfeiture to Washington County." The Act of 1840 contains the same idea; it remits a forfeiture. In the Act of 1835, different expressions are used in the 7th and 9th sections, where it is declared that "the company shall bind itself by an instrument to pay," &c.; and in the 14th section, where the duty of providing transportation is imposed upon the company, they are made liable to an action by any party aggrieved. In the 5th section, it is not the less a penalty because the amount is ascertained. If the legislature meant the obligation in the 5th section to rest on contract, can it be accounted for that they did not use the appropriate terms, when they did so in the 7th and 9th sections? It has been said, that the Railroad Company assented to the act, and that it thus became a contract. But the assent was given to the act as it stood, with the penalty in it. Assent to it did not change a penalty into a contract. The Act of Virginia contained penalties for wronging persons, but by accepting this the company left it optional

with the proper authorities of Virginia whether to enforce the penalties or not.

2. If it be a penalty, has the legislature the power to release it?
Whether injustice was or was not done to Washington County, was
a question for the legislature to decide, but not for this court, which
must *jus dicere* and not *jus dare*. In England, the king cannot remit a penalty where private rights are involved, but parliament can.
2 Black. Com. 437, 446; 1 Wm. Black. Rep. 451.

Where a forfeiture is imposed by Act of Congress, and the law
expires, the forfeiture cannot be enforced, although there was a
judgment below. 1 Cranch, 104; 5 Cranch, 281; 6 Cranch, 203,
329.

Decisions in the different States are uniform on this point. 2 Mc-
Cord, 1; 2 Bailey, 584; 1 Missouri, 169; Breese, 115; 1 Murphy,
465; 1 Stew. Ala. Rep. 346; Allen, N. H. 61; 4 Yates, 392.

It is clear, therefore, that if this provision is in the nature of a penalty, the law of 1840 is valid.   .

3. Suppose, however, that the stipulation is in the nature of a
contract, had the legislature power to release it? The Act of 1840,
professes to release it, whether it be contract or penalty. It is not
denied that a State may make a contract, and if she does, that she
cannot break it. The Constitution intended to protect private
property, whether of corporations or individuals. Is Washington
County such a person? We say, that she can have no interest separate from the State. She is a component part of Maryland, and
is separate only for the purpose of executing the sovereign will of
the State. The distinction between public and private corporations
must exist in such a case, if it exists at all. In 1804 the Levy
Court was incorporated, the justices of which were appointed by
the State, but they had no power to levy taxes, nor any other power,
except that which was conferred upon them by law. In 1839,
commissioners were authorized by law to supersede the Levy Court,
with the same powers. They cannot be the *cestui que use* of the
State, for they had no authority to accept such a use, and could not
appropriate the money, if it were given to them. The State could
pass a law, directing the purpose for which it should be expended,
and even order it to be paid over to the Railroad Company. Maryland can abolish Washington County. Suppose that on the day after
the forfeiture the county were to be annihilated or broken up, and
partitioned amongst the adjacent counties, what would be done with
the funds on hand? It would be for the State to prescribe their direction. 9 Cranch, 43, 52, 292.

If the distinction between public and private corporations be that interests are protected, all are protected, because there can be no litigation without interests. 4 Wheat. 629, 630, 659, 660, 693, 694; 13 Wend. 325, 334, 337.

Was a right of action such a property as is protected? The penalty was never reduced into possession, and the State had a right to defeat the remedy when it was sought by a suit in its own name. All the points in this case are covered by 1 Missouri Rep. 169. Counties are public corporations, and can be changed or modified at the pleasure of the State. Breese, (Illinois Rep.) 115.

In the case of the town of Pawlet private interests were involved; it was not intended to throw the shield of protection over public property. The public may do what they please with their own. A legislature cannot repeal a charter, and take the property of individuals; but if you refuse to it the power to control public funds, you strip it of a useful and legal authority.

R. Johnson argued upon the same side, but of his argument the reporter has no notes.

Sergeant, for plaintiff in error, in conclusion, stated the facts in the case, referred to the Acts of Assembly, and then argued that the proviso in the Act of 1835 was not a penalty. There was an alternative, an option given to the railroad company, either to make the road as directed, or to pay the money. The nature of the proviso was perfectly understood by the legislature. The previous part of the law enacted, that the company should pass through three towns. Had the law stopped there, the obligation would have been complete, under the penalty, as it is said by the other side, of forfeiting their charter. But the proviso makes a difference. If the company choose to pay the money, they may decline to obey the enacting clause. The difference between a law and an agreement is, that the one is binding absolutely, and the other not without an assent. But here the company were required to signify their assent to the law, which shows that the legislature thought they were making a contract. When a State becomes a contracting party, she acts with no higher power than an individual, except that sometimes persons are made able to contract who would be unable, without the assistance of legislation. A confusion arises in some cases from the same power making laws and contracts; and the different mode of action must be steadily kept in view. A treaty is binding, and yet there is no exercise of a legislative power. In the case before us, the company were not bound to adopt any certain route. All that the legislature said was, that if they did not agree to pass through the three towns, they should not have the subscription of $3,000,000. It makes no difference, in a legal point of view, whether it was or was not difficult to construct the road along that route. This circumstance did not alter the contract. If they had agreed to pay the $1,000,000, the legislature could not have compelled them to pass through the towns.

The Act of 1840 does not declare what that of 1835 was, but professes to annihilate it. But the legislature cannot do this. They cannot even construe the law, which is the peculiar province of a court. There is nothing in this disability derogatory to the dignity of Maryland, because it is common to all the States. Courts may look at acts which are *in pari materia*, but the examination is only to guide their judgment, and not because the legislature has a right to construe a contract already made. When the Constitution of the United States protects contracts, it means that they shall be defined and construed according to received and settled principles; there is no exception of implied contracts or those made by States or corporations, public or private. Public corporations have a right to make contracts and to sue, and there is no exception of a penalty by contract, such, for example, as a bond. This court has always acted up to the letter and spirit of the Constitution, and it is a subject of rejoicing that its opinions have found their way into the hearts of the people, and become guides of action. In a convention of the people of Pennsylvania, which met not long since, an argument addressed to that body, founded on the decisions of this court, settled a question which had been much debated. It is a principle that contracts must be interpreted by the judiciary, and this is equally true of contracts made by individuals or States. All the incidents of contracts are protected also, and no equivocation or subterfuge will be allowed. The only distinction which can be made amongst penalties, is regarding crimes and contracts. No one can contract to commit a crime; it would be void. If the Act of 1840 impairs the obligation of a contract, it is nugatory. Between individuals, this would be considered a case of contract, and there is in the law no exercise of the legislative power, which would have been the case if Washington county, by it, had been empowered to make a contract. But this was not necessary. The State could contract, undoubtedly, and so could the railroad company, and a third party is introduced with the consent of both. A charter is a contract; but provisions are sometimes introduced into it which are not matters of contract. 4 Wheaton, 235. In the present case, the acceptance completed the contract. If you strike out of the law the words, "for the use of Washington county," there is nothing to show what was. to be done with the money. But when these were inserted, it prevented the State from claiming it for herself; if she had done so, the railroad company would have been justified in refusing to pay. Here then were two parties, each capable of contracting; and as to the capacity of Washington county so to do, it was held in the case of Terrett and Taylor, that the recognition of a power to contract is equivalent to a fresh grant of power. A bond between A. and B., for the use of C., admits C.'s interest, and suit must be brought in the name of the obligee. When a bond is assigned, there is an implied engagement that the assignor will do nothing to impair the interest of the other party. A *cestui que trust* has, in equity, a control of the fund. Black *v.* Zacharie, decided at this term.

The Act of 1835 is, in fact, a stipulation for a license to depart. from a prescribed route. It has been said, by the other side, that it is a penalty, that the legislature can release it, and that if it is a contract, the legislature can annul it. If it is a penalty, and the State has released it, the question cannot come up here. We have no desire to say any thing as to the power of a State over criminal penalties, such as that in 10 Wheaton. It is said that Washington county was not a party to the contract. But it seems to be conceded that if it were not for the Act of 1840, there would be no opposition to the claim. There was a time then, when Washington county had an interest, and this remained at the institution of the suit. If the State of Maryland were to receive the money as the plaintiff in the cause, perhaps we could not legally coerce her to pay it to Washington county. But she would be morally bound to do so. The moment that the railroad company determined not to pass through the three towns, Washington county acquired a right. The trustee and the party bound have concurred to destroy the contract, and it is only in consequence of this, that Washington county does not stand as it did at first. It has been said that the legislature could take away the remedy by which the contract was to be enforced. But the decisions of this court are uniform, that a legislature cannot take away a right, under pretence of affecting the remedy. The last case upon this point is Bronson *v.* Kenzie, 1 Howard, 311.

If the law impairs a remedy, or varies a contract a hair's breadth, it is void; and it makes no difference whether it is a general or a special law. In the case before us, the plaintiffs are put in a worse situation than they were before, and the same thing is intended to be accomplished as if a law had been passed forbidding them to bring a suit.

It is said that Washington county is a public municipal corporation, and therefore within the control of the legislature. But in the

Act of 1835, there was no reservation of power upon this ground. It may be .that the votes of some few persons were required to pass the law, who would not have voted for it if any such reservation had been made. Men cannot be such general philanthropists as to give up the interests of their own immediate neighborhood. Suppose Washington county to have said, if you take away the road from us, you must make compensation. In such case, the law would not have been passed with a reservation in it like the one just spoken of. And if it be a contract, it is violated for the benefit of the railroad company. The argument on the other side goes to the extent that every contract, made by a public municipal corporation, is beyond the pale of the Constitution. There is no decision of this court that such a charter and property can be taken away. One of the complaints in the Declaration of Independence is, that charters were taken away; and this practice, in part, produced a revolution in England. By this argument, they may be all swept off; and such corporations may, moreover, be asked what they are going to do with their property. It has been said, that, supposing it to be a contract, it cannot inure to the benefit of Washington county. But an implication cannot be made contrary to what is expressed, or what is just and right. What Washington county is going to do with the money is of no concern to the railroad company, the true defendant in this case. It may educate the poor with it; it may pay debts; or it may erect a monument to that glorious clause in the Constitution which enables it to assert its rights in this court.

Mr. Chief Justice TANEY delivered the opinion of the court.

The question brought before the court by this writ of error depends upon the construction and effect of an Act of the General Assembly of Maryland, passed at December session, 1835, entitled "An act for the promotion of internal improvement."

The original charter of the Baltimore and Ohio Railroad Company authorized it to construct a railroad from Baltimore to some suitable point on the Ohio River, without prescribing any particular route over which the road was to pass; leaving the whole line to the judgment and discretion of the company. But by the act above mentioned the State proposed to subscribe $3,000,000 to its capital stock, provided the company assented to the provisions of that law; and, among other provisions, this Act of Assembly required the road to pass through Cumberland, Hagerstown, and Boonsborough; and provided also that, if the road was not located in the manner therein pointed out, the company " should forfeit $1,000,000 to the State for the use of Washington county."

The towns of Cumberland, Hagerstown, and Boonsborough, are, all situated in Maryland; the first in Alleghany county and the two latter in Washington.

This law was assented to by the company, and became obligatory upon it, and the sum proposed was subscribed by the State; but for reasons which it is not necessary here to mention, the company did not locate the road through Hagerstown or Boonsborough, nor pass through any part of Washington, on its way from Harper's Ferry to Cumberland, to which point the road has been made; and this suit was thereupon brought, at the instance of the commissioners of Washington county, in the name of the State, for the use of the county, to recover the $1,000,000 above-mentioned. After the suit had been instituted, the State, at December session, 1840, passed a law repealing so much of the Act of 1835 as required the company, to locate the road through Hagerstown and Boonsborough, and remitting the forfeiture of the $1,000,000, and directing any suit instituted to recover it to be discontinued.

The commissioners of Washington county, however, at whose instance the action was brought, insisted that the money was due to the county by contract; and that it was not in the power of the State, to release it; and upon that ground continued to prosecute the suit; and the Court of Appeals of the State, having decided against the claim, the case is brought here by writ of error.

Undoubtedly, if the money was due to Washington county by contract, the Act of 1840, which altogether takes away the remedy, would be inoperative and void. But even if the provisions upon this subject in the Act of 1835 could be regarded as a contract with the railroad company, it would be difficult to maintain that the county was a party to the agreement, or that it acquired any private or separate interest under it, distinct from that of the State. . It was certainly, at that time the policy of the State to require the road to pass through the places mentioned in the law, and if it failed to do so, to appropriate the forfeiture to the use of the county. But it cannot be presumed that, in making this appropriation, the legislature was governed merely by a desire to advance the interest of a single county, without any reference to the interests of the rest of the State. On the contrary, the whole scope of the law shows that it was legislating for State purposes, making large appropriations for improvements in different places; and if the policy which at that time induced it to prescribe a particular course for the road, and, in case it was not followed, to exact from the company $1,000,000, and devote it to the use of Washington county, was afterwards discovered to be a mistaken one, and likely to prove highly injurious to the rest of the State, it

2 *

had unquestionably the power to change its policy, and allow the company to pursue a different course, and to release it from its obligations both as to the direction of the road and the payment of the money. For, in doing this, it was dealing altogether with matters of public concern, and interfered with no private right; for neither the commissioners, nor the county, nor any one of its citizens, had acquired any separate or private interest which could be maintained in a court of justice.

As relates to the commissioners, they are not named in the law, nor were they in any shape parties to the contract supposed to have been made, nor is the money declared to be for their use. They are a corporate body, it is true, and the members who compose it are chosen by the people of the county. But like similar corporations in every other county in the State, it is created for the purposes of government, and clothed with certain defined and limited powers to enable it to perform those public duties which, according to the laws and usages of the State, are always intrusted to local county tribunals. Formerly they were appointed in all of the counties annually, by the executive department of the government, and were then denominated the Levy Court of the county; and in some of the counties they are still constituted in that manner, the legislature commonly retaining the old mode of appointment, or directing an election by the people, as the citizens of any particular county may prefer. But, however chosen, their powers and duties depend upon the will of the legislature, and are modified and changed, and the manner of their appointment regulated at the pleasure of the State. And if this money had been received from the railroad company, the commissioners, in their corporate capacity, would not have been entitled to it, and could neither have received nor disbursed it, nor have directed the uses to which it should be applied, unless the State had seen fit to enlarge their powers and commit the money to their care. If it was applied to the use of the county, it did not by any means follow that it was to pass through their hands, and the mode of application would have depended altogether upon the will of the State. This corporation, therefore, certainly had no private corporate interest in the money, and indeed the suit is not entered for their use, but for the use of the county. The claim for the county is equally untenable with that of the commissioners. The several counties are nothing more than certain portions of territory into which the State is divided for the more convenient exercise of the powers of government. They form together one political body in which the sovereignty resides. And in passing the law of 1835, the people of Washington county did not and could not act as a community having separate and distinct interests of their own, but as a portion of the sovereignty; their delegates to the General Assembly acting in conjunction with the delegates from every other part of the State, and legislating for public and State purposes, and the validity of the law did not depend upon their assent to its provisions, as it would have been equally obligatory upon them, if every one of their delegates had voted against it, provided it was passed by a constitutional majority of the General Assembly. And whether the money was due by contract or otherwise, it must, if received and applied to the use of the county, have yet been received and applied by the State to public purposes in the county. For the county has no separate and corporate organization by which it could receive the money or designate agents to receive it or give an acquittance to the railroad company, or determine upon the uses to which it should be appropriated. We have already seen that the corporation of commissioners of the county had no such power; and certainly no citizen of the county had any private and individual property in it. It must have rested with the State so to dispose of it as to promote the general interest of the whole community, by the advantages it bestowed upon this particular portion of it.

Indeed, if this money is to be considered as due, either to the commissioners or to the county, by contract with the railroad company, so that it may be recovered in this suit, in opposition to the will and policy of the State, it would follow necessarily that it might have been released by the party entitled, even if the State had desired to enforce it. And if the State had adhered to the policy of the act in question, and supposed it to be for the public interest to insist that the road should pass along the line prescribed in that law, or the company be compelled to pay the million of dollars, according to the construction now contended for, the commissioners or the county might have counteracted the wishes of the State, and, by releasing the company from the obligation to pay this money, allowed them to locate the road upon any other line. And if the construction of the plaintiff in error be right, the Legislature of Maryland, in a case where the whole people of the State had become so deeply concerned by the large amount subscribed to the capital stock of the road, that its success or failure must seriously affect the interests of every part of the State; and where the improvement was regarded as of the highest importance to its general commercial prosperity; it deliberately deprived itself of the power of exercising any future control over it, and left it to a single county or county corporation to decide upon the course of the road, and either to insist on the line prescribed by the legislature, or to release the company from the obligation to pursue it, without regard to the wishes or interest of the rest of the State. Whether the million of dollars was reserved by contract, or inflicted as a penalty, such a construction of the law cannot be maintained.

But we think it very clear that this was a penalty, to be inflicted if the railroad company did not follow the line pointed out in the law. It is true, that the Act of 1835, which changed in some important particulars the obligations imposed by the original charter, would not have been binding on the company without its consent; and the 1st section, therefore, contains a provision requiring the consent of the company in order to give it validity. And when the company assented to the proposed alterations in their charter, and agreed to accept the law, it undoubtedly became a contract between it and the State; but it was a contract in no other sense than every charter, whether original or supplementary, is a contract, where rights of private property are acquired under it. Yet, although this supplementary charter was a contract in this sense of the term, it does not by any means follow that the legislature might not, in the charter, impose duties and obligations upon the company, and inflict penalties and forfeitures as a punishment for its disobedience, which might be enforced against it in the form of criminal proceedings, and as the punishment of an offence against the law. Such penal provisions are to be found in many charters, and we are not aware of any case in which they have been held to be mere matters of contract. And in the case before the court, the language of the law requiring the company to locate the road so as to pass through the places therein mentioned, is certainly not the language of contract, but is evidently mandatory, and in the exercise of legislative power; and it is made the duty of the company, in case they assent to the provisions of that law, to pass through Cumberland, Hagerstown, and Boonsborough; and if they fail to do so, the fine of $1,000,000 is imposed as a punishment for the offence. And a provision, as in this case, that the party shall forfeit a particular sum, in case he does not perform an act required by law, has always, in the construction of statutes, been regarded not as a contract with the delinquent party, but as the punishment for an offence. Undoubtedly, in the case of individuals, the word forfeit is construed to be the language of contract, because contract is the only mode in which one person can become liable to pay a penalty to another for a breach of duty, or the failure to perform an obligation. In legislative proceedings, however, the construction is otherwise, and a forfeiture is always to be regarded as a punishment inflicted for a violation of some duty enjoined upon the party by law; and such, very clearly, is the meaning of the word in the act in question.

Philadelphia and Wilmington Railroad Co. v. Maryland.

In this aspect of the case, and upon this construction of the Act of Assembly, we do not understand that the right of the State to release it is disputed. Certainly the power to do so is too well settled to admit of controversy. The repeal of the law imposing the penalty, is of itself a remission. 1 Cranch, 104; 5 Cranch, 281; 6 Cranch, 203, 329. And in the case of the United States v. Morris, 10 Wheat. 287, this court held, that Congress had clearly the power to authorize the Secretary of the Treasury to remit any penalty or forfeiture incurred by the breach of the revenue laws, either before or after judgment; and if remitted before the money was actually paid, it embraced the shares given by law in such cases to the officers of the customs, as well as the share of the United States. The right to remit a penalty like this stands upon the same principles.

We are, therefore, of opinion, that the law of 1840, hereinbefore mentioned, did not impair the obligation of a contract, and that the judgment of the Court of Appeals of Maryland must be affirmed.

The Philadelphia and Wilmington Railroad Company, *Plaintiff in Error, v.* The State of Maryland.[1]

December Term, 1850.

Taxation — Exemption of Road.

The Philadelphia, Wilmington, and Baltimore Railroad Company was formed by the union of several railroad companies, which had been previously chartered by Maryland, Delaware, and Pennsylvania, two of which were the Baltimore and Port Deposit Railroad Company, whose road extended from Baltimore to the Susquehanna, lying altogether on the west side of the river, and the Delaware and Maryland Railroad Company, whose road extended from the Delaware line to the Susquehanna, and lying on the east side of the river.

The charter of the Baltimore and Port Deposit Railroad Company contained no exemption from taxation.

The charter of the Delaware and Maryland Railroad Company made the shares of stock therein personal estate, and exempted them from any tax, "except upon that portion of the permanent and fixed works which might be in the State of Maryland."

Held, that under the Maryland Law of 1841, imposing a tax for State purposes upon the real and personal property in the State, that part of the road of the plaintiff which belonged originally to the Baltimore and Port Deposit Railroad Company, was liable to be assessed in the hands of the company with which it became consolidated, just as it would have been in the hands of the original company.

------

[1] 10 Howard's Reports, 376.

Also, that there is no reason why the property of a corporation should be presumed to be exempted from its share of necessary public burdens, there being no express exemption.

This Court holds, as it has on several other occasions held, that the taxing power of a State should never be presumed to be relinquished, unless the intention is declared in clear and unambiguous terms.

ERROR to the Court of Appeals for the Western Shore of Maryland.

This was an action of *indebitatis assumpsit*, brought by the defendant in error, in the Baltimore County Court, to recover certain State taxes assessed upon the real and personal property of the plaintiff in error, being in Harford County, in the State of Maryland.

The suit was docketed by consent, with an agreement that a judgment. *pro forma* should be entered for the plaintiff, now defendant in error, upon a statement of facts. An appeal was taken from this judgment to the Court of Appeals, where it was affirmed *pro forma*, and the present writ of error was afterwards sued out. The statement of facts was as follows : —

" The Philadelphia, Wilmington, and Baltimore Railroad Company" was formed by an agreement of union, duly made and entered into between the following corporations, to wit, the Baltimore and Port Deposit Railroad Company, the Wilmington and Susquehanna Railroad Company, and " the Philadelphia, Wilmington, and Baltimore Railroad Company," of Pennsylvania. This agreement of union was made on the day of its date, under the authority claimed under and in pursuance of the directions of the several acts of assembly therein recited, and was entered into after the primary meetings of stockholders, as required by said several acts. A copy of said agreement is herewith produced, as a part of this statement, marked exhibit A. " The Baltimore and Port Deposit Railroad Company" was incorporated by the Act of 1831, chap. 288, of the General Assembly of Maryland; "the Wilmington and Susquehanna Railroad Company," (one of the parties to said agreement marked exhibit A,) was formed by an agreement of union duly made and entered into on the 18th·day of April, 1835, between the Delaware and Maryland Railroad Company and the Wilmington and Susquehanna Railroad Company, (of Delaware,) in virtue and in strict pursuance of the several acts in said agreement of union recited, to wit, an, act of the · General Assembly of. the State of Delaware, passed on the 24th day of July, 1835, and an act of the General Assembly of the State of Maryland, passed at December session, 1835, chap. 93, and was certified and recorded, as directed by said several acts. The said corporation, " the Delaware and Maryland Railroad Company," was incorporated by the Act of 1831, chap.

296, of the General Assembly of Maryland; "the Wilmington and Susquehanna Railroad Company," (of Delaware,) was incorporated by an act of the General Assembly of the State of Delaware, passed on the 18th day of January, 1832; "the Philadelphia, Wilmington, and Baltimore Railroad Company," (of Pennsylvania,) was originally chartered by an act of the General Assembly of the Commonwealth of Pennsylvania, approved on the 2d day of April, 1831, by the name of "the Philadelphia and Delaware County Railroad Company," which, by a supplement to said act, passed the 14th day of March, 1836, was changed to the corporate name of the Philadelphia, Wilmington, and Baltimore Railroad Company. The agreement of union, by which "the Philadelphia, Wilmington, and Baltimore Railroad Company," the party to this suit, was formed, (of which said exhibit A is a copy,) was made by the authority and in pursuance of the act of the General Assembly of Maryland, passed at December session, 1837, chap. 30, and other corresponding acts of the General Assembly of the State of Delaware and the Commonwealth of Pennsylvania, recited in said agreement of union, marked exhibit A. All which said acts of assembly of the States of Maryland, Delaware, and Pennsylvania, above referred to, or referred to in said exhibit A, relating to the incorporation and charter of the defendant, are to be regarded as part of this statement, and, to save the trouble of transcribing them, either party may read them from the printed statutes; to have the same effect as if they were transcribed into this statement, or regularly certified copies of the same filed herewith.

The railroad of the defendant extends from the city of Baltimore, in Maryland, to the city of Philadelphia, in Pennsylvania, passing through the counties of Baltimore, Harford, and Cecil, in Maryland, and thence over a part of the States of Delaware and Pennsylvania. That portion of said railroad which lies west of the Susquehanna River, that is to say, between the city of Baltimore and the said river, lying partly in Baltimore county and partly in Harford county, was made and constructed, (prior to the agreement of union of which exhibit A is a copy,) and owned in severalty by "the Baltimore and Port Deposit Railroad Company." That portion of said railroad which lies east of the Susquehanna, and between that river and the divisional line between the States of. Delaware and Pennsylvania, was made by the Wilmington and Susquehanna Railroad Company, and (prior to the said agreement of which exhibit A is a copy,) was owned in severalty by said last-mentioned company. Previous to the consolidation of "the Delaware and Maryland Railroad Company," and "the Wilmington and Susquehanna Railroad Company," (of Delaware,) into one company, the line of the road which the said corporation, "the Delaware and Maryland Railroad Company," was authorized to make, was that part of said road which lay east of the Susquehanna, and between that river and the divisional line between the States of Maryland and Delaware, and that part of the said road which the said corporation, "the Wilmington and Susquehanna Railroad Company," (of Delaware,) was authorized to make, is that part of said road which lies between the divisional lines of the States of Maryland and Delaware and the Commonwealth of Pennsylvania; each of said last mentioned corporations, prior to the consolidation, had commenced the location and construction of their said several parts; but at the time of their consolidation, under their agreement of union aforesaid, neither part was completed, but the whole was completed by the Wilmington and Susquehanna Railroad Company, after their agreement of union aforesaid. The River Susquehanna is passed over by the use of a steamboat belonging to the defendant, the said Philadelphia, Wilmington, and Baltimore Railroad Company, and used by said defendant for the sole and exclusive purpose of transporting persons and property across said river, from shore to shore, from the terminus of the railroad track on the other shore; said steamboat is especially constructed for its use, in connection with said railroad, and has rails laid on its upper deck, which are so constructed that the said rails are placed in juxtaposition with the railroad track of the railroad, when the boat is in place for use, in connection with the terminus of the road on either shore; cars are received upon the said deck of said steamboat from the railroad track on one shore, and passed over the river by the said steamboat, and on to the railroad track on the other shore, from off said boat, as the means of passing cars, &c., across the river; and prior to the agreement of union, of which exhibit A is a copy, was owned jointly, but in unequal parts, by the Baltimore and Port Deposit Railroad Company and the Wilmington and Susquehanna Railroad Company, and was managed and kept in repair at the joint expense, in proportion of their respective interest therein, by the said last mentioned two companies. The said steamboat, before and since the said agreement of union, of which exhibit A is a copy, usually remained, and still usually remains, in a dock constructed in the Susquehanna River by protecting piers projecting from the Harford shore, when not actually in use; which dock is on the west shore of the Susquehanna River, and within the limits of Harford County. That part of said road which lies east of the divisional line between the States of Delaware and Pennsylvania, and thence extending to the city of Philadelphia, was, prior to the said agreement of union of which exhibit A is a copy, constructed and owned in severalty by the said corporation, called the Philadelphia, Wilmington, and Baltimore Railroad Company (of Pennsylvania.) The principal office of the defendant, (ever since the agreement of union of which exhibit A is a copy,) for the transaction of the business of said company, has been established and held in the city of Philadelphia, at the eastern terminus of said railroad.

The stated meetings of the board-of directors, by the terms of said agreement of union, are to be held alternately at Wilmington and Philadelphia. There are offices at Philadelphia, Wilmington, and Baltimore, at any one of which transfers of stock may be made; the stated meetings of the stockholders were to be held in the city of Wilmington. Prior to said agreement of union, the principal office of the Baltimore and Port Deposit Railroad Company was held in the city of Baltimore, and the principal office of the defendant within the State of Maryland has been, and is now, in said city, at which place one of the vice-presidents of the said corporation resides. All the corporate funds and capital stock of said defendant have been expended and contained in the location and construction of said road, and in the construction of such works and improvements as were necessary and expedient to the proper completion and use of said road, and in the purchase of cars and machinery of transportation, &c., necessary and indispensable to the completion and use of said road; and the said company has not, at any time, since the said agreement of union, owned or held, and does not now own or hold, any estate, real, personal, or mixed, other than what forms a part of, or necessarily appertains to, the construction and completion of said road, and its works and improvements, and in the purchase of cars and machinery of transportation, &c., necessary and indispensable to its use; and over and beyond its actual capital, it was found necessary to raise by loan a large additional amount for the purposes aforesaid, and which amount has been so applied. The defendant was assessed, under the act of the General Assembly of Maryland of March session, 1841, chap. 23, by the assessors, appointed under said act, for Harford County, with the sum of $127,000, as shown by a copy of said valuation and assessment, filed herewith as a part of this statement, marked exhibit B. The several parcels or tracts of land, valued for 200 acres at $10 per acre, as held and occupied by said company from the Gunpowder Falls to the Susquehanna River, lie within the limits of Harford County, and consist of the land held and occupied by said company for the bed of its railroad, water stations, depots, and ticket-offices of said company; portions of which said land were acquired under condemnations for the use of said company, under the provisions of the said act of the General Assembly of Maryland, of December session, 1831, chap. 233, and other portions of which were acquired by agreement with the owners thereof. The title acquired in each case of agreement with the owner being consummated by deed of bargain and sale to the president and directors of said company and their successors, in the ordinary terms of a conveyance in fee. The houses and other improvements on the road, and at Havre de Grace, and the depots, ticket-offices, and water stations of said company, lie within the limits of Harford County. The railroad track iron, within the limits of Harford County, valued at $95,000, consists of the rails actually laid down and in use as the track of said railroad within the limit aforesaid. And the steam ferry-boat at Havre de Grace, valued at $15,000, is the steamboat hereinbefore mentioned, used as aforesaid for the sole and exclusive purpose of transporting persons and property across the River Susquehanna, from the terminus of the railroad track on one shore to the terminus of the railroad track on the other shore, in the manner hereinbefore mentioned; said steamboat is, and continually since its use as aforesaid has been, duly enrolled and licensed at the custom-house in Baltimore, according to the act of Congress. The capital stock of the defendant, under the agreement of union, (of which exhibit A is a copy,) is divided into 45,000 shares of $50 each, which stock is held by various persons, many of whom reside in the State of Maryland, and others of whom, and a large majority of whom, reside in other States, and in Europe, and was so held at the time of said union. The stockholders residing in the city of Baltimore, in Maryland, had actually been assessed to the extent of the stock by them respectively held, no objection being taken to said assessment, nor any appeal prosecuted therefrom; no assessment has been made on the stock of any of the stockholders residing in Harford County, or Cecil County, if any reside there, nor on the stock of non-resident stockholders. It is further admitted, that the taxes assessed and levied upon the said property of the said defendant were for State purposes for the years 1842, 1843, 1844, and 1845; and that the same were assessed and levied by the commissioners of Harford County, under the act of the General Assembly of the State of Maryland, passed at March session, 1841, chap. 23, and that the said paper, marked exhibit B., filed as a part of this statement, is a correct statement of the rate and amount of taxes so assessed and levied, and that said rate of taxation is the same as that imposed for said years upon all real and personal property (not expressly exempted by said act of assembly) in said State. It is further agreed, that if the court

shall be of opinion, on the aforegoing statement, that the said property of the said defendant is liable to be assessed for taxes for
general State purposes, under the act of assembly aforesaid, that
then judgment be rendered for the plaintiff for $1,455.19 and costs ;
but if the court shall be of opinion that the said property of the said
defendant is not liable to be assessed and taxed as aforesaid, but the
same is exempt from such assessment and taxation under the charter
of the defendant, or the said act of the General Assembly of Maryland of March session, 1841, chap. 23, then judgment to be given for
defendant.

GEO. R. RICHARDSON, *Attorney for Plaintiff.*
REVERDY JOHNSON, *for Defendant.*

Exhibit A, referred to in the aforegoing statement, is as follows, to
wit : —

"Agreement between the Wilmington and Susquehanna Railroad
  Company, the Baltimore and Port Deposit Railroad Company, and
  the Philadelphia, Wilmington, and Baltimore Railroad Company.

"Copy. — Articles of union made and concluded this 5th day of
February, in the year of our Lord 1838, between the Wilmington
and Susquehanna Railroad Company, the Baltimore and Port
Deposit Railroad Company, and the Philadelphia, Wilmington, and
Baltimore Railroad Company, by virtue and in pursuance of an act
of the General Assembly of the State of Delaware, entitled ' A further supplement to an Act entitled an Act to incorporate the Wilmington and Susquehanna Railroad Company,' and of an act of the
General Assembly of Maryland, entitled 'An Act to authorize the
union of the Baltimore and Port Deposit Railroad Company, the
Wilmington and Susquehanna Railroad Company, and the Philadelphia, Wilmington, and Baltimore Railroad Company,' and of an act
of the General Assembly of Pennsylvania, entitled ' an Act supplementary to the Act incorporating the Philadelphia, Wilmington, and
Baltimore Railroad Company.'
  " First. The said three corporations are hereby united, and from
and after the first election of directors hereinafter provided for
in the third article shall be merged into one body corporate,
under the name and style of the Philadelphia, Wilmington, and
Baltimore Railroad Company, and the stocks of the said three corporations so united shall form one common stock, and all the estate,
real, personal, and mixed, and the rights, privileges, advantages, and
immunities belonging to each of the said corporations, become and
be vested in the said body corporate, and the debts and liabilities of

each of the said corporations shall be deemed, and are hereby declared to be, the debts and liabilities of the said body corporate.

" Second. The stock of the said body corporate is hereby divided into shares of fifty dollars each, of which the present stockholders of the Wilmington and Susquehanna Railroad Company are hereby declared to be entitled in all, to sixteen thousand shares, the present stockholders of the Baltimore and Port Deposit Railroad Company to nineteen thousand shares, the present stockholders of the Philadelphia, Wilmington, and Baltimore Railroad Company .to ten thousand shares, including those forfeited heretofore, which are to be held for the use of this corporation ; and certificates of stock, as may be regulated by the president and directors of the said body corporate, shall be granted and issued accordingly to each of the said stockholders so soon as the said stockholders shall have paid up all instalments due upon the shares of stock held by them respectively, and shall have surrendered the certificates previously issued to them as stockholders in the respective companies hereby united ; and the capital stock of the said corporation shall consist of such number of shares as aforesaid, subject to the right and privilege of increasing the same from time to time, according to the provisions of the respective charters of the said companies hereby united.

" Third. There shall be fifteen directors to manage the affairs and business of the said body corporate, and a meeting of the stockholders of the three corporations hereby united for the election of the first directors shall be held at Wilmington on Wednesday, the 14th day of February, instant, of the time and place of which meeting notice shall be given by the present president of the Wilmington and Susquehanna Railroad Company by advertisement in at least three newspapers, at which meeting fifteen directors shall be elected by the said stockholders, voting in person or by proxy, and each share being entitled to one vote ; and the directors so elected shall hold their offices until the ensuing annual meeting of the stock-holders, and until their successors are elected.

" Fourth. The stated meetings of the stockholders shall be held in the city of Wilmington, on the second Monday of January in each and every year hereafter, at which time and place an annual election of directors shall be made by the stockholders, and fifteen days' notice of the time and place of each stated meeting shall be given by advertisement in at least three newspapers ; the election shall be by ballot, and each share of the stock shall entitle the holder thereof to one vote, to be given either in person or by proxy, pro-vided it has been held for three calendar months before the time of voting ; the directors shall, after the first and each subsequent election, choose by ballot one of their own number to be president of the said body corporate, who shall serve one year, or until the election of a successor; the omission to hold an election for directors at the time prescribed shall in no wise affect the said body corporate, but such election may be had upon due notice from the said president and directors, published as aforesaid, at any time within three months after the time so prescribed as aforesaid.

"The directors shall hold their offices for one year, and until a new election shall take place, and the powers of the said president and directors shall be the same as are now vested in the president and directors of the Wilmington and Susquehanna Railroad Company; the president may be removed from his office by a vote of two thirds of all the directors. The directors may, in each year that they may deem it advisable, elect a vice-president from their own number, who, in the absence of the president, shall have all the powers of the president, and shall be liable to removal in like manner as the president. Five directors shall constitute a quorum for the transaction of business. The directors may, if they shall deem it advisable, appoint an executive committee, consisting of six members, from the States of Pennsylvania, Delaware, and Maryland, for such time, and for the performance of such duties, as any resolutions of the directors, or any by-law, may prescribe and assign; and the president, or vice-president, and any two members of said committee, shall constitute a quorum thereof. All officers and agents of the corporation, other than directors, shall be appointed by the directors, who may prescribe and exact such security as they may deem proper for the performance of their duties.

"Fifth. The stated meetings of the board of directors shall be held alternately at Wilmington and Philadelphia, and special meetings may be held either at Wilmington, Philadelphia or Baltimore. The corporation shall have offices opened at Wilmington, Philadelphia, and Baltimore, at either of which transfers of stock may be made, under such regulations as the board of directors may prescribe.

"Sixth. All by-laws shall be made, altered, or repealed only by a majority, consisting of not less than two thirds of all the directors; it being understood that no by-law shall contravene any of these terms or stipulations; and the existing by-laws of the Wilmington and Susquehanna Railroad Company shall, until altered or repealed as aforesaid, be the by-laws of this corporation; and all rules and regulations necessary for the management and conduct of the business of the company, not provided for in a by-law, may be made by the directors.

"In witness whereof, the said corporations, parties to this agree-

3 *

ment, have caused their respective corporate seals, attested by the signatures of their respective presidents, to be hereunto affixed, the day and year first hereinbefore written.

JAMES PRICE,   [L. S.]
Pres. Wilm. and Susq'a Railroad Co.
J. I. COHEN, JR.,   [L. S.]
Pres. Balto. and Port Deposit Railroad Co.
M. NEWKIRK,   [L. S.]
Pres. Philad., Wilm., and Balto. Railroad Co.

" In pursuance of the provisions of an act of the General Assembly of Maryland, entitled ' An Act to authorize the union of the Baltimore and Port Deposit Railroad Company, the Wilmington and Susquehanna Railroad Company, and the Philadelphia, Wilmington, and Baltimore . Railroad Company,' said corporations do hereby certify, under their respective corporate seals, attested by their respective presidents, that the within and foregoing instrument of writing is a true copy of an agreement for the union of the said company, made and concluded on the 5th day of February, 1838.

JAMES PRICE,   [L. S.]
Pres. Wilm. and Susq'a Railroad Co.
J. I. COHEN, JR.,   [L. S.]
Pres. Balto. and Port Deposit Railroad Co.
M. NEWKIRK,   [L. S.]
Pres. Philad., Wilm., and Balto. Railroad Co.

" Received to be recorded the 12th day of February, 1838, at 5 o'clock, P. M.; same day recorded and examined.

Per THOMAS KELL, *Clerk.*

" In testimony that the foregoing is a true copy, taken from liber T. K, No. 276, folio 392, &c., one of the land records of [L. S.] Baltimore County, I hereto subscribe my name and affix the seal of Baltimore County Court, this 3d day of December, 1846.

A. W. BRADFORD, *Clerk of Balto. Co. Court.*"

Exhibit B, referred to in said statement, is as follows, to wit: —

"A list of the real and personal property of the Philadelphia, Wilmington, and Baltimore Railroad Company, as per the assessors' books on file in the office of the Commissioners of Harford County, on which taxes are due for the years of 1842, 1843, 1844, and 1845, to wit: —

Different tracts of land, from the Gunpowder Falls to the
   Susquehanna, containing 200 acres, at $10 per acre, .$2,000
Track iron, &c., &c., ... 95,000
Houses and other improvements on the road, and at Havre
   de Grace, ... 15,000 ·
Steamboat at Havre de Grace, ... 15,000

                                     $127,000

    " I hereby certify, that the above is a true transcript of the property
of the Railroad Company from the assessors' books.

    " Given under my hand and seal of the Commissioners of Harford
County, this

1842. To State tax on $127,000, at 25 cents per $100,		$317.50
Commission at 1½, _.		19.05
Interest for three years, ...		60.57
1843. To State tax on the same, at 25 cents per $100,	.	317.50
Commission at 1½, ...		22.22
Interest for two years, ...		40.75
1844. To State tax on the above, 25 cents per $100,	.	317.50
Commission at 1½, ...		22.22
Interest for one year, ...		20.38
1845. State tax on the above, 25 cents in $100,	.	317.50

                                     $1,455.19
              JAMES SPICER, *Collector.*"

    It is agreed that any errors in the foregoing statement may be cor-
rected by counsel, at the trial of the cause, either in the County
Court, Court of Appeals, or Supreme Court of the United States;
and that said statement may be added to or amended, by agreement,
at any time.
           GEORGE R. RICHARDSON, *Attorney for Plaintiff.*
           REVERDY JOHNSON, *for Defendant.*

    The following is a summary of the act imposing the tax, as well
as of the acts incorporating the different companies, so far as they
bear upon the question before the court.
    The first section of the Act of 1st April, 1841, imposing the tax
sought to be recovered, after enumerating the several kinds of property which are to be the subject of taxation, including " all stocks
or shares, owned by residents of this State, in any bank, institution,
or company incorporated in any other State or Territory," also " all
stocks or shares in any bank, institution, or company incorporated

by this State," declares that such "and all other property of every description whatsoever shall be valued agreeably to the directions of this act, and shall be chargeable according to such valuation with the public assessments provided," &c.

The ninth section makes it the duty of the assessor to inform him-self of all property liable to assessment, and to make a return thereof under prescribed heads, the fifth of which was, "Bank stocks and other stocks particularly specified, with their respective values."

The sixteenth section provided, that, for the valuing of stock in private corporations held by non-residents, the locality of such stock should be deemed to be at the place where the principal place of business of such corporation should be situate.

The seventeenth section enacted that the president or proper offi-cers of corporations should make out and deliver to the assessors of the proper county an account of stock in such corporation.

The forty-fifth section made it the duty of the levy court or com-missioners of the several counties to impose a tax of twenty cents in every $100 of assessable property, according to their valuation.

The fifty-third section provided that the tax imposed "shall be collectable and payable into the State treasury according to the pro-visions of this act, and be in all respects subject thereto."

The second section of the Act of 1831, ch. 288, entitled "An Act to incorporate the Baltimore and Port Deposit Railroad Company," enacted that "the subscribers of the said stock, their successors and assigns, shall be, and they are hereby declared to be, incorporated into a company, by the name of the Baltimore and Port Deposit Railroad Company, and by that name shall be capable in law of purchasing, holding, selling, leasing, and conveying estates, real, per-sonal, and mixed, so far as shall be necessary for the purposes here-inafter mentioned, and no further, and shall have perpetual succes-sion, and by said corporate name may sue and be sued."

The twelfth section gave authority to construct a road one hundred feet wide from the City of Baltimore to Port Deposit, &c.

The twentieth section declared that "the shares of the capital stock of said company shall be deemed and considered personal estate."

The Act of 1831, ch. 296, entitled "An Act to incorporate the Dela-ware and Maryland Railroad Company," gave a perpetual charter, and authorized the construction of a road one hundred feet wide "from some point on the Delaware and Maryland line" "to Port Deposit, or any other point on the Susquehanna River."

The nineteenth section, after giving authority to purchase property, charge tolls, &c., and declaring that the property specified should be vested in said company and their successors for ever, proceeds: "And the shares of the capital stock of said company shall be deemed and considered personal estate, and shall be exempt from the imposition of any tax or burden by the State's assenting to this law, except upon that portion of the permanent and fixed works of said company which may lie within the State of Maryland; and that any tax which shall hereafter be levied upon said section shall not exceed the rate of any general tax which may at the same time be imposed upon similar real or personal property of this State for State purposes."

The Act of 14th March, 1836, ratifies and adopts the act of the General Assembly of Delaware, passed 24th July, 1835, which provided for the union of the Wilmington and Susquehanna Railroad Company (incorporated by the General Assembly of Maryland) into one company, to be styled " the Wilmington and Susquehanna Railroad Company," and which also provided that " the holders of the stock of the said railroad companies, so united as aforesaid, shall hold, possess, and enjoy all the property, rights, and privileges, and exercise all the power granted to and vested in the said railroad companies, or either of them, by this or any other law or laws of this State, or of the State of Maryland."

The Act of 1837, ch. 30, authorizes the union of the Baltimore and Port Deposit Railroad Company, and the Wilmington and Susquehanna Railroad Company, with the Philadelphia, Wilmington, and Baltimore Railroad Company, and provides that said " body corporate so formed shall be entitled within this State to all the powers and privileges and advantages now belonging to the two first abovenamed corporations."

The cause was argued by *Meredith*, for the defendant in error, and submitted on printed points by *Reverdy Johnson*, for the plaintiff in error.

Meredith, for defendant in error.

It will be contended by the defendant in error, —

1st. That the property assessed for the State taxes, for the recovery of which this suit was brought, was, at the time of said assessment, liable to State taxation. Laws of Maryland, March Session, 1841, ch. 23; McCulloch *v.* State of Maryland, 4 Wheaton, 436; Providence Bank *v.* Billings, 4 Peters, 563, 564; Passenger Cases, 7 Howard, 402; Nathan *v.* State of Louisiana, 8 Howard, 80; Battle *v.* Corporation of Mobile, 9 Alabama, 234; Howell *v.* State of Maryland, 3 Gill, 14.

2dly. That the property so assessed was not exempted from taxa-tion by any contract or agreement binding on the State of Maryland. Laws of Maryland, 1831, ch. 288 ; 1831, ch. 296 ; 1835, ch. 93 ; 1837, ch. 30 ; Providence Bank v. Billings, 4 Peters, 514 ; Charles River Bridge v. Warren Bridge, 11 Peters, 420 ; McCulloch v. State of Maryland, 4 Wheaton, 436 ; Bulow v. City Council, 1 Nott & McCord, 527 ; Angel and Ames on Corporations, 435, 459, 462, 467, and cases referred to ; Blatchford v. Mayor of Plymouth, 3 Bingham, N. C. 691 ; Dwarris on Statutes, 9 Law Library, 50 et seq. ; Kirby v. Potter, 4 Vesey, 751 ; Wildman v. Wildman, 9 Vesey, 177 ; Raw-lins v. Jennings, 13 Vesey, 45 ; Page v. Leapingwell, 18 Vesey, 467 ; Reed v. McGrew, 5 Hammond, 380 ; Pembroke v. Duxbury, 1 Pick-ering, 199.

There are several questions which might be raised in the court below, but which would not be properly raised here. The only ques-tion is that which gives this court jurisdiction.

The Baltimore and Port Deposit Railroad Company had granted to them a perpetual charter, without any *bonus* to the State. But the charter contained no exemption from State taxation.

The Act of 1831, ch. 296, gave to the Delaware and Maryland Railroad Company a perpetual charter. The nineteenth section declares that the shares of the capital stock shall be considered per-sonal estate. There is obscurity in this section. The object would seem to have been to convert the *shares* into personal estate in order to subject them to execution, Maryland not having passed any law till after this charter subjecting stocks, &c., to execution. The same section also declares, that such shares shall be exempt from the im-position of any tax, &c. It would seem from this that the legisla-ture meant to exempt stock in the hands of the stockholders. Then comes the exception, that the legislature reserves the right to tax the permanent and fixed works of the company, which would indicate that every thing else was exempted. And yet that would be a grant of an exemption by implication, there being no express words.

The plaintiffs claim an exemption which was not originally granted to them, but was granted to another company, which was subse-quently merged in the present company. How was this exemption transferred ?

The Act of 1835, chap. 93, incorporates the legislation of Delaware on the same subject. That act *creates* a new corporation. In 1837, when the last union was asked for, Maryland provided that the three corporations should be merged in and form one body corporate, and that it should have all the powers, privileges, and advantages of the two former companies, namely, the Baltimore and Port Deposit Railroad Company, and the Wilmington and Susquehanna Railroad Company. Now the only exemption which could be transferred was that of the Delaware and Maryland Railroad Company, (because the other company had no exemption,) which had been merged in the Wilmington and Susquehanna Railroad Company. But the exemption of the former was gone necessarily, because it was only the *stock* of that company which was exempted. The moment, then, the stock was destroyed by the merger of that company in another, or the transfusion or intermingling of it with that of the other companies, its distinctive character was destroyed. Reed *v.* McGrew and Pembroke *v.* Duxbury are full to the point. And in the Charles River Bridge case this court held, that, by the charter to the Charles River Company, the franchise which had originally existed in Harvard College was extinguished. So here, by these new charters, the original exemption was extinguished.

But suppose it to have been transferred, how will it avail the present company? The property here assessed was not that which originally belonged to the Delaware and Maryland Company, but to the Baltimore and Port Deposit Company, which latter had, as I have shown, no exemption at all.

The only doubt is as to the steamboat. But it has been decided that a tax of this kind does not interfere with the regulations of commerce. It does not appear that this steamboat ever belonged to the exempted company. On the contrary, from the kinds of property authorized by the charter, it would seem otherwise. The charter was to construct a road from the divisional line *to the* Susquehanna River, and no farther. The property to be used was such as was required for this road, not for crossing the river. *Non constat*, then, that this steamboat ever belonged to the exempted company.

Johnson, for the plaintiff in error.

The only question is, whether, by contract between the plaintiff in error and the State, the plaintiff was not exempt from the taxation, the amount of which it was the purpose of the suit to exact. The judgment being against the plaintiff in error, who claimed the exemption under the alleged contract, and its protection under the Constitution of the United States, it must be reversed if their ground can be maintained.

First, Was there a contract, and second, is it impaired by the tax in question?

This is to be ascertained by referring to the several acts of Maryland, under which the plaintiff's franchise is held. If these contain the contract relied upon, the point is made out. That a State may contract in the form of a legislative act, and so as to deprive herself in a particular instance of the right to exercise her taxing power, are not now open questions. It is the settled doctrine. Dartmouth College v. Woodward, 4 Wheaton, 518; New Jersey v. Wilson, 7 Cranch, 164.

Is there, then, such a contract in this case?

Before the present company existed, the right to make the road from Baltimore to Philadelphia was in various companies, chartered for certain portions of the road, by Maryland, Delaware, and Pennsylvania. These, by an agreement authorized by laws of the same States, were united into one on the 5th of February, 1838, under the name of the plaintiff in error; the agreement is in the record.

By the terms of this association, and the several acts legalizing it, it will be seen that *all the privileges and exemptions* possessed by any one of the companies under its own charter became vested in the united body, and coextensive with the entire route of the road.

The Act of Maryland of 1831, chap. 288, contains the exemption from taxation upon which reliance is placed. The tax levied is not on the real or fixed property only, owned by plaintiff in error, and being within the limits of Harford County, but upon the iron rail, &c., and the steamboat at Havre de Grace.

The land is taxed, and also three other items; this, it is submitted, is a clear violation of the exemption referred to. That the exemption, but for its qualification in the section making it, would have embraced the entire property, real and personal, of the company, is perfectly clear. The question then is, Was it the object of the qualification to take out of the exemption any thing else than the new land? It is submitted, that the rail-track, iron and wooden, and the steamboat, are the fixed property, within the meaning of the exemption. To give it that interpretation, would be to make the exemption annul the entire section, and render the exemption altogether nugatory.

Mr. Chief Justice TANEY delivered the opinion of the court.

The plaintiff in error is a corporation composed of several railroad companies which had been previously chartered by the States of Maryland, Delaware, and Pennsylvania; and which, by corresponding laws of the respective States, were united together, and form one corporation under the name and style of the Philadelphia, Wilmington, and Baltimore Railroad Company. The road of this corporation extends from Philadelphia to Baltimore.

One of the companies which now forms a part of this corporation was originally the Baltimore and Port Deposit Railroad Company, and was chartered by Maryland by an Act passed in 1831, chap. 288.

The road constructed by this company extended from Baltimore to the Susquehanna, lying altogether on the west side of the river.

The Delaware and Maryland Railroad Company was another of the original corporations, and was also chartered by Maryland by the Act of 1831, chap. 296. It extended from the Delaware line to the Susquehanna, and lies on the east side of the river. This company was afterwards, by the Act of 1835, chap. 93, and a corresponding law passed by the State of Delaware, united with the Wilmington and Susquehanna Railroad Company, which had been previously chartered by Delaware; the two companies when united taking the corporate name of the latter.

Afterwards, by an Act of Assembly of Maryland, of 1837, chap. 30, and corresponding laws passed by Delaware and Pennsylvania, the last-mentioned company, together with the Baltimore and Port Deposit Railroad Company, was authorized to unite with the Philadelphia, Wilmington, and Baltimore Railroad Company, which had been previously chartered in the States where it was situated; and these united companies were incorporated into one, under the name and style of the last-mentioned company, and the corporation thus formed is the plaintiff in error.

In 1841, since the union of these companies, an act of Assembly of Maryland was passed, imposing a tax for State purposes upon the real and personal property in the State. Under this law, the portion of the road which belonged to the Baltimore and Port Deposit road, before the union last above mentioned, has been assessed as a part of the taxable property in the State, in the manner set forth in the schedule contained in the record. It is admitted that it has been assessed at the same rate with that of individuals, and as prescribed by the law.

The question submitted to this court is, whether this property of the plaintiff in error is liable to be so taxed, under the grants contained in the different charters above referred to.

The charter of the Baltimore and Port Deposit Railroad declared that the property in this road when constructed should be vested in the company, and that the shares of the company should be deemed and considered as personal property. But there is no provision in law exempting its stocks or its property, real or personal, from taxation. And certainly there is no reason why the property of a corporation should be presumed to be exempted, or should not bear its share of the necessary public burdens, as well as the property of individuals. This court on several occasions has held, that the taxing power of a State is never presumed to be relinquished, unless the intention to relinquish is declared in clear and unambiguous terms.

In the act incorporating this company, there is nothing from which such an inference could possibly be drawn; and, standing upon this charter alone, the tax was without doubt lawfully imposed.

Neither can such an inference be drawn from any thing contained in the subsequent law by which this company became finally consolidated with the plaintiff in error. It remained a separate corporation, without any alteration in its charter in this respect, until the union was formed by the Act of 1837. It was situated altogether in the State of Maryland. The Wilmington and Susquehanna Railroad Company was partly in Maryland and partly in Delaware, and owed its existence to a separate charter. And the law which authorizes these two companies to unite themselves with the plaintiff in error declares that this new corporation, that is, the Philadelphia, Wilmington, and Baltimore Railroad Company, shall be entitled within this State to all the powers and privileges and advantages at that time belonging to these two companies. It grants it nothing more.

Now, as these companies held their corporate privileges under different charters, the evident meaning of this provision is, that whatever privileges and advantages either of them possessed should in like manner be held and possessed by the new company, to the extent of the road they had respectively occupied before the union; that it should stand in their place, and possess the power, rights, and privileges they had severally enjoyed in the portions of the road which had previously belonged to them. And this intention is made still more evident by the fourth section of the law, which makes the new corporation responsible for the contracts, debts, obligations, engagements, and liabilities at law or in equity of the several companies, and declares that it shall hold and be entitled to all the estate, real, personal, and mixed, choses in action, &c., belonging to or due to the several companies. The plaintiff in error, therefore, took the property of the Baltimore and Port Deposit Railroad Company with all the liabilities to which it was subject in the hands of that company.

The act which incorporated the Delaware and Maryland Railroad provided that the shares in that company should be deemed and considered personal extate, and should be exempt from any tax or burden, " except upon that portion of the permanent and fixed works which might be in the State of Maryland." And the law of 1835, which authorized the union of this company with the Wilmington and Susquehanna Railroad Company, secured to the united company the property, rights, and privileges which that law or other laws conferred on them or either of them. The original exemption, therefore, of the Delaware and Maryland Railroad Company, as far as it went, was extended to the Wilmington and Susquehanna Railroad Company, and has been continued to the plaintiffs in error. But as the right of taxation on that part of the road is not in question in this suit, we forbear to express an opinion upon it. For if this restriction could be supposed to exempt from taxation the description of property enumerated in the schedule, or any part of it, it could not affect the question before us. The provisions of this charter have never been extended to the portion of the road on the west side of the river, which was constructed under the charter of the Baltimore and Port Deposit Railroad. As that company held it, so it is now held by the plaintiff in error, with the same privileges, powers, and liabilities. And as the property assessed was liable to taxation in the hands of the original corporation, it is equally liable in the hands of the company with which it is now consolidated.

The judgment must therefore be affirmed.

Order.

This cause came on to be heard on the transcript of the record from the Court of Appeals for the Western Shore of Maryland, and was argued by counsel. On consideration whereof, it is now here ordered and adjudged by this court, that the judgment of the said Court of Appeals in this cause be, and the same is hereby, affirmed, with costs and damages at the rate of six per centum per annum.

THE BALTIMORE AND SUSQUEHANNA RAILROAD COMPANY, Plaintiff in in Error, v. ALEXANDER NESBIT and PENELOPE D. GOODWIN.[1]

December Term, 1850.

Taking of Land — When Land vests in Company — Assessment of Damages — Setting aside Assessment.

The State of Maryland granted a charter to a railroad company, in which provision was made for the condemnation of land to the following effect; namely, that a jury should be summoned to assess the damages, which award should be confirmed by the County Court, unless cause to the contrary was shown.

The charter further provided, that the payment, or tender of payment, of such valuation should entitle the company to the estate as fully as if it had been conveyed.

---

[1] 10 Howard's Reports, 395.

Baltimore and Susquehanna Railroad Co. v. Nesbit.

In 1836, there was an inquisition by a jury, condemning certain lands, which was ratified and confirmed by the County Court.

In 1841, the legislature passed an act directing the County Court to set aside the inquisition and order a new one.

On the 18th of April, 1844, the railroad company tendered the amount of the damages, with interest, to the owner of the land, which offer was refused; and on the 26th of April, 1844, the owner applied to the County Court to set aside the inquisition, and order a new one, which the court directed to be done.

The law of 1841 was not a law impairing the obligation of a contract. It neither changed the contract between the company and the State, nor did it divest the company of a vested title to the land.

The charter provided, that, upon tendering the damages to the owner, the title to the land should become vested in the company. There having been no such tender when the act of 1841 was passed, five years after the inquisition, that act only left the parties in the situation where the charter placed them, and no title was divested out of the company, because they had acquired none.

The States have a right to direct a re-hearing of cases decided in their own courts. The only limit upon their power to pass retrospective laws is, that the Constitution of the United States forbids their passing ex post facto laws, which are retrospective penal laws. But a law merely divesting antecedent vested rights of property, where there is no contract, is not inconsistent with the Constitution of the United States.

THIS case was brought up from Baltimore County Court by a writ of error issued under the twenty-fifth section of the Judiciary Act.

The facts in the case are stated in the opinion of the court, to which the reader is referred.

It was argued by *Campbell* and *Yellot*, for the plaintiff in error, and *Johnson*, for the defendants in error.

The counsel for the plaintiff in error made the following points:—

1st. That the charter was a contract between the State of Maryland and the railroad company, and that the Act of 1841, which varies the terms of that contract without the company's assent, is a law impairing the obligation of the contract, and therefore unconstitutional and void. Green v. Biddle, 8 Wheat. 84; Dartmouth College v. Woodward, 4 Wheat. 647, 663, 668, 669, 699, 710, 711, 712.

2d. That the title to the land condemned having vested by the confirmation of the inquisition, and the tender of the money anterior to the action by the Baltimore County Court, under the Act of 1841, that act is unconstitutional, because it divests vested rights, and in this way impairs the obligation of contracts.

Johnson contended,—

That there is nothing of the character of a contract in the charter, that, by the Constitution of the United States, deprives the legislature of the State of the power to order a rehearing of the case.

Satterlee *v.* Matthewson, 2 Pet. 380; Livingston's Lessee *v.* Moore et al., 7 Pet. 469; Wilkinson *v.* Leland, 2 Pet. 627; s. c., 10 Pet. 294; Watson *v.* Mercer, 8 Pet. 88; Charles River Bridge *v.* Warren Bridge, 11 Pet. 420.

Mr. Justice DANIEL delivered the opinion of the court.

This case comes before us from the District of Maryland, upon a writ of error to the court of Baltimore County, prosecuted under the twenty-fifth section of the Judiciary Act.

The facts from which the questions to be adjudged arise are the following.

The legislature of Maryland, by a law of the 18th of February, 1828, incorporated the plaintiff in error by the name and style of the Baltimore and Susquehanna Railroad Company, for the purpose of constructing a railroad from the city of Baltimore to some point or points on the Susquehanna River. To enable this company to acquire such land, earth, timber, or other materials as might be necessary for the construction and repairing of the road, the law above mentioned, by its fifteenth section, authorized the company to agree with the owners of the land and other materials wanted for the purchase or use thereof; and in the event that the company could not agree with the owners, or that the owners were femes covert under age, insane, or out of the county, this section provided that a justice of the peace of the county, upon application, should thereupon issue his warrant to the sheriff, to summon a jury, who, in accordance with the directions contained in the same section of the statute, should value the damages which the owner or owners would sustain, and that the inquisition, signed and sealed by the jury, should be returned by the sheriff to the clerk or prothonotary of his county, to be filed in court, and that the same should be confirmed by said court at its next session, if no sufficient cause to the contrary be shown.

The section further provides, that " such valuation, when paid or tendered to the owner or owners of said property, or to his, her, or their legal representatives, shall entitle the company to the estate and interest in the same thus valued, as fully as if it had been conveyed by the owner or owners of the same; and the valuation, if not received when tendered, may at any time thereafter be recovered from the company without costs by the said owner or owners, his, her, or their legal representatives."

It appears that, under the authority of the statute above cited, an inquisition was (upon the application of the plaintiff in error) held by the sheriff of Baltimore County, on the 13th of December, 1836,

4 *

upon the lands of the defendants in error as possessed by Alexander
Nesbit in the character of *trustee*, and by Penelope D. Goodwin as
cestui que trust, and the damages assessed by the jury upon that
inquisition, for the land to be appropriated to the use of the plaintiff
in error, were to the said Alexander Nesbit *nothing*, and to the said
Penelope Goodwin *five hundred dollars;* that this inquisition having
been returned to the court of Baltimore County, the following order
in relation thereto was made on the 24th of April, 1837: " Ordered,
That this inquisition be ratified and confirmed, no cause to the contrary having been shown." Subsequently to this order of confirmation, it appears that payment of the money assessed for damages to
the lands of the defendants was not tendered by the plaintiff, nor any
measure whatever in relation to this inquisition adopted by them,
prior to the 18th day of April, 1844, on which last day the plaintiff
by its agent tendered to the defendant Penelope D. Goodwin the
sum of $500, the principal of the damages assessed, with $220.42
as interest for seven years four months and five days on the amount
of that assessment, making an aggregate of $720.42. In the mean
time, between the date of the inquisition and the tender just mentioned, namely, at their December session of 1841, the legislature of
Maryland passed a statute, by which they directed, " that the Baltimore County Court should set aside the inquisition found for the
Baltimore and Susquehanna Railroad Company condemning the
lands of Penelope D. Goodwin of said county, and that the said
court direct an inquisition *de novo* to be taken, and that such proceedings be had as in cases where inquisitions in similar cases are set
aside." In obedience to the statute last cited, the court of Baltimore
County, upon the petition of the defendants in error, presented to
them on the 26th of April, 1844, entered a rule upon the plaintiff in
error to show cause, on the 11th day of May succeeding, why the
inquisition should not be set aside, and an inquisition *de novo*
directed as prayed for, and, after hearing counsel for and against the
application, did, on the 13th of May, 1847, order and adjudge, that
the inquisition returned in that case be set aside, and that hereafter
the court will upon application of the petitioners provide for the
taking of an inquisition *de novo*, according to law.

The court of Baltimore County is admitted to be the highest in
the State in which a decision upon this matter could be had, there
being no appeal allowed from its judgment.

The plaintiff in error insists, —

1st. That, its charter being a contract between itself and the State,
the Act of 1841, having varied that contract without the assent of the

company, was a law impairing the obligation of a contract, and therefore unconstitutional and void.

2d. That, the title to the land condemned having vested by the confirmation of the inquisition, and the tender of the money anterior to the judgment of the Baltimore County Court under the Act of 1841, this act of the legislature is unconstitutional, because it divests vested rights, and in this way impairs the obligation of contracts.

In considering the two propositions here laid down by the plaintiff in error, the first criticism to which they would seem to be obnoxious is this, that they assume as the groundwork for the conclusions they present, that which remains to be demonstrated by a fair interpretation of the legislative action which it is sought to impugn. For instance, with respect to the first proposition, admitting the charter of the plaintiff to be a contract, the reality and character of any variation thereof by the legislature must be shown, before it can be brought within the inhibition of the Constitution. So, too, with respect to the second charge, it must certainly be shown that there was a perfect investment of property in the plaintiff in error by contract with the legislature, and a subsequent arbitrary divestiture of that property by the latter body, in order to constitute their proceeding an act impairing the obligation of a contract.

The mode of proceeding prescribed by the fifteenth section of the charter of incorporation, for the acquiring of land and other materials for constructing the road, has been already stated. Let us now inquire by what acts to be performed by the company, and at what period of time, the investiture of such land and other property in them was to become complete,—what conditions or stipulations were imposed on the plaintiff in error as necessary to the completion of their contract. This will be indispensable in order to ascertain whether any variation of these conditions, amounting to an infraction of the contract, has been made by the Maryland legislature. After declaring that the inquisition, when returned, if no objection be made, shall be recorded, the fifteenth section provides that the *payment* or *tender* of the valuation to the owner of the land, &c., shall entitle the company to the estate and interest in the same as fully as if it had been conveyed by the owner or owners thereof. Thus it appears that it is the payment or tender of the value assessed by the inquisition which gives title to the company, and consequently, without such payment or tender, no title could, by the very terms of the law, have passed to them. Have the legislature by any subsequent arrangement abrogated or altered this condition, or the consequences which were to flow from its performance? From the period of the assessment to the 18th of April, 1844, this record discloses no evidence of any acceptance by the company of the proceedings under the inquisition, or such at least as could bind them. It can hardly be questioned, that, without acceptance by the acts and in the mode prescribed, the company were not bound; that if they had been dis- satisfied with the estimate placed upon the land, or could have pro- cured a more eligible site for the location of their road, they would have been at liberty before such acceptance wholly to renounce the inquisition. The proprietors of the land could have no authority to coerce the company into its adoption. This being the case, there could up to this point be no mutuality, and hence no contract, even in the constrained and compulsory character in which it was created and imposed upon the proprietors by the authority of the statute. This view of the matter seems to accord with the opinion of the Chancellor of Maryland in his construction of this very charter, in the case of Compton v. The Baltimore and Susquehanna Railroad Company, where he uses this language: "In the taking of an inqui- sition under this and similar statutory provisions, it must appear that the authority given has been pursued; and as under a writ of *ad quod damnum* there should be no unreasonable delay, much less could any fraudulent practice be allowed to pass without check or rebuke." 3 Bland's Chancery Reports, 391. Five years after this inquisition, during all which interval this company neglects or omits the fulfilment of the essential condition on performance of which its title depended, the legislature again interposes; and it may be asked in what respects this interposition amounted to an abrogation or variation of any contract which the legislative body itself, rather than the proprie- tors of the land, had been instrumental in making. We think this interposition in no respect impaired or contravened the contract alleged to have been previously existing; that it is perfectly consist- ent with all its conditions, and leaves the parties precisely as they stood from the passage of the charter, and at full liberty to insist upon whatever rights or interests that law had granted. It divested no rights of property, because, as we have shown, none had been vested. This intervention was simply the award of a new trial of the proceedings under the inquisition, which proceedings were of no avail as a judgment, after such new trial was allowed. This inter- vention, too, was the exercise of power by the legislature supposed by that body to belong legitimately to itself; whether this authority was strictly legislative or judicial, according to the distribution of power in the State government, was a question rather for that government than for this court to determine.

What exact partition of powers, legislative, executive, or judicial, the people of the several States in their domestic organization may or should apportion to the different departments of their respective governments, is an inquiry into which this court would enter with very great reluctance.

It might seem advantageous to some of the States that the judicial and legislative authorities or functions of the government should be blended in the same body; and that the legislature should in all cases exercise powers similar to those now vested in one branch of the British Parliament, and, as in some specified instances, in one of the houses of our own national legislature. Should such an organization be adopted by a State, whatever might be thought of its wisdom, where beyond the body politic of the State would exist any power to impugn its legitimacy? But in truth no such inquiry regularly arises upon this record. The only questions presented for our consideration, the only questions we have authority to consider here, are, — 1st, Whether under their charter of incorporation and the proceedings therein directed, and which have been had in pursuance of that charter, the plaintiff in error has, by *contract with the State*, been invested with certain perfect absolute rights of property? And, 2dly, Whether such contract, if any such existed, has been impaired by subsequent legislation of the State, by a divestiture of those rights? To each of these questions we reply in the negative; because, as has already been shown, the conditions of the charter, — conditions indispensable to the vesting of a title in the plaintiff in error, — never were in due time and in good faith fulfilled; nor, until after the new trial had been ordered by the legislature, pretended to be complied with.

If it were necessary to sustain by precedent the authority or practice of the State legislature in awarding a new trial, or in ordering a proceeding in the nature of an appeal, after litigation actually commenced, or even after judgment, and as to which provision for a new trial or appeal had not been previously made, a very striking example from this court might be adduced in the case of Calder and wife *v.* Bull and wife, decided as long since as 1798, and reported in the 3d of Dallas, p. 386. The facts of that case are thus stated by Chase, Justice, in delivering his opinion : — "The legislature of Connecticut, on the 2d of May, 1795, passed a resolution or law, which, for the reasons assigned, set aside a decree of the Court of Probate for Hartford on the 21st of March, 1794, which decree disapproved of the will of Norman Morrison, made the 21st of August, 1779, and refused to record said will; and granted a new hearing by the said Court of Probate, with liberty of appeal therefrom within six months. A new hearing was had in virtue of this resolution or law, before the said Court of Probate, who, on the 27th of July, 1795, approved the will, and ordered it to be recorded. In August, 1795, appeal was had to the Superior Court of Hartford, who, at February term, 1796, affirmed the decree of the Court of Probate. Appeal was had to the Supreme Court of Errors of Connecticut, who, in June, 1796, adjudged that there were no errors."

" The effect," says this same judge, " of the resolution or law of Connecticut above stated is to revise a decision of one of its inferior courts, and to direct a new hearing of the case by the same Court of Probate that passed the decree against the will of Norman Morrison. By the existing law of Connecticut, a right to recover certain property had vested in Calder and wife in consequence of a decision of a court of justice, but in virtue of a subsequent resolution or law, and the new hearing thereof, and the decision in consequence, this right to recover certain property was divested, and the right to the property declared to be in Bull and wife, the appellees." Upon a full examination of this case, the court being of the opinion that the resolution or law of Connecticut awarding the new trial, with right of appeal, did not fall within the technical definition of an *ex post facto* law, and there being no contract impaired or affected by that resolution, they by a unanimous decision sustained the judgment founded upon that resolution.

That there exists a general power in the State governments to enact retrospective or retroactive laws, is a point too well-settled to admit of question at this day. The only limit upon this power in the States by the Federal Constitution, and therefore the only source of cognizance or control with respect to that power existing in this court, is the provision that these retrospective laws shall not be such as are technically *ex post facto*, or such as impair the obligation of contracts. Thus, in the case of Watson et al. *v.* Mercer, 8 Peters, 110, the court say : " It is clear, that this court has no right to pronounce an act of the State legislature void, as contrary to the Constitution of the United States, from the mere fact that it divests antecedent vested rights of property. The Constitution of the United States does not prohibit the States from passing retrospective laws generally, but only *ex post facto* laws. Now it has been solemnly settled by this court, that the phrase *ex post facto* is not applicable to civil laws, but to penal and criminal laws." . For this position is cited the case of Calder *v.* Bull, already mentioned ; of Fletcher *v.* Peck, 5 Cranch, 138 ; Ogden *v.* Saunders, 12 Wheat. 266 ; and Satterlee *v.* Matthewson, 2 Peters, 380. Now it must be apparent that the act of the Maryland legislature of December, 1841, simply ordering a new trial of the inquisition, does not fall within any definition given of an *ex post facto* law, and is not therefore assailable on that account. We have already shown that this law impaired the obligation of no

Baltimore and Susquehanna Railroad Co. v. Nesbit.

contract, because at the time of its passage, and in virtue of any proceeding had under the charter of the company, no contract. between the company on the one hand, and the State or the proprietors of the land on the other, in reality existed. We therefore adjudge the act of the legislature of Maryland of December, 1841, and the proceedings of the court of Baltimore County had in pursuance thereof, to be constitutional and valid, and order that the judgment of the said court be, and the same is hereby, affirmed.[1]

Order.

This cause came on to be heard on the transcript of the record from the Baltimore County Court, and was argued by counsel. On consideration whereof, it is now here ordered and adjudged by this court, that the judgment of the said Baltimore County Court in this cause be, and the same is hereby, affirmed, with costs.

---

[1] In England it is held that after a railway company has given notice of its intention to take land, it is not at liberty to recede from the step, but is bound to go forward with the proceedings necessary to ascertain the price and complete the transfer. The relation of vendor and purchaser is established by the notice, the transaction being regarded as strictly analogous to a sale by the owner himself. It is, indeed, called a Parliamentary contract. The consent of the legislature takes the place of the owner's consent. The legislature, on behalf of the owner, offers the land to the company upon certain conditions, and a notice of the intention of the company to take the land is regarded as an acceptance of the terms. The contract then is complete, and the owner may insist upon a specific performance in the same manner as though the offer had emanated from himself, and he had given the company the refusal of the land upon the condition prescribed by the legislature. Rex v. The Hungerford Market Company, 4 Barnewall & Adolphus, 327; Doe v. The London and Croydon R. Co., 1 English Railway Cases, 257; Stone v. The London and Croydon R. Co., Id. 375; Tawney v. The Lynn & Ely R. Co., 4 English Railway Cases, 615; Burkinshaw v. The Birmingham & Oxford Junction R. Co., 4 English Law & Eq. Rep. 489. In the latter case Baron Alderson in delivering the judgment of the court, said, "We entirely concur in the opinion, that when a company, as here, give notice to a party that they require his lands for their works, it amounts to an agreement by them for a purchase of those lands, assented to by the opposite party, on the terms of making the compensation in the way appointed by the act, under which such notice is given, and binds both parties finally."

In Massachusetts it was determined, in the case of Harrington v. The Commissioners of Berkshire, 22 Pickering, 263, that where the county commissioners had assessed the damages to a land-owner for laying out a highway across his land, he was entitled to such damages notwithstanding the road was discontinued before it was built, and the land was never actually taken. And in Maine and New Hampshire it has also been held, that where a road was so discontinued without being built, an action could not be maintained to recover back damages which had been paid to the land-owner. Westbrook v. North, 2 Greenleaf's Rep. 179; Hampton v. Coffin, 4 New Hampshire, 517.

THE RICHMOND, FREDERICKSBURG, AND POTOMAC RAILROAD COMPANY, Plaintiffs in Error, v. THE LOUISA RAILROAD COMPANY.[1]

December Term, 1851.

Grant of Exclusive Privileges — Contract of the State — How far subsequent Grant is a violation of.

The legislature of Virginia incorporated the stockholders of the Richmond, Fredericksburg, and Potomac Railroad Company, and in the charter pledged itself not to allow any other railroad to be constructed between those places, or any portion of that distance ; the probable effect would be to diminish the number of passengers travelling between the one city and the other upon the railroad authorized by that act, or to compel the said company, in order to retain such passengers, to reduce the passage-money.

Afterwards the legislature incorporated the Louisa Railroad Company whose road came from the West and struck the first-named company's track nearly at right angles, at some distance from Richmond ; and the legislature authorized the Louisa Railroad Company to cross the track of the other, and continue their road to Richmond.

In this latter grant, the obligation of the contract with the first company is not impaired within the meaning of the Constitution of the United States.

In the first charter, there was an implied reservation of the power to incorporate companies to transport other articles than passengers ; and if the Louisa Railroad Company should infringe upon the rights of the Richmond Company, there would be a remedy at law, but the apprehension of it will not justify an injunction to prevent them from building their road.

Nor is the obligation of the contract impaired by crossing the road. A franchise may be condemned in the same manner as individual property.

(Mr. Justice DANIEL, did not sit in this cause.)

THIS case was brought up from the Court of Appeals of the State of Virginia, by a writ of error, issued under the 25th section of the Judiciary Act.

The facts in the case are stated in the opinion of the court.

It was argued by *Robinson,* for the plaintiffs in error, and *Lyons* and *Johnson,* for the defendants in error.

Robinson, for the plaintiffs in error, made the following points : —

1. That, under the Act passed the 25th of February, 1834, incorporating the stockholders of the Richmond, Fredericksburg, and Potomac Railroad Company, Sess. Acts, 1833 – 4, p. 127, there is, by force of the 38th section, copied in the record, at p. 165, and of what

has been done under the act, a contract, the obligation of which can.
not be impaired.by any State law. Fletcher v. Peck, 6 Cranch, 135,
136, 137; Terret, &c. v. Taylor, &c. 9 Id. 50; Wilkinson v. Leland,
&c. 2 Pet. 657; State of New Jersey v. Wilson, 7 Cranch, 166;
Green v. Biddle, 8 Wheat. 92; Providence Bank v. Billings, &c. 4
Pet. 560; Dartmouth College v. Woodward, 4 Wheat. 637; State of
New Jersey v. Wilson, 7 Cranch, 164; Armstrong, &c. v. Treasurer
of Athens Co. 16 Pet. 289; Gordon v. The Appeal Tax Court,
3 How. 133.

2. That a court of equity has jurisdiction to protect the plaintiffs
.in the enjoyment of their chartered privileges, and should award an
injunction to restrain the defendants from any acts which would
impair the obligation of the contract under which the plaintiffs
claim; from any acts which the defendants are bound (whether by
contract or duty) to abstain from. Green v. Biddle, 8 Wheat. 91;
Opinion of Kent, J., in Livingston v. Van Ingen, 9 Johns. 585 to
589; Coats v. Clarence Railway Company, 1 Russ. & Mylne, 181;
4 Cond. Eng. Ch. Rep. 378; Frewin v. Lewis, 1 Mylne & Craig, 255;
18 Eng. Ch. Rep. 255; Canal Company v. Railroad Company, 4 Gill
& Johns. 3; Osborn v. United.States Bank, 9 Wheat. 838, 841; Stevens v. Keating, 2 Phillips, 334; 22 Eng. Ch. Rep. 334; The Attorney-General v. The Great Northern Railway, 3 Eng. Law & Eq.
263; The Great Western Railroad Company v. The Birmingham and
Oxford Railroad Company, 2 Phillips, 597; Williams v. Williams,
2 Swanst. 253; Dietrichsen v. Cabburn, 2 Phillips, 52; 22 Eng. Ch.
Rep. 52, and class of cases there referred to; Kemp v. Sober, 4 Eng.
Law & Eq. R. 64.

3. That the exercise of such jurisdiction should not be declined,
because of the provision in the 18th section of the act incorporating
the stockholders of the Louisa Railroad Company, Sess. Acts, 1835-6,
p. 174, sect. 18, or in the 13th section of the act prescribing general
regulations for the incorporation of railroad companies. Sess. Acts,
1836-7, p. 107, sect. 13. For even if those provisions apply to the
defendants' work between the junction and Richmond, (and the
plaintiffs, p. 22, insist they do not,) yet following, as they do,
sections relating to proceedings for ascertaining the damages to a
proprietor for the condemnation of his land, it is manifest they were
only intended for the case of such a proprietor, asking for an injunction to stay the proceedings of a company which is taking his land
for its work, and though under the case of the Tuckahoe Canal
Company v. The Tuckahoe and James River Railroad Company,
11 Leigh 42, cited in the answer, p. 169, 174, they may apply to land
of one corporation taken for the work of another, yet they are not

intended for, and are inapplicable to the case of a company enjoying
a right under a contract with the State, which asks to be protected
in that enjoyment against another company, claiming, not under a
prior but a subsequent grant.   And 2, whatever may have been the
intention of those acts, yet being passed after the grant in the 38th
section of the plaintiff's charter, they cannot be allowed to impair
the obligation of the contract arising under that grant; but the
plaintiffs claiming under it, are entitled to whatever is necessary to
make that grant effectual and protect them in the enjoyment of their
rights.   Babcock v. Western Railroad Corporation, 9 Met. 556;
Blakesley v. Whieldon, 1 Hare, 180; 23 Eng. Ch. Rep. 180; Green
v. Biddle, 8 Wheat. 75; Bronson v. Kinzie et al. 1 How. 319;
McCracken v. Hayward, 2 How. 612.

4. That the court, in respect to those matters which are distinctly
raised, should declare the rights of the plaintiffs, and upon such
declaration decree an injunction in terms ascertaining the extent of
the right.   Cother v. The Midland Railway, 2 Phil. 472; 22 Eng.
Ch. Rep. 472.

5. That from the facts stated in the bill, and not denied, and also
from the map of Mr. Crozet, it is obvious that the probable effect of
allowing the defendants to have a railroad between the city of Richmond and the city of Washington, for that portion of said distance
which is from the junction to Richmond, will be to diminish the
number of passengers travelling between the city of Richmond and
the city of Washington, upon the plaintiffs' railroad, or to compel
them, in order to retain such passengers, to reduce the passage-
money. And if such would be the probable effect, the defendants
(as is contended in the petition, as well as in the bill,) should, until
the expiration of the thirty years mentioned in the plaintiffs' charter,
have been enjoined from constructing their railroad for said portion
of the distance.   Rankin v. Huskisson, 4 Sim. 13; 6 Eng. Ch. Rep. 7;
Blakemore v. Glamorganshire Canal Navigation, 1 Myl. & Keen, 154;
6 Eng. Ch. Rep. 544, and cases before cited.   And the defendants
having, notwithstanding the warning given by the letter of the 18th
of December, 1848, and by the institution of this suit, proceeded with
such construction, they might and should at the hearing, have been
enjoined, and ought now to be enjoined from further constructing or
using their railroad for that portion of the distance.   Lane v. Newdigate, 10 Ves. 192.   And if the construction has been completed,
the injunction against the use should continue not only until the expiration of said thirty years, but for such time after the thirty years
as it may reasonably be supposed would be occupied in the construction, if it had not taken place within the thirty years.   For, as

the bill insists, the protection will not be preserved to the extent to which it is granted, if immediately on the expiration of the thirty years there can be opened for transportation, a railroad constructed within that period.

6. That although an injunction to the extent mentioned in the preceding point would, as contended in the petition, give no higher security to the plaintiffs than was intended by the legislature, yet if the court do not grant it to that extent, it should, at least, prohibit acts, the probable effect of which would be to diminish the number of passengers travelling between the city of Richmond and the city of Washington, upon the plaintiffs' railroad, or to compel the plaintiffs, in order to retain such passengers, to reduce the passage-money; it should make such prohibition to whatever extent may be necessary to protect the plaintiffs in the enjoyment of their rights.

7. That the prohibition should be of all transportation of passengers on the defendants' railroad between Richmond and the junction; 1st, upon the ground taken in the bill, and the answer, that he who travels only over a portion of the railroad, equally with him who travels over the whole line, is, within the meaning of the 38th section of the plaintiffs' charter, a passenger travelling between (that is, over the whole, or some part of the intermediate space between) the cities of Richmond and Washington; a ground sustained in part by the judge, and strongly fortified by the views presented in the petition, and, 2d, upon the ground that such prohibition is necessary to protect the plaintiffs in respect to passengers travelling the whole distance between those cities. For, in the absence of such prohibition, the Louisa Company may take passengers at reduced rates between Richmond and the junction, as pointed out in the bill, and between the junction and Washington or Alexandria give through tickets in conjunction with the Orange and Alexandria railroad.

8. That if the court do not prohibit all transportation of passengers on the defendants' railroad between Richmond and the junction, it should, at the least, prohibit the transportation by the defendants on their railroad of passengers travelling between the city of Richmond and the city of Washington. The necessity for an injunction to this extent is not at all obviated by the concession remarked on in the answer. Nor is the remark of the judge, that "to award the injunction now, would be to inflict a present, certain, and serious injury upon one party, to prevent a remote, uncertain, and possible injury to the other," well founded as to the injunction here proposed. For no injury is inflicted on the defendants by requiring them to abstain from what it is their duty to abstain from. While on the other hand, a remedy far more effectual than any at law can be had

in equity through its restraining power, which, besides awarding the injunction as here proposed, may, and it is submitted, should, in aid of such injunction, prohibit through tickets between Richmond and Washington, at points south of Richmond and north of Washington, by the Louisa road.

9. That the final decree in these suits in the State court should be reversed in the Supreme Court; and this court should proceed to pass such decree as the State court which made such final decree should have passed, to wit: in the second case, for obvious reasons, some of which are stated in the answer to the bill in that case, it should dissolve the injunction and dismiss the bill with costs; and in the first and principal case, it should award such injunction as is proper, and decree against the defendants the costs. The writ of error issued under the Act of Congress, is to be so used as to effect the object. Gelston v. Hoyt, 3 Wheat. 303. The mandate for execution should issue to the Circuit Court of Chancery for the county of Henrico. Clerke v. Harwood, 3 Dall. 342.

The points made by the counsel for the defendants in error, were the following:

1. That this court has no jurisdiction of the case, the court of final resort in Virginia not having pronounced a final decree or judgment, but having simply refused to relieve the complainants by injunction, in the face of the statute of the State. This refusal to allow an appeal is no affirmance of the reasons of the court below.

2. That the appellants have not such a monopoly as they claim. That the grant which they insist upon as contained in the 38th section of their charter is void: 1. Because it is unintelligible. 2. Because it is impracticable, as no standard is furnished in the charter, or elsewhere, by which any tribunal can determine what is the extent of the grant or its limitation; and, therefore, no means exist by which to determine when the grant is violated, and when not, according to its terms; no distance being furnished within which, to the right or left of the existing road, another road shall not be made. The franchise claimed is, therefore, undefined, and therefore void; or, if defined, as the appellants insist, it confers upon them an unlimited power over the territory, highways, and people of Virginia, and over the legislative power of the State, and the power to advance and improve the State, which the legislature had no power to confer, and therefore, it is void.

One legislature had no power to say to all future legislatures that there should never be more than one railroad between Richmond and Washington, without regard to the wants of the country and the capacity of this road to meet them; or that there should be but one for thirty years; and still less could it transfer the right so to declare to a petty corporation. The change of the form does not increase the power; the defect still is a want of power. The name of "contract" cannot conceal or justify the usurpation. The power of internal improvement over the State generally, or over a large portion of it, cannot be bartered away by the legislature. The legislature is clothed with power for the benefit of the people, and the improvement of the State, and a law declaring that it shall not be improved, would be a gross abuse, a usurpation, in fact, of power, which would be void. To that extent the monopoly here claimed goes, if sustained.

III. If the grant is worth any thing, it is only by giving it a reasonable interpretation, having regard to the end proposed; the general interest of the community, and the power of the legislature; and thus interpreted, it only means that the appellants should have a monopoly of the passengers travelling from Richmond to Washington directly, or to such intermediate point as the Fredericksburg railroad could carry them to. This interpretation the appellants deny, and thus make their grant unintelligible. It was not intended to forbid the construction of a railroad to Winchester, or the Ohio, because, when a passenger reached either of those points, he might get on the Baltimore and Ohio road, and thus get to Washington. Nor was it intended that the people residing five, ten, or twenty miles east and west of the Fredericksburg road, should be denied for thirty years the use of a railroad, unless they would first travel to, and then travel upon, the Fredericksburg railroad.

Taking this view, the most favorable for the appellants which can be taken, the decree in Virginia is correct.

IV. The grant to the appellants, under the most enlarged and extravagant view of it, relates only to the profits of passengers. It has no reference to freights, and was never intended to have, and if intended, cannot, by its words, have the effect to denude the legislature of the power to authorize a railroad to carry agricultural products, and other freights; and therefore the decree in Virginia was right. The court had, therefore, no power to prevent the construction of the road. If it could do any thing, it could only restrain the improper use of it, when a proper case should be made, which was not made by the appellants.

V. There was no violation of the rights of the appellants in authorizing the Louisa Company to cross their road, because they could do so only upon condition of paying the value of the privilege, even to the extent, if necessary, of the entire value of the franchise. A franchise is but a qualified property, and cannot, therefore, be more

5 *

sacred and inviolable than the unqualified property of the owner in fee, whose property is condemned for the purposes of the franchise; over every franchise the "*jus publicum*" must prevail, as it does over all other property. 3 Leigh, 318; 11 Leigh, 42; 11 Peters, 544, 549, 567, 638, 641, 646; 6 How. 507.

If the opposite conclusion can be maintained, then the monstrous result follows, that the railroad of the appellants is an impassable barrier between Eastern and Western Virginia, which can never, at any point, be crossed by another railroad. The legislature never intended to erect such a barrier, and had not the power to do it if they would.

VI. If the appellants sustained any wrong, their remedy was not by injunction. 1. Because an injunction must have inflicted enormous and certain mischief upon the appellees, while the injury to the appellants, if it was denied, was uncertain, hypothetical, and might never occur, and could be redressed without an injunction. In such cases an injunction is never awarded.

2. Because the chancery courts in Virginia have, by law, no jurisdiction to grant an injunction in a case like the present. (See acts referred to in the answer, viz., 13th sect. of Gen. Railroad Law, 1837, and 18th sect. of the Charter of the Louisa Company.) And Virginia alone can prescribe the jurisdiction of her own courts. She can mould her remedies as she pleases. She can abolish her chancery courts as New York has done, or she can define their jurisdiction at pleasure; and this court has no power to say that she shall have chancery courts, or, if she has them, they shall exercise a jurisdiction forbidden by her laws. She may be bound to provide some remedy · for wrong, but she is the exclusive and sovereign judge of the form of the remedy. But she is not bound to furnish any remedy for the courts of the United States. The judiciary act of the United States applies only when she does provide a remedy.

VII. As to the last bill filed by the appellants, this court can have no jurisdiction. A refusal of an injunction is not a final decree under any interpretation of those words, for a new bill may be presented every day, and the refusal of one is no bar to another. A court may refuse an injunction, and yet at the hearing decide for the plaintiff.

The Supreme Court of the United States does not sit to revise the Virginia Chancellors upon applications for injunctions.

The following authorities will be relied upon in the argument by the counsel for the appellees, viz : —

I. 6 Howard, 209; Gibbons v. Ogden, 6 Wheaton, 448.

II. 11 Peters, 467, 547; 6 Cranch, 133, 135; 3 Dall. 388; Vattel, 4, 14, 40, 41; Domat, book 1, tit. 6, sect. 1; Puffend., book 8, c. 5, sect. 7; Attorney-General v. Burridge, 10 Price, 372, 373; Locke on Government, 304, 307.

III. Johnson's Dictionary — " Between."

V. Vattel 40, 41, 103 ; Hawkins v. Barney's Lessee, 5 Peters, 457 ; Coats v. The Clarence Railway Co., 1 Russell & Mylne, 181.

VI. Eden on Injunction, 236; Earl of Ripon et al. v. Hobart, 3 Mylne & Keen, 169, 174 ; Attorney-General v. Nichol, 16 Vesey, 342; Bonaparte v. The Camden & Amboy Railroad, 1 Baldwin, C. C. Reps., 205 ; Jackson v. Lamphire, 3 Peters, 280.

Mr. Justice GRIER delivered the opinion of the court.

This case comes before us on a writ of error to the Court of Appeals of Virginia.

The appellants filed their bill in the Superior Court of Chancery for the Richmond Circuit, setting forth that, on the 25th of February, 1834, the General Assembly of Virginia passed an act entitled " An act to incorporate the stockholders of the Richmond, Fredericksburg and Potomac Railroad Company." That in order to induce persons to embark their capital in a work of great public utility, the legislature pledged itself to the said company, that, in the event of the completion of the said road from the city of Richmond to the town of Fredericksburg, within a certain time limited by said act, the General Assembly would not, for the period of thirty years from the completion of said railroad, allow any other railroad to be constructed between those places, or any portion of that distance, the probable effect of which would be to diminish the number of passengers travelling between the one city and the other upon the railroad authorized by said act, or to compel the said company, in order to retain such passengers, to reduce the passage-money ; that the stock was afterwards subscribed, the charter issued, and the road constructed, within the time limited by the act; that on the 18th of February, 1836, an act was passed incorporating " The Louisa Railroad Company, for the purpose of constructing a railroad from some point on the line of the Richmond, Fredericksburg, and Potomac Railroad, in the neighborhood of Taylorsville, passing by or near Louisa court-house to a point in the county of Orange, near the eastern base of the southwest mountains, with leave to extend it to the Blue Ridge, or across the same to Harrisonburg; that on the 28th of December, 1838, this railroad was opened from Louisa court-house to the junction with complainants' road.   The bill then gives a history of the several contracts made between the two companies for the transportation of the freight and passengers of the Louisa Railroad from the junction to Richmond, and of the frequent and protracted disputes and difficulties which arose between the two corporations on the subject of the compensation to be paid to the complainants for such services, the particulars of which it is unnecessary to mention ;, the result being, that the respondents insisting that the demands made by complainants for this service were exorbitant and oppressive, finally petitioned the legislature for leave to extend their road from the junction to the city of Richmond. That complainants resisted, and protested against the passage of such an act, as an infringement of the rights guaranteed to them by their act of incorporation. Nevertheless, the legislature on the 23d of March, 1848, passed an act authorizing the respondents to extend their road from the junction to the dock, in the city of Richmond, unless the complainants would comply with certain terms which were deemed reasonable ; and these terms being refused by complainants, the respondents commenced the construction of their road to Richmond, and to extend it across the road of complainants at the junction.

The bill insists that the grant of the Act of the 27th of March, 1848, to the Louisa Railroad Company, is inconsistent with the previous grant to the complainants, and impairs the obligation of the contract made with them; that the lands condemned for their franchise cannot be taken from the complainants for the use of the respondents, and that they have, therefore, no right to build their road across the road of complainants. It prays, therefore, that the respondents may be enjoined: 1st. From entering upon any lands which have been condemned for the use of complainants' road, for the purpose of constructing a railroad across it; 2d. That the respondents may be enjoined from all further proceedings towards the construction of a railroad between the junction and the city of Richmond; and, 3d. That they may be enjoined from " transporting on the railroad so proposed, persons, property, or the mail, and especially from transporting passengers travelling between the city of Richmond and the city of Washington."

The respondents, in their answer, deny " that the act of Assembly which authorizes them to construct their road from its terminus at the city of Richmond, in any manner violates the bill of rights, or Constitution of Virginia, or the Constitution of the United States, or any right guaranteed to the complainants by their act of incorporation., They deny also, that it is their purpose to invade or violate any right or privileges of the complainants by the manner in which they shall use their road if they are permitted to construct it."

The State court decided : 1st. That the privilege or monopoly guaranteed to the complainants by the 38th section of their act of incorporation, was that of transporting passengers between Richmond and Washington; but that the legislature, by that enactment, did not part with the power to authorize the construction of railroads between

Richmond and Fredericksburg for other purposes; that they had, therefore, the right to authorize the extension of respondents' road to the dock in the city of Richmond, and consequently the court refused to enjoin the respondents from constructing their road. 2d. That a grant of a franchise to one company to make a railroad or canal, is not infringed by authorizing another railroad or canal to be laid across it, on paying such damages as may accrue to the first, in consequence thereof. The injunction for this purpose was therefore refused.

3d. "That if the Louisa Company shall hereafter use their road by transporting passengers in violation of the rights guaranteed to complainants by the 38th section of their charter, the remedy at law seems to be plain, easy, and adequate; if, however, it should, from any cause, prove to be inadequate, it may be proper to interpose by injunction, and that will depend on the facts which may then be made to appear."

The decree having dismissed the complainants' bill, was "a final decree or judgment;" and that decree having been affirmed by the Court of Appeals by their refusal to entertain an appeal; and, moreover, the record showing that "there was drawn in question the validity of a statute and authority exercised under the State of Virginia," "on the ground of their being repugnant" to that clause of "the Constitution of the United States" which forbids a State to pass "any law impairing the obligation of contracts;" and "the decision of the court being in favor of their validity," there can be no doubt of the jurisdiction of this court to review the decision of the State court.

For this purpose, it will be necessary to set forth, at length, the 38th section of the act of incorporation of the company complainant, which contains the pledge or contract which their bill claims to have been impaired or infringed by the Act of 1848, authorizing the respondents to continue their road from the junction to the dock in Richmond. It is as follows: —

"And whereas the railroad authorized by this act will form a part of the main northern and southern route between the city of Richmond and the city of Washington, and the privilege of transporting passengers on the same, and receiving the passage-money, will, it is believed, be a strong inducement for individuals to subscribe for stock in the company, and the General Assembly considers it just and reasonable that those who embark in the enterprise should not be hereafter deprived of that which forms a chief inducement to the undertaking:

"38. *Be it therefore enacted and declared, and the General Assembly pledges itself to the said company,* That, in the event of the completion of the said railroad from the city of Richmond to the town of Fredericksburg, within the time limited by the act, the General Assembly will not, for the period of thirty years from the completion of the said railroad, allow any other railroad to be constructed between the city of Richmond and the city of Washington, or for any portion of the said distance, the probable effect of which would be to diminish the number of passengers travelling between the one city and the other, upon the railroad authorized by this act, or to compel the company, in order to retain such passengers, to reduce the passage-money: *Provided, however*, That nothing herein contained shall be so construed as to prevent the legislature, at any time hereafter, from authorizing the construction of a railroad between the city of Richmond and the towns of Tappahannock or Urbana, or to any intermediate points between the said city of Richmond and the said towns: *And provided, also*, That nothing herein contained shall be construed to prevent the General Assembly from chartering any other company or companies to construct a railroad from Fredericksburg to the city of Washington."

Two objections were made by the counsel to the validity of this act, on which we do not think it necessary to express an opinion. They are: 1st. That one legislature cannot restrain, control, or bargain away the power of future legislatures, to authorize public improvements for the benefit of the people. 2d. That the grant made by this section is void for uncertainty, being both unintelligible and impracticable, furnishing no standard by which any tribunal can determine when the grant is violated and when not, according to its terms.

For the purposes of the present decision, we shall assume that the legislature of Virginia had full power to make this contract, and that the State is bound by it; and moreover, that the franchise granted is sufficiently defined and practicable for the court to determine its extent and limitations.

It is a settled rule of construction adopted by this court, "that public grants are to be construed strictly."

This act contains the grant of certain privileges by the public to a private corporation, and in a matter where the public interest is concerned; and the rule of construction in all such cases is now fully established to be this: "That any ambiguity in the terms of the contract must operate against the corporation, and in favor of the public; and the corporation can claim nothing but what is clearly given by the act." See Charles River Bridge v. Warren Bridge, 11 Pet. 544.

Construing this act with these principles in view, where do we find that the legislature have contracted to part with the power of constructing other railroads, even between Richmond and Fredericksburg, for carrying coal or other freight? Much less can they be said to have contracted, that no railroad connected with the western part of the State, shall be suffered to cross the complainant's road, or run parallel to it, in any portion of its route. Such a contract cannot be elicited from the letter or spirit of this section of the act.

On the contrary, the preamble connected with this section shows that the complainants' road was expected to " form a part of the main northern and southern route between the city of Richmond and the city of Washington;" and the inducement held out to those who should subscribe to its stock, was a monopoly " of transporting passengers " on this route, and this is all that is pledged or guaranteed to them, or intended so to be by the act. It contains no pledge that the State of Virginia will not allow any other railroad to be constructed between those points, or any portion of the distance for any purpose; but only a road, " the probable effect of which would be to diminish the number of passengers travelling between the one city and the other, upon the railroad authorized by the act," or to compel the company to reduce the passage-money.

That the respondents will not be allowed to carry the passengers travelling between the city of Richmond and the city of Washington, is admitted; and they deny any intention of so exercising their franchise as to interfere with the rights secured to complainants. That the parties will differ widely as to the construction of the grant, owing to the ambiguity created by the use of the word " between," as it may effect the transportation of passengers travelling to or from the west, is more than probable. But on this application for an injunction against the construction of the respondents' road, the chancellor was not bound to decide the question, by anticipation : And, although he may have thrown out some intimation as to his present opinion on that question, he has very properly left it open for future decision, to be settled by a suit at law, or in equity, " upon the facts of the case as they may then appear." But, however probable this dispute or contest may be, it is not for this court to anticipate it, and volunteer an opinion in advance.

The Act of 1848, authorizing the extension of the complainants' road, is silent as to any grant of power to transport passengers, so as to interfere with the pledge given to complainants; and it is sufficient for the decision of the case before us, to say, that the grant of authority to respondents to extend their road from the junction to the dock at the city of Richmond, does not, *per se*, impair the obligation of the contract contained in the 38th section of the complainants' charter. The conditions annexed to the grant to respondents, by which the complainants were enabled to defeat it, cannot effect the question in any way. If the 38th section of the act of incorporation of complainants does not restrain the legislature from constructing another railroad for any purpose, parallel or near to the complainants', the respondents have a right to proceed with the construction of their road, and the State court was justified in refusing the injunction.

The counsel, very properly, have not insisted in their argument in this court, on this point made in their bill, that the legislature had no power to authorize the construction of one railroad across another. The grant of a franchise is of no higher order, and confers no more sacred title, than a grant of land to an individual; and, when the public necessities require it, the one, as well as the other, may be taken for public purposes on making suitable compensation; nor does such an exercise of the right of eminent domain interfere with the inviolability of contracts. See West River Bridge Company v. Dix, 6 How. 507.

Leaving, therefore, the question, as to the proper construction of the contract or rights guaranteed to the complainants, by this section of their charter, to be settled when a proper case arises, we are of opinion that the State court did not err in refusing to enjoin respondents from constructing their road according to the authority given them by the Act of Assembly of 27th March, 1848, and that said act does not impair the obligation of the contract made with the complainants, in the 38th section of their act of incorporation. The judgment of the Court of Appeals of Virginia is therefore affirmed, with costs.

Mr. Justice McLEAN, Mr. Justice WAYNE, and Mr. Justice CURTIS, dissented.

Mr. Justice CURTIS. I have been unable to agree with the majority of the court in this case, and some of the principles on which a decision depends are of so much importance, as affecting legislation, that I think it proper to state my opinion and the reasons on which it rests.

That the 38th section of the complainants' charter contains a contract between the corporation and the State, the obligation of which the latter cannot impair by any law, must, I think, be admitted. Whether " An act for the extension of the Louisa Railroad to the dock in the city of Richmond," does impair that obligation, depends upon the interpretation which the contract requires; and, inasmuch as it is the duty of this court to determine whether the obligation of

.the contract has been impaired, it is necessarily its duty to decide what is the true interpretation of the contract.

The 38th section, with its preamble, are as follows:

" And whereas the railroad authorized by this act will form a part of the main northern and southern route between the city of Richmond and the city of Washington, and *the privilege of transporting passengers on the same*, and receiving the passage-money, will, it is believed, be a strong inducement to individuals to subscribe for stock in the company, and the General Assembly considers it just and reasonable that those who embark in the enterprise should not be hereafter *deprived of that* which forms a chief inducement to the undertaking.

"38. *Be it therefore enacted and declared, and the General Assembly pledges itself to the said company*, That in the event of the completion of the said railroad from the city of Richmond to the town of Fredericksburg, within the time limited by this act, the General Assembly will not, for the period of thirty years from the completion of the said railroad, allow any other railroad to be constructed between the city of Richmond and the city of Washington, *or for any portion of the said distance, the probable effect of which would be to diminish the number of passengers travelling between the one city and the other, upon the railroad authorized by this act*, or to compel the company, in order to retain such passengers, to reduce the passage-money. *Provided, however*, That nothing herein contained shall be so construed as to prevent the legislature, at any time hereafter, from authorizing the construction of a railroad between the city of Richmond and the towns of Tappahannock or Urbana, or to any intermediate points between the said city of Richmond and the said towns; *And provided, also*, That nothing herein contained shall be construed to prevent the General Assembly from chartering any other company or companies to construct a railroad from Fredericksburg to the city of Washington."

The preamble in effect declares what general object the parties have in view, and the section makes known to what extent and by what means that subject is to be accomplished. That general object is to secure the corporation from being deprived of the passenger travel on its railroad; and the means of prevention are, to prohibit for thirty years the existence of any other road, the probable effect of which would be to diminish the number of passengers travelling between Washington and Richmond upon the railroad of the complainants.

.The first question is, whether what is called the extension of the Louisa road, is a railroad, the probable effect of which would be to diminish those passengers; and this depends on what passengers are, referred to in the contract.

It is maintained by the appellees that only passengers travelling the distance between Washington and Richmond are intended; but this is not consistent either with the substantial object of the parties, or with the language they have employed to make known their agreement. " The privilege of transporting passengers *on the same* and receiving the passage-money," and protection from being " deprived of *that* which forms the chief inducement of the undertaking," would be but imperfectly secured, if limited to one particular class of passengers only. Such a limitation, inconsistent with the apparent object of the parties, is not to be engrafted on the contract unless clearly expressed. It is said that the words, " passengers travelling between the one city and the other," contain this limitation, their meaning being passengers travelling from one city to the other. The word " between," in this clause, admits of that interpretation, but does not require it. That word may also designate any part of the intermediate space, as well as the whole. It may be correctly said that the complainants' railroad is between Richmond and Washington, though it does not traverse the whole distance from one of those cities to the other, and the words which immediately follow, certainly tend strongly to show that it was in this last and more comprehensive sense the word " between " was here used. The whole clause is, " passengers travelling between one city and the other, *upon the railroad authorized by this act.*" But the railroad there referred to, upon the completion of which this contract was to take effect, was only to be from Richmond to Fredericksburg, so that, strictly speaking, passengers could not travel to or from the city of Washington upon the railroad authorized by the act; they could thus pass over only a part of the intermediate space between Washington and Richmond. This clause therefore does not control the evident general intent of the parties to protect the passenger travel, but rather tends to make that general intent more clear. The question being whether the travellers referred to are only those going the whole distance; and one part of the descriptive words, designating where they are travelling, being ambiguous, and the other part, which points out how they are travelling, being clear, the result of the whole is to include all who travel in the intermediate space between the two cities, upon the complainants' railroad. And this construction is still further strengthened by the stipulation that the State will not authorize another road " to be constructed between the city of Washington and the city of Richmond, *or for any portion of the said distance ;*" for if the object of parties was merely to protect the enjoyment by the complainants of the tolls derivable from passengers going from one of those cities to the other, it is highly improbable that the State would have agreed to this broad restriction. Construing the preamble and the section together, I think it was the intention of the parties to secure to the complainants, for the period of thirty years, the exclusive enjoyment of all the railroad passenger travel over every part of the line between Washington and Richmond; and that the mode of security agreed on by the parties was, that the State should not authorize the construction of any such railroad as might probably interfere with that exclusive enjoyment.[1]

In coming to this conclusion I have not overlooked the rule, that grants from States to corporations of such exclusive privileges, are to be construed most strongly against the grantees. But this rule, like its converse, *fortius contra proferentem*, which applies to private grants, is the last to be resorted to, and never to be relied upon, but when all other rules of exposition fail. Bac. Max. reg. 3; 2 Bl. Com. 380; Love v. Pares, 13 East. 86. In Hindekoper's Lessee v. Douglass, 3 Cranch 70, Chief Justice Marshall says: " This is a contract; and although a State is a party it ought to be construed according to those well-established principles which regulate contracts generally." A grant such as is now in question, in consideration of the grantees risking their capital in an untried enterprise, which, if successful will greatly promote the public good, in no proper sense confers a monopoly. It enables the grantees to enjoy, for a limited time, what they may justly be considered as creating. It is in substance and reality, as well as in legal effect, a contract, and in my judgment it is the duty of the court to give it such a construction as will carry it into full effect; imposing on the public no restriction, and no burden, not stipulated for, and depriving the company of no advantage, which the contract, fairly construed, gives. This is required by good faith; and

---

[1] The meaning of the word "*between*," was considered in The Grantham Canal Co. v. The Ambergate, Nottingham, &c. R. Co., 6 Eng. Law & Eq. Rep. 328. The railway company were authorized to build a road from Grantham to Ambergate. From Grantham to Nottingham, the road would compete with the Grantham Canal Company, and from Nottingham to Ambergate, with the Nottingham Canal Co. The statute of incorporation required the railway company, "from and immediately after the opening of the railway *between* Ambergate and Grantham," to purchase all the shares of both the canal companies. The railway company having constructed and opened their road from Grantham to Nottingham, the Grantham Canal Co. brought an action for the price of the shares which the railway company were required to purchase. But the court held that the contingency had not arisen upon which the money was to become payable; that the road having been built only a part of the distance from Grantham to Ambergate was not opened "*between*" those places within the meaning of the statute.

to its demands all technical rules, designed to help the mind to correct conclusions, must yield. Having come to the conclusion that the intentions of the parties to this contract was to secure to the complainants exclusive enjoyment of all railroad passenger travel over every part of the distance between Richmond and Washington, for thirty years, and that the means adopted to effect this object was the promise of the State to authorize the construction of no railroad which might probably interfere with that exclusive enjoyment, the next inquiry is, whether the extension of the Louisa Railroad to the dock in the city of Richmond would probably have that effect. This act enables the Louisa Railroad Company to extend their road, from its junction with the complainants' road, at a point about twenty-four miles from Richmond, to that city, and thus to make another railroad between Richmond and that point on the complainants' road.

That this authority comes within that part of the restrictive stipulation, which describes the route over which another railroad is not to be built, is clear; for it does authorize " another railroad," " for a portion of the distance" "between the cities of Richmond and Washington." But it is said that it does not come within the residue of the restrictive clause, because its probable effect will not be to diminish that passenger travel designed to be secured to the complainants. To this I cannot assent. The Louisa Company, by their original charter, are expressly authorized to carry passengers on their railroad, and when they are empowered by the act now in question to extend their road, it is a necessary implication that the extension is for the same uses, and subject to the same rights, and powers, and privileges as the original road, to which it is to be annexed. And accordingly we find, that by the 5th section of this act, the legislature has prescribed a limit of tolls, as well for passengers as for merchandise, coming from or going to another railroad and passing over the whole length of the Louisa road and each part of it, including the extension.

Passengers using the complainants' road between Richmond and the junction, may be divided into three classes. Those who travel the whole, or a part of the distance between Richmond and the junction, and do not go beyond the junction; those who do go to, or come from points beyond the junction on the complainants' road; and those who travel on the Louisa road, beyond the junction, going west, or coming east. The extension of the Louisa road is adapted to carry all these, and, by the act complained of, the Louisa Company is authorized to construct a road to carry them. It may certainly be assumed, that a corporation, created to conduct a particular business for profit, will do all such business as it is its clear interest, and within its authority to do, and which it was created for the very purpose of doing. And if so, the effect of this extension must be, to transport thereon a part of all these classes of passengers, and thus to diminish the number of those same classes of passengers, who, at the time of the passage of the act in question, used the complainants' road.

As to those passengers who do not use the Louisa road beyond the junction, I am at a loss to perceive any reason why they are not within the description of passenger travel designed to be secured to the complainants; and if they are excluded therefrom, I know of none who would be included, unless upon the interpretation already considered and rejected, that the contract was designed to embrace only passengers travelling the entire distance between Richmond and Washington. It is not absolutely necessary to go any further to find that this extension act impairs the obligation of the contract, by authorizing another road to be built, the probable effect of which would be to diminish the number of passengers travelling on the complainants' road between the junction and Richmond. But it is clear to my mind, that the third class of passengers using the Louisa road, are as much within the contract as any others. To explain my views on this point it is necessary to refer to a few dates.

The complainants were incorporated in February, 1834, and their act of incorporation contained the compact now relied on. Their road was completed and opened for use in January, 1837. In February, 1836, an act was passed incorporating the stockholders of the Louisa Railroad Company. In December, 1838, the Louisa road was opened for use to the Louisa court-house; and from that time to March, 1848, the passengers using the Louisa road, going to or coming from Richmond, and points between that city and the junction, passed over the road of the complainants. In March, 1848, the complainants and the Louisa Company having differed concerning the tolls to be charged by the former on passengers and merchandise going to or coming from the Louisa road, the legislature passed the "Act for the extension of the Louisa Railroad," which contains the following section:—"Be it further enacted, that in case the Richmond, Fredericksburg, and Potomac Railroad Company shall, at the next annual meeting of the stockholders, stipulate and agree, from and after the expiration of the present contract with the Louisa Railroad Company, to carry all passengers and freight coming from the Louisa Railroad from the junction to the city of Richmond, at the same rate per mile as may at the same time be charged by the Louisa Railroad Company on the same passengers and freight; and shall also agree to carry all passengers and freight entered at the city of Richmond for any point on the Louisa Railroad, at the same rate per mile as is charged at the time for the same, by the Louisa Railroad

6 *

Company; and shall also agree to submit to the umpirage of some
third person or persons, to be chosen by the said companies, the compensation to the Richmond, Fredericksburg, and Potomac Railroad
Company for collecting at the depots in Richmond the dues of the
Louisa Railroad Company, and any other matters of controversy,
which may arise between the said companies owing to the connection between them, then this act to be void, or else to remain in full
force." It will thus be seen that the passenger travel, which it is the
object of this act to take away from the complainants' road, had been
de facto a part of its passenger travel between Richmond and the
junction for about ten years. It is maintained that as the Louisa
Railroad, from the junction westward, was the cause of the existence
of this travel upon the complainants' road, between Richmond and
the junction, the Louisa corporation might be empowered to construct another road between those points for the purpose of doing
that business. In other words, that passenger travel actually existing
on the complainants' road, may properly be diminished by the construction of another road for a part of the distance between Richmond and Washington, provided it be done by a party who at some
prior time was instrumental in increasing the passenger travel; that
we are to inquire whether by this new and competing road any more
is to be taken away than was brought by the corporation which
builds it, and if not, then the competing road does not diminish the
number of passengers, travelling on the complainants' road, within
the fair meaning of this contract. I cannot give to this contract
such a construction. It seems to me to be at variance with its express
terms and with what must have been within the contemplation of the
parties when it was entered into. The promise not to authorize any
other railroad between Washington and Richmond, or for any part of
that distance, the probable effect of which would be to diminish the
number of passengers travelling on the complainants' railroad is absolute and unqualified. It contains no reservation in favor of parties
who have been instrumental in bringing that travel to the complainants' road. It extends over the period of thirty years, and applies to
the travel actually existing thereon during every part of that period,
to whatever causes its existence there may be attributable. It must
have been contemplated by the parties that the number of travellers on the complainants' road would increase during the long period
of thirty years; it must have been known to them that this increase
would be likely to arise, among other causes, from the increased number of passengers coming laterally to the line, in consequence of the
construction of other railroads, as well as from increased facilities of
access by other means. They enter into a contract which by its terms

protects this increased travel during the whole period, and by whatever causes produced, just as much as it protects the travel existing
during the first month after the opening of the road. How then can
we engraft upon the contract an exception not found there, and say,
that when it speaks generally of passengers travelling upon the road,
it does not mean passengers which another railroad corporation has
brought there? I am unable to see why not, as much as if a steamboat or stage company had brought them. In my opinion this class
of passengers on the complainants' road, are as truly within the contract as any others; and a railroad, the object of which is take away
this class of passengers from the complainants' road, is one which the
State has promised it would not authorize to be built.

Parties may agree, not only on the substantial rights to be protected, but on the particular mode of protecting them; and if they
do agree on a particular mode, it becomes a part of their contract,
which each party have a just right to have executed. In this compact the parties have agreed on the mode of protection. It is that
the State will not authorize to be built any other railroad, which
would probably have the effect to diminish the number of passengers
on the complainants' road. It is the right to construct, and not the
right to use which the contract restrains. To say that the State
may properly authorize a road to be built, the purpose of which is to
carry passengers, and thus diminish the number of passengers on
the complainants' road, but that the road thus authorized must
not be used to the injury of the complainants' rights, is to strike
out of the contract the stipulation that such a road should not
be authorized to be built.[1] The power of the State to enable a corporation to build another road to carry merchandise only, seems to
me to have nothing to do with this question. When the legislature

---

[1] In Farrar v. Vansittart, 1 Eng. Railw.
Cas. 602, the court granted an injunction
to restrain the defendant and others from
constructing a railway for an unauthorized
purpose, to the injury of the plaintiff. The
plaintiff had leased a farm, the lessor reserving the right to construct and lay down
such ways as might be necessary for carrying away the coal on the granted premises. Under this reservation the lessor
granted to the defendants the right to construct a railway, the object of which appeared to be, not only to carry coal, but
incidentally, at least, to carry on other traf-
fic. The Vice-Chancellor granted an injunction in the first instance, but afterwards, upon the showing of the defendants,
that there was a large body of coal which
it was their primary object to remove, he
dissolved the injunction on the ground that
there was a lawful purpose for which the
road might be used, but he gave leave to
the plaintiff to apply for an injunction if
the defendant should attempt to use the
road for any other purpose. But, upon
appeal, the Lord Chancellor renewed the
injunction until the legal rights of the parties could be determined in a suit at law.

shall adjudge that the public convenience requires another railroad there, to carry merchandise only, and that therefore the power of eminent domain may be exercised to build it, and when a company is found ready to accept such a charter, and risk their funds in its construction, then a case will arise under the power of the legislature to authorize a road for the transportation of merchandise only. But in the law now in question the legislature has not so adjudged; no such charter has been granted, or accepted, and no such road built; but one which the State is by its own promise restrained from autho-: rizing. It seems quite aside from the true inquiry, therefore, to urge that the State might have empowered a company to make a railroad on which to transport merchandise only; for it has not done so.

It has been suggested by one of the defendants' counsel, that though the power of the legislature to enter into a compact for some exclusive privileges is not denied, yet that the legislature had not power to grant such privileges as are here claimed by the complainants, and therefore the State is not bound thereby. This is rested, not upon any express restriction on the powers of the legislature, contained in the Constitution of Virginia, but upon limitations resulting by necessary implication from the nature of the delegated power confided by the people of that State to their government. But if, as must be, and is admitted, it is one of the powers incident to a sovereign State to make grants of rights, corporeal and incorporeal, for the promotion of the public good, it necessarily follows that the legislature must judge how extensive the public good requires those rights to be. Whether the State shall grant one acre of land, or one thousand acres; whether it shall stipulate for the enjoyment of an incorporeal right, in fee, for life or years; whether that incorporeal right shall extend to one or more subjects; and what shall be deemed a fit consideration for the grant in either case, is intrusted to the discretion of the legislative power, when that discretion is not restrained by the constitution under which it acts. This has been the interpretation by all courts, and the practice under all constitutions in the country, so far as I know, and it seems to me to be correct. See Piscataqua Bridge v. New Hamp. Bridge, 7 N. H. Rep. 35, and cases there cited; Enfield Bridge v. The Hart. & N. H. R. R. Co., 17 Conn. R. 40; Washington Bridge v. State, 18 Conn. R. 53.

It remains to consider whether this court has jurisdiction to reverse the decision of the State court.

The Court of Appeals having refused to entertain an appeal, the superior Court of Chancery of the Richmond Circuit, was the highest court of the State, to which the complainants could carry the case; and it is to the decision of that court we must look. The questions are whether that court erroneously decided against a right claimed by the complainants under the Constitution of the United States, and whether the bill was dismissed by reason of that erroneous decision. The points decided are set out with great clearness upon the face of the decree. Their substance is, that the construction of this extension road is lawful, the legislature having power to authorize it; that it may lawfully be used for the transportation of passengers, who, but for the existence of the Louisa road would never have come on the line of the Fredericksburg road; that whether the Louisa Company will use the extension for the transportation of any other passengers, and thus infringe complainants' rights, does not appear; when the supposed case shall occur, it may be proper to interfere by injunction, if, upon the facts of that case, as they shall appear, there is not a plain, adequate, and complete remedy at law.

It is clear, then, that the Chancellor decided, against the right claimed by the complainants, under the Constitution, that this extension should not be constructed. In my opinion, this decision was erroneous. It is clear, also, that he decided against their right, under the Constitution, to be protected in the enjoyment of the passenger travel coming upon their road, in consequence of the existence of the Louisa road. I think this was also erroneous. By reason of these decisions the bill was dismissed. They left nothing but a case of contingent damage, which would not happen at all, if the Louisa Company should carry only passengers coming upon the line of the complainants' railroad by reason of the existence of the Louisa road; there was no certainty to what extent, or under what circumstances, or whether at all, the complainants' rights would be infringed.

Upon these views of the contract of the State, and the rights of the complainants, it necessarily followed that the bill was to be dismissed: for equity would not interfere in a case where the defendants had valuable rights and powers, which they might not exceed, and which they ought not to be restrained from exercising. But on the other hand if the defendants had no such rights or powers; if they were claiming them and about to exercise them, in a manner certain to inflict great and continuing injury on the complainants, the extent of which injury a court of law could not fully ascertain, and could redress, even partially, only by a great multiplicity of suits, then no court of chancery would hesitate to grant relief. It is certain therefore that this bill was dismissed, by reason of, what I consider, the erroneous views taken by the Chancellor, of the rights claimed by the complainant under the Constitution of the United States.

It has been argued that by the local law of Virginia, contained in the general railroad act of that State, the Chancellor had not jurisdiction to grant an injunction to restrain the construction of the extension road. If the Chancellor had so decided and dismissed the bill, for that reason the court could not reverse that decision. But he did not so decide; and I cannot infer that he would so decide if this case were to be remanded, because I am of opinion that the statute relied on has no application to this case.

My opinion is that the decree of the Superior Court of Chancery should be reversed and the case remanded, with such directions as would secure to the complainants the remedy to which they are entitled, to prevent the violation of rights secured to them by the Constitution of the United States.[1]

Order.

This cause came on to be heard on the transcript of the record from the Court of Appeals of the Commonwealth of Virginia, and was argued by counsel. On consideration whereof, it is now here ordered, adjudged, and decreed, by this court, that the decree of the said Court of Appeals in this cause be, and the same is hereby affirmed with costs.

———◆———

THE PHILADELPHIA, WILMINGTON, AND BALTIMORE RAILROAD COMPANY, Plaintiffs in Error, v. SEBRE HOWARD.[2]

December Term, 1851.

Covenant to Pay as work progresses — Right to declare the Contract at an end — Extent of Forfeiture — Variation of work by Direction of Engineer.

In Maryland, the clerk of a county court was properly admitted to prove the verity of a copy of the docket-entries made by him as clerk, because, by a law of Maryland, no technical record was required to be made.

And, moreover, the fact which was to be proved being merely the pendency of an action, proof that the entry was made on the docket by the proper officer was proof that the action was pending, until the other party could show its termination.

Where the question was, whether or not the paper declared upon bore the corporate seal of. the defendants, (an incorporated company,) evidence was admissible to show that, in a former suit, the defendants had treated and relied upon the instrument as one bearing the corporate seal. And it was admissible, although the former suit was not between the same

---

[1] See The Boston & Lowell R. Co. v. The Boston & Maine R. Co. 5 Cush. 375; s. c. *post*; and Tucker v. The Cheshire R. Co. 1 Foster, 29; s. c. *post*.
[2] 13 Howard's Reports, 307.

Philadelphia, Wilmington, & Baltimore Railroad Co. v. Howard.

parties; and although the former suit was against one of three corporations, which had afterwards become merged into one, which one was the present defendant.

The admission of the paper as evidence only left the question to the jury. The burden of proof still remained upon the plaintiff.

The evidence of the president of the company, to show that there was an understanding between himself and the plaintiff, that another person should also sign the paper before it became obligatory, was not admissible, because the understanding alluded to did not refer to the time when the corporate seal was affixed, but to some prior time.

In order to show that the paper in question bore the seal of the corporation, it was admissible to read in evidence the deposition of the deceased officer of the corporation, who had affixed the seal, and which deposition had been taken by the defendants in the former suit.

If the defendants had relied upon the paper in question to defeat the plaintiff in a former suit, they are estopped from denying its validity in this suit. It was not necessary to plead the estoppel, because the state of the pleadings would not have justified such a plea.

Where the covenant purported to be made between two persons by name, of the first part, and the corporate company, of the second part, and only one of the persons of the first part signed the instrument, and the covenant ran between the party of the first part and the party of the second part, it was proper for the person who had signed on the first part to sue alone; because the covenant enured to the benefit of those who were parties to it.

In this particular case a covenant to finish the work by a certain day, on the one part, and a covenant to pay monthly on the other part, were distinct and independent covenants. And a right in the company to annul the contract at any time, did not include a right to forfeit the earnings of the other party, for work done prior to the time when the contract was annulled.

A covenant to do the work according to a certain schedule, which schedule mentioned that it was to be done according to the directions of the engineer, bound the company to pay for the work, which was executed according to such directions, although a profile was departed from which was made out before the contract was entered into.

So, also, where the contract was, to place the waste earth where ordered by the engineer, it was the duty of the engineer to provide a convenient place; and if he failed to do so, the other party was entitled to damages.

Where the contract authorized the company to retain fifteen per cent. of the earnings of the contractor, this was by way of indemnity, and not forfeiture; and they were bound to pay it over, unless the jury should be satisfied that the company had sustained an equivalent amount of damage by the default, negligence, or misconduct of the contractor.

Where, in the progress of the work, the contractor was stopped by an injunction issued by a court of chancery, he was not entitled to recover damages for the delay occasioned by it, unless the jury should find that the company did not use reasonable diligence to obtain a dissolution of the injunction.

If the company annulled the contract merely for the purpose of having the work done cheaper, or for the purpose of oppressing and injuring the contractor, he was entitled to recover damages for any loss of profit he might have sustained; and of the reasons which influenced the company, the jury were to be the judges.

THIS case was brought up, by writ of error, from the Circuit Court of the United States, for the District of Maryland.

It was a complicated case, the decision of which involved numerous points of law, as will be seen by the syllabus prefixed to this statement.

There were six exceptions to the admissibility of evidence taken during the progress of the trial in the Circuit Court. The plaintiff below then offered eleven prayers to the court, and the defendant, thirteen. The court laid aside all the prayers and embodied its instructions to the jury in thirteen propositions.

The facts of the case, out of which all these points of law arose, were the following:

Prior to 1836, there existed, in Maryland a company called the Delaware and Maryland Railroad Company, which, by an act of the legislature, passed on the 14th of March, 1836, was united with the Wilmington and Susquehanna Railroad Company; the two united taking the name of the latter.

It will be perceived that this company is not *eo nomine*, one of the parties to the present suit, and it may as well be now mentioned that afterwards a further union of companies took place by virtue of a law of Maryland, passed on 20th of January, 1838. The following companies were united, viz.: The Baltimore and Port Deposit Railroad Company; The Wilmington and Susquehanna Railroad Company; The Philadelphia, Wilmington, and Baltimore Railroad Company; — the three, thus united, taking the name of the latter company, which was the plaintiff in error.

On the 12th of July, 1836, whilst the Washington and Susquehanna Railroad Company had a separate existence, a contract was entered into between them and Howard for the prosecution of the work in Cecil county, in the State of Maryland. Two copies of this paper were extant. They were substantially alike except in this: that one of them (the one referred to as marked B) was sealed by Sebre Howard, and was signed by James Canby, President, with his private seal affixed. It was not sealed by the Railroad Company. The other (referred to as marked A) was signed and sealed by Howard, and signed also by Canby, as president. It also bore an impression which purported to be the seal of the company.

This latter paper was the basis of the present suit, which was an action of covenant. Some of the points of law decided in the case refer to the paper, which makes it necessary to insert it, viz.:

Agreement between Sebre Howard and Hiram Howard, of the first part, and the Wilmington and Susquehanna Railroad Company, of the second part.

The party of the first part, in consideration of the matters hereinafter referred to and set out, covenants and agrees, to and with the party of the second part, to furnish and deliver, at the proper cost of the said party of the first part, the building materials which are described in the annexed schedule, to the said party of the second part, together with the necessary workmanship and labor on said railroad, and at such times, and in such quantities, as the party of the second part shall designate; and faithfully, diligently, and in a good and workmanlike manner, to do, execute, and perform the office, work, and labor in the said schedule mentioned.

And the party of the second part, in consideration of the premises, covenants and agrees to pay the party of the first part the sums and prices in the said schedule mentioned, on or before the first day of November next, or at such other times and in such manner as therein declared.

Provided, however, that in case the party of the second part shall at any time be of opinion that this contract is not duly complied with by the said party of the first part, or that it is not in due progress of execution, or that the said party of the first part is irregular, or negligent; then, and in such case, he shall be authorized to declare this contract forfeited, and thereupon the same shall become null; and the party of the first part shall have no appeal from the opinion and decision aforesaid, and he hereby releases all right to except to, or question the same in any place or under any circumstances whatever; but the party of the first part shall still remain liable to the party of the second part, for the damages occasioned to him by the said noncompliance, irregularity, or negligence.

And provided, also, that in order to secure the faithful and punctual performance of the covenants above made by the party of the first part, and to indemnify and protect the party of the second part from loss in case of default and forfeiture of this contract, the said party of the second part shall, notwithstanding the provision in the annexed schedule, be authorized to retain in their hands, until the completion of the contract, fifteen per cent. of the moneys at any time due to the said party of the first part. Thus covenanted and agreed by the said parties, this twelfth day of July, 1836, as witness their seals.

SEBRE HOWARD, [SEAL.]

[SEAL.]

[SEAL.]

[SEAL.]

JAMES CANBY, *President.* [SEAL.]

Sealed and delivered in the presence of —

WILLIAM P. BRÒBSON. [SEAL.]

Schedule referred to above.

The above-named Sebre Howard and Hiram Howard contract to do all the grading of that part of section No. 9, in the State of Maryland, of the Wilmington and Susquehannah Railroad, which extends from station No. 191, to the end of the piers and wharf in the River Susquehanna, opposite Havre de Grace, according to the directions of the engineer, and according to the specification hitherto annexed, for the sum of twenty-six cents per cubic yard, for every cubic yard excavated; the said section to be completed in a workmanlike manner, viz., one mile from station No. 191, by October 15, 1836, and the residue by November 1, ensuing.

They also contract to make the embankment at the river from the excavation of the road, provided the haul shall not exceed a distance of eight hundred feet from the eastern termination of the said embankment; all other portions of the hauling together not to exceed an average of eight hundred feet; and for any distance exceeding the said average the price is to be one and a half cents per cubic yard for each hundred feet.

The party of the second part contracts to pay to the said Sebre and Hiram Howard, the said sum of twenty-six cents per cubic yard, in monthly payments, according to the measurement and valuation of the engineer, retaining from each payment fifteen per cent. until the final completion of the work. If any additional work, in consequence of water, grubbing, or hard material, is required on the side ditch or ditches, or through Cowden's woods, the same is to be decided by the engineer, as in case of rock, &c.

Specification of the manner of grading the Wilmington and Susquehanna Railroad.

Before commencing any excavation or embankment, the natural sod must be removed to a depth of three inches from the whole surface occupied by the same, for the purpose of afterwards sodding the slopes thereof, and all stumps, trees, bushes, &c., entirely removed from the line of road as directed by the engineer. In cases of embankment a grip must be cut about one foot deep, for footing the slopes, and preventing them from slipping. The embankments must be very carefully carried up in layers of about one foot in thickness, laid in hollow form, and in so doing, all hauling or wheeling, whether loaded or empty, must be done over the same. The slopes of excavations and embankments will be one and a half horizontal to one perpendicular, except where otherwise ordered by the engineer, and are to be sodded with the sods removed from the original surface.

Side ditches and back drains must be cut wherever ordered by the engineer, at the same price as the common excavation. The side ditches will on an average be about nine feet wide on top, and about two feet deep, and will extend along a great portion of the road. In most places where embankments are to be made, the cutting of the adjacent parts is about sufficient for their formation, and as the contractor is supposed to have examined the ground and profiles, and to have formed his estimates accordingly, no allowance will be made for extra hauling. Where more earth is required than is procured from the excavations, the contractor shall take it from such places as the engineer may direct, the cost per cubic yard being the same as the other parts. Where there is any earth from the excavations, more than is required for the embankments, it shall be placed where ordered by the engineer.

All the estimates will be made by measuring the excavations only.

Loose rocks, boulders, ironstone, or other pebbles, of a less weight than one fourth of a ton, are to be removed by the contractor at the same price as the common excavation; but in cases of larger size, or for blasting, the price shall be a matter of special agreement between the contractors and engineer, and if the former should not be willing to execute it for what appears to the engineer a fair price, the latter may put the same into other hands.

No extra allowance will be made for cutting down trees, grubbing, bailing, or other accidental expenses.

Measurements and estimates will be taken about once a month, and full payment will be made by the directors, after deducting 15 per cent., which deduction on each estimate will be retained until the entire contract is completed, which must be on or before the

It is distinctly understood by the contractors that the use of ardent spirits among the workmen is strictly forbidden.

> WILLIAM STRICKLAND,
> *Chief Eng. of the Wil. & Sus. R. R.*

(*Indorsed.*) — *S. & H. Howard's Contract.*

Sebre Howard went to work alone, Hiram Howard never having signed or participated in the contract.

On the 17th of September, 1836, he was served with an injunction issued by the High Court of Chancery of Maryland, against the Maryland and Delaware Railroad Company, its agents and servants, commanding them to desist from the prosecution of a particular part of the work.

On the 30th of October, 1835, the injunction was dissolved.

On the 18th of January, 1837, the directors of the company passed the following resolution :

A communication was received from the chief engineer representing that the contract of S. & H. Howard for section No. 9, was not in due progress of execution, and recommending that it should be forfeited, which was read, and on motion of Mr. Gilpin, the following resolution was adopted, viz.:

" Whereas a contract was duly executed between S. Howard (acting for himself and H. Howard) and the Wilmington and Susquehanna Railroad Company, bearing date the 12th day of July last, whereby the said S. & H. Howard contracted, for the consideration therein mentioned, to do all the grading of that part of section No. 9, of the said railroad which extends from station No. 191 to the end of the piers and wharf in the River Susquehanna, opposite Havre de Grace, according to the directions of the engineer of the said railroad, and to the specification thereto annexed, and to complete the same by the time therein mentioned; and whereas, the times appointed for the completion of said contract have elapsed, and the work is not yet completed, and the party of the second part is of the opinion that the contract is not duly complied with by the party of the first part, and that the said contract is not in due progress of execution: — Therefore, resolved, that the said contract be, and the same is hereby declared to be forfeited."

A suit was then brought in Cecil County Court, by Sebre and Hiram Howard, against the Wilmington and Susquehanna Railroad Company, which was finally disposed of at October term, 1847. The result of the suit is shown in the following copy of the docket-entries, which were admitted in evidence by the Circuit Court, but the admissibility of which constituted the subject of the first bill of exceptions.

In Cecil County Court, October Term, 1847.

S. & H. Howard, use of Charles Howard, use of Hinson H. Cole, $5,000, use of Daniel B. Banks, $1,000,

v.

The Wilmington and Susquehanna Railroad Company.

Procedendo and record for the court of appeals; leave to amend pleadings; nar. filed; pleas filed: similiter; replication and demurrer; leave to defendant to amend pleadings; amended pleas; replication and demurrer; rejoinder; agreement; leave to defendants to issue commission to Wilmington, Delaware; agreement filed; jury sworn; jury find their verdict for the defendants, under instructions from the court, without leaving their box; December 3d, 1847, judgment on the verdict.

In testimony that the above is a true copy of the docket-entries taken from the record of Cecil County Court, for October term, 1847,

I hereunto set my hand, and seal of said court affix, this 12th of November, A. D. 1849.   R. C. HOLLYDAY, [SEAL.]
                            Clerk of Cecil County Court.

This suit having thus failed, Sebre Howard, a citizen of the State of Illinois, brought an action of covenant in his own name, in the Circuit Court of the United States for the District of Maryland. The declaration set out the following breaches which were filed short by agreement of counsel.

1st breach. In not paying the estimate of the first of January.

2d breach. Damages resulting from the injunction sued out by John Stump.

· 3d breach. ·For not building the bridge over Mill creek, and the culvert in·Cowden's woods, whereby the plaintiff was damaged by the necessity of making circuitous hauls.

4th breach. For omission seasonably to build the wharf and cribs on the Susquehanna, whereby the plaintiff was prevented from hauling the earth from the excavations made by him upon said road.

5th breach. For refusal to point out a place or places to permit plaintiff to waste or deposit the earth from the excavations of the road.

6th breach. For refusal to pay for the overhaul.   •

7th breach. For fraudulently declaring contract forfeited, and thereby depriving plaintiff of gains which would otherwise have accrued to him on the completion of the contract, and refused to pay the amount of 15 per cent. retained by the defendants under the several estimates.

8th breach. For not paying said fifteen per cent. so retained upon the several estimates.

The defendants put in the following pleas :

Pleas. And the said defendant, by William Schley, its attorney, comes and defends the wrong and injury, when, &c., and says, that the said supposed agreement in writing, in the said declaration mentioned, is not the deed of this defendant. And of this the said defendant puts itself upon the country, &c.

And the said defendant, by leave of the court here, for this purpose first had and obtained, according to the form of the statute in such case made and provided, for a further plea in this behalf, says, that the said supposed agreement in writing, in the said declaration mentioned, is not the deed of the Wilmington and Susquehanna Railroad Company, in the said declaration mentioned. And of this the said defendant puts itself upon the country, &c.

And the said defendant, by leave of the court here for this purpose

7 *

first had and obtained, according to the form of the statute in such case made and provided, for a further plea in this behalf to the said declaration, says, that the said Wilmington and Susquehanna Railroad Company, in the said declaration mentioned, did not make, or enter into, an agreement in writing with the said plaintiff, sealed with the corporate seal of the said Wilmington and Susquehanna Railroad Company, in manner and form as the said plaintiff hath above in his said pleading alleged. And of this the said defendant put itself upon the country, &c.   WILLIAM SCHLEY,
Attorney for Defendant.

It was agreed that leave was given to the defendants to give in evidence any matter of defence which could be specially pleaded.

Upon this issue the cause went to trial, when the jury, under the instructions of the court, which will be hereafter set forth, found a verdict for the plaintiff for twenty-four thousand four hundred and twenty-five dollars and twenty-four cents damages, with costs.

It has been already mentioned that the defendants took six exceptions, during the progress of the trial, to the admission of evidence. They were as follows :

First Exception. At the trial of this cause, the plaintiff, to maintain the issue on his part joined, proved by Richard T. Hollyday, a competent witness, that he is the present clerk of Cecil County Court, and that the following is a true copy of the docket-entries under the seal of Cecil County Court in a case heretofore depending in that court.

(Then followed the docket-entries above quoted.)

The plaintiff then offered to read said docket-entries in evidence to the jury, for the purpose of showing that such a suit was depending in said court, as shown by said docket-entries, and for no other purpose ; but the defendant, by its counsel, objected to said docket-entries as legal and competent evidence in this cause, and insisted that the same ought not to be read to the jury as evidence in this cause, for the purpose for which they were offered, or for any other purpose. But the court overruled the said objection, and permitted the said docket-entries to be read in evidence in this cause, and the same were accordingly read to the jury. To the admission of which said docket-entries in evidence, the defendant, by its counsel, prayed leave to except.

Second Exception. The plaintiff then further proved, by said Richard T. Hollyday, that he was present in the month of December, 1847, at the trial in Cecil County Court of the said cause, specified in the said docket-entries referred to in the first bill of exceptions, and being shown the paper marked A, of which the following is a true copy :

(The paper marked A has been already described in this statement.)

He was asked whether or not he had ever seen said paper before, and particularly whether or not he had seen the paper A exhibited as a paper of defendant's, and in the possession of the counsel for the defendant in said case, specified in said docket-entries at the said trial in December, 1847; but the defendant, by its counsel, objected to said question, and to the admission of evidence of any answer to the same, on the ground that that suit was between different parties; but the court overruled the objection to said question, and to the answer to the same, and permitted the said witness to answer the same, who deposed that the plaintiff in said case, at said trial in Cecil County Court, relied upon another paper, shown to the witness marked B, and which is as follows.

(The paper marked B has been heretofore described in the statement.)

But that one of the counsel for the defendant had then and there in his possession, at said trial, the said paper, marked A, and handed the said paper to Judge Chambers as the real contract in the case, and spoke of it as the real and genuine contract between the parties.

To which said question to said witness and to the answer given by the said witness thereto, the defendant by its counsel prayed leave to except.

Third Exception. The said Richard T. Hollyday being further examined, stated that whether the impression on said paper, marked A, is or is not the seal of the Wilmington and Susquehanna Railroad Company, he does not know, not having seen at any time the seal of the said company; but that the witness thinks that said paper A was offered in evidence by the defendant in said cause, in Cecil County Court, as the deed of said company, and that evidence of that fact that it was such deed was offered by said defendant. The plaintiff then offered to read in evidence to the jury the said paper marked A, but the defendant, by its counsel, objected to the admissibility of the said paper in evidence to the jury. But the court overruled the said objection, and permitted the said paper to be read in evidence to the jury, as *primâ facie* proved to be the deed of the said Wilmington and Susquehanna Railroad Company; to the admission of which said paper in evidence, the said defendant, by its counsel, excepted.

Fourth Exception. The plaintiff then further proved by Francis W. Ellis, a competent witness, that he is a member of the bar of

Cecil County Court, and that he was present at said court in December, 1847, at the trial of said case, specified in said docket-entries set out in the first bill of exceptions; that at said trial no evidence whatever was given by the defendant; but that, at the conclusion of the plaintiff's case, an objection was made by the counsel for the defendant in the case, to the plaintiff's right of recovery, and he thinks the ground of objection was that the action should not have been brought in the names of Sebre Howard and Hiram Howard. The said witness further stated that, at said trial, one of the counsel for the defendant in that case had in his hands the paper marked A, offered in evidence in this case by the plaintiff, and that he stated, not only to those around him at the bar, but also in conversation with the presiding judge, that said paper was the real contract between the parties.

Evidence of Henry Stump. The plaintiff further proved by Henry Stump, a competent witness, that he was present at the trial, in December, 1847, in Cecil County Court, of the said case, specified in the said docket-entries set out in the first bill of exceptions, and that he was so present as one of the counsel for said plaintiff, and that he took part in the trial. That at said trial the said paper, marked A, was offered in evidence by the defendant, and relied on by the counsel for the defendant in that case, the same having been proved by a witness, to be sealed with the corporate seal of said defendant; and that the objection to the right of recovery in that case was based on said paper, marked A, as a deed; and that the production and proof of said paper A, as the sealed deed of the defendant, at once satisfied him that said suit could not be maintained, and that he therefore suffered the verdict to be taken for the defendant.

The plaintiff then read the agreement of union, dated 5th February, 1838, between the Wilmington and Susquehanna Railroad Company, the Baltimore and Port Deposit Railroad Company, and the Philadelphia, Wilmington, and Baltimore Railroad Company, under the last mentioned name. He then offered to read in evidence a copy of an injunction, issued from the Court of Chancery of Maryland, on the 13th September, 1836, at the suit of John Stump against the Delaware and Maryland Railroad Company. The defendant objected to the admissibility of the copy so offered; but the objection was overruled, and the court permitted said paper to be read in evidence to the jury, "for the purpose of showing the fact that an injunction had issued, which it was admitted had been served on Howard, on the 17th September, 1836, and as furnishing evidence of excuse, on the part of said Howard, for his failure to complete the work to be done, under his contract, by the time therein specified."

Fifth Exception. After evidence, on various points, had been given on both sides, the defendant offered to prove by James Canby, " that when the two papers, respectively marked A. and B, were signed by him and by Sebre Howard, and sealed by the latter, that it was then understood between them, that both said papers were also, thereafter to be signed and sealed by Hiram Howard. The plaintiff objected to the evidence, so offered to be given; and the court sustained the objection, and refused to allow the question to be propounded to the said witness, or to be answered by said witness, and rejected as inadmissible the evidence so proposed to be given.

[Mr. Canby had previously proved that he was then the president of the Wilmington and Susquehanna Railroad Company, and that both the papers, A and B, were signed and sealed by him, and by Sebre Howard. He had also proved that, although the impression on paper A was the seal of said company, yet that it was never placed there by his authority, or by the authority of the board. He had also proved that the section was let to Sebre and Hiram Howard. Evidence had also previously been given, that all the estimates were made in the names of S. & H. Howard; and that all receipts, for payments made, were given in their joint name.]

The object of the defendant, by the evidence proposed to be given, was to confirm the evidence of the said witness, that the seal of the company impressed on paper A, was not placed there by his authority, or by the authority of the board; and further, and, more especially, to show that, in point of fact, said paper A was not intended, sealed or unsealed, as it then stood, to be the complete and perfect contract of the company; and that the actual execution of the contract by Hiram Howard, also, was a condition precedent to its existence as the contract of the company.

Sixth Exception. This exception covered upwards of an hundred pages of the printed record. The evidence offered by the plaintiff and objected to by the defendant, consisted principally of so much of the record of the case in Cecil County Court, as preceded the appeal, in that case, to the Court of Appeals; and it was offered by the plaintiff below, for the purpose of introducing, as evidence against the defendant below, the deposition of William P. Brobson, taken in that case, on behalf of the defendant in that case, and whose subsequent decease was proved. The defendant objected to the admission of said deposition in evidence in this case. The court, however, admitted the deposition, and it was accordingly read. The deposition was taken 7th April, 1840.

Seventh Exception. This included an exception to the refusal of the court to grant the prayers offered by the counsel for the defendants, and also an exception to the instructions given by the court to the jury. It has been already stated that the court laid aside the prayers offered by the counsel on both sides, and gave its own instructions to the jury; but by way of illustration, the prayers offered by the counsel for the plaintiff are here inserted also.

Plaintiff's Prayers.

1st. If the jury believe that Sebre Howard made with the defendants the contract in question, and went on to perform the work under the same, and so continued the same until the month of January, 1837, when the company declared his contract forfeited, and that the engineers of the company made an estimate of the work so done, showing a balance due the contractor, Howard, of   , then plaintiff is entitled to recover that sum with interest.

2d. If the jury believe the facts stated in the foregoing prayer, and further find that the plaintiff was stopped by the officers of the defendant from proceeding in the work, which stoppage was induced by the injunction issued and given in evidence; and if they further find that the defendant had neglected to procure any title to the land worked upon until after such injunction was laid and dissolved, then the plaintiff is entitled to recover such amount of damages as the jury may find from the evidence that he sustained by reason of his being turned off from said work.

3d. If the jury find the facts stated in the preceding prayers, then by the true construction of the contract the plaintiffs are entitled to the excess of overhaul, resulting from going off the company's lands, and descending to and ascending from Mill creek, in the construction of the embankment east of Mill creek.

4th. If the jury find all the facts stated in the preceding prayers, and further find that the plaintiffs were obstructed in the performance of their work by the absence of proper cribs at the River Susquehanna, where plaintiff was at work at the time; and if they further find that he was, in consequence of such non-performance by defendants, turned away from this work, then plaintiffs are entitled to recover such amount as the jury may find he sustained damage by reason of such omission of defendant.

5th. That by the true construction of the contract in this case, the defendants were bound to furnish ground to waste the earth upon which was to be dug out of the hills through which the road was to be cut by the plaintiff; and if they find that the defendant refused to do so, plaintiff is entitled to recover such sum as the jury may find he sustained loss by not being furnished with ground to waste such earth upon.

6th. That plaintiff is entitled to recover for any and every overhaul exceeding an average of 800 feet.

7th. That if the jury find that the plaintiff faithfully performed his work under this contract, and was only prevented from finishing it by the misconduct of the defendant, then plaintiff is entitled to recover such sum as he would have made by completing said contract.

8th. If the jury believe that the defendant wilfully and fraudulently, and without any reasonable or proper cause, declared the contract given in evidence forfeited, then the plaintiffs are entitled to recover, notwithstanding such declaration of forfeiture, for any damages arising to them, after such declaration of forfeiture, in consequence thereof.

9th. That by the true construction of the contract given in evidence, it was the duty of the defendant to have all the culverts and bridges upon the route of said road, within the limits of plaintiffs' contract, prepared for the free pursuance of his work; and if the jury believe that the defendants or persons employed by them neglected so to do, they, defendants, are liable for such damages as plaintiffs show they sustained in consequence of such omission or neglect of defendant.

10th. That by the true construction of this contract, it was the duty of defendants to prevent or remove all obstructions to the plaintiffs' work which it was within their power to remove; and it was their duty to have obtained a right to work on the road before said plaintiffs commenced their work; and if they find that, in consequence of legal proceedings against said company, plaintiffs were obstructed and hindered in the performance of their work, and thereby seriously damaged, the plaintiffs are entitled to recover for such damage.

11th. That plaintiffs are entitled to recover for all work and labor actually done and performed under said contract, including the 15 per cent. retained upon the several estimates, after deducting the payments shown to have been made.

And the defendant offered the following.

Defendant's Prayers.

1st. The defendant, by its counsel, prays the court to instruct the jury that if they shall find, from the evidence in this cause, that the seal upon the contract, offered in evidence by the plaintiff, dated 12th July, 1836, was not affixed to the said contract by the authority of the Wilmington and Susquehanna Railroad Company, and was affixed without the authority of the defendant in this suit, and was so affixed after the execution of the agreement of union, offered in evidence by the plaintiffs, dated the 5th of February, 1838, the plaintiff is not entitled to recover upon it in this suit.

2d. If the jury shall find, from the evidence in this cause, that at the trial in Cecil County Court, in December, 1847, of the case of Sebre Howard and Hiram Howard against the Wilmington and Susquehanna Railroad Company, spoken of in their testimony, by Mr. Hollyday, Mr. Ellis, Mr. Stump, and Mr. Scott, the plaintiffs in said suit offered in evidence to the jury, in support of the issue joined on their part, the contract offered in evidence in this cause, marked exhibit B, and shall further find, from the evidence in the cause, that the defendant in said suit offered no evidence whatever in support of the issue joined on its part, and that the counsel for the defendant in that suit, when the plaintiffs offered to read in evidence the contract, marked B, objected to the admissibility of the same in evidence upon the issue joined in said suit, upon the ground that whereas the plaintiffs in that suit declared on an alleged contract, made by the said plaintiffs with the said defendant in that suit, yet the said paper so offered to be read in evidence by the said plaintiffs, being executed only by said Sebre Howard, and under his seal, was the contract alone of said Sebre Howard, and was not the same contract alleged by the plaintiffs in the pleadings in that case ; and shall further find, from the evidence in the cause, that this was the only objection made and argued in the trial of said cause on the part of the defendant, and was the only point then and there decided by the said court, then the reliance on said objection does not estop or debar the defendant in this suit from denying that the paper, marked exhibit A, now offered in evidence in this suit by the plaintiff, is not the deed of the Wilmington and Susquehanna Railroad Company, even if the jury shall find, from the evidence in the cause, that the said paper A was then and there in court, in the possession of the defendant's counsel in that suit, and was spoken of by him, as stated by the witnesses, as the real contract between the parties ; provided, they shall also find, from the evidence in the cause, that the counsel who appeared for the defendant in said suit were then wholly ignorant of the fact that said seal had been placed on the said contract, without any authority, as aforesaid.

3d. If the jury shall find, from the evidence in the cause, that the work done on the 9th section of the Wilmington and Susquehanna Railroad on and after the 12th day of July, 1836, so far as done by the plaintiff, Sebre Howard, was so done by said plaintiff as one of the firm of Sebre and Hiram Howard, and that all the estimates were made out as in favor of said firm, and received and receipted for by the plaintiff, so far as any moneys were received by him from the said company in the name and on behalf of said firm; and that the plaintiff, in his dealings and transactions with said company, professed to act as one of said firm, and for and on behalf of said firm, and never notified the said company, or any of its officers, whilst engaged in work on said road, that he was not acting as a member of said firm, and for and on behalf of said firm, then the plaintiff is not entitled to recover in this case upon the first breach by him assigned in his declaration.

4th. If the jury shall find, from the evidence in the cause, that the resolution of the board of the Wilmington and Susquehanna Railroad Company, dated 18th January, 1837, offered in evidence in this cause, was duly passed by said board, and shall not find from the evidence in the cause that the same was fraudulently passed by said board, or by said company, then the plaintiff is not entitled to recover on the 7th breach of his declaration.

5th. If the jury shall find with the defendant on the fourth prayer, and shall also find, from the evidence in the cause, that notice was given on the same day, to the plaintiff in the suit, of the passage of said resolution, then the said contract was thereby rendered null so far as concerned any liability thereunder on the part of the defendant; and that the plaintiff is not entitled to maintain this suit.

6th. If the jury shall find, from the evidence in the cause, that the first mile of said section No. 9 was not finished on or before the 15th day of October, 1836, and was not, in fact, finished at any time, nor accepted by the defendant as fully and completely graded by the plaintiff, or by the said firm of Sebre Howard and Hiram Howard; and shall further find, from the evidence, that the alleged excuses, alleged in pleading by the plaintiff, were not in any respect the cause of, or contributory to the failure on the part of the said plaintiff, or of the said plaintiff and said Hiram Howard, to finish the same in the time limited for that purpose in said contract, then the plaintiff is not entitled to recover in this case on said first breach in his said declaration.

7th. If the jury shall find from the evidence, that the injunction issued by John Stump, offered in evidence in this cause, was issued without any justifiable cause, and without any basis in right, and that the issuing of said injunction was not based on any actual omission of duty on the part of said company, then the plaintiff is not entitled to recover on the second count of his declaration.

8th. If the jury shall find, from the evidence in the cause, that the plaintiff was contractor on another section of the road of the said company, and that said former section was completed by him before the making of the contract offered in evidence in this case; and shall further find, that in the execution of said former contract the plaintiff .provided bridges and other modes of intercommunication from one part of his work to another, without any complaint; and shall further find that it was the known usage of said company to leave to the contractors the business of construction of their bridges so as to pass with materials and excavation from one part of their work to another, and that such is the known and uniform usage of other public works, then the plaintiff is not entitled to recover on the second breach of his declaration.

9th. If the jury shall find, from the evidence in the cause, that the plaintiff, at the time he was stopped by the assistant engineer, Mr. Farquhar from throwing more earth against the outer crib of the embankment at the river, might readily and conveniently have deposited many thousand cubic yards of earth within the limits of said embankment, if he had chosen so to do; and that the plaintiff perversely and stubbornly refused so to do; then the plaintiff is not entitled to recover on the 4th breach of his declaration.

10th. If the jury shall find, from the evidence, that the excavations made by the plaintiff, in the month of December, 1836, were needed by the defendant for the embankment at the river; and shall also find that the same could have been conveniently deposited there by the plaintiff, and that the plaintiff knew these facts, then the plaintiff is not entitled to recover on the fifth breach of his declaration.

11th. If the jury shall find that fair and proper estimates were made by defendant for all the overhaul of earth made by the plaintiff, over the average haul of 800 feet, then the plaintiff is not entitled to recover on the 6th breach of his declaration.

12th. If the jury shall believe that, at the time of the execution of the agreement, the road to be excavated and graded was staked out and marked upon the ground, and that a profile was shown, showing the depth of excavation to be made, and the height of the embankments, and that afterwards the plan of the road was altered and changed, by which the excavations were to be deeper and wider, and some of the embankments higher and some lower, to suit the altered plan of the road, and that the work done by the plaintiff, and for which he claims damages, was in grading the road according to the altered plan, then the plaintiff is not entitled to recover in this action.

13th. If the jury shall believe that all the work done in pursuance of the agreement stated in the declaration was done by Sebre and Hiram Howard, and not by Sebre Howard alone, that then the plaintiff is not entitled to recover.

The court thereupon rejecting the respective prayers on both sides, gave the jury the following instructions :

Court's Instructions to the Jury.

SEBRE HOWARD
vs.
THE PHILADELPHIA, WILMINGTON, AND
BALTIMORE RAILROAD COMPANY.

1st. If the corporate seal of the Wilmington and Susquehanna Railroad Company was affixed to the instrument of writing upon which the suit is brought, with the authority of the company, while it had a separate existence for the purpose of making it at that time, and as it then stood the contract of the company, then the said instrument of writing is the deed of the said corporation, although it was never delivered to the plaintiff nor notice of the sealing given to him; and although no seal was affixed by the corporation to the duplicate copy delivered to him; and the defendant in the present action is equally bound by it, and in like manner.

2d. If the jury find from the evidence that this instrument of writing was produced in court, and relied upon by the present defendant, as a contract under the seal of the Wilmington and Susquehanna Railroad Company, in an action of *assumpsit* brought by Sebre and Hiram Howard against the last-mention [ed] company in Cecil County Court; and that the said suit was decided against the plaintiffs upon the ground that this instrument was duly sealed by the said corporation as its deed, then the defendant cannot be permitted in this case to deny the validity of the said sealing, because such a defence would impute to the present defendant itself a fraud upon the administration of justice in Cecil County Court.

3d. If upon either of these grounds the jury find the instrument of writing upon which this suit is brought to be the deed of defendant, then the plaintiff is entitled to recover in this suit any damage he may have sustained by a breach of the covenants on the part of the corporation; but if they find that it is not the deed of the defendant upon either of these grounds, then their verdict must be for the defendant.

4th. The omission of the plaintiffs to finish the work within the times mentioned in the contract, is not a bar to his recovery for the price of the work he actually performed; but the defendant may set off any damage he sustained by the delay, if the delay arose from the default of the plaintiffs.

5th. If the defendant annulled this contract, as stated in the testimony, under the belief that the plaintiff was not prosecuting the work with proper diligence, and for the reasons assigned in the resolution of the board, they are not liable for any damage the plaintiff may have sustained thereby, even although he was in no default, and the company acted in this respect under a mistaken opinion as to his conduct.

6th. But this annulling did not deprive him of any rights vested in him at that time, nor make the covenant void *ab initio,* so as to deprive him of a remedy upon it for any money then due him for his work, or any damages he had then already sustained.

7th. The increased work, occasioned by changing the width of the road and altering the grade, having been directed by the engineer of the company under its authority, was done under this covenant, and within its stipulations, and may be recovered in this action, without resorting to an action of *assumpsit.*

8th. If the jury find for the plaintiff upon the first or second instructions, he is entitled to recover the amount due on the work done by him in December, 1836, and January, 1837, according to the measurements and valuation of the engineer of the company, and cannot go into evidence to show that they were erroneous, or that he was entitled to a greater allowance for overhaul than the amount stated in the estimates of the engineer.

9th. Also, if from any cause, without the fault of the plaintiff, the earth excavated could not be used in the filling up and embankments on the road and at the river, it was the duty of the defendant to furnish a place to waste it. And if the company refused, on the application of the plaintiff to provide a convenient place for that purpose, he is entitled to recover such damages as he sustained by the refusal, if he sustained any; and he is also entitled to recover any damage he may have sustained by the delay of his work or the increase of his expense in performing it, occasioned [by] the negligence, acts, or default of the defendant.

10th. Also, the plaintiff is entitled to recover the fifteen per cent. retained by the company, unless the jury find that the company has sustained damage by the default, negligence, or misconduct of the plaintiff. And if such damage has been sustained, but not to the amount of the fifteen per cent., then the plaintiff is entitled to recover the balance, after deducting the amount of damage sustained by the company.

11th. The corporation was not bound to provide bridges over the streams to enable the plaintiff to pass conveniently with his carts from one part of the road to another.

12th. The decision of the Court of Appeals is conclusive evidence that the injunction spoken of in the testimony, was not occasioned by the default of the defendant; and the plaintiff is not entitled to recover damages for the delay occasioned by it, unless the jury find that the company did not use reasonable diligence to obtain a dissolution of the injunction.

13th. If the jury find that the resolution of the company annulling the contract was not in truth passed for the reasons therein assigned, but for the purpose of having the remaining work done upon cheaper terms than those agreed upon in the contract with the plaintiff, or for the purpose of oppressing and injuring the plaintiff, then he is entitled to recover damages for any loss of profit he may have sustained by the refusal of the company to permit him to finish the work he had contracted to perform, if he sustained any.

The defendant, by its counsel, prayed leave to except, in respect of all and each of the prayers offered on the part of the defendant, to the court's refusal to grant said several prayers respectively, and also prayed leave to except to the instructions given by the court to the jury, and to each one of said instructions, severally and respectively, and prayed that the court here would sign and seal this, its seventh bill of exceptions, according to the form of the statutes in such case made and provided; and which is accordingly done this 16th day of November, 1850.

R. B. TANEY, [SEAL.]
U. S. HEATH, [SEAL.]

Upon all these exceptions the case came up to this court, and was argued by *Schley*, for the plaintiffs in error, and *Nelson* and *Johnson*, for the defendant in error.

The reporter has not room to notice the arguments of Mr. Schley, for the plaintiffs in error, upon the points of evidence brought up in the six first exceptions. The points made by him upon the 7th exception which included the rulings of the court as instructions to the jury were the following:

1. The defendant in error cannot, as sole plaintiff in the action, maintain the suit. Whether the contract be the deed of the company, or a mere contract by parol, the covenantees or promisees, as the case may be, are Sebre Howard and Hiram Howard. This point, if well taken, is decisive of the case. Platt on Covenants, 18; Clement *v.* Henley, 2 Rolle's Abr. 22; Faits (F.) Pl. 2; Vernon *v.* Jeffreys, 2 Stra. 1146; Petrie *v.* Bury, 3 Barn. & Cress. 353, (10 Eng. C. L. Rep. 108); Rose *v.* Poulton, 2 Barn. & Ad. 822, (22 Eng. C. L. Rep. 194); Scott

v. Godwin, 1 Bos. & Pul. 67 ; Anderson *v.* Martindale, 1 East, 497 ;
1 Wms. Saunders, 201, f. and cases cited there ; 1 Saunders, Pl. &
Ev. 390 ; Wetherell *v.* Langton, 1 Exch. Rep. (Welsby, Hurl. &
Gord.) 634 ; Foley *v.* Addenbrooke, 4 Q. B. 197, (45 Eng. C. L. Rep.
195) ; Hopkinson *v.* Lee, 6 Q. B. 964, (51 Eng. C. L. Rep. 963) ;
Wakefield *v.* Brown, 9 Q. B. 209, (58 Eng. C. L. Rep. 217) ; Smith
v. Ransom, 21 Wend. 204.

. 2. Unless the instrument, on which the action is founded, was, in
fact, the deed of the Wilmington and Susquehanna Railroad Company, existing and operative as such, at the time of the union of the
companies, an action of covenant cannot be maintained thereon,
under the Act of 1837, against the plaintiff in error. This point, if
well taken, is decisive of the case.

3. If the last preceding proposition cannot be supported, in its
full extent, still, upon the issue joined on the plea of *non est factum,*
the plaintiff in error was not estopped, in law, from showing, that the
paper was not, in fact, the deed of the Wilmington and Susquehanna
Railroad Company. Wilson *v.* Butler, 4 Bing. N. Cas. 748, (33 Eng.
C. L. Rep. 521) ; 1 Chitty's Plead. 603 ; and cases referred to in the
notes.

4. The alleged production of the instrument, in the former suit, as
a deed, would not, as matter of law, have been a fraud upon the
administration of justice. Fraud or no fraud was a question of fact
for the jury ; and the application of the doctrine of estoppel ought
to have been only upon the hypothesis, that the jury would find fraud,
as a fact in the case. 'Accident, mistake, or surprise, might afford
good ground for relief in equity, under very peculiar circumstances ;
but not for the application of estoppel *in pais,* in the absence of all
intention to perpetrate a fraud. Reference is made to the various
cases collected in the notes, in 44 Law Lib. 467 ; Conard *v.* Nicholl,
4 Pet. 295 ; United States *v.* Arredondo, 6 Pet. 716.

5. Even if the instrument was properly held to be the deed of the
said company, yet, upon its true construction, time was of the essence
of the contract. As the evidence clearly showed that the work was
not performed, within the time limited in that behalf, and as there
was no valid excuse for the default, the plaintiff below could not
recover on the basis of said agreement. The proper form of action
would have been *assumpsit,* upon a *quantum valebat,* for the work and
labor done. This objection, if well taken, is decisive of the case.
1 Chitty's Plead. 340, and cases in note (4.) Watchman *v.* Crook, 5
Gill & Johns. 254 ; Watkins *v.* Hodges & Lansdale, 6 Harr. & Johns.
38 ; Bank of Columbia *v.* Hagner, 1 Pet. 455, 465 ; Longworth *v.*
Taylor, 1 M'Lean's Rep. 395 ; Fresh *v.* Gilson, 16 Pet. 327, 334 ;

Notes to Cutter v. Powell, Smith's L. C. 44 Law Lib. 17, 27; Gibbon's Law of Contracts, § 20 to § 47; and the cases there stated.

6. By force of the declaration of forfeiture, if validly made, (that is, if made under the circumstances stated as the hypothesis of the fifth instruction,) the instrument was annulled, so far as it imposed any obligation upon the company. It could not be made, thereafter, the basis of an action against said company. Whilst conceding that the plaintiff below was not thereby deprived of any rights, completely vested in him before forfeiture; yet, it will be insisted, that the remedy, for the enforcement of such rights, is not by an action upon the instrument itself. *Assumpsit*, upon a *quantum valebat*, would have been the appropriate form of action, or relief could have been had in equity. It will, therefore, be respectfully insisted, that the sixth instruction, (which is founded on the same hypothesis as the fifth,) confounds the distinction between right and remedy. As to the first branch, *vide* Mathewson v. Lydiate, 5 Co. 22 b.; s. c. Cro. Eliz. 408, 470, 546. As to second branch, 1 Chitty's Plead. 340, note 4; and cases there cited.

7. At all events, no action at law can be maintained against the plaintiff in error, on said annulled contract, (if validly annulled,) under the provisions of the Act of 1837, c. 30. The forfeiture was declared on the 18th January, 1837. The act was passed on the 20th January, 1838. The instrument, therefore, was not a subsisting obligation of the Wilmington and Susquehanna Railroad Company, when the act of union was passed.

8. The claim to the fifteen per cent. retained by the company was not a vested right, at the time the contract was annulled. Even if the sixth instruction was correct, the tenth instruction was erroneous. By the express terms of the agreement, the retained per cent. was not demandable until the completion of the contract. As the contract was never fulfilled by the contractor, the retained per cent. cannot be demanded, in an action based on the contract.

9. No recovery can be had, in this suit, in respect of any matter, not embraced in the contract. The subject-matter of the contract is to be limited and confined to the original plan of the work, as contemplated and established, when the contract was made. The obligation of the contract cannot be extended beyond the subject-matter. It had not the capacity of expansion or contraction, in accordance with any changes that the company might choose to make. Such additional work cannot be recovered in this action, as declared in the seventh instruction of the court, as work done under the covenant, and within its stipulations. 2 Stark. Ev. 768; Fresh v. Gilson, 16 Pet. 327.

10. There was no implied covenant on the part of the company, to

procure a place for the waste of the surplus excavations, if any. But even if there was such implied covenant, there was no evidence in the cause from which it could reasonably be inferred, that there was any excavation to be wasted as surplus.

11. The defendant below was not liable, in any manner, for the consequences of the injunction issued from chancery. The action was grounded on the alleged covenant; and the company, by its contract, had not warranted against interruption by the wrongful acts of any stranger. There is a wide difference between allowing the interruption to avail to the plaintiff below, as an excuse on his behalf for non-performance of the work within the prescribed time; and in making the delay of the company, in removing the cause of interruption, a ground of action against the defendant below, as being a violation by the company of its covenant. Platt on Covenants, 601, (3 Law Lib. 269,) and case referred to in the notes there.

12. It will be insisted, that there was no evidence in the cause to justify the hypothesis of the thirteenth instruction of the court; that there was nothing from which the jury could legitimately find the facts of fraud and oppression, which are made the basis of that instruction.

13. And it will also be insisted, that the thirteenth instruction is erroneous, in this, that thereby it is laid down, that the loss of profits, if any, sustained by the plaintiff, is the proper measure of damages to be allowed by the jury, if they should find that the company improperly refused to permit the plaintiff to perform his work. Gilpins v. Consequa, Peters, C. C. Rep. 85. Hopkins v. Lee, 6 Wheat. 109; Bell v. Cunningham, 3 Peters, 69, 86; 2 Greenleaf on Evidence, sect. 261; Fairman v. Fluck, 5 Watts, 516, 518; Story on Agency, 216; Short v. Skipwith, 1 Brock. Rep. 108.

14. The third prayer of the defendant ought to have been granted. Even if, in fact, or by estoppel, the paper A was the deed of the company; yet, if the work was really performed by, or on behalf of, the firm of S. & H. Howard, and the dealings and transactions of the company, in relation to said work, were with the said firm, (without notice of any proposed or actual separate performance of the work by the plaintiff, individually, as under said paper A,) then the defendant had a right to insist, that as the work was done by said firm, the privity of contract, in relation thereto, was with said firm, and that the estimate was payable only to the firm, under the paper B, as the subsisting contract between the parties, or otherwise upon an assumpsit to said firm.

15. The ninth and tenth prayers of the plaintiff ought to have been granted. The evidence of Mr. Heckert shows that "the embank-

ment under the change of grade was 650 feet long and 100 feet wide, and there was much space wherein Howard could have placed the earth from his excavations to make the said embankment." Besides this, there was express directions from the engineer to the plaintiff below, to place the embankment (not against the crib, but) on each side of the centre-line of the embankment for the width of twenty-five feet on each side of said centre-line. His conduct in throwing the embankment against the outer crib was wilful and perverse.

The counsel for the defendants made the following references to authorities, to show that the exceptions were not sustainable :

On the First Exception. Act of Assembly of Maryland, 1817, c. 119; Peake's Evidence, 34; Jones *v.* Randall, Cowper's Rep. 17.

On the Second and Third Exceptions. Acts of Assembly of Mary-land, 1831, c. 296; 1835, c. 93; 1837, c. 30; Agreement of Union, 1838, February 5th, (page 29th of the Record); 4 S. & R. 246; 2 Hill, 64; 1 Metcalf, 27; 5 Monroe, 530; 17 Conn. 345, 355; 18 Id. 138, 443; Fishmonger *v.* Robertson, 5 Mann. & Grang. 131, 192, 193.

On the Fourth Exception. Same authorities cited in support of the 4th instruction.

On the Sixth Exception. 1 Greenleaf's Evidence, sect. 553, p. 618; 1 Adolphus & Ellis, 19.

On the Seventh Exception. In support of the 1st, 2d and 3d instructions. Coke's Lit. Lib. 1, sect. 5, 36, (a.) note 222; 2 Leonard, 97; 1 Ventr. 257; 1 Levinz, 46; 1 Siderfin, 8; Carthew, 360; 3 Keble, 307; 1 Kyd on Corporations, 268.

In support of the 4th Instruction. Terry *v.* Dance, 2 H. Black. 389; 1 East, 625, 631; 2 Johns. 272, 387; 5 Johns. 78; 15 Mass. 500; 19 Johns. 341; 2 Wash. C. C. Rep. 456; Campbell *v.* Jones, 6 T. R. 570; Fishmonger *v.* Robertson, 5 Mann. & Granger, 197; How-ard *v.* Philadelphia Railroad Company Co. 1 Gill, 311; Goldsborough *v.* Orr, 8 Wheat. 217; 1 Williams's Saund. 320 b.; Pordage *v.* Cole, Id. 220, n. 4.; Carpenter *v.* Creswell, 4 Bing. 409; Boon *v.* Eyre, 1 H. Bla. 273.

Mr. Justice CURTIS delivered the opinion of the court.

Sebre Howard brought his action of covenant broken, in the Circuit Court of the United States for the district of Maryland, and upon the trial, the defendants took seven bills of exception, which are here for consideration upon a writ of error. Each of them must be separately examined.

The first, raises the question, whether Howard could prove that a certain suit was pending in Cecil County Court by the testimony of the clerk of that court to the verity of a copy of the docket-entries made in that suit by him, as clerk.

It is not objected that a copy of the docket-entries was produced instead of the original entries, because no court is required to permit its original entries to go out of the custody of its own officers, in the place appointed for their preservation; but the objection is, that a formal record ought to have been shown. There are two distinct answers to this objection, either of which is sufficient.

By the act of Assembly of Maryland, (1817, c. 119,) the clerk of the County Court is not required to make up a formal record. The docket-entries and files of the court stand in place of the record. When a formal record is not required by law, those entries which are permitted to stand in place of it are admissible in evidence. Several judicial decisions in England have been referred to by the counsel of the plaintiff in error, to the effect, that the finding of an indictment at the sessions cannot be proved by the production of the minute-book of the sessions, from which book the roll, containing the record of such proceedings, is subsequently made up. See 2 Phil. Ev. 194. But the distinction between those cases and a case like this is pointed out in a recent decision of the Court of King's Bench in Regina v. Yeoveley, 8 Ad. & El. 806, in which it was held, that the minute-book of the sessions was admissible to prove the fact that an order of removal had been made, it appearing that it was not the practice to make up any other record of such an order; and Lord Denman fixes on the precise ground on which the evidence was admissible in this case, when he says, "the book contains a caption, and the decision of the sessions; and their decision is the fact to be proved."

So in Arundell v. White, 14 East, 216, the plaintiff offered the minute-book of the Sheriff's Court in London, containing the entry of the plaint, and the word "withdrawn," opposite to the entry, and proved it was the usual course of the court to make such an entry when the suit was abandoned by the plaintiff; it was held to be competent evidence to prove the abandonment of the suit by the plaintiff, and its final termination. In Commonwealth v. Bolkhom, 3 Pick. 281, it was decided that the minute-book of the sessions, showing the grant of a license to the defendant, was legal evidence of that fact, there being no statute requiring a technical record to be made up.

And in Jones v. Randall, Cowper's R. 17, copies of the minute-book of the House of Lords were admitted in evidence of a decree because it was not the practice to make a formal record.

The principle of all these decisions is the same. Where the law which governs the tribunal, requires no other record than the one, a copy of which is presented, that is sufficient. In Maryland, no tech-

nical record was required by law to be made up by the clerks of the
county courts; and, therefore, no other record than the one produced
was needful to prove the pendency of an action in such a court.

But there is another point of view in which this evidence was
clearly admissible.

The fact to be proved was the pendency of an action.   An action
is pending when it is duly entered in court.   The entry of an action
in court is made, by an entry on the docket, of the title of the case,
by the proper officer, in the due course of his official duty.   Proof of
such an entry being made by the proper officer, accompanied by the
presumption which the law entertains, that he has done his duty in
making it, is proof that the action was duly entertained in court, and
so proof that the action was pending; and if the other party asserts
that it had been disposed of, at any particular time after it was entered,
he must show it.   The docket-entry of the action was therefore admissible for this special purpose; because it was the very fact which,
when shown, proved the pendency of the action, until the other party
showed its termination.

The second bill of exceptions was taken to the ruling of the court
admitting a witness to testify that he was present at the trial of the
above-mentioned case in Cecil County Court, in December, 1847, in
which Sebre Howard and Hiram Howard were shown by the docket-
entries to have been plaintiffs, and the Wilmington and Susquehanna
Railroad Corporation defendant; that the plaintiffs at that trial relied
on a paper writing, shown to the witness, and set out in the bill of
exceptions; that one of the counsel of the defendant had in his possession another paper writing, also shown to the witness, and being
the deed declared on in this suit; and that the defendant's counsel
handed this last mentioned paper to the presiding judge, and spoke
of it as the true and genuine contract between the parties.

To render the ruling, to which this bill of exceptions was taken,
intelligible, it is necessary to state, that the Wilmington and Susquehanna Railroad Corporation was the defendant in that action, which
was assumpsit, founded on the paper first spoken of by the witness,
which did not bear the seal of the corporation; that by the Act of Assembly of 1837, c. 30, the Baltimore and Susquehanna Company, the
Baltimore and Port Deposit Company, and the Philadelphia, Wilmington, and Baltimore Company, were consolidated, under the name
of the Philadelphia, Wilmington, and Baltimore Railroad Company,
and that this action being covenant, against the Philadelphia, Wilmington, and Baltimore Railroad Company, and the plea *non est
factum*, the plaintiff was endeavoring to prove, that the paper declared
on bore the corporate seal of the Wilmington and Susquehanna Railroad Company.   This being the fact to be proved, evidence that the

'corporation, through its counsel, had treated .the instrument as bearing the corporate seal, and relied upon it as a deed of the corporation,
was undoubtedly admissible.   It is objected that the parties to that
suit were not the same as in this one; but this is wholly immaterial.
The evidence does not derive its validity from any privity of parties.
It tends to prove an admission by the corporation, that the instrument was sealed with its seal.   It is further objected that the admission was not made by the defendants in this action, but by the Wilmington and Susquehanna•Corporation.   It is true the action in the
trial of which the admission was made, being brought before the
union of the corporations, was necessarily in the name of the original
corporation; but as, by virtue of the act of union, the Wilmington
and Susquehanna Company, the Baltimore and Port Deposit Company, and the Philadelphia, Wilmington, and Baltimore Company
were merged in and 'constituted one body corporate, under the name
of the Philadelphia, Wilmington, and Baltimore Railroad Company,
it is very clear that at the time the trial took place in Cecil County
Court, all acts and admissions of the defendant in that case, though
necessarily in the name of the Wilmington and Susquehanna Company, were done and made by the same corporation which now defends this action.   This exception must therefore be overruled.[1]

---

[1] The relations which a company formed
by the consolidation of two or more companies sustains to parties who have contracted with the original companies, has
been considered by the English courts in
several cases.   Thus far the courts have
held that a consolidated company is bound
to discharge the obligations of the several
original companies, though in a recent case
it was strongly urged by the counsel, and
admitted by the court, that there would be
great difficulty in many cases, in holding
contracts with the old companies to be
binding upon the new company ; such, for
instance, as a contract to supply all the
rails which a company should require.
The Eastern Union R. Co. v. Cochrane, 17
Jurist, 1103; s. c. 20 Eng. Law & Eq. Rep.
The defendant had become surety upon a
bond given to a railway company, for the
faithful discharge of his duties, by a person
in the employment of the company as clerk.
This company and another were afterwards amalgamated.   The person for whom
the defendant had become bound continued
in the employment of the new company.

The action was brought for a breach of the
bond after the consolidation, and was defended upon the ground that by the change
in the companies, the duties of the clerk
were so changed and increased that the
surety ought to be discharged.   But the
court held the defendant liable on his bond.
A previous case, presenting the same facts,
except that the alleged breach was committed before the consolidation of the companies, was decided in the same manner.
London, Brighton, &c. R. Co. v. Goodwin,
6 Eng. Rail. Ca. 177.   And where a company provisionally organized, but not incorporated, has entered into an agreement
with a land-owner for the purchase of so
much of his land as may be needed for the
proposed road, and afterwards the contemplated company has amalgamated with
other companies, the new consolidated
company has been held bound to carry out
the agreement.   Preston v. The Liverpool,
Manchester, &c. R. Co. 7 Eng. Law & Eq.
Rep. 124; Stanley v. The Chester and
Birkenhead R. Co. 1 Eng. Rail. Ca. 58,
See also Capper v. The Earl of Lindsay,

The third exception is that the court permitted the deed to be read to the jury, although only vague and inconclusive evidence had been given, that it bore the corporate seal.   We do not consider the evidence was vague, for it applied to this particular paper, and tended to prove it to be the deed of the company.   Whether it would turn out to be conclusive, or not, depended upon the fact whether any other evidence would be offered to control it, and upon the judgment of the jury.   But the deed was rightly admitted to be read as soon as any evidence of its execution, fit to be weighed by the jury, had been given by the plaintiff.   It was argued that this evidence was not sufficient to change the burden of proof; and it is true that, upon the issue whether the paper bore the corporate seal, the burden of proof remained on the plaintiff throughout the trial, however the evidence might preponderate, to the one side or the other, (Powers v. Russell, 13 Pick. 69); but the court did not rule that the burden of proof was changed, but only that such *primâ facie* evidence had been given as enabled the plaintiff to read the deed to the jury.

The subject-matter of the fourth exception became wholly immaterial in the progress of the cause, and could not be assigned for error, even if the ruling had been erroneous.   Greenleaf's Lessee v. Birth, 5 Pet. 132.   But we think the ruling was correct.

The fifth exception was taken to the refusal of the court to allow a question to be answered by James Canby, one of the defendant's witnesses.   This witness had already testified as follows :

" Leslie and White were the first contractors, and they were induced to relinquish it at the instance of the board, and it was then let to Sebre and Hiram Howard ; the terms and price, and other essentials of the contract, were entered into on the 12th July, 1836 ; and on that same day two papers were prepared and were then signed by him, and also signed by Sebre Howard ; and deponent, as presi-

---

14 Eng. Law & Eq. Rep. 9 ; Greenhaghl . The Manchester and Birmingham R. Co. 1 Eng. Railw. Ca. 68.

The English courts have repeatedly held that a railway company is bound by contracts entered into for the benefit of a company before its incorporation by its projectors, on the principle that " whenever a third party enters into a contract with the plaintiff, and the defendant takes the benefit of it, he is bound to give the plaintiff the advantage he has stipulated for.   Gooday

v. The Colchester and Stour Valley R. Co. 15 Eng. Law & Eq. Rep. 596 ; Preston v. The Liverpool, Manchester, &c. R. Co. 7 Eng. Law & Eq. Rep. 124 ; Edwards v. The Grand Junction R. Co. 1 Mylne & Craig, 650 ; Lindsay v. The Great Northern R. Co. 19 Eng. Law & Eq. Rep. 87. And this principle alone would seem, in most cases, to be sufficient to render a consolidated company liable to discharge all the duties and obligations of the original companies.

dent of the company, expressly directed the secretary, Mr. Brobson, that the seal of the company was not to be fixed to either paper until Hiram Howard signed and sealed both of them. The two papers, respectively marked A and B, being shown to him, he stated that they are the two papers to which he refers; that the impression of the seal on said paper A, is the seal of the Wilmington and Susquehanna Railroad Company, but that said seal was not placed there, he is very positive, at any time whilst he was president of said company, and was never placed there by his authority or by the authority of the board.

The defendant now insists he had a right to prove by this witness, that although the paper bore the corporate seal of the company, it was not its deed, because of an understanding between the witness and the plaintiff that Hiram Howard was to execute the paper. If the offer had been to prove that at the time the corporate seal was affixed, it was agreed that the instrument should not be the deed of the company, unless, or until Hiram Howard should execute it, the evidence might have been admissible. Pawling et al. v. The United States, 4 Cranch, 219; Derby Canal Company v. Wilmot, 9 East, 360; Bell v. Ingestre, 12 Ad. & El. N. S. 317. But the understanding to which the question points, was prior to the sealing, and in no way connected with that act, of which the witness had no knowledge. It did not bear upon the question whether the instrument was the deed of the company, and was properly rejected.

The sixth exception rests on the following facts: The plaintiff offered to read the deposition of a deceased witness taken by the defendants in the case in Cecil County Court, to prove that the paper in question bore the seal of the corporation placed there by the deponent, an officer of the corporation. The defendant objected, but the court admitted the evidence. We consider the evidence was admissible upon two grounds; to prove that in that case the defendant had asserted this instrument to be the deed of the corporation, and relied on it as such; and also, because the witness being dead, his deposition, regularly taken in a suit in which both the plaintiff and defendant were parties, touching the same subject-matter in issue in this case, was competent evidence on its trial. It is said the parties were not the same. But it is not necessary they should be identical, and they were the same, except that Hiram Howard was a co-plaintiff in the former suit, and this diversity does not render the evidence inadmissible. 1 Greenl. Ev. 553; 1 Ad. & El. 19.

The seventh and last bill of exceptions covers nine distinct propositions given by the court to the jury as instructions. The first of the instructions excepted to, was as follows:

" If the jury find from the evidence that this instrument of writing was produced in court, and relied upon by the present defendant, as a contract under the seal of the Wilmington and Susquehanna Railroad Company, in an action of *assumpsit* brought by Sebre and Hiram Howard, against the last mentioned company in Cecil County Court; and that the said suit was decided against the plaintiffs upon the ground that this instrument was duly sealed by the corporation as its deed, then the defendant cannot be permitted in this case to deny the validity of said sealing, because such a defence would impute to the present defendant itself a fraud upon the administration of justice in Cecil County Court."

It is objected that this instruction applied the doctrine of estoppel, where the matter of the estoppel had not been relied on in pleading. The rules on this subject are well settled. If a party has opportunity to plead an estoppel and voluntarily omits to do so, and tenders or takes issue on the fact, he thus waives the estoppel and commits the matter to the jury, who are to find the truth. 1 Saund. 325 a., n. 4; 2 B. & A. 668; 2 Bing. 377; 4 Bing. N. C. 748. But if he have not opportunity to show the estoppel by pleading, he may exhibit the matter thereof in evidence, on the trial, under any issue which involves the fact, and both the court and the jury are bound thereby. 1 Salk. 276; 17 Mass. 369. Now the plea in this case was *non est factum*, which amounts to a denial that the instrument declared on was the defendant's deed at the time of action brought. If sealed and delivered, and subsequently altered, or erased, in a material part, or if the seal was torn off, before action brought, the plea is supported. 5 Coke, 23, 119 b.; 11 Coke, 27, 28; Co. Lit. 35 b., n. 6, 7. It follows that a replication to the effect that on some day, long before action brought, the instrument was the deed of the defendant, would be bad on demurrer, for it would not completely answer the plea.

The plaintiff cannot be said to have opportunity to plead an estoppel, and voluntarily to omit to do so, when the previous pleadings are such that if he did plead it, it would be demurrable.

Besides, a plea of *non est factum* rightly concludes to the country, and so the plaintiff has no opportunity to reply specially, any new matter of fact. He can only join the issue tendered, and if he were prevented from having the benefit of an estoppel, because he has not pleaded it, it would follow that the plaintiff can never have the benefit of an estoppel when the defendant pleads the general issue, for in no such case can he plead it. This was clearly pointed out in Trevivan *v.* Lawrence, 1 Salk. 276, where the court say, " that when the plaintiff's title is by estoppel, and the defendant pleads the general issue, the jury are bound by the estoppel." And it is in this way that the numerous cases of estoppels *in pais* which are in the recent books of reports, have almost always been presented.

It is further objected, that the facts supposed in the instruction, did not amount in law to an estoppel. We think otherwise. Hall *v.* White, 3 C. & P. 137, was detinue for certain deeds. The defendant wrote to the plaintiffs' attorney, and spoke of the deed as in his possession under such circumstances as ought to have led him to understand a suit would be brought upon the faith of what he said. Best, C. J., ruled: " If the defendant said he had the deeds, and thereby induced the plaintiffs to bring their action against him, I shall hold that they may recover, though the assertion was a fraud on his part." In Doe *v.* Lambly, 2 Esp. 635, the defendant had informed the plaintiffs' agent that his tenancy commenced at Lady-day, and the agent gave a notice to quit on that day. This not being heeded, ejectment was brought, and the tenant set up a holding from a different day. But Lord Kenyon refused to allow him to show that he was even mistaken in his admission, for he was concluded. Mordecai *v.* Oliver, 3 Hawks, 479; Crocket *v.* Lasbrook, 5 Mon. 530; Trustees of Congregation, &c. *v.* Williams, 9 Wend. 147, are to the same point.

These decisions go much further than this case requires, because the defendant not only induced the plaintiff to bring this action, but defeated the action in Cecil County Court, by asserting and maintaining this paper to be the deed of the company; and this brings the defendant within the principle of the common law, that when a party asserts what he knows is false or does not know to be true, to another's loss, and his own gain, he is guilty of a fraud; a fraud in fact, if he knows it to be false, fraud in law, if he does not know it to be true. Polhill *v.* Walter, 3 B. & Ad. 114; Lobdell *v.* Baker, 1 Met. 201.

· Certainly it would not mitigate the fraud, if the false assertion were made in a court of justice and a meritorious suit defeated thereby. We are clearly of opinion, that the defendant cannot be heard to say, that what was asserted on the former trial was false, even if the assertion was made by mistake. If it was a mistake, of which there is no evidence, it was one made by the defendant, of which he took the benefit, and the plaintiff the loss, and it is too late to correct it. It does not carry the estoppel beyond what is strictly equitable, to hold that the representation which defeated one action on a point of form should sustain another on a like point.

The next instruction is objected to on the ground that Hiram Howard ought to have been joined as a co-plaintiff. By reference to the indenture, it will be seen that it purports to be made between Sebre Howard and Hiram Howard, of the first part, and the Wilmington and Susquehanna Railroad Company, of the second part. The cove-

Philadelphia, Wilmington, & Baltimore Railroad Co. *v.* Howard.

nants are not by or with these persons *nominatim*, but throughout the party of the one part covenants with the party of the other part. Sebre Howard alone and the corporation sealed the deed.

It is settled that if one of two covenantees does not execute the instrument, he must join in the action, because whatever may be the beneficial interest of either, their legal interest is joint, and if each were to sue, the court could not know for which to give judgment. Slingsby's case, 5 Coke, 18, b.; Petrie *v.* Bury, 3 B. & C. 353. And the rule has recently been carried so far as to hold, that where a joint covenantee had no beneficial interest, did not seal the deed, and expressly disclaimed under the seal, the other covenantee could not sue alone. Wetherell *v.* Langton, 1 Wels. H. & G. 634. But this rule has no application until it is ascertained that there is a joint covenantee, and this is to be determined in each case by examining the whole instrument. Looking at this deed, it appears the covenant sued on was with " the party of the first part," and the inquiry with whom the covenant was made, resolves itself into the question, what person, or persons, constituted "the party of the first part," at the moment when the deed took effect?

The descriptive words, in the premises of the deed, declare Sebre and Hiram Howard to be the party of the first part; but, inasmuch as Hiram did not seal the deed, he never in truth became a party to the instrument. He entered into no covenant contained in it. When, in the early part of the deed, the party of the first part covenants with the party of the second part to do the work, it is impossible to maintain that Hiram Howard is there embraced, under the words " party of the first part," as a covenantor. And when, in the next sentence, the party of the second part covenants with the party of the first part to pay for the work, it would be a most strained construction to hold, that the same words do embrace him as a covenantee. There can be no sound reason for the construction, that the words party of the first part mean one thing, when that party is to do something, and a different thing, when that party is to receive compensation for doing it. The truth is, that the descriptive words are controlled by the decisive fact, that Hiram did not seal the deed, and so *error demonstrationis* plainly appears. An examination of the numerous authorities cited by the counsel for the plaintiff in error will show that they are reconcilable with this interpretation of the covenants; for, in all the cases in which one of the persons named in the deed did not seal, he was covenanted with *nominatim*. Our conclusion is, that the action was rightly brought by Sebre Howard alone.

The next instruction excepted to was as follows: " The omission of the plaintiffs to finish the work within the times mentioned in the contract, is not a bar to his recovery for the price of the work he actually performed; but the defendant may set off any damage he sustained by the delay, if the delay arose from the default of the plaintiffs."

· The time fixed for the completion of the contract was the first day of November, 1836. The company agreed to pay twenty-six cents per cubic yard, in monthly payments, according to the measurements and valuation of the engineer. · These monthly payments were made up to December, 1837; and when the contract was determined by the company, January 18th, 1838, under a power to that effect in the instrument, which will be presently noticed, there remained due the price of the work done in December, and on eighteen days in January.

The question is, whether the covenant to pay was dependent on the covenant to finish the work by the first day of November. So far as respects each monthly instalment, earned before breach of the covenant to finish the work on the first day of November, it is clear the covenants were independent. Or, to state it more accurately, the covenant to pay at the end of each month, for the work done during that month, was dependent on the progress of the work so far as respected the amount to be paid; but was not dependent on the covenant to finish the work by a day certain. The only doubt is, whether, after the breach of this last mentioned covenant, the defendants were bound to pay for work done after that time.

There is an apparent, and perhaps some real conflict, in the decisions of different courts, on this point. 2 Johns. 272, 387; 10 Johns. 203; 2 H. Bl. 380; 8 Mass. 80; 15 Mass. 503; 5 Gill & Johns. 254. We do not deem it needful to review the numerous authorities because we hold the general principle to be clear, that covenants are to be considered dependent, or independent, according to the intention of the parties, which is to be deduced from the whole instrument; and in this case we find no difficulty in arriving at the conclusion, that the covenants were throughout independent. There are, in this instrument, no terms which import a condition, or expressly make one of those covenants in any particular dependent on the other. There is no necessary dependency between them, as the pay for work done may be made, though the work be done after the day. The failure to perform on the day does not go to the whole consideration of the contract, and there is no natural connection between the amount to be paid for work after the day, and the injury or loss inflicted by a failure to perform on the day. Still it would have been competent for the parties to agree that the contractor should not receive the monthly instalment due in November, if the work should not be then finished, and that he should receive nothing for work done after that time.

But we find no such agreement. On the contrary, the covenant to pay for what shall have been done during each preceding month is absolute and unlimited, and the parties have provided a mode of securing the performance of the work and the indemnification of the company from loss, wholly different from making these covenants in any particular dependent on each other. They have agreed, as will be presently more fully stated, that the company may declare a forfeiture of the contract in case the work should not proceed to their satisfaction, and may retain fifteen per cent. of each payment to secure themselves from loss. Without undertaking to apply to this particular case any fixed technical rule, like that held in Terry v. Duntze, 2 H. Bl. 389, we hold it was not the intention of these parties, as shown by this instrument, to make the payment of any instalment dependent on the covenant to finish the work by the first day of November; and that consequently the instruction given at the trial was correct.

The sixth instruction, which is also excepted to, must be read in connection with the fifth and the provision of the contract to which they refer. The contract contains the following clause:

"Provided, however, that in case the party of the second part shall at any time be of opinion that this contract is not duly complied with by the said party of the first part, or that it is not in due progress of execution, or that the said party of the first part is irregular or negligent, then, and in such case, he shall be authorized to declare this contract forfeited, and thereupon the same shall become null, and the party of the first part shall have no appeal from the opinion and decision aforesaid, and he hereby releases all right to except to, or question the same in any place under any circumstances whatever; but the party of the first part shall still remain liable to the party of the second part for the damages occasioned by the said non-compliance, irregularity, or negligence."

The instructions thereon were:

5th. "If the defendant annulled this contract, as stated in the testimony, under the belief that the plaintiff was not prosecuting the work with proper diligence, and for the reasons assigned in the resolution of the board, they are not liable for any damage the plaintiff may have sustained thereby, even although he was in no default, and the company acted in this respect under a mistaken opinion as to his conduct."

6th. "But this annulling did not deprive him of any rights vested in him at that time, or make the covenant void *ab initio*, so as to deprive him of a remedy upon it for any money then due him for his work, or any damages he had then already sustained."

The law leans strongly against forfeiture, and it is incumbent on the party who seeks to enforce one, to show plainly his right to it. The language used in this contract is susceptible of two meanings. One is the literal meaning, for which the plaintiff in error contends, that the declaration of the company annulled the contract, destroying all rights which had become vested under it, so that if there was one of the monthly payments in arrear and justly due from the company to the contractor, and as to which the company was in default, yet it could not be recovered, because every obligation arising out of the contract was at an end.

Another interpretation is, that the contract, so far as it remained executory on the part of the contractor, and all obligations of the company dependent on the future execution by him of any part of the contract might be annulled. We cannot hesitate to fix on the latter as the true interpretation.

In the first place, the intent to have the obligation of the contractor, to respond for damages, continue, is clear. In the next place, though the contractor expressly releases all right to except to the forfeiture, he does not release any right already vested under the contract, by reason of its part performance, and *expressio unius exclusio alterius*. And finally, it is highly improbable, that the parties could have intended to put it in the power of the company, to exempt itself from paying money, honestly earned and justly due, by its own act declaring a forfeiture. The counsel for the plaintiff in error seemed to feel the pressure of this difficulty, and not to be willing to maintain that vested rights were absolutely destroyed by the act of the company; and he suggested that though the covenant were destroyed, *assumpsit* might lie upon an implied promise. But if the intention of the parties was to put an end to all obligation on the part of the company arising from the covenant, there would remain nothing from which a promise could be implied; and if this was not their intention, then we come back to the very interpretation against which he contended; for if the obligation arising from the covenant remains, the covenant is not destroyed. We hold the instruction of the court on this point to have been correct.[1]

---

[1] In Ranger *v.* The Great Western R. Co., 1 Eng. Rail. Ca. 1, and 3 Ib. 298, under an agreement providing that a certain proportion of the amount found, by the engineer of the company, at stated times to be due to the contractor for the work then completed, it was held that the company, after putting an end to the contract, were still liable to pay any sums which became due to the contractor under the

The next instruction, excepted to, was in these words : — "The in-creased work occasioned by changing the width of the road and alter-ing the grade having been directed by the engineer of the company under its authority, was done under this covenant, and within its sti-pulations, and may be recovered in this action, without resorting to an action of assumpsit."

The covenant of the plaintiff was " to do, execute, and perform the work and labor in the said schedule mentioned." And the sche-dule mentions " all the grading of that part of section 9, &c., accord-ing to the directions of the engineer," &c. We think this instruction was correct. The plaintiff in error insists that the covenant was to do the grading precisely as shown by a profile made before the contract was entered into. If this were so, the company would have been disa-bled from making any change either of width or grade, without the consent of the defendant. We do not think this was the meaning of the contract, and both the company and the contractor having acted on a different interpretation of it, the company must now pay for the increased work of which they have had the benefit.

The ninth instruction was as follows :

9th. "Also, if from any cause, without the fault of the plaintiff, the earth excavated could not be used in the filling up and em-bankments on the road and the river, it was the duty of the defend-ant to furnish a place to waste it. And if the company refused, on the application of the plaintiff to provide a convenient place for that purpose, he is entitled to recover such damages as he sustained by the refusal, if he sustained any ; and he is also entitled to recover any damage he may have sustained by the delay of his work or the increase of his expense in performing it, occasioned [by] the negli-gence, acts, or default of the defendant."

To this the plaintiff in error objects, " that it assumes that the company was bound to provide a place on which to waste the earth." The contract says the contractor is to place earth, not wanted for embankment, " where ordered by the engineer." He can rightfully place it nowhere until ordered by the engineer, and if such an order was refused, or delayed, and the contractor was thereby injured, he had a clear right to damages. It cannot be supposed such an order was to be given or obeyed, if obedience to it would be a trespass. Be-fore giving it, the company was bound to make it a lawful order, the

---

agreement, and that the estimates of the engineer were not conclusive upon the contractor. His decision was held con-clusive as to the quality of the work only, the measurements and calculations might be disputed by the contractor and exa-mined by a court of equity in taking the accounts between the parties.

execution of which would not subject the parties to damages, for a wrong, and therefore was bound to provide a place, and, of course, a reasonably convenient place, as well as seasonably to give the order.

The plaintiff in error also excepted to the tenth instruction, which must be taken together with the clause of the contract to which it relates, to be intelligible. The contract contains the following provision :

"And provided, also, that in order to secure the faithful and punctual performance of the covenants above made by the party of the first part, and to indemnify and protect the party of the second part from loss in case of default and forfeiture of this contract, the said party of the second part shall, notwithstanding the provision in the annexed schedule, be authorized to retain in their hands, until the completion of the contract, fifteen per cent. of the money at any time due to the said party of the first part; thus covenanted and agreed by the said parties, this twelfth day of July, 1836; as witness their seals."

The instruction was :

10th. "Also, the plaintiff is entitled to recover the fifteen per cent. retained by the company, unless the jury find that the company has sustained damage by the default, negligence, or misconduct of the plaintiff. And if such damage has been sustained, but not to the amount of fifteen per cent. then the plaintiff is entitled to recover the balance, after deducting the amount of damage sustained by the company."

It is argued that here is a stipulation that the fifteen per cent. may be retained by the company until the completion of the contract by the defendant; that it never was completed by him, and so the time of payment had not arrived when this action was brought.

Now, it is manifest that one of the events contemplated in this clause was a forfeiture such as actually took place; that in that event the contract never would be completed by the defendant, and so its completion could not with any propriety be fixed on as to the limit of time during which the company might retain the money, unless it was the intention of the parties that the fifteen per cent. so retained should belong absolutely to the company in case of a forfeiture of the contract. But the parties have not only failed to provide for such forfeiture of the fifteen per cent. but have plainly declared a different purpose. There language is, that this money is retained, " to indemnify and protect the party of the second part from loss, in case of default and forfeiture of this contract."

There is a wide difference both in fact and in law, between indemnity and forfeiture; yet it is the former and not the latter which the parties had in view. Whether an express stipulation for a forfeiture of this fifteen per cent. could have been enforced, it is not necessary to decide.

But when the parties have shown an intent to provide a fund for indemnity merely, the legal, as well as the just result is, that after indemnity is made and the sole purpose of the fund fully executed, the residue of it shall go to the person to whom it equitably belongs. Rightly construed, the words, "until the completion of the contract," refer to the time during which all monthly payments were to be made, and give the right to retain the fifteen per cent. out of each and every payment, rather than fix an absolute limit of time during which these sums might be retained. In neither event, contemplated by this clause, would this limit of time be strictly proper. If a forfeiture of the contract took place, it was manifestly inapplicable; and if a forfeiture did not take place, but damage were suffered by the company, from default of the contractor, equal to the fifteen per cent., it cannot be supposed their right to retain was to cease with the completion of the contract. This objection, therefore, must be overruled.[1]

The plaintiff in error also excepts to the 12th instruction. We do not deem it needful to determine whether there was evidence to go to the jury, that the company did not use reasonable diligence to obtain a dissolution of the injunction, because we consider so much of the instruction as relates to this subject, to be a proper qualification of the absolute and peremptory bar, asserted in the first part of the instruction; and if the company desired to raise any question concerning the proper tribunal to decide on the matter of diligence, or respecting the evidence competent to justify a finding thereon, some prayer for particular instructions respecting these points should have been preferred. But we consider there was some evidence bearing on this

---

[1] That a reserved fund may be absolutely forfeited by a contractor who fails to perform his agreement to the satisfaction of the company, if such was the intention of the parties, appears from the case of Macintosh v. The Midland Counties R. Co., 3 Eng. Rail. Ca. 780. The contract in that case provided that a portion of the instalments becoming due to the plaintiff should be reserved till a fund of £15,000 should be created, and that in case of a failure of the contractor to complete the works by a certain day he should forfeit the sum of £300 per day till this completion. The contract not having been performed by the specified time, the court held that the forfeiture took effect, notwithstanding the company had failed to supply in season certain materials which it was bound to furnish. See also Ranger v. The Great Western R. Co., 1 Eng. Rail. Ca. 1; 1, and 3 Ib. 298. And it seems that not only a reserved fund, retained from the compensation-money, may be thus forfeited, but the tools and materials of the contractor also. Rouch v. The Great Western R. Co. 2 Eng. Rail. Ca. 505; Hawthorn v. The Newcastle-upon-Tyne, &c. R. Co. Ib. 288.

question of diligence, and that it was for the jury and not the court to pass thereon.

Two objections are made to the thirteenth instruction. The first is, that this instruction assumed the existence of evidence, competent to go to a jury, to prove that the defendants fraudulently terminated the contract under the clause which enabled them to declare it forfeited. To this objection, it is a conclusive answer that the defendants themselves prayed for an instruction substantially like that given. The other objection is, that the jury were instructed to allow by way of damages, such profit as they might find the plaintiff had been deprived of by the termination of the contract by the defendants, if they should find the act of termination to be fraudulent.

It is insisted that only actual damages, and not profits, were in that event to be inquired into and allowed by the jury. It must be admitted that actual damages were all that could lawfully be given in an action of covenant, even if the company had been guilty of fraud. But it by no means follows that profits are not to be allowed, understanding, as we must, the term profits in this instruction as meaning the gain which the plaintiff would have made if he had been permitted to complete his contract. Actual damages clearly include the direct and actual loss which the plaintiff sustains *propter rem ipsam non habitam.*

And in the case of a contract like this, that loss is, among other things, the difference between the cost of doing the work and the price to be paid for it. This difference is the inducement and real consideration which causes the contractor to enter into the contract. For this he expends his time, exerts his skill, uses his capital, and assumes the risks which attend the enterprise. And to deprive him of it, when the other party has broken the contract and unlawfully put an end to the work, would be unjust. There is no rule of law which requires us to inflict this injustice. Wherever profits are spoken of as not a subject of damages, it will be found that something contingent upon future bargains, or speculations, or states of the market, are referred to, and not the difference between the agreed price of something contracted for and its ascertainable value, or cost. See Masterton *v.* Mayor of Brooklyn, 7 Hill's R. 61, and cases there referred to. We hold it to be a clear rule, that the gain or profit, of which the contractor was deprived, by the refusal of the company to allow him to proceed with, and complete the work, was a proper subject of damages.

We have considered all the exceptions; we find no one tenable, and the judgment of the court below is affirmed with costs.

Order.

This cause came on to be heard on the transcript of the record from the Circuit Court of the United States for the District of Maryland, and was argued by counsel. On consideration whereof, it is now here ordered and adjudged by this court, that the judgment of the said Circuit Court in this cause be, and the same is hereby, affirmed with costs and damages at the rate of six per centum per annum.

PHILADELPHIA AND READING RAILROAD COMPANY, Plaintiff in error, v. ELIAS H. DERBY.[1]

December Term, 1852.

Collision — Negligence — Gratuitous Passengers — Liability of Company.

Where a suit was brought against a railroad company, by a person who was injured by a collision, it was correct in the court to instruct the jury, that, if the plaintiff was lawfully on the road, at the time of the collision, and the collision and consequent injury to him were caused by the gross negligence of one of the servants of the defendants, then and there employed on the road, he was entitled to recover, notwithstanding the circumstances, that the plaintiff was a stockholder in the company, riding by invitation of the President, paying no fare, and not in the usual passenger cars.

And also that the fact that the engineer having the control of the colliding locomotive, was forbidden to run on that track at the time, and had acted in disobedience of such orders, was no defence to the action.

A master is liable for the tortious acts of his servant, when done in the course of his employment, although they may be done in disobedience of the master's orders.

THIS case was brought up, by a writ of error, from the Circuit Court of the United States for the Eastern District of Pennsylvania.

It was an action on the case brought by Derby, for an injury suffered upon the railroad of the plaintiff in error.

The declaration, in ten counts, was, in substance, that on the 15th day of June, 1848, the defendants, being the owners of the railroad, and of a certain car engine called the Ariel, received the plaintiff into the said car, to be safely carried therein, upon, and over the said railroad, whereby it became the duty of the defendants to use proper

---

[1] 14 Howard's Reports, 468.

care and diligence that the plaintiff should be safely and securely carried, yet, that the defendants, not regarding their duty in that behalf, conducted themselves so negligently by their servants, that, by reason of such negligence, while the car engine Ariel was upon the road, and the plaintiff therein, he was precipitated therefrom upon the ground, and greatly injured. Defendants pleaded not guilty.

On the 22d of April, 1851, the cause came on to be tried, and the evidence was, in substance, as follows :

In the month of June, 1848, the plaintiff, being a stockholder in the said railroad company, came to the city of Philadelphia, for the purpose of inquiring into its affairs, on his own account and as the representative of other stockholders. On the 15th of June, 1848, the plaintiff accompanied John Tucker, Esq., the President of the said company, over the railroad, for the purpose of viewing it and the works of the company.

They proceeded in the ordinary passenger train of the company, from the city of Philadelphia, (the plaintiff paying no fare for his passage,) as far as the city of Reading.

On arriving at Reading, the plaintiff inspected the machine-shops of the defendants, there situate, and remained for that purpose about half an hour after the departure of the passenger train towards Pottsville, which latter place is about the distance of ninety-two miles from Philadelphia.

By order of Mr. Tucker, a small locomotive car engine, called the Ariel was prepared for the purpose of carrying the plaintiff and Mr. Tucker further up the road. This engine was not constructed, or used, for the business of the said defendants, but was kept for the use of the President and other officers of the company, their friends and guests.

On this engine, the plaintiff and Mr. Tucker, accompanied by the engineer and fireman, and a paymaster of defendants, proceeded, following the passenger train, until they reached Port Clinton, a station on the line of the railroad.

After leaving Port Clinton, when about three miles distant from it, going round a curve, the passengers of the Ariel saw another engine called the Lycoming, of which S. P. Jones was the conductor, approaching on the same track. The engineer of the Ariel immediately reversed the engine, and put down the break. Mr. Tucker, the plain-tiff, and the fireman, jumped from the Ariel, to avoid the impending collision. After they had jumped, the engineer also left the Ariel, having done all he could to stop it. The plaintiff, in attempting to jump, fell, and received the injury of which he complains.

The engineer of the Lycoming, when he saw the approach of the

Ariel, reversed his engine and put down the break. He did not leave the Lycoming till after the collision. At the time of the collision, the Lycoming was backing. The engines were but slightly injured by it.

On the night of the 14th or the morning of the 15th of June, a bridge, on the line of the railroad above Port Clinton, was burnt. In consequence of this, one of the tracks of the railroad was blocked up by empty cars returning to the mines, and stopped by the destruction of the bridge. For this reason a single track only could be used for the business of the road between Port Clinton and the burnt bridge.

Lewis Kirk, an officer of the said company, (master machinist and foreman,) went on the passenger cars from Reading, towards Pottsville, informing the plaintiff and Mr. Tucker, that he would give the proper orders to have the track kept clear for the Ariel. On arriving at Port Clinton he did give an order to Edward Burns, despatcher at Port Clinton, (an officer of said company, charged with the duty of controlling the starting of engines,) that no car should be allowed to go over the road until he the said Kirk returned.

This order was communicated in express terms by Burns to Jones, the conductor of the Lycoming. Jones replied that he would go, and would take the responsibility, and, contrary to his order, did go up the road towards the burnt bridge, and on his return met the Ariel, and the collision ensued, as above stated. Jones had the reputation of being a careful and competent person, no previous disobedience of orders by him had ever occurred, and he was discharged by the defendants immediately after the accident, and because of it.

On the trial the plaintiff below requested the court to charge the jury —

I. That if the plaintiff was lawfully upon the railroad of the defendants at the time of the collision, by the license of the defendants, and was then and there injured by the negligence or disobedience of orders of the company's servants, then and there employed on the said railroad, the defendants are liable for the injury done to the plaintiff by such collision.

II. That if the defendants, by their servants, undertook to convey the plaintiff along the Reading Railroad, in the car Ariel, and while so conveying him, through the gross negligence of the servants of the company then and there employed on the said railroad, the collision occurred, by which the plaintiff was injured, that the defendants are liable for the injury done to the plaintiff by such collision, although no compensation was to be paid to the company for such conveyance of the plaintiff.

III. That if the collision, by which the plaintiff was injured, was occasioned by the locomotive Lycoming, then driven negligently or in disobedience of orders upon the said road by J. P. Jones, one of the company's servants, then having control or command of said locomotive, that the defendants are liable for the injury to the plaintiffs, caused by such collision.

And the counsel for the defendants below requested the court to charge the jury, —

1. That the damages, if any are recoverable, are to be confined to the direct and immediate consequences of the injury sustained.

2. That if the jury believe the plaintiff had paid no fare, and was passing upon the railroad of the defendant as an invited guest, in order to entitle him to recover damages he must prove gross negligence, which is the omission of that care which even the most thoughtless take of their own concerns.

3. That the defendants would be liable in damages to a passenger who had paid passage-money upon their contract to deliver him safely, for slight negligence; but to an invited guest, who paid no fare or passage-money, they will not be responsible unless the jury believe that there was not even slight diligence on the part of the agents of the defendants.

4. That the employer is not responsible for the wilful act of his servant.

5. That if the jury believe that the conductor of the engine Lycoming wilfully, and against the express orders of the officer of the company, communicated to him, by running his engine upon the track above Port Clinton, caused the collision, the defendants are not responsible for any injury or loss resulting from such wilful disobedience.

6. That if the jury believe that every reasonable and proper precaution was taken to have the track of the railroad clear for the passage of the Ariel, and collision ensued solely by reason of the wilful disobedience of the conductor of the Lycoming, and of the express orders duly given by an agent of the company, the plaintiff cannot recover.

7. That if the jury believe that the conductor of the Lycoming, and all the officers of the company in any wise connected with the collision, were carefully and prudently selected, and that the collision ensued and the injury resulted to the plaintiff, an invited guest, by the wilful disobedience of one of them to an order duly communicated, then the plaintiff cannot recover.

The learned Judge charged the jury as requested, on all the points offered by the plaintiff.

And the learned Judge charged on the first and second points offered by the defendants, as requested, and also on the third point of the defendants, with the explanation, that though all the other agents

of the defendants acted with diligence, yet if one of the agents used
no diligence at all, then the defendants could not be said to have
shown slight diligence.

As to the fourth point, the learned Judge charged as requested by the
defendants, with this explanation, that though the master is not liable
for the wilful act of his servant, not done in the course of his employment as servant, yet if the servant disobeys an order relating to his
business, and injury results from that disobedience, the master is liable, for it is his duty to select servants who will obey. The disobedience in this case is the. *ipsa negligentia*, for it is not pretended by
the defendants that the Lycoming was intentionally driven against
the Ariel.

On the fifth, sixth, and seventh points of the defendants, the learned
Judge refused to charge as requested.

The learned Judge further said, that it is admitted that the plaintiff was injured through the act of Jones, the conductor of the Lycoming, that the plaintiff was lawfully on the road by the license of
the defendants; then, in this view of the case, whether he paid fare
or not, or was the guest of the defendants, made no difference as to
the law of the case.

The jury found a verdict for the plaintiff, and assessed the damages
at three thousand dollars.

A writ of error brought the case up to this court.

It was argued by *Campbell* and *Fisher*, for the plaintiff in error,
and *Binney* and *Wharton*, for the defendant in error.

The points made by the counsel for the plaintiff in error, were the
following:

I. The plaintiff stood in such relation to the defendants at the
time of the accident, that he cannot by law recover.

II. The plaintiff suffered no damage from any act with which the
defendants are by law chargeable.

These propositions cover the whole case; yet it may be proper to
direct the attention of the court to two others, which, although included in the latter, are made more specific by referring to the points and
charge of the court.

III. That the learned Judge erred while affirming the third and
fourth points of the defendants, in the explanation by which that
instruction was accompanied. The points and explanations referred
to, were,

3. That the defendants would be liable in damages to a passenger
who had paid passage-money, upon their contract to deliver him
safely, for slight negligence; but to an invited guest, who paid no

fare, or passage-money, they will not be responsible, unless the jury believe that there was not even slight diligence on the part of the agents of the defendants.

4. That the employer is not responsible for the wilful act of his servant or agent.

The learned Judge charged as requested on the third point, with the explanation, that though all the other agents of the defendants acted with diligence, yet, if one of the agents used no diligence at all, then the defendants could not be said to have shown slight diligence.

The learned Judge also charged as requested on the fourth point, with this explanation, that though the master is not liable for the wilful act of his servant, not done in the course of his employment as servant, yet, if the servant disobeys an order relating to his business, and injury results from that disobedience, the master is liable; for it is his duty to select servants who will obey. The disobedience in this case is the *ipsa negligentia*, for it is not pretended by the defendants that the Lycoming was intentionally driven against the Ariel.

IV. The learned Judge erred in refusing to charge as requested by the 5th, 6th, and 7th points of the defendants.

5. That if the jury believe that the conductor of the engine Lycoming wilfully, and against the express orders of the officer of the company, communicated to him, by running his engine upon the track above Port Clinton, caused the collision, the defendants are not responsible for any injury or loss resulting from such wilful disobedience.

6. That if the jury believe every reasonable and proper precaution was taken to have the track of the railroad clear for the passage of the Ariel, and the collision ensued solely by reason of the wilful disobedience of the conductor of the Lycoming, and of the express orders duly given by an agent of the company, the plaintiff cannot recover.

7. That if the jury believe that the conductor of the Lycoming, and all the officers of the company, in any wise connected with the collision, were carefully and prudently selected, and that the collision ensued, and the injury resulted to the plaintiff, an invited guest, by the wilful disobedience of one of them to an order duly communicated, then the plaintiff cannot recover.

I. The plaintiff stood in such relation to the defendants at the time of the accident, that he cannot by law recover.

The plaintiff was a stockholder of the defendants; he was on the road an invited guest, and paid no fare; was not carried in the way of their business, nor in a car used for such purpose. He voluntarily left the passenger train at Reading, and took his seat in the Ariel, with full knowledge of the service to which he was devoted, and the character of the engine itself. He was himself the president of a railroad company.

Being no passenger, and not carried by the company, even gratu-itously, in the way of their business, he was in the car and was carried as a stockholder and a guest.

What were his legal rights, and what the obligations of the defend-ants?

It was contended:

1. That no cause of action can arise to any person by reason of the occurrence of an unintentional injury while he is receiving or partaking of any of those acts of kindness which spring from mere social relations. No contract exists, and no such duty as can give a cause of action, is by law cast upon either party in such relation. Such was the position of the plaintiff.

Upon principles somewhat analogous to the one now presented it has been ruled, " Si un hoste invite un al supper, et le nuit esteant farr spent et luy invite a stayer la tout le nuit, fit soit apres robbe uncore le hoste ne serra charge pur ceo, car cest guest ne fuit ascur traveller." 1.Rolle's Abr. 3.

" And if a man set his horse at an inn, though he lodge at another place, that makes him a guest, for the innkeeper gains by the horse, and therefore that makes the owner a guest, though he be absent. Contra, if goods left there by a man, because the innkeeper hath no advantage by them." York v. Grenaugh, 2 Ld. R. 868.

" So where one leaves his horse at an inn, to stand there by agree-ment at livery, although neither himself nor any of his servants lodge there, he is reputed a guest for that purpose, and the innkeeper hath a valuable consideration, and if that horse be stolen, he hath an action upon the common custom of the realm. But, as in the case at bar, where he leaves goods to keep, whereof the defendant is not to have any benefit, and goes from thence for two or three days, although he saith he will return, yet he is at liberty, and is not a guest during that time, nor is the innkeeper chargeable as a common hostler for the goods stolen during that time, unless he make a special promise for the safe keeping of them, and the action ought to be grounded upon it." Greeley v. Clarke, Cr. Jac. 188.

" For if a man be lodged with another who is not an innholder on request, if he be robbed in his house by the servants of him who lodged him, or any other, he shall not answer for it." Cayle's case, 4 Rep. 32.

" And therefore, if a neighbor who is no traveller, as a friend, at the request of the innholder, lodges there, and his goods be stolen, &c., he shall not have an action." Cayle's case. Id. 33.

The principles on which rights and obligations, arising from particular relations, are founded, are stated by Shaw, C. J., in Farwell v. Boston & Worcester Railroad Co. 4 Metcalf, 58.

And it may be proper to refer to that class of cases based upon the principle, that unless the parties met upon the terms of contract, none can be inferred, or, in the words of Mr. Justice Williams, in Davies v. Davies, (38 Engl. C. L. R. 46,) that the evidence must show " that the parties came there on the terms that they were to pay and be paid, but if that was not so, there can be no *ex poste facto* charge made on either side."

And to the same effect are the actions brought upon claims for services rendered, when the relations of the parties do not justify the inference of contract. Strine v. Parsons, 5 Watts & S. 357. The case of a woman who lived with the decedent (whose estate was sued) as his wife. Walker's Estate, 3 Rawle, 343. An action by a son for services rendered after he arrived at full age. And also Candor's Appeal, 5 Watts & S. 216 ; Hacks v. Stewart, 8 Barr, 213.

2. The plaintiff, being a stockholder as well as guest, and availing himself of an opportunity to inspect, for his own interest as for that of others, the line of the road, their shops, &c., he cannot, by reason also of this relation recover.

He was in the car, as already stated, as a stockholder, and not carried by the company in the way of their business, but for his own benefit, and for the interest of other stockholders whom he represented, and for whom he was acting as agent. No contract was entered into with him, and he occupied, in this regard, no other relation than any other officer or agent of the company or co-proprietor of the road.

One agent injured by another agent, cannot recover from their common principal. Farwell v. Boston & Worcester Railroad Co. 4 Metcalf, R. 49; Brown v. Maxwell, 6 Hill, 592 ; Murray v. South Carolina Railroad Co. 1 McMullan, 385 ; Coon v. Railroad Co. 6 Barbour, 231; Priestly v. Fowler, 3 Mees. & Welsb. 1.

If the defendant in error owned half the stock of the road, or being so the owner, the company was unincorporated, (its charter cannot affect this relation,) or if the charter had created an individual liability in the shareholders, what duty did the law impose upon the other proprietors towards him, while he was on the road by their license, without compensation, to inspect its condition for his own benefit ? It is submitted he went there like any other tenant in common, or joint proprietor, without right to claim against his co-proprietors for the negligence of any of their common servants.

II. The plaintiff suffered no damage from any act with which the defendants are by law chargeable.

The gist of the action is, the neglect of the servant of the defendants of some duty imposed upon them by law, for which negligence they are sought to be held responsible.

1. It is first to be observed, that this liability of the defendants, if any, is not affected by their corporate character, and if under like circumstances an individual would not be liable, a corporation will not.

"A corporation will be liable for an injury done by its servants, if under like circumstances an individual would be responsible." The First Baptist Church v. Schenectady & Tr. R. R. Co. 5 Barb. Sup. Ct. Rep. N. Y. 79. " Indeed the same rule should be applied to a corporation as should be applied to an individual who carries on a business solely through the medium of agents and servants." Pratt, J., Coon v. The Utica R. R. Co. 6 Barb. Sup. Ct. R. 231; Philadelphia R. R. Co. v. Wilt, 4 Wharton, R. 146.

" The power and duty of an engine driver must be the same, simply as such, whether he be employed by a corporation, or a joint stock company, or an ordinary partnership, or an individual. The driver appointed by a corporation, or company, or partnership, carrying on the business of carriers of passengers or goods, must, as such, have the same duties and powers." Per Parke, B. 3 Welsby, H. & G. 277; Con. v. R. R. Co.

2. That an individual would not, under the facts in this case, have been liable, is, it is submitted, clear, from the following authorities, and the principles upon which the decisions are based:

"A master is chargeable with the acts of his servant, but when he acts in the execution of the authority given him by his master, and then the act of the servant is the act of the master." Per Holt, C. J., Middleton v. Fowler, 1 Salk. 282.

" In civil matters, to render one man amenable for another's misconduct, it must ever be established that the latter, in committing the injury, was all the while acting under the authority, and with the assent, express or implied, of the former." Hammond's Nisi Prius, 80.

" Hence it is, that the principal is never liable for the unauthorized, the wilful, or the malicious act or trespass of the agent." Per Story, J., Princip. and Agt. § 456.

In McManus v. Crickett, Lord Kenyon cites these cases, as illustrating the rule:

" If my servant, contrary to my will, chase my beasts into the soil of another, I shall not be punished."

" If I command my servant to distrain, and he ride on the distress, he shall be punished, not I." 1 East, 106.

" In order to render a master liable for a trespass committed by the servant, it is necessary to show that the acts were done while the servant was acting under the authority of the master. . . . To render him liable, it must be shown that the commission of the trespasses was in the execution of his order, or with his assent, or approbation." Per Waite, J., Church v. Mansfield, 20 Conn. 287.

In Armstrong v. Cooley, (5 Gill's Rep. 512,) it was said, by Treat, C. J., " Even when the act is lawful, the principal is responsible for the manner of its performance, if done in the course of his employ- ment, and not in wilful violation of his instructions." Thus declaring that, in the latter case, he would not be liable.

" It should here be observed, that the ground of the principal's lia- bility cannot be that he has selected an agent who is more or less unworthy, and placed him in a situation which enables him to be- come the instrument of mischief to his neighbor, because that would hold him responsible ; not alone for the acts done by the other, in his capacity *quatenus* agent, but even for a wilful default." Ham. N. P. 81.

This principle is exemplified in the case next cited, which, with the following, it is submitted, rule the cause now before the court.

Joel v. Morrison, 25 Eng. C. L. Rep. 512. In this case, the plain- tiff was knocked down by the defendant's horse and cart, then driven by one of his servants accompanied by another. The defendant proved that his horse and cart were only in the habit of being driven out of the city, and did not go into the city (where the act happened) at all. Thesiger, counsel for the plaintiff, suggested that the defend- ant's servants might have gone out of their way, for their own pur- poses, or might have taken the cart at a time when it was not wanted for the purpose of business, and have gone to pay a visit to some friend. He was observing that, under these circumstances, the defend- ant was liable for the acts of his servants — but, per Parke, B., " He is not liable, if, as you suggest, these young men took the cart without leave."

Wilson v. Peverally, (2 N. Hamp. Rep. 548,) was an action on the case against the master. It appeared that, by the defendant's orders, a fire was set on his land, and the charge of it given to a hired laborer. That the defendant left home, directing the laborer, after setting the fire, to employ himself in harrowing other land in the neighborhood. That the laborer, after his master's absence, and before he commenced harrowing, carried brands from that fire into the ploughing field, to consume some piles of wood and brush there collected, and on his way dropped some coals, from which another fire arose, and did all the injury complained of. That carrying fire from one field to another was dangerous, and was not in conformity to any express authority of his master; that the laborer was accustomed to work under the particular directions of his master, and could conveniently have harrowed, without first burning the piles of wood, though to burn them first is the usual course of good husbandry.   A verdict was taken for the plaintiff, subject to the opinion of the court.   Judgment was afterwards given for the defendant, and the Judge (Woodbury) said : " The next ground on which a master is liable for wrongs of his servant, is, that the wrongs are performed by the servant in the negligent and unskilful execution of business specially intrusted to the servant, but the principle does not reach wrongs caused by carelessness in the performance of an act, not directed by the master, as a piece of business of some third person, or of the servant himself, or of the master, but which the master did not, either expressly or impliedly, direct him to perform. . . . Thus a piece of labor might be very properly performed at one time, and not at another; as, in this case, the setting of a fire in the neighborhood of much combustible matter.   And if the master, when the fire would be highly dangerous in such a place, forbore to direct it to be kindled, and employed his servant in other business, it would be unreasonable to make him liable, if the servant, before attending to that business, went in his own discretion, and kindled the fire to the damage of third persons.   The master *quoad hoc*, is not acting in person, or through the servant, neither *per se*, nor *per aliud*, and the doctrine of *respondeat superior*, does not apply to such an act, it being the sole act of the servant."

It appears by the evidence, as applied to these rules :

1. Jones was not acting in execution of the authority given him by his master, the company, which is deemed essential by Lord Holt.

2. In committing the injury, he was not all the while, or at any time, acting under the authority, or with the assent of the company, things, says Hammond, ever to be established to make the principal liable.

3. His act was contrary to the will and express direction of the company, which, under the cases approved by Lord Kenyon, in McManus *v.* Crickett, would discharge the master from liability.

4. The company directed him to do one thing, and not to do another; yet, he did the latter, and did not do the former; therefore, according to the rule approved by Lord Kenyon, he, and not the company, is liable to the plaintiff.

5. His whole conduct was unauthorized by the defendants, who are, therefore, not liable, under the authority of Story and Waite, Js.

6. His acts were "in wilful violation of his instructions," and therefore, as stated in the opinion of Treat, C. J., the defendants are not liable.

7. He took and run the car " without leave," in which case, says Parke, B., the principal is " not liable."

8. Nor are the defendants liable because Jones was in the perform-ance of a piece of business of the defendants, because they did not, either expressly or impliedly, direct him to. perform it; and if, as Judge Woodbury said, it would be unreasonable to make the princi-pal liable for an act done by the servant, without authority, but only on his own discretion, with what reason can the principal be made responsible for the wilful violation of his orders ?

It is hence submitted, that the defendants are not by law charge-able with the damages resulting from the wilful and disobedient act of one of their servants, and that the second point is maintained.

(The argument upon the remaining points, is necessarily omitted.) ·

The points made by the counsel for the defendant in error, were the same ruled by the court below, and were stated as follows :

The three points made by the defendant in error, and affirmed by his honor, Judge Grier, who tried the cause, are found on the record. They are as follows:

I. That if the plaintiff, was lawfully upon the railroad of the defendants, at the time of the collision, by the license of the defend-ants, and was then and there injured by the negligence or disobe-dience of orders of the company's servants, then and there employed upon the said railroad, the defendants are liable for the injury done to the plaintiff by such collision.

Two principles sustain this point.

I. That every person (or corporation) whose negligence or careless-ness causes damage to another person, is *primâ facie* responsible to such person therefor.

II. That a corporation is liable to third persons for the damage done by its servants through negligence or disobedience of orders, in the course of their employment.

I. To the first principle, as an axiom of the law, it is not deemed necessary to cite authorities.

II. In support of the second, the authorities which follow are cited, the principles being first given as stated by eminent text-writers.

In Story on Agency, p. 465, ch. 17, § 452, the rule is laid down as follows :

" It is a general doctrine of law, that, although the principal is not ordinarily liable, (though he sometimes is,) in a criminal suit, for the acts or misdeeds of his agent, unless, indeed, he has authorized or coöperated in those acts or misdeeds ; yet he is · held liable to third persons in a civil suit for the frauds, deceits, concealments, misrepre-sentations, torts, negligences, and other malfeasances or misfeasances and omissions of duty of his agent in the course of his employment, although the principal did not authorize, or justify, or participate in, or, indeed, know of such misconduct, or even if he forbade them, or disapproved of them. In all such cases, the rule applies, *Respondeat superior;* and it is founded upon public policy and convenience; for in no other way could there be any safety to third persons in their dealings, either directly with the principals, or indirectly with him through the instrumentality of agents. In every such case, the principal holds out his agent as competent, and fit to be trusted; and thereby, in effect, he warrants his fidelity and good conduct in all matters of the agency." And in note 2, the learned author, in commenting upon a passage in 1 Blackstone's Comm. 432, adds, " for the master is liable for the wrong and negligence of his servant, just as much when it has been done contrary to his orders and against his intent, as he is, when he has coöperated in, or known the wrong."

"A master is ordinarily liable to answer in a civil suit for the tortious or wrongful acts of his servant, if those acts are done in the course of his employment in his master's service; the maxims applicable to such cases, being, *Respondeat superior*, and *Qui facit per alium, facit per se.* This rule, with some few exceptions, is of universal application, whether the act of the servant be one of omission or commission, whether negligent, fraudulent, or deceitful, or even if it be an act of positive malfeasance or misconduct; if it be done in the course of his employment his master is responsible for it, *civiliter*, to third persons. And it makes no difference that the master did not authorize, or even know of the servant's act or neglect; for even if he disapproved of or forbade it, he is equally liable, if the act be done in the course of the servant's employment. Smith on Master and Servant, p. 152; Law Lib. Jan. 1852, p. 130.

" If a servant is acting in the execution of his master's orders, and by his negligence causes injury to a third party, the master will be responsible, although the servant's act was not necessary for the proper performance of his duty to his master, or was even contrary to his master's orders." Smith on Master and Servant, p. 157; Law Lib. Jan. 1852, p. 134.

The following authorities establish conclusively the principles above stated. Sleath *v.* Wilson, 9 Carrington & Payne, 607, (38 E. C. L. 249.).

If a servant, without his master's knowledge, take his master's carriage out of the coach-house, and with it commit an injury, the master is not liable; because he has not in such case intrusted the servant with the carriage. But whenever the master has intrusted the servant with the control of the carriage, it is no answer that the servant acted improperly in the management of it; but the master, in such case, will be liable, because he has put it into the servant's power to mismanage the carriage by intrusting him with it. Therefore, where a servant, having set his master down in Stamford street, was directed by him to put up in Castle street, Leicester Square; but instead of so doing, went to deliver a parcel of his own, in the Old Street Road, and in returning along it, drove against an old woman, and injured her; it was held, that the master was responsible for his servant's act.

Mr. Justice Erskine states the law in the clearest manner. " Whenever the master has intrusted the servant with the control of the carriage, it is no answer that the servant acted improperly in the management of it. If it were, it might be contended that if a master directs his servant to drive slowly, and the servant disobeys his orders and drives fast, and through his negligence occasions an injury, the master will not be liable. But that is not the law: the master, in such a case, will be liable, and the ground is that he has put it in the servant's power to mismanage the carriage, by intrusting him with it."

The case of Joel v. Morrison, (6 Carrington & Payne, 501, 25 E. C. L. 511,) is to the same point, — but the servant in that case was acting against his master's implied commands, and not his express. The master was held liable. In Brown v. Copley, (7 Mann. & Granger, 49 E. C. L. 566,) Sergeant Talfourd arguendo, puts the case, previously put by way of illustration by Mr. Justice Erskine, in Sleath v. Wilson, — "As, if a coachman were driving his master, and were ordered not to drive so fast, but he nevertheless continued to do so, the master would be responsible for the injury." To which Mr. Justice Cresswell assents, saying, — " In that case, the coachman would still be driving for his master, though driving badly."

It is not pretended, in the present case, that Jones disobeyed the order given him, to attend to any private business of his own; he was still " driving " (his locomotive) " for his master," " though driving badly."

Nor did the damage ensue from the breach of the express order not to run up the railroad until the Ariel had passed. Jones ran his locomotive up the road without harming any one. It was on his return down the road that he encountered the Ariel.

And in Croft v. Alison, (4 Barn. & Ald. 590, 6 E. C. L. 528,) in an action for the negligent driving of the defendant's coachman, whereby the plaintiff's carriage was upset, it appeared that the accident arose from the defendant's coachman striking the plaintiff's horses with his whip, in consequence of which they moved forward, and the carriage was overturned. At the time when the horses were struck, the two carriages were entangled. The defendant was held liable for the damage caused by his servant's act, although wanton, as it was done in pursuance of his employment. And *per curiam*, " The distinction is this; if a servant driving a carriage, in order to effect some purpose of his own, wantonly strikes the horse of another person, and produce the accident, the master will not be liable. But if, in order to perform the master's orders, he strikes, but injudiciously, and in order to extricate himself from a difficulty, that will be negligent and careless conduct, for which the master will be liable, being an act done in pursuance of the servant's employment."

The third point of the defendant in error, and sustained by his Honor who tried the cause, is as follows :

III. That if the collision by which the plaintiff was injured was occasioned by the locomotive Lycoming, then driven negligently, or in disobedience of orders, upon the said road, by J. P. Jones, one of the company's servants, then having control or command of the said locomotive, that the defendants are liable for the injury to the plaintiff, caused by such collision.

This point merely applies the general principles of the first point to the facts proved, and is virtually comprehended in it. It therefore needs no further notice.

The second point of the defendant in error, sustained by his Honor who tried the cause, is as follows :

II. That if the defendants, by their servants, undertook to convey the plaintiff along the Reading Railroad, in the car Ariel, and while so conveying him, through the gross negligence of the servants of the company, then and there employed upon the said railroad, the collision occurred by which the plaintiff was injured, that the defendants are liable for the injury done to the plaintiff by such collision, although no compensation was to be paid to the company for such conveyance of the plaintiff.

The principle of this point is identical with that of the second point presented by the plaintiffs in error themselves, and which was duly affirmed by his Honor in his charge, and the principle is in entire harmony with the third point of the plaintiffs in error, which was also duly affirmed by his Honor.

As both parties, therefore, seem to have agreed in their views on these points as presented as above to his Honor for adoption, and which was duly adopted by him, it can hardly be necessary to refer to the authorities on which the doctrines are based.

The leading case in point is that of Coggs v. Barnard, (Lord Raymond, 909,) the celebrated case under the law of bailments. The principle of that case is that, " if a man undertakes to carry goods safely and securely, he is responsible for any damage they may sustain in the carriage through his neglect, though he was not a common-carrier, and was to have nothing for the carriage."

This case has been commented upon with great ability, and at much length in 1 Smith's Leading Cases, p. 82, and the American authorities upon the point are collected by Messrs. Hare and Wallace, p. 227.

Mr. Smith states the general principle in these words, viz. " The confidence induced by undertaking any service for another, is a sufficient legal consideration to create a duty in the performance of it."

Among the numerous American cases affirming this principle, is Thorne v. Deas, 4 Johns. 84, in which Chief Justice Kent says, " If a party who makes this engagement," (the gratuitous performance of business for another,) " enters upon the execution of the business, and does it amiss, through the want of due care, by which damage ensues to the other party, an action will lie for this misfeasance."

A principle to which the defendant in error's second point also refers, is the liability of an unpaid agent for gross negligence only.

In the later cases, the English courts have found considerable difficulty in distinguishing with precision between negligence and gross negligence. In Wilson v. Brett, 11 Mees. & Wels. 113, Baron Rolfe observes, " that he could see no difference between negligence and gross negligence ; that it was the same thing, with the addition of a vituperative epithet."

And see Hare and Wallace's American note, p. 242, with the American cases there cited, and which are collected and commented on at much length, and the true principle stated, that any negligent conduct, which causes injury or loss, is actionable.

The defendant in error might perhaps have been entitled to ask the benefit of a rule less rigid in its bearing upon himself; but as the conduct of the railroad company in discharging Jones, the conductor, showed their own estimate of the grossness of the negligence in question, the defendant in error was content to ask the ruling of the point in its milder form, and the finding of the jury established the grossness of the negligence. The question of what is gross negligence being for the jury, see Storer v. Gowen, 6 Shepley, 174 ; Whitney v. Lee, 8 Metcalf, 91 ; Angell on Carriers, p. 12.

Mr. Justice GRIER delivered the opinion of the court.

This action was brought by Derby, the plaintiff below, to recover damages for an injury suffered on the railroad of the plaintiffs in error. The peculiar facts of the case, involving the questions of law presented for our consideration are these :

The plaintiff below was himself the president of another railroad company, and a stockholder in this. He was on the road of defendants by invitation of the president of the company, not in the usual passenger cars, but in a small locomotive car used for the convenience of the officers of the company, and paid no fare for his transportation. The injury to his person was caused by coming into collision with a locomotive and tender, in the charge of an agent or servant of the company, which was on the same track, and moving in an opposite direction. Another agent of the company, in the exercise of proper care and caution, had given orders to keep the track clear. The driver of the colliding engine acted in disobedience and disregard of these orders, and thus caused the collision.

The instructions given by the court below, at the instance of plaintiff, as well as those requested by the defendant, and refused by the court, taken together, involve but two distinct points, which have been the subject of exception here, and are in substance as follows:

1. The court instructed the jury, that if the plaintiff was lawfully on the road at the time of the collision, and the collision and consequent injury to him were caused by the gross negligence of one of the servants of the defendants, then and there employed on the road, he is entitled to recover, notwithstanding the circumstances given in evidence, and relied upon by defendant's counsel as forming a defence to the action, to wit: that the plaintiff was a stockholder in the company, riding by invitation of the president — paying no fare, and not in the usual passenger cars, &c.

2. That the fact that the engineer having the control of the colliding locomotive, was forbidden to run on that track at the time, and had acted in disobedience of such orders, was not a defence to the action.

1st. In support of the objections to the first instruction, it is alleged, "that no cause of action can arise to any person by reason of the occurrence of an unintentional injury, while he is receiving or partaking of any of those acts of kindness which spring from mere social relations; and that as there was no contract between the parties, express or implied, the law would raise no duty as between them, for the neglect of which an action can be sustained."

In support of these positions, the cases between innkeeper and guest have been cited, such as 1 Rolle's Abr. 3, where it is said, "If a hoste invite one to supper, and the night being far spent, he invites him to stay all night, and the guest be robbed, yet the host shall not be chargeable, because the guest was not a traveller;" and Cayle's case, 4 Rep. 52, to the same effect, showing that the peculiar liability of an innkeeper arises from the consideration paid for his entertain-

11*

ment of travellers, and does not exist in the case of gratuitous lodging of friends or guests. The case of Farwell v. The Boston and Worcester Railroad Company, 4 Metcalf, 47, has also been cited, showing that the master is not liable for any injury received by one of his servants, in consequence of the carelessness of another, while both are engaged in the same service.

But we are of opinion, that these cases have no application to the present. The liability of the defendants below, for the negligent and injurious act of their servant, is not necessarily founded on any contract or privity between the parties, nor affected by any relation, social or otherwise, which they bore to each other. It is true, a traveller, by stage-coach, or other public conveyance, who is injured by the negligence of the driver, has an action against the owner, founded on his contract to carry him safely. But the maxim of " *respondeat superior*," which, by legal imputation, makes the master liable for the acts of his servant, is wholly irrespective of any contract, express or implied, or any other relation between the injured party and the master. If one be lawfully on the street or highway, and another's servant carelessly drives a stage or carriage against him, and injures his property or person, it is no answer to an action against the master for such injury, either, that the plaintiff was riding for pleasure, or that he was a stockholder in the road, or that he had not paid his toll, or that he was the guest of the defendant, or riding in a carriage borrowed from him, or that the defendant was the friend, benefactor, or brother of the plaintiff. These arguments, arising from the social or domestic relations of life may, in some cases, successfully appeal to the feelings of the plaintiff, but will usually have little effect where the defendant is a corporation, which is itself incapable of such relations or the reciprocation of such feelings.

In this view of the case, if the plaintiff was lawfully on the road at the time of the collision, the court were right in instructing the jury that none of the antecedent circumstances, or accidents of his situation, could affect his right to recover.

It is a fact peculiar to this case, that the defendants, who are liable for the act of their servant coming down the road, are also the carriers who were conveying the plaintiff up the road, and that their servants immediately engaged in transporting the plaintiff were not guilty of any negligence, or in fault for the collision. But we would not have it inferred, from what has been said, that the circumstances alleged to the first point would affect the case, if the negligence which caused the injury had been committed by the agents of the company who were in the immediate care of the engine and car in which the plaintiff rode, and he was compelled to rely on these counts of his declaration, founded on the duty of the defendant to carry him safely. This duty does not result alone from the consideration paid for the service. It is imposed by the law, even where the service is gratuitous. " The confidence induced by undertaking any service for another, is a sufficient legal consideration to create a duty in the performance of it." See Coggs. v. Bernard, and cases cited in 1 Smith's Leading Cases, 95. It is true, a distinction has been taken, in some cases, between simple negligence, and great or gross negligence; and it is said, that one who acts gratuitously is liable only for the latter. But this case does not call upon us to define the difference, (if it be capable of definition,) as the verdict has found this to be a case of gross negligence.

When carriers undertake to convey persons by the powerful but dangerous agency of steam, public policy and safety require that they be held to the greatest possible care and diligence. And whether the consideration of such transportation be pecuniary or otherwise, the personal safety of the passengers should not be left to the sport of chance or the negligence of careless agents. Any negligence, in such cases, may well deserve the epithet of " gross."

In this view of the case, also, we think there was no error in the first instruction.

2. The second instruction involves the question of the liability of the master where the servant is in the course of his employment, but, in the matter complained of, has acted contrary to the express command of his master.

The rule of " *respondeat superior*," or that the master shall be civilly liable for the tortious acts of his servant, is of universal application, whether the act be one of omission or commission, whether negligent, fraudulent, or deceitful. If it be done in the course of his employment, the master is liable ; and it makes no difference that the master did not authorize, or even know of the servant's act or neglect, or even if he disapproved or forbade it, he is equally liable, if the act be done in the course of his servant's employment. See Story on Agency, § 452 ; Smith on Master and Servant, 152.

There may be found, in some of the numerous cases reported on this subject, dicta, which, when severed from the context, might seem to countenance the doctrine that the master is not liable if the act of his servant was in disobedience of his orders. But a more careful examination will show that they depended on the question, whether the servant, at the time he did the act complained of, was acting in the course of his employment, or, in other words, whether he was or was not at the time in the relation of servant to the defendant.

The case of Sleath v. Wilson, 9 Car. & Payne, 607, states the law in such cases distinctly and correctly.

In that case a servant, having his master's carriage and horses in his possession and control, was directed to take them to a certain place; but instead of doing so he went in another direction to deliver a parcel of his own, and, returning, drove against an old woman and injured her. Here the master was held liable for the act of the servant, though at the time he committed the offence, he was acting in disregard of his master's orders; because the master had intrusted the carriage to his control and care, and in driving it he was acting in the course of his employment. Mr. Justice Erskine remarks, in this case: "It is quite clear that if a servant, without his master's knowledge, takes his master's carriage out of the coach-house, and with it commits an injury, the master is not answerable, and on this ground, that the master has not intrusted the servant with the carriage; but whenever the master has intrusted the servant with the control of the carriage, it is no answer, that the servant acted improperly in the management of it. If it were, it might be contended that if a master directs his servant to drive slowly, and the servant disobeys his orders, and drives fast, and through his negligence occasions an injury, the master will not be liable. But that is not the law; the master, in such a case, will be liable, and the ground is, that he has put it in the servant's power to mismanage the carriage, by intrusting him with it."

Although, among the numerous cases on this subject, some may be found (such as the case of Lamb v. Palk, 9 C. & P. 729) in which the court have made some distinctions which are rather subtile and astute, as to when the servant may be said to be acting in the employ of his master; yet we find no case which asserts the doctrine that a master is not liable for the acts of a servant in his employment, when the particular act causing the injury was done in disregard of the general orders or special command of the master. Such a qualification of the maxim of *respondeat superior*, would, in a measure, nullify it. A large proportion of the accidents on railroads are caused by the negligence of the servants or agents of the company. Nothing but the most stringent enforcement of discipline, and the most exact and perfect obedience to every rule and order emanating from a superior, can insure safety to life and property. The intrusting such a powerful and dangerous engine as a locomotive, to one who will not submit to control, and render implicit obedience to orders, is itself an act of negligence, the "*causa causans*" of the mischief; while the proximate cause, or the *ipsa negligentia* which produces it, may truly be said, in most cases, to be the disobedience of orders by the servant so intrusted. If such disobedience could be set up by a railroad company as a defence when charged with negligence, the remedy of the injured party would in most cases be illusive, discipline would be relaxed, and the danger to the life and limb of the traveller greatly enhanced.   Any relaxation of the stringent policy and principles of the law affecting such cases, would be highly detrimental to the public safety.[1]

The judgment of the Circuit Court is therefore affirmed.

Mr. Justice DANIEL dissents from the decision of this court in this cause, upon the ground that the said railroad company being a corporation, created by the State of Pennsylvania, is not capable of

---

[1] The liability of a railway company for injuries to passengers does not arise from contract, but is "founded on the great principle of social duty, that every man, in the management of his own affairs, shall so conduct them, as not to injure another." The promise is implied from the duty, not the duty from the promise. See the language of Shaw, C. J., in Farwell v. Boston & Worcester R. Co. *post.*

See also Mc'Elroy v. Lowell & Nashua R. Co. *post.*

The principle was recently discussed in Marshall v. The York, Newcastle, &c. R. Co. 7 Eng. Law & Eq. Rep. 519. The plaintiff was a servant travelling with his master, who had purchased tickets for both. The servant's baggage was lost, and he brought an action against the company. It was objected that he could not maintain the action, on the ground that the loss was a breach of contract, and the contract was not with the servant, but with his master. But the court held the company liable, and Chief Justice Jervis in delivering his opinion, used the following language. "It was admitted, in the course of the argument, that if the plaintiff, instead of losing his property had broken his leg, he could have had an action for his personal suffering, and his master might have sued for the loss of his service. But in what respect could the plaintiff have an action for his personal suffering? Not because there was a contract between him and the company, *but by reason of a duty irrespective of the contract.*" And Justice Williams says in the same case, that the allegation of contract, in the declaration, is not necessary.

In Collett v. the London & Northwestern R. Co. 6 Eng. Law & Eq. Rep. 305, the plaintiff was a mail agent in charge of the mails. The action was for personal injuries received while the plaintiff was passing over the road in the discharge of his duty as mail agent. The action was resisted on the ground that there was no contract between the plaintiff and the company which rendered the latter liable to the former for the injuries which he had received. Lord Campbell, C. J., in the course of the argument, observed to the counsel for the defendants, "The question is, what is the duty of the company? Is it not to carry safely and securely, if they carry at all?" The company were held responsible.

If the liability of the company in such case does not arise from their contract to carry safely, but from the duty springing from the relation which they sustain to their passengers, it would seem to be a matter of no consequence as regards their liability, whether a person was conveyed gratuitously or for a consideration. In the management of their business, they are bound, like natural persons, to exercise *reasonable* care and diligence to avoid injuring others; but the *degree* of care which may reasonably be required of a company varies with circumstances, and whether a person rightfully upon the road as a gratuitous passenger may require the observance of the same rule as a passenger for hire, is not decided in the above case.

See Gladwell v. Steggall, 5 Bingham N. C. 733; Pippin v. Sheppard, 11 Price, 400.

pleading or being impleaded, under the 2d section of the third article of the constitution, in any of the courts of the United States ; and that therefore the Circuit Court could not take cognizance of the controversy between that corporation and the plaintiff in that court.

Order.

This cause came on to be heard, on the transcript of the record, from the Circuit Court of the United States for the Eastern District of Pennsylvania, and was argued by counsel. On consideration whereof, it is now here ordered, and adjudged, by this court, that the judgment of the said Circuit Court, in this cause be, and the same is hereby, affirmed, with costs and interest until the same is paid at the same rate per annum that similar judgments bear in the courts of the State of Pennsylvania.

CASES

IN THE

SUPREME COURT OF MAINE.

BANGOR AND PISCATAQUIS RAILROAD COMPANY *v.* ELBRIDGE HARRIS.[1]

June Term, 1842.

Taxation of the Real Estate of Company.

The act incorporating the Bangor and Piscataquis Railroad Company, among other things, authorized them to "procure, purchase, and hold in fee simple, improve and use for all purposes of business, to be transacted on or by means of said railroad, lands, or other real estate, and to manage and dispose thereof, as they may see fit;" and provided, "that the capital stock of said company may consist of three hundred thousand dollars, and shall be divided into shares of one hundred dollars each, *to be holden and considered as personal estate.*" *It was held,* that the real estate owned and used by the company, either as a railroad or as a depot, was not subject to taxation, otherwise than as personal estate, unless the legislature should specifically prescribe differently.

THIS case was submitted for the opinion of the Court, without argument, upon the statement of facts found at the commencement of the opinion.

Cutting, for the plaintiffs.

Coney, for the defendant.

The opinion of the court was drawn up by

WHITMAN, C. J. By the statement of facts agreed upon by the parties, it appears, that this is a writ of entry, wherein the plaintiffs

---

[1] 21 Maine Reports, 533.

are seeking to obtain possession of two lots of land of which, it is conceded, they are the rightful owners unless the defendant has obtained a title paramount to theirs by a sale for taxes, assessed thereon by the inhabitants of Orono. It is admitted that the modes of proceeding by the assessors and collector were correct; and the only question in controversy is, whether the inhabitants of Orono had a right to levy a tax upon the lots. These lots, it is also agreed, were the depots of the plaintiffs' railroad, at the villages of Oldtown and Upper Stillwater in said town.

By the act incorporating the plaintiffs, (c. 307, § 8,) they were authorized to " procure, purchase, and hold in fee simple, improve and use, for all purposes of business, to be transacted on or by means of said Railroad," among other things, " lands or other real estate, and to manage and dispose thereof, as they may see fit." § 11 of the same act provides, " that the capital stock of said company may consist of three hundred thousand dollars, and shall be divided into shares of one hundred dollars each, *to be holden and considered as personal estate.*"

The property in the railroad, being thus converted, by statute, into personal estate, was no longer subject to taxation, otherwise than as personal estate unless the legislature should think fit, by the tax act or otherwise, specifically to prescribe. And we are not aware that in 1840, when the tax in question was imposed, any such provision was in existence. The inhabitants of Orono, might as well tax the whole of the land within their town, taken for the railroad, as to tax the two depots in question; and any other town through which it passes might, with equal propriety, do the same. The interest in this railroad, being personal estate, was no otherwise taxable as such. Each shareholder was taxable for the amount of his interest in it, in the town where he resided, and not elsewhere; and to allow the inhabitants of the towns, through which it might pass, to tax it, would be subjecting it to a double taxation which could be tolerated neither by the policy, nor justice of the law, and the legislature never could have designed any such thing.

The defendant must be defaulted, and judgment be thereupon entered, that the plaintiffs recover seisin and possession of the demanded premises.

THE ATLANTIC AND ST. LAWRENCE RAILROAD COMPANY *v.* THE CUM-
BERLAND COUNTY COMMISSIONERS.[1]

Cumberland Co. April Term, 1848.

Costs in Assessment of Land Damages — Services of Commissioners.

There is no provision of law, by which the Atlantic and St. Lawrence Railroad Company,
can be compelled, by an order of the County Commissioners, to pay for the " services of
the commissioners and for their expenses," incurred while they were employed on petitions
presented by the company to have the damages assessed, sustained by persons, by the location of that railroad over their lands.

THIS case came before the court, upon the facts stated in a petition
for a *certiorari* to the county commissioners, of which the following
is a copy : —

" To the Hon. Justices of the Supreme Judicial Court, next to be
holden at Portland, within and for the County of Cumberland, on
the Tuesday next but one preceding the last Tuesday of April, A. D.
1848 : —

The petition of the President, Directors, and Company of the Atlantic and St. Lawrence Railroad Company, respectfully represents, that
on divers days and times in the years 1846 and 1847, your petitioners
made application to the County Commissioners for said county of
Cumberland, under and by virtue of the first section of the Act to
establish the Atlantic and St. Lawrence Railroad Company, to establish and determine the damages sustained by divers individuals by
the location of said railroad over their land in said county, and that
said commissioners in compliance with said application, did on divers
days and times in said years 1846 and 1847, proceed to examine said
lands and to ascertain said damages and made report thereof, in
which report final adjudication has been made and the damages so
ascertained have been paid by said company in all cases, whether said
reports were accepted without appeal, or whether on the petition of
any of such individuals said damages were ascertained by a jury, or
a committee, according to the provisions of law, in which last mentioned cases all costs recovered against said company have also been
paid by said company.

Your petitioners would further represent, that in none of the cases

---

[1] 28 Maine Reports, 112.

134   AMERICAN RAILWAY CASES.

Atlantic and St. Lawrence R. Co. *v.* Cumberland County Commissioners.

where the damages aforesaid were ascertained and established by said county commissioners, was the said company ordered or adjudged by the said county commissioners to pay the costs and expenses of said commissioners for their services, travel, or other expenses in ascertaining and establishing the damages aforesaid.

Your petitioners would further represent, that at a court of county commissioners, holden on the 4th day of January last, being an adjournment of the last December term of said court, an order was passed by said court, and made a part of the records thereof, in the words and figures following, viz. : —

STATE OF MAINE.

CUMBERLAND, ss. At the court of county commissioners, begun and holden at Portland, within and for the county of Cumberland, on the 4th day of January, 1848, being an adjournment from December term, 1847, it was ordered, that the Atlantic and St. Lawrence Railroad Company pay into the County Treasury of the county of Cumberland the sum of six hundred sixty-eight dollars and sixty-two cents, being the amount of costs and expenses of the board of county commissioners, officers, jurors, and committees for estimating the damages on lands over which the road of said company passes, and for other costs and expenses, and also for the amount of the bill of the clerk of the judicial courts, against said company, which costs and expenses have been examined and allowed and ordered to be paid out of the County Treasury of said county. And that the Clerk of this court cause a copy of this order to be served upon the Treasurer of said company."

"And your petitioners further represent, that in the sum of six hundred and sixty-eight dollars and sixty-two cents, named in said order, are included large sums of money allowed to Lemuel Rich, 3d, Richard Greenleaf, Daniel Merrill, and Daniel M. Cook, for their services and expenses, in ascertaining and establishing the damages aforesaid in compliance with the applications, so as aforesaid by said company made, and the particular items and amount of which will appear by the schedule hereunto annexed, and all which make a part of the records of said court of county commissioners.

And your petitioners say, that said records and order are erroneous and illegal in this, that said commissioners have no right to make their services and expenses in ascertaining and establishing damages aforesaid, a charge upon said company, or to order that said company pay the same into the Treasury of said county of Cumberland.

Whereupon your petitioners pray this Hon. Court to issue their writ, ordering the said court of county commissioners to certify their records aforesaid, relating to the damages so as aforesaid ascertained and established, and the amount allowed said Rich, Greenleaf, Merrill, and Cook for their services and expenses in ascertaining and establishing such damages, and their order aforesaid, directing said company to pay the same, for the inspection of this Court, and that the order aforesaid, or so much thereof as relates to the services and expenses of said commissioners aforesaid, be quashed.

By WILLIS & FESSENDEN, their Attorneys."

Swasey, county attorney, for the respondents.

The respondents contend that the writ should not be granted; because, they say —

1st. That there is no *substantial* error in their proceedings; and if there be any error, it is merely in the form of their proceedings.

2d. The question as to awarding that the corporation pay such costs is one within the discretion of the commissioners. If so, no error has been committed.

By the 6th sect. chap. 81, Rev. Stat. entitled, " of railroads," the commissioners are authorized upon the application of the corporation or the owner of the land, for an estimation of damages, to require the corporation to give security for the payment of all such damages and costs as shall be awarded, &c.

It is contended, that this provision extends to all costs incident to the examination and determination by the commissioners; their own fees, as well as any other costs; and that the commissioners, acting under the provision of the statute referred to, may well require the corporation to give security for the payment of their fees as a part of the costs. If the commissioners thus take security, the corporation would be bound to pay. If they act without the security, they may, within their discretion, award and adjudicate that the corporation pay such fees as they may tax as a compensation for their services. There is no provision of law or of the statutes, relating to the subject which restricts them.

·3d. That the county commissioners, in cases of application to them to determine the damages caused by the taking of land belonging to private persons, by a railroad corporation, have a legal right, and it is their duty, to award and order that the railroad corporation pay all legal costs, including their own fees.

The owner of the land can, in no event, be charged with them. Such costs, therefore, are a legal charge, either upon the corporation or upon the county. If they cannot be legally charged, by the commissioners, to the county, they are a proper charge upon the corporation. It is contended that the commissioners have no right or power to charge the county with their fees for such service. They are not paid by a salary, for their official services, but in a manner somewhat peculiar.

Rev. Stat. chap. 99, sect. 13. ' The compensation of each commissioner shall be two dollars and fifty cents a day, &c., actually employed in the service of the county." And each commissioner shall keep an accurate account, specifying the kind of service, &c., which shall be audited by the county attorney and clerk. They cannot therefore legally charge to and be paid by the county for any services excepting as the statute has authorized. The commissioners are not employed in the service of the county, when they act upon applications such as have been referred to. A railroad is not a public highway. It is the property of the corporation. It is not a county road. The county is not liable to the owner of the land for the damages awarded ; they are to be paid by the corporation. The county should not be made liable for costs, by virtue of a charge against the county, by the commissioners for their fees.

If it be said that the county commissioners constitute a tribunal to which the petitioners may apply for specified purposes, without subjecting themselves to liability to pay the commissioners their fees for official services ; the reply is, that for every day the commissioners may be employed in the service above referred to, they have a right to charge a given sum, either to the county, or such a sum, as may compensate them, to the company. It is believed they cannot charge the county. And further, that they do not in the case alluded to, act by virtue of their office, but by virtue of a special designation by the statute ; and again, that there are other cases where the services of county commissioners are brought into requisition by virtue of statute regulations and provisions, for which services the county is not to be taxed. Rev. Stat. chap. 25, § 32, 33, 34. In certain cases, they are authorized and required to lay out town ways, to discontinue town ways, to approve of town ways, &c.

For services rendered by commissioners for either of these purposes, they cannot legally claim of the county. They are not services rendered for the county. And the practice has been for the commissioners to order their fees, in such cases, to be paid by the town or by the individuals who applied, according to the result of the case.

This practice has been acquiesced in as a legal and proper one. The court will pardon me for referring to the fact, that the proceedings of the county commissioners here complained of as being erroneous are, as I believe, in conformity to what has been the practice in Massachusetts ; and with what has heretofore been the practice in this State, in the counties of York and Cumberland.

W. P. Fessenden, for the petitioners.

In answer to the foregoing, the counsel for the petitioners would observe, that the 6th sect. of chap. 81, manifestly refers only to the damages and costs of the party, where land is taken. If the company applies to the commissioners to estimate damages, how can the owner of the land require the company to give him security for costs with which he has no concern?

As to the 13th sect. of chap. 99, it is replied, that the commissioners are in the service of the county, when they are performing the duty imposed on them as county commissioners.

But it is further replied, that if the commissioners are entitled to be paid for such services, by the company, they have no right to charge it to the county, take their pay out of the county treasury, and then order the company to pay the amount into the county treasury. They cannot fix the amount of their own compensation, and fix it by judicial decision; order a third party to pay it, and then order the company to pay that third party.

If they act merely because they, as individuals, are specially designated, then, as the law fixes no rate of pay, they must receive a *quantum meruit,* like any body else. They cannot first act as individuals, and then, as a court, judicially decide their pay.

The statute gives them, nowhere, the power to fix their pay as a court of county commissioners; and we object, that their attempt to do so is extra-judicial.

The opinion of the court was drawn up by

SHEPLEY, J. The question presented for consideration is, whether the railroad company can be compelled by an order made by the county commissioners, to pay for the services of the commissioners and for their expenses, incurred while they were employed on petitions presented by the company, to have the damages assessed, sustained by persons, by the location of the railroad over their lands.

The statute, c. 99, § 13, provides, that "compensation of each county commissioner shall be two dollars and fifty cents a day, and in that proportion for any part of a day actually employed in the service of the county." They are authorized and required by that statute to perform many duties for the county. They are also authorized to perform many duties not particularly beneficial to the county. In some of those cases, provision is made for the payment of their services by those who are specially benefited by them, and in other cases no such provision appears to have been made.

They are authorized to lay out and alter town and private ways,

12*

when the selectmen of towns have unreasonably refused or neglected to do so. In such cases the costs of the proceeding, which would include compensation for their services, are to be paid by the persons for whose benefit private ways are laid out or altered, and by the town, when town ways are laid out or altered. c. 25, § 32.

When such ways have been laid out or altered by the selectmen, and towns have unreasonably refused or delayed to approve the same, the county commissioners are authorized to approve them, and to direct the proceedings to be recorded by the town clerk. But no special provision is made for the payment of their services. c. 25, § 34.

They are also authorized to discontinue town and private ways, when any person is aggrieved by the refusal of a town to discontinue them; and no special provision is made for the payment of their services. c. 25, § 33.

They are required to perform certain duties on applications made by individuals for the assessment of damages sustained by them, by the laying out, alteration, or discontinuance, of town and private ways; and there is no special provision made for the payment of such services. c. 25, § 36.

They are required to cause town and private ways accepted by them to be opened, when the towns have neglected to open them; and there is no special provision made for the payment of their services. c. 25, § 40.

They are authorized to ascertain and determine the damages to be paid by railroad corporations for any real estate taken by them, under the same conditions and limitations, as are by law provided in case of damages for laying out highways. c. 81, § 8.

A like provision exists in the first section of the charter of the corporation, which has presented this petition. But in neither of those enactments is there any special provision made for the payment of the services of the commissioners. And yet those services are not performed for the particular benefit of the county.

If requested by the owners of real estate taken by railroad corporations, the commissioners are authorized to require those corporations to give security for the payment of all such damages and costs, as shall be awarded for the real estate so taken, whether the application for the assessment of the damages be made by the corporation or by the owner of the land. c. 81, § 6. In behalf of the respondents it is contended, that the amount to be taxed for the services of the commissioners would be included in the costs to be thus secured. The owner of the estate taken surely could not be liable to pay for the services of the commissioners in those cases, in which the application was made by the corporation, and yet in such cases they are authorized to require security to be made for the payment of the damages and costs. Those damages and costs are such only as are awarded to the owner of the estate, and can include the amount to be paid for the services of the commissioners only, when the owner of the estate is liable to pay them. There is no provision, that he shall be liable to pay them, even when the application is made by him.

The result of an examination of the several statute provisions is, that there are indications of a purpose or design, that the commissioners should be paid by the county, while employed in business, in which the county has a particular interest; and that they should be paid by towns, corporations, or individuals when employed in business, in which such town, corporations, or individuals, had a particular interest, and in which the county had no such interest. But there are no statute provisions suited to carry into effect in certain cases the design thus indicated. And among them is the cases of services rendered for railroad corporations to estimate the damages to be paid by them for real estate taken for their use. As the county commissioners cannot exercise any power not conferred upon them by statute, they cannot compel payment for their services performed for the benefit of railroad corporations, unless some statute provision is found authorizing them to do so. It may be highly probable, if not clearly perceived, that the legislature would have conferred authority to do so, if the defective provisions of the statutes had been noticed and considered.

While judicial tribunals should so interpret legislative enactments as to cause the intention of the legislature to be carried into effect, if it be possible, they are not authorized to supply obvious defects, when by their supply alone power would be granted to enable those intrusted with the exercise of it, to carry into effect the purposes contemplated by the general course of legislation.

The writ prayed for is granted.

ANDROSCOGGIN AND KENNEBEC RAILROAD COMPANY *v.* ISAAC T. STEVENS,[1]

Cumberland Co. May Term, 1848.

Place of Business — Residence of Company — Where Suit may be Brought.

,Where a railroad passes over parts of two counties, the Railroad Corporation may maintain an action of assumpsit in that county wherein they have an office which is "made the depositary of the books and records of the company by a vote of the directors, and a place where a large share of the business is transacted," although the company may at the same time have another office in the other county, where the residue of their business is transacted, and in which the treasurer and clerk reside.

THIS case came before the court upon the following statement of facts: —

This is an action of assumpsit on a note of hand, given by the defendant to the plaintiffs, for the amount of sundry assessments laid upon his stock in that company, and which at the date of said note were due and unpaid. The plaintiffs are a corporation, duly established in this State. Said note was made payable at the office of the treasurer of said company at Waterville. The writ is dated February 22d, 1848, and may be referred to. The plaintiffs were organized as a corporation on the 6th March, 1847, by the choice of directors, some of whom reside in the county of Kennebec, some in the county of Cumberland, and others in the counties of Lincoln, Somerset, Franklin, and Penobscot. The clerk, who keeps the records of said company, resides in Winthrop, but keeps no office there, but is required by vote of the directors to keep the books and records of the corporation at their office in said Danville, for the transaction of business. The treasurer of said company resides in Waterville, and has his office there. The company have an office in Waterville, and one also in Danville, in the county of Cumberland, both of which are established places of business of the company. A large share of the business of said company is transacted at the company's office in Danville, where the agent of said company resides. The residue of the business of the company is transacted at their office in Waterville. One quarter part of the stockholders live in the county of Cumberland, and the residue in the counties of Kennebec, Franklin, Somerset, Oxford, York, Lincoln, Penobscot, and Piscataquis.   The assessments are all made payable to the treasurer of the company at his office in Waterville.   The directors hold their meetings sometimes at Winthrop, sometimes at the company's office in Waterville, and sometimes at the company's office in Danville.   The railroad which the company are constructing lies partly in the county of Cumberland and partly in Lincoln and Kennebec counties.

It is agreed, that if upon the foregoing facts this action is not rightly commenced in the county of Cumberland, the plaintiffs shall become nonsuit, otherwise the defendant shall be defaulted.   And it is further agreed, that the above agreed statement of facts shall have the same effect as if a plea had been filed to the jurisdiction of the court, and an issue made thereon.

W. Goodenow, for the plaintiffs.

E. Noyes, for the defendant.

The opinion of the court was drawn up by

TENNEY, J.   The only question presented in this case is, whether the action being commenced in the county of Cumberland can be maintained.   Every corporation instituted under the authority of this State, shall keep the office of its clerk, together with its records and papers, at some place within this State.   Rev. Stat. c. 76, § 2. When one of the parties is a corporation, not a town, parish, or school district, an action may be brought in any county in which such corporation shall have a place of business.   Rev. Stat. c. 114, § 11, 12, and 13.

The residence of the plaintiff's clerk and treasurer is in the county of Kennebec, but the clerk has no office in that county, but is required by a vote of the corporation to keep the books and records at their office in Danville, in the county of Cumberland, for the transaction of business, where the corporation have such office, at which a large share of their business is transacted, their agent having his residence there.   Another office is established at Waterville, in the county of Kennebec, where the residue of the business is done.   The directors hold meetings at Winthrop, and also at the company's offices in Danville and Waterville.

The plaintiffs are a corporation under the authority of this State, duly organized; the office at Danville, being made the depositary of the books and records of the company by a vote of the directors, and

Androscoggin and Kennebec Railroad Co. v. Stevens.

the place where a large share of the business is transacted, is " an established place of business " of the corporation, and the action is maintainable in the county of Cumberland. By the agreement of the parties the defendant is to be defaulted.[1]

[1] The *place of business* of a corporation has for many purposes the same legal incidents as the *residence* of a natural person.

It gives to the courts jurisdiction over the company, and determines the legality of service of process, and the sufficiency of notice.

Maclaren v. Stainton, 15 Eng. Law & Eq. Rep. 500 ; Cromwell v. The Charleston Insurance and Trust Co. 2 Richardson, 512 ; Allen v. The Pacific Insurance Co. 21 Pickering, 125 ; Louisville, &c. R. Co. v. Letson, 2 Howard, 497 ; Glaize v. The South Carolina R. Co. 1 Strobhart, 70 ; Bank of the United States v. M'Kenzie, 2 Brockenbrough, 393.

In the case of Maclaren v. Stainton the plaintiff prayed an injunction in England, to restrain a Scotch manufacturing company from proceeding with a suit in Scotland against an English citizen. The corporation had an office in London for the transaction of business in that city, and the notice for the motion for an injunction was served upon the company at that office. The defendant denied the jurisdiction of the English court over the company, it being a foreign corporation. But the Master of the Rolls determined that the company became amenable to the courts of England by coming into that country and establishing an agency and a *place of business*, and that a notice left at such place of business was sufficient. But where an Irish company had no place of business in England, the court held, on the contrary, that no suit could be maintained against the company, in England, although the writ was served upon some of the directors in England. Evans v. The Dublin & Drogheda R. Co. 3 Eng. Rail. Ca. 760. From the case of Pilbrow v. Pilbrow, 4 Eng. Rail. Ca. 683, it appears that the " office " or " place of business " of a company is regarded as its

residence, so far as the service of process is concerned ; and Wilson v. The Caledonia R. Co. 1 Eng. Law. & Eq. Rep. 415, shows that where a road extends into two countries, the courts of each have jurisdiction over the company. The road of the company in this case was partly in England and partly in Scotland ; and by the act of incorporation the company was subjected to the general railway acts of each country as to that portion of the road which was located within it. Subsequently another Scotch company was amalgamated with it, and the plaintiffs sued in England upon a claim arising from that amalgamation, and served the writ upon this secretary of the company while he was in London. It was objected that, as to this claim, at least, the company was a Scotch corporation, and therefore not within the jurisdiction of the English courts. But the court held, that the residence of the company was determined not by the origin of the claim upon which suit was brought, but by the location of the road, and the act of incorporation, and that this company, therefore, filled a double character, being both an English company and a Scotch one, and liable to be sued in both countries.

A foreign railway company suing in England, is compellable as an absent plaintiff to give security for costs, although all its business may be transacted in England, and though it may have property within the jurisdiction of the English courts. Limerick & Waterford R. Co. v. Fraser, 4 Bingham, 394 ; Edinburgh & Leith R. Co. v. Dawson, 3 Jurist, 55 ; Kilkenny R. Co. v. Fielding, 2 Eng. Law & Eq. Rep. 388.

In Rex v. Gardner, Campbell, 79, Lord Mansfield held, that, for purposes of rating, the occupancy of land by a corporation made it an inhabitant of the parish where the land was situated.

In this country the *place of business* of a corporation is considered its *residence*, and brings such a company within the operation of statutes relating to the residence of natural persons.

In The Bank of the United States *v.* M'Kenzie, 2 Brockenborough, 393, Chief Justice Marshall decided that the Bank, though located at Philadelphia, and having its principal banking house there, must still be considered as residing at Richmond, within the spirit of the statute of limitations. The suit was upon a promissory note, and the defendant pleaded the statute of limitations. The replication alleged that the Bank was located at Philadelphia, and so was within the provision exempting parties out of the State from the operation of the statute. A branch bank was located at Richmond, and the contract upon which the suit was brought was entered into there. The opinion of the court is thus laid down : "The banking house of the president and directors of the office at Richmond is as fixed and notorious as the banking house at Philadelphia. The agents of the company, acting at Richmond, are as notoriously, and as completely its agents, as those who act at Philadelphia. If, then, the residence of the corporate body is fixed and ascertained by the residence of its agents, or their place of doing business, it resides in Richmond as truly as in Philadelphia. So far as respects this particular contract, it may, with entire propriety, be said to reside in Richmond. The contract was made here, with agents who reside here, at a banking house established here, and is to be performed at this place. In equity and in reason, the plaintiff cannot, I think, as to this contract, if as to any, be placed at Philadelphia."

In Cromwell *v.* The Charleston Insurance Company, 2 Richardson, 512, the court held the corporation to be within the operation of a statute giving jurisdiction to the city courts over *persons residing* in the city. In Glaize *v.* The South Carolina R. Co. 1 Strobhart, 70, the court held the following language upon the re-

sidence of a corporation : — "The residence of a company, if local residence can be affirmed of it, is most obviously where it is actively present in the operations of its enterprise." For the purposes of a suit, the residence of a corporation was said to be in all parts of the State, which created it, and within which it carried on its business.

In the case of the Louisville, &c. R. Co. *v.* Letson, 2 Howard, 497, it was decided that the railway company is a citizen of the State which granted its charter, and in which it transacts its business, within the meaning of the provision of the constitution which determined the jurisdiction of the federal courts. "A corporation," say the court, "created by, and doing business in a particular State, is to be deemed to all intents and purposes as a person, though an artificial one, capable of being treated as a citizen of that State as much as a natural person. Like a citizen, it makes contracts, and though in regard to what it may do, in some particular it differs from a natural person, and in this especially, the manner in which it can sue and be sued, it is substantially within the meaning of the law a citizen of the State which created it, and where its business is done for all the purposes of suing and being sued."

In Massachusetts an insurance company, located in Boston, and doing business there, was held liable, like a natural person, to be sued in any county in the State, by a plaintiff living out of the State. Allen *v.* The Pacific Insurance Co. 21 Pickering, 125.

In The Taunton and South Boston Turnpike Corporation *v.* Whiting, 9 Massachusetts, 321, the court held, on the contrary, that the company did not *reside* in the county where the suit was brought within the meaning of the statute requiring actions to be brought in the county where one of the parties resided.

This case cannot, however, be justly considered to contradict the current of the authorities that the place of business of a company is to be regarded as its residence,

ELISHA PERKINS v. THE EASTERN RAILROAD CO. AND THE BOSTON
AND MAINE RAILROAD CO.[1]

York Co. April Term, 1849.

*Fences — Obligation to Maintain — Negligence — Injury to Cattle
Running at Large.*

A railroad company is not bound to maintain fences on the lines of their road, except when
the same passes through inclosed or improved land.

If an injury to another's cattle happen, (through want of such fences,) upon common and
uninclosed land, it is not legally imputable to the negligence of the company.

Cattle are not to be presumed as lawfully going at large. There must be proof that the
town gave permission.

CASE for killing plaintiff's cow, by negligence of the defendants in
not maintaining fences on the line of their railroad.

The declaration alleges that the defendants had the exclusive use
and management of the Portsmouth, Saco, and Portland railroad,
with its cars and engines ; that they were bound to maintain fences
or other safeguards, to prevent cattle from passing upon said railroad ;
that the defendants had neglected to maintain such fences or safeguards at a certain spot in Biddeford ; that the plaintiff's cow,
through that neglect, passed upon the railroad and was killed by a
collision with the defendants' engine.

It appeared in evidence, that there was (near the depot in Biddeford) an open, unfenced street, called Chestnut street, leading from
the main highway, by which cattle from the adjoining lands, (which
are common and uninclosed,) may pass into the railroad ; that,
for a few rods on each side of the junction of Chestnut street with
the railroad, and adjoining said common and unimproved land, the
fence on the southerly line of the railroad, had recently been removed
by the defendants, and that the plaintiff's cow was killed by collision
with the defendant's engine, not far from said junction.

since the case was decided upon demurrer, perhaps be safely concluded, that, for the
and the pleadings did not aver that the administration of justice, the *place of busi-
company had a place of business in the ness* of corporation will give the courts
county, but merely alleged that several of jurisdiction over it in the same manner as
the stockholders dwelt there. the *place of residence* does over the natu-
    As the result of all the cases, it may ral person.

[1] 29 Maine Reports, 307.

The trial was had in the District Court, GOODENOW, J., who ordered a nonsuit, and the plaintiff excepted.

Statute of 1842, ch. 9, § 6, provides that "every railroad corporation shall erect and maintain substantial, legal, and sufficient fences on each side of the land taken by them for their railroad, where the same passes through inclosed or improved lands."

Luques, for plaintiff.

1. The defendant's negligence and carelessness caused the injury. It was their duty to maintain the fences. Their road was formerly fenced, and they had recently removed the fence. They knew that cattle were on the adjoining land. The omission to keep up a fence on the line of their road was a heedless disregard to the rights of others. Their intention is of no consequence. If one injures his neighbor, the natural and legal inference is, that he intended it. Let the defendants show some justification. Johnson v. Patterson, 14 Conn. 1.

2. The plaintiff is not chargeable with want of care. It does not appear that he knew there was a want of fences on the railroad lines. The legal presumption is, that the cow was rightfully on the adjoining lands. 1 Greenl. Ev. 39. But it is not incumbent on plaintiff to prove himself entirely without fault. Even a trespasser is not out of the protection of law. Good faith must still be preserved toward him. No more force shall be used toward a trespasser, than is necessary to accomplish the object. Bennett v. Appleton, 25 Wend. 371; 15 C. L. R. 91; Maule & Selwyn, 198; Illidge v. Goodwin, 24 C. L. R. 272; Lynch v. Nurdin, 41 C. L. R. 422; Stephen's Nisi Prius, vol. 2, 1013; Cook v. C. T. Com. 1 Denio, 91. In this last case, the court say, "that if the plaintiff's negligence concurs with that of the defendant in producing the injury, the law will not aid him in obtaining redress. This principle, however, admits of qualifications and exceptions." Our case is within the exceptions.

HOWARD, J. It appears by the evidence stated in the exceptions, that the defendants had the entire and exclusive use and management of the Portland, Saco, and Portsmouth railroad, with all its structures, cars, and engines, by their servants and agents, when the alleged injury occurred. They were liable, therefore, in this form of action, for all damages sustained by any person, in consequence of the neglect of their agents or the mismanagement of their engines. R. S. c. 81, § 21; Yarborough & al. v. The Bank of England, 16 East, 6; Mathews v. West Lond. W. W. Co. 3 Camp. 403; Gibson v.

Inglis, 4 Camp. 72; Smith v. B. & S. Gas Light Co. 1 Adolph. & Ellis, 526; Riddle v. The Prop. of Locks, &c. on Merrimack River, 7 Mass. 186.; Foster & al. v. The Essex Bank, 17 Mass. 502, 503; Lowell v. Boston & Lowell Railroad, 23 Pick. 24; Harlow v. Humiston, 6 Cowen, 189; Beach v. Fulton Bank, 7 Cowen, 485; Hawkins v. The Dutchess & Orange Steamboat Co. 2 Wend. 452; Dater v. Troy Turnpike & Railroad Co. 2 Hill, 629; The Rector of the Church of Ascension v. Buckhart, 3 Hill, 193; Bailey & al. v. The Mayor of New York, 3 Hill, 351; 2 Kent's Comm. 284.

It was proved that the plaintiff's cow was killed upon this railroad, by the engine of the defendants, about one hundred rods westerly of the depot in Biddeford; that there was not any fence on the southern side of said railroad, for about ten rods easterly and three rods westerly of the depot; that Chestnut street, leading from the depot, southerly to Maine street, was the only road leading from the depot to Maine street; that there was not any fence across, or on either side of Chestnut street; and that the lands on either side of this street, were " common and uninclosed, or vacant," to the extent at least, of the deficiency of the fences upon the railroad.

To sustain his action, the plaintiff must prove negligence, wilful or otherwise, on the part of the defendants, and ordinary care on his own part; or if he did not exercise ordinary care, that this did not contribute to the alleged injury.

The only evidence of negligence or misconduct by the defendants was the deficiency of the fence, before mentioned. Every railroad corporation is required by law to erect and maintain sufficient fences, on each side of the land taken by them for a railroad, where the same passes through inclosed or improved lands. Stat. 1842, c. 9, § 6. In this case the lands adjoining the railroad, where there was no fence, being common or vacant and uninclosed, and there being no evidence that they were improved, under existing laws, the defendants were not bound to fence against them; and omitting to erect and maintain a fence on that portion of their road, cannot be imputed as negligence.

But if required to fence the entire track, the defendants would not be responsible for killing the plaintiff's cow, if she were wrongfully upon the adjoining close. The animal was not lawfully at large unless under permission from the town. R. S. c. 30, § 3, 5, 6. There was no evidence that the town gave any such permission, and none could be inferred, as an exemption from the operation of the general law. The burden was on the plaintiff, to prove the permit, or establish the exemption; and, as he failed to do either, he cannot recover for the loss which his own want of ordinary care and prudence has

contributed to produce.   Little *v.* Lothrop, 5 Greenl. 359; Kennard
v. Burton, 25 Maine, 49; Rust *v.* Low, 6 Mass. 90; Lane *v.* Crombie
& al. 12 Pick. 177; Howland *v.* Vincent, 10 Metc. 371; Hartfield *v.*
Roper & al. 21 Wend. 615; Bush *v.* Brainard, 1 Cowen, 78; Brownell
v. Flaglee, 5 Hill, 282; Rathburn & al. *v.* Payne & al. 19 Wend. 399;
Chaplin *v.* Hawes, 3 C. & P. 554; Pluckwell *v.* Wilson, 5 ib. 375;
Williams *v.* Holland, 6 ib. 23.

Admitting all the testimony offered by the plaintiff to be true, with
all admissible inferences, he failed to make out his case in law and
fact; and there being no other testimony offered at the trial, a nonsuit
was properly ordered by the District Judge.

Exceptions overruled.[1]

CHARLES PEAVEY *v.* THE CALAIS RAILROAD COMPANY.[2]

Washington Co. 1849.

Location of Road — Expiration of Time limited by Charter.

Under a charter authorizing the construction of a railroad " to the place of shipping lumber,"
on a tide-water river, the right of location is not limited to the upland or to the shore, but
the road may be extended across the flats and over tide-water, to a point, at which lumber
may conveniently be shipped.

After the time has expired, within which a railroad company were, by their charter, to complete their road, they have no authority to take additional lands for the extension of their
road, except by consent of the owner.

WRIT OF ENTRY.   The tenants disclaimed a portion of the land.
The part, not disclaimed, is a strip four rods wide, extending from
the shore of the St. Croix river, one hundred and fifty-three feet upon
the flats in tide-water.   The first, or inner ninety-five feet from the
shore was taken by the tenants under claim of a right conferred by
their railroad charter; and it is covered by a wharf which they erected.
The remaining, or outer fifty-eight feet, is covered by a wharf which
the St. Croix Manufacturing Company built for their own convenience, and which they sold to the tenants in 1842.

After the evidence was exhibited, the case was submitted to the
court for a decision on legal principles.

---

[1] WELLS, J., being a proprietor in the railroad, took no part in this decision.
[2] 30 Maine Reports, 498.

T. J. D. Fuller, for plaintiff.

1. The defendant is entitled to the whole of the one hundred and fifty-three feet. The charter gave no authority to take land, covered by tide-water. The terminus, fixed in the charter, is " the place of shipping lumber on the St. Croix river." This excludes the flats. The Colonial ordinance does not reach this case. If the road could extend over any of the tide-water, it might, at the discretion of a private corporation, for their own use, be extended indefinitely, making no provision for the purposes of navigation.

2. In no event can the tenants hold the land, beyond the first ninety-five feet. That part was never taken or claimed as a railroad.

Downes and *Cooper*, for the tenants.

By the charter, the tenants were authorized to establish their road quite to low-water mark. But they have not extended it so far. The outer portion of the wharf has been, and yet is, occupied by the defendants, and, it being flats, they may hold it as incident to their rights in the inner portion of the wharf or in the upland itself.

WELLS, J. The company disclaimed the land demanded except a strip four rods wide, extending from the bank of the river into the same, and to the end of certain erections, claimed by them. This portion of the premises, they claim a right to hold, under their act of incorporation.

By the act of 1836, c. 204, and also by the Rev. Stat. chap. 80, railroad corporations have the right to take so much of the land, and other real estate of private persons, as may be necessary for the location, construction, and convenient operation of their railroads. But the land so taken, shall not exceed four rods in width, except in certain cases.

The company by their charter were authorized to construct " a railway within the town of Calais, in the county of Washington, from the still water at Milltown, so called, to the place of shipping lumber on the St. Croix river."

The demandant contends, that the company have not the right, by their charter to extend their road beyond the bank of the river and over the flats to its channel, and that the legislature have not granted authority to make the road over any portion of tide-waters.

The grant gives the power to make the road, to the place of shipping lumber on the river, in the town of Calais. The company were empowered to extend it to the place where their lumber could be shipped. The use to which the railroad was intended to be appropriated, was the transportation of lumber to a place of shipping.

The lumber was to be brought to the ships or the ships to the lumber. But the ships could not pass over the flats, and to effect the purpose contemplated by the charter, the road must be extended to the ships. The flats could then be taken by virtue of the rule, that a grant of a thing includes the means necessary to attain it. Babcock v. W. R. Road Corporation, 9 Metc. 553.

If the road were limited to the bank or the shore of the river, it would fall short of the place of shipping, the place from which the lumber could be directly taken on board the ships.

The act does not indicate, that the lumber should be boated from the shore to the vessels. Nor to the company is the use of tide-waters forbidden. They may take flats as well as upland, unless the charter precludes them.

It is true, that highways cannot be located over tide-waters, without the consent of the legislature. But it is believed to be a fair construction of the charter, in the present case, that the road might be continued, as far as was necessary to reach the vessels, which were to receive the lumber, and that the corporation has obtained the consent of the legislature for that purpose.

It is unnecessary to consider what would be the construction, if the language had been only that the road should be located on the river, for the import of that used is more comprehensive, although a grant of land bounded on a navigable river, embraces the flats as well as the upland. Lapish v. Bangor Bank, 8 Greenl. 85.

It is no uncommon event for railways to run over tide-waters, and where they lie within the line of the grant, such must be the case unless words of limitation or exclusion are used.

By the act of Feb. 22, 1838, two years further were allowed to the company, to complete their road.

After the expiration of that period, they could not take the land of individuals, without their consent, for the extension of their road. They must act within the time given to them by the legislature.

It appears by the testimony, that in June, 1838, the wharf was finished, and the road completed, extending ninety-five feet from the shore, over the flats. And that subsequently the St. Croix Manufac-turing Company continued the wharf fifty-eight feet further, for their own private accommodation.

The St. Croix Company sold their erections to the tenants, in November, 1842.

The tenants not having authority to extend their road, after the expiration of the two years, limited for its completion, could not by law, under their charter, take the premises, upon which those erections had been made.

13 *

The St. Croix company held the premises, occupied by them, under Isaac Clapp, who had mortgaged them to Joseph Whitney, in 1836.

The demandant's title is derived from Whitney, and the tenants cannot lawfully withhold from him that portion of the demanded premises, which extends from the termination of the ninety-five feet, before mentioned, towards the channel of the river. And judgment is to be rendered accordingly.[1]

---

[1] The powers of a railway company to take the land of individuals for the construction of the road may be determined, either by the expiration of the time limited for their exercise, or by being once exercised.

In England the compulsory powers of a company to take land are usually limited to three years, and after the expiration of the prescribed period, a company, if it has failed to secure the necessary lands, cannot prosecute its undertaking except with the consent of all the land-owners, whose lands are required. It has accordingly been held a good return to a mandamus requiring a company to go forward and complete its road, that the period limited for the compulsory purchase of lands has expired. Regina v. The London and Northwestern R. Co. 6 Eng. Law & Eq. Rep. 220.

But it is not a good return to such a writ that the powers of the company to purchase lands *will* expire before all the requisite proceedings can be completed. Regina v. The York, Newcastle, &c. R. Co. 6 Eng. Law & Eq. Rep. 259.

And it seems not to be requisite to a valid exercise of the company's powers, that all the proceedings incident to the taking of land should be completed within the prescribed period. It was, indeed, held by the Vice-Chancellor of England in Brocklebank v. The White Haven Junction R. Co. 5 Eng. Rail. Ca. 373, that if the necessary steps for ascertaining the price of land were not taken before the expiration of the time limited, all the proceedings became null and void, and he accordingly granted an injunction to

restrain the defendants from acquiring possession of the plaintiff's premises. But the Lord Chancellor, upon appeal, though he continued the injunction upon other grounds, expressed great doubt whether the position assumed by the Vice-Chancellor could be sustained. And it was afterwards held by the Queen's Bench, and, upon error, by the Exchequer Chamber that the limitation did not apply, at least as against the land-owner, and that he might compel the company to go forward after the expiration of the prescribed period, and complete a purchase begun before. Regina v. The Birmingham and Oxford Junction R. Co. 6 Eng. Rail. Ca. 628, s. c. in error, 4 Eng. Law & Eq. Rep. 276. And, in a still later case, the Court of Queen's Bench denied the soundness of the opinion of the Vice-Chancellor, above referred to, and held that the true construction of the statute is, that the proceedings for ascertaining the amount of the compensation, are not strictly a part of the compulsory powers of the company, but are rather auxiliary powers to be exercised upon taking land either before or after the expiration of the compulsory powers. Doe d. Armstead v. The North Staffordshire R. Co. 4 Eng. Law & Eq. Rep. 216.

It has accordingly been held a bad return to a mandamus, commanding a company to complete its road, that before the necessary steps for effecting a compulsory purchase could be taken the powers of the company would expire. Where actual possession may be obtained before the expiration of the time, the compensation may be ascertained afterwards either at the instance of the land-owner or the company. Regina v. The York, Newcastle, and Berwick R. Co. 6 Eng. Law & Eq. Rep. 259. But in Kinnersly v. The North Staffordshire R. Co. 6 Eng. R. Ca. 660, the Vice-Chancellor of England expressed great doubt whether a company which had not acquired actual possession of land, could, three days before the expiration of its powers, commence proceedings to ascertain the price of land, with a view to acquiring the possession afterwards.

The powers, also, of a railway company, to take land, when once exercised are exhausted, and cannot be restored except by the legislature. A company being authorized to construct a road, may, for that purpose, within certain limits exercise a discretion as to the location, and may take the requisite land and materials without the owners' consent, but it cannot after the road is actually located make a relocation or abandon a route once adopted for a more eligible one. Moorehead v. The Little Miami R. Co. 17 Ohio Rep. 340, s. c. post. And a power to change the location during the progress of work does not, impliedly, give the power to change it after the completion of the road. Ib.

In England this principle was strongly asserted in the case of Blakemore v. The Glamorganshire Canal Co. 1 Mylne & Keene, 154. The company was empowered to construct a canal between two places. The surplus water of the canal was to be returned to the river from which it was drawn, for the use of certain manufactories thereon. The dimensions of the canal were not fixed by the act authorizing its construction, nor the amount of water which might be appropriated by the company. Several years after the completion of the canal, the company determined upon an enlargement, the effect of which would be to abstract a portion of the water used by the manufacturing establishments. Upon a bill to restrain the company from proceeding with the enlargement an injunction was granted upon the ground that the company had no power

to reconstruct the canal after its original completion. Lord Eldon held the following language upon the case : — " When was the canal, which this act authorized to be made, completed ? If, after the canal was completed, the proprietors are to be at liberty to widen and deepen and alter the canal just as they please, what was the use of the act of parliament which gave them power, within certain limits to make the canal ? The proprietors are by this act empowered to buy the land, we will suppose of A. B.; they are also empowered to buy land of C. D. and E. F. Well, if those parties, A. B., C. D., and E. F., give their consent to the bill, or withhold their opposition while it is passing through parliament, and if the bill be passed into a law, that thing is to be done, and nothing but that which is specified in the act is to be done. But if that is done, and the canal is completed in the sense which the act of parliament means by the word completed, and in the sense put upon the words by the defendants themselves (as is shown by their going about to levy their tolls upon the whole course of the canal), and if, notwithstanding, they may afterwards widen and deepen the canal, what is there to hinder them from carrying it from sea to sea. Why, there would be no end to it. When the canal is completed, the powers of the company are exhausted ; and, in making the canal, the proprietors are not at liberty afterwards to injure the interests of parties by making what is quite a different canal." His lordship also denied that the power to improve the canal gave any power to effect a radical change in the work by enlarging it.

The plaintiff afterwards brought an action at law against the company to recover damages for the injury he had sustained, by the enlargement which had been made before the injunction was granted ; and judgment being given in his favor in the Court of Exchequer, the defendant appealed to the House of Lords, where the judgment was affirmed. Lord Lyndhurst fully sustained the opinion of Lord Eldon, that the powers of the company for con-

JAMES DEERING, *in Equity, v.* THE YORK AND CUMBERLAND RAIL-
ROAD COMPANY.[1]

Cumberland Co. 1850.

*Injunction — Right of Party to Immediate Relief — Presumption as
to Constitutionality of a Law.*

Upon a bill in equity, praying for an injunction and for relief, an Act of the Legislature
ought not to be adjudged unconstitutional, on a mere preliminary hearing for the injunction, and before an examination into the general merits of the bill.

Thus, upon such a bill, calling for an immediate injunction against a railroad corporation,
to stay their operations, under their charter, upon the plaintiff's land, upon the allegation
that the powers, granted by the charter, were in violation of the constitution, it was *held*,
that, until the general merits of the bill should be examined, the injunction must be
denied.

BILL for an injunction and for relief.

The bill, in substance, alleges *that* the plaintiff is owner and occupant of improved and valuable lands, upon which he resides ; *that*

---

structing the canal were exhausted when
once fully exercised.

" The question then," his lordship observed, " comes to this, whether after
these works have been so made and completed, under the authority of the legislature ; after the water for the *Merlin Griffith Works* had been provided for in the
manner I have stated ; after the apportionment of the water had been made, as
it was made, in pursuance of the provision
in the act of parliament : — whether the
right of the parties were not, from that
moment, fixed, ascertained, and determined. I am of opinion that they were ; and
that the company of proprietors of Glamorganshire canal had no right afterwards to enlarge, and extend, and widen,
and deepen their canal so as to draw a
larger quantity of water from the river
Taff, and thereby to interfere with the
Merlin Griffith Works, and injuriously to
affect their use."

But where no limitation is imposed by
the legislature upon a company as to the
time within which its powers shall be exercised, there is no implied limitation that
they shall be exercised in a reasonable
time. Thicknesse *v.* The Lancaster Canal
Co. 4 Meeson & Welsby, 472, s. c. 1 Eng.
Rail. Ca. (American Edition,) App. 612.
Lord Abinger seemed to think that under
some circumstances, where a company,
having an unlimited charter, neglected for
a long time to exercise its rights and
powers, it might be restrained by a court
of equity from going forward with its
works to the injury of private individuals
who have, in the mean time, with the
knowledge of the company, made important improvements which would be
destroyed by the exercise of the company's powers. At law, however, he held
that the injured party could have no
relief.

---

[1] 31 Maine Reports, 172.

defendants were incorporated with power to construct a railroad, and to purchase or to take, hold, and use lands necessary for said purpose; provided, that when lands should be taken without purchase or contract, the company should pay damages, to be ascertained and determined by the county commissioners, in the same manner and under the same conditions and limitations as are by law provided in the case of damages by the laying out of highways, and that the lands so taken by the corporation shall be held as lands taken and appropriated for public highways; *that*, by said charter, the defendants were invested with all the powers, privileges, and immunities, and made subject to all the duties and liabilities, provided respecting railroads, in chapter 81 of the Revised Statutes, not inconsistent with the express provisions of their charter.

The plaintiff's bill further alleges *that*, acting under said charter, the defendants have caused a portion of the route of said railroad to be located upon and over said lands of the plaintiff, and have commenced using the same, and have cut down his fences and trees, and dug up and defaced his grounds, and are still committing great waste, and threatening to continue so to do, to his great annoyance, and to the prevention of his future improvements of the lands, and to the ruin of the same, *in the character in which they have long been enjoyed by him; that* there has been no agreement between the plaintiff and defendants, as to the price to be paid for said appropriation of the plaintiff's lands; *that* the damages thereby created have never been ascertained and determined by the county commissioners, or in any other way, nor have the defendants paid or offered to pay any thing for the same; and *that* said injurious acts have been done without any purchase from or consent of the plaintiff, and without any pretence of right, except under said charter.

The plaintiff's bill further alleges *that*, whatever may be the purport of the defendant's charter, it cannot have conferred upon them the right to do the injurious acts aforesaid, because it makes no adequate and certain provision for the payment of damage or compensation for the lands taken as aforesaid, and is therefore unconstitutional and void; *that* the aforesaid doings of the defendants are wholly of their own wrong, and contrary to equity and good conscience, for which there is no adequate remedy at law. Wherefore the plaintiff prays that the defendants may be enjoined from further appropriation of, or operation upon, the said lands of the plaintiff, and for further relief.

For the purpose of a hearing at the present term, so far as relates to the injunction prayed for, the defendants admit the facts stated in the bill to be true.

W. P. Fessenden, for plaintiff.

John A. Poor, for defendants.

For the plaintiff, it was contended, *that* the defendant's proceedings, (unless justified by their charter,) are acts of waste, even under the strictest definitions of the ancient law ; and *that, à fortiori,* they are such within the mitigated doctrines of modern times; also that they are, to the plaintiff, a nuisance from which he is entitled to be exempted ; and *that,* for such waste and such nuisance, the appropriate and only adequate remedy is at equity.

The counsel then contended, that the defendant's acts are not justified by their charter, because it is merely an unconstitutional and void enactment, inasmuch as it does not provide a "just compensation" for the private property which it authorizes to be taken for public uses.

These positions were enforced with much strength of argument, and a voluminous citation of authorities.

By the defendant's counsel, the provisions of the charter were vindicated with much force, and by a learned reference to adjudged cases.

WELLS, J. The plaintiff, by his bill in equity, charges the defendants with having committed waste upon his lands, and the doing of certain acts upon the same, which are denominated in the bill a nuisance to him. He also prays for an injunction to restrain the defendants from doing any further acts upon his premises, by virtue of their charter. The injunction is asked for at the present time without a hearing upon the general merits of the bill and the defendants, without making an answer to the bill, admit, for the purposes of the hearing, in relation to the injunction, that the facts stated in the bill are true.

It is contended by the plaintiff that if the act incorporating the defendants, allows them to take and use his land, before compensation is made to him, that then the act is so far unconstitutional and void.

It is quite manifest that the act, by a fair construction of its language, does authorize the taking and using of the land, before compensation is made, and in case the parties cannot agree upon the damages, they are to be determined by the county commissioners, in the same manner and under the same conditions and limitations, as are by law provided in the case of damages by the laying out of highways. The statute, chap. 81, sect. 6, when real estate is taken by a

Deering *v.* The York and Cumberland Railroad Co.

railroad corporation, directs the commissioners, upon the request of the owner of such real estate, to require the railroad corporation to give security to the satisfaction of the commissioners, for the payment of damages and costs, which may be awarded by jury or otherwise, and it further provides that the authority of the corporation to enter upon or use such real estate, except for making surveys, shall be suspended until the security is given. And the character of the defendants confers upon them all the rights, and subjects them to all the liabilities, provided in chap. 81, before mentioned, not inconsistent with the provisions of the charter. Any party aggrieved by the doings of the commissioners, in estimating damages, may have a jury to determine the matter of his complaint, agreeably to chap. 25, sect. 8.

By the charter and the provisions of the statute, the defendants may continue to use the real estate taken, by giving the required security.

By the constitution of this State, it is provided, art. 1, sect. 21, that "private property shall not be taken for public uses, without just compensation; nor unless the public exigencies require it."

The constitution does not prescribe that the compensation shall be made before the property is taken, nor when it shall be made.

In times of war and civil commotions, the government may need the property of its citizens for public uses, when the exigency is so pressing, that there is neither opportunity nor means for making compensation at the time when it is taken.

Lands are required for highways, turnpikes, canals, and ferries, and the acts authorizing them to be taken have uniformly, so far as they have come to our notice, provided for compensation subsequently to be made.

But it is conceded, that in cases where the owner of the land has a claim upon a town or county for his damages, that there is then such a degree of certainty as will insure the eventual payment, and that it would not be in violation of the constitution to allow the property to be taken, when a public corporation would be liable for the compensation subsequently to be made.

But even in those cases, the compensation would not be absolutely certain, for governments are subject to revolutions, and they may fail of making payment. As all future earthly events are doubtful, if the payment provided, though not absolutely certain, may still be constitutional, can any thing more be required than a reasonable certainty of it?

The law does not prescribe the kind of security with which the commissioners may be satisfied. They may require a deposit of public stocks and securities of a town, city, State, or of the United States. But they may require security of a less satisfactory character, and it may entirely fail and the owner be subject to great injury, though not to the ultimate loss of his land.

This is strictly a constitutional question of great magnitude, not only affecting the plaintiff but having an important bearing upon the interests of others. Before the injunction can be granted, we must decide the act incorporating the defendants to be unconstitutional and void. And this decision we are called upon to make, upon a mere interlocutory proceeding, without sufficient opportunity for examination and deliberation.

In the case of Moor v. Veazie, the plaintiff asked for an injunction on the ground that the charter under which he acted was constitutional, and it was presumed to be so, so far as to authorize a temporary injunction. There the charter was claimed to be valid; here, invalid. There we could grant what was asked, assuming the act to be in accordance with the constitution, here we cannot do it, without deciding the act to be in opposition to the constitution.

As we assumed in that case the constitutionality of the legislative act, so we must in this, so far as relates to the application for an injunction at the present time. The same rule, which authorized it to be granted in that case, requires in this, that it should be refused. We base our conclusion upon the rule, that an act of the legislature ought not to be decided to be unconstitutional upon a preliminary hearing of this nature, before an examination of the general merits of the bill.

We therefore decline at present from expressing any opinion in relation to the validity of the defendants' charter. We have stated enough to show what the question is, and that it is one requiring very great consideration, and the most careful and attentive investigation. It must take the ordinary course of judicial proceedings, and will be decided, if the nature of the case requires it, upon the final disposition of the plaintiff's bill.

The injunction is denied.

FOWLER *et al. v.* KENNEBEC AND PORTLAND RAILROAD COMPANY.[1]

Cumberland Co. 1850.

Construction of Contract.

The plaintiffs had contracted to build for the defendants certain sections of their railroad, at agreed prices. While the work was progressing, the defendants, with a view to some change in their location, desired a suspension of the work. Thereupon the contract was modified by the parties. For an agreed compensation, the work was to cease, till the further order of the defendants, and if the work should not be resumed within two years, the defendants were to pay the plaintiffs $750; if resumed within that time, the former contract was to apply to a residue part only of the said road sections; and upon such resumption, the plaintiffs were, upon notice, to proceed with the work upon said residue sections, in the manner and at rates of price originally agreed. In the modified contract, a quantity of stones for the road, which the plaintiffs had procured, were purchased by the defendants, upon a stipulation that, if such resumption should take place, the stones should be repurchased by the plaintiffs.

The location of the road having been altered, as to some of its sections, the defendants, within the two years, recommenced operating upon some of its unchanged parts. They gave notice to the plaintiffs of their intention, but employed another company to do the work: *Held*, that, as the work was resumed within the two years, the plaintiffs were not entitled to recover the $750. *Held*, also, that the plaintiffs were entitled to do the work, when resumed, and to recover damages for not being called upon and employed to do it.

COVENANT BROKEN.

The facts are sufficiently stated in the opinion of the court. The case was submitted for nonsuit or default.

Shepley and *Dana*, for the plaintiffs, urged the following positions.

1. Where one party to an executory contract puts an end to it by refusing to fulfil, the other party is entitled to an equivalent in damages for the gains he would have realized from the performance. Masterton *v.* Mayor, &c. of Brooklyn, 7 Hill, 61.

2. By the resumption of the work, the original contract, which had been merely suspended, was revived.

3. By necessary construction, the defendants were bound to that contract.

R. Williams, for the defendants.

The contract was not mutual and was not intended to be. It left, and was intended to leave, the election with the defendants, whether again to employ the plaintiffs.

The road, after the plaintiffs retired from the work, was located upon a different bed. The plaintiffs were not bound to build it there. It was therefore necessary to employ others to do it.

Upon the road, as contemplated in the contract, there has been no resumption of the work by the defendants.

The plaintiffs therefore are entitled to the $750, as stipulated, though not in this action.

TENNEY, J. On Nov. 29, 1847, the plaintiffs, with one Cassidy, entered into a contract with the defendants to do certain work upon sections No. 1 to 11 inclusive, of their railroad, in a specified manner and within a given time. The defendants in the same instrument contracted with the plaintiffs to pay the consideration agreed upon, for their services. The work was commenced and continued to be prosecuted by the plaintiffs according to the agreement, till the defendants, having determined to suspend all further work upon the part of the road embraced in the contract, entered into a further agreement on April 29, 1848; by which the original contract was to be suspended for the present; and that the work agreed therein to be done was to cease until the further order of the company; upon the resumption of the work at any time within two years from the date of the last agreement, by the defendants, the former contract was to apply only to sections No. 1 to No. 11, inclusive; Cassidy ceased to be a party; but the former contract was to remain in force against the other parties thereto, as it regarded sections Nos. 3 to 11 inclusive; and if the construction of said road from North Yarmouth to Portland was not resumed by the defendant within two years, they were to pay the plaintiffs the sum of $750, in addition to the sums which had been paid at the time of the execution of the latter contract. In consideration of the before-mentioned agreement to modify the original contract, and the sum of $1,000, paid to Cassidy, and of $2,250, paid to the plaintiff, and the full payment of the amount of the stipulated price for their work, which had been done, the plaintiffs covenanted and agreed with the defendants, that upon the request of the latter at any time within two years, they would resume the work, upon the several sections to be done according to the latter agreement, and would do and perform all the covenants and agreements in the contract of November 29, 1847, which they and Cassidy had therein contracted to do upon the several sections, from No. 3 to No. 11 inclusive, upon the same terms and conditions, for the same prices and terms of payment, and in the same manner in every particular, as-is provided for, in said contract, to be fully completed within two years from the time of such resumption. And it was further agreed between the parties, that the plaintiff should purchase a quantity of stone, lying upon the line of. the road, sold by them to the defendants, at the time of the suspension of the work, if the work should be resumed within two years, in the manner provided in the contract of April 29, 1848, and to allow the defendants the amount which they paid therefor, in part payment of the work.

In September, 1849, and within two years from the date of second contract, the company resumed operations on a part of that portion of the road embraced in the modified agreement, and contracted with Nash and others to do the work thereon; and gave the plaintiff no opportunity of performing the work which they had contracted to do, although they were ready and willing to execute the agreement on their part.

The defendants contend, that, by the contract of April 29, 1848, they were at liberty to employ others and not the plaintiffs to do the work, after they had resumed it, without incurring any liability therefor.

The intention of the parties must be ascertained from their contract, including the original agreement, and the subsequent modification. It is believed that their language and spirit are clear, and free from any ambiguity. The validity of the original contract is fully recognized in that made afterwards, excepting so far as it is changed by the latter. The parties do not undertake to cancel it, or to substitute therefor, entirely another. The agreement last made is expressly termed a modification of the one first made, which is referred to therein, as containing the several obligations of each party. Such being the character of the contract of April 29, 1848, that of November 29, 1847, would be binding upon the parties, so far as their duties remained unchanged by the modification.

But the design of the parties is apparent from language which is still more direct and positive. Cassidy, for a consideration mentioned, was released from the contract, in which he had been interested as a party; " but the same shall remain in force against the other parties thereto, as regards sections three to eleven inclusive." The contracting parties to the original agreement are obviously the parties here referred to excepting Cassidy, and the term cannot be limited so as to apply to the individuals only, who composed one of the parties to the contract, unless from other parts of the instrument, such was manifestly the intention. Upon an examination of the whole contract, the restrictive construction contended for by the defendants cannot be admitted. It would not only pervert the plain meaning of the language quoted, but would not comport with the general purpose, evidently entertained by both parties.

Upon the resumption of the work, as provided in the contract of April 29, 1848, the plaintiffs were bound to take the stone and allow their value in part payment of the work to be done, after the renewal of the labor. It was for the company to determine, whether the work should be recommenced within two years or not; and if it was, the resumption by the defendants, which was to impose this duty upon the plaintiffs, without any obligation of the other party to employ them by making the request, to do the work, this provision in the agreement was absurd, and under the circumstances disclosed in the contract and the case, hostile to the interest of both parties.

The contract last entered into assumes that the omission of the company to resume the work within the period of two years, would occasion a loss to the plaintiffs of $750, which loss would be avoided by an opportunity of doing the work. It is not easy to understand, that the plaintiffs could be induced to surrender without consideration, all claim under the first contract, to the privilege of finishing the work, if the defendants should resume it within two years, and should employ others to their exclusion, and should at the same time exact the sum agreed upon, in the event, that the suspension should continue. It is remarkable that the discontinuance of the farther construction of the road, which the company might feel compelled to prolong for the period of two years, should require them to make the payment of this sum, when upon a resumption, they might employ others instead of the plaintiffs, who were bound to do the work if requested, they were under no liability to compensate the plaintiffs for the loss of the benefit which was expected to accrue to them from a fulfilment of the agreement. It cannot be believed that such results were contemplated.

The defendants rely upon the language of the contract, that upon *the request* of the company at any time within two years, the plaintiffs were to resume the work, &c., insisting that it was only upon such request, which the defendants were at liberty to make or withhold, the plaintiffs were entitled to any of the advantages, which they might otherwise expect under their agreement.

It was for the company alone to elect, whether they would proceed with the construction of the road within two years; and if so, at what time. They had the right to call upon the plaintiffs to reenter upon the work at any time during that period. The plaintiffs had no right to move therein without notice from the other party after the suspension. Before their liability would be revived, they were entitled to know the design of the company touching their future labors under the contract. This condition was for the purpose of giving the information to the plaintiffs, that the work was to be recommenced, and of creating a liability in them to perform it; they could be under none without a request from the company to that affect. This request was not intended as a step to be taken by the defendants, necessary to give the plaintiffs *a right* to perform what they had contracted to do, and to receive upon the performance, the benefits anticipated, but to perfect their *obligation* under the contract. This right of the plaintiffs' was fully secured to them in other parts of the agreement, and cannot be taken away by another clause, which admits of a construction, which renders the whole harmonious, and according with the manifest intention, designed to be carried into effect.

It is again contended by the defendants, that they not having resumed the construction of the road in all its parts, as it was described in the contract after its modification, the plaintiffs were not entitled to perform the work.

In one part of the contract of April 29, 1848, it is agreed, " that in the event the construction of said road from North Yarmouth to Portland be not resumed," by the defendants within two years, they will pay the plaintiffs the sum of $750, &c. In another part of the instrument, the language is, " that in the event, the said work shall not be resumed within the period of two years, the defendants will pay, &c. From this there can be no doubt, that the parties intended, when the company recommenced operations upon the road, the privileges and obligations of each party under the contract and its modification would be revived, and would be the same as if the suspension had not taken place. The road which the plaintiffs were to do the work upon, was so described in the instruments, that it is not suggested that it could be misunderstood, or its identity be matter of dispute. The work which the plaintiffs were to do was specified with sufficient precision; and when done the company was bound to pay the consideration according to the agreement. It was not in their power by any change in the location or mode of construction of the road, without the consent of the plaintiffs, to take from them the benefit of their contract, unless that right was secured to them. The written agreement contains no such provision; but on the contrary material changes were provided for, and the force of the contract was not to be thereby annulled or essentially impaired.

It is not to be supposed, that the defendants in resuming the construction of the road, would do so by simultaneous acts upon every minute portion of it. If the work was renewed upon a part of the road referred to in the agreement, it cannot with propriety be denied, that " the construction of said road" or that " said work was resumed," without some explanation, to be found in the contract, that the language was used in a different sense, from its generally received

14 *

meaning. No such explanation is found. And when the company are admitted to have resumed operations on a part of that portion of the road, embraced in the modified agreement of April 29, 1848, and to have contracted with Nash and others to do work thereon, it cannot be doubted, that it was such a resumption, as would come within the meaning of the contract. Whether there were any changes, which were so great that the road to be made by the plaintiffs, and that on which the company resumed their operations were not identical, the case is silent. We cannot assume that it was so. The decision must be upon the facts agreed, and which are before us. It does not appear from them, that any change took place after the modification. It is manifest from the case, that the construction of the road was resumed by the defendants within two years from the date of the contract of April 29, 1848.

The resumption having taken place by the company within the period of two years, they are not liable for the sum agreed upon by the parties as an equivalent for the loss, which was expected to result to the plaintiffs from an omission to resume the work within two years. But having broken their covenant they are liable for the loss, which has accrued to the plaintiffs in consequence thereof. These damages are to be determined in the manner provided for in the agreed statement of facts.

According to the agreement of the parties,

Defendants defaulted.

MASON *v.* THE KENNEBEC AND PORTLAND RAILROAD COMPANY.[1]

Cumberland Co. 1850.

*Damages — What should be included in Estimating — Statute Remedy
to Recover, exclusive.*

The charter of the Kennebec and Portland Railroad Company provides a remedy for the land-owner, to recover damage for the location and construction of the track across his land.

The remedy, thus provided, is exclusive of the remedy at common law.

In the estimate of that damage, is to be included the injury which may be done to the owner

---

[1] 31 Maine Reports, 215.

by the erection of an embankment upon the site of the road, whereby the communication is destroyed between the parts of the land which lie upon the opposite sides of the track.

An action to recover damage for destroying such communication, either by taking the strip of land for the site of the road, or by the erection thereon of such an embankment, proceeds, not upon the ground that the land for the road was illegally taken, but upon the ground that the power, granted by the charter, had been transcended or abused. It therefore presents no basis for a decision as to the constitutionality of that power.

TENNY, J. This action is case, in which the plaintiff alleges, that he was seised as in his demesne of fee of a certain farm described, from April 14, 1845, to October, 1848, and during that time ought to have had a private way from his house to another part of his farm; that the defendants in October, 1848, built a railroad with a deep fill and high embankments, intending unjustly to disturb him, across the entire width of said farm, and thereby wholly obstructed and deprived the plaintiff of his way, up to the day of the date of the writ, which was May 16, 1849.

The defendants pleaded the general issue with a brief statement, justifying under their charter.

The plaintiffs offered to prove among other things that the defendants by their railroad, caused a separation of the part of his farm on which his house was situated from another portion, containing about twenty-four acres, on which is the most of his wood and timber, and some of his best pasture land; that a quantity of wood has been cut thereon, and is there ready to be hauled to his dwelling-house and to market; and that by reason of the railroad he has been made unable to remove the same, and also a quantity of timber; that the twenty-four acres are entirely surrounded by land, owned, cultivated, and inclosed, belonging to others, excepting on the side bounded by the railroad; that the distance over which loads must be carried upon the lands of others, from one portion of his farm to the other, is increased by means of the railroad from one hundred and sixty rods to three miles; that the only place, where a passage from one part of the farm to the other, separated by the railroad, was practicable, before its construction, has been thereby obstructed, a fill of twenty feet in depth, with no passage-way under or over the road on his land, having been interposed. The defendants admit, for the purpose of settling certain legal questions raised, that the facts so offered to be proved, can be established.

The plaintiff contended, under another count, that he was entitled to damages for the land taken as alleged.

If the act of incorporation gave power to the company to locate and construct the road, and in doing so they did not exceed the authority granted, their acts were not tortious; and the mode for

settling the damages for any real estate taken for the purposes contemplated by the statute, when not agreed upon, are to be ascertained and determined by the County Commissioners, under the
same conditions and limitations, as are by law provided in case of
damages by laying out highways. The land so taken, is to be
held as lands taken and held for public highways. R. S. chap. 81,
sect. 3.

It is well settled by decisions of Massachusetts, before our separation from that Commonwealth, and other States, that when the legislature have authorized the laying out of highways, or the establishment
of other works, deemed by them to be of public necessity and convenience, or when, in their opinion, it is for the public benefit, and in
the construction thereof damages are supposed to result to the property of others, and a mode is provided by statute for the assessment
and payment of the same, the party so authorized is not a wrongdoer; and the remedy for the person injured, is confined to the mode
provided by the statute, and none exists at common law. Stowell v.
Flagg, 11 Mass. 364; Stevens v. Middlesex Canal, 12 Mass. 446;
Cushing v. Baldwin, 4 Wend. 667. And if an injury is done to the
property of an individual not situated upon the land, taken for the
road, in the operations for its construction, the means not being inap-
propriate for the purpose, the damages therefor are to be estimated
by the County Commissioners, under the same authority by which
they determine the more direct injury. Dodge v. County Commissioners of Essex, 3 Metc. 380.

The necessity for a way from one portion of the plaintiff's farm to
the other does not change the principle. The owner of land has all
the rights incident to his title thereto, not inconsistent with the right,
which has been conferred upon others for public use, by a legislative
act. The statute provision for the assessment of damages, extends to
the injury occasioned by the interruption of the proprietor's passage
from one part of his land to another, as well as to any other injury,
which may be caused by the construction and use of the road, and
when such damages as may be anticipated from its future construction, if it has not been made, are assessed, they are made up, on the
whole injury done or expected to be done, including not only the loss
of the use of the land produced by the road, but the probable expense
of fences, and the diminution of the value of the land, by a separation from each other of different parts. If the ground has been excavated or elevated at the place where the communication between the
two parts must be, the expense of a way under or over the road is to
be considered, and if from the situation one portion cut off from the
other will be greatly diminished in value, or rendered worthless, such
facts may properly make an element in the computation.

The corporation entitled to the road, will be confined to those acts, which are necessary for the accomplishment of the object of the act. If they exceed their powers under their charter, and do injury to the individuals over whose lands the road may pass, they are not protected thereby. The construction of a passage-way across the railroad, which passes through the plaintiff's land, is not made a duty of the defendants, either by the general statute on the subject of railroads, or by the act of incorporation; and the omission to provide such means of communication is not in violation of their charter. There was no offer to prove, that any injury was done to the land separated from the residue of the farm, beyond that necessarily arising from construction of the road.   •

It is contended by the plaintiff, that the acts under which the defendants justify as to the building the road, furnishes no protection, being so far unconstitutional, and in violation of the twenty-first section of the declaration of rights of this State, that "private property shall not be taken for public uses, without just compensation; nor unless the public exigencies require it." It is insisted that the law cannot be upheld, because no adequate provision is made for compensation; and that the security which is provided by R. S. chap. 81, sect. 6, if from a private corporation, does not meet the requirement of the constitution.

For reasons which are sufficient, the constitutional question, which the plaintiff has attempted to present, cannot in this action be entertained. It is unnecessary to advert to more than one of these reasons.

It is true, that, according to the report of the case, the plaintiff in the third count of his writ claimed damages for taking three acres of his land, the same on which the railroad is constructed. · In looking at the writ, which is made a part of the case, this count is not for the recovery of damages arising from an alleged unauthorized appropriation of the land covered by the railroad, or for any injury, which the plaintiff has sustained by a supposed trespass thereon; but is confined to damages, which the plaintiff alleges he has sustained by being deprived of the former and accustomed use of the part of his farm cut off from the residue by the railroad, and the facilities for going to and from the same. The action in none of the counts in the writ is for taking the land for the road, or for an invasion of the rights of the plaintiff in any manner, to the portion of the farm covered thereby. But it is for the construction of the road in such a mode, that the plaintiff has been limited in the proper enjoyment of his land *not* covered by it. The issue, whether the land, on which the road is built has been unlawfully taken, does not appear to have been designed by the plaintiff, in making his writ, to be presented, and it is not before us. There is no allegation, that the defendants placed any obstructions mentioned in the writ, *upon the land of the plaintiff;* and consequently there is no basis for a decision of the question, whether the act under which the defendants justify is in contravention of that part of the constitution referred to or otherwise. It is manifest that the injury of which the plaintiff complains, was one which he had sustained by acts of the defendants, which the charter did not authorize, and not that the charter conferred no power to appropriate so much of the plaintiff's property as was contemplated by the legislature.

The action not being maintainable, according to the agreement of the parties, the plaintiff is to become nonsuit.[1]

True, for the plaintiff.

Shepley and *Dana*, for the defendants.

---

[1] In Carr *v.* The Georgia R. Co. 1 Kelly, 524; s. c. *post*, the Supreme Court of Georgia held in direct opposition to the above case, that the remedy provided by statute for the assessment of land damages, is not exclusive, and that the owner may maintain an action at common law for the injury which he sustains. The court relied mainly upon the authority of Crittenden *v.* Wilson, 5 Cowen, 165, where it was decided, that a party whose lands had been overflowed by the erection of a dam, might maintain an action for the injury he had sustained, although the stream was a public highway, and the defendant had erected the dam under the special authority of the legislature, and although a mode for assessing the damages which individuals might sustain was also provided by the act.

These cases are based upon the principle, that "If a statute gives a remedy in the affirmative, (without a negative expressed or implied,) for a matter which was actionable at common law, the party may sue at the common law as well as upon the statute, for this does not take away the common-law remedy." 2 Inst. 200; Com. Dig. Action upon Statute C.

It admits of doubt whether these cases properly came within the operation of this principle. The question is not whether an action might, at common law, be maintained against a party for doing injurious acts unlawfully, but whether an action can be maintained for acts done judiciously, and with reasonable care, under the authority and sanction of law, but which prove injurious to other parties. In the examination of this question all those cases arising in this country, under statutes which are void as being contrary to the constitutional restrictions against taking private property for public uses without compensating the owner, may be excluded from consideration. In such cases, the law being void, the common-law rights of the parties remain unaffected.

The question is simply, in the language of the Lord Chancellor of England, "Whether an action will lie on behalf of a man who has sustained a private injury, by the execution of parliamentary powers, exercised judiciously and cautiously." The London and North-Western R. Co. *v.* Bradley, 5 Eng. Law & Eq. Rep. page 104. His lordship, in that case, expressed a very decided opinion (which he, however, admitted might possibly be erroneous,) that such an action could not be sustained. But in a later case, before the Court of Queen's Bench, one of the judges expressed a decided opinion that an action in some form might be maintained in such a case, either concurrently with the statute remedy, or at least upon a failure of such remedy. See The Kennet & Avon Canal Co. v. Witherington, 11 Eng. Law & Eq. Rep. page 479.

If any remedy at common law exists, in such a case, it must be either an action of tort for the injuries, or an action of assumpsit upon an implied promise arising from the duty of the party to make compensation for the injuries he commits. The remedy in tort will be first considered. Without the authority of the legislature, the acts of a railway company in entering upon lands, taking materials, and encroaching upon roads, bridges, and rivers, would be wholly unjustifiable, and would render it liable in trespass at the suit of the party injured, to public prosecution by indictment, or to be restrained by injunction from prosecuting its illegal enterprises. But under the sanction of the law, the *legal character* of such acts is changed, and consequently the rights and duties of the parties. The company may lawfully prosecute its works without restraint, and in some cases may even be compelled to do it, at the suit of a party whose lands would be required in the construction of the road; it is no longer liable to indictment, and cannot be restrained by injunction; and it would seem that, upon principle, it would be no longer liable to a suit which in its very nature presupposes the unlawful character of the acts complained of. The proceedings of a company being rendered legal by the statute, the common-law remedy, based upon their illegality, becomes inapplicable, and is by necessary implication taken away. The case is therefore taken out of the rule relied upon in the above-mentioned cases of Crittenden v. Wilson, and Carr v. The Georgia R. Co., and comes, more properly, under the principle, that " If an affirmative statute which is in-

troductive of a new law, direct a thing to be done in a certain manner, that thing shall not, even although there are no negative words, be done in any other manner." Dwaris on Statutes, 641.

So far from being a trespasser when acting under the authority of a special statute or charter, a railway company is in England regarded as a *purchaser*, in exercising its compulsory powers for acquiring lands. The company and the land-owner are said to occupy the position of *vendor and purchaser*. If this is the true relation which they sustain to each other, an action in tort is clearly inapplicable to the case, and unavailable as a remedy. And an examination of the cases will show the weight of the authorities to be clearly that a railway company, while acting within the scope of its powers, is not a trespasser or wrongdoer, and consequently not liable to an action of tort. The leading case upon this subject is the Plate Manufacturers v. Meredith, 4 Term Rep. 794. This was an action upon the case against paving commissioners for an injury to the plaintiffs' premises caused by elevating the adjacent streets. It appeared that the proceedings of the commissioners were clearly within the powers conferred upon them by the statute under which they acted, and the court unhesitatingly decided that no action could be supported. " If this action," said Lord Kenyon, " could be maintained, every turnpike act, paving act, and navigation act, would give rise to an infinity of actions. If the legislature think it necessary, as they do in many cases, they enable the commissioners to award satisfaction to the individuals who happen to suffer. But if there be no such power, the parties are without a remedy, provided the commissioners do not exceed their jurisdiction." There was a clause in the act empowering the commissioners to make satisfaction to parties injured, and Justice Buller, after remarking that there was no principle of law which would enable a party to maintain an action for damages, in the absence of any express provision for compensation, went on to say, that " This is one of those cases to which the maxim applies, *salus populi suprema est lex.* If the thing complained of were lawful at the time, no action can be sustained against the party doing the act. In this case express power was given to the commissioners to raise the pavement; and not having exceeded their power they are not liable to an action for having done it." Two of the judges in this case laid some stress upon the circumstance that the act provided a mode for injured parties to obtain compensation. This remedy, they held, must be exclusive of the common-law remedy, if any such existed. But Lord Kenyon treated this as of no account, and it appears to have been entirely disregarded in the subsequent cases. The distinction here taken, that persons acting under the sanction of a statute are protected while they act within the powers granted, but become liable the moment they exceed them, although they act under the color of the law, has been closely observed in all the later English cases.

The next case is that of Sutton v. Clarke, 6 Taunton, 29, in which the court, after consideration, affirmed the principle of the above case from Term Reports. The action was against the trustees of a turnpike company for so constructing the road as to throw the flood waters from a brook upon the plaintiff's land. The act, which conferred their powers upon the trustees, prescribed their duties in general terms, but did not prescribe the precise manner in which the road should be constructed. The decision of the court is best given in the language of the reporter, that, " One who, in the exercise of a public function without emolument, which he is compellable to execute, acting without malice, and according to his best skill and judgment, and obtaining the best information he can, does a work which occasions consequential damage to a subject, is not liable to an action for such damage."

The question was distinctly presented by the court in Bolton v. Crowther, 2 Barnewall & Cresswell, 703, " Whether an action could be maintained against persons who, in the exercise of a public trust,

and for a public benefit, do an act which by law they may do, but which act works some special injury to a particular individual." The court unanimously decided that the action could not be sustained, one of the judges saying, that " It would be absurd to hold that an action would lie against them for doing an act which they are empowered by the act of the legislature to do." .

The question has been presented and discussed in the following cases, and the application of the principle pointed out and its limitations defined. Lister v. Lobley, 7 Adolphus & Ellis, 124 ; Rex v. The Hungerford Market Company, ex parte, Yeates, 2 Neville & Manning, 340 ; Rex v. Scott, 3 Adolphus & Ellis, 543 ; Rex v. Pease, 4 Barnewall & Adolphus, 30 ; s. c. 1 Eng. Rail. Cas. app. 551 (Am. ed.) ; Ramsden v. The Manchester South Junction R. Co. 5 Eng. Rail. Cas. 552 ; Rex v. The Hungerford Market Company, ex parte Eyre, 3 Neville & Manning, 622 ; Brown v. Clegg, 6 Eng. Law & Eq. Rep. 334.

In the case of the Grand Junction R. Co. v. White, 2 Eng. Rail. Cas. 559, the court held, that the defendant was justified in removing the fences of a railway in order to cross the road, the company having neglected to provide a crossing, and the statute in such case allowing a party to cross the road wherever he pleased. .

One of the consequences of holding that a party could be held liable as a trespasser or a wrongdoer while executing powers conferred by the statute would be, that the party complaining of the injury might, in the exercise of his rights of peaceably redressing his own wrongs, enter upon a railway, and abate it as a nuisance. 3 Bl. Com. 5.

The case above referred to of the Kennet & Avon Canal Co. v. Witherington, 11 Eng. Law & Eq. Rep. 472, presents this question in a novel aspect. The defendants were chartered for the purpose of improving the navigation of a river. A board of commissioners was created by the act of incorporation to determine the compensation which should be due to persons who might be injured by the company in the execution of their powers. It was made the duty of the surviving commissioners in case a vacancy occurred to appoint a new commissioner, and no provision was made for preserving the existence of the board in any other way, or for assessing the damages in any other manner. The commissioners neglected to supply the vacancies as they occurred from time to time, and the board became extinct. The company afterwards, for the purpose of further improving the navigation, made erections which diverted the water from the defendant's mill. An assessment of the damages in the mode prescribed by the statute being impossible the defendant destroyed the new works of the company, and restored the water to its previous state. The company brought an action of trespass, and the question before the court was, whether the company could lawfully exercise the powers conferred by the statute after it became impossible to ascertain the compensation to be paid, in the prescribed mode, and whether, therefore, the defendant had been guilty of a trespass in destroying the company's works. A majority of the court held, that the company might still lawfully exercise the powers of their act, two or three of the judges intimating that the common law would furnish a remedy in the place of that provided by the statute. Lord Campbell, however, dissented from the majority of the court, holding that the company could not lawfully do acts to the prejudice of others, in a case where it was clearly the intention of the legislature that complete satisfaction should be made, after it became impossible to enforce satisfaction under the statute. And his lordship was, also, clearly of the opinion that no other remedy was known to the law.

There are several American cases no less decisive on the subject. In Stowell v. Flagg, 15 Mass. 364, the action was brought for injuries caused by the defendant in erecting a dam whereby the plaintiff's land was overflowed. The defendant relied upon the mill act, authorizing the erection of dams. Chief Justice

Parker in delivering the opinion of the court after admitting the defendant's liability at common law, said, "As the common-law action is founded on a wrong done by the defendant, and the process itself presupposes a tort, when the legislature has authorized the act itself complained of we cannot conceive that the action remains."

In Stevens v. The Middlesex Canal Co. 16 Mass. 466, the plaintiff sued the canal company for damage which he had received from the construction of the canal through his land. The court held, that the action could not be sustained, laying down the principle, that " When the legislature authorizes an act, the necessary and natural consequence of which is damage to another, he who does the act cannot be complained of as a trespasser or wrongdoer." So in Piscataqua Bridge v. New Hampshire Bridge, 7 New Hampshire Rep. 35, the principle is strongly asserted that no action in tort, can be maintained against a party for acts done under the authority of a valid statute. The plaintiffs prayed for an injunction to restrain the defendants from erecting a bridge which the legislature had authorized, and they alleged the act to be unconstitutional, as a violation of their chartered rights, the bridge being an encroachment upon their franchise, and the act making no provision for compensation. The defendants contended that they might legally erect the bridge, and that the plaintiffs could obtain compensation by an action at common law. But the court emphatically denied the soundness of the position. "Such a proposition," said Chief Justice Parker, "may be said to be felo de se. The plaintiffs have a grant of certain exclusive limits. The defendants claim a right to erect a bridge within those limits, upon the ground that their charter gives them a right to erect such a bridge, and that the plaintiffs may have compensation for the injury done to them by a suit at law. But if the defendants have a right to erect such a bridge, what wrong or injury is done ? If the plaintiffs might have an action on the case for the injury, ⋅ ⋅

that negatives the idea of a right. It presupposes an interference contrary to law. The legislature cannot empower any one to do a wrong; and the right to take by wrong would be a solecism. So far as the defendants may act lawfully under their charter, they will not subject themselves to an action for an injury. So far as they cannot lawfully act, they ought to refrain from acting. Whenever lawful authority is given to take property for public use the act of taking is justifiable. There is no injury to the rights of the party; and no action as for a *tort* can accrue. Recompense is made for what is legally taken, and the party cannot complain that a wrong is done, for his property has been taken according to the laws of the land." See also Rogers *v.* Bradshaw, 20 Johnson, 735; Knorr *v.* The Germantown, R. Co. 5 Wharton, 256; Aldrich *v.* The Cheshire R. Co. *post.*

In a recent case in Vermont, (Hatch *v.* The Vermont Central R. Co. Livingston's Law Mag. vol. 2, p. 39, not yet reported in the reports of that State,) the Supreme Court held that no action could be maintained against a railroad company for consequential injury to lands near their track but no part of which is taken by them, no compensation being given by statute, and the injury not being attributable to the improper manner of constructing the road, but resulting necessarily from the location of the road in the vicinity of the plaintiff's land. The court held, that the plaintiff could not recover in such case unless he could show that the statute authorizing the construction of the road without making compensation for such injuries to be invalid, either as being a violation of the constitutional provisions against taking private property, or of some fundamental maxim of justice which the legislature have no power to set aside. In other words, if the law is valid, it justifies the company in doing the work upon the very conditions which it prescribes. No implied conditions can be imposed upon the company. The subject has been ably discussed in Connecticut, and the principle fully sustained that upon no principle of the common

law can an action be maintained against parties executing a public trust under the authority of a statute, for injuries which may be occasioned by a proper exercise of the statute powers. Hollister *v.* The Union Company, 9 Connecticut, 436.

An application of the principle is made in Borroughs *v.* The Housatonic R. Co. 15 Connecticut Rep. 124; s. c. *post,* and a limitation of it in Hooker *v.* The New Haven & Northampton Company, 14 Connecticut Rep. 146.

A distinction was taken in Sickinson *v.* Johnson, 2 Harrison, 129, between the case of a party executing a public trust under the authority of a statute, and that of a private individual doing acts to the injury of others for his own benefit, but under the sanction of a legislative grant. In the former case it was admitted that the statute authority afforded a complete justification, but in the latter it was held, that the statute only protected the party from public prosecution, and that he was liable, notwithstanding, to a suit for any injury which he might inflict upon others in the exercise of the rights granted by the legislature. The action was for overflowing the lands of the plaintiff by the erection of a dam under the authority of a special statute. The case closely resembled that of Stowell *v.* Flagg, 15 Mass. 364, except that no provision was made for compensation. It was admitted that if such provision had been made, the party injured would have been compelled to rely upon the statute remedy.

The principle admitted in this case, that parties acting under the authority of statute in the execution of a public trust cannot be held liable as wrongdoers in carrying out the objects of the law, is important, since railway companies fall within that class. They are, so far as this question is concerned, public agents or trustees, for the execution of public works. Upon no other principle, and in no other character, could they, under the constitutional restrictions in this country, be lawfully authorized to take property at all. It is, therefore, unnecessary here to inquire whether the principle can properly be ex-

SAGER *v.* THE PORTSMOUTH, S. & P. & E. RAILROAD COMPANY.[1]

Cumberland Co. 1850.

Common Carrier — Restriction of Liability by Notice — Effect of Special Contract by Owner to bear all Risks.

The common-law liability of a carrier, may be restricted by a notice from him, brought home to the knowledge of the customer, as to the extent of the liability to be borne by the carrier.

But no *notice* or *contract* can exonerate a common-carrier from liability for damage, occasioned by his *negligence* or *misconduct.*

The want of suitable vehicles, in which to transport articles, is negligence on the part of a carrier.

tended to the case of private persons exercising privileges specially granted for the grantee's personal interest. But see the case of Fletcher *v.* The Auburn & Syracuse R. Co. 25 Wendell, 462.

If, therefore, a railway company cannot be treated as a trespasser or wrong-doer in exercising its statutory powers, it follows that no action founded in tort, and which presupposes that the acts complained of are unjustifiable, can be maintained.

The only other inquiry which it is necessary to make is, whether an action of assumpsit can be maintained upon an implied assumpsit, springing from the duty to make compensation for the injury inflicted. Although it has been often intimated by counsel, and perhaps by judges, that such an action might be maintained, all the cases which have been brought before the court appear to have been in tort. This of itself would furnish reason to believe that no such action could be supported.

It may be further observed, that the cases already cited, show that no liability exists at common law to make compensation, where no provision to give it is made by statute. The obligation to make it in such cases, if any exists, is a purely moral one, which cannot be enforced by

action. The question is simply, whether the common law furnishes a remedy to enforce a statute obligation in addition to the statute remedy. In Boulton *v.* Crowther, before cited, Justice Littledale, after showing that in the nature of the case an action of trespass could not be maintained against public trustees acting under the sanction of the statute, says, " If any action could be maintainable it must be assumpsit upon an implied promise. But surely the law would not imply a promise in them to pay for that from which they derived no benefit, and which the legislature authorized them to take."

Only in those cases where a party is acting for his own benefit could a promise in any way be implied against him. And, though a railway company acts for its own interests, yet, so far as this question is concerned, the remark already made in regard to the remedy in tort, will apply equally well to this proceeding, that a railway company must, as to the subject of compensation, be regarded as a public agent or trustee. And it is difficult to see how any obligation can be implied against a company, or any process be employed to enforce it, without the authority of the legislature, which would not exist against the direct agents of the government.

Sager *v.* Portsmouth, S. & P. & E. Railroad Co.

A common-carrier will be liable for damage to goods, resulting from disobedience of the directions, given by the owner and assented to by the carrier, respecting the mode of conveyance.

If, with a *bailee* employed to carry goods for him, the owner stipulate to take upon himself the risk of "all damages, *that may happen*" to the goods in the course of transportation, such stipulation will not exonerate the bailee from liability for damage to the goods, resulting from his *negligence* or *misconduct.*

The damages, which, within the meaning of that stipulation, *might happen* to the goods, would not include such as resulted from *negligence* or *misconduct.*

Such stipulation, however, would cast upon the owner, the burden of proving that the damage was *so* occasioned.

ASSUMPSIT. The plaintiff's horse was transported upon the defendants' railway from Boston to Portland, for which the plaintiff paid freight, $2.75. It was upon a cold day in November, 1848. The horse was carried in an open car, and suffered serious injury from the exposure to the cold. This action is brought to recover for that injury.

A witness for the plaintiff testified, that he took the horse to the depot in East Boston, and requested one of the defendants' servants there to have the horse carried in a close car. He did not know the name of the servant, nor whether he had any charge in the transportation department.

The defendants introduced a paper, made in 1845, signed by the plaintiff and many other dealers in horses and cattle, as follows: " We the undersigned, hereby agree to exonerate the P., S. & P. & E. Railroad Company from all damages that may happen to any horses, oxen, or other live stock that we send or may send, over said company's railroad; meaning by this, that we take the risk upon ourselves of all and any damages, that may happen to our horses, cattle, &c.; and that we will not call upon said railroad company or any of their agents for any damages whatever."

The trial was before HOWARD, J. He instructed the jury *that,* by the common-law, common-carriers for hire were always bound to obey special directions given them as to the manner of transporting property intrusted to them; *that* they were bound to provide themselves with suitable carriages and conveyances; *that* they were bound to guard against improper hazards and injury to the property by storms; *that* they were liable for losses which might happen by injuries of every kind to such property, except those which occur from the act of God or public enemies; *that* the burden of proof is on the defendants to show, when any loss happens, that it is not occasioned by their fault; *that* they are held to give and prove the excuse; and *that* this is the law, unless otherwise provided by special contract, between the parties; *that,* by special contract, they might guard against such an extent of liability; *that* the paper, signed by the plaintiff, might not excuse the defendants for every sort of accident, though happening without their fault; but that the same is a binding contract and excuses the defendants from liability for such losses as are incurred by the running off of the cars from the track, breaking the legs of live stock and the like accidents, but does not excuse them for their own malfeasance, misfeasance, or negligence; *that* this contract shifts the burden of proof to the plaintiff, and requires of him to prove that the loss was occasioned by the misconduct or neglects of the defendants; *that* parties have the right thus to change their liabilities; *that*, if the plaintiff gave the defendants special directions as to the mode of carrying this horse, the defendants were bound to follow them, if they undertook to transport the property, or they could not avail themselves of the change of liabilities, provided for in the said paper; and *that* it would be such negligence, if they did not conform to these directions, as would make them liable for the loss, notwithstanding this written agreement; *that* such an omission to follow the orders given, again shifted the burden of proof to the defendants to make good their excuse, and they would be bound to show that the loss was suffered without their fault; *that*, if the plaintiff relied upon having given directions to have the horse carried in a close car, he must prove that such orders were given to the defendants or their officers, or to some agent of the company; *that* it was not necessary that this order should be proved to have been given to *that* officer of the company who had in charge the carrying of such freight to Portland, but it was enough if such order was given to any agent of the company there acting for them, whatever may have been the particular duty of such agent; but that the plaintiff was bound to bring the knowledge of the special directions home to the company; *that*, if no special directions were given to carry this horse in a close car, the jury would next consider and find, whether it was an act of negligence to transport the horse in an open car; *that*, if it was known to be the custom of the defendants to transport horses in either kind of car indiscriminately, the plaintiff would be bound by such custom, if there were no special directions; *that* the jury would next inquire, if they came to the question of damages, whether the horse was injured in the course of his transportation to Portland, and whether such injury was occasioned by the neglect of the defendants; *that* this was the rule, whether the special directions were given or not.

The jury returned their verdict for the plaintiff and assessed the damages at $155.

By agreement of the parties, the case was submitted to the court for a decision upon the principles of law.

Deblois, for defendants.

Two points are here presented.

. 1. Upon the effect of the paper signed by the plaintiff. Whatever be its import, it is binding upon the plaintiff.

That paper expressly relieves˜the defendants from the liability charged. He thereby became his own insurer, and the employees of the defendants became his servants.

Fraud alone could make the company liable. Bean *v.* Green & al. 12 Maine,. 422; Parker *v.* Flagg, 26 Maine, 181; Holliston *v.* Nowland, 19 Wendell, 247; Bingham *v.* Rogers, 6 Watts & Sergent, 495; Story on Bailments, sect. 554, 555, and note to 557; Riley *v.* Horn, 5 Bingham, 217; Mayhew & al. *v.* Eames & al. 3 Barnewall & Creswell, 601; Clark *v.* Hutchins, 14 East, 475; Beck *v.* Evans, 16 East, 245 and 247.

As to the plaintiff, the defendants are not bound by the rules relative to common-carriers.

The making of such a contract, impugns no policy or law.

The law of common-carriers arose from the necessities of a semi-barbarous age. The progress of events has removed the occasion for it, and its rigors have been mitigated, so far as to give a qualified effect to notices. The question now arises, whether by *express contract*, a party can cast off the obligations of a common-carrier.

A party may waive any right, except as to immoral tendencies, or such *crassa negligentia* as amounts to fraud. An owner of goods has the right to say to a carrier, you may transport goods for me, exempt from the rigors of the ancient law.

The charge to the jury in this case, restricted that right. The . plaintiff's stipulation protected us against " all damage," the judge limited it to damage from common and ordinary accident. Except for the protection, given by that paper, the defendants would not have carried the horse; at least not for that price.

If mere *notice* of a restricted obligation on the part of a carrier, protects him, surely a written contract will be no less available.

If *notice* takes away the character of a common-carrier, *à fortiori* a contract may do it.

Suppose a notice would relieve merely from common and ordinary accidents, yet a *contract* may relieve from losses even through gross neglect.

The defendants dislike to carry such freight. They consent only upon the owners assuming the risk. This is no invasion of policy, of law, or of justice.

2. The direction to carry in a covered car, was not so given as to create an obligation on the company. They have five or six hundred

employees in many various departments. To whom was the direction-given? No one can tell. It should have been given to some one having charge of the freight business. A notice to the baggage-master could have been of no use to the company. The company has usages. People employing them must deal according to those usages, and they must take time to know and to conform to them. This is the more requisite, from the rapidity of railroad movements. 22 Pick. 24; 1 Metc. 294; 4 Paige, 127.

Fessenden, on the same side.

How far the rigid law of England is in force here has never been presented, on solemn argument, to this court.

Cessante ratione cessat lex, is a sound rule.

From the half-barbarism which gave rise to the old law, this nation has emerged into civilization and moral light. If parties, by their silence, acquiesce in the rigors of the old rule, let it be so. But I have yet to learn, that, in modern days, (when the chief dangers, against which that rule was adopted, have passed away,) the party may not, *by contract*, relieve himself from an insurance upon property conveyed.

The law of common-carriers does not apply to the carrying of cattle and horses. It related only to money and merchandise. The transporting of live stock is of modern origin. Defendants are not bound to carry it. As well may it be required of them to transport meeting-houses and ships. Must they take caravans of wild animals? Is a steamboat or railway, bound as they are to carry *passengers*, compellable to mix them up with *lions, hyenas*, and *monkeys?* Suppose a person becomes a carrier to distribute newspapers; is he compellable to transport rocks and piles of manure?

Besides, their charter itself, section three, gives the defendants the right to decide what description of articles to carry. They are not bound to provide, beforehand, vehicles for every possible sort of property. They have indeed provided cars for cattle, but to be used only on condition that the insurance is taken by the owners.

The contract made by the plaintiff with the defendants, was not void for want of consideration; it sanctions no immorality, is not *contra bonos mores*. Suppose it should be thought the better policy to uphold the old rule, and to set aside the contract, I submit to this honorable court, that they have no right to do it. Such a decision would impair the obligation of a contract. Such a decision is forbidden by an express provision of our constitution. Public policy may change. But that provision is unalterable.

Even the ancient law had one qualification. The owner might go with his goods and take charge of them, at his own risk. I suppose, too, he might send his servant. So in this case, the plaintiff having taken the risk, made the defendants' employees his servants. At any rate, the contract protects the defendants against all but fraud or gross neglect. That either of these occurred, there is no pretence.

Shepley and *Dana*, for plaintiff.

SHEPLEY, C. J. It cannot be useful to notice or to attempt to reconcile the very numerous opinions and decisions respecting the responsibility of common-carriers for the loss of property intrusted to them for conveyance. Most of the cases were collected or referred to in the opinion of Mr. Justice Cowen, in the case of Cole v. Goodwin, 19 Wend. 251.

It will be sufficient to state the law established by the progressive and decisive weight of authority.

By the common law they were liable for all losses not occasioned by the act of God or the public enemy. They could not refuse to carry a package, and when its contents were not made known to them, they were often subjected to heavy damages without receiving any adequate compensation for the risk incurred. To obtain relief by a limitation of their liability, it became a very general practice to give notice, that they would not be answerable for the loss or damage of goods above the value of five pounds, unless the nature and value were specified and entered, and a premium paid accordingly. The effect of notices of this description was soon presented for judicial determination.

The conclusion, to which the courts ultimately came, was, that they could have no effect, unless brought to the knowledge of the owner of the goods, before he had intrusted them to the care of the carrier. That in such case they would have the effect to prevent a recovery of damages, for a loss not occasioned by the misconduct or negligence of the carrier or his servants, when the owner had not complied with the terms of the notice.

This conclusion appears to have been formed by a consideration, that a person informed of the notice, who intrusted goods to their care without making known their nature and value, consented that they should be carried upon the terms proposed in the notice, and that a contract to that effect was thus made between the parties, by a proposal for their carriage upon certain terms stated, and by an acceptance of them. Lyon v. Mells, 5 East, 428.

The notices were usually given in terms so general, that a literal construction of the contract thus arising out of them, would have exonerated the carriers from liability for their own misfeasance or negligence and from that of their servants. Yet the well-established construction of them has been, that they were not thereby relieved from their liability to make compensation for losses thus occasioned. Beck v. Evans, 16 East, 244; Smith v. Horne, 8 Taunt. 144; Newborn v. Just, 2 C. & P. 76; Birkett v. Willan, 2 B. & A. 356; Garnett v. Willan, 5 B. & A. 53; Sleat v. Flagg, 5 B. & A. 342; Duff v. Budd, 3 Brod. & Bing. 177; Brooke v. Pickwick, 4 Bing. 218; Riley v. Horne, 5 Bing. 217; Bodenham v. Bennet, 4 Price, 34; Story on Bailm. (4th ed.) § 570, where it is said, " it is clear, that such notices will not exempt the carrier from losses by the misfeasance or gross negligence of himself or servants," " for the terms are uniformly construed not to exempt him from such losses." Kent also states, " it is perfectly well settled, that the carrier, notwithstanding notice has been given and brought home to the party, continues responsible for any loss or damage resulting from gross negligence or misfeasance in him or his servants." 2 Kent's Com. 607. Mr. Justice Cowen, in the case of Cole v. Goodwin, while speaking of the decisions in Westminster Hall, respecting the liability of a common-carrier, says, " it is equally well settled, that he cannot either capriciously, by a single instance, or by public notice, seen and read by his customer, nor even by special agreement, exonerate himself from the consequences of gross neglect.

In many of the cases, the words " gross neglect," were used without any definite explanation of their meaning, and for some time it was considered to be doubtful, whether the carrier was not exonerated from losses occasioned by negligence or a want of that ordinary care, for which bailees are responsible. This doubt was removed by the decisions made in Wyld v. Pickford, 8 Mee. & Welsb. 443, and Hinton v. Dibbin, 2 Ad. & El. N. S. 646. In the former case, Baron Parke, speaking of a carrier who had given notice, says, " he still undertakes to carry for hire, and is therefore bound to use ordinary care in the custody of goods and their conveyance to and delivery at their places of destination, and in providing proper vehicles for their carriage. It is enough to prove an act of ordinary negligence." In the latter case, Lord Denman observes, " again, when we find ' gross negligence ' made the criterion to determine the liability of a carrier, who has given the usual notice, it might perhaps have been reasonably expected, that something like a definite meaning should have been given to the expression. It is believed, however, that in none of the numerous cases upon this subject is any such attempt made; and it may well be doubted, whether between gross negligence and negligence, any intelligible distinction exists." In his first edition of

the treatise on Bailments, the law was regarded by Story to be uncertain whether a carrier would be liable without proof at least of
gross negligence. After the case of Wyld v. Pickford was decided,
he says, in the fourth edition, § 571, " the question may however be
now considered at rest by an adjudication entirely satisfactory in its
reasoning, and turning upon the very point, in which it was held,
that in cases of such notice the carrier is liable for losses and injuries
occasioned, not only by gross negligence, but by ordinary negligence;
or, in other words, is bound to ordinary diligence."

The cases of Clarke v. Hutchins, 14 East, 475, and of Mayhew v.
Eames, 3 B. & C. 601, cited by the counsel for the defendants, did
not turn upon the question of negligence; and, upon the ground on
which the nonsuits were ordered, they are opposed to the general current of the authorities.

A change was made in the law of England, as thus established, by
the statute, 11 G. 4, and 1 W. 4, chap. 68. The first section of this
statute relieved carriers from their responsibility for the loss or
damage of certain enumerated valuable goods, contained in packages
or parcels of the value of more than ten pounds, unless their nature
and value were at the time of their delivery made known to the
carrier, and his increased charge paid or agreed to be paid. The
fourth section provided that no public notice should exempt a carrier
from his liability at common law, for the loss or injury of goods not
enumerated in the first section. By the construction of this statute,
adopted in the case of Hinton v. Dibbin, a carrier is not liable for a
loss of valuable goods exceeding ten pounds, occasioned by the gross
negligence of his servants, unless their nature and value are made
known according to the provisions of the statute.

Although the doctrines established before the enactment of this
statute were received in the State of New York, her courts appear
since to have denied, that the responsibility of a common-carrier can
be restricted by any notice or agreement. Hollister v. Nowlen, 19
Wend. 234; Cole v. Goodwin, idem, 251; Gould v. Hill, 2 Hill, 623.
Some of the considerations leading to such a conclusion appear to
have been, that many of the English judges and jurists doubted the
propriety of the admission of a restriction by notice, and lamented
its introduction; that it had been removed and the rule of the com.
mon law restored by the statute, with certain exceptions introduced
by it; that the decisions respecting the effect of notices rested upon
the unsound foundation, that the carrier could and had divested him.
self of his public character, and assumed that of a bailee for hire; and
that he was not obliged to receive goods for carriage, except upon
terms prescribed by himself.

However strongly such and other considerations might have operated, had they been presented to this court at an earlier time, it is not now at liberty to entertain them, without overruling a former decision, (Bean v. Green, 3 Fairf. 422,) in which it is said, that the attempt on the part of common-carriers to limit and qualify the liability imposed on them by the common law, although sustained, is not to be favored or extended. To admit them to be exonerated from liability for losses occasioned by negligence, would be to extend the limitation of it.

Another form of notice, often given by the proprietors of railways and stage coaches, " all baggage at the risk of owners," has, when made known to them, been construed not to exempt the proprietors from losses occasioned by negligence. In the case of the Camden and Amboy Railroad v. Burke, 13 Wend. 611, Savage, C. J., says, " where notice is given, that all baggage is at the risk of the owners, such notice excuses them from losses, happening by theft or robbery," " but not from losses arising from actual negligence." In the case of Dwight v. Brewster, 1 Pick. 50, Parker, C. J., says, when speaking of a similar notice, " it was intended to guard the proprietors from liability in case the trunks, &c., should be stolen."

Nor do such notices prevent the proprietors from being liable for losses occasioned by neglect to provide sufficient and suitable vehicles and machinery. Lyon v. Mells, 5 East, 428; Sharp v. Grey, 9 Bing. 457; Wyld v. Pickford, 8 M. & W. 651; Cam. & Am. Railroad v. Burke, 13 Wend. 611; Story on Bailm. (4th ed.) § 557, where it is said, " but at all events such notices will not exempt the carriers from responsibility for losses occasioned by a defect in the vehicle or machinery used for the transportation."

A carrier will be liable for disobedience of directions given and assented to respecting the mode of conveyance. Streeter v. Horlock, 1 Bing. 34; Hastings v. Pepper, 11 Pick. 41; Demseth v. Wade, 2 Scam. 285; Story on Bailm. § 509.

If a literal construction of the agreement signed by the plaintiff would exonerate the defendants from losses occasioned by the negligence of their servants, it will be perceived, that it could not be permitted to have that effect without a violation of established rules of construction and without a disregard of the declared intention of this court not to extend the restriction of the liability of common-carriers. The very great danger to be anticipated, by permitting them to enter into contracts to be exempt from losses occasioned by misconduct or negligence, can scarcely be over estimated. It would remove the principal safeguard for the preservation of life and property in such conveyances.

It however requires no forced construction of that agreement, to regard it as effectual to place the defendants in the position of bailees for hire, and as not exoneratimg them from liability for losses occasioned by misfeasance or negligence. The latter clause, " we will not call upon the railroad company or any of their agents for any damages whatsoever," considered without reference to the preceding language, would be sufficiently broad to excuse them from making compensation for losses occasioned by wilful misconduct. It is most obvious, that such could not have been the intention ; and that the true meaning and intention was, that they would not call upon them for any damages whatsoever, " that may happen to any horses, oxen, or other live stock, that we send or may send over said company's railroad." The intention of the parties, by the use of the language contained · in this last clause, is then attempted to be explained as follows : — " meaning by this, that we will take the risk upon ourselves of all and any damages, that may happen to our horses, cattle," &c. The meaning of damages happening to live animals is to be sought.

The word happen is defined by the words, to come by chance, to fall out, to befall, to come unexpectedly. An accident, or that which happens or comes by chance, is an event, which occurs from an unknown cause, or it is the unusual effect of a known cause. This will exclude an event produced by misconduct or negligence, for one so produced is ordinarily to be expected from a known cause. Misconduct or negligence under such circumstances would usually be productive of such an event. Lord Ellenborough, in the case of Lyons v. Mells, speaking of what " may or may not happen," explains it as " that which may arise from accident and depends on chance." An injury occasioned by negligence, is the effect ordinarily to be expected as the consequence of· that negligence, without reference to any accident or chance. A correct construction of the agreement will not, therefore, relieve the defendants from their liability for losses occasioned by the misfeasance or negligence of their servants.

It will have the effect to change the burden of proof, and to require that the owner shall prove, that the loss was thus occasioned.

The instructions respecting the liability of the defendants for losses were therefore correct.

It is alleged, that those respecting the directions given by the plaintiff, for the conveyance of his horse, were erroneous.

If the only instruction had been, that " it was enough if such order was given to any agent of the company, there acting for them, whatever may have been the particular duty of such agent," there might have been just cause for complaint. The true rule would seem to be, that an order should be given to some servant or agent, who is acting upon the subject-matter, or whose duty it is to act upon it, or to communicate to some one, whose duty it is to act upon it. Fulton Bank v. New York Canal Company, 4 Paige, 127. But the instructions also stated, " that the plaintiff was bound to bring the knowledge of the special directions home to the company." If this was done through a servant whose duty did not require him to act upon, or to communicate the directions, the company would become sufficiently informed of them ; and it could not have been aggrieved by the instructions.

The testimony appears to have been sufficient to authorize the jury to find, that the officers of the company, especially charged with the transportation of freight, were informed of those directions; and that is all that could have been intended by the instruction, that a knowledge of them should be brought home to the company.[1]

Judgment on the verdict.[2]

[1] Several cases have been decided in England upon the liability of railway companies for injuries to live stock carried under special contracts similar to that in the above case. These agreements have there been held to exempt the companies from all responsibility for damages arising from defective cars, or the gross negligence of their servants. The above case is in direct conflict with the English decisions, and in several cases in this country it has been either decided or intimated that such contracts would not be so construed as to exempt common-carriers from responsibility for their own gross negligence. Swindler v. Hilliard, 2 Richardson, 286 ; Camden &c. R. Co. v. Baldauf, 4 Harris, 67; Dorr v. The New Jersey Steam Navigation Co. 4 Sandford, 136 ; Laing v. Colder, 8 Barr, 479 ; New Jersey Steam Navigation Co. v. Merchants' Bank, 6 Howard, U. S. R. 344; Slocum v. Fairchild, 7 Hill, 292.

An examination of the English cases will, however, show, that they differ in several important particulars from all the American cases in which the question has yet been presented, and that they are based upon principles which have been recognized as sound in this country. In Shaw v. The York and North Midland R. Co. 6 Eng. Rail. Ca. 87, the plaintiff declared in case against the defendants for a breach of their duty as common-carriers. The defendants had undertaken to transport the plaintiff's horses under the following special agreement : — " This ticket is issued subject to the owner's undertaking all risks of conveyance whatever, as the company will not be responsible for any injury or damage (however caused) occurring to horses or carriages while travelling, or loading or unloading."

One of the horses was killed through a defect in the car. The court decided that the company could not, under the agreement, be held liable as common-carriers, and that the declaration must be upon the special agreement for a breach of such duties as arose upon the contract, the company being special bailees simply.

The next case was that of Austin v. The Manchester & Sheffield R. Co. 5 Eng. Law & Eq. Rep. 329. The declaration was against the company as common-carriers, for an injury to the plaintiff's horses, which they were transporting. At the trial, it was proved that the horses were carried under the following agreement: — This ticket is issued subject to the owner undertaking all the risks of injury by conveyance and other contingencies, and the owner is required to see to the efficiency of the carriages before he allows

[2] Wells, J., took no part in this decision.

his horses or live stock to be placed therein. The charge being for the use of the railway carriages and locomotive power only, the company will not be responsible for any alleged defects in their carriages or trucks, unless complaint be made at the time of booking, or before the same leave the station; nor for any damage however caused, to horses, cattle, or live stock of any description travelling upon their railway or in their vehicles.

"I have examined the carriages, and am satisfied with their sufficiency and safety.

"(Signed)   } Owner, or on
——,   } behalf of Owner."

In this case, too, the court held that the company were not liable as common-carriers, and that the action must be upon the special agreement.

Another attempt was made to fasten upon the companies the common-law liabilities of carriers in Austin v. The Manchester, Sheffield, &c., R. Co. 11 Eng. Law & Eq. Rep. 506. The declaration alleged the company to be common-carriers, and that it was, therefore, their duty to exercise due and proper care in the carriage of horses over their road; that the plaintiff's horses were delivered to them as such carriers, to be carried according to the due and ordinary course of business, except so far as the duty was altered by the terms of the special agreement, which was the same as that set out last above. The declaration then alleged that the horses were injured through the gross negligence of the defendants. In the cases above referred to the courts had only decided that under these agreements, the defendants were not liable as common-carriers, but as special bailees, under the terms of the contracts. It now became necessary to give a construction to these agreements, and to determine the responsibilities of the companies under them, and after mature consideration it was decided that the company was not liable for damages occasioned even by gross negligence. It should, however, be observed, that the English courts have in many cases disregarded the distinction between gross negligence and ordinary negli-

gence, as respects the civil liabilities of parties, and in this case the court clearly did not consider the allegation of gross negligence to be equivalent to a charge of wilful misconduct, misfeasance, or of a renunciation of the character in which the defendants received the goods.

Subsequently the case of Carr v. The Lancashire and Yorkshire R. Co. 14 Eng. Law & Eq. Rep. 340, came before the Court of Exchequer. The declaration was upon the special agreement, alleging the defendants to be common-carriers, and charging them with gross negligence. The contract was in the same form as that given above from Shaw v. The York and North Midland R. Co., and the court gave it the same construction and legal effect, as the Court of Common Pleas had previously done to that in the last case of Austin v. The Manchester, Sheffield, &c., R. Co., holding the defendants to be free from responsibility for gross negligence.

In the Court of Queen's Bench, the same principles have also been asserted, and the same construction given to these agreements by Justices Coleridge and Erle in Chippendale v. The Lancashire and Yorkshire R. Co. 7 Eng. Law & Eq. Rep. 395, and Morville v. The Great Northern R. Co. 10 Eng. Law & Eq. Rep. 366.

It is important to observe, in regard to these English cases, 1st, That they all relate to the transportation of live stock; and 2d, That the English railway companies are under no legal obligation to become common-carriers, but like natural persons may assume the character or not at their option.

1st. The transportation of horses, cattle, &c., has sprung up since the introduction of railways, and the English judges in the cases above cited lay considerable stress upon the reasonableness of allowing parties to relax the rigor of those common-law rules which were established in reference to a state of circumstances widely different from those to which they are now applied.

In three of these cases it appears that the owners or their servants accompanied the trains with the horses; and it is probably customary both in England and in this country for the owners of live stock transported by railway to provide for its personal attendance by some one besides the servants of the company. The feeding and other care which such freight requires are duties unknown to the common-law.

And it may admit of doubt whether, in such cases, there is so complete a delivery of the property into the custody of the company as to impose upon them all the duties and liabilities of common-carriers. It has been decided that the owners of steamboats employed to tow other vessels are not common-carriers, on the ground that there is not that delivery of the vessels or their cargoes which the law requires to fasten upon carriers their common-law liabilities. Caton v. Rumney, 13 Wendell, 387; Alexander v. Greene, 3 Hill, 9; Wells v. The Steam Navigation Co. 2 Comstock, 204. These cases are somewhat analogous to those of the transportation of cattle on a rail as respects the care and custody of the property; for though the conductors of a train have a more complete possession of the cattle in their charge, than the managers of a towboat have over the vessels committed to their care, it seems, nevertheless, to fall short of that exclusive control which carriers usually have over the ordinary articles of transport. In some of the English cases above cited the companies have endeavored to free themselves from the character of common-carriers by a stipulation in the agreement that the charge is made only for motive power and the use of the carriages. The effect of this provision has not, however, been determined by the English courts.

2d. As to the duty of a railway company to assume the character and liabilities of a common-carrier, the English courts have decided that no such obligation exists. Like a natural person a company may become a common-carrier or not, at its option; and in the same manner it may become a carrier generally of all things which may be offered for transportation, or it may restrict its business in that capacity to certain articles, or to carrying between certain places, even on the line of its own road. Johnson v. The North Midland R. Co. 6 Eng. Rail. Ca. 61. It may be doubtful whether this decision would be followed in this country, but it has an important bearing upon the question which we are considering in two respects; 1st, Upon the *right* or *power* of a company to contract for such an exemption from responsibility as is claimed under these agreements; 2d, Upon the *true construction* of the agreements themselves.

If a railway company is legally bound to become a common-carrier, it may be a matter of doubt how far it can restrict its liabilities as such; but if like a natural person it may wholly decline to engage in the carrying business, it would seem to follow as a necessary consequence, that it might contract to perform services for others upon just such terms as the parties can agree. The distinction between the right of common-carriers, and other bailees, to free themselves wholly from responsibility is noticed in Wells v. The Steam Navigation Co. 2 Comstock, 204, and Alexander v. Greene, 3 Hill, 9. In the former case the court say, "There is no room for doubt that other bailees, and persons engaged in other employments, may contract for either a larger or a more restricted liability than the law would imply against them in the absence of a special contract. They are not, like common-carriers and innkeepers, bound to accept employment when offered; nor, like them, are they tied down to a reasonable reward for their services. They are at liberty to demand an unreasonable price before they will undertake any work or trust, or to reject employment altogether; and they may make just such stipulations as they please concerning the risk to be incurred. They may become insurers against all possible hazards, or they may say, we will answer for nothing but a loss happening *through our own fraud or want of good faith.* In short, the parties stand on equal terms, and can in this matter, as they may in others, make just such a bargain as they think will answer their purpose."

It is upon this ground that the English cases referred to are decided, and in Carr v. The Lancashire and Yorkshire R. Co. Lord Campbell expressly says, that with the defendants in their character as common-carriers they have nothing to do.

2d. The position, which, under the English decisions, a railway company occupies in making these agreements may have an important bearing upon their construction. If the company is bound to accept all goods which are offered, and to transport them as common-carriers, if required to do so by the owner, it may, perhaps, in the light of this circumstance, be the true construction of these contracts that they affect only the peculiar liabilities of the company as a common-carrier, and not those which devolve upon it as a simple bailee. If, on the contrary, a company may rightfully refuse to act as a common-carrier, and may legally make such terms as it pleases as to a special bailment, then, perhaps, the true construction of the same language might exempt the company from all liability whatever, or at least from all except such wilful misfeasance or gross negligence as would amount to a renunciation of the bailment.

This distinction seems to have been judicially recognized in England. In Wyld v. Pickford, 8 Meeson & Welsby, 443, the question arose as to the effect of a notice which the court treated as a special contract. The defendants were common-carriers, and had (according to the pleadings in the case) given notice to the plaintiff, that they would not be responsible for his goods, unless they were insured according to their value and paid for, which was not done. The court, in relation to the effect of such a notice, said, "We agree, that if the notice furnished a defence, it must be either on the ground of fraud, or of a limitation of the liability by contract, which limitation it is competent for a carrier to make, because being entitled by

common law to insist upon the full price of the carriage being paid beforehand, he may, if such price be not paid, refuse to carry upon the terms imposed by the common law, and insist upon his own ; and if the proprietor of the goods still chooses that they should be carried, it must be on those terms; and *probably the effect of such a contract would be only to exclude certain losses, leaving the carrier liable as upon the custom of England for the remainder.*" And after an examination of the case the court further say, "The weight of the authorities seems to be in favor of the doctrine, that, in order to render a carrier liable after such a notice, it is not necessary to prove a total abandonment of that character, or an act of wilful misconduct, but that it is enough to prove an act of ordinary negligence — gross negligence in the sense in which it has been understood in the last mentioned cases; and that the effect of the notice in the form stated in the plea is, that the carrier will not, unless he is paid a premium, be responsible for all events (other than the act of God and the king's enemies,) by which loss or damage to the owner may arise, against which events he is by the common law a sort of insurer ; but still, he undertaking to carry from one place to another, and for some reward in respect of the carriage, *is therefore bound to use ordinary care in the custody of the goods and in their conveyance to, and delivery at their place of destination, and in providing proper vehicles for their carriage.*" See also Dorr v. The New Jersey Steam Navigation Co. 4 Sandford, 136.

It may be added, that the question, whether a special agreement shall be held to exempt a party from the gross negligence of his servants is entirely different from that which arises when he is charged with personal negligence of his own. The first question is the one which is usually presented in railway cases.

PORTER AND BENSON v. BUCKFIELD BRANCH RAILROAD.[1]

Kennebec Co., May Term, 1851.

Construction of Contract by Referees — Conclusiveness of Award — Damages for Non-fulfilment of Agreement to pay in Stock.

The construction of a contract by referees, appointed under a submission at common law to *settle the dispute in relation to that construction*, is not reëxaminable in this court.

Thus the plaintiffs contracted with the defendants to construct for them a railroad; the defendant reserved the right to alter the line or the gradients of the road, without the allowance of any extra compensation, if the engineer should judge such alterations necessary or expedient; alterations were accordingly made, involving a large increase of expense; for that increase of expense, the referees allowed compensation to the contractors; *Held*, by the court, that the allowance of that compensation did not transcend the authority of the referees.

Thus, again; the defendants in the contract reserved the right to substitute *piling* instead of *embankment*, on a specified part of the road; and the substitution was made, creating to the contractors an increased expense, for which the referees allowed a compensation; *Held*, that that allowance did not transcend the authority of the referees.

The submission stipulated, that the referees should take the contract, *as the basis of their action.* The contract required, that a fixed proportion of the cost of the road should be paid to the contractors, in the stock of the company. The referees, having ascertained the amount of that proportion, awarded that certificates for the same should be issued to the contractors; *Held*, by the court, that this part of their award did not transcend their authority.

The certificates of the stock were demanded, but were not furnished. *Held*, the measure of damage is, not their *par value*, but their *marketable value*.

It is not within the province of referees to award costs, unless so authorized by the submission.

The part of an award by which costs are allowed without authority, may be set aside, without invalidating the residue of the award.

The report of a case from *Nisi Prius* will be dismissed, though signed by the Judge, if it be found defective in any essential particulars.

On a report from *Nisi Prius*, HOWARD, J., presiding.

On the 24th of October, 1848, the plaintiffs contracted in writing with the defendants to construct a railroad upon a specified location, and in a prescribed manner. The contract contained many specifications. Among them were the following: —

" The line of road or gradients may be changed, if the engineer shall consider such change necessary or expedient, and no extra allowance shall be claimed therefor.

The company reserve the privilege of substituting piling for embankment, across the intervale land on a portion of sections No. 5 & 6.

In reference to the quantities of excavation and embankment, as shown in the estimate, it is to be observed that they are but such an approximation as could be made from centre levels, and the company do not consider themselves bound to assure the contractor, that those quantities will not exceed the estimate, but desire that he will base his bid upon his own examination of the ground and profile as to the quantities, the.character of the material to be excavated, as well as all other circumstances connected with the work."

For the foregoing work the defendants agreed, by the same contract, to pay the plaintiffs $40,000. The plaintiffs were " to receive fifteen per cent. of the total amount on their contract in the capital stock of said company." . . . the said stock to be issued on the final completion of this contract, and the full and entire assessments on such amount of stock to be retained by the said company from any moneys remaining in their hands, then due and payable to the plaintiffs.

The plaintiffs, as they now contend, completed the road as agreed; and also did other and extra work, not required by the contract, except for additional compensation.

Difficulties arose between the parties, each claiming compensations as will herein appear; whereupon they agreed " to submit the matters in dispute " to certain referees, *from whose decision there should be no appeal*, upon the following stipulations, viz.: —

" The matter in dispute is in relation to the true construction of the contract between them for the building of the Buckfield Branch Railroad, and for several violations of the contract.

It is also agreed that P. S. Noxon, Esq., as engineer, shall be engaged to examine the work and measure the work, and report the result of his examinations to the referees mentioned in this agreement, at such time and place as the referees may appoint. It is understood that the contract shall be presented for examination, as a basis for a settle. ment, and such damage as either party has sustained by non-fulfil. ment of contract to be so awarded."

The referees accepted the trust. Their report presented the follow. ing views and results: —

" By the original estimate exhibited to the contractors and referred to in the contract, the estimate cost of the whole work embraced in the contract was $41,711, which work Messrs. Porter & Benson, by their written tender, promised to do, and to build and complete the whole road according to the plans and specifications exhibited, including the ballasting where necessary, but not the superstructure, for the gross or round sum of $40,000.

The contract having been entered into, and the construction of the road commenced under it, the chief engineer of the company so changed and altered the alignment of the road, that the former proposed line on the original plan and profile was so departed from, that the proposed and actually located lines seldom coincided, and at the same time the engineer also raised the general grade line of the road above what was originally proposed and contemplated, and furthermore the company claimed and exercised the privilege of substituting piling for embankment across the intervale lands already referred to; all of which changes, alterations, raising of the grade line, and substitution of piling for embankment were adopted and carried out for the general improvement of the road, and in the supposed interest of the company.

The effect of these changes, alterations, and modifications upon the interests of the contractors, was to increase the expense of construction on masonry some seventeen per cent.; on excavation and embankment, some thirty per cent.; and on the total cost of the whole work under the contract some twenty-five per cent.

By the terms of said contract the said company undertook and covenanted, that on or about the first day of each month during the progress of the work, an estimate of the relative value of the work done under the contract should be made, and that three fourths of the amount of said estimate should be paid to the contractors, and it fully appeared in evidence that said contractors did commence their work under said contract, and followed up the same with all due diligence until they became embarrassed for the want of the necessary funds and capital to carry on the work advantageously, occasioned by the failure of said railroad company to pay said contractors the seventy-five per cent. estimated value of work done, which said neglect on the part of said company to furnish the stipulated funds, in accordance with their contract, continuing, the said Porter and Benson, in the month of October, A. D. 1849, abandoned the further prosecution of the work, and left the same unfinished, without having completed the road, and performed on their part the stipulations of the contract of October 24, A. D. 1848.

And the undersigned further report and award, that in view of the whole evidence laid before them, and of the state of facts as proved, the neglect of said Porter and Benson to finish and complete all the graduation, masonry, and other work on said Buckfield Branch Railroad, required by the terms and stipulations of their contract, arose from and was wholly owing to the previous neglect of said railroad company to fulfil the covenants of said company in not making the payments as stipulated in and by said contract on their part.

And the undersigned further report and award that, according to the true construction of said contract, the changes in the line of road and gradients, which the company reserved to itself the power to make, when considered necessary or expedient by the engineer, and for which no extra allowance should be claimed by the contractor, must *in foro conscientiæ* be restricted to such proper changes and modifications as would not materially increase the expense and enhance the cost of constructing said proposed railroad, and that material and expensive changes and alterations, such as those subsequently made and adopted in this case, were not in the contemplation of the contracting parties at the time of entering into said contract; because, among other reasons, it would place one of the contracting parties wholly at the mercy of the other, and because the consideration of $40,000 which said Porter and Benson were to receive from said company for the work to be done, under the circumstances of the case exclude the idea of all expensive changes and modifications of the line of gradients in the proposed road, their tender or bid being expressly based upon the estimates of the originally proposed alignment and gradients.

And the undersigned further report and award, that although by the terms of the contract, the company reserved to itself the privilege of substituting piling for embankment across certain intervale lands, should a further examination of the ground render such a course advisable, yet according to the true construction of said contract, and on a careful collation of its several provisions, — while said company had such right to make their election as they should deem it most for the interest of the company itself, they had no right to impose an additional burden and expense upon the contractors for the sole and exclusive benefit of the company, without indemnifying the contractors therefor.

With these views in relation to the true construction of the contract between the Buckfield Branch Railroad Company, on the one part, and Messrs. Porter and Benson, contractors, on the other part, for the building of the Buckfield Branch Railroad, the undersigned further report and award, that there be allowed to said railroad company, for the non-fulfilment of the covenants and stipulations in said contract of Oct. 24, 1848, on the part of said Porter and Benson, the following sums, to be computed and taken and charged in set-off, against any claims on the part of said Porter and Benson against said company for damages or otherwise, to wit : —

1. The amount of the estimate made by Mr. Noxon, as engineer, Nov. 17, 1840, at the special request of the directors of the company as sufficient in his judgment to bring the road-bed in such shape as to fulfil all the requirements of the contract, being $1,150.

2. Also a further sum to be added to said estimated amount for imperfections in masonry, in piling, in clearing and grubbing, in covering up stumps and rubbish in embankments, and for other deficiencies of ballasting, &c., being $1,350. Which two sums being charged as damages against said Porter and Benson, amount in the whole to the sum of $2,500. And the undersigned further report and award, that there has been paid to said Porter and Benson, by said railroad company, for and on account of work done under said contract of Oct. 24, 1848, the amount of $32,874.15, of which one hundred dollars was paid by one share in the capital stock of said company.

And the undersigned further report and award, that the said railroad company stand chargeable to said Porter and Benson in the following sums, to wit : —

1. In the sum of forty thousand dollars, being the price stipulated to be paid by said company to said Porter and Benson, according to the terms of the contract of Oct. 24, 1848.

2. In a further sum to be added to said forty thousand dollars for the excess of work and enhanced cost occasioned by the new alignment of the road, the raising of the road-bed, the increase of masonry, of excavation and embankment, of trestle work, &c., and also for the increased expense of piling across the intervale lands mentioned, over embankment, which enhanced cost of construction, after a careful examination and computation, assuming the contract of Oct. 24, 1848, as a basis for a settlement, the undersigned have estimated at $9,500.

And the undersigned further report and award, that on a final adjustment of all claims, as well for moneys due as damages sustained by either party, for non-fulfilment of the contract of Oct. 24, A. D. 1848, and for violations of said contract by either party, there now remains due to said Porter and Benson from said railroad company the sum of fourteen thousand one hundred and twenty-five dollars and eighty-five cents ; which said sum of $14,125.85, according to the terms of said contract, and upon the basis of the same, is payable in manner following : — that is to say, seven thousand three hundred dollars in the capital stock of the company at par, of one hundred dollars a share, — said seven thousand three hundred dollars, part of the aforesaid $14,125.85, is to be retained and applied by said company to the payment in full of all assessments made, and to be made, to the amount of one hundred dollars per share, of said capital stock. And the undersigned award that the said railroad company forthwith issue to said Porter and Benson certificates of seventy-three shares in the capital stock of said company, the whole amount of one hundred dollars on each share being paid in the manner above mentioned. Such certificates to be delivered at the office of said company on demand there.

And the undersigned further report and award, that the said railroad company pay to the said Porter and Benson on demand, after being notified of this award, the sum of six thousand eight hundred and twenty-five dollars and eighty-five cents, being the balance of $14,125.85, after deducting the aforesaid sum of $7,300 which said sum, when paid, the undersigned award, is to be received by said Porter and Benson, in full satisfaction and discharge of all claims and demands whatsoever against said company, growing in any manner out of said agreement of Oct. 24, A. D. 1848, and of all claims and demands for material or supplies furnished, or work done by or on behalf of said Porter and Benson, in the construction of the Buckfield Branch Railroad.

And the undersigned further report and award, that the respective parties in this case, each pay their own witnesses, counsel, and expenses, and furthermore, under the peculiar circumstances of the case, as presented to the undersigned by the evidence adduced, it appearing to the undersigned that the elucidation of the case was for the mutual interest of both parties, and necessary for the common understanding of their respective rights. The undersigned, therefore award, that the expense of survey authorized and required of Mr. Noxon, as engineer, by the instrument of reference, amounting to sixty-six dollars, and the further expense of certain calculations made by Mr. Arrowsmith, amounting to thirty dollars, should be at the charge and expense of both parties.

And the undersigned further award that the compensation of the referees in this case for fifteen days' service each, at the rate of $5,00 per day each, together with five dollars each for incidental expenses, and twenty dollars more in addition for notifying the parties and referees, and drawing this report and award, be also at the joint expense of the parties.

In accordance with these views and adjudications, the undersigned further award that the said Porter and Benson, paying to the undersigned, for the use of the parties interested, the amount of the aforesaid mentioned sums, being three hundred and fifty-six dollars, the said Porter and Benson shall have the right to claim and demand of the aforesaid railroad company, the one moiety of said sum, being one hundred and seventy-eight dollars, which sum the undersigned award to be paid to said Porter and Benson, in addition to the sums hereinbefore awarded.

Done at Portland, this 26th day of January, A. D. 1850.

All which is respectfully submitted by   WM. P. PREBLE,
                                                 JOHN ANDERSON,
                                                 P. S. NOXON."

The defendants were duly notified of the award, and a demand was made upon them for the certificates of stock which were not delivered.

This action is Assumpsit upon the award.

The defendants pleaded the general issue with a brief statement; alleging no such award as set forth in the plaintiff's writ.

The defendants objected to the said award as exceeding the authority given to the arbitrators, and as defective and illegal on its face, and generally to its sufficiency, admissibility, and effect, and to the introduction of these papers, but the court admitted them to be read, subject to all legal exceptions, and for the purpose of carrying forward the case, ruled *pro forma*, that 'the submission and award might be read to the jury, and were sufficient to maintain the action.

The defendants proposed to show that said stock was of less value than one hundred dollars per share, and contended that if the plaintiffs were entitled to receive the said stock, that their claim was limited to the actual market value of said stock at the time of the demand. But for the purpose of this trial, the court ruled that the measure of damages, if any were recoverable, on account of not delivering the same on demand, would be the par or full amount of one hundred dollars for each share of stock not delivered.

The defendants then called John Anderson, one of the arbitrators, who testified in relation to the hearing before the referees, that the referees in making up the award, adopted the report of P. S. Noxon, engineer, as the basis of the award. That they took Noxon's report of the quantities of work and applied the contract prices, and made up the amount in that way; — that much testimony was before them that Noxon had been engineer of the company ; — that no objection. was made to the correctness of his report, and that the referees took it for granted that the admeasurement was correct.

The defendants also called W. P. Preble to the same points, who confirmed the statements of Mr. Anderson, and also testified that the company brought on testimony to show that there was not so much work as represented by Noxon, and that he directed Noxon to make all the surveys either party wanted.

The defendants then called A. P. Robinson, civil engineer, and proposed to show by him and other witnesses that the report of Noxon was untrue in every essential particular, and that the basis on which the arbitrators made their award was false and untrue ; — that so far from there having been any excess of work done on the road by the contractors, beyond the requirements of the contract, the entire amount of all work done on the road was less than the original estimates on which the work was let, and less than the amount which would have been required to have completed the contract upon the original line and survey.

The case was then withdrawn from the jury and submitted to the court; judgment to be entered according to the rights of the parties.

Codman and *May*, for the plaintiffs.

Parris and *Poor*, for the defendants.

HOWARD, J. This report was not drawn up, and presented for signature, until several months after the trial; and, although then signed and allowed, it was subsequently discovered, that it did not contain a full statement of the case, and of the rulings of the presiding Judge, and it must be dismissed. But two questions were presented at the argument, upon which an expression of the opinion of the court, in this stage of the proceedings, has been strongly urged. 1. Whether the award is void upon its face. 2. What would be the measure of damages, if the plaintiffs should recover in this action upon the award.

This was a submission at common law, and by its terms, the referees had power to award conclusively, upon " the matter in dispute " between the parties; which is stated to be " the true construction of the contract between them, for the building of the Buckfield Branch Railroad, and for several violations of the contract." The agreement of submission recites, that, " it is understood, that the contract shall be presented for examination, as a basis for a settlement, also all the receipts given to the company by Porter and Benson, on account of said contract, and all other legal evidence which either party can produce, in relation to this matter in dispute; and such damage as either party has sustained by non-fulfilment of contract to be so awarded."

The referees accepted the trust confided to them; met and heard the parties and their counsel; gave a full and deliberate construction to the contract of October 24, 1848, which was submitted to them, and awarded such damages as in their opinion, either party had sustained by non-fulfilment of that contract. Such construction, if honestly and fairly made, must stand, as the decision of the tribunal selected by the parties for that purpose, and this court can neither change or reverse it. But it is contended, that the referees exceeded their authority, and extended their decision beyond the scope of the submission, and that the award is, therefore, void.

The articles of agreement, or contract, as it is termed, of October 24, 1848, provide, that the plaintiffs " should construct and finish in the most substantial and workmanlike manner " the railroad according to the specifications stated, for $40,000. It is specified, that " the line of the road or gradients may be changed, if the engineer shall consider such change necessary or expedient, and no extra allowance shall be claimed therefor." And " the company reserve the privilege of substituting piling for embankment across the intervale land on a portion of sections No. 5 and 6, should a further examination of the ground render such a course advisable." After awarding to the defendants the amount of payments made to the plaintiffs and $2,500, for "non-fulfilment of the covenants and stipulations in said contract of Oct. 24, 1848, on the part of said Porter and Benson, to be computed and taken and charged in set-off against any claims, on the part of said Porter and Benson, against said company for damages, or otherwise," the referees " further report and award, that the railroad company stand chargeable to said Porter and Benson, in the following sums, to wit," $40,000, being the price stipulated to be paid to them in the contract, and a further sum to be added to said $40,000, for the excess of work and enhanced cost occasioned by the new alignment of the road, the raising of the road bed, the increase of masonry, of excavation and embankment, of trestle work, &c., and also for the increased expense of piling across the intervale lands mentioned, over embankment, which enhanced cost of construction, after a careful examination and computation, assuming the contract of October 24, 1848, as a basis for a settlement, the undersigned have estimated at $9,500."

Whether there was excess of work done, and whether the work was performed at enhanced cost, occasioned by such new alignment and substitution of piling for embankment, and whether the plaintiffs were entitled to increased compensation therefor, under the contract, were questions to be determined upon a true construction of the contract, by the referees, and taking that as the basis for the settlement contemplated by the agreement of submission.

So, the neglect, on the part of the company, to furnish funds, in accordance with the contract, might constitute a violation of it, and it was, therefore, competent for the referees to " report and award on a final adjustment of all claims, as well for moneys due as damages sustained by either party for non-fulfilment of the contract of October 24, 1848, and for violations of said contract by either party."

• It is objected, further, that the referees had no authority to award in what manner the damages should be paid. This objection would have more force if the agreement of submission had not stipulated that the contract should be presented as the basis of the settlement; or if the terms of that contract had been invaded by the adjudication. As it is, the award provides that the defendants may, or shall pay in accordance with their contract and agreement, and the objection fails.

If the method of payment, thus provided, is more favorable to the defendants, than the payment in money, they may not suffer on that account; but if less favorable, and even if not authorized by the submission, such provision, as to the manner of payment, would not necessarily invalidate the whole award. It might be good in part, and bad in part; valid for the amount awarded, and void for the provision prescribing the manner of payment, if by annulling that provision, the rights of neither party to the award are impaired. Pope v. Brett, 2 Saund. 293, note 1; Banks v. Adams, 23 Maine, 259.

In thus awarding, the referees appear to have acted within the scope of the authority conferred upon them, in giving a construction to the contract, and awarding upon its basis the damages either party had sustained by its non-fulfilment; and their award is not rendered invalid by any thing presented by these objections.

At common law, referees or arbitrators have no power to award costs, unless conferred by the agreement of submission. The award in this case, respecting costs, was not authorized, and is not binding upon the parties. But as this does not affect the substance of the award of damages, or the substantial justice of the case, it cannot impair the validity of the award in other respects. Chandler v. Fuller, Willes, 62; Fox v. Smith, 2 Wilson, 267; Addison v. Gray, 2 Wilson, 293; Gordon v. Tucker, 6 Maine, 247; Walker v. Merrill, 13 Maine, 173.

It has been held that, if no provision be made by the award respecting costs of reference and award, they are to be paid by the parties equally. Grove v. Cox, 1 Taunt. 165.

On the subject of damages the referees " report and award, that on a final adjustment of all claims, as well for moneys due, as damages sustained by either party, for non-fulfilment of the contract of October 24, 1848, and for violations of said contract by either party, there now remains due to said Porter and Benson from said railroad company, the sum of fourteen thousand, one hundred and twenty-five dollars and eighty-five cents, — which said sum of $14,125.85, according to the terms of said contract, and upon the basis of the same, is payable in manner following: — that is to say, seven thousand, three hundred dollars in the capital stock of the company, at par, of one hundred dollars a share; — said seven thousand, three hundred dollars, part of the aforesaid $14,125.85, is to be retained and applied by said company to the payment in full of all assessments made, and to be made, to the amount of one hundred dollars per share, of said capital stock. And the undersigned award that said railroad company forthwith issue to said Porter and Benson certificates of seventy-three shares in the capital stock of said com.

pany, the whole amount of one hundred dollars on each share being paid in the manner above mentioned. Such certificates to be delivered at the office of said company on demand. And the undersigned further report and award that the said railroad company pay to said Porter and Benson, on demand, after being notified of this award, the sum of six thousand, eight hundred and twenty-five dollars, and eighty-five cents, being the balance of $14,125.85, after deducting the aforesaid sum of $7,300, which said sum when paid, the undersigned award, is to be received by said Porter and Benson, in full satisfaction of all claims and demands whatsoever, against said company, growing in any manner out of said agreement of October 24, 1848, and of all claims and demands for material or supplies furnished, or work done, by or on behalf of said Porter and Benson, in the construction of the Buckfield Branch Railroad."

This is not an award that the defendants should pay to the plaintiffs $14,125.85, as claimed by them, but that they should pay that sum, less $7,300, and issue to the plaintiffs, seventy-three shares of the stock of the company, exempt from assessment, in accordance with the contract of the parties. The sum of $7,300 being nominally retained as an equivalent for such assessments, though in fact never due to the plaintiffs upon the contract, or by the award.

The measure of damages, then, will be $6,825.85, and the value of seventy-three shares of the stock, thus circumstanced, with interest from the date of the demand proved. Any other rule would cast upon the defendants a burden not imposed by the award, and wholly inconsistent with the terms and spirit of the contract, upon which the award was to be based, and upon which it was in fact made. But, for the reasons given, the report must be dismissed, and the cause may be submitted to a jury.

CASES

ARGUED AND DETERMINED

IN THE

SUPREME COURT OF NEW HAMPSHIRE.

TUCKER *v.* THE CHESHIRE RAILROAD COMPANY.[1]

Cheshire Co. July Term, 1850.

Bill for an Injunction — Answers — Impertinent Allegations.

A statement in an answer explanatory of and showing the reason for another statement in the answer is not impertinent.

A bill prayed for an injunction against a railroad corporation, upon the ground that a certain railroad bridge which the respondents intended to build across the Connecticut River would injure the orator's bridge, which had been erected under a charter from the Legislature. The answer stated that the orator and his wife owned certain land adjacent to the bridge and held it and the franchise of the bridge by the same title. It was then stated that the assessment of damages to them was for injuries sustained by them as owners of the bridge and franchise, and also as owners of the land. *Held*, that the statement of the ownership of the land was not impertinent, because it explained the reason of the assessment.

The court will not strike matter out of an answer as impertinent unless its irrelevancy be clearly shown.

If the matter excepted to, be such as may require examination in some future stage of the case it will not be stricken out, but the benefit of the exception will be reserved to the orator upon the final hearing of the cause.

A bill prayed that the respondents might be enjoined from erecting a railroad bridge across the Connecticut River upon the ground that it would injure the orator's bridge by infringing the vested rights conferred by his charter. The answer stated that railway communications were not discovered and brought into use until long after the date of the orator's charter. *Held*, that this statement was not impertinent, because in order to determine the rights of the parties it might become necessary to inquire whether the orator's bridge were intended and calculated to answer the purposes of a railway bridge, and whether the latter

---

[1] 1 Foster's Reports, 29.

were so different from the former that it could not be considered as violating the exclusive privileges conferred by the orator's charter.

The respondents are bound to deny or admit all the facts stated in the bill, with all their material circumstances, without special interrogatories for that purpose.

IN EQUITY.   The following case was stated in the bill.

On the 30th day of December, 1783, the Legislature of New Hampshire granted to Enoch Hale, of Rindge, and his heirs forever, " the exclusive right and privilege of building and keeping a bridge over the Connecticut, anywhere between the upper end of Bellows Falls on a certain rock in said Falls, and the exclusive right of receiving from any persons who might pass over the bridge, either by themselves or with horses, carriages, cattle, or creatures of any kind, or any other thing, such tolls as should be allowed by the Justices of the Quarter Sessions."

An act passed on the 15th day of June, 1797, provided that no person without the consent of the owners of the grant, should build or keep any bridge over the Connecticut, at any place between the southerly bounds of the grant, and a point distant two miles down the river, and from the northerly bound, to a point two miles up the river.

Certain specific rates of toll were given by the Act of June, 15th, 1804.

On or about the 14th day of May, 1790, Frederick W. Geyer became the owner of the grant, and died on the 18th day of March, 1821.

By his will, dated on the 12th day of October, 1820, he devised this property to Rufus G. Amory and Richard D. Tucker, in trust for the use of Mrs. Nathaniel Tucker for her life, but subject to an annuity payable to a son of the testator, and after her death to the use of her children, or such of them as she might appoint.

On the 21st day of March, 1848, the trustees named in the will having died, the orator was appointed trustee under the will by the Court of Probate.

A bridge was erected under the charter by Enoch Hale, the original grantee, and since his death the trustees have kept it in repair, and there has been a large amount of travel across it, from which very considerable profits have been derived.

The defendants were chartered on the 27th day of December, 1844, and under the charter of that date they have acted.   They deny the exclusive right of the orator; and have laid a railway to a point within his exclusive bounds, and, without making or causing to be assessed to the orator, trustee as aforesaid, any compensation, threaten to build a bridge by the side of the orator's bridge, in violation of his rights. They allege that they have the right so to do, and that the erection of the bridge would not injure him, or deprive him of his rights ; that he, as trustee, would be entitled to no compensation or damages therefor, and therefore they have not offered it. They allege that damages have been awarded to the orator and to Mrs. Tucker by the commissioners, but the orator alleges that they were not awarded for any injury done to the franchise, but for other property taken by the defendants.

The bill also alleges that the several acts of the Legislature created a contract between the grantees and the State, and that the franchises were private property, which could not be taken away without the consent of the orator, or without compensation.

It was also averred in the bill that Messrs. Howland and Farrar, two of the railroad commissioners by whom the damages for the land were assessed, were interested in the Cheshire Railroad Company, and therefore were incompetent to act upon the matter.

The case stated by the answer was, that the respondents, acting under their charter and the laws of New Hampshire, have proceeded in all things according to law; that the orator and Mrs. Tucker were duly notified; that they were the occupants and owners in the same right, of the adjacent land and the franchise of the bridge, and that damages were awarded them for the injury to the land and the franchise together, which damages have been duly paid or tendered.

Various exceptions were taken to the answer, as follows :

For impertinence.

1. Because it is alleged in the answer that the orator and Mrs. Tucker, on the 8th day of May, 1847, occupied the land adjacent to the bridge, and on the easterly side of the Connecticut River, near to, and adjoining the bridge, which land the respondents aver was then held in the same right and under the same title as the franchise of the bridge, and were believed to be the true and only proprietors and owners of the land and bridge.

2. Because it is alleged in the answer that the mode of travel and transportation by railroad was not discovered and brought into use until long after the alleged grant to Enoch Hale.

For insufficiency.

3. Because it is charged in the bill that the building of a railroad, as contemplated by the respondents, within the exclusive limits of the orator, and the use of the bridge to be constructed in connection with the railroad of the respondents, will be productive of great and irreparable injury to the franchise of the orator, by diverting travel and transportation from the bridge of the orator to the railroad bridge, resulting in a great loss of tolls and profits to the orator, and

the respondents have not in any wise answered the matters thus charged.

4. Because the bill alleges that the respondents threaten to build, and have made preparations for building a railroad bridge over the Connecticut River, within the exclusive limits of the orator, without causing to be assessed, in any manner prescribed by law, any compensation for the injury which would be caused thereby to the franchise ; and it is also charged, that a certain assessment, made by the railroad commissioners of such damages, is void, for the reason that Messrs. Howland and Farrar, two of the commissioners, were, at the time the assessment was made, interested in the stock of the Cheshire Railroad and in its value. And the respondents have not, to the best and utmost of the knowledge, remembrance, and belief of Thomas M. Edwards, the President of the corporation, by whom they have answered, disclosed, and set forth whether, at the time aforesaid, the said Howland and Farrar were or were not interested in the stock as above-mentioned.

Vose, and *Shafter* (of Vermont) for the orator. Any thing not material, and not responsive to the allegations in the bill, is impertinent.

The answer states that there were lands easterly of the bridge, owned by Mr. and Mrs. Tucker. The object of the bill is to restrain the respondents from injuring the franchise. The answer does not state that these lands were affected in any way by the franchise, but merely says that they were held under the same title as the franchise, and that the damages were assessed as well for the lands, as for the franchise. As the lands are recognized as not being within the franchise by the answer, they have nothing to do with it, and the statement about them is impertinent.

The answer is also impertinent in stating that railways were invented and brought into use since the year 1782. This was not called for by the bill, and is not responsive to it. Perhaps the respondents mean to allege that a railroad bridge is not a violation of our charter. In the case of the Enfield Co. v. Hartford and N. H. Railroad Co. 17 Conn. 50, the respondents said that a railroad bridge was not such a bridge as the parties contemplated should not be built. The court said that it was not strickly speaking a bridge, because it was not meant to accomplish the ordinary purposes of a common bridge. But it did much of the business which the orators would otherwise have had the benefit of.

The answer is insufficient, because it does not answer the matters stated in the bill as to the injury to the orator by diminishing the tolls, and this the answer should do.

The bill alleges that no damages were assessed for the franchise. The attempt to assess damages failed because two, of the commissioners were interested in the road.

The answer alleges that the commissioners were competent. This is not an answer to the charges in the bill, because the facts therein stated should be answered according to the knowledge, information, and belief of the respondents. 2 Dan. Ch. Pr. 835. A general denial is not enough. There should be a specific, positive, and precise denial, and the answer contains no such denial of the interest of the commissioners. The competency is a question of law, and is a conclusion to be made by the court from the facts. The answer may state that the commissioners are competent, because it may be the opinion of counsel that an interest in the stock does not disqualify them from acting as commissioners.

Wheeler for the respondents. As to the first exception for impertinence, we merely stated the facts as they were. The reason for stating the ownership of the land, as well as of the franchise, and the joint appraisal, was, that they were so connected by the title and the appraisal of the commissioners, that no full and intelligible statement could be made which did not include these facts. The respondents are not to be confined, in their answer, to a naked admission or denial of the allegations in the bill. They may state such matters as will explain their position fully, and show the nature of their justification. All the facts stated are necessarily connected, they show the nature and reason of the assessment, and must come out in the proof.

As to the second exception, relating to the discovery of the mode of transportation by railroads subsequent to the grant to Hale, the allegations in the answer are pertinent in reference to the alleged infringement of the rights secured by the original charter. The court are called upon to give a construction to the charter, and it is a part of the respondent's case that the grant to Hale does not include all possible modes of transportation not then known. It seems to us that it would be an extraordinary interpretation of this grant, to hold that Hale and his grantees were thereby clothed with the exclusive right of providing all the means of crossing the river within the chartered limits, and that, in all coming time, the public are to be confined to the orator's bridge, although they may have occasion to pass in other modes and for other purposes, than originally contemplated, and for which the bridge is adapted.

The respondents believe that they may, without subjecting themselves to the objection of impertinence, allege the fact that the discovery and use of railroads and railroad bridges are of recent date, and that it could not have been the intention of the legislature to exclude from the chartered limits, such a bridge as is to form a part of the railroad — a bridge not intended for the public travel in the sense in which these words were used at the time of the grant. Both structures may, in common language, be called *bridges*, but they are intended for different purposes, and might well be designated by different names. The erection of a bridge within the exclusive limits of a ferry, if it do not obstruct the convenient use of the latter, is no infringement upon the rights of the ferry. Piscataqua Bridge *v.* N. H. Bridge, 7 N. H. Rep. 35. Grants of this character are not to be extended by construction.

An exclusive right to make communications by post, would not be infringed by the incorporation of a line of telegraphic communication. It does not follow that any thing is impertinent because its bearing cannot be seen at once. The court will not order it to be struck out, unless it be clearly out of place in the answer. Story, Eq. Pl. 661. If there be any doubt whether the statement be impertinent, the court allows it to remain.

As to the alleged insufficiency of the answer in relation to the possible injury to the franchise by the railroad, the statements of the bill on this point are answered for all purposes the orator can have in view. The intention to build the bridge is admitted. If enough be stated, so that the orator can have a decree if he be entitled to one by law, this is all that can be required. He cannot say what effect our bridge may have upon the orator's interests. Perhaps it will cause the erection of buildings, and an increase of population, so that the orator's bridge will be more profitable. Our crossing between the limits of the grant does no more injury than would be caused by crossing above or below them. We do not think this material. 7 Paige, 517. As to the other exception, relating to the interest of the commissioners, the bill states that they are interested, and we say they are competent. The orator cannot take evidence of the interest as he has attempted to do, after the filing of his bill, and bring the matter into our answer, and so ask us to weigh his evidence. It is enough that the answer denies the allegations in the bill.

The bill contains no interrogatories, and we are not bound to answer to any particular matter, unless we are specially interrogated in relation thereto. Such we understand to be the English rule, and the rule of the Supreme Court. 2 Dan. Ch. Pr. 820, (Perkins's Ed.)

We also contend that the orator's bridge does not accommodate the public, in the way in which the public now require to be accommodated. We then, by our bridge, do not deprive the orator of any profit; for he could not furnish the public with the mode of transportation which we propose, and which our charter authorizes.

Shafter, in reply. . The respondents say that where an incidental advantage would arise to our bridge by reason of the erection of theirs, their erection will not be within the exclusive words of our charter, unless it be such an advantage as the parties might anticipate. But a bridge means now what it meant in 1783. It is a structure of wood or other material for passage and transportation. Its material is not an element of the definition, nor is the mode in which it is crossed. It is still a bridge, although it may be a foot bridge ; and we have a right to take toll for every thing that may pass over a bridge. We might erect a bridge for the transportation of locomotives, but the respondents could not do so. A bridge and a ferry are generally different things ; and there is no analogy between communications by telegraph and by the post.

There is enough disclosed in the case to entitle us to a decree. But the respondents say that we should show irreparable damage, something that amounts to a nuisance. If they know nothing but what appears in the answer they should have so stated. But they deny the incompetency of the commissioners and thereby assume that they know the facts relating to their interest, or else they have jumped at a conclusion. If they know the facts, they should have stated them, that the court might draw the conclusion.

As to the interrogatories, we understand the practice to be that a general interrogatory is broad enough to draw out specific answers.

GILCHRIST, C. J. The bill alleges that the damages assessed to Mr. and Mrs. Tucker, were not awarded as compensation for any injury to the orator's franchise, but entirely for other and distinct property taken by the respondents.

The answer states that Mr. and Mrs. Tucker, on the 8th day of May, 1847, occupied the land adjacent to the bridge on the east side of the river, and held it under the same right, and by the same title as the franchise of the bridge, and are believed to be the true and only proprietors of the land and bridge.

This is excepted to as impertinent. The answer also states that the damages were assessed to them, as well for injuries sustained by them, as owners of the bridge and franchise, as of the land.

It is relevant to the case of the respondents to state that the assessment included the damages done to the franchise. This is responsive to the bill, and is not excepted to.

But the statement that the franchise and land were owned in the same right, is explanatory of the averment that the assessment included the damages both for the franchise and the land, and shows the reason for it. The damages were thus included because the franchise and the land were owned in the same right.

An exception to a part of an answer as impertinent, which refers to and explains the meaning of a schedule annexed to such answer, without also excepting to the schedule itself, must be disallowed. McIntyre v. Union College, 6 Paige, 240. If exceptions would mutilate the answer unnecessarily, by breaking up sentences or clauses which ought to stand or fall together, they should be disallowed. Franklin v. Keiler, 4 Page, 382.

We think that this exception must be disallowed. An exception for impertinence must be supported *in toto*, or it must fail altogether. Story, Eq. Pl. § 266.

There is another ground for disallowing the exception. If Mr. and Mrs. Tucker owned the land and the franchise in the same right, there could be no reason for awarding the damages separately. If they owned the property in different rights, the damages should have been separated. The allegation is that they owned them in the same right. This is relevant. If made out in proof, it may dispose of the orator's allegation that no damages were awarded for the franchise.

By § 5, ch. 128, Rev. St., railroad commissioners are to assess damages in the same way as road commissioners, and they, by ch. 51, § 2, are to proceed as selectmen do. By ch. 49, § 3, the selectmen are to give notice to the owner if known and resident in the State, otherwise to him who has the care and possession of the land; to the occupant.

The answer states that the belief of the respondents to be that Mr. and Mrs. Tucker were " the true and only proprietors and owners of the land and bridge."

. Amory and R. D. Tucker, the original trustees, having died, on the 21st day of May, 1848, the orator was made trustee.

It appears that at the time when the respondents began to build their bridge, or to take the preliminary steps thereto, the legal title to the franchise was in Amory and R. D. Tucker, both of whom lived out of this State.

It became necessary to allege that the orator and Mrs. Tucker were the occupants, because the respondents desired to show the reason why the damages were assessed together, without specifying what was for each right; that is the right to the land and to the franchise.

The second exception for impertinence, is because the answer alleges that the mode of travel by railroad was not discovered and brought into use until after the grant to Hale.

The court, in cases of impertinence, ought, before expunging the matter alleged to be impertinent, to be especially clear that it is such as should be struck out of the record; for this reason, that the error on one side is irremediable, on the other it is not. If the court strikes

it out of the record it is gone, and the party may then have no opportunity of placing it there again ; whereas, if it is prolix or oppressive,
and is left on the record, the court, at the hearing of the cause, has
the power to set the matter right in point of costs.   Davis *v.* Cupps,
2 Younge & Coll. New Rep. 443 ; Story, Eq. Pl. § 268.   If the fact
stated is wholly immaterial, the answer may be excepted to for
impertinence, or the complainant will have the benefit of the objection on the hearing.   Clissold *v.* Powell, 2 Madd. Ch. 355 ; Spencer
v. Van Duzen, 1 Paige, 566.   It ought to be clear to demonstration
that the matter complained of is impertinent, before that which if
wrong, is irremediable, is done.   Story, Eq. Pl. § 268.   The court will
always feel disposed to give the answer a liberal consideration on this
point of matter irrelevant, and to consider whether it can have any
real and proper influence on the suit, having regard to the nature of
it, as made by the bill.   Woods *v.* Morrill, 1 Johns. Ch. 106.   If the
matter of an answer is relevant, that is, if it can have any influence
whatever in the decision of the suit, either as to the subject-matter of
the controversy, the particular relief to be given, or as to the costs, it
is not impertinent.   Van Rensselaer *v.* Bruce, 4 Paige, 177 ; Hawley
v. Wolverton, 5 Paige, 522.[1]

Applying, then, the principles recognized by these authorities to
the question raised by this exception, it is evident that in order to
determine the rights of the parties it may become necessary to inquire
whether the bridge, proposed to be erected by the respondents, be a
violation of the orator's charter, and the exclusive privileges conveyed
thereby.   What kind of travel it is calculated to accommodate, how
far the purposes it is designed to accomplish, are the same with those
intended by the orator's bridge, are matters which we may be called
upon to examine.   And in this view it is by no means clear that we
may not find it proper to consider the allegation that railway communications were not brought into use until after the grant to Hale.
Does a railroad bridge subserve the purposes for which the orator's
bridge was erected ?   They are both bridges, that is, both are structures of wood, iron, and stone, crossing the river.   But although
generically the same, the specific difference between them may be

---

[1] This proposition as to striking out matter which is alleged to be material is sustained by Reeves *v.* Baker, 17 Eng. Law
& Eq. Rep. 509, and the Attorney-General *v.* Richards, 6 Beavan, 444.   In the
latter case the Master of the Rolls laid
down the principle, "that exceptions for
impertinence, in respect to matters alleged
to be immaterial, cannot be maintained,
when the question of the materiality is so
connected with the merits of the cause,
that it cannot be decided without going
into the consideration of the whole merits
of the cause."

very great; so great that one may not be considered as infringing upon the province of the other. We shall, therefore, not allow the second exception for impertinence, but shall give the orator the benefit of it upon the final hearing of the cause.

The other exceptions to the answer, are, that it is insufficient in omitting to state the knowledge, information, and belief of the respondents in relation to certain facts stated in the bill.

The rule is that the respondents should state the point of substance, positively and certainly. No rule however, can provide for all the various difficulties in cases of this sort, but each case must be decided upon its own circumstances. Story, Eq. Pl. § 855. In general a respondent must answer " as to his knowledge, information, and belief." 2 Dan. Ch. Pr. 830; Woods v. Morrill, 1 Johns. Ch. 107. In this case Chancellor Kent says, that " As to facts not within his knowledge, he must answer as to his information, or belief, and not to his information or hearsay merely, without stating his belief one way or the other. The general rules on the subject of exceptions to answers, are founded in good sense and sound justice, and they cannot be too well understood, nor too strictly enforced. If the respondent is not compelled to a full, frank, and explicit disclosure of every thing properly required of him, and resting in his knowledge, information, or belief, one of the most salutary ends of the jurisdiction of this court would be defeated. But if the matter be charged as within the respondent's own knowledge, he must answer positively, and not to his information or belief only. Ibid.; Hall v. Hood, 1 Paige, 404.

It is necessary, to the trial of the orator's case, that it should be proved, whether the road commissioners were interested, and whether the respondent's bridge would be injurious, and the orator therefore has a right to the respondent's best knowledge and belief. The answer is silent on both these points. The exceptions for insufficiency therefore must be sustained, and upon these points the respondents must answer further.

The respondents contend that they are not bound to answer any particular matter charged in the bill, unless they are specially interrogated in relation thereto. But we do not apprehend the rule to be so. If there be enough to call for a full, and frank disclosure of the subject-matter of the bill, it will be sufficient. The respondents are bound to deny or admit all the facts stated in the bill, with all their material circumstances, without special interrogatories for that purpose. Plain sense, and a good conscience will, without any difficulty, in most cases teach a respondent how far it is requisite to answer to the contents of a bill, and to meet the *gravamen* alleged. Methodist Epis. Church v. Jaques, 1 Johns. Ch. 65.

ALDRICH v. CHESHIRE RAILROAD COMPANY.[1]

Cheshire Co., December Term, 1850. .

Damages — Assessment by Commissioners not Cumulative Remedy — Unforeseen Injury Presumed to have been Considered.

When the legislature has authorized an act, the necessary and natural consequence of which is injury to the property of another, and at the same time has prescribed the mode of compensation, he who does the act cannot be liable as a wrongdoer.

Where damages have been assessed by the commissioners to a land-owner for injury done him by excavations in his land for the purposes of a railroad, an action on the case to recover further damages cannot be sustained against the railroad corporation.

The assessment of damages by commissioners is not a cumulative remedy, but is the substitution of one mode for another, and their decision is final upon the merits, subject only to the right of appeal.

The plaintiff's buildings were supplied with water from a permanent spring. After an excavation had been made in his land for the purpose of a railroad, water appeared in the excavation, about fifteen feet below the surface of the ground, and the spring disappeared. Damages were assessed to him before the excavation was made. *Held,* that the injury to the spring must be presumed to have been considered by the commissioners, and that an action to recover damages therefor could not be sustained.

CASE. The declaration alleged, that upon the plaintiff's farm in Westmoreland, there was a permanent spring, which supplied the plaintiff's house and barn with water and irrigated his land; and that the corporation by excavations, &c., diverted the water from its accustomed course, &c., to the injury of the plaintiff.

At the trial upon the general issue, the plaintiff's evidence tended to prove that, until the excavations complained of, there was an abundant supply of water from a spring upon the plaintiff's land for all his purposes; that directly upon the excavation being made, the water disappeared from the spring, and a stream of water began to flow in the excavation, at a point about fifteen feet below the surface of the ground and about a foot and a half above the grade of the railroad. It was admitted that the corporation were authorized to construct the road, that it passed through the plaintiff's land, and that damages were duly assessed to him as a land-owner. The question of damages was submitted to the jury, who returned a verdict for the plaintiff for the sum of $300. The defendants moved to set aside the verdict upon the following grounds:

1. The injury complained of by the plaintiff necessarily resulted

from the construction of the railroad through his land, and the damages awarded by the commissioners must be presumed to have included damages for the injury in question.

2. The defendant, having the right to make the excavations in the plaintiff's land necessary in constructing the road, cannot be liable for interrupting or cutting off any underground springs or runs of water in making their excavations.

Wheeler, for the defendants. If the commissioners have a right to assess damages for any thing, it is for the injury which naturally and necessarily results from the proper construction and use of the railroad. They are not merely to assess the value of the soil taken, or the injury to the land, but " the damages sustained by the owners of land." N. H. Laws, Act of November, 1844, ch. 128, § 5. By the assessment and payment of damages, the corporation acquired the right to construct the road, and, of course, the right to use the proper, usual, and necessary means to accomplish that object. As the water in the excavation flowed from a place considerably above the bed of the road, the injury to the plaintiff's spring must be presumed to result from the grading of the road. The writ contains no allegation of negligence or malicious injury on the part of the corporation or its agents. It may be said that the injury of which the plaintiff complains could not have been foreseen, and so could not have been considered by the commissioners. In no case, perhaps, can the exact nature and extent of the injury be foreseen and considered ; but that, surely, cannot affect the principle upon which the damages are to be assessed. If we could go behind the award, and inquire what was or was not considered by the commissioners, and whether they were or were not fully aware of the nature and extent of the injury sustained by the land-owner, there would be opened a field of endless litigation, certainly not contemplated by the statute. And if these questions could be considered in any case, they do not arise under the mode of redress which the plaintiff has adopted in this action. If the land-owner is dissatisfied with the assessment of damages, he has his remedy by appeal under the statute, and not by an action on the case.

It is to be presumed that the commissioners, having acted in the matter, did their whole duty, and assessed damages for all injuries which they might lawfully take into consideration. And it must be a very narrow construction of the law which would exclude from their consideration an injury to a spring of water under the circumstances of this case.

The corporation had the right to make the necessary excavations, although the plaintiff's supply of water was thereby diminished or diverted from its former course. Greenleaf v. Francis, 18 Pick. 117; Acton v. Blundell, 12 Mees. & W. 324. Under the facts in this case no adverse rights to the water could be acquired against adjoining owners, much less against the defendant who claims under the plaintiff. 18 Pick. 122.

Chamberlain, for the plaintiff.

GILCHRIST, C. J. The Act of November, 1844, requires the commissioners " to assess the damages sustained by the owners of land." Whether the commissioners take into consideration all the circumstances proper to be adverted to by them, depends on their attention to the subject, and their capacity to come to a correct conclusion. But the result they reach is conclusive upon the party, unless there be an appeal from their decision. This is plainly the intent of the statute, for the institution of this tribunal would be useless, unless their estimate should be regarded as final. Any other view of the question would lead to great practical difficulties ; for if we might go behind their assessment, it would be impossible to draw any line beyond which we might proceed. There would be scarcely any injury a land-owner could sustain, which might not be said with more or less plausibility, to be one which the commissioners did not take into consideration. They are not bound to specify each injury and the sum awarded for it, and thus enable us to ascertain in what manner and upon what grounds their judgment has been made up, and when this is not done it is obviously impossible for the Court to say, that for this or that special injury the land-owner has received no compensation. To require this of them would take from them all power of action as an independant tribunal. It would not permit them to exercise their own judgment without any supervision over the merits of a case, as the statute intended, unless where an appeal had been interposed; but would compel them to be interrogated, and in a manner cross-examined as to the mode in which they had discharged their duties. Having the power to consider all the injuries the owner has sustained, and having made an assessment, the presumption is that they have done their duty, and have considered all matters worthy of their attention.

It is a well-settled principle in this State, that when the legislature has authorized an act, the necessary and natural consequence of which is damage to the property of another, and at the same time has prescribed the particular mode in which the damage shall be ascertained and compensated, he who does the act cannot be liable as a wrongdoer. Lebanon *v.* Olcott, 1 N. H. Rep. 339; Woods *v.* Nashua Man. Co. 4 N. H. Rep. 527. Both these cases were actions on the case for erecting dams, and causing injury thereby to the respective plaintiffs, and in each of them damages were awarded by a committee designated in the charter of incorporation, and the position above stated was not denied by the plaintiffs.

If we were to consider the remedy by the award of the commissioners as merely cumulative, we should defeat the manifest object of the legislature, which was, not to give an additional remedy to the party injured, but to substitute one proceeding for another, in the first instance; and this mode of indemnity was supposed to be more convenient than the other and usual remedy at common law. In other States the decisions have been similar to those in this State. Stevens *v.* The Middlesex Canal, 12 Mass. 466. In the case of Steel *v.* The Western Inland Co. 2 Johns. 283, the legislature authorized the defendants to dig a canal through the property of individuals, and provided for the appointment of appraisers to assess the damages. The plaintiff brought an action on the case against the defendants to recover damages, among other things, for the injury occasioned by stopping up his cross-ditches and drains. But it was said by Mr. Justice Thompson, that this must necessarily have been taken into consideration in the appraisement of the damages and compensation to be made to the plaintiff in the first instance. "The law required the appraisers to ascertain the value of the land, and the damages sustained by the owner in consequence of the appropriation of it to the use of the company. The injury on this score was inseparable from the very act of making the canal, and not occasioned by any neglect of a duty enjoined by law."

There is nothing in the present case to show, that the damage complained of was not the necessary consequence of a lawful act. That the commissioners could not probably have anticipated, as a matter of fact, the cutting off the stream of water in the place excavated for the railroad and the consequent injury to the plaintiff, may be an argument against the expediency, but not against the obligation of the law in question. As it does not appear that the cuttings and excavations were not made in a proper and reasonable manner, we think the action cannot be maintained upon these facts.

Verdict set aside.

TOWNS *et al. v.* CHESHIRE RAILROAD COMPANY.[1]

Cheshire Co., December Term, 1850.

Fences — Obligation to Maintain — Injury to Cattle Straying upon Railroad from Highway.

By the Rev. Stat. ch. 142, § 6, railroad corporations are not bound to make or keep fences, except against the land of persons adjoining the railroad, nor are they bound to keep cattle-guards.

The plaintiffs' mare escaped from their pasture into an adjoining highway, which was crossed by a railroad, in land not owned by the plaintiffs, and went thence upon the track at a place where it crossed the highway and where there was no cattle-guard or fence, and was killed by the engine: *Held*, that the corporation was not liable.

CASE. The parties agreed to submit this action to the decision of the Court upon the following statement of facts.

On the 3d of September, 1849, the plaintiffs' mare escaped from their pasture in the westerly part of Keene, distant about one fourth of a mile from the railroad, into an adjoining highway which is crossed by the railroad at grade, in lands not owned by the plaintiffs; and went along in the highway till she came to the crossing, when she turned upon the railroad and passed down it for about one fourth of a mile. She was within the limits of the railroad, by the side of the embankment, when a passenger train came along at its usual time in the afternoon, and at its usual speed.

As the train approached, the engineer discovered the mare about ten rods distant, and gave the usual signal by the steam-whistle for breaking up and stopping the cars, and the breaks were applied. The mare immediately went upon the embankment and ran along upon the track for a short distance, was overtaken by the engine, thrown from the track by the cowcatcher down the bank and killed. The train could not have been stopped, after she was seen by the engineer, before reaching her.

There was no cattle-guard or fence across the railroad at the crossing where the mare passed from the highway upon the railroad.

The mode of preventing animals from passing from highways upon railroads is usually by cattle-guards, so called, across the railroad on each side of the highway.

If the Court should be of opinion that the plaintiffs are entitled to recover, judgment is to be rendered for them for such sum as shall be assessed by the jury; otherwise for the defendants for costs.

Vose, for the plaintiffs.

We contend, that by implication from the Rev. Stat. page 276, the corporation is bound to fence the railroad; that cattle-guards or some equivalent fence are usual and necessary at the intersections of railroads with common highways, and cannot be omitted without danger to the lives of passengers in the cars, and to the property transported by them, as well as to animals passing on the roads. The public highways are open to all for the purposes of passing along them, and the plaintiffs' mare was rightfully there at the time. No question as to the right of adjoining land-owners arises in this case.

We contend, that the failure of the corporation to construct the usual cattle-guard at the crossing in question was dangerous negligence, which deprived them of any right they might otherwise have had to run over and destroy the plaintiffs' mare. The corporation, as occupants, were bound to fence against every thing lawfully in the highway. Tewksbury *v*. Bucklin, 7 N. H. Rep. 521.

Wheeler and *Faulkner*, for the defendants.

We contend, that we are not bound in law to fence *across* the railroad at places where highways intersect it. It is enough that the sides of the railroad were fenced. Even if the corporation were required by law to construct cattle-guards or fences at the crossings of highways, this action cannot be maintained, for the reason that the plaintiffs' mare was wrongfully in the highway. She was not in the service of her owners, or under their control.

Since the case of Rust *v*. Low, 6 Mass. 90, the decisions have been numerous and uniform, that the owner of a close is bound to fence only against cattle which are rightfully in the adjoining close. Thayer *v*. Arnold, 4 Met. 589, and the authorities there cited. When cattle stray from the owner's pasture into the highway where the right of soil is in another, they become trespassers. Mills *v*. Stark, 4 N. H. Rep. 512; Avery *v*. Maxwell, 4 N. H. Rep. 36. And they are not the less trespassers when they pass from such highway into the close of another.

GILCHRIST, C. J. It is provided by the Rev. Stat. ch. 142, § 6, that if any railroad corporation shall neglect to keep a sufficient and lawful fence on each side of their road, any person against whose land such fence is insufficient may notify the agent of the corporation, and if the fence shall not be made sufficient within twenty days, the

owner of the land may repair the fence and may recover of the corporation double the amount of the expense.

This section gives a remedy in terms, only to the owners of land
adjoining the railroad, and it was accordingly held, in the case of
Woolson v. The Northern Railroad Corporation, decided in the
county of Merrimack at the December term, 1848, that railroad corporations were not bound to build fences except against the land
adjoining the road, and that they were not bound to make "cattle-
guards," so called, where the railroad intersected a highway. In the
case referred to, the action was case to recover the value of three
calves killed on the railroad track by the engine, and it appeared that
the animals escaped from the plaintiff's land and wandered along the
highway until they came to the track, where they were killed by the
engine at a point distant from the plaintiff's land.

Since the decision of that case, the Act of July 13th, 1850, has
been passed, making it the duty of railroad corporations to maintain
cattle-guards, &c.; but as the injury sustained in this case was before
the passage of the act, its provisions are not applicable here, and the
decision in Woolson v. The Northern Railroad Corporation settles
that the plaintiffs, in this suit, cannot recover.

It is said in this case that the mare was rightfully in the highway.
The rule of the common law is, that a man is bound to keep his cattle
on his own land at his peril. Avery v. Maxwell, 4 N. H. Rep. 36 ;
Mills v. Stark, Ib. 514. But a person is not bound to fence against
cattle unlawfully in the highway. Tewkesbury v. Bucklin, 7 N. H.
Rep. 518. In this case the mare escaped from the pasture. She was
not driven along the road by her owner, for which purpose the road
might lawfully be used, but was straying upon it, and went from it
upon the track where she was killed. It cannot therefore be said that
she was lawfully in the highway, and we are of opinion that there
should be

Judgment for the defendant.[1]

---

[1] It is a well-established proposition that
at common law the owner of land was not
obliged to fence against the cattle of other
persons. The owner of cattle was bound
to keep them upon his own premises, and
if they strayed upon the land of his neighbor, he was held liable for any damage
they might commit, and he could not in
general recover for any injuries they might
receive while thus unlawfully upon another's land.

Where no statute regulations exist defining the duties of railway companies as to
fences, they are governed by this common-
law rule, and are under no obligations to
erect fences between their road and the
adjoining lands. Fawcett v. The York and
North Midland R. Co. 2 Eng. Law & Eq.
Rep. 289 ; Rickett v. The East and West
India Docks Co., 12 Eng. Law & Eq.
Rep. 520 ; Perkins v. The Eastern R. Co.
Maine 307, s. c. *ante* p. 144; The Ton-

awanda R. Co. v. Munger, 5 Denio, 255; s. c. *post;* affirmed on appeal, 4 Comstock 349; s. c. *post.* Brooks v. The New York & Erie R. Co. 13 Barbour, 594; s. c. *post.*

Justice dictates that the burden of fencing should be borne by the company. Quimby v. The Vermont Central R. Co. 23 Vermont, 387; s. c. *post.* But unless the duty to fence is imposed directly upon the company by statute, the just claim of the land-owner must be satisfied in the compensation allowed him for the taking of his land. It was held in one case, indeed, that in the absence of a special statute upon the subject, a railway company ought to be governed by the general statute regulating the right of adjoining land-owners in respect to fences, and, therefore, that a company could be compelled to maintain one half of the division fence, while one half the estimated expense of maintaining the requisite fences should form an element in the estimate of damages. *Ex parte* The Renssellaer & Saratoga R. Co. 4 Paige, 553. It is intimated in Quimby v. The Vermont Central R. Co. 23 Vermont, 387, s. c. *post,* that a railway company might be charged with negligence in not providing fences, if injury resulted therefrom; and there is a similar intimation in Vanderkar v. The Renssellaer and Saratoga R. Co. 13 Barbour, 390, but there is no adjudged case to support such a proposition. On the contrary it has been held that a railway company is not liable for damage done to cattle entering upon the road through the want of fences which the land-owner was bound to erect, although at the immediate time of the injury the company was guilty of actual negligence. Clarke v. The Syracuse and Utica R. Co. 11 Barbour, 112; s. c. *post.*

So, too, a company has been held not liable for killing cattle not belonging to the owner of the adjoining land, which, while straying upon such land have entered upon the railway through the defect of fences, which the company was bound to maintain. Ricketts v. The East and West India Docks Co. 12 Eng. Law & Eq. Rep. 520. It is only against cattle lawfully in the adjoining close that the company is re-

quired to fence. Where the statute required a company to provide cattle-guards at road-crossings the company was held free from liability in not providing guards at a private farm-crossing. Brooks v. The New York and Erie R. Co. 13 Barbour, 513; s. c. *post.* The liability of a company has in all cases been held to be exactly coextensive with the statute requirements, and in no instance has a company been charged upon any common-law liability, or upon any allegations of negligence in not providing the safeguards of fences. The case in the text shows how strictly the liability of a company is limited to the statute requirements. So in Perkins v. The Eastern R. Co. 29 Maine, 307; s. c. *ante,* 144, the defendants, though required to fence against inclosed lands, were not by statute required to fence against *uninclosed* lands, and in consequence were held free from blame in killing a cow, which entered upon their road from a common, through the want of a fence at that place.

In Vanderkar v. The Renssellaer and Saratoga R. Co. 13 Barbour, 390; s. c. *post,* the court held, that the company were not bound to provide gates and cattle-guards at the street-crossings in a village, the statute, in the opinion of the court, making a distinction between common road-crossings and street-crossings.

Where the statute has imposed upon a company the duty to fence, the company may, nevertheless, by contract with the adjoining land-owner, relieve itself from this duty; Talmadge v. Rensselaer and Saratoga R. Co. 13 Barbour, 493; s. c. *post.*

To make a company liable for injuries resulting from a want of fences, it is not necessary that the duty should be imposed in express terms by the statute. See the next case, (Dean v. The Sullivan Railroad Co.) A provision that in case a company neglects to keep suitable fences, the adjoining land-owner may, after notice to the company of the defect, make or repair the fence and recover of the company double the amount necessarily expended, is sufficient to show that the duty devolves upon the company.

DEAN v. THE SULLIVAN RAILROAD COMPANY.[1]

Sullivan Co., July Term, 1851.

Fences — Obligation of Railway Company to Maintain — Action for Injuries resulting from Neglect to Maintain.

At common law, the owners of adjoining lands are under no obligations to maintain division fences. But by the statute of New Hampshire they are bound, if the lands are improved, to maintain the partition fence equally.

Railroad companies, where they own their own track, are subject to the same liabilities as other owners.

But where they do not own the track, and have merely a right of way, neither the companies or the land-owners are bound to fence the road.

But the statute of New Hampshire which provides, that, if a railroad company shall neglect to keep a suitable fence, the adjoining land-owner may, after notice to the company, make or repair the fence, and recover double the amount necessarily expended in so doing, imposes upon the company the duty to maintain fences in all cases, except where the land-owner has been paid for assuming it.

And a party who has suffered special injury from the neglect of a company to maintain proper fences may recover damages for such injury in an action on the case.

CASE. The plaintiff declared against the defendants, "in a plea of the case, for that the plaintiff heretofore, to wit, on the 10th day of June, 1848, was and from thence hitherto hath been and still is lawfully possessed and in the occupation of a certain close, situated in Claremont, &c.; and the said defendants, during the time aforesaid, were and still are in possession of, and in the use and occupation of a certain railroad passing over and across the plaintiff's said close; and the said corporation, by reason of their said railroad passing over and across the plaintiff's said close, on the day first above mentioned, ought to have erected, and, during all the time aforesaid, to have kept and maintained a sufficient and lawful fence on each side of their said railroad, against the plaintiff's said close, to prevent cattle, lawfully feeding, or depasturing, or being in said close, from erring or escaping from and out of said close, into and upon the defendants' said railroad, and into and upon other lands of the said plaintiff, and into and upon the adjoining closes, and to prevent cattle of other persons, lawfully feeding and depasturing in adjoining closes, from escaping into the said close of the said plaintiff; yet the defendants, well knowing the premises, but continuing, &c., to wit: on the day and year first above mentioned, neglected, and refused, and from thence hitherto have neglected and refused, and still neglect and refuse, to erect and keep a sufficient and lawful fence on each side of their railroad, against the plaintiff's said close, whereby the said close was, and has been, during all that time, laid open and exposed, and thereby, divers cattle, to wit: three horses, ten cows, and one hundred sheep, lawfully feeding and depasturing in said close, on the several days and times aforesaid, went, erred, and escaped from and out of the same, in and upon the adjoining closes, and upon other lands of the said plaintiff, and to other places unknown to the plaintiff; and the cattle of persons unknown to the plaintiff, by reason of said close being and remaining so open and exposed, on divers days and times between the day first above mentioned and the day of the purchase of this writ, entered into the said close of the plaintiff, and greatly injured the same, and spoiled the grass and grain thereon growing, and being, and by all which the plaintiff lost the profits of his said close for the time aforesaid, and was put to great trouble and expense in finding his said horses, cows, and sheep, so erring and escaping from his said close as aforesaid ; to the damage, &c.

The defendants demurred generally.

Gates and *Fuller*, for the plaintiff.

Freeman and *Cushing*, for the defendants.

BELL, J. At common law, owners of adjoining lands owe each other no duties, and are subject to no obligations to maintain fences. By our statute, they are bound, if the lands are improved, to maintain the partition fence equally. Rev. Stat. chap. 136. As owners of land, where they own their track, railroad companies are subject to the same liabilities as other owners. But these statute provisions do not apply to such corporations, where they own nothing in their track, but an easement, a right of way merely. In such a case, neither the company nor the owner, by this statute, would be bound to fence. The interest of both requires that the road generally should be fenced. And the safety of the travelling community demands, that such roads should be effectually guarded against the hazards arising from animals passing on the track. We can, therefore, hardly suppose, that the legislature could intend to leave in any doubt, upon whom the duty rested of maintaining such fences.

The question is of great importance, both to the land-owners and to the railroad companies ; since upon its decision depends, in a great degree, the liability of the one or the other, for injuries to the animals and crops of the land-owner, and to the engines and cars of the rail-roads, and to the persons and property borne upon the road, arising from such defects of the fences. In construing the statutory provisions, we are to regard the state of the common law, and the evils to be remedied, and the mischiefs to be guarded against by legislation, to which we have adverted, and the previous enactments on the subject. By the statute of 1840, (p. 434,) chap. 498, § 4, it was made " the duty of every railroad corporation to erect, or cause to be erected, and keep, or cause to be kept, in good and sufficient repair, a proper and sufficient fence on each side of the track," &c. ; and this provision was inserted in the report of the Committee of Revision. It ·was omitted, while the statutes were passing through the legislature, and the existing provision inserted in its stead. The section is as follows : " If any railroad corporation shall neglect to keep a sufficient and lawful fence on each side of their road, any person against whose land such fence is insufficient, may notify the agent of such corporation thereof, and if such fence shall not be made sufficient within twenty days after such notice, the owner may make or repair such fence, and may thereupon recover of such corporation in an action of assumpsit, double the amount necessarily expended in making or repairing the same, as aforesaid ; provided, however, that the foregoing provisions of this section shall not apply to any case where such corporation shall have settled with and paid the owner of such land for building and maintaining such fence." Rev. Stat. chap. 142, § 6.

It is contended that this statute imposes on the railroad companies no such general duty to maintain fences along the sides of their road, as the declaration alleges ; and that the repeal of the statute of 1840, shows that the design of the legislature was, to change the duty and the responsibility, in relation to fences, and to exonerate the corporations from any liability, except that of paying double the amount expended by the land-owner in building or repairing the fence, after due notice to the corporation, &c.

Upon this view the responsibility for damages, arising from neglect to build and keep up the fence, whether to the land-owner, the corporation, or to third persons, would be shifted from the corporation, who are chiefly interested in the railroad, and who are, by their charters, impliedly relieved from the risk consequent upon very rapid travelling, upon the land-owner, who would thus be made to bear, without compensation, one of the most serious risks of railroad travelling. There is a very strong presumption that the legislature could not have contemplated such consequences, nor intended to make such a change of the law. And we have carefully considered this statute provision, with a view to trace the principle on which the legislature designed to settle the rights of the corporations and of the land-owners, on this subject. The result of our examination is an undoubted conviction, that the legislature intended to continue the burden already imposed by the previous statute, upon railroad corporations, of erecting and maintaining proper fences upon each side of their track; and to exonerate the land-owner from any liability to maintain such fences, and to provide him a stringent remedy to enforce the performance of their duty by the railroad companies.

We think this conclusion is apparent, upon the language of the act: " If any railroad corporation shall neglect to keep a sufficient fence," &c. With what propriety can the corporation be said to *neglect* to do what is no part of their duty, by contract or by law. The idea of neglect is based entirely upon the existence of a duty or obligation, and this expression, we think, most strongly implies, that it was designed to be the duty of the corporation to maintain such fences, especially when it is followed by a provision, that if, upon being notified, the neglect is continued for twenty days, the corporation shall be liable to pay double the cost of building it. The duty necessarily results from a penalty being imposed upon its neglect. The same conclusion follows from the proviso, which exonerates the corporation from the provisions of the section, "in any case where the corporation shall have settled with and paid the owner of such land, for building and maintaining such fence." We are wholly unable to imagine, upon what view this clause could be introduced, unless it was, that the duty of maintaining the fence rested, of course, on the railroad, unless the owner was settled with and paid for building it. The same result seems to us naturally to follow from the succeeding (7th) section, which provides, that " if any person, having been thus settled with and paid for keeping any such fence in repair, shall neglect to do so, such railroad corporation may make such repairs, and recover the necessary expense thereof, of the person liable." If the legislature designed to leave the land-owner under the general liability to fence against the road, with a limited recourse to the corporation only in certain events, it is inconceivable, that when making this provision, it should not have been extended to every neglect to repair the fence, by which the interests of the railroad company might be prejudiced, whether the party had been settled with and paid, or not. It seems evident, from this section, that the legislature contemplated the duty of erecting and maintaining such fences, as resting exclusively on the corporation, in all cases, except where the land-owner has been paid for assuming it. There is manifestly no third case contemplated, in which the duty rests upon no one. There are clearly many cases supposable where the land-owner has no interest to compel the corporation to fence, and where they have no interest to pay him for fencing; where the public safety requires that the road shall be fenced, and where no supposition can be admitted that the legislature did not intend to provide against this source of danger.

The same view is confirmed by the consideration of the interest which railroads have in the ground over which their railway is laid. By the charters, as well as by the general railroad law, it is evidently supposed, they are to acquire a right of way only. They can attain no other, or higher interest, except by a voluntary conveyance. Now, it is evident, that no right to erect or maintain fences results from a mere right of way, and if a railroad corporation can *neglect* to erect fences, it can only be, where they have a right to erect them. Such a right necessarily results from the duty imposed on them by law, if that is the true construction of the statutes; but if it were otherwise, it would seem to be clear that they were subjected to a penalty for not doing an act, the performance of which would be a trespass.

We are by no means sure that, upon the same principle upon which towns, and turnpike, and bridge companies are subjected to the duty of guarding dangerous causeways, side-hills, cuts, and bridges by railings, for the safety of travellers, the duty would not be implied at common law, that is, by an extension of legal principles to a new case falling *in pari ratione*, upon railroad corporations to maintain everywhere, where they were needed, such fences as would prevent any danger to travellers from the animals, either of neighboring land-owners, or others, escaping upon the track. This point it is at present unnecessary to decide, because we are satisfied the same duty is necessarily implied from the revised statutes.

It has been suggested that where a new right is given by a statute, or a new duty imposed, and by the same statute a remedy is provided for any violation of such right, or neglect of such duty, the party whose rights are affected, is confined to the statute remedy. Admitting the general principle, we think it has no application to this case. If, in cases of that class, the remedy is, in its nature, coextensive with the injury, to which the party is exposed, the rule as stated would not be unreasonable. But it is apparent here, that the remedy provided is not general, but limited to a single object, that of obtaining compensation for building the fence after notice. It is in the nature of a provision to enable a party to anticipate and prevent the mischiefs that might result from neglect to build a fence; but it contains no provision whatever, for any adjustment of the damages which may have already resulted from neglect of duty. So far as there is a statute remedy provided, it may not be unreasonable to confine a party

Dean *v.* The Sullivan Railroad Company.

to it.   But it can surely be no answer to an action for an injury to a
man's cattle, when, through the neglect of the railroad to fence, they
have escaped upon the track and have been injured, that the statute
has provided a different remedy for neglect to build the fence.   The
statute remedy applies to no case, where twenty days' notice has not
been given to build the fence.   The railroad company may, at any
time, remove their fence, or any third person may do so, and thus expose a man's fields to injury, or his cattle to escape and loss.   The
owner, by the statute, may give twenty days' notice to the agent
of the company to rebuild the fence; if they do not, he may rebuild
it for them at their expense.   Is there no remedy for the damage and
loss the land-owner may sustain during those twenty days?   Certainly, the legislature have been very unfortunate in their enactments,
if this is the true result.

The duties of the owners of adjoining lands as to fences, depend
upon the statutes; and in case of neglect by one owner to build his
fence after notice, the other may build the fence and recover, as in
this case, double the expense of building.   But it has never been supposed that this remedy, designed to effect the single object of having
the fence built, barred, or cut off in any way, or to any extent, any of
the common-law remedies for injuries resulting from the neglect of the
owner to build the fence, as required by the statute.

Judgment for the plaintiff on demurrer.[1]

---

[1] The distinction taken in this case between the acts of a company in respect to
which the statute remedy for an injury is
the only one which can be pursued, and
those in respect to which relief may be obtained by the ordinary common-law remedies, is supported by the case of The
Mayor of Lichfield *v.* Simpson, 8 Adolphus & Ellis, N. S. 65.   This was an action against the clerk of the borough for
neglecting or refusing after his removal
from office to deliver as required by statute an account of all matters committed
to his charge, the vouchers for his disbursements, and a list of the delinquent
persons.   The statute provided a summary mode for compelling the party to do
his duty, and for obtaining possession of
books and papers which might be with-
held.   The court held, that the action
might be maintained, the statute remedy
not being coextensive with the injury, but
being in fact a process for compelling a
party to do his duty, and not for obtaining satisfaction for injuries resulting from
his neglect.   See also the *nisi prius* case
of Collinson *v.* Newcastle & Darlington
R. Co. 1 Carrington & Kirwan, 546.

CASES

SUPREME COURT OF VERMONT.

WILLIAM GOLD, JR., *v.* THE VERMONT CENTRAL RAILROAD COMPANY.[1]

Washington Co, April Term, 1847.

Appraisement of Land Damages — Right to a Jury — Construction of the Word " Court."

The provision in the charter of the Vermont Central Railroad Company, which authorizes a person, whose land has been taken for the use of the company, and who feels aggrieved by the appraisal of the damages by the commissioners appointed in pursuance of the charter, to appeal to the county court, and which provides that the decision of the county court shall be final in the matter, does not entitle the person thus appealing to have his damages assessed in the county court by a jury.

The term " Court " may be construed to mean the *judges* of the court, or to include the *judges and jury*, according to the connection and the object of its use. Resort must be had for the purpose of determining the form of trial, where there is no express legislative provision, other than the use of the general term, to the nature of the question submitted to the court, and the mode, heretofore in use, of determining similar questions.

In cases analogous to those where land has been taken by a railroad corporation, pursuant to the provisions of their charter, it has never been the practice in this state, where the matter has been pending in the county court, to assess the damages by a jury, — but by commissioners, or perhaps by the judges of the court.

The statute of November 2, 1846, which provides, that, when it becomes necessary to assess damages, *and no other provisions are made by law* for such assessment, the same shall be assessed by a jury upon the request of either party, does not entitle a person, whose land has been taken by the Vermont Central Railroad Company, and who has appealed from the

---

appraisal of his damages by the commissioners appointed under the charter,. to have his damages assessed by a jury in the county court; — since the general terms used in the charter of the company must be construed to have provided that the damages, in such cases, should be assessed in the mode usual in this State in analogous cases, which is by the appointment of commissioners by the county court, or perhaps by the judges of the court, — but never by a jury.

PETITION for a writ of mandamus. The petitioner set forth, that certain of his lands had been taken by the Vermont Central Railroad Company, for the purpose of building their road; that the commissioners, appointed in pursuance of the provisions of the charter of the company, had appraised his damages at sixty-five dollars; that, feeling aggrieved by this decision, he had appealed to the county court, and had filed in that court a motion in writing, to be allowed to have his damages assessed by a jury; and that the county court had refused to allow the same, but had proceeded to assess his damages by the judges of the court; — and he prayed, that a writ of mandamus might issue, directed to the county court, and commanding them to grant to him a trial by jury for the assessment of his damages.

J. L. Buck, for petitioner.

1. We insist, that the Constitution and laws of this State, as well as the settled practice under them, give the petitioner a right of trial by jury, unless it is taken away by the charter of the company. The true interpretation of the 15th Article of the Constitution is, that when any question of fact, to be decided upon the testimony of witnesses, is raised, or presented, the parties have a right to a jury trial. 3 Pet. 446. 1 D. Ch. 247. We deny, that the act of incorporation prescribes the *mode* of trial. The eighth section declares, "that the decision of the county court shall be final;" — but it is not declared, whether the trial shall be had, or the damages assessed, by the judges, or by the jury. It might as well be claimed, that the judges should try all civil suits; for the statute, in defining the jurisdiction of the county court, is entirely silent upon the subject of a jury. Rev. St. 160, § 7.

2. The statute of November 5, 1846, upon the subject of the appraisement of damages, is applicable to this case, and was intended by the legislature to embrace such cases. The act of incorporation does not prescribe the mode of trial; and no rights can be claimed by the company, except such as are given by its charter, or are incident to its existence. Ang. & Am. on Corp. 2; 5 Conn. 560. The forms of administering justice and the powers of courts must ever be subject to legislative enactment. Bank of Columbia *v.* Okely,

19*

4 Wheat. 235; Young *v.* Bank of Alexandria, 4 Cranch, 384; Mc-Laren *v.* Pennington, 1 Paige, 107.

L. B. Peck, for defendants.

1. By the act of incorporation the damages, on an appeal, are to be determined by the court. The eighth section provides, that either party may appeal from the decision of the commissioners to the county court, " and the decision of such court shall be *final.*" If the jury fix the amount of damages, the court do not pass on the question; for it will not be insisted, that the court can change the verdict. The term "county court," as here used, must mean that tribunal which is described as such in the Constitution and laws of the State. The third section of chap. 25, of the Revised Statutes, provides, that " there shall be, in each county, a *county court,* to consist of one chief judge," &c., " and two assistant judges, to be appointed for each county;" and when the act of incorporation provides, that the party may appeal to the " county court," and that the decision of *such* court shall be *final*, it must mean that tribunal above described, composed of a judge of the supreme court and two assistant judges. From the whole structure and language of this chapter it is evident, that these judges are the "county court;" p. 161, §§ 11 – 13; p. 164, § 36. It has been the uniform practice in this State, in all cases where damages were claimed by land-owners for the location of turnpikes and common highways over their lands, to have them assessed by committees appointed by the legislature, or by some judicial tribunal. It is fair to presume, that, if the legislature had intended, in the present case, to change this practice and provide for the assessment of damages by a jury, they would have used language, which could leave no reasonable doubt of that intention. The whole legislation in this State, in reference to this subject, and those of a kindred character, shows that the whole matter has been studiously excluded from the consideration of a jury. Acts of 1794, p. 26, § 3. Acts of 1803, p. 129, § 2.

2. But the party claims, that he is entitled to a jury trial by the Constitution. That article in the Constitution, upon which he relies, has no application to this case. It has reference to an issue of fact, joined in a cause or proceeding known to the common law. The proceeding in this case is not known to the common law. It is a proceeding created by statute only. The case of Huntington *v.* Bishop, 5 Vt. 186, is decisive of this question. See, also, Beekman *v.* Saratoga R. Co. 3 Paige, 45; Backus *v.* Lebanon, 11 N. H. 19.

3. The statute of November 2, 1846, does not affect the present question. That statute applies only to those cases, where no mode

for assessing damages is prescribed. The act of incorporation has made provision "for such assessment." And in any view that can be taken of this statute, the question must rest upon and be determined by the provisions of the act of incorporation. 3 Vt. 507 ; 2 D. Ch. 77 ; Stamford *v.* Barre, 1 Aik. 321,; 1 N. H. 199.

The opinion of the court was delivered by

DAVIS, J. This is an application to this court by William Gold, Jr., for a writ of mandamus, to be directed to the county court for the county of Washington, setting forth, substantially, that the Vermont Central Railroad Company have located their road through the petitioner's land in Northfield, in said county, taking and appropriating for that purpose about four acres and thirteen square rods; that, the parties failing to agree upon the price of said land, these commissioners, duly appointed in pursuance of the act incorporating said company, assessed the petitioner's damages at the sum of $65,— from which assessment, being aggrieved thereat, he appealed to the county court, and duly entered his appeal at the term of said court holden at Montpelier in November, 1846 ; that at the same term he filed a motion in writing, requesting the court to direct that his damages should be assessed by a jury, duly impanelled, — which request said court declined to grant; but, on the contrary, proceeded to assess such damages by the judges of said court, and did assess them at the sum of ————. The petitioner thereupon, believing this proceeding of the county court to be a violation of his legal rights, prefers this petition to this court, — notice of which having been duly served upon the railroad company, they appear by attorney to resist the application.

Practically the question may be considered one of considerable importance ; and it has undergone a full discussion at the bar, by the counsel of the respective parties. No question is made with respect to the power of this court to issue such a writ, in a case of this kind, directed to the county court, provided the ground assumed by the petitioner be correct, as to his right to insist on having his damages ascertained in that mode. We shall therefore consider the case as involving that question alone.

We are not disposed to attach any importance to the peculiar phraseology of the act of incorporation, authorizing the *county court* to decide finally upon appeal. The term " *court* " may be construed to include a jury, as well as judges and a clerk, or as used in contradistinction from a jury, according to the connection and object of its use. When the statute speaks of the county court generally, its powers and jurisdiction, it is to be understood in the former sense.

When it authorizes the court, upon the agreement of parties, to try issues of fact, it is to be understood in the latter sense.

In this case nothing can be predicated, as to the sense in which the term " court," is to be used, from the mere language and connection. Resort must be had, for that purpose, to the nature of the question submitted to the county court, and to the mode of determining similar questions heretofore in use. If any uniform mode exists, which has been recognized since the establishment of a judiciary in the State, it will be a reasonable presumption, that, in the absence of any express provision to the. contrary, the legislature intended that the same mode should continue to be pursued.

No matter precisely similar has heretofore been brought under cognizance of the court. Railroad corporations are new bodies with us; and the taking and holding another's land *in invitum*, for the purpose of constructing such roads, is a novel proceeding, now for the first time authorized by our laws. Easements for the use of turnpike corporations, and for common roads, have, however, long been established, upon a compensation rendered; and the mode of ascertaining the compensation to be paid in such cases would seem, from the close analogy in the subjects, the proper one to be applied here. What, then, has been that mode? By commissioners, by committee-men, by appraisers, and perhaps by the county court judges, — but never by a jury. It has not been hitherto supposed, that it was a subject coming within the scope of the appropriate duties of a traverse jury. The issue to be tried, if it can, with any propriety, be called such, is altogether unlike that presented by the counter allegations between party and party, in which the truth of the facts in controversy is to be ascertained. The duty imposed is rather one of appraisement merely. As such it appropriately belongs to one man, or a board of competent men, qualified properly to discharge it.

This view of the subject necessarily leads us to the conclusion, that the legislature, in transferring to the county court, upon the dissatisfaction of either party at the decision of the commissioners, the appraisement of damages in cases under this act, intended that the question should be tried without the intervention of a jury. If any innovation had been intended, it would doubtless have been indicated in express terms.

A similar view was taken by the Supreme Court of New Hampshire, in Backus v. Lebanon, 11 N. H. 20, in which case a turnpike corporation claimed to have the damages, occasioned by an appropriation of a portion of their road to the purposes of a free road, assessed by a jury. Chief Justice Parker, in denying the application, observed, " that, by a long course of legislation, the damages occasioned by the laying out of highways.were to be assessed by the court, or by a committee; and ·no provision is found for the intervention or a jury in cases of that character." The same remark is equally applicable to our own legislation.

On similar grounds the Chancellor of New York, in Beekman *v.* S. R. Co. 3 Paige, 45, determined, that a legislative provision for the ascertainment of damages, on laying a railroad by a committee was not an infringement of the right of trial by jury, guaranteed by the Constitution.

The case under consideration is, in fact, in another particular, stronger than the ordinary one of laying out highways. Here the fee of the land is taken and paid for, — whether with a reversionary right to the former proprietor, on the extinguishment of the corporation, it is not necessary now to consider; and the question is simply one involving an appraisement of the value of the land, — taking into view, indeed, the uses to which it is to be applied. It was competent for the legislature to provide, that this revision of the primary appraisement should be made by the county court judges, or supreme court judges, or by a jury, or by another board of commissioners. No doubt the tendency of our legislation is in favor of extending the scope of the duties of traverse juries. County courts have been invested with a discretionary power to grant jury trials in trustee proceedings; and such mode of trial is now, in some cases, made imperative, on the request of either party when before it was matter of discretion. A similar tendency may be discovered in the legislation of the general government, in a provision contained in the late bankrupt act, authorizing jury trials in certain cases under the act.

It only remains to be considered, whether the statute of November 2, 1846, can be considered as in any manner affecting this question. We are all agreed, that it does not. .It simply provides, that in any *case* then pending, or which might afterwards occur, when it should become necessary to assess damages, *when no other provisions by law are made* for such assessment,. the same shall be assessed by a jury, on the request of either party. Now, not to place any stress upon the word *case*, as here used, — for perhaps that term may as well comprehend this proceeding, as an ordinary common-law suit, — and in common parlance it has a more extended meaning than the word *suit*, or *action*, and may include application for divorce, applications for the establishment of highways, applications for orders of support of relatives, and other special proceedings unknown to the common law, — yet if the views already expressed are well founded, there was no absence of provision by law for the assessment of damages in this case, already provided. The act of incorporation expressly provides it, in requiring the county court to perform that duty, — construing the language of the act, as we have done, to require it to be done in those modes only heretofore known and practised.

The result is, the application for a mandamus must be denied, with costs.

VERMONT CENTRAL RAILROAD COMPANY *v.* GEORGE CLAYES.[1]

Chittenden Co., December Term, 1848.

Subscription for Stock — Payment of Assessment by Promissory Note to Commissioners — Action by Company.

By section four of the statute incorporating the Vermont Central Railroad Company, certain persons named are constituted commissioners for receiving subscriptions to the capital stock of the company; and it was enacted as follows, — "And every person, at the time of subscribing, shall pay to the commissioners five dollars on each share for which he may subscribe, and each subscriber shall be a member of said company;" and it was farther enacted, that when one thousand shares should be subscribed, the commissioners might issue a notice for the stockholders to meet and elect directors. The defendant, after some other shares, but less than one thousand, had been subscribed for, subscribed for fifty shares, and, instead of paying to the commissioners, in money, five dollars upon each share at the time of subscribing, he gave them his promissory note for that amount, being two hundred and fifty dollars, which was made payable to "The Commissioners of the Vermont Central Railroad Company" on demand, for value received. This note was received from the commissioners by the corporation, upon its organization. And it was held, that the note was giving upon sufficient consideration, and that it was a valid note in the hands of the corporation.

And it was also held, that an action might be sustained upon the note in the name of the corporation.

And it was also held, that the provision in the charter, that each subscriber should be a member of the company, and the fact that others had subscribed for stock previous to the defendant's subscription, were sufficient to show, that the corporation was *in esse* at the time of making the note, and so capable of taking the promise, through their agents, the commissioners, notwithstanding their right to organize was made to depend upon certain conditions, which were not fully complied with until after the note was executed.

ASSUMPSIT upon a promissory note. Plea, the general issue, and trial by the court, November adjourned term, 1847, — BENNETT, J., presiding.

On trial the plaintiffs gave in evidence the note declared upon, signed by the defendant, and dated July 18, 1845, and which was in these words, — " On demand, for value received, I promise to pay the Commissioners of the Vermont Central Railroad Company two hundred and fifty dollars." The plaintiffs also gave in evidence a subscription list to the capital stock of, the corporation, upon which it appeared the defendant had subscribed for fifty shares, and that other individuals had subscribed for stock, previous to the defendant, amounting in all to six hundred and thirty-one shares. The plaintiffs also gave in evidence their act of incorporation, enacted by the legislature of Vermont in 1843, by the fourth section of which Charles Paine and others, who were named, were constituted commissioners to receive subscriptions to the capital stock of the corporation, and by which it was enacted as follows, — "And every person, at the time of subscribing, shall pay to said commissioners five dollars on each share for which he may subscribe, and each subscriber shall be a member of said company ;" and by which it was also enacted, that when one thousand shares should be subscribed, or as soon thereafter as the commissioners should deem proper, a meeting of the stockholders might be called by the commissioners for the purpose of electing directors ; and that, when directors were so elected, the commissioners should deliver to them the books of subscription, and all sums of money deposited with them on all shares subscribed. It appeared, that the note in suit was given by the defendant in settlement for the first five dollars on each share subscribed by him, which was required, by the charter, to be paid at the time of subscribing, and that he paid nothing in any other form.

Upon these facts the county court rendered judgment in favor of the plaintiffs, for the amount of the note. Exceptions by defendant.

C. Russell, for defendant.

1. It is insisted, that the note in suit is without consideration and of no validity. By the act of incorporation the duties of the commissioners are defined, and they must conform to its provisions ; it does not authorize them to take notes, either to themselves, or to the corporation, but only to receive five dollars in money upon each share, at the time of subscribing ; and if, acting under a statutory authority, the commissioners did not conform to its provisions, their acts are invalid. The subscribing for the stock, merely, without making the payment required, did not entitle the defendant to the stock ; and it does not appear, that any stock was ever issued to him. Union Turnp. *v.* Jenkins, 1 Caines's Cas. in Error, 86.

2. The plaintiffs cannot maintain this action. The note is upon

its face, the note of the defendant to the commissioners, and contains an absolute promise to pay the commissioners, and no other. If valid, the commissioners must be considered as having taken it to themselves, in lieu of money. The corporation had a legal right to require the money from the commissioners, and the commissioners took upon themselves to pay the corporation in money, and received the note for their own security and benefit. The words " Commissioners of the Vermont Central Railroad Company," are merely descriptive of the persons named in the act; and therefore the persons composing the commissioners are the proper persons to sue upon the note.

The instrument cannot be·deemed a promissory note to the corporation, for the reason, that, at the time it was executed, the one thousand shares, required by the statute as preliminary to organization, had not been subscribed. At that time it was wholly uncertain, whether such a corporation would ever exist, so as to have capacity to enter into legal contracts. The corporation, then, cannot adopt such an instrument and declare upon it as a promissory note, but must declare upon it, if at all, as a special contract, alleging the consideration.

Platt, Peck, and *A. Peck*, for the plaintiffs.

1. The provision in the act of incorporation does not make the actual payment of the five dollars indispensable to the validity of the subscription; it is directory, and is introduced for the benefit of the corporation, and may be waived. The note, being giving for this sum, rests on good consideration; and as the plaintiffs have adopted the note, no question as to the power of the commissioners can arise.

2. The consideration for the note passed from the plaintiffs; and the rule is, that, if the principal and agent are named in the contract, and the consideration moves to the other party from the principal, the contract is with the latter, and he may sue upon it. The promise moves upon the consideration, and to the party from whom it flows. Whitelaw *v.* Cahoon, 1 D. Ch. 295; Arlington *v.* Hinds, Ib. 431; Piggott *v.* Thompson, 3 B. & P. ,147; Gilmore *v.* Pope, 5 Mass. 491; Commercial Bank *v.* French, 21 Pick. 486; 1 Am. Lead. Cas. 460; Irish *v.* Webster, 5 Greenl. 171; 1 Fairf. 341; State *v.* Boies, 2 Fairf. 474.

3. The defendant having pleaded the general issue only, the existence of the corporation is admitted. Besides, by the act of incorporation the company has a legal existence on·the first subscription of stock, even before organization; and the note, being given for a consideration moving from the corporation, is, in legal effect, payable

to the corporation, — especially as the *office* of commissioners, and not the persons, is named in the note.

The opinion of the court was delivered by

BENNETT, J. It is claimed by the defendant, that the note now in controversy is *without consideration*. The defendant and others had signed an instrument, by which the subscribers agreed to take, and did take, the number of shares of the capital stock of the company, affixed to their respective names; and this defendant sub⸗ scribed for fifty shares of the stock. The note in suit was given for the first five dollars payablé on each respective share, which, by the terms of the charter of incorporation, was to be paid to the commis⸗ sioners at the time of the subscription. This, it is said, cannot con⸗ stitute a sufficient consideration to sustain the note; but we think otherwise.

By the terms of the charter each subscriber becomes a stock⸗ holder and a member of the company; and the interest thereby acquired is a sufficient consideration to support an action for the amount subscribed, against the person subscribing, upon an express promise to pay the subscription. See Wordsworth on Joint Stock Companies, 317; 39 Law Lib. 85; Worcester Turnp. Co. v. Wilson, 5 Mass. 80; Goshen Turnp. Co. v. Hurtin, 9 Johns. 217; Dutchess Cotton Manf. Co. v. Davis, 14 Johns. 238; Baltimore Turnp. Co. v. Barnes, 6 Har. & Johns. 57. The defendant, having given his note for the first instalment to be paid upon his shares, cannot stand in any more favorable light, than if the action had been upon a subscription containing an express promise to pay the amount subscribed, as the same should be assessed. Though the corporation was not in point of fact organized at the time when this defendant subscribed for his stock, yet his concurrence in obtaining and accept⸗ ing the charter of incorporation, and thereby becoming himself a member of the corporation, raises a *mutuality* in his contract; and gives efficiency to his subscription.

We do not think, that the simple fact, that the commissioners accepted the note of the defendant in lieu of so much money, or, as the case finds, in *settlement* of the sum which was to have been paid upon the making of the subscription, can have the effect to give the defendant the right to repudiate his contract, or render it void for want of consideration. The corporation, having accepted this note as so much cash, could not certainly deny to the defendant the rights and privileges of a corporator.

The act does not, as in the case of bank charters, require the first instalment to be paid in specie; and no good reason is perceived, why it should. If it is paid in money's worth, every valuable purpose of a payment is answered; and we see no objection to the commissioners regarding the defendant's note as money's worth, if they saw fit. There is no pretence, that the public have an interest in this subject, as in the case of moneyed corporations, which needs protection, and which might lead the court to require a strict performance of the provisions of the charter. There is no pretence that this note was taken in bad faith, or to the injury of any of the corporators. It is quite another question, whether the corporation might have declined to have received this note of the commissioners, and required of them to have advanced the money, if they had thought proper. But we are not called on to pass upon any such question. Neither are we required to determine, what would have been the rights of the defendant, as a corporator, if the corporation had declined to receive the note from the commissioners; but, having received it, the defendant must be entitled to all the rights he would have had, if he had paid the money upon subscribing; and, upon the principle of *mutuality*, the note must be held valid in the hands of the corporation.

In the case of The Union Turnp. Co. *v.* Jenkins, 1 Caines, 381, the act of incorporation required the payment of ten dollars on a share at the time of subscription. The defendant subscribed for two hundred and eighty shares, but paid nothing; neither was any thing demanded by the commissioners. It was in that case urged, that, as the first instalment of ten dollars was not paid, the contract was incomplete, and not obligatory upon the company, and consequently not binding upon the defendant. But the supreme court held, that this did not affect the validity of the subscription. Though the Court of Errors reversed that decision, (see 1 Caines's Cases in Error, 86,) it may well be questioned, which is the better opinion. But in the case now before us, not only was *the five dollars* on a share demanded by the commissioners at the time of subscription, but it was in fact paid to them in the defendant's note, which the case finds was received in *settlement* of the first instalment payable on the shares subscribed for. If the present note is not valid, the whole subscription is void, and neither party acquired any rights by means of it. This, we think, can hardly be contended for.

The more important question would seem to be, can the present plaintiffs maintain an action on this note? It is said, the corporation was not *in esse* at the time of making the promise. If this be so, it would be difficult to get over the objection. But the first section of the plaintiffs' act of incorporation declares, in express terms, that such persons, as shall thereafter become stockholders of said company, *are* constituted a body corporate, &c. Though it is necessary, that every corporation should have corporators, yet we find by the fourth section of the act, that every subscriber for stock becomes *per se* a corporator; and by the subscription paper, which is made a part of the case, it appears, that there were several subscribers for stock prior to the defendant's becoming one. Each subscriber for stock *per se* becomes a member of the corporation, and *all*, as fast as they subscribe, become *corporators*, under the provisions of the act. To justify an organization of the corporation, certain things are made necessary; but in the eye of the law this corporation should be regarded *in esse* before they have the right to organize. It is the statute, which creates the subscribers for stock a corporation, and not their organizing under it. It is usual, in acts of incorporation, to designate the names of certain individuals as corporators; but that was not done in this instance. As the act incorporates all, that shall thereafter become stockholders, it may be taken, for the purpose of giving *vitality* to the charter of incorporation, that the defendant, as well as other subscribers for stock, became such on the day the act of incorporation passed, although in point of fact they did not subscribe until some time subsequent. See Chester Glass Co. *v.* Dewey, 16 Mass. 94. If this be not so, the charter must, at all events, have *vitality* from the time individuals became stockholders in point of fact, by an actual subscription; and this is sufficient for present purposes.

The note contains a promise, "to pay the commissioners of the Vermont Central Railroad Company," two hundred and fifty dollars. It is claimed, that this is a promise to pay the individuals, who were appointed the commissioners for receiving subscriptions for the company, and not a promise to the corporation, and that such individuals alone have the right of action. Although it may be true, that, as to bills of exchange, the person named as payee has the right of action, and not the person who has the beneficial interest, and that it is to be determined upon the inspection of the bill alone, who has the right of action, or, in other words, who is the promisee, and although we should concede, that the same principle should apply to promissory notes, yet the important inquiry is, who is the payee, upon the face of this note? Is it the Railroad Company, or the individuals who constituted the board of commissioners? The commissioners are not named in the note as individuals, but only referred to officially, as the commissioners of the " Vermont Central Railroad Company." If the promise had been to A. B. and C., Commissioners of the Vermont Central Railroad Co., the question would have been quite a different one from what is raised in this case.

I think the authorities well sustain the position, that where the principal is named in a bill of exchange, or promissory note, and the agent is not, except officially, — as a promise to pay "the cashier of the Bank of Burlington," — the principal, who is named, is to be taken to be the promisee, rather than the agent, who is not named; and this, too, upon the face of the instrument. In the case of the New York African Society v. Varick et al., 13 Johns. 38, the bond was executed to the *standing committee*, of that society; and it was claimed, that the society could not sustain an action on it; but it was held otherwise. So in Bailey v. The Onondaga County M. Ins. Co., in error, 6 Hill, 476, the bond was given to the *directors* of the company, to be paid to the *said directors, their successors and assigns;* and yet it was held, in legal effect, to be a bond to the company. In the case of The Commercial Bank v. French, 21 Pick. 486, the promise in the note was to pay "the cashier of the Commercial Bank, Boston, or his order;" and the action was sustained on the note by the bank. See, also, the case of Bank of United States v. Lyman et al., 20 Vt. 669, where this subject is ably and fully considered. Also, 1 Am. Lead. Cas. p. 461.

Our own courts have gone much farther than is necessary to go to sustain the present action, and that, too, in the case of promissory notes. In Arlington v. Hinds, 1 D. Ch. 431, the promise was ".to pay Luther Stone, town treasurer, or his successors in office;" and yet it was held, that the town of Arlington might maintain the action. In the case of Bank of Manchester v. Slason, 13 Vt. 334, the bill was indorsed thus, "pay to M. Clark, Esq., cashier;" and yet, it appearing in evidence that Clark was at the time cashier to the Bank of Manchester, and that this was the uniform mode of indorsing paper to banks, it was held, that the action was well brought in the name of the bank. It may be remarked, that in both of these cases the agents are designated by name, as well as officially, and there is no designation of their principals, in either case, upon the face of the paper. In the case before us the commissioners are a part of the necessary machinery for getting this corporation into operation, and are *quasi* agents of the corporation, necessarily acting in their behalf, prior to an organization. We think, that upon this note, the company are the proper persons to bring this action, and especially as it appears that the consideration, for which the note was given, was stock subscribed for by the defendant. In effect, it is a promise to the corporation, through the commissioners.

No question was raised in the county court as to the existence of the plaintiffs as a corporation, and none has been raised in argument in this court, excepting whether they were *in esse* at the time the note was executed; and probably none could be raised, under the present pleadings.

The result is, the judgment of the county court is affirmed.

WHITE RIVER TURNPIKE COMPANY *v.* VERMONT CENTRAL RAILROAD COMPANY.[1]

Windsor Co. March Term, 1849.

IN CHANCERY.

Eminent Domain — Right of State to take the Franchise of a Corporation — Compensation — Location of Road — Right to cross Turnpike.

It is now settled law, that there is no implied contract by the State in a charter of a turnpike or other private corporation, that their property, or even their franchise, shall be exempt from the common liability of the property of individuals to be taken for the public use; that it may be taken, on proper compensation being made; that a railroad is an improved highway, and that property, taken for its use by authority of the legislature, is property taken for the public use, as much as if taken for any other highway; and that the legislature may delegate its power to a railroad corporation, to take private property for public use in the construction of their railroad, as well as to a turnpike corporation to take the like property for the public use in the construction of a turnpike road.

It is also settled, that where there has been a legislative grant to a private corporation to erect a bridge, a turnpike, or other public convenience, which is not in its terms exclusive, there is no constitutional obligation on the legislature, not to grant to a second corporation the right to erect another bridge, or turnpike, for a similar purpose, to be constructed so near the former, as greatly to impair, or even to destroy, the value of the former, — and this without making compensation to the first corporation for the consequential injury.

But so far as the real estate of such private corporation, or their interest in real estate, is concerned, they are entitled to the same constitutional protection that an individual would be. The property of either may be taken for public use by authority of the legislature, if compensation be made therefor, but not otherwise.

Although the charter of the Vermont Central Railroad Company does not in terms empower the corporation to locate their road along the valley of White River, yet it must be taken, in the absence of evidence to show that there was any other practicable route to the proper point on the Connecticut River, designated in the charter, or that the route adopted was unsuitable, that the road was properly located in the valley of White River.

Under the tenth section of the statute incorporating the Vermont Central Railroad Company, that corporation have power to enter upon and cross a turnpike road, as well as any other highway, making compensation to the turnpike corporation for the injury they should sustain.

And the provisions of the charter of that corporation, prescribing a mode for making compensation by appraisal, for injuries to land entered upon by them, may be fairly construed to apply to the property and interest of a turnpike corporation in the land embraced by their road, and in the road itself, as tangible property.

APPEAL from the court of chancery. The allegations in the bill and answer and 'the facts proved are fully stated in the opinion delivered by the court. The court of chancery dismissed the bill; from which decree the orators appealed.

Tracy and *Converse*, for orators.

1. The defendants had no legal right to lay their road over or in any way interfere with the plaintiffs' road. The State had granted the right for the turnpike, without reserve; and the legislature had no constitutional power to revoke, or resume, the rights and privileges granted to the plaintiffs. It was a contract, upon good and sufficient consideration. Dartmouth College v. Woodward, 4 Wheat. 518; [4 U. S. Cond. R. 562]; West Boston Bridge v. Middlesex, 10 Pick. 270; 11 Vt. 380. But if the government have power to resume the rights thus granted for public use, it cannot transfer those rights to another private corporation, established, not for merely public objects, but confessedly for private emolument. The Chesapeake & Ohio Canal Co. v. The Baltimore & Ohio R. Co. 4 Gill & J. 1; 10 Pick. 270.

2. The legislature have no power, under any circumstances, to interfere, or authorize any other person to interfere, with rights and privileges already granted, except upon payment of damages. No damages are directed to be paid in this case. See charter of defendents, Acts of 1843, sec. 7. The defendants, by their charter, are not authorized to interfere with the plaintiffs' road; and without such authority it will not be contended, that they had that right. So important a power cannot be implied; and certainly not in this case, as the charter specially provides for taking the Winooski turnpike. If the legislature have power to take turnpike roads and make them free roads, it is upon compensation, and to make them public property. Armington v. Barnet et al., 15 Vt. 745. But in such cases they must give the power to take the franchise. 15 Vt. 745; West River Bridge Co. v. Dix, 16 Vt. 446. There is nothing in the defendants' charter, which by implication can be construed to authorize this.

L. B. Peck for the defendants.

By the provisions of the act of incorporation, under which the defendants justify, they had the right to locate their road in the valley of White River, and within the limits of the turnpike. Acts of 1843, p. 43, § 1; p. 45, § 4; p. 46, § 7; p. 48, § 9. This power is expressly given by the tenth section of the act, which declares, that

When it shall be necessary, in the construction of said road, to cross any stream of water, watercourse, road, or way, intersecting said railroad route, or line, said company may construct said railroad across or upon the same, provided said company shall restore the stream, watercourse, road, or way, thus intersected, as near as practicable to its former state and usefulness," &c.   The terms " *road or way* " are very broad and comprehensive, and most clearly include turnpikes.   This construction is strongly aided by the last clause of the proviso to section eight, which provides for the payment of consequential damages to the Winooski Turnpike Co.; — but the tenth section is left operative upon that company and the defendants.

If it be said, that the act is silent as to the right of the defendants to interfere with the property of another corporation, we answer, that this right is clearly to be inferred.   The eighth section and its proviso would seem to remove all doubt.   Though the act names the right of taking *land*, its provisions are to be construed liberally, and will therefore include easeholds, easements, and other interest in land, as well as land itself.   Ellis v. Welch, 6 Mass. 246 ; Parks v. Boston, 15 Pick. 203 ; Boston Water Power Co. v. Boston & Worcester R. Co. 23 Ib. 360, 395 ; s. c. *post* ; Rogers v. Bradshaw, 20 Johns. 715 ; Enfield Toll Bridge Co. v. Hartford & New Haven R. Co. 17 Conn. 454, 466 ; s. c. *post* ; Rev. St. 53, § 8.

There is no constitutional objection to the act, in this view of the case.   It does not deprive the orators of their franchise.   The only effect is, to diminish its value.   Charles River Bridge v. Warren Bridge, 11 Pet. 420 ; 23 Pick. 360, 395 ; 17 Conn. 454 ; 20 Johns. 735 ; 6 Paige 554 ; 15 Vt. 745 ; 15 Wend. 114 ; 11 N. H. 20.

The opinion of the court was delivered by

HALL, J.   This was an appeal from the court of chancery.   The bill, which was filed in 1846, states, that the plaintiffs were incorporated by the legislature of this State in the year 1800 and authorized to lay out and make a turnpike road from the mouth of White River to the second branch of that river; that the corporation was duly organized, and built the road, and have ever since kept it in good repair, and have rightfully, in conformity to their charter, kept gates upon it, and received tolls from travellers over it, and that no person, or corporation, has a right to injure the road, or interrupt the plaintiffs, or travellers, in the use of it ; — that the defendants, a corporation chartered by the General Assembly of this State in October, 1843, have laid out and surveyed a line for a railroad, and are preparing to build the same, in the valley of said White River, along and over the plaintiffs' turnpike road, in many places crossing it in such manner as to stop all passing upon it, and in other places embracing the whole of the turnpike road, thereby interrupting, or entirely preventing, all travel or passing on the same; and that, if the road is permitted to be built, it will entirely destroy the plaintiffs' turnpike road, and prevent all passing upon it with any kind of teams or carriages whatever. The bill prays for a perpetual injunction against the defendants, from taking any real estate of the plaintiffs for their railroad, and from locating or building it across or within the limits of the plaintiffs' road, and from encroaching upon it in any manner.

From the answer of the defendants, and the facts shown and agreed upon, it appears that the turnpike company laid out their road four rods wide, agreeably to their charter; that the railroad in many places is within the limits of the turnpike road, and that it crosses the turnpike road in four places, — in three of the places by means of bridges, the abutments of which stand within the limits of the turnpike road, but not within the travelled part of it, and once upon the track of the road; that some two or three acres of the turnpike road, in the whole, are. covered by the railroad; that the turnpike road is in places, for considerable distances, made narrower by the encroachments of the railroad, but that from eighteen to thirty feet is in all places left for the travelled part of the turnpike; that in locating the railroad the defendants avoided passing over or within the limits of the turnpike road, whenever it could be avoided without great inconvenience and almost ruinous expense; and that no other route along White River for the railroad could have been adopted, without greatly increased expense and difficulty. It is admitted by the plaintiffs, that the proceedings of the defendants in locating their road were regular, if they might locate it along White River, except in so far as they have encroached upon the plaintiffs' turnpike road. Since the filing of the bill the railroad has been in the process of construction; and the defendants have offered to agree with the plaintiffs upon the damages done to their road, and failing to do so, have caused their damages to be appraised by the Railroad Commissioners; and from their appraisal the plaintiffs have appealed to the county court, where the appeal is now pending.

The ground, upon which the plaintiffs claim relief, is, that the defendants have no right to build their road in such manner, as to cross or touch upon the limits of their turnpike road.

The first objection to the right of the defendants thus to construct their road rests upon an alleged want of constitutional power in the legislature of the State, to confer authority on the railroad company to take the plaintiffs' property for the use of their railroad. It is said, that the charter to the plaintiffs was a contract of the State with the turnpike corporation, which would be impaired by the execution of the grant to the defendants, and that such grant to the defendants cannot therefore be carried into effect, but in violation of that clause of the tenth section of the first article of the Constitution of the United States, which prohibits any State from passing " a law impairing the obligation of contracts."

Upon this question it is deemed sufficient to say, that it now appears to be too well settled by authority to be controverted, that there is no implied contract by the State, in a charter of a turnpike or other private corporation, that their property, or even their franchise itself, shall be exempt from the common liability of the property of individuals to be taken for the public use; that it may be taken, on proper compensation being made; that a railroad is an improved highway, and that property, taken for its use by authority of the legislature, is property taken for the public use, as much as if taken for any other highway; and that the legislature may delegate its powers to a railroad corporation, to take private property for public use in the construction of their railroad, as well as to a turnpike corporation to take the like property for the public use in the construction of a turnpike road. Armington v. Barnett, 15 Vt. 745; West River Bridge Co. v. Dix, 16 Vt. 446; Boston Water Power Co. v. Boston & Worcester R. Co. 23 Pick. 360; s. c. post; Enfield Toll Bridge Co. v. Hartford & N. Haven R. Co. 17 Conn. 454; s. c. post.

It appears, also, to be equally well settled, that where there has been a legislative grant to a private corporation to erect a bridge, turnpike, or other public convenience, which is not in its terms exclusive, there is no constitutional obligation on the legislature, — however strong a moral one there may be, — not to grant to a second corporation the right to erect another bridge, or turnpike, for a similar purpose, to be constructed so near the former as greatly to impair, or even to destroy, the value of the former; and this, without making compensation to the first corporation for the consequential injury. Charles River Bridge v. Warren Bridge, 11 Pet. 420; Enfield Bridge Co. v. Hartford & New Haven R. Co. 17 Conn. 454; s. c. post; Mohawk Bridge Co. v. Utica & Schenectady R. Co. 6 Paige, 544; s. c. post, vol. 2. It is therefore unimportant to inquire, whether the defendants' railroad charter contains any provision, by virtue of which the plaintiffs' corporation can obtain compensation for an injury to their franchise, by the diversion of travel from their turnpike road; and we have not looked into the defendants' charter with a view to determine that question.

The plaintiffs' bill does not, however, complain, that the value of their franchise is likely to be destroyed, or impaired, by the diversion of the travel from their turnpike to the railroad, or that their right under their charter to maintain a turnpike road and to collect tolls upon it along White River, has been in any manner invaded. The injury complained of is an actual encroachment upon the plaintiffs' real estate, — or interest in real estate, — which they hold under and by virtue of their charter. It is precisely such an injury as an individual, having a similar interest in real estate, might complain of; and it must be conceded, that the plaintiffs are entitled to the same constitutional protection to their property, that an individual would be. The property of either may be taken for public use by authority of the legislature, if compensation be made therefor, but not otherwise. Constitution of Vermont, Bill of Rights, Art. 2. The question, then, arises, whether the legislature have conferred the power on the defendants to take the plaintiffs' property in the manner it has been shown to have been taken, and have provided a compensation therefor ?

The defendants' act of incorporation does not *in terms* empower them to lay out their road along the valley of White River, but to construct it from some point on Lake Champlain, up the valley of Onion River, and extending to a point on Connecticut River most convenient to meet a railroad, either from Concord, New Hampshire, or Fitchburg, Massachusetts. But it not being shown that there was any other practicable route to the proper point on Connecticut River, or that the route adopted was an unsuitable or improper one, we think it is to be taken, that the road was properly located in the valley of White River; and from the evidence it must also be taken, that it was located in the proper place in that valley, unless its location has invaded the legal rights of the plaintiffs.

It being conceded, that the requisitions of the charter, so far as the forms of proceeding were concerned, were pursued in laying out the railroad, the only remaining question is, whether it is to be fairly inferred from the defendants' charter of incorporation, that they might enter upon and cross a turnpike road, making compensation to the turnpike corporation for the injury they should sustain ?

The tenth section of the act of incorporation provides, " that when it shall be necessary, in the construction of the road, to cross any stream of water, watercourse, *road*, or *way*, the company may construct their railroad across the same, provided said company shall restore the stream, watercourse, *road*, or *way*, thus intersected, as near as practicable to its former state and usefulness, to the acceptance of the selectmen of the town, where the same is situated."

The language of the section is sufficiently comprehensive to allow an entry of the corporation upon a turnpike road, and it would, indeed, seem to embrace such a road, as well as any other highway. It also provides a compensation for the injury to the way itself, by requiring the company to restore it, as near as may be, to its former state and usefulness. It is objected, however, that the board of selectmen, though suitable to determine the sufficiency of the restoration of the road, when the public only are concerned, would be an unfit tribunal to decide upon the right, in such case, of a turnpike corporation; and that therefore the section could not have been intended to apply to the road of such a corporation. It does not appear to us, that the argument from this provision is entitled to any great weight. Some tribunal must necessarily be provided; and the selectmen, being the ordinary representative of the public in regard to highways, might well be supposed to feel a sufficient interest in the preservation of convenient facilities for public travel, to take care that the road was properly restored.

But if the construction of the tenth section were doubtful, we think the doubt would be removed by reference to the eighth section. That section, after prescribing a mode by which the Winooski Turnpike Corporation should be compensated for the injury to their franchise by the construction of the railroad, provides, that, upon a compliance of a railroad company with the requisitions in regard to such franchise, such company " shall not be subject to any damages or liabilities to the turnpike companies, *excepting such as is provided in section ten of the act.*" Thus clearly implying, that the provisions of the tenth section were designed to apply to turnpike roads, as well as to other highways.

This clause of the eighth section may also be considered as implying, that there were other damages, besides those provided for by the restoration of the 'road under the tenth section, that the turnpike company might be entitled to, if their franchise remained to them; such, perhaps, as damages to the turnpike company occasioned by the impracticability of restoring the road to its former state of usefulness for travel, as well as for the occupancy of a portion of the land covered by the easement in the turnpike corporation, — which, when the public only were concerned, might be overlooked, but which, in the case of a road owned by a corporation, might be proper to be regarded.

But without such implication, we think the provisions of the charter, prescribing a mode for making compensation by appraisal for injuries to land entered upon by the railroad company, may be fairly construed to apply to the property and interest of a turnpike corporation, in the land embraced by their road and in the road itself, as tangible property. The terms *land* and *real estate,* which are both used in reference to compensation for damages, when found in statutes whose object seems to require it, are often construed as embracing not only the soil itself, but an easement, or other interest, arising out of and depending upon what is termed land in its limited sense. Such is the defined meaning of the terms *land* and *real estate* as used throughout the Revised Statutes; and a legislative definition having been expressly given them, they may well be considered as retaining that sense in subsequent statutes, unless there is a clear indication to the contrary. Rev. St. chap. 4, sec. 8; Boston Water Power Co. *v.* Boston & W. R. Co. 23 Pick. 395; s. c. *post.* We are therefore satisfied, that the defendants' charter of incorporation did authorize them to enter upon the plaintiffs' turnpike road in the manner they are shown to have done, and did provide a mode for making compensation to the plaintiffs for the injury thereby occasioned to them. We are not called upon to lay down any specific rule for the government of commissioners in making an appraisal of the plaintiffs' damages, and we do not intend to do so. We merely decide, that the commissioners appointed in pursuance of the railroad charter have the power to award to the plaintiffs such damages as they may legally and justly claim.

We are all agreed, that the plaintiffs are not entitled to the injunction prayed for, and that the decree of the chancellor dismissing the bill should be affirmed.

VERMONT CENTRAL RAILROAD COMPANY *v.* CHESTER BAXTER.[1]

Windsor Co., March Term, 1850.

Right to take Materials beyond Limits of Road — Damages for so taking — Jurisdiction of Commissioners.

The commissioners need not be called upon to appraise damages for materials taken by the Vermont Central Railroad Co., without the limits of their survey, under section sixteen of their charter,[2] for the construction of their road, until after the materials are ascertained.

---

[1] 22 Vermont Reports. 365.

[2] Which is in these words, — "Said company may, by their engineers, agents, or workmen, with such teams and carriages and tools, as they may find convenient, enter upon any lands contiguous to said railroad, or the works connected therewith, to dig, blast, and carry away and use such stone, gravel, earth, and other materials, as may be

The commissioners have jurisdiction to determine the damages for acts of the corporation, where those acts are such as the corporation, by their engineers, agents, or workmen, may rightfully do, by virtue of their charter, and the parties cannot agree upon the amount of damages; and it makes no difference, in this respect, whether the corporation admit or deny their liability.

The corporation have power, under section sixteen of their charter, when necessary for the construction of their road, to take stone from land contiguous to the line of their survey, and to use land for the purpose of cutting and hewing stone thereon.

The power of the corporation to take the land and other materials adjoining the line of the road, for the purpose of constructing their road, is conferred upon them by their charter, and is as necessary to exist in and be exercised by all the contractors on the road as by the corporation. This power, to be exercised within reasonable limits and in a proper manner, is necessarily delegated from the corporation to the contractor, and for this purpose the contractor is the agent of the corporation, and the corporation is liable to the land-owner, for the damages occasioned by the exercise of this power on the part of the contractor.

And the liability of the corporation to the land-owner, in such case, is not affected by any stipulation in the agreement between the corporation and the contractor.

The commissioners, who are called upon to assess damages in such case, may award costs to the land-owner.

PETITION for a writ of *certiorari* to the commissioners appointed to appraise damages for land and materials taken by the Vermont Central Railroad Company.

The petitioners alleged, that the defendant applied to the commissioners to appraise and award damages, which had accrued to him on land held by him in his own right and as administrator of Hiram Shepard, and that the commissioners, after giving due notice to the parties, had met, and, upon hearing, had made their award. The award was recited in the petition, and was, in substance as follows; — that the corporation had contracted with Sewall F. Belknap to construct their railroad, by a written agreement, a copy of which was annexed to the award; that it did not appear, that Baxter had knowledge of the provisions of this contract; that Belknap, for the purpose of procuring stone to build culverts for the road, by his servants, agents, and workmen, entered upon the land of Baxter, and upon the land of Shepard, contiguous to the railroad, and laid open the fields, and blasted and drew away stone, and occupied the land for hewing stone, and used the stone in the construction of the

necessary for building or repairing said road; doing as little damage thereby, as the nature of the case will admit; and in case damage shall be claimed by the owner of land thus entered upon, and for the stone, gravel, and other materials carried away as aforesaid, and the owner and said company do not agree upon the sum to be paid therefor, the same shall be assessed by commissioners in the manner before prescribed in this act; and all persons, aggrieved by any decision of said commissioners, shall have the right to appeal, as herein before provided." Act of 1843, p. 49.

railroad, claiming to do so by virtue of the provisions of the charter of the corporation ; that the corporation denied their liability to pay for the damages so occasioned, and the parties being unable to agree upon the amount of damages, the commissioners, upon the applica· tion of Baxter, after giving due notice and hearing the parties, awarded to Baxter $63.00, as his damages, viz., for stone taken from the land of Baxter $28.00, — for laying open his fields and drawing stone across his land $10.00, — for the use of land for cutting and hewing stone, $12.00, — and for stone taken from the land of Shepard, $13.00 ; and that they allowed to Baxter $10.98 for his costs in the matter. It was farther alleged in the petition, that the petitioners did not authorize or direct the acts committed by Bel· knap upon the land of the defendant, but that Belknap, in so doing, was acting for himself, under the stipulations in the contract between him and the corporation; and the petitioners denied that the commissioners had authority to make the award in question.

The fourteenth specification, in the contract between the corpora· tion and Belknap was in these words, — " The price per yard, for masonry shall in every case include the furnishing of all materials, and the transportation of the same to the place where wanted, the cost of all scaffoldings, centerings, &c., and the preparation of all roads and bridges that may be required, in order to transport the stone, or other materials, to the work." The seventeenth specifica· tion was in these words, — ".The corporation . will assure a right of way over the premises of land-owners, so far as may be necessary to afford the contractors convenient access to their work ; but the con· tractors shall be responsible for all damage done to such premises, in consequence of leaving gates or fences open, and also for all depredations upon fences, wood lots, or other property, by the work· men in their employ." By the sixth specification it was provided, that " in cases where the quantity of materials taken from the exca· vations in any section shall be not sufficient for the formation of the requisite embankments, the deficiency shall be supplied by materials taken from the adjacent grounds, at such places as the engineer may designate." By the fourth specification it was provided, that in case "land or gravel cannot be obtained from land-holders on terms satis· factory to the corporation, then such sections shall be finished off ac· cording to such grades as the engineer shall establish."

Peck & Colby, Tracy, Converse & Barrett, for petitioners.

The award shows, that no such entry, or taking of materials, as the charter contemplates was made or done by the corporation. Belknap was neither engineer, agent, or workman, of the corpora.

tion, but a contractor, having no other relation to the corporation, than such as was created by the contract; and by the terms of the contract the price for masonry was to include the *furnishing all materials.* The claim, or pretence, of Belknap, or his workmen, to act under the charter, conferred no authority to enter and take and use the stone, and cannot bind the corporation; third persons deal with a professed agent at their peril, and cannot charge the supposed principal by reason of ignorance or want of information in respect to the pretended agency. Nor can it be said, that the corporation have become liable to Baxter, by reason of adopting such agency and enjoying the benefit of the materials taken by Belknap. They had no knowledge, or means of knowing, that Belknap procured the materials by claiming to represent the company, nor of the fact, that he procured any of Baxter; and the ratification of the act of an agent, previously unauthorized, must, in order to bind the principal, be with a full knowledge of all the material facts. Owings *v.* Hull, 9 Pet. 606; Davidson *v.* Stanley, 2 M. & G. 721; Bell *v.* Cunningham, 3 Pet. 69; Paley on Agency, 172.

By the fourth and sixth specifications all questions as to borrowing *earth,* or *gravel,* are deferred to the order of the corporation, and their engineer, and without such order the contractor is not authorized to take materials without the limits of the section. In regard to *stone,* procured off the road, the contract has no provision, subjecting the selection to the engineer, as that, by the fourteenth specification, was to be furnished by the contractor. If, then, the corporation are liable for stone thus taken and used by a contractor, it is not by force of the contract, in its terms, but from the fact that he was contractor and had agreed to construct the road. The argument, that the corporation, by contracting with Belknap to build the road, thereby gave him the rights, which the corporation have to take property without the consent of the owner, and to render the corporation chargeable, is certainly opposed to settled and well established principles. If this be so, the corporation is also liable for the debts and acts of *sub-contractors,* for all materials, and even perhaps for the wages of the laborers. The inconveniences and utter impracticability of such a doctrine are ample reasons against its reception. For a class of injuries by the fault, or the negligence of a sub-contractor, or his servant, the law is stringent enough; Bush *v.* Steinman, 1 B. & P. 409; but even the doctrine of this case is greatly shaken in Quarman *v.* Burnett, 6 M. & W. 499; Rapson *v.* Cubitt, 9 M. & W. 710; Dunlap's Paley on Ag., notes, 297.

If the taking by Belknap was a tort, and he the servant of the corporation, they are not liable. Dunlap's Paley, 306; Schmedt *v.*

Blood, 9 Wend. 268; Foster *v.* Essex Bank, 17 Mass. 479; 6 Com. Dig. 393.

The right of taking materials under the charter is a *privilege* in derogation of the rights of the owners of the property, and therefore not to be extended by implication; it is a right *personal* to the corporation, and not to be transferred.

The commissioners have no authority to determine a question like this; their powers are restricted to the single inquiry, as to the " sum to be paid," and they are called upon only when the " parties do not agree" upon that question, and that only; they are not a tribunal for litigation, when the corporation deny their liability and repudiate all connection with the matter.

The commissioners have no authority to award costs to the landowner.

W. C. French and *O. P. Chandler*, for defendant.

The contract between the corporation and Belknap had no effect as to third persons, who had no knowledge of its provisions. Belknap claimed to enter upon the land and take the stone by virtue of the provisions of the charter. He was the general agent, for the purpose of building the road; and land-owners could in no way resist his so entering upon their lands, as the charter gave him the right. His acts, as general agent for the purpose of building the road, bind the corporation, whatever may have been the *private* contract between him and the corporation. 2 Kent. 624. No action could have been maintained against Belknap for taking the stone. Calking *v.* Baldwin, 4 Wend. 667. The corporation are equally liable for laying open fields and drawing stone across them and for damages in consequence of hewing the stone upon the land. It was necessary, for the purpose of enabling Belknap to construct the road. Dodge et al. *v.* Co. Com'rs of Essex, 3 Met. 380. Stevens *v.* Prop'rs Middlesex Canal, 12 Mass. 466; Stowell *v.* Flagg, 11 Mass. 364.

The opinion of the court was delivered by

REDFIELD, J. This is a petition to this court for a writ of *certiorari* to the commissioners of the Vermont Central Railroad Company for appraising land damages, to certify to us a judgment, or appraisal, which they made against the company for damages in taking stone, drawing them across land, and hewing them on land of the petitionee, — also allowing him costs, — that its correctness may be determined by this court. If their proceedings were substantially correct, we should refuse the writ. We must therefore inquire into their legality. We must be very brief, in regard to most of the points raised.

1. We think the commissioners need not be called out to appraise damages under the sixteenth section, for materials taken to build the road, out of the limits of the survey, until after the materials are ascertained. This seems to us to be the only practicable mode of proceeding in such case, if they would come at a reasonable and just determination in regard to such damages. And it is admitted such, from necessity, has been the practical construction put upon this section.

2. We think, if the company are liable at all in this case, under the facts set forth in the award of the commissioners, it is a proper case for the determination of the commissioners. As is said by Ch. J. Shaw, in Dodge v. County Com'rs of Essex, 3 Metc. 380, if the company keep " within the scope of their authority, they are not wrongdoers," but are justified by their act of incorporation, and liable to pay damages in the mode there pointed out. We see no good reason, why the right to refer this question to the determination of the commissioners should depend upon the company admitting their liability, and differing only as to the *amount* of damages, to which the land-owner is entitled. It seems to us, that such a rule would be liable to a very great abuse. If the company, by their agents, or servants, have so conducted, as to be in fact liable for damages, and the parties cannot agree upon them, then the commissioners are constituted the only proper tribunal, in the first instance, to determine that question, and either party may apply to them and set their action in motion.

Of course it is not intended to say here, that the jurisdiction of the commissioners extends beyond those cases where the company are rightfully subjected to damages, under the charter provisions, for acts which they may rightfully do, by virtue of the authority therein conferred. Beyond that, if they incur liabilities, either for torts, or by way of contract, they are liable like other persons. So that the question, how far this matter comes within the jurisdiction of the commissioners, depends upon the prior question, whether the liability is one for an act, which they had the right to do by the charter, or is a mere tort. And as it seems to be supposed on all hands, that the act itself is clearly within the charter rights of the company, if done in such a manner, as to be the act of the company, the questions of liability and jurisdiction are identical.[1]

[1] NOTE BY REDFIELD, J. Since the decision of this case, it has been somewhat questioned, by some, whether the company itself has any right to take materials for building its road, beyond the limits of the survey. That question was not made or

3. In regard to this question, which is the important inquiry in the case, no doubt, it does not appear to us, that the determination upon the general principles of the law of agency wholly reaches the true merits. involved. If it were so, I could have no hesitation in saying, the company are not liable for the act of Belknap. One who simply lets a job of work to another is not ordinarily liable, I think, for the acts of that other, whether of tort, or contract, unless there be something in the contract, or the conduct of the work, whereby the act becomes that of the principal, — although there is, I know, some apparent conflict in the cases, not important to be here examined.

It is clear, that these stones were not taken by any express direction of the company, nor for their benefit, as between them and Belknap. And if Baxter had the legal right to resist Belknap, so that he must be considered as having acquiesced in what Belknap did, without informing himself of the nature of the contract between Belknap and the company, it is, in my opinion, his own folly, and he is in the same position, as if he had notice of the contract. For he, no doubt, knew enough to put him upon inquiry, and is therefore affected with the notice of such facts, as he might have ascertained upon reasonable inquiry. And if it be viewed as a mere tort of Belknap, it is very questionable, in my mind, how far, upon common principles, the company could be made answerable for the act, as being in effect the act of their agent. Some of the cases, perhaps, go that length. But those entitled to the most consideration seem to stop somewhat short of that point. It would seem, from some of the recent cases, — Rapson v. Cubitt, 9 M. & W. 709, and cases there referred to, and Millegin v. Wedge, 12 Ad. & El. 177, — that the relation of master and servant must exist, in order to make one liable for the torts of the other, unless there is an express or implied permission to do the act. The case of obstructions on one's premises of the nature of nuisances, by which injury occurs to others, rests upon different grounds.

But we think the case before us is entitled to a different consideration. The power conferred upon railroad corporations, to take the

considered by the court, in this case, and, if it be a question, is one involving constitutional considerations of a character which might require serious discussion and grave inquiry. But at present I should be inclined to suppose it must depend upon the *necessity* for taking such materials, and that it is therefore a question of fact mainly. But in a case like the present, where the land-owners preferred the responsibility of the corporation, they would naturally decline contracting with the contractors for building the road, which would create the necessity, contemplated in the charter.

land and other materials adjoining the line of the road, for the purpose of constructing the road, is one in derogation of the ordinary
rights of land-owners, and one which could only be conferred by
the legislature by virtue of the right of eminent domain, and because it is necessary to the reasonable exercise of sovereignty.
And we think it is one, which is as necessary to exist in and be
exercised by all the contractors on the road, as by the corporation.
Indeed, it is only for that purpose that it is important. And whether
the corporation construct their road themselves, or by contract with
others, is unimportant. This is a power which must go with the
contract, which is indispensable to the building of the road, which
must be understood to go with the contract, which is in fact never
exercised by the board of directors of the company, but always by
the builders, under the supervision of the engineers, and which must
of course be exercised only within reasonable limits and in a proper
manner. The very words of the statute show by whom it was expected this power would be exercised, — " by *engineers, agents, or
workmen.*"

This, then, being a power, which was conferred by charter upon
the company, and which of necessity pertains to the contractors, as
a necessarily delegated office from the company to the contractor,
and which they must expect him to exercise, it is the same, as if in
express terms it were stipulated, that he may exercise it. For this
purpose, then, the contractor is the agent of the company. And as
the proprietors of the land cannot resist the contractor, because he
is clothed with the authority of the company, it would be hard, if
they could be compelled to look to any and every contractor, to whom
the company might see fit to turn them over. Any stipulation between the contractor and the company is of no importance to the
land-owners. It is merely a private arrangement between the company and contractor, as to the mode of coming at the price of the
work.

This subject may be very well illustrated, by supposing that the
land-owners had, *by contract,* conferred upon the company the same
rights and privileges, as to building their road, and upon the same
conditions, stipulated in the charter, and the company had let the
building of the road to this contractor, and he and the land-owners
had proceeded, in all respects, as they now have. There could be no
doubt, I apprehend, that the contractor would have acquired the
rights of the company, as to taking and working materials for the
road, and, as between himself and the company, would be bound to
pay for them; but the land-owners might well claim to look to the
stipulations in their own contract, and could not, without their own

consent, be turned over to the contractor. This illustration, which, as far as we can see, is every way a fair one, brings the whole subject within a very narrow compass, and renders it sufficiently simple.

Costs seem to be given by the statute, and we do not see that they are unreasonable.

The petition is dismissed with costs.

NATHAN B. HASWELL *v.* VERMONT CENTRAL RAILROAD COMPANY.[1]

Chittenden Co., May Term, 1851.

Railroad — Deposit of Land Damages — Order of Chancellor — Appeal.

The Vermont Central Railroad Company took land in Burlington, under their charter, to which there were conflicting claims, and, upon petition to the chancellor, under the provisions of the statute of 1846, [Comp. St. 196,] were ordered to deposit in the Farmers' and Mechanics' Bank the amount of the land damages, as appraised by the commissioners, subject to the future order of the chancellor ; and, upon petition subsequently preferred by one who claimed to be entitled to the money so deposited, the chancellor, upon notice given to the company, no adverse claimants of the fund appearing, ordered the money so deposited to be paid to the petitioner. And it was held, that the statute contemplated, that the proceedings before the chancellor, in reference to the deposit of the money, should be summary and final ; and that, upon the petition being preferred by the claimant, the company had no interest in the question, and could not appeal from the order of the chancellor.

PETITION to the chancellor of the third judicial circuit, setting forth, that the Vermont Central Railroad Company had taken certain land in Burlington, under the provisions of their charter, to which there were conflicting claims, and caused the damages to be duly appraised by the commissioners, and had been ordered by the chancellor, upon petition preferred by them pursuant to the provisions of the statute of November 3, 1846, to deposit the amount of the award in the Farmers' and Mechanics' Bank at Burlington, subject to the future order of the chancellor, and had deposited the money accordingly, and that the petitioner was rightfully entitled to the money so deposited, and praying, that an order be made for the payment of the money to him. Notice of the petition having been given to the company to appear before the chancellor at the office of

[1] 23 Vermont Reports, 228.

Smalley & Phelps, in Burlington, on the 16th day of July, 1850, and shows cause why the prayer of the petition should not be granted, the company appeared, and a hearing was had, and, no adverse claimant to the fund appearing, the chancellor decided, that the·petitioner was legally and equitably entitled to a certain portion of the fund, and ordered that part to be paid to him accordingly. From this order the corporation appealed.

In the Supreme Court the petitioner moved to dismiss the appeal, for the reason that no appeal could be taken from such order of the chancellor.

D. A. Smalley, for petitioner.

J. Maeck, for defendant.

The opinion of the court was delivered by

REDFIELD, J. The question now to be determined is, whether this case can be entertained in this court, upon the present appeal. This includes the inquiry, —

1. Whether, under the statute conferring this power upon the chancellor, any appeal can be had in any case. It seems to us, that the purpose of the statute was to give railroad companies a certain and expeditious mode of relieving themselves from any further responsibility in the matter by depositing the money, according to the order of the chancellor; and that, so far as the mere order of deposit of the money was concerned, it was intended to be summary and final. The object of the application and of allowing the deposit is to give the company a more expeditious mode of acquiring title to the land. And the form of the proceeding, being by petition, indicates, that it was not expected to be by bill and answer in the common course of proceeding in the Court of Chancery. And the practice in this case, and in other cases under the statute, so far as we know, has been in accordance with this law.

2. It seems to us, that the manner of this proceeding is such, that it must be regarded as a matter within the summary jurisdiction or discretion of the chancellor, if it be in conformity with the statute. The general laws of the State only allow an appeal from the chancellor upon a final decree, and such decree is required to be made at a regular term of the court, or an adjournment from such term. This proceeding is clearly not of this character. If it is the proceeding contemplated by the statute, it does not seem to us, it could have been intended to be subject to appeal; and if it be not such a proceeding as the statute contemplates, it will conclude the rights of no

one and for that reason should be dismissed. If the statute contemplated a proceeding by bill and answer, then here has been no such
proceeding and nб such decree as the statute requires, and it is
therefore a mere nullity, and should be dismissed for that reason. In
either of these views, it seems difficult to hold, that it comes within
the appropriate sphere of our duties, to hear and determine this
matter, as to the rights of the respective claimants to this fund. In
the particular claim, which was under consideration before the
chancellor, there is nothing to show, that there is any adverse claim.
From all that does appear, it would seem probable, there is no such
claim.

As a general thing, where a fund is to be distributed according to
the order of a specified person, the order of such person is considered
sufficient warrant for the depositary to act upon. In regard to this
class of cases, it is not important here to inquire, how far a regular
chancery proceeding by bill and answer would be regarded as appropriate. That is the least, which would induce the court to entertain
an appeal in the matter. But it may not be improper to say, that it
does seem to us desirable, where any such matter is finally to be determined, and where there may be adversary claims, either to give
some kind of general notice, by publication, or to take security by
way of bond, that the money shall be refunded, in case other persons
should show, in the opinion of the chancellor, superior claims.

3. Finally, it seems to us, that the defendants, although cited in
by the claimant, were not bound to appear, and that, having no interest in the matter, they could not properly bring the case here by
appeal.

The case is dismissed from the docket.

COLCORD QUIMBY, JR., v. VERMONT CENTRAL RAILROAD COMPANY.[1]

Windsor Co., March Term, 1851.

Interest of Railroad Corporation in Land taken for their Road — Obligation to maintain Fences — Care required in management of Locomotive Engines — Evidence to charge Defendants for want of Care.

The charter of the Vermont Central Railroad Company provides, that the company, upon complying with the conditions upon which they may take land for the use of their road, shall be " *seised and possessed of the land.*" This does not make them owners of the fee, but gives them a right of way merely. Hence, although the charter makes no provision in reference to the obligation to maintain fences upon the line of the road, the general law of the State, in reference to the obligation of adjoining land-owners to maintain the division fences between them, does not apply, but the obligation to maintain the fences rests primarily upon the company, and until they have either built the fences or paid the land-owner for doing it, a sufficient length of time to enable him to do it, the mere fact, that cattle get upon the road from the land adjoining is no ground for imputing negligence to the owners of the cattle.

The owner of cattle, which stray upon a railroad track by reason of the insufficiency of a fence, which the railroad company are under obligation to maintain, and who brings an action upon the case against the company for killing the cattle by means of a locomotive engine, is entitled to have the degree of care, which the company are bound to exercise, defined in a more strict manner, than by instructing the jury that the company are bound to the exercise of such care, as a man of ordinary prudence would use, who was the owner of both the railroad and the cattle ; but if such instructions are given to the jury, the defendants cannot complain.

It is not incumbent upon the plaintiff, in such case, to prove, in opening his case, the customary and usual conduct and practice in the management of locomotive engines and trains on railroads under similar circumstances ; but if the defendants desire the benefit of the rules of engineering, under such circumstances, for their exculpation, they may show the custom, and if not unreasonable, — of which the jury must judge, — it will avail them.

TRESPASS on the case for want of care by the defendants' servant in the management of their locomotive engine, whereby the plaintiff's mare and colt were killed. Plea, the general issue, and trial by jury, December Term, 1850, — Collamer, J., presiding.

On trial the plaintiff gave evidence tending to prove, that in July, 1849, he was the owner of a mare and colt, which were in the possession of his father, Colcord Quimby ; that Colcord Quimby resided on a farm in Sharon, through which the defendants' railroad was located and constructed ; that in constructing their railroad the de-

fendants had excavated a part of his barnyard, and he had erected
on that side a temporary fence of poles, which he regarded as sufficient; that the mare and colt were placed by Colcord Quimby in
this yard, and that, in his absence, they escaped through or over this
fence on to the defendants' railroad, where, through the neglect or
want of care of the defendants' engineer, in the management and
control of their locomotive engine, upon the railroad, the mare was
killed, and the colt was so injured, as to be of little or no value. No
evidence was introduced, tending to show the customary and usual
conduct and practice in the management of locomotive engines and
trains under similar circumstances.

The defendants gave in evidence the record. of the proceedings
and judgment of the county court, upon an appeal taken by Chester
Baxter from the decision of the commissioners for appraising the
damages. occasioned by the location of the defendants' railroad
through the farm in question, — of which Baxter was then the owner,
and which had since been purchased of Baxter by Colcord Quimby, —
from which it appeared, that commissioners were appointed by the
county court to re-appraise the damages, and that they reported that
they assessed the damages to said Baxter at $650.00, upon the repre-
sentation of the defendants, among other things, that good and sufficient fences would be built and maintained by the defendants upon
both sides of the railroad, but that, in case such fences were not to
be built and maintained by the defendants, then the farther sum of
$540.40 should be added to the assessment, for the purpose of build-
ing and keeping in repair suitable fences, as the land-owner should
choose, upon the line of the road through the farm; and it appeared
by the record, that the county court, November term, 1847, rendered
judgment in favor of Baxter, upon the report, for the amount of both
sums, with interest, — being in the whole $1,304.24. The defendants
also gave evidence tending to prove, that their engineer was using
diligence and care at the time the plaintiff's mare was killed.

The plaintiff gave evidence tending to prove, that immediately
after the rendition of the judgment of the county court, evidenced
by the record above mentioned, the defendants commenced proceedings at law and in chancery, by which the collection thereof, of the
defendants, was superseded and enjoined, and so remained until
June, 1850, when a settlement was effected between the defendants
and Baxter, and the amount of the judgment was paid to him by the
defendants, except a sum agreed to be discounted therefrom.

The plaintiff requested the court to charge the jury, that it was the
duty of the defendants, by their servants to exercise the highest degree of care, and to erect and maintain a sufficient fence upon the

line of their road, to prevent animals from passing from the adjoining land on to the railroad.

The defendants requested the court to charge the jury; — 1. That under and by virtue of the said appeal and proceedings, judgment and execution thereon, the duty of making and maintaining the whole fence, through the farm in question, along the railroad, devolved upon Baxter and his grantees of the farm, and that the defendants were absolved from any liability or duty to make or maintain the fence. 2. That the owner of the farm was bound to make and keep such a fence, as would have kept the mare and colt from the railroad; and that, if they escaped from his inclosure on to the railroad, over or through the said line of fence, it was at his own risk, and the plaintiff was not entitled to recover in this action for the injury, which happened to them in consequence of their so being upon the railroad. 3. That if the court should hold, that the owner of the premises and the defendants were under equal obligation to make and maintain a sufficient fence along the railroad, through said premises, each one half, yet, if the mare and colt came upon the railroad for want of such sufficient fence to restrain them, the plaintiff was not entitled to recover. 4. That the defendants were bound to exercise only ordinary care, such as is ordinary and customary in the use and management of such engines and trains on railroads generally; and unless the defendants were shown not to have exercised that kind and degree of care in this instance, they were not liable in this action. 5. That if the accident occurred in any part or degree through any negligence or fault on the part of the plaintiff, through his father, who was keeping and had care of the mare and colt, or through any fault of said animals, the plaintiff was not entitled to recover.

The court charged the jury, that in July, 1849, before the judgment of the county court, above mentioned, was paid, it was no more the duty of the defendants than of Colcord Quimby to erect and maintain a fence between the adjoining lands possessed by them respectively, — the same being the duty of both; that the defendants were bound, in the direction, management, and control of their locomotive engine, by their engineer and servant, running on their railroad, to the exercise of ordinary prudence and care, such as a man of ordinary prudence and care would exercise in such business and service, — such, for instance, as a man of ordinary prudence would use, who was the owner of both the road and the mare; and that, if the jury found, that there was a neglect, by the defendants' engineer, of that degree of care in the management and control of the defendants' locomotive engine, and thereby the plaintiff's mare was killed, the plaintiff was entitled to recover; but that, if they found that ordinary care was exercised by the engineer, their verdict should be for the defendants.

Verdict for plaintiff. Exceptions by defendants.

Tracy, Converse & Barrett, for defendants.

The defendants were in no legal fault, in respect to the fence. The statute being silent on the subject, the parties stand on common-law rights and liabilities. At common law adjoining owners are not obliged to fence, but each is bound to keep his beasts from the other's close. 3 Kent, 438; 5 Greenl. 356; 4 N. H. 36; 6 Mass. 90; Vin. Ab., Fences A.; Dyer, 372, *b.*

All legal and equitable duty was taken from the defendants by the award, appeal, and judgment, made part of the case. The grantee of Baxter is in privity of estate and interest, and bound by the proceedings affecting the premises, the same as Baxter, had he remained the owner. The best that could be said for the plaintiff is, that the beasts were there by the mutual fault of the parties; the plaintiff, being implicated and chargeable with that fault, cannot recover for an injury, to which that fault contributed. Flower v. Adam, 2 Taunt. 314; Cogswell v. Baldwin, 15 Vt. 404; Washburn v. Tracy, 2 D. Ch. 128; Noyes v. Morristown, 1 Vt. 353; Briggs v. Guilford, 8 Vt. 264. Even if it were the defendants' duty to build the fence, it does not follow that the plaintiff could put his beasts in a yard insufficient to restrain them, regardless of the danger of their escaping and exposing themselves to injury, and thus cast the whole hazard of damage upon the defendants. Under the evidence it should have been submitted to the jury, whether the plaintiff was in fault in putting the beasts into that yard, and whether that contributed to the happening of the injury.

The defendants were entitled to the charge asked in the fourth request. The managing of an engine and train requires and combines scientific and practical skill, and under the state of circumstances and incidents often occurring and likely to occur, becomes matter of rule and usage, to be applied and followed as the emergency may require. The idea of exercising *common and ordinary* care involves the necessity of doing, in the given case, as is commonly and ordinarily done in similar circumstances. The plaintiff, alleging the want of care, must show affirmatively all that is necessary to enable the jury to determine the truth of the allegation. This can only be done, by showing what facts constitute and indicate care, under the circumstances.

The illustration, explaining and applying the rule, was an extraordinary one, and tended to mislead the jury.

W. C. French, for plaintiff.

1. Whatever may have been the relation between Baxter and the defendants, it does not affect the plaintiff; he can only enforce his remedy against the defendants, and they must seek their remedy over, if they have any, against Baxter.

2. In July, 1849, at the time of this accident, the defendants had no right to the land appropriated to their use across the premises of the plaintiff's father, and were mere trespassers; as such, they were liable for all the consequences of their acts. Bloodgood *v.* Mohawk and Hudson Railroad Co. 18 Wend. 9; Presb. Soc. *v.* Auburn and Rochester Railroad Co. 3 Hill, 567; Dater *v.* Troy Turnp. and Railroad Co. 2 Hill, 629; Acts of 1843, pp. 43 – 46, § 7.

3. Even if the defendants had done all that was legally required of them by their charter, to become legally possessed of the land, it was their duty to have fenced the road for the protection of the public. We do not claim this by virtue of any statute, but under the well-known principle of the common law, that a man must so use his own property and rights, as not to interfere with the rights of others. 1 Sw. Dig. 552; 2 H. Bl. 350.

4. The statute in relation to division fences does not apply to such cases. The defendants' charter differs from the New York charters. It is very doubtful, whether the legislature intended to convey, by this charter, a fee in the land; most probably the intention was simply to convey an easement. 4 Paige, 553.

5. The charge in reference to the degree of care required was in accordance with the defendants' request, except the illustration, which makes more in favor of the defendants, than of the plaintiff. A case might occur, where the defendants would be liable under the general principle, as stated, but not under its illustration.

6. The plaintiff was not bound to introduce evidence as to the custom and practice of railroad corporations, in the management of trains. The question of negligence is always one of fact; and it was distinctly submitted to the jury. Leicester *v.* Pittsford, 6 Vt. 245.

7. The defendants were not entitled to the charge asked in the fifth request. There was no evidence tending to prove any negligence on the part of the plaintiff's father. The plaintiff could only be holden to the exercise of ordinary care. If the plaintiff were in some fault, it does not dispense with the exercise of such care, as the law requires, on the part of the defendants. Butterfield *v.* Forrister, 11 East, 60; 2 Taunt. 314; 1 Sw. Dig. 550; 4 Paige, 553; 2 D. Ch. 128.

The opinion of the court was delivered by

REDFIELD, J. 1. The court have not deemed it · necessary to go into the inquiry, in this case, whether, upon the facts stated in the bill of exceptions, the defendants' right to the land, where the injury occurred, had so vested, that they might rightfully occupy the same· The very action pre-supposes, that the company were rightfully occupying the land; else the action must be *trespass*, and not *case*.

2. ·In regard to the obligation to fence the land, we think the rule adopted by the court below was as favorable as the defendants could ask. That is treating them as owners in fee of adjoining lands. This is the view taken of the subject by the New York courts. In the railroad charters in that State it is provided, that the company may take *the fee* of the land. The charter of the defendants' company, although copied, in the main, from the New York charters, adopts different language, as to the defendants title,— only saying, that they shall be " seised and possessed of the land ; " that is, seised of such an estate as is necessary for their uses, — a right of way. This form of expression seems to have been adopted by design, and with a view to .limit the estate of the company strictly to their necessities. Indeed, we do not well see, how the legislature could assume to vest in the company any greater estate than their necessities required.

This being so, then the general laws of the State, as to adjoining land-owners, would not apply, and the defendants' charter being silent in regard to the obligation to fence, it becomes a question of reason and justice, growing out of the relations of the parties. And in this view it would seem, that no two persons could give different answers to the inquiry. The company have taken a strip through the land. Shall the proprietor have only the value of the estate taken from him, without regard to the form in which it is taken, the form in which it leaves the remainder, and the risk of losses and the necessity of fencing? ·An affirmative answer to such an inquiry would be not a little startling to the moral sense! The truth is, the *expense* of fencing rests primarily upon the company, — whether as a part of the land damages, or as a necessary precaution to running their engines, with safety, as is said by the Chancellor of New York in the matter of the Rensselaer and Saratoga Railroad Co. 4 Paige, 553, is immaterial. And whether the whole expense of fencing is to be assessed in the land damages, as was done in this case, or half, as was held in the last case cited, or none at all on the ground, that, from the necessity of the case, the obligation to fence must rest upon the company, is not necessary now to inquire. It is sufficient to say, that, until the company had either built the fence, or paid the land. owner for doing it, a sufficient length of time to enable him to do it, we do not think, that the mere fact, that cattle get upon the road from the lots adjoining, is any ground of imputing negligence to the owners of the cattle.

3. We think, then, there being no testimony in the case tending to show want of ordinary care on the part of the plaintiff, in regard to the horses injured, the court properly refused to charge upon that point.

4. The charge in other respects seems to have been altogether unobjectionable, and the illustration not objectionable, so far as the defendants are concerned. If the jury had given a verdict for the defendants, it might have been more questionable. That illustration is one, which has often occurred to me, as applicable to the ordinary cases of injuries to property, through alleged want of care, and in most cases just. It is but requiring one to do by others, as he would in the same circumstances do by himself, or wish others to do by him. It is but a paraphasis upon the exposition of Jones in his treatise on Bailments, where he defines common diligence to be that degee of diligence, which common men exercise in their own affairs. But we do not think the illustration entirely applicable to the present subject, — for the reason stated at the bar, that the company might, as matter of expediency, choose to endanger the life of their own beast, rather than check their train. But if they did that to another's property, they should make good all loss to the owner and to all others injured by such rashness. But this is matter of which the plaintiff, only, has reason to complain.

5. We do not think it was incumbent upon the plaintiff, in opening his case, to show, that by the laws of railroad companies, the defendants were guilty of want of ordinary care. If he saw fit to trust that question to the good sense and judgment of the jury, he might. It is not one of those mere scientific subjects, whose laws, like that of botany and geology, or medicine, or surgery, are matters of settled principle and accurate knowledge. If the defendants desired the benefit of the rules of engineering for their exculpation, they might show the custom ; and if not unreasonable, of which the jury must judge, it would avail them.

There being no error in the case, the judgment is affirmed.

OLIVER CURTIS *v.* THE VERMONT CENTRAL RAILROAD COMPANY.[1]

Second Circuit, June Term, 1851.

Merger of Contract — Right of Recovery for Performance of Contract after Merger.

The defendants, a railroad corporation, agreed with the plaintiff, that they would pay him four shillings per rod for constructing the fence upon each side of their railroad through the land of the plaintiff, according to a specified plan. Subsequently the plaintiff having appealed from the decision of the commissioners assessing the land damages for the crossing of his land by the railroad, commissioners were appointed by the county court, who, after appraising the damages to the land, reported, that an additional sum of one dollar per rod should be allowed to the plaintiff, for the purpose of building and keeping in repair such suitable fences on the line of the road over his land, as he might elect, unless such fences were to be built and maintained by the defendants. Upon this report being returned, the plaintiff took judgment for the full amount of the appraisal, including the allowance for fences, and the amount of the judgment was paid by the defendants. *Held,* that the judgment upon the report must be regarded as a merger of the previous contract made by the parties for the construction of the fence.

And the plaintiff having proceeded, subsequent to the rendition of the judgment, and constructed the fence according to the contract, it was held, that he was not entitled to recover of the defendants the difference between the contract price and the actual value of the fence to him for farming purposes, although he proved, that the fence so constructed by him under the contract was not such as he should have built for himself upon the line of the road through his farm, for his farming purposes, but that he would have built different fence, which would have been no more expensive, and would have been more durable and worth at least thirty cents a rod more than the fence constructed by him under the contract.

BOOK ACCOUNT. The suit was commenced in the county of Windsor. Judgment to account was rendered in the county court, and an auditor was appointed, who reported the facts substantially as follows.

The plaintiff's account was for building one hundred and eighty-five rods of fence, at four shillings per rod. It appeared, that on the tenth day of August, 1847, the plaintiff contracted with the defendants, that he would construct the fence upon both sides of their railroad through his land, according to a specified plan of construction, for the price of four shillings per rod, and that the fence was built by the plaintiff, according to the contract. The commissioners originally appointed to appraise the land damages occasioned by the location of the railroad of the defendants having appraised the damages to the plaintiff at $350, the plaintiff appealed, and commissioners were appointed by the county court, who reported, that they examined the premises, October 19, 1847, and that they appraised the damages to the plaintiff, occasioned by the location of the railroad across his land, at $450, upon a representation by the agents of the defendants, among other things, that good and sufficient fences would be built and maintained by the defendants upon both sides of their railroad, but that, in case such fences were not to be built and maintained by the defendants, a farther sum of $180, should be added to their appraisal, " for the purpose of building and keeping in repair such suitable fences, on the line of said railroad over the land [of the plaintiff] as the owner of said land may elect;" and that interest should be added, upon both sums, from October 13, 1846. At the November Term, 1847, of the county court, this report was accepted, and judgment was rendered in favor of the plaintiff for the full amount of both sums assessed by the commissioners, with the interest, and execution was thereupon issued, and the amount of the judgment was paid by the defendants. The fence built by the plaintiff, and mentioned in the contract made in August between the parties, was constructed upon both sides of the railroad upon the same land mentioned in the report of the commissioners above referred to. The plaintiff proved, that the fence, so built by him under the contract of August 10, 1847, was not such as he should have built for himself on the sides of the railroad through his farm, for his farming purposes, at his own expense and on his own plan, without regard to the contract, but that he should have built different fence, which would have been far more durable, and less likely to decay and become out of repair, while it would not have been any more expensive, and that the fence, which he should have built for his farming purposes, on his own plan, would have been worth at least thirty cents *per* rod more than the fence built according to the contract; and that he commenced preparing the materials for the fence, built by him under the contract, before the commissioners appointed by the county court made their examination and appraisal, and had made considerable progress in the preparation of materials. The auditor submitted to the court the question as to the plaintiff's right of recovery upon these facts.

The county court, December Term, 1850, — COLLAMER, J., presiding, — decided, that the plaintiff was entitled to recover the difference of thirty cents per rod between the value of the fence built by him and such as he would have built for himself, as reported by the auditor. Exceptions by defendants.

Tracy, Converse & Barrett, for the defendants.

If the defendants were bound to make the fence, they have so done, under the contract with the plaintiff, and have paid him therefor, and more than the price stipulated in the contract, viz., $180, for 185 rods of fence, and interest from Oct. 13, 1846. If the company were not bound to make the fence, independently of the contract, yet they have made it, by the plaintiff, under the contract, and the plaintiff has received his pay, and more than the stipulated price. In either case, the form and mode of enforcing the payment cannot alter the legal effect of the fact of the payment. Although the plaintiff has thought proper, indirectly, and through the machinery of an award of commissioners and a judgment of court, to enforce the payment, yet it is a payment, and for the very subject-matter of the contract. Granting that the fence built under the contract was not worth so much by thirty cents per rod, as the fence the plaintiff would have built at the same expense without regard to the contract, the county court erred in allowing a recovery. The plaintiff has already received payment, more than thirty cents per rod above the contract price. The making of the award and enforcing it was a proceeding *in invitum*, as against the defendants, and wholly within the control of the plaintiff. His accepting and enforcing the award must be treated as showing his assent to treat the fencing the same as if no contract had been made. That the plaintiff has built such a fence, as is described in the contract, is no fault of the defendants. He did it so at his own option, having elected to take the judgment for the larger sum.

J. S. Marcy, for the plaintiff.

The fence built under the contract became the sole property of the defendants, as soon as completed. They have the entire control of it, and may at any time remove it, or otherwise render it useless to the plaintiff; wherefore they ought to pay the plaintiff the whole price agreed for it, and are legally bound to do so. But if (as was supposed by the court below) the fence is legally the joint property of the parties, and is therefore to remain where it is for the benefit of both, while it lasts, yet the plaintiff has, in law and in equity, a claim to recover the thirty cents per rod difference in value. The allowance by the appeal commissioners, on account of the fence, was not for the fence in question, nor any particular fence; but the allowance was made upon the ground, that the plaintiff, in consequence of the road's passing through his land, was subjected to the necessity of maintaining " such fence as he should elect " through all future time; and the auditor's report shows, the plaintiff could, and would, (without regard to the contract,) have built a fence no more expensive

than this, while it would equally, if not better, have subserved his
farming purposes, and would have been worth thirty cents *per* rod
more than this. Although the defendants, as between them and the
plaintiff, are not bound to maintain a fence, yet by their promise to
pay, the plaintiff has been induced to build a fence according to a
plan and of a quality prescribed by the defendants, which cost, and
for which they agreed to pay, more than it is worth to the plaintiff;
and, as an unavoidable consequence, unless he recover the difference
between the agreed price and the value of the fence to him, he suffers
a loss equal to that difference, although the defendants should permit
the fence to remain, and the plaintiff to have the benefit of it, while
it lasts.

The opinion of the court was delivered by

REDFIELD, J. This is an action of book account, in which the
plaintiff seeks to recover for building fence upon his own land,
through which the defendants' road runs, by virtue of a special contract with the defendants, dated August 10, 1847. In October, 1847,
and before the plaintiff had built the fence, the parties had a hearing
before the appeal commissioners for appraising land damages, and
the plaintiff obtained a hypothetical report for the amount of the
expense of building and maintaining the same fence, which he had
contracted with the defendants to build at four shillings per rod, at
one dollar per rod. At the November Term, 1847, of the county
court, the plaintiff obtained judgment for the full sum reported; which
he has since collected.

The plaintiff, subsequently to the rendition of the judgment, finished building the fence according to the previous contract made
with the defendants, and proved, on the trial, that he might, at the
same cost, have built a fence worth thirty cents a rod more for his
purposes, if he had not built it in conformity with the contract. He
now seeks to recover the agreed price of the fence, or else the difference between that and its value to him.

We think, the judgment on the report must be regarded as a merger of the contract. Any other view of the subject involves, it seems
to us, very manifest absurdities. If one is not to recover pay twice
for the same thing, then it is clear the plaintiff ought not to recover
the *full price.*

And it seems to us, that the claim of thirty cents a rod is a most
remarkable claim to be allowed in this form of action, and under the
state of facts involved in the present case.

·1. It seems to have been altogether at the suggestion and against
the will of the defendants, that the plaintiff obtained an adjudication,

imposing upon him the burden of maintaining the fence. 2. After that judgment, the contract was no longer subsisting, and the plaintiff was in reality building the fence for himself, and might build it as he chose. It was his own folly to build it according to the contract, unless that was the best mode of building it. 3. It seems a rather remarkable asking to have pay for the difference between the *value* and the *agreed price* of a fence, which the plaintiff himself built, if there was nothing more in the case. But it is supposable, this might occur in consequence of the fence being built upon some defective model, or of unsuitable materials. But that does not appear in the case, but only the bare fact of the difference is stated.

But the two former grounds are to us altogether invincible. We think, that if the plaintiff, under the circumstances, could satisfy himself that he was really building this fence for the defendants, he must certainly possess a very remarkable moral sense. And we are not surprised, that the counsel felt compelled to admit, that he considered the claim somewhat inequitable, and altogether *strictissimi juris.* And the claim for the thirty cents a rod seems to be a claim for special damage for building his own fence in a particular form, which the plaintiff mistakenly felt compelled to do, in consequence of a contract, which had been merged by a judgment obtained at the solicitation of the plaintiff, against the earnest remonstrances, it may be safely presumed, of the defendants. The mere statement of the claim affords a sufficient answer to it.

Judgment reversed and judgment on the report for the defendants.

THE VERMONT CENTRAL RAILROAD COMPANY *v.* ESTATE OF ZERAH HILLS.[1]

Fourth Circuit, September Term, 1851.

Parol Evidence to Control Deed — What will pass by a Deed — Disturbance of Right — Appraisal of Damages by Railroad Commissioners.

A deed, absolute in its terms, cannot be controlled by oral evidence of conversation between the parties, previous to its execution.

---

[1] 23 Vermont Reports, 681.

A deed, which is absolute in its terms, and without conditions or reservations, will have the effect to convey the land described in it, with all the privileges of drawing water from other portions of the grantor's land, which were then in use, as appurtenant to the land.

And if water is conveyed in an aqueduct from a spring upon another portion of the grantor's land to the land conveyed, and there used at the time of the conveyance, any diversion of the water by the grantor, although upon that portion of his land not conveyed by the deed, will be a disturbance of the right of the grantee, for which an action may be sustained. The grantor cannot be allowed to say, in defence, that the grantee did not desire to use the water, or that he has suffered no detriment.

The defendant was the owner and occupant of a messuage, to which water was conducted, for use, by an aqueduct, from a spring upon another portion of his land, and the Vermont Central Railroad Company having located their railroad across the same, the commissioners were called upon to appraise the damages thereby occasioned to the defendant. At the hearing before the commissioners, the defendant stated, that he should use the water for the purpose of supplying a new house, which he contemplated erecting, and that the commissioners need not take the water into the account in assessing the damages. The president and engineer of the company were present, and heard this statement, and made no claim to the use of the water; and the water was not taken into consideration by the commissioners, in assessing the damages. The defendant received from the company the amount of damages assessed by the commissioners, and executed to the company an absolute deed of the premises, without condition or reservation. And it was held, that the right to use the water upon the premises passed by the deed.

THIS case was referred, under a rule from the county court of the county of Washington; and the referee reported the fact substantially as follows:

In 1846, Zerah Hills, now deceased, owned a building lot, with buildings thereon, in the village of Middlesex, through which lot the railroad of the Vermont Central Railroad Company was located. From about the year 1830, Hills had supplied the house upon the premises with water, brought in a wooden aqueduct a distance of about thirty rods. On the first day of April, 1839, Hills, by written lease, duly executed, granted to Jesse Johnson, Jr., who resided on the opposite side of the road, and southerly, from the house of Hills, the privilege of taking water for his house from Hills' penstock, when there should be a greater quantity of water run there, than what was necessary for the use of a family and barn on the premises of Hills, for the term of 999 years; and Hills bound himself not to take water between his house and the head of the aqueduct or spring, from where the water was taken, so as to deprive Johnson of the full privilege of the grant; and Johnson, having sold his premises to one McIntyre, afterwards duly assigned to McIntyre the lease. The Vermont Central Railroad Company, having located their railroad across the premises of Hills in such manner as to require the removal of the buildings, in the spring of 1846 called upon the commissioners, appointed for that purpose, to appraise the damage to Hills occasioned by such location. Hills appeared before the commissioners, and stated, among other things, to the commissioners, that he should use the water, then running there, for a new house, to be erected northerly of the one then standing there. The president and engineer of the company were present, and heard this statement, and made no claim to the water; and the water was not taken into consideration by the commissioners, in estimating the damages. Afterwards, on the sixteenth day of June, 1846, in consideration of receiving the amount of money awarded to him by the commissioners for the premises, the whole of the premises being taken by the company, Hills executed to the company a warrantee deed of the premises, without reservation or exception. Hills claimed to have the water reserved, but the agent of the company, who received the deed, would not do it, saying he knew nothing of such reservation, and that Hills must trust to their understanding of that matter and the good faith of the company. Soon after giving the deed, the water ceased to run in the aqueduct, by reason of its decay, to the premises so deeded, but was taken out at a point north of the leak, by all who used water from the aqueduct, until Hills diverted it, and conducted it to his new house, which was about thirty rods northerly of the premises deeded to the company. In the spring of 1848, Hills, having moved into the new house, took the water from the aquedect near that house, and conducted the water by a new aqueduct to the new house, and thence by a new route to the house of McIntyre. This diverting of the water is the injury sued for in this action. Hills died in September, 1848. During the summer of 1848, the company, having previously removed the house from the premises deeded to them by Hills, constructed their railroad through the premises, and in doing so excavated about twelve feet deep, in doing which they cut off and took out the old logs of the aqueduct, which they never offered to restore; nor have they ever repaired, or offered to repair the decayed part of the aqueduct, northerly of the railroad track, so as to have the water run to the premises, after it stopped in 1846. The company have all the while owned, and still own, a small dwelling-house, which stood on a lot adjoining to the premises deeded to them by Hills, which would be more accommodated and be of more value, if its occupants could get their water at the place where the old penstock stood on the premises deeded to the company by Hills. The company made no complaint to Hills, during his lifetime, in regard to what he had done, nor did they give any assent to it.

The County Court, May Term, 1850, — REDFIELD, J., presiding, — accepted the report, and rendered judgment thereon for the plaintiffs for one dollar damages. Exceptions by defendant.

J. A. Vail, for defendant.

1. The plaintiffs have no just claim to the water, for the reason, that it was not appraised by the commissioners. It was distinctly understood by the parties, that Hills was to have the water for his new house.

2. The spring, from which the water was taken, was upon another and distinct piece of land, which was not conveyed to the plaintiffs, and for that reason, the privilege of taking the water, or the spring, not being mentioned in the deed, the spring would not pass by the deed, and Hills might lawfully take water from it, or from the old aqueduct, for his new house. Manning *v.* Smith, 6 Conn. 289.

3. If the plaintiffs have a right to draw water from the spring for the use of one family, it was time enough for them to complain, when Hills refused to permit them to exercise the right. Hills had no notice, that the plaintiffs wanted or claimed the right to take water from the spring.

4. Hills virtually had a license from the plaintiffs to take the water, which was not countermanded in his lifetime.

Peck and *Colby*, for plaintiffs.

1. The plaintiffs acquired a right, by deed, to have the water conveyed across the defendant's land, in the aqueduct, to the premises purchased of the defendant, in the manner it had been done previous to the conveyance. Nichols *v.* Chamberlin, Cro. Jac. 121; Nitzell *v.* Paschal, 3 Rawle, 76.

2. As to the question of damages, — "if water is wrongfully diverted, from the plaintiff's mill, nominal damages may be recovered though no actual injury be proved." "An unoccupied mill has a value, which is under the protection of the law." 2 Hill, 133; Butman *v.* Hussey, Fairf. 407; Blanchard *v.* Baker, 8 Greenl. 268. But the referee finds actual injury, by diverting the water from the aqueduct.

By THE COURT. It is very obvious, that oral evidence of conversations between the parties, previous to the execution of the deed, cannot, in a court of law, be allowed to control the deed. The party must be content to abide by the deed, as he gave it. That is general, without condition, or reservation. We think it must have the effect to convey the land, with all the privileges of drawing water from other portions of the grantor's land, which were then in use, as appurtenant to the land. It would be wonderful, if this were not so, in ordinary cases of deeds of land with artificial ponds and aqueducts. It is admitted, such a right is acquired by fifteen years use.

If conveying the land would not convey the right, it would revert to the dominant proprietor, even after he had granted it away, or lost it by adverse use, which would be absurd. And even if the owner of the land had acquired no perfect right, it seems to us, that a general conveyance of the land, with all its privileges and appurtenances, the aqueduct being in use, would bind the grantor to defend the title to it, if he gave covenants of warranty, &c. And if so, then clearly, when he owned the spring, the right will pass by the deed. The case of Manning *v. Smith, 6 Conn. 289, is certainly very much in point, and if it were to be regarded as full authority, must certainly govern the present. But it seems to us opposed to the early English cases, and to have been decided upon too narrow ground, and not fully consonant to the soundest principles.

And the grantor, in the present case, having diverted the entire watercourse, it is not for him to say, that the plaintiffs did not desire to use it, or that they have suffered no detriment. They had the right to insist, that it should flow in its accustomed artificial channel, and any diversion, although not upon their land, is a disturbance of their rights, and in contemplation of law, affords a cause of action, the same as diverting the water from a natural stream subjects the party to an action, at the suit of all the proprietors below.

CASES

SUPREME COURT OF MASSACHUSETTS.

The Boston Water Power Company *v.* The Boston and Worcester Railroad Corporation *et al.*[1]

Suffolk Co., March Term, 1835.

Franchise, what constitutes — Conflicting Rights of Corporations — Nuisance — Parties to a Suit to restrain Railway Company from proceeding with its works.

In order to sustain a demurrer for want of jurisdiction, pleaded to the whole of a bill in equity, it must appear that no substantial and essential part of the complaint is within the equity jurisdiction of the Court.

The plaintiffs in a bill in equity praying for an injunction, allege that a corporation was authorized by its act of incorporation, to build a dam over an arm of the sea, (the shores of which were owned by individuals,) and from this main dam to certain upland above it to run a cross dam, so as to make on one side of the cross dam a full basin, and on the other an empty or receiving basin, and to cut raceways from the full basin to the receiving basin, and to use, sell, or lease the water power thus created; that the corporation erected the dams and created thereby a water power sufficient to turn twenty pairs of common mill-stones, and performed all the duties required of them by the legislature, and thereby became entitled to certain exclusive privileges; that the corporation, with the assent of the legislature, transferred all the water power and all their rights, privileges, and duties respecting the same, to the plaintiffs; that the plaintiffs thereby became entitled to the exclusive right and privilege of forever using the soil included within the limits of the full basin, for the purpose of flowing the same by the tide waters, and of keeping the soil included within the limits of the receiving basin uncovered by the tide waters, and of using it to receive and carry off the waters flowing from the full basin, and of holding and using all the water power which can be and is created by the dams, without any hindrance,

---

[1] 16 Pickering's Reports, 512.

obstruction, or diminution of the capacity of the basins, or of the right to cut raceways in the cross dam; and that the defendants, pretending to act under the authority of certain statutes, threaten to build a railroad through the basins and over the cross dam, and have actually commenced building the same by driving piles in both of the basins, and that the building of it will diminish the capacity of the basins and destroy two mill sites on the cross dam, whereby the water power will be diminished and the franchise of the plaintiffs abridged. It was *held*, that the right of using the land of others in the basins, for the purpose of creating water power, was a franchise or easement; that such a franchise or easement in the basins was sufficiently set forth in the bill; that the acts of the defendants in filling up portions of the basins for the purpose of making a railroad, were, if illegal, a disturbance of the plaintiffs in the enjoyment of their franchise, for which the remedy at law would be an action on the case; that such an injury is, in strict legal consideration, a nuisance, and therefore is within St. 1827, c. 88, giving this Court jurisdiction in equity in cases of nuisance; that it did not appear on the face of the bill, that the plaintiffs had an adequate and complete remedy at law, and that the matter of complaint was a more fit subject for a bill in equity.

To a bill in equity, in which it was alleged that the plaintiff was the owner of a water power, and that he had leased a part of it, and that the defendant had by a nuisance diminished the water power, the defendant demurred because the lessee was not made a party plaintiff; but as it did not appear on the face of the bill, that the interest of the lessee would be affected by the diminution of the water power, there being a surplus beyond the quantity leased, the demurrer was not sustained.

BILL in equity, filed in March, 1833, containing the following allegations.

By St. 1814, c. 39, divers persons were incorporated by the name of the Boston and Roxbury Mill Corporation, and by that statute and those of 1816, c. 40, 1819, c. 65, and 1822, c. 34, the corporation was authorized to purchase and hold real and personal estate; to build a dam from Charles street at the westerly end of Beacon street, in Boston, to Sewall's Point, in Brookline, so as to exclude the tide water and form a reservoir or receiving basin of the space between the dam and Boston Neck; to build another dam from Gravelly Point, in Roxbury, to the dam first mentioned, so as to inclose the tide water within Tide-Mill Creek; to cut any number of convenient raceways from the full basin to the receiving basin; to maintain and keep up all their works forever; and to lease or sell the right of using the water upon any terms and in any manner they might think proper; and it was provided, that no other person should have a right to dispose of the water, without the consent of the corporation. The corporation was authorized to make over the main dam a good and substantial road, and to receive toll for passing over it; and it was provided, that the legislature might suspend the right of taking toll until the dam should be so far completed as that mills could be established, employing a power equal to turning twenty pairs of common mill-stones, and until the corporation, or its assigns, should have erected mills employing a power equal to ten pairs. It was further provided, that any person sustaining any damage by the building of the dams, or from the exercise of any of the powers given to the corporation, might apply to the Court of Common Pleas for the county in which the land lies, for a committee to estimate the damage, &c. Certain duties and obligations in favor of the public, set forth at large in the bill, were imposed upon the corporation, and certain penalties and forfeitures created to secure the performance of its undertakings.

These acts were accepted by the corporation, whereby a contract conformable to the terms of the acts, was created between the corporation and the Commonwealth.

This contract was performed on the part of the corporation, by the erection of the works required, being works of great magnitude and expense, and of great public convenience and utility, wholly constructed out of the private funds of the corporation, and since maintained at great expense in like manner, and a water power was created sufficient for the turning of twenty pairs of common mill-stones, and mills were erected employing a power equal to turning ten pairs, and all the other duties and obligations imposed by the statutes were performed; and thereby the corporation became entitled to the exclusive right and privilege of forever using the soil included within the limits of the full basin, for the purpose of flowing and keeping the same covered with water to the height and extent of surface to which the tide naturally flowed the lands surrounding the basin before the building of the dam, and also the exclusive right and privilege of forever keeping the soil included within the limits of the receiving basin free from, and uncovered by the tide waters, and of using the same as and for a reservoir or receiving basin to receive and carry off the waters flowing from the full basin through the raceways cut, or which should thereafter be cut, through the cross dam, and the exclusive right and privilege of cutting raceways through any part of the cross dam, and of using or disposing of the water power thereby created by lease or otherwise; and the corporation, relying upon this contract, erected and put in operation mills requiring a quantity of water equal at all times to the turning of three pairs of common mill-stones, and leased, on long terms yet unexpired, the privilege of drawing water equal to the turning of fourteen pairs of common mill-stones, receiving from the lessees valuable rents, liable to be suspended or lost by insufficiency of water power, and the lessees erected and put in operation mills using the whole water power so granted to them.

The complainants were incorporated by the name of the Boston Water Power Company, on June 12, 1824, (St. 1824, c. 26,) with power to purchase and hold any quantity of the water power created

23 *

by the establishment of the dams above mentioned.· They accepted the act of incorporation, and entered into an indenture dated May 9, 1832, (and which is made a part of the bill,) between themselves and the Boston and Roxbury Mill Corporation.

By this indenture the Boston and Roxbury Mill Corporation made a division of their property, retaining the main dam for the purpose of the road, and covenanting to keep it in repair except as to the gates and sluices, and, for the sum of 175,000 dollars,·transferring to the plaintiffs all the grantors' right to the land on the south side of (above) this dam, and all the water power, and ˜all their privileges, contracts, duties, and obligations respecting the water power; and the plaintiffs allege that they thereby, so far as regards the water power, became entitled to the exclusive right and privilege of forever using the soil included within the two basins, for the purposes before mentioned, and to all the water power which can be and is created by the constructing and maintaining of the dams, without any hindrance, obstruction, interruption, or diminution of the capacity of the full and receiving basins respectively, and to all the exclusive rights and privileges above mentioned as belonging to the Boston and Roxbury Mill Corporation.

But the Boston and Worcester Railroad Corporation, which has no funds to respond to damages recovered at law, except such as are raised by assessments limited to the expense of constructing their railroad, and incidental expenses, and the South Cove Corporation, and other persons, confederating together under various groundless pretences, deny and disregard these vested rights, and openly threaten to build a railroad through the full basin, and over the cross dam, and through the receiving basin, and have actually commenced building the same by driving piles in both of the basins ; and have taken for their road a strip of twenty-six feet wide through the full basin, and five rods wide through the receiving basin.

The building of the railroad over the cross dam destroys two valuable mill sites, and takes away the right of cutting raceways in that part of it. The construction of the railroad through the full basin will directly diminish its capacity, and will also obstruct the flow of water to the southerly part of it. In ordinary tides, the receiving basin is now just sufficient in capacity to hold all the water which flows from the full basin, until its escape by the ebb tide, without throwing back-water on the mills, and, in neap tides, is now insufficient, and back-water is actually created ; the space taken for the railroad is nine acres and upwards, and a great part of it is to be filled up with solid embankment, which will greatly diminish the capacity of the basin, and so increase the back-water. The building of the railroad, therefore, through and across the two basins and cross dam, will greatly diminish the water power, and abridge the franchise vested in the complainants, of using the soil and space between their main dam and Boston Neck for their basins, to their irreparable injury, and so far as their rights are concerned, will be a nuisance.

The pretences of the Boston and Worcester Railroad Corporation are, that they are authorized by their act of incorporation and the acts. additional thereto, to locate and construct their railroad in or near Boston and thence to Worcester, in such manner and form as they should think expedient, and that as they thought it expedient to adopt this location, they are justified in it; and that the public necessity and convenience requiring this location, the legislature might authorize it, notwithstanding the prior grant of the franchise now owned by the complainants.

The bill concludes with a prayer for a perpetual injunction and other relief.

The act incorporating the Boston and Roxbury Mill Corporation, and the several acts in addition thereto, and the act incorporating the Boston Water Power Company, are made a part of the complainants' bill.

The Boston and Worcester Railroad Corporation demur to the bill, assigning for cause, that this Court has not jurisdiction by the statutes of the Commonwealth, or otherwise; that the lessees named in the bill are not made parties thereto; and that the complainants have not stated such a case as entitles them to relief.

Greenleaf. Fletcher, and *F. Dexter*, in support of the demurrer, contended that the lessees of the water power were interested in the subject-matter of the bill, as it stated that in neap tides the power is not sufficient for the present mills, and they ought therefore to have been made parties, in order that the judgment might conclude all persons. London v. Richmond, 2 Vern. 422; Penn v. Baltimore, Ridgw. 335; West v. Randall, 2 Mason, 189; Cornish v. Gest, 2 Cox, 27; 3 Swanston, 139, 150, notes; Poore v. Clark, 2 Atk. 515; Green v. Poole, 5 Bro. P. C. 504; Elmendorp. v. Taylor, 10 Wheat. 166; Mallow v. Hinde, 12 Wheat. 197; Hallett v. Hallett, 2 Paige, 15; St. 1833, c. 187; Ellis v. Welch, 6 Mass. R. 251; Boston and Roxbury Mill Corp. v. Gardner, 2 Pick. 33; Mitf. Pl. 133, 146; Brown v. Ricketts, 3 Johns. Ch. R. 553; Wiser v. Blachly, 1 Johns. Ch. R. 437; Davoue v. Fanning, 4 Johns. Ch. R. 199.

This case does. not come within the St. 1827, c. 88, giving the Court power to " hear and determine in equity, any matter touching waste or nuisance, in which there is not a plain, adequate, and complete remedy at law." It is not a case of nuisance, but of trespass *quare clausum fregit.* The question is not whether a court having full chancery power would interfere, but whether the bill presents a case of nuisance *at common law.* And the criterion of this is, whether the remedy at law would be by an action of the case, or an action of trespass; if *trespass* will lie, *case* will not, and the cause of action is not a nuisance. 3 Bl. Com. 216, c. 13; Com. Dig. Action on the case, B. 8. The basins are the complainants' *close;* St. 1814, c. 39, § 2; the complainants have, as they allege, the exclusive right to the soil, for the purpose of creating water power; and so it was determined in the case of Boston and Roxbury Mill Corporation *v.* Newman, 12 Pick. 467; and this is sufficient to enable them to maintain trespass *quare clausum* against a party who enters upon the soil and with direct force interferes immediately (not consequentially) with the water power. In Clap *v.* Draper, 4 Mass. R. 268, Parsons, C. J., says, " It appears to be a principle of law well settled, that where a man has a separate interest in the soil for a particular use, although the right of soil is not in him, if he be injured in the enjoyment of his particular use of the soil, he may maintain trespass *quare clausum fregit."* And this is the doctrine from the time of the Year Books. 1 Rol. Abr. 105, pl. 6; Co. Lit. 4 *b.*; Ashmead *v.* Ranger, 2 Salk. 638; The King *v.* Watson, 5 East, 486; Welden *v.* Bridgewater, Cro. Eliz. 421; Burt *v.* Moore, 5 T. R. 329; Wilson *v.* Macreth, 3 Burr. 1824; Crosby *v.* Wadsworth, 6 East, 602; Harker *v.* Birkbeck, 3 Burr. 1563; White *v.* Moseley, 8 Pick, 356; Shapcott *v.* Mugford, 1 Ld. Raym. 188; Reynolds *v.* Clarke, 2 Ld. Raym. 1403; Wilson *v.* Smith, 10 Wendell, 324; Stewart *v.* Doughty, 9 Johns. R. 113; Austin *v.* Sawyer, 9 Cowen, 39; Tompkinson *v.* Russell, 9 Price, 287; 2 Saund. Pl. and Evid. 867; Rehoboth *v.* Hunt, 1 Pick. 224; Dyer, 285 *b.*; Erie &c., Turnpike *v.* Cochran, 2 Hall's Law Journal, 88; Smith *v.* Rutherford, 2 Serg. & Rawle, 360; Cotteral *v.* Cummins, 6 Serg. & Rawle, 349; Dyson *v.* Collick, 5 Barn. & Ald. 600; 2 Rol. Abr. 545, pl. 1; 1 Wms.'s Saund. 24, note 1.

Admitting that the facts alleged show a nuisance, still the complainants cannot maintain a bill in equity, because they have a plain, adequate, and complete remedy at law; for past damages, by compensation in money, for prospective, by abatement of the nuisance. Charles River Bridge *v.* Warren Bridge, 6 Pick. 395, 397; Messiter *v.* Wright, *ante,* 151; Fishmongers' Co. *v.* East India Co. 1 Dickens, 164; New York *v.* Mapes, 6 Johns. Ch. R. 46; Jerome *v.* Ross, 7 Johns. Ch. R. 315; Newburgh Turnp. Co. *v.* Miller, 5 Johns. Ch. R. 101.

J. Mason and *C. G. Loring,* for the plaintiffs. The acts of the legislature respecting the Boston and Roxbury Mill Corporation and the

.Boston Water Power Company, are a part of the bill, and taken in connection with the rest of the bill, they show a possessory right to the soil so far as to allow the erection of the dams, and for an injury to them the plaintiffs may maintain trespass; but to the soil in the basins the plaintiffs have no right, except for the purpose of maintaining a water power, by using one of them for a full basin, and the other for a receiving basin; in other words, they have only an easement in the basins.

In the statute under which the bill is brought, the word *nuisance* is used in a popular sense. 3 Bl. Comm. 5, 216, 218. A continued trespass is a nuisance. But we contend, that from the nature of the plaintiffs' property, the facts alleged present a technical nuisance.. They show an injury to an easement or incorporeal hereditament, for which the remedy at common law is *case*, and not *trespass*. Com. Dig. Action on the case for disturbance, A 2; Cook v. Hull, 3 Pick 269; Baker v. Sanderson, 3 Pick. 348; Sumner v. Tileston, 7 Pick. 198; Fiske v. Framingham Manuf. Co. 12 Pick. 68; Boston and Roxbury Mill Corp. v. Newman, 12 Pick. 467; Challenor v. Thomas, Yelv. 143; Monckton v. Pashley, 2 Ld. Raym. 974; Wetmore v. Robinson, 2 Connect. R. 529.

If the acts of the defendants do not constitute a nuisance at common law, they do in equity, and the rules of equity are to be resorted to in construing the statute under which the bill is brought. Jeremy on Eq. Jurisd. 310; Coulsoun v. White, 3 Atk. 21; Eden on Injunctions, 163; Mitchell v. Dors, 6 Ves. 147; Hanson v. Gardiner, 7 Ves. 305; Mogg v. Mogg, 2 Dickens, 670. Injuries to watercourses are a well-known subject of chancery interference in England, on the ground of nuisance, and the legislature must be supposed to have referred to them in this statute. Lane v. Newdigate, 10 Ves. 194; Robinson v. Byron, 1 Bro. C. C. 588; Gardner v. Newburgh, 2 Johns. Ch. R. 162; Chalk v. Wyatt, 3 Meriv. 688; Van Bergen v. Van Bergen, 3 Johns. Ch. R. 282; Angell on Watercourses, 21 to 28.

The plaintiffs have not an adequate remedy at law. The injury will be irreparable. Jeremy on Eq. Jurisd. 310, 424; Crowder v. Tinkler, 19 Ves. 622; Att. Gen. v. Nichol, 16 Ves. 342; Bathurst v.. Burden, 2 Bro. C. C. 64; Charles River Bridge v. Warren Bridge, 6 Pick. 396, 397, 398.

It does not appear by the bill, that the rights of the lessees will be affected by the acts of the defendants, and the Court therefore will not call them in on demurrer to the bill for want of parties.. Townsend v. Auger, 3 Connect. R. 354; Wendell v. Van Rensselaer, 1 Johns. Ch. R. 349; Wiser v. Blachly, 1 Johns. Ch. R. 437. And it was not necessary to join them in the bill, as their interests are represented by

those who are made plaintiffs.   Adair v. New River Co. 11 Ves. 429 ;
Wilkins v. Fry, 1 Meriv. 244.

SHAW, C. J., delivered the opinion of the Court. Both parties in
the present controversy are incorporated companies, claiming rights
under several acts of the legislature, professing to have one common
design and purpose, that of promoting public improvements; and as
the powers respectively claimed by them, under the acts and grants
of the sovereign authority of the State, have come into conflict, it
becomes necessary for the Court to decide between them. Two
general questions naturally present themselves for consideration;
namely, what those rights are, and whether the remedy now sought
by the complainants, in the form of a suit in equity, is the proper
mode of redress. Upon the preliminary objection taken to the jurisdiction of the Court as a court of equity, by a general demurrer to the
bill, the latter question alone is now open; but as the form of the
remedy must essentially depend upon the nature of the rights violated, both questions must, to a certain extent, be considered. The
direct question is, whether this Court has jurisdiction of the cause,
under the statute vesting in this Court the powers of a court of
equity, in all cases of waste and nuisance. St. 1827, c. 88. The
authority is to " hear. and determine in equity any matter touching
waste or nuisance, in which there is not a plain, adequate, and complete remedy at law."

Several grounds are taken by the complainants, to show that the
subject-matter of their complaint is within the true meaning and construction of the statute, and so is within the jurisdiction of the Court
as a court of equity ; one of which is, that it is technically and strictly
a nuisance, at common law, that the legal remedy for the injury done
to their rights, by the acts complained of, would be an action on the
case, and not an action of trespass, and therefore that the equity
jurisdiction of the Court extends to and embraces it, by the plain
words of the statute.

It may be proper, by way of preliminary remark, to state, that as
this is a general demurrer to the bill, in order to sustain it, it must
appear that no substantial and essential part of the complaint is
within the provisions of the statute.[1]   And, therefore, if the plaintiffs
set forth mixed rights, consisting in part, of a right of soil, and of
possession, in certain parts of the land described in their bill, as those
upon which their dams and permanent structures are erected, in order

---

[1] See Livingston v. Story, 9 Peters, Supr. C. Rep. 633.

to pen up the water, and use and appropriate it to the purposes of creating and maintaining mill powers, and in part, of a franchise and easement, consisting in a right to have the water flow freely and unobstructed over other lands, and the acts complained of are an injury to both these rights, the demurrer cannot be sustained, because the injury to the easement and incorporeal hereditament, is technically a nuisance, and within the statute.

The rights claimed by the plaintiffs, depend entirely upon the acts of the legislature, and the nature and character of them must be determined by those acts. They do not purport to make a grant of land, or the general right of property in any land whatever, and therefore the legal character of the right, interest, or property, which the plaintiffs acquire, must be inferred from the uses, to which it appears by the acts, to have been intended to appropriate it. As they were authorized to erect certain dams, sluices, and other permanent structures, it may well be inferred, that as an exclusive possession of the soil would be necessary both to erect and maintain these structures, it was intended to vest in them a right of possession, so far as might be necessary to protect and preserve those works, and for so long a time as might be necessary for that purpose. If, therefore, the only damage complained of, were the damage done to these works, it would certainly afford strong ground to contend, that the damage complained of was a violation of the plaintiff's right of possession, for which trespass *quare clausum* is the appropriate remedy. Wilson *v.* Smith, 10 Wendell, 324. But the injury done to the plaintiffs' works, forms but a very small part of the plaintiffs' complaint. The *gravamen* of the complaint is, the filling up with solid materials a considerable portion both of their full and receiving basins, thereby to diminish their capacity, to check the free current and flow of the water from one part of these respective inclosures to another, and thereby to diminish the plaintiffs' water power. But the right of making use of the land of others, whether it be that of the public or of individuals, for a precise and definite purpose, not inconsistent with a general right of property in the owner, especially where it is for a public use, is in legal contemplation an easement, or franchise, and not a grant of the soil, or general property. And, upon the best consideration which we have been able to give to these statutes, the Court are all of opinion that, so far as the right of flowage is concerned, the right conferred was a franchise.

It seems to be no valid objection to this view of the case, that the easement is of such a character as to deprive the owner of all useful or available beneficial interest in the land. In case of land appropriated to the use of a turnpike corporation, although the corporation obtains the entire use of the surface of the land, as well for use as a travelling path, as for collecting gravel, earth, and materials for constructing it, and although in point of fact, in assessing damages for the owner in such case, the whole value of the land is usually given, deducting nothing for the general right of ownership, yet it is clearly held, that such right of property in the original owner is not divested, the right of the corporation is an easement only. Adams v. Emerson, 6 Pick. 57.

So it seems to us in the present case, the legislature intended to confer upon the plaintiffs a franchise or easement, for public purposes, two of which are prominently set forth in the acts; the one, to have an extensive right of flowage for mill purposes; the other, for a right of way. The original grantees, under the sanction of the legislature, have divided these distinct interests, and the plaintiffs now claim all those rights, which were conferred on the original grantees, so far as they relate to the grant for mill purposes. As the acts of the legislature purport to confer upon the plaintiffs a right of flowage only, and the rights necessarily incident thereto, as the enjoyment of such right of flowage does not necessarily draw after it a right of property or an exclusive right of possession, and as these are not necessary to its enjoyment, no rule of construction requires, that a larger grant should be considered as conferred by it, than that of an easement, which fully satisfies it.

The Court are also of opinion, that the manner in which the plaintiffs have stated their rights in their bill, is not inconsistent with this view as constituting a franchise, and not an exclusive right of possession. There is certainly much weight in the suggestion, that they have set out the acts of the legislature at large, and made them part of their bill, and profess to claim such rights only as these acts confer, and therefore if in summing them up, they should state them in terms which, if they stood alone, might be deemed the averment of a right of property or of possession, still this statement is to be qualified by this reference to the acts of the legislature, and this statement must be deemed to be the statement of an inference from all the foregoing particulars, and therefore to be restrained and made definite, by the several provisions in their acts. But without relying much upon this suggestion, we are of opinion, that the statement in the conclusion of the bill, taking it as it must be taken, in connection with the subject-matter of the bill, is the statement of a franchise and not of a right of property in the reservoirs.

After setting forth the acts of the legislature, the acts of the Boston and Roxbury Mill Corporation under them, and the assignment by the Boston and Roxbury Mill Corporation, to them, the Boston

SUPREME COURT OF MASSACHUSETTS. 277

Boston Water Power Co. v. Boston and Worcester Railroad Corporation.

Water Power Company they proceed to state their right to have and enjoy the exclusive right and privilege of forever using the soil included within the limits of the full basin for the purpose of flowing, &c., and of keeping the soil included within the limits of the receiving basin free from and uncovered by the tide waters, and using the same to carry off, &c., and of holding and using all the water power, &c., without any hindrance, &c., or diminution of the capacity of the full and receiving basins respectively, &c., referring to the acts of the legislature. The exclusive right claimed, is not a right to the soil, exclusive of all other persons for all other purposes, but a right exclusive of that of all others to use for a like purpose, or a purpose inconsistent with their right thus to use it.

The manner in which the disturbance is stated, and the damage occasioned by the defendants' contemplated works, confirm this view of the nature of the plaintiffs' complaint, and of the rights which they allege to have been interrupted. They aver, indeed, as one of the incidental injurious consequences of the defendants' works, that the plaintiffs are prevented from occupying two valuable mill-sites; but the *gravamen* of the complaint is the filling up, with piles and other solid-materials, a considerable portion of the full and receiving basins, diminishing their respective capacities and the mill power derived from them, preventing the free current of the water from one part to another of these basins; so that the subject-matter of complaint, is an injury to the plaintiffs in their right of flowage.

Taking the whole bill together, the Court are of opinion, that the principal right set out by the plaintiffs, is a franchise, an easement or incorporeal hereditament; that it is sufficiently set out and described as such; that the injury complained of is an injury to such incorporeal hereditament, by a disturbance of the plaintiffs, in the enjoyment of such franchise; that the remedy for such an injury at law, would be an action on the case for a disturbance, and not an action of trespass *quare clausum;* that such an injury is in strict legal consideration a nuisance, and is therefore within the provisions of the statute giving the Court jurisdiction in equity, in all cases of nuisance. This opinion renders it unnecessary to consider the question, whether in any case, the words of the statute can be construed in a more enlarged sense, so as to include wrongs not regarded at law as nuisances, thereby using the term nuisance in a more generic or popular sense, and as equivalent to hurt or damage.

2. It has been contended that this is not a case within the statute, because the plaintiffs have a plain, adequate, and complete remedy at law.

Where it appears upon the face of the bill, that a plaintiff has such remedy, it shows such a want of equity, as may be taken advantage of by general demurrer. But as this relief is given in all cases where there is not such remedy, it must plainly appear upon the bill, before the jurisdiction can be considered as taken away upon this ground.

There appear to be several grounds upon which this bill for an injunction, so far as the rights of the parties appear upon the bill, may be sustained.

It has often been held, that where a party claims a franchise under a statute, and is in the possession and enjoyment of such franchise, equity will interpose to protect and secure the enjoyment of such franchise, because it affords the only plain and adequate remedy. Newburgh Turnpike Co. v. Miller, 5 Johns. Ch. R. 101. In the present case, certain rights and franchises were granted to the plaintiffs, by the legislature, upon the ground that the enjoyment and exercise of them would not only be a benefit to the persons incorporated, but would also contribute to the public benefit.

Another ground is, where the party complained against professes to act by public authority, to enter upon, and to a certain extent to use the land of third persons, and exceeds his authority, it is held to be a peculiarly proper case for the interposition of a court of equity. Agar v. The Regent's Canal Co., Cooper's Eq. Rep. 77 ; Shand v. Henderson, 2 Dow's R. 519.

In this case both these conditions concur; the plaintiffs claim a statute franchise of which they are in possession, and the defendants claim to act under a legislative provision vesting in them the power to do what they have done.

It is also another ground for the interposition of a court of equity, that what the defendants proposed to do, and claim a right to do, is the erection of a work, which is in its nature permanent and perpetual. It is not like the case of a single or temporary disturbance, the injury arising from which can be measured and estimated and compensated in damages in a single suit; the plaintiffs would be compelled to bring successive suits, from time to time. This is more especially a ground · of interference, where the party complained against professes to exercise a public authority, and where the claim is to appropriate the property or franchises of the complainant, to a purpose claimed to be public, and where the plaintiff denies and contests the right of the defendants to exercise such power. Gardner v. Newburgh, 2 Johns. Ch. R. 162; Belknap v. Belknap, 2 Johns. Ch. R. 473.

Without going at large into the authorities, the Court are of opinion, that this is a case where the rights of the plaintiffs, being fixed and settled by the statutes, where both parties are corporations claiming certain rights, but claiming them as granted by the public, and to be exercised and carried into effect for the use and benefit of the public, it is fit, that 'the plaintiffs, instead of being left to a suit at law, in which relief in damages only could be obtained, should be entitled to the more adequate and complete remedy furnished by a court of equity, where the relative rights of the parties with their just limits and qualifications, may be declared and fixed, and under which the parties may enjoy specifically the very rights, immunities, and franchises which the public intended to grant to them respectively with an ultimate view to the public benefit and accommodation. A suit at law would only enable the plaintiff corporation to recover and distribute a sum of money by way of damages for the violation of those rights, among the members of that corporation, as individuals, but would not empower them to accomplish the specific public objects, for attaining which these franchises were conferred on them.

If it be contended in answer to this suggestion, that by a recent statute, the court have the power, where judgment is rendered in an action on the case for a nuisance, on motion, to award and issue a warrant to the sheriff or his deputy to abate and remove the nuisance at the expense of the defendant, in like manner as common nuisances are abated and removed, (St. 1828, *c.* 137, § 6) we think it may be well-replied, that this statute power is not equally adequate and beneficial. Under the statute, the power is to prostrate and remove only, whereas the decree of a court of equity may be modified and adapted to the case with a due regard to the rights of both parties, securing the rights of the one, and diminishing as little as possible the advantages of the other. It may therefore be more beneficial for the defendants, as well as for the plaintiffs.

It is hardly necessary to add, that this view is taken on a demurrer to the plaintiffs' bill, which admits, for the purpose of presenting the question of jurisdiction, that the plaintiffs have all the rights which they claim, and that all the grounds upon which the defendants claim to justify their proceedings, as warranted by the acts of the legislature, are untenable. We have not taken into consideration, and, for obvious reasons, upon this preliminary proceeding, could not consider the merits of the respective claims of the parties.

3. As to the last point, that the demurrer will be sustained on the ground that the lessees are not made parties to the bill, we think it is apparent that this affords no sufficient ground for a demurrer, unless it also appears that the persons indicated are necessary parties. It is not sufficient, that it may turn out upon further inquiry, that they have an interest. But we think this does not appear upon the bill.

The *gravamen* is, that the acts complained of tend to diminish and reduce the amount of the water power, which the plaintiffs are entitled to enjoy, and but for the works of the defendants, would enjoy, under their grants. But it does not appear that the power will thereby be reduced to so low an amount as to prevent the lessees from enjoying that which has been granted them, under their respective leases.

The case of a lessee of land taken for public use, does not apply. A lease gives the lessee the enjoyment of the estate, for a term of time; and this is necessarily impaired and taken away for such term, by appropriating the land to public use. Such lessee has a real interest, a proprietary title and ownership, for the time being, of the estate taken. But we are to understand from the statement in this bill, and the nature of the right granted, that it is the use of a certain quantity of water, out of a much larger quantity, from which it is taken, the residue of which remains to the lessors. As between lessors and lessees, therefore, the lessees are to be first fully served to the extent of the quantity granted, whether any thing remains to the lessors or not. The substance of the complaint is, not the destruction but the diminution of the power. But it may be diminished, so as to be greatly injurious to the plaintiffs, and yet there may be enough to satisfy the rights of the lessees, and if so, they have not necessarily an interest in the subject-matter of the controversy. Should it appear in the further progress of the cause, that the lessees have an interest in the subject-matter of the suit, there will then be time to make them parties. But at present, it not appearing that they are necessarily parties, the demurrer cannot be sustained on that ground.

Demurrer overruled.

DAVIS CARPENTER *v.* THE COUNTY COMMISSIONERS OF THE COUNTY OF BRISTOL.[1]

Plymouth Co. October Term, 1838.

Damages — Ownership of Land — Mandamus to Commissioners to Summon Jury.

In the case of land taken for a railroad, if the county commissioners refuse to assess damages on the ground that the party applying for them does not own the land, he is entitled

---

[1] 21 Pickering's Reports, 258.

to have their judgment revised by a jury; and a mandamus will lie in his behalf, to com.
pel them to grant a warrant for a jury.

THE petitioner alleges, that he is, and for more than ten years last
past has been, seised of a parcel of land in Seekonk; that the Boston and Providence Railroad Corporation have laid out and constructed their railroad over the land, to his injury; that he petitioned
the county commissioners to estimate the damages, and they made
report of their doings thereon, but did not estimate or award him
damages; that being dissatisfied with their doings, he applied to
them for a jury to assess the damages, but the commissioners refused
to grant him a warrant for a jury; and he therefore prays that this
Court will issue a writ of mandamus to the commissioners, commanding them to issue their warrant for a jury.

By the records of the commissioners it appeared, that they were
of opinion that the petitioner failed to show that the use of the land
belonged to him in such manner as to authorize them to award him
any damages for the loss thereof.

A. Bassett and *Warren*, in support of the petition, cited Revised
Stat. c. 39, § 56, 57; and c. 24, § 13; Commonwealth *v.* Sessions of
Hampden, 2 Pick. 414.

Coffin and *Cushman,* for the respondents, contended that a party is
entitled to a jury only in a case in which there has been an assessment of damages by the commissioners; Revised Stat. c. 39, § 57,
62; that the commissioners may pass upon the title to the land, and
the Revised Stat. c. 24, § 12, 32, provide, that in the case of a highway, their decisions may be revised by a jury, but there is no such
provision in respect to a railroad. If the commissioners have decided
erroneously upon the petitioner's title, he has a remedy by certiorari.

MORTON, J., delivered the opinion of the Court. There is no doubt
that the petitioner has sought the proper remedy. If this process will
not lie, he can have no relief. Mandamus lies to all inferior tribunals,
magistrates, and officers, and extends to all cases of neglect to perform a legal duty, where there is no other adequate remedy. It
applies to judicial as well as ministerial acts. If the duty be judicial,
the mandate will be to the officers to exercise their official discretion
or judgment, without any direction as to the manner in which it shall
be done. If it be ministerial, then the mandamus will direct the
specific act to be performed. Commonwealth *v.* Sessions of Hampden, 2 Pick. 414; Springfield *v.* Commissioners of Highways of

Hampden, 4 Pick. 68; Strong, Petitioner, &c. 20 Pick. 484. Were application made to county commissioners, to estimate damages caused by the laying out of a railroad, turnpike, or common highway, the duty required of them would be a judicial duty. If they refused or neglected to perform it, this court would issue a mandamus, commanding them to do it; that is, to exercise their judgment upon the matter. But when they had performed this duty, it being within their discretion, no other tribunal would have a right to interfere with, or complain of, the manner in which they had performed it.

But having estimated damages, if either party should be dissatisfied, and apply for a jury, the granting a warrant would be a ministerial duty. It is a process to which the complaining party is entitled as a right, and which does not depend on the discretion of any tribunal. If the county commissioners refused this application, this Court would issue a mandate, commanding them to grant the proper process for a jury in such case.

In the case at bar, the county commissioners undertook to decide, that the petitioner had no such estate in the land over which the railroad passed, as would entitle him to damages. Now, whether their decision on this point was right or wrong, we think the petitioner had a right to have their judgment revised by a jury.

By the 56th section of the 39th chapter of the Revised Statutes, "every railroad corporation shall be liable to pay all damages that shall be occasioned by laying out and making and maintaining their road;" "and such damages shall be estimated by the commissioners in the manner provided in the case of laying out highways." This, by necessary implication, gives to the commissioners authority to inquire whether any damages have been sustained by the applicant, and consequently whether he owned the property, for an injury to which damages were claimed.

By the 57th section, "either party, if dissatisfied with any *estimate* made by the commissioners, may apply for a jury to assess the damages," "and the like proceedings shall be had thereon as are provided for the recovery of damages for laying out highways." The respondents contend that the complainant is entitled to a jury, only when *damages* are estimated; but that, where the commissioners decide against the party's claim altogether, their decision is final and he is not entitled to a revision of it by a jury. But we think this is too narrow a construction of the statute. Trial by jury is a favorite of our laws and constitutions, and we will not suppose it to be taken away by inference. The estimate, from which the party *is entitled* to appeal, may fairly be construed to import, not only a *valuation of damages*, but also a *judgment* on the party's *claim for damages;* and such, we have no doubt, was the intention of the legislature. Otherwise, a party might be deprived of his right to a trial by jury in a very important controversy concerning his property. Bill of Rights, art. 15.

For the mode of applying for and obtaining a jury, we are referred to the chapter regulating the laying out of highways, &c. By the 13th section of this chapter it is provided, that " any party who shall be aggrieved by the doings of the commissioners," " may have a jury to determine the matter of his complaint, on application therefor by petition in writing to the commissioners." This is imperative and leaves nothing to the discretion of the commissioners. However plain it may appear to them that the party has suffered no damage, or that he has no title to the land injured, or that his interest in it is not affected, they have no power to reject an application for a jury. The party has a right to have these questions reëxamined by that constitutional tribunal, and whether he will exercise that right or not, must depend entirely on his own discretion. The powers of the jury in this case, in relation to the assessment of damages and the questions incident thereto, will be co-extensive with those of the commissioners. Merrill et al., Petitioners, v. The Inhabitants of Berkshire, 11 Pick. 269.

We have not examined the several points presented in the statement made by the commissioners in answer to this application; because they do not properly come before us at this time, and because we have not the means of giving them that full investigation which they may deserve. Whether the vote of the proprietors passed the fee of the land, or only its usufruct, and if the latter, whether a partial or total use was granted, whether a perpetual servitude would not be an injury to the owner of the fee, as well as the occupant of the use, are questions raised, or at least suggested in the statement, which present intrinsic difficulties, and upon which we do not deem it proper to give any opinion.

Alternative mandamus ordered.

THE INHABITANTS OF LOWELL v. THE BOSTON AND LOWELL RAIL-
ROAD CORPORÁTION.[1]

Middlesex Co., October Term, 1839.

*Negligence — Responsibility of Company for the Negligence of the
Servants of a Contractor.*

A railroad corporation was authorized to construct its railroad across a highway, and in the
progress of the work it became necessary from time to time to remove certain barriers,
which were placed across the highway for the protection of travellers,
but were adopted by the town in which the highway was situated, and in consequence of
the neglect of the workmen to replace the barriers, at night, a traveller, in 1832, sustained
an injury, and subsequently, under St. 1786, c. 81, recovered double damages against the
town. It was held, that the railroad corporation was bound to cause the barriers to be
replaced at night, although its charter contained no express provision on this point; as
otherwise an accident might have happened before the town had notice, actual or constructive, and no one would have been liable for the damages.
Held, also, that the corporation was responsible for the negligence of such workmen, although
they were employed by an individual, who had contracted to construct this portion of the
railroad, for a stipulated sum, the work being done by the direction of the corporation.
Held, also, that an action might be sustained against the corporation by the town for
indemnity, the parties not being *in pari delicto;* but, that the town was only entitled to
recover the single damages, as, beyond that extent, it had suffered from its own *constructive*
negligence; and that the corporation was not liable for the costs and expenses of the action
brought against the town by such traveller, it not appearing that such action was defended
at the request of the corporation, or for its benefit.

ACTION on the case. The declaration set forth, in substance, that
the plaintiffs were bound by law to keep in repair a highway leading
from Thorndike street, in Lowell, to Chelmsford; that the defend-
ánts, in constructing their railroad in Lowell, cut through and across
such highway; that in the progress of the work, it became necessary
for the defendants to make use of such highway for the purpose of
removing stone and rubbish from the deep cut made for the passage
of the railroad; that while using the highway for this purpose, they
removed certain barriers which had been placed across the highway
to prevent travellers from falling into the deep cut, and neglected to
replace the same; that in consequence thereof two persons, named
James Currier and Mary Smith, while driving along such highway,
on the 11th of December, 1832, in the night time, were precipitated
into the deep cut, and greatly injured; and that by reason thereof
those persons brought their actions and recovered large sums of
money against the plaintiffs, which the plaintiffs had been compelled

[1] 23 Pickering's Reports, 24.

to pay, together with witness fees, counsel fees, and other expenses attending the defence of such actions, amounting in the whole to more than $8,000. (See Currier v. Lowell, 16 Pick. 170.)

The trial was before Morton, J. Joshua Swan, one of the select-men of Lowell, in 1832, testified that he was at the place in question shortly before the accident happened; that the barriers were gone; and that he told the person who was there giving directions about the work, that the barriers must not be down an hour; and that such person answered, that he would replace them.

William A. Swan testified, that he worked for the plaintiffs in the autumn of 1832; and that shortly before the accident happened he found the poles, which constituted a part of the barriers, down, and that he replaced them.

It appeared, that on the 1st of October, 1832, John Noonan con-tracted with the defendants to construct that portion of the railroad where the accident happened.

It was admitted, that the deep cut across the road, was made by the persons employed by the defendants in constructing the railroad; and that no surveyors had been chosen by the town of Lowell, for that year.

It was also admitted, that Morris Slatterly would, if present, have testified, that the barriers were put up and maintained by him, as a servant or agent of the defendants, and by their orders; that none were put up or maintained by the plaintiffs; that no engagement or promise was made by him with or to the plaintiffs, in relation to the barriers; and that he had the care and supervision of them.

It was agreed between the parties, that the case should be sub-mitted to the jury upon the question, whether, or not, the barriers were removed and left down by the servants of the defendants, while employed in the construction of the railroad.

The jury returned a verdict for the plaintiffs for the sum of $10,000. But it was agreed by the counsel, that the verdict should be increased, diminished, or set aside, and judgment entered, as the court should direct.

Hoar and *C. G. Loring*, for the defendants.

The defendants were under no obligation to erect the barriers. All their rights and duties are created and distinctly prescribed by their act of incorporation; but it contains no provision imposing such an obligation on them. If the plaintiffs had chosen surveyors of high-ways, and those surveyors had erected the barriers, it would have been illegal for the defendants to take them down without putting them up again when they left off work; but as the defendants erected them originally, they had a right to remove them and leave them down. The judgments recovered against the plaintiffs prove that they were not relieved by the acts of the defendants, from the duty of erecting such barriers. The defendants were authorized by their act of incorporation to cut through the highway, and they are liable for its consequences only in the manner provided by the statute. Stevens v. Middlesex Canal Co. 12 Mass. R. 466; Stowell v. Flagg, 11 Mass. R. 364; Thurston v. Hancock, 12 Mass. R. 220; Callender v. Marsh, 1 Pick. 418. But it will be contended, that the barriers having been once erected, the duty of the plaintiffs was discharged, and the defendants were bound to maintain them, or had no right to remove them. But there was no such privity between these parties as would constitute the defendants the servants or agents of the plaintiffs in this matter. Their interests were adverse. But if it be conceded, that the defendants were bound to erect barriers, it does not follow that they are responsible to the plaintiffs for their neglect of the same duty; for it was, at least, a concurrent duty. The plaintiffs are precluded from denying that they were in fault; for Currier and Smith could not have recovered against them if they had not had reasonable notice of the existence of the deep cut, and reasonable time to guard travellers against it. The policy of the law forbids the recovery of any indemnity by one party against another, where both are equally in fault; especially where, as in the present case, indemnity is sought against a penalty. Holman v. Johnson, Cowp. 343; Morck v. Abel, 3 Bos. & Pul. 38; Griswold v. Waddington, 16 Johns. R. 487; Harlow v. Humiston, 6 Cowen, 189; Vose v. Grant, 15 Mass. R. 505; Peck v. Ellis, 2 Johns. Ch. R. 137; Farebrother v. Ansley, 1 Campb. 343; Merryweather v. Nixon, 8 T. R. 186; Smith v. Smith, 2 Pick. 621; Riddle v. Proprietors of Locks and Canals, 7 Mass. R. 169; Waterhouse v. Waite, 11 Mass. R. 207; Wood v. Waterville, 4 Mass. R. 422; S. C. 5 Mass. R. 294; Drew v. New River Co. 6 Carr. & Payne, 754.

The defendants were not responsible for the negligence of the persons employed in the construction of that section of the railroad where the accident happened, because it was let out to Noonan, who had contracted to construct it for a stipulated sum, and employed the workmen.

But if these workmen are to be deemed the servants or agents of the defendants, still, if the barriers were tortiously removed by them, the defendants would not be responsible for the consequences.

The plaintiffs cannot recover, because the damages sustained by them were the remote and not the immediate or natural consequence of the acts of the defendants. The positive negligence of the plaintiffs, after notice, must have supervened, to render them liable to Currier and Smith. Salem Bank v. Gloucester Bank, 17 Mass. R. 31; Jackson v. Adams, 9 Mass. R. 484; Harris v. Baker, 4 Maule & Selw. 27.

If the defendants are liable at all, they are not responsible for the double damages; for the persons injured could, at any rate, have recovered only single damages against them. Jackson v. Adams, 9 Mass. R. 484.

Dexter, Robinson, Smith, and *Ames,* for the plaintiffs.

The claim of the plaintiffs is founded on the negligence of the defendants in doing an act authorized by their charter. They were intrusted, by the legislature, with the execution of a public work, and were bound, in the construction of it, to take special precautions to protect the public against danger. Com. Dig. (Day's ed.) Action on the Case for Negligence, A. 2, A. 3, note; Com. Dig. Action on the Case for Nuisance, C.; Sutton v. Johnstone, 1 T. R. 509; Weld v. Gas Light Co. 1 Stark. R. 189; Drew v. New River Co. 6 Carr. & Payne, 754; Jones v. Bird, 5 Barn. & Ald. 837; Boulton v. Crowther, 2 Barn. & Cressw. 703; Matthews v. West London Water Works Co. 3 Campb. 403; Townsend v. Susquehanna Turnpike Co. 6 Johns. R. 90; Chestnut Hill Turnpike Co. v. Rutter, 4 Serg. & Rawle, 6; Bush v. Steinman, 1 Bos. & Pul. 404.

This case is analogous to that of a master who has been made responsible for the negligence of his servant, and who, it is well settled, may recover over against the servant. So here, the plaintiffs having been compelled to pay for a constructive wrong, have their remedy over against the actual wrongdoer. 1 Bl. Comm. (Chitty's ed.) 431, note 24; Green v. New River Co. 4 T. R. 589; 2 Stark. Ev. 768, 769; 3 Stark. Ev. 982, 983; Brucker v. Fromont, 6 T. R. 659.

It is true, that a party cannot lay a foundation for an action, in a wrong on his own part. But that principle is not applicable, unless *actual* negligence is proved. Burckle v. New York Dry Dock Co. 2 Hall's (N. York) R. 151. The defendants cannot say, that the plaintiffs were barred by their own negligence. The plaintiffs had no control over the highway, although their liability for damages sustained by travellers was not suspended. The defendants *inherited* the rights and duties of the town for the time being.

The barriers having been once placed across the highway, were adopted by the plaintiffs, and their duty in this behalf was discharged; the defendants, therefore, were not authorized to remove them. If they had not been erected by the defendants, it must be presumed, that they would have been by the town.

If, however, there was *actual* negligence on the part of the plaintiffs, they cannot recover. The defendants, in order to prove such negligence, rely on the judgments recovered by Currier and Smith. Our answer is, that the plaintiffs were not sued for *actual* negligence, but because a certain state of facts existed which, by the statute, made them liable, to wit, the highway was out of repair, and they had notice of it.

The agents of the defendants were the last who used the highway, and it was therefore their duty to see that it was properly secured when they left off work. Milne *v.* Smith, 2 Dow, 390.

The damage sustained by the plaintiffs was not too remote and consequential to be the foundation of an action against the defendants. Com. Dig. Action upon the Case for Nuisance, C.

It is suggested that though single damages may not be remote and consequential, yet that double damages are so. But if the fault of the defendants creates the plaintiff's liability to double damages, they are not more remote and consequential than single damages.

WILDE, J., delivered the opinion of the court. Several important and interesting questions are involved in the decision of this case, which have been ably argued by counsel, and which we have taken time to consider with the attention and deliberation that their importance and difficulty seemed to require.

Our first impressions as to one of the questions, on which the decision of the case depends, were not free from doubt. No adjudged case has been found in all respects similar; but reasoning from analogy, taking into consideration the principles of law, and the decided cases which have the closest application to the question in dispute, we have been brought to a conclusion which appears to us satisfactory, and which will enable us to administer justice between the parties without violating any known rule of law.

The facts on which the plaintiffs rest their claim, have not been disputed except in one particular, which has been ascertained by the jury in favor of the plaintiffs.

By the report of the case it appears, that the defendants being authorized by law to construct a railroad from Boston to Lowell, had occasion, in so doing, to cut across and through one of the highways situated in Lowell, and which the plaintiffs were bound by law to keep in repair, whereby it became necessary to place barriers across the highway to prevent travellers from falling into the chasm or deep cut made by the defendants. Barriers were accordingly so placed by them. Afterwards it became necessary for the defendants to make use of the highway for the purpose of removing stone and rubbish from the deep cut, and the barriers were removed by persons in the defendants' employ, who neglected to replace them ; in consequence whereof, two persons driving along the highway in the night time, were precipitated into the deep cut, and were greatly injured, and, on account thereof, recovered large damages against the plaintiffs, which the plaintiffs have been compelled to pay. The amount thus paid they claim the right to recover of the defendants in this action, they having become liable by law to pay, and this liability having been incurred, in consequence of the negligence of the defendants' agents.

The defendants resist this claim on several grounds.

1. The principles, or most of the principles, on which the defendants rely, as the first ground of defence, may well be admitted ; but they furnish no criterion by which we can be guided to a legal and just decision. It is undoubtedly true, that the defendants had a right to make the excavation in the highway. And they were not bound to erect barriers across the way, provided they had given seasonable notice to the officers of the town of their intended operations. So, after barriers were erected, the defendants might take them down from time to time, if necessary, for the purpose of removing rocks and rubbish, which could not be otherwise removed. These acts the defendants were authorized to do, and cannot be responsible to any one for consequential damages. But the plaintiffs' claim of indemnity is not for damages arising from these acts; they do not controvert the defendants' right to make the excavation in the highway, or to take down the barriers when necessary. The action is founded on the negligence of the defendants' agents and servants, in not replacing the barriers when the works were left, the day before the accident happened. These barriers, although voluntarily erected by the defendants, were approved and adopted by the selectmen of the town ; and if the defendants were under the necessity of removing them for the purpose of making use of the road, they were bound to replace them when the necessity of using the road ceased, or, at least, every evening when their agents or laborers left the works. This was imperatively required by a due regard to public safety ; otherwise an accident might happen before the town had notice, actual or constructive, and no one would be responsible for the damages. It is not true, as has been contended by the defendants' counsel, that all the defendants' duties and liabilities are created and prescribed by their act of incorporation. Corporations as well as individuals, by the principles of the common law, are bound so to exercise their rights as not to injure others. The principle, *sic utere tuo, ut alienum non lædas*, is of universal application.

2. But the defendants deny their responsibility for the negligence of the persons employed in the construction of that part of the rail-

road where the accident happened, because this section thereof had been let out to one Noonan, who had contracted to make the same for a stipulated sum, and who employed the workmen. We do not, however, think that this circumstance relieves the defendants from their responsibility. The work was done for their benefit, under their authority, and by their direction. They are, therefore, to be regarded as the principals, and it is immaterial, whether the work was done under contract for a stipulated sum, or by workmen employed directly by the defendants at day wages. This question was very fully discussed and settled in the case of Bush v. Steinman, 1 Bos. & Pul. 403. In that case it appeared, that the defendants had contracted with A to repair his house for a stipulated sum. A contracted with B to do the work; and B contracted with C to furnish the materials. The servant of C brought a quantity of lime to the house and placed it in the road, by which the plaintiff's carriage was overturned. And it was held, that the defendant was answerable for the damage. This decision is fully supported by the authorities cited and by well-established principles.

3. Another objection to the plaintiffs' claim was made in arguments which cannot be sustained. It is objected, that the defendants are not answerable for the tortious acts of their agents or servants. And this is true, if the acts were accompanied with force, for which an action of trespass *vi et armis* would lie, or were wilfully done. But the acts complained of were not so done. The defendants' workmen had a right to remove the barriers for a necessary purpose. Their only fault was their neglect in not replacing them at night when they left their work. For this negligence or non-feasance the defendants were clearly answerable.

Thus far then the case is free from all difficulty. The defendants were answerable to the parties injured for all damages. But the doubt is, whether they are responsible to the plaintiffs.

4. It has been urged that the plaintiffs or their officers have been guilty of neglect, as well as the agents of the defendants; that it was their especial duty to see to it that their roads and streets were kept in good repair and safe for travellers; and that they, therefore, being culpable, and *participes criminis*, are not, by the policy of the law, allowed to recover damages, as an indemnity, against their co-delinquents.

This objection is certainly entitled to much consideration. The general rule of law is, that where two parties participate in the commission of a criminal act, and one party suffers damage thereby, he is not intitled to indemnity, or contribution, from the other party. So also is the rule of the civil law. *Nemo ex delicto consequi potest actionem.* The French law is more indulgent, and allows a trespasser, who has paid the whole damage, to maintain an action for contribution against his co-trespasser. Pothier on Oblig. 282. Whether the latter rule be or be not founded on a wiser policy and more equal justice, is a question which we are not called upon to decide. This case, like all others, must be decided by the law as it is, whether it be consonant with sound policy or not.

Our law, however, does not in every case disallow an action, by one wrongdoer against another, to recover damages incurred in consequence of their joint offence. The rule is, *in pari delicto potior est conditio defendentis.* If the parties are not equally criminal, the principal delinquent may be held responsible to his co-delinquent for damages incurred by their joint offence. In respect to offences, in which is involved any moral delinquency or turpitude, all parties are deemed equally guilty, and courts will not inquire into their relative guilt. But where the offence is merely *malum prohibitum,* and is in no respect immoral, it is not against the policy of the law to inquire into the relative delinquency of the parties, and to administer justice between them, although both parties are wrongdoers.

This distinction was very fully considered in a case recently decided by this court. White *v.* Franklin Bank, 22 Pick. 181. In that case the plaintiff had deposited in the bank a large sum of money payable at a future day, in violation of a provision in the Revised Statutes, which prohibits any such deposit or loan. Both parties were culpable, but as the defendants were deemed the principal offenders, it was held, that the plaintiff was entitled to recover back his deposit.

No one will question the manifest justice of that decision; and it is fully sustained by the authorities. The cases, for instance, where persons who had paid more than lawful interest on usurious contracts, have been allowed to recover back the surplus, although they were parties in illegal transactions, were decided on the same distinction. So, in Smith *v.* Bromley, 2 Dougl. 696, which is a leading case on this point. The plaintiff, who was the sister of a bankrupt, was persuaded to pay the defendant a certain sum of money, which he exacted as the condition upon which he would consent to sign the bankrupt's certificate; and it was held, that although the transaction was illegal, the plaintiff was entitled to recover back the money paid, she not being *in pari delicto* with the defendant. So money paid to a plaintiff in a *qui tam* action, in order to compromise the action contrary to the prohibition of the St. 18 Eliz. c. 5, was recovered back in the case of Williams *v.* Hedley, 8 East, 378. So in Jaques *v.* Golightly, 2 Wm. Bl. 1073, it was held, that money paid to a lottery-office keeper, as a premium for an illegal insurance, might be recovered back in an action for money had and received.

In all these instances, the defendants were deemed the principal offenders, and the cases were decided on the distinction already stated. This distinction, Chief Justice Parker says, " is founded in sound principle, and is worthy of adoption as a principle of common law in this country." Worcester v. Eaton, 11 Mass. R. 377.

The principle established by these cases arising from illegal contracts, has long been admitted in certain cases of torts, where the parties were not *in pari delicto*. If a servant, in obedience to the command of his master, commits a trespass upon the property of another, not knowing that he is doing any injury, he is, nevertheless, answerable for the tort as well as his master, to the party injured; yet he is entitled to an action against his master for the damages he may suffer, although the master also was ignorant that the act commanded was unlawful; because he is deemed the principal offender. So, if a sheriff's deputy takes the property of A on a writ or execution against B, and A recovers damages of the sheriff for the trespass, he may maintain an action for indemnity against his deputy; and, in a like case, if the property be taken by the command of the plaintiff in the writ or execution against B, under a promise of indemnity, the deputy may maintain an action against the creditor on his promise, although the deputy be himself a trespasser. So, also, if A, with a forged warrant, should arrest B, and command C, to whom he shows his warrant, to confine B a reasonable time, until he could carry him to prison, and C, being ignorant of the forgery, confines him accordingly, an action for indemnity by C against A would lie, notwithstanding both parties were trespassers. Fletcher v. Harcot, Hutt. 55; 1 Roll. Abr. 95, 98. The distinction in all these cases is the same. The parties are not *in pari delicto*, and the principal offender is held responsible.

This distinction is manifest in the case under consideration. The defendants' agent, who had the superintendence of their works, was the first and principal wrongdoer. It was his duty to see to it that the barriers were put up when the works were left at night; his omission to do it was gross negligence; and for this, the defendants were clearly responsible to the parties injured.

In this negligence of the defendants' agent, the plaintiffs had no participation. Their subsequent negligence was rather constructive than actual. The most that can be said of it is, that one of their selectmen confided in the promise of the defendants' agent to keep up the barriers; and by this misplaced confidence the plaintiffs have been held responsible for damages to the injured parties. If the defendants had been prosecuted instead of the town, they must have been held liable for damages, and from this liability they have been relieved by the plaintiffs. It cannot, therefore, be controverted, that the plaintiff's claim is founded in manifest equity. The defendants are bound in justice to indemnify them so far as they have been relieved from a legal liability; and the policy of the law does not in the present instance interfere with the claim of justice. The circumstances of the case distinguish it from those cases where both parties are *in pari delicto*, and one of them, having paid the whole damages, sues the other for contribution.

From a view of the evidence reported, and the finding of the jury, we are to consider, that the defendants' agents or servants were, while employed in the construction of the railroad, the principal, if not the only, actual delinquents, and that for their delinquency the defendants are responsible to all persons suffering damage thereby; and they, in their turn, may maintain an action for indemnity against their negligent agents or servants. Unless, therefore, the plaintiffs are estopped by some inflexible principle of law, they are entitled to indemnity, so far as they have suffered a loss by the fault of the defendants' servants; and holding as we do, for the reasons stated, that they are not so estopped, we are of opinion that they are entitled to recover.

They are not, however, entitled to a full indemnity, but only to the extent of single damages. To this extent only were the defendants liable to the parties injured; and so far as the plaintiffs have been held liable beyond that extent, they have suffered from their own neglect; and whether it was actual or constructive, is immaterial. The damages were doubled by reason of the neglect of the town; and although there was, in fact, no actual negligence, yet constructive negligence was sufficient to maintain the action against them; and they must be responsible for the increased amount of damages, and cannot throw the burden on the defendants.

The only remaining question relates to the costs of the former action against the town. And we are of opinion, that the plaintiffs are not entitled to recover any part of those costs. The ground of defence in that action, on the part of the town, was, that they had no sufficient notice of the defect in the road, and that the remedy for the injured party was against the present defendants. The suit, therefore, was not defended at the request of the defendants or for their benefit; at least, no such request has been proved; and the ground of defence taken by the town in the former action, is well remembered, although it does not appear in the present report. If the claim of the injured parties had been made on the defendants, or if they had had notice that the town defended the suit against them in behalf of the defendants, they might have compromised the claim.

But however this may be, we think there is no ground on which the defendants can be held liable for the costs and expenses of the suit against the town.

Judgment for the plaintiffs.

THE NEWBURYPORT TURNPIKE CORPORATION *v.* THE EASTERN RAILROAD COMPANY.[1]

Essex Co., November Term, 1839.

Crossing Turnpike — Right to Cross on same Level.

Under Revised Stat. c. 39, § 67, providing that every railroad corporation may raise or lower any turnpike or way for the purpose of having their railroad *pass over or under* the same," a railroad corporation may raise a turnpike road for the purpose of constructing the railroad across it *upon the same level.*

THIS was a bill in equity praying for an injunction against the respondents.

By the bill and answer, it appeared, that on the 8th of February, 1839, the complainants received notice from the respondents, that they proposed to construct their railroad over the turnpike road of the complainants upon a level therewith, and, for this purpose, to raise the turnpike road to the height of three feet and a half above its existing level at the point of intersection; that upon the complainants objecting thereto, the respondents applied to the county commissioners, to determine in what manner the railroad should cross the turnpike road; that the county commissioners, after hearing the parties, reported, that the respondents should be permitted to raise the turnpike road to the height of three feet and a half above its existing level, for the purpose proposed, and in a mode specified by the commissioners; which report was accepted; and that the respondents had commenced operations on the turnpike road.

The respondents, in their answer, averred that it was their intention to complete the crossing in conformity with the directions contained in the report of the county commissioners.

[1] 23 Pickering's Reports, 326.

Lunt, for the complainants, cited Revised Stat. c. 39, § 66, 67, 69, 72, 79 ; St. 1836, c. 232, § 1 ; St. 1837, c. 226, § 1.

Saltonstall and *Lord,* for the respondents, cited Revised Stat. c. 39, § 66, *et seq.;* Rowe *v.* Granite Bridge Corporation, 21 Pick. 344.

SHAW, C. J., afterward drew up the opinion of the court. This case presents a question of considerable interest, in regard to the powers of railroad companies, in cases where they necessarily intersect other ways, including turnpike roads, highways, town ways, and private ways. Turnpike roads, highways, and town ways, are all public, and designed, as well as railroads, to promote public accommodation. For, although turnpike roads are originally constructed, and subsequently maintained, by a company of stockholders, who advance their own capital for the purpose, and are reimbursed by a toll, still, when constructed, they are public works, the right to use them is secured to the public, an injury to them is a public injury, (Commonwealth *v.* Wilkinson, 16 Pick. 175,) and the public benefit is the ultimate end and purpose of all the powers and privileges conferred upon them. This alone justifies and warrants the authority conferred on them to take private property when necessary for the construction of such turnpike road. These, therefore, as well as highways, townways, and railroads, are to be regarded as public works, intended in their various modes to promote public accommodation, and all alike entitled to consideration and respect, in all legislative regulations ; and we are to presume, that in granting, limiting, and modifying the powers and rights of each, the legislature had in view that common public good, which is the object of them all. In cases, therefore, where some interference is unavoidable, and where legislative provisions have been made with reference to such interference, such construction ought to be put upon them if possible, as that the powers and privileges of each shall be no further limited or restrained, than may be reasonably necessary to enable the other to accomplish the public purpose for which it was established. Such must be presumed to have been the intention of the legislature ; and such intention may be often usefully referred to, in expounding provisions which are general and comprehensive in their nature, or doubtful in their terms.

The complainants insist, that the defendants had no authority by law to alter the level of the turnpike road, so that the railroad might cross it at the same level, without the consent of the turnpike corporation, and that the county commissioners had no authority to adjudicate or act in the premises. This depends upon the construction of the Revised Statutes. Revised Stat. c. 39, § 66, provides, that if any railroad shall be so laid out as to cross any turnpike road, or other way, it shall be so made as not to obstruct such turnpike road or way.

The word "obstruct," in its ordinary sense, means to stop up, and wholly prevent travel, upon a road, or render it unfit for travel. In this section, it cannot be so construed, as to say, that the travel on such turnpike road or highway, shall not be rendered in any degree more inconvenient, because it is clearly implied, in a subsequent section, § 72, that the railroad corporation may erect a bridge over the railroad, or a tunnel under it, for the travel on the turnpike road, and such elevation or depression of the road must, to some extent, impede the travel upon it, and render it less convenient. We think, therefore, that this section intended to provide, that the travel upon a turnpike road or public or private way, already established, should not be stopped by a railroad, but that its continuance should be provided for, by alterations in the road itself, which should increase the impediment and inconvenience of travel upon it as little as possible, and the subsequent provisions were made with a view to such alterations. It is obvious, that, in many cases, it would be necessary to effect this object, by alterations in the turnpike road or highway itself, because, from the nature of the work, it is important, and often necessary, that the railroad should be kept on a given level and not be varied so as to adapt it to the existing levels of other roads.

But the question mainly turns on the construction of the 67th section, which provides, that every railroad corporation may raise or lower any turnpike or way, for the purpose of having their railroad pass over or under the same; it then goes on to provide, that before proceeding to make any alterations in such way, they shall give notice to the turnpike proprietors or selectmen, that the latter may then give notice what alterations they require, or, if the parties do not agree, they may apply to the county commissioners, to determine whether any and what alterations shall be made, and their decision shall be final.

The complainants contend, that it was not the intention of the legislature, to authorize the railroad corporation to raise the turnpike road a few feet to bring it up to the level of the railroad, and thus let it pass over the railroad on the same level, but so to raise it, as to pass above the railroad, by means of a separate and independent bridge. The argument is this, that the words "raise" and "lower," as applied to the turnpike road, are relative and opposite; so, the corresponding words "under" and "over" are to be construed as applying to the railroad; and as they can only lower the turnpike road to pass under the railroad, by an independent passage, so it was only intended that they should raise the turnpike road to pass over the railroad at a higher grade and by an independent bridge. But it seems to us, that this reasoning is far from being conclusive. The words "over" and "under," as applied to the surface, are not precisely opposites. One passes over a road, if he crosses it on the surface, as well as when he crosses above it, on a bridge; but he cannot be said to pass under it, unless on another surface at a lower level. We think the words are to be applied, according to the subject-matter. It may be necessary to lower or to raise the turnpike road, to let the railroad pass over; in the former case, where the surface of the turnpike is higher than the grade of the railroad at the place of intersection, in the latter, where it is lower. And if so, why should it not have been contemplated by the legislature? The words are sufficient to warrant this construction, and the power is as useful and necessary in the one case as in the other. To raise the turnpike road to permit the railroad to pass over it at the same level, is then as much within the words and intent of the statute, as the power of raising it much higher to carry the travel above the railroad by an independent bridge. This latter power is undoubtedly granted, but does not, in terms, or by implication, exclude the other. And it may be remarked as tending to strengthen this conclusion, that raising the turnpike road three feet, to pass on the level of the railroad, is a much less impediment to traveling on the turnpike road than to raise it eighteen or twenty feet, to pass above it by a bridge. The former would create a slight rise in the road, easily relieved; the other would require the ascent and descent of a considerable elevation. The construction which is thus put on the statute, is calculated to promote the execution of one of these public works, that is, the railroad, with the smallest amount of inconvenience to the travel on the other, the turnpike road. The court are therefore of opinion, that the railroad company were authorized, without the consent of the proprietors of the turnpike road, to pass the turnpike road and to raise the turnpike road sufficiently at the place of intersection to pass on the same level with the railroad, having the sanction and approbation of the county commissioners therefor, and making the alterations in the manner directed and required by those commissioners; which was done in the present case.

Decree for the respondents accordingly, with costs.

THE BOSTON WATER POWER COMPANY *v.* THE BOSTON AND WORCESTER RAILROAD CORPORATION *et al.*[1]

Suffolk Co., November Term, 1839.

Eminent Domain — Franchise of a Company subject to — Conflicting Grants.

A corporation was empowered by its charter, to build a dam westerly from Boston to Brookline, over an arm of the sea, and from this main dam to run a cross dam southerly to the shore, so as to make on one side of the cross dam a full basin, and on the other an empty or receiving basin, and to cut raceways from the full basin to the receiving basin, and to have the use of the land in the basins, derived partly from the Commonwealth and partly from individuals, either by purchase or by taking it for public use, at an appraisement; and to use, sell, or lease the water power thus created; and the corporation built the dams accordingly, and erected mills.   It was *held*, that it was within the constitutional power of the legislature to authorize a railroad corporation to construct their road across the basins, making compensation to the water power corporation for the diminution and injury caused thereby to the water power.

Held also, that the grant of this authority to the railroad corporation could not be considered as annulling or destroying the franchise of the water power corporation ; and the right of the water power corporation to use the land constituted an interest and qualified property therein not larger nor of a different nature from that acquired by a grant of land in fee, and did not necessarily withdraw it from a liability to which all lands in the Commonwealth are subject, to be taken for public use, for an equivalent, when in the opinion of the legislature the public exigency requires it ; and·that the effect of the railroad act was merely to appropriate to another and distinct public use a portion of the land over which the franchise of the water power company was to be used.

If the whole of a franchise should become necessary for the public use, it *seems* that the right • of eminent domain would authorize the legislature to take it, on payment of a full equivalent.

An act of the legislature, in the exercise of the right of eminent domain, appropriating to public use, on payment of a full equivalent, property or rights in the nature of property granted by the State to individuals, is not a law impairing the obligation of contracts, within the meaning of the Constitution of the United States.

It was *held*, that the act authorizing the railroad is not liable to the objection that it does not provide for compensation for the damage done to the franchise of the water power corporation, for the franchise was not taken but only a portion of the land over which it extended, and for all damages occasioned by the taking of land the act makes provision.

The act empowered the railroad corporation to locate and construct a railroad " in or near the city of Boston and thence to any part of the town of Worcester, in such manner and form as they should deem expedient." It was *held*, that the act sufficiently declared the public necessity and convenience of the railroad and fixed the general *termini*, and that the delegations to the corporation, of the power to fix the precise *termini* and the intermediate course between them, and thus to take private property for public use, did not render the act unconstitutional and invalid.

---

[1] 23 Pickering's Reports, 360.

Boston Water Power Co. v. Boston and Worcester Railroad Corporation.

Where a corporation was empowered by the legislature, in general terms, to locate and construct a railroad between certain *termini,* and between these *termini* lay an extensive tract of land already appropriated, under the authority of the legislature, to a distinct public use, namely, for mill ponds, by another corporation, and this tract might be crossed by the railroad, with some diminution indeed of the mill power, and which might be compensated in damages, but without essential injury, it was considered that there was nothing in the nature of such public use, and in the extent to which it would be impaired or diminished, from which the power of constructing the railroad over it might be presumed to have been restrained by the legislature.

It was *held,* that if the water in the basins above mentioned was once a part of the Charles river, it ceased to be so after it was effectually separated by the dam and rendered unfit for the general purposes of navigation ; and consequently, that a prohibition to the railroad corporation to build a bridge over the water of Charles river, connected with Boston, or to place any obstruction therein, was not intended to apply to the basins, but only to the waters of Charles river below the dam and open to navigation, and was designed mainly to protect this navigation.

BILL in equity, filed in March, 1833, containing the following allegations.

By St. 1814, c. 39, divers persons were incorporated by the name of the Boston and Roxbury Mill Corporation, and by that statute and those of 1816, c. 40, 1819, c. 65, and 1822, c. 34, the corporation was authorized to purchase and hold real and personal estate; to build a dam from Charles street, at the westerly end of Beacon street, in Boston, westerly to Sewall's Point, in Brookline, so as to exclude the tide water on the northerly side of the dam and form on the southerly side a reservoir or receiving basin of the space between the dam and Boston Neck ; to build another dam from Gravelly Point, in Roxbury, to the dam first mentioned, so as to inclose the tide water within Tide-Mill Creek, on the westerly side of this cross dam ; to cut any number of convenient raceways from the full basin to the receiving basin; to maintain and keep up all their works forever; and to lease or sell the right of using the water, upon any terms and in any manner they might think proper; and it was provided, that no other person should have a right to dispose of the water, without the consent of the corporation.   The corporation was authorized to make over the main dam first mentioned a good and substantial road, and to receive toll for passing over it.   Certain duties and obligations in favor of the public, set forth at large in the bill, were imposed upon the corporation, and certain penalties and forfeitures created to secure the performance of its undertakings.   These acts were accepted by the corporation, whereby a contract conformable to the terms of the acts was created between the corporation and the Commonwealth.

This contract was performed on the part of the corporation by the erection of the works required, being works of great magnitude and expense, and of great public convenience and utility, and thereby the corporation became entitled to the exclusive right and privilege of forever using the soil included within the limits of the full basin, for the purpose of keeping it covered with water to the height and extent of surface to which the tide naturally flowed it, and the exclusive right and privilege of forever keeping the soil included within the limits of the receiving basin uncovered by the tide waters, and using it for a reservoir to receive and carry off the waters flowing from the' full basin through the raceways cut, or which should thereafter be cut, through the cross dam, and the exclusive right and privilege of cutting raceways through any part of the cross dam, and of using or disposing by lease or otherwise, of the water power thereby created.-

The plaintiffs were incorporated by the name of the Boston Water Power Company, on June 12th, 1824, (St. 1824, c. 26,) with power to purchase and hold any quantity of the water power created by the establishment of the dams above mentioned, and by an indenture, dated May 9th, 1832, the Boston and Roxbury Mill Corporation transferred to them, for the sum of $175,000, all the grantor's right to the land above the main dam, and all the water power, and all their privileges, contracts, duties, and obligations respecting the water power; and the plaintiffs thereby, so far as regards the water power, became entitled to the exclusive right and privilege of forever using the soil included within the two basins, for the purposes before mentioned, and to all the water power which can be and is created by the constructing and maintaining of the dams, without any hindrance, obstruction, interruption, or diminution of the capacity of the basins respectively.

The plaintiffs allege, that the Boston and Worcester Railroad Corporation deny and disregard these vested rights, and threaten to build a railroad through the full basin, and over the cross dam, and through the receiving basin; and have actually commenced building the same, by driving piles in both of the basins; and have taken for their road a strip of land twenty-six feet wide through the full basin, and five rods wide through the receiving basin.

The construction of the railroad through and across the two basins and cross dam will, it is alleged, greatly diminish the water power, and abridge the franchise vested in the plaintiffs, of using the soil and space between the main dam and Boston Neck for their basins, to their irreparable injury, and, so far as their rights are concerned, will be a nuisance.

The bill concludes with a prayer for a perpetual injunction and other relief.

The defendants filed an answer, in November, 1835, in which they deny, that the Boston and Roxbury Mill Corporation have complied with certain essential conditions of their act of incorporation, and that the plaintiffs, as their successors, or assigns, are or ever were entitled to the exclusive right of forever using the soil included within the basins, for the purposes and to the extent set forth in the bill, or for any other purpose, or to any other extent; and they allege, that the soil in the basins is, and ever has been, subject to the lawful rights of the proprietors of the lands bordering on and extending into the basins to use the same, and subject to the right of the Commonwealth to take any property for public use. They deny that the several rights and privileges of the Boston and Roxbury Mill Corporation were ever so far perpetual and exclusive as to deprive or abridge the Commonwealth, or the legislature, of the right and power of taking, or causing to be taken, for public uses, the soil of the basins and dams, and any and all of the property, rights, privileges, and franchises of that corporation, or their assigns, making to the corporation, or their assigns, reasonable compensation therefor.

The defendants allege, that the legislature, prior to granting the charter to the Boston and Worcester Railroad Corporation, chose a board of directors of internal improvements, with authority to appoint engineers, whose duty it should be to examine and survey routes for railroads between Boston and the Hudson River, and between Boston and Providence, and that in January, 1829, that board made a report of the doings of themselves, and of an engineer appointed by them, to the legislature, stating the various routes which they recommended, accompanied with plans and estimates of the same, and that in this report they contemplated and referred, among other routes, to a route between Boston and Providence through these basins; and that this report was accepted by the legislature, and, with the plans and estimates, was printed and published at the public expense; that in consequence of the information thus disseminated, and of the belief that the construction of the railroad to Worcester would be of great public benefit, the original applicants for the charter of the Boston and Worcester Railroad Corporation were induced to apply therefor; that the legislature accordingly, on the 23d of June, 1831, passed an act establishing this corporation, and on March 22d, 1832, March 11th, 1833, March 28th and 31st, 1834, and April 8th, 1835, passed additional acts, all of which are made a part of the answer; that by their act of incorporation, the railroad corporation were authorized and empowered to locate, construct, and finally complete a railroad in or near the city of Boston, and thence to any part of the town of Worcester, in such manner and form as they should deem to be most expedient, and for this purpose were authorized to lay out their road not exceeding five rods wide, through the whole length, and for the purpose of cutting embankments and procuring stone and gravel, to

take as much more land as might be necessary for the proper construction and security of the road, provided that all damage that
might be occasioned to any person or corporation by the taking of
such land or materials for these purposes should be paid for by the
railroad corporation, in the manner provided in the act; and that by
the seventh section, it was enacted, that the railroad corporation
should be holden to pay all damages that might arise to any person
or persons, corporation, or corporations, by taking their land for the
railroad, when it could not be obtained by voluntary agreement, to.
be estimated and recovered in the manner provided by law for the
recovery of damages suffered by the laying out of highways ; and the
defendants aver, that the property of the plaintiffs in the water power
is comprehended under the term land; and that in the additional
act of March 11th, 1833, provision is made for compensating the
owners of land or other property, for all damages by them sustained
by the construction of the railroad; and that by a general law of
March 26th, 1833, a similar provision is made for compensating
owners of land or other property, for all damages by them sustained
by the construction of any railroad.

They further state, that by the fifteenth section of the act incorporating the railroad corporation, it was provided, that nothing contained in the act should be construed as giving them authority to
erect a bridge over the waters of Charles River, connected with the
city of Boston.

They allege, that before the location of any part of the railroad,
the act of incorporation and the additional acts were accepted by the
persons incorporated, and they thereby become entitled to exercise
all the powers, and enjoy all the rights granted therein ; that the corporation thereupon proceeded to survey a great variety of routes, and
after a full view and consideration thereof, they were of opinion, that
it was most expedient, on account of the public benefit and accommodation, to adopt the route which they have adopted, and that it
was, in fact, for the public benefit that the road should pass in that
direction, and that it was accordingly so located; that about the 1st.
of May, 1833, they laid out and took as and for a part of their rail-
-road, a strip of land running across the basins and cross dam, as by
virtue of the authority granted to them they lawfully might do, and
since the filing of the bill, they have completed and put in operation
their railroad from Boston through and across the basins and cross
dam to Worcester.

The defendants admit that two mills might be erected on the part
of the cross dam taken for the railroad, but they allege that the
plaintiffs have other mill sites more than sufficient for the employ-

ment of all the water power; and they admit, that the driving of piles and laying of stones, necessary for the support of the railroad, and making the embankment through and across the basins, must necessarily and directly, but not in any great degree, diminish the capacity of the basins, namely, by about one two hundredth part of the area of the basins; but they allege, that the increase of the capacity by the excavations which the railroad corporation have made, is much greater than such diminution.

The defendants aver, that the railroad corporation have been always and are ready to pay the plaintiffs the full amount of damages which they have sustained, if they are entitled to any, and have attempted to agree with the plaintiffs in respect to the amount of such damages, but without success; and that the plaintiffs have never applied to the county commissioners of Norfolk, or to the mayor and aldermen of Boston, as provided by law, for the purposes of having the damages ascertained.

The defendants deny, that the building of the railroad has operated, or can operate, as an irreparable damage to the plaintiffs, or is or will be in derogation of any of the lawfully vested rights of the plaintiffs, or is or will be in any way a nuisance to them.

The defendants deny, that the waters of the basins are a part of the waters of Charles River, connected with the city of Boston, according to the meaning and intent of the fifteenth section of the charter of the railroad corporation, but they aver, that they are tide waters separated and excluded from the waters of Charles River, and rendered innavigable by the main dam; they aver, that the location and building of the railroad across the basins, is fully authorized by the general powers conferred by their act of incorporation, and not in any manner restricted or forbidden by any section or clause thereof, or of any subsequent act; and that if such power and authority had not before been conferred, or was before restrained and prohibited, yet such power and authority were, by necessary implication, conferred upon the corporation by the act passed on the 31st of January, 1833, establishing the South Cove Corporation; by which act, the South Cove Corporation were authorized and empowered to purchase and hold certain lands and flats, called the South Cove, and to take measures to procure the railroad from Worcester to be located on the same; that a majority of the directors of the railroad corporation have at all times considered the route across the basins, and thence to deep water by the South Cove, as the most expedient that could be adopted, so far as the convenience and accommodation of the public was concerned, as well as for all other reasons except the expense thereof, and that while they were deliberating upon the relative expediency of the different routes, they received a communication from persons residing in the south part of Boston, representing that it would be for the public interest that the railroad should terminate in that quarter, and that afterwards the South Cove Corporation and the railroad corporation made a compact, wherein it was agreed, that the South Cove Corporation should prepare a suitable termination and place of deposit for the railroad within the limits of the South Cove, and should pay the damages which should be sustained by the owners of lands and buildings lying between the receiving basin and the South Cove, by reason of building the railroad through and over the same, and should moreover pay to the railroad corporation $75,000, whereupon the railroad corporation determined to make its termination and place of deposit within the limits of the South Cove; and the railroad corporation admit, that upon these inducements held out by the South Cove Corporation, which enabled them to do so, and because they believed it the most expedient route for the public use and accommodation, the railroad corporation located their road as above mentioned; but they deny, that in consideration of those inducements, the railroad corporation did, without regard to the general public expediency in that behalf alter any course or direction before purposed for the railroad; and the defendants further say, that in making this contract and in so locating the railroad, the railroad corporation were well warranted and authorized by their own act of incorporation; but they further say, that in the charter of the South Cove Corporation such a contract and location were expressly authorized.

C. G. *Loring*, (with whom were J. *Mason* and *Gardiner*,) for the plaintiffs.

By the exercise of the right of eminent domain, the soil in these basins, belonging in part to individuals, and in part to the Commonwealth, has been appropriated to the exclusive use of the plaintiffs' grantors, for the purpose of creating mill powers; and a valid and binding contract was made between them and the Commonwealth, by which the perpetual enjoyment of the privileges thus granted has been secured. It is to be remarked, that the privileges and powers of the plaintiffs, and the territory in which they were to be exercised have been *expressly defined* by the legislature; and they have been fully recognized by this court. Boston and Roxbury Mill Corporation v. Newman, 12 Pick. 467. But the charter of the railroad corporation confers a general power, not definite or precise as to the *termini* of the railroad, excepting by the exclusion provided in reference to Charles River, and there is no specific exercise of the right of eminent domain over any particular or described lands. Under this power the defendants have laid out and made their railroad through the basins, and confessedly, to a certain extent, impaired the plaintiffs' water power; thereby creating a nuisance, unless justified by law. And the question is, whether the law will warrant their proceedings.

That the right of using these lands for basins for the creation and maintenance of water power, is a franchise, cannot be questioned, the point having been judicially determined in a former stage of this case. 16 Pick. 512; 2 Bl. Comm. 37; 3 Kent's Comm. (3d edit.) 458. And it is to be observed, that the exercise of the right assumed by the defendants, goes to the existence of the whole franchise; for if they may obstruct a portion of the basins, they or others may acquire like rights over the residue.

The plaintiffs contend, that the defendants had no right to locate and build their road across these basins in such manner as to lessen, injure, or repair the water power, or any of the privileges or franchises held by the plaintiffs by virtue of legislative grants : —

1. Because the legislature cannot constitutionally destroy, nor essentially injure or repair, by a subsequent grant, a franchise which it had previously created, and thus in effect vacate its own contract; and this, whether there be or be not a provision for compensation.

The principle upon which this position rests is, that the creation of a franchise, involving great expenditures, is a contract between the legislature and the corporators, which by the Constitution of the U. S. art. 1, § 10, the legislature is prohibited to revoke or impair. That the grant of a charter is a contract, is well settled; and the only question is, whether the right of eminent domain will extend to the abrogation or resumption of franchise. No case has been found where this point has been decided. The case of Bradshaw v. Rogers, 20 Johns. 103, 735, cannot be deemed an exception to this remark, for the point was not judicially before the court. The eminent domain belongs to the sovereign, the people, and not to the legislature, except so far as it is delegated by the people; and by the Constitution of the United States, that part of the eminent domain which consists in the power of vacating contracts, is expressly surrendered by the States. If it be asked what is to be done in cases of extreme necessity, as where land is required for a fortress, &c., the answer is, that such cases fall under the rule of self-preservation and make a law for themselves; and further, that such cases, being of national concern, come within the power of the United States; which are not restrained from abrogating a contract between a State and a citizen. Const. U. S., 5th art. of Amendments; Chesapeake and Ohio Canal

26 *

Co. v. Baltimore and Ohio Railroad Co. 4 Gill & Johns. 1, 108, 109, 144, 145, 165; Enfield Bridge v. Connecticut River Co. 7 Connect. R. 52; Charles River Bridge v. Warren Bridge, 7 Pick. 459, 494; s. c. 11 Peters, 577; West Boston Bridge v. County Commissioners, &c. 10 Pick. 272; Wales v. Stetson, 2 Mass. R. 146; Dartmouth College v. Woodward, 4 Wheaton, 628; Terrett v. Taylor, 9 Cranch, 52; Day v. Stetson, 8 Greenleaf, 369. It may be said that every franchise must be held subject to the right of eminent domain, in the same manner as land granted by the legislature. But all land is in theory held under a grant from the State, and the right of appropriating it for public uses is founded as well upon the principle of absolute necessity, as upon immemorial usage; so that every one who takes a grant of land from the State is presumed to know that he takes it subject to the eminent domain. But there is no such preexisting necessity or usage in relation to a pure franchise, and no such presumptive notice as to the power of the public to resume the grant. We do not deny the right of eminent domain over lands granted by the State to a corporation, subsequently to its incorporation, nor even over lands granted by the charter, where they are not essential to the existence of the corporation or the enjoyment of its franchise. But there is an obvious distinction between those cases and one like the case at bar, where the existence of the franchise depends upon the subject-matter granted or acted upon. Even in the case of a grant of land, should the legislature covenant never to exercise the right of eminent domain over it, we do not perceive why the covenantee would not be protected by the Constitution of the United States. It will perhaps be said, that it is incompetent for the legislature to part with that right; but to maintain this position, the provision in the Constitution of the United States must be regarded as of no effect. Nor can it be said that a State does not impair a contract when it makes compensation for rescinding it. Commonwealth v. Cambridge, 7 Mass. R. 167.

Now we contend, that the charter of the plaintiffs constituted a continuing executory contract between them and the State, totally distinct from a mere grant of land. It was a grant in the exercise of eminent domain, of a right over these lands for peculiar uses, those uses requiring constantly a vast expenditure of money, and being in their nature exclusive of all other uses as well by the grantees as others. It was a special contract, in which the State stipulated for the continued exercise of its right of eminent domain upon condition of the plaintiffs performing their part of the contract, and the plaintiffs stipulated to keep the works in repair and in a state to benefit the public, and it resembles any other contract made for a special purpose and which the State cannot revoke.

The second ground, under this first point, is, that the legislature having granted to the plaintiffs the right of exercising the eminent domain over these lands for a specific purpose, and for a valuable consideration, and they having entered upon the enjoyment of the grant and paid the consideration, the legislature could not grant the same right to the defendants for a different purpose. In this point of view the case stands rather as a question of title than one of constitutional power, and rests upon the common-law axiom, that a second grant of the same thing is void. To give validity to the second grant would not be a taking for the public use, for the public already had the benefit of the subject of the grant, but it is only shifting the private benefit. Chesapeake &c. Canal v. Baltimore &c. Railroad, 4 Gill & Johns. 1.

2. If the legislature had themselves this power to impair or revoke the plaintiffs' franchise, in whole or in part, they could not constitutionally delegate to private individuals the power of determining upon the expediency of doing so; and especially not to persons directly interested to impair or revoke it.

That these defendants, if they have the right claimed, do hold or take it under a delegated authority to exercise the legislative functions in this behalf, is manifest, because upon reference to the acts under which they claim, it appears that no legislative action was ever had upon the question of resuming or impairing this franchise, and the plans and reports of engineers and of the board of directors of internal improvement, show that the railroad might have been constructed and carried to the depot on the South Cove by a different route; and the actual determination of the question between the comparative importance of this franchise to the public, and of the construction of the railroad here rather than elsewhere, was made by the railroad corporation themselves. We are aware of the usage which existed in this State, of granting to corporations general powers to lay out turnpike roads, without prescribing the precise limits, and which has been modified by St. 1804, c. 125, § 1; but this course of legislation is anomalous and peculiar to this country. It arose, probably, from the newness of our settlements, and the comparative worthlessness of land and paramount value of roads to the owners of lands; and the question has never been the subject of a direct judicial decision. If it were a new question, we should insist that a power of so solemn a nature, and involving consequences so important to the public and to individuals, could not be so delegated. And if our case required it, we should even now appeal to the first principles of law, and deny that a power resting in a body appointed by the public, and to be exercised solely for the public, could be dele-

gated to private and irresponsible individuals, not impartial and disinterested, but acting from motives of direct personal, private, pecuniary interest. Commonwealth v. Parker, 2 Pick. 556 ; Declaration
of Rights, art. 10 ; 1 Bl. Comm. 139. The power of taking land for
highways is delegated to courts of sessions and municipal corporations, but they are public bodies and governed by general laws.
Bloodgood v. Mohawk and Hudson Railroad Corporation, 18 Wendell, 69 ; Commonwealth v. Charlestown, 1 Pick. 185. It is an axiom
of our government, that the legislature acts by a delegated authority
and merely as servants of the people; and it is an axiom of the common law, that *delegatus non potest delegare.* Charles River Bridge
v. Warren Bridge, 7 Pick. 445 ; Marr v. Enloe, 1 Yerger, 452 ; Boston v. Schaffer, 9 Pick. 415.

But though a usage may have prevailed, of delegating to individuals the power of appropriating private property in this way, it has
never yet been acknowledged by practice or by precedent, that the
power of taking public property, or of revoking public contracts, has
been or can be thus delegated. It cannot be contended that under
this act for laying out a railroad, power is given to the corporation to appropriate arsenals, dock-yards, public buildings, colleges,
and other establishments created for the public defence, instruction,
or ornament; but all franchises created by the exercise of the eminent domain, are to all intents public works and equally sacred.
The franchise in question involved a great exercise of this sovereign
power, over a vast territory, and was created at a vast expense;
the grant was made on the ground that the public good to be produced justified and required this appropriation of the private property of individuals; and can it be supposed that the legislature
ever delegated to private individuals the power of determining upon
the continuance of this great public establishment? Further, the
legislature, by the charter to the plaintiffs, entered into a solemn
contract, that in consideration of vast sums of money to be contributed by them, they should perpetually enjoy the benefit of this
franchise, and the public faith was pledged. It cannot be pretended
that the legislature, by the grant of a general power, has acted upon
the question of abrogating this franchise; for it is obvious that the
question, whether it was more for the public good to have the road
pass in this direction and thus sacrifice this franchise, or to have it
pass in another, so that the public might enjoy both, has never been
acted upon by the legislature, nor by any public body acting under
general laws.

3. If it were competent to the legislature to delegate to the defendants the power of revoking or impairing the plaintiffs' franchise,

yet according to the rules of legal construction the charter of the defendants does not purport to delegate to them any such power. It being a branch of the sovereign power the exercise of which affects the rights of private individuals by the appropriation of their property, and the public by impairing a franchise previously established for the public good, and most of all, involves the integrity and good faith of the government in regard to its contracts, any delegation of it into the hands of third persons, and especially those who are under no responsibility to the public, and who have pecuniary interests at stake, should, upon all laws of interpretation, be by express terms or by necessary implication. And if the terms and object of the grant in which such delegation is alleged to be found, can be answered by any other interpretations, so that both may stand together, this latter interpretation is to be adopted. This is the more obviously necessary conclusion here, because if the construction contended for by the defendants is sound, they would have an equal right to destroy the arsenal, pass through public fortifications, or cross navigable rivers, under their charter, as to take this public franchise. Now there can be no pretence of any express grant of the power claimed; no mention is made of any right to appropriate public property, or to take or destroy a previously granted franchise; the only terms used in the original act, under which alone the railroad corporation can claim, designating the property to be taken, are *lands* and *materials;* no specific route is prescribed; general *termini* are alone given; and the case finds that various other routes were practicable. The only ground therefore upon which the power can be asserted, is by implication. But such implication cannot be said to be necessary, where the terms can be answered and the objects of the act obtained by a different construction; as is clearly the case here.

The first ground we take under this point is, that grants of this sort are to be construed strictly, and not as passing any powers which are not necessary for carrying the purposes of the charter into effect. 2 Kent's Comm. (3d ed.) 298, 299; Charles River Bridge *v.* Warren Bridge, 11 Peters, 465, and case sthere cited; s. c. 7 Pick. 464, 468, 469, 557; Providence Bank *v.* Billings, 4 Peters, 514; The Elsebe, 5 Rob. Adm. R. 183; Chesapeake &c. Canal *v.* Baltimore &c. Railroad, 4 Gill & Johns. 123, 175; Kingston-upon-Hull Dock Co. *v.* Lamarche, 8 Barn. & Cressw. 42; Stourbridge Canal *v.* Wheeley, 2 Barn. & Adolph. 792; Commonwealth *v.* Coombs, 2 Mass. R. 492; Arundel *v.* M'Culloch, 10 Mass. R. 70; Martin *v.* Commonwealth, 1 Mass. R. 356; United States *v.* Arredondo, 6 Peters, 738; Rutherford *v.* Green's Heirs, 2 Wheaton, 203; Beattee *v.* Knowles's Lessee, 4 Peters, 168; Jackson *v.* Lanfear, 3 Peters, 289; 19 Vin. Abr. 525, pl. 132. Upon this general principle we should contend, that as the defendants could have laid out their road in various other directions, and the right to go through these basins and thus injure the plaintiffs' franchise was not necessary, no such power to injure or destroy a franchise created for the benefit of the public, as well as of individuals, and to impair works of such vast importance, could be implied.

Another ground on which the defendants' charter shall be held not to authorize the destruction of our franchise, is, that the grant of the use of these lands to the plaintiffs for the purposes specified in their charter, was a dedication and appropriation of them to the public use; and no subsequent grant can be construed to impair or destroy that use, unless by its express terms or necessary implication such construction is unavoidable. Boston and Roxbury Mill Corporation v. Newman, 12 Pick. 476; Commonwealth v. Coombs, 2 Mass. R. 489; Arundel v. M'Culloch, 10 Mass. R. 70; Hood v. Dighton Bridge, 3 Mass. R. 267; Keen v. Stetson, 5 Pick. 494; Commonwealth v. Stevens, 10 Pick. 248; Wales v. Stetson, 2 Mass. R. 146; West Boston Bridge v. County Commissioners &c. 10 Pick. 272; Wellington, Petitioner &c. 10 Pick. 105.

Another reason against the defendants' construction of their charter is, that no compensation is therein provided for the injury which might be done to the *public* by the destruction of this beneficial franchise. The legislature might undoubtedly surrender this benefit, but a surrender without consideration will not be implied except by an inevitable construction. Here, as before remarked, the public might well have had the benefit of the water power and of the railroad, without the interference of one with the other. Commonwealth v. Stevens, 10 Pick. 248. It will be said that the compensation to the public lies in the greater benefit to arise from taking this route rather than any other; but it may not be so great; and the legislature cannot be presumed to have given to an interested corporation the power of determining the question.

A further ground on which we contend that the railroad charter does not confer the power claimed under it, is that a subsequent statute or grant shall not be construed to revoke a previous one, if capable of a different construction. By the plaintiffs' charter the legislature had granted and appropriated to them the exclusive use of these lands for a particular purpose; and now the defendants assert a right to the use and enjoyment of the same lands for a different purpose, destructive entirely of the use of the land taken, and consequentially injurious to the whole franchise of the plaintiffs. 3 Kent's Comm. (3d ed.) 459; United States v. Arredondo, 6 Peters, 738, 740; Rutherford v. Green's Heirs, 2 Wheaton, 203; Jackson v.

Muzzy, 7 Johns. R. 5; Chesapeake &c. Canal v. Baltimore &c. Railroad, 4 Gill & Johns. 108, 109, 134, 136, 144, 145, 149, 154, 190; Pease v. Whitney, 5 Mass. R. 382; People v. Platt, 17 Johns. R. 195; M'Cartee v. Orphan Asylum, 9 Cowen, 507; Charles River Bridge v. Warren Bridge, 11 Peters, 619, and cases cited; s. c. 7 Pick. 527; Terrett v. Taylor, 9 Cranch, 50; Williams v. Pritchard, 4 T. R. 2; Gibson v. Buck, 15 East, 371; Scales v. Pickering, 4 Bingh. 450; 2 Wms's Saund. 175, note 2; 5 Bac. Abr. 385, Prerog. F.; 19 Viner, 525, pl. 132; People v. Tibbetts, 4 Cowen, 392; Enfield Bridge v. Connecticut River Co. 7 Connect. R. 28; United States v. Harris, 1 Sumner, 42; Coolidge v. Williams, 4 Mass. R. 145. If it be alleged in reply to these authorities, that they are cases of subsequent acts impairing prior grants without providing compensation, we answer that this consideration is of no avail, for the taking of the prior grant or vested right is nevertheless *in invitum*, and as much a revocation and destruction of the right as if no indemnity were provided, and the rule of construction must therefore be the same. Commonwealth v. Cambridge, 7 Mass. R. 167; Commonwealth v. Sawin, 2 Pick. 547.

4. The charter of the defendants does not in terms, nor by any just interpretation, purport to vest in them the power of revoking or impairing a franchise; nor is any compensation provided for such an injury. The only power given is to lay out their road not exceeding five rods wide, and for the purpose of cuttings and embankments and procuring stone and gravel, to take as much more *land* as may be necessary; and the compensation for damages is limited to such as are occasioned by the taking of land, and is to be made to those whose lands are taken. And so far from there being any power to take, or destroy, or impair any other franchise, provision is made to prevent it in all cases where the conflict could be anticipated. St. 1831, c. 72, § 11. *Land* and *materials* clearly do not embrace franchises or easements. A grant of land does not pass the easement; nor does a grant of the easement pass the land. West Boston Bridge v. County Commissioners &c. 10 Pick. 272; Charles River Bridge v. Warren Bridge, 7 Pick. 385, 502, 529. It is plain, too, that as between the plaintiffs and the defendants the latter have not taken any land belonging to the plaintiffs, but merely their easements. 16 Pick. 512. The defendants may rely upon the additional act of the 11th of March, 1833, (St. 1833, c. 91, § 2,) which provides that in case the railroad corporation shall " not be able to obtain the land or *other property* which they may take for said road, or for the proper construction and security thereof, by voluntary agreement with the owner," the corporation, as well as the owner,

may apply to the county commissioners of the county where the property is situate, to estimate the damages' occasioned by taking the same. But the object of this provision was, not to give new power to take, but merely to give to the corporation the privilege of applying to the county commissioners for an estimate of the damages; which, in the original act, was given only to the party whose land should be taken. Further, the words *other property*, in the additional act, must be construed to have the same meaning as in the original act; where they are used (§ 8) to embrace the estates of minors, &c., in lands held in trust for them, and not as embracing any distinct and different estates from those in lands which the corporation was, by a previous section, authorized to take. And this act does not apply to land or property in Boston, because it gives a remedy only by application to county commissioners, and there are no such commissioners in Boston; and the St. 1834, c. 437, authorizing a similar application to the mayor and aldermen of Boston, contains a provision that it shall not affect existing rights. It may be contended, that it is not necessary that compensation should be provided in the act giving the power to take; and the case of Bonaparte v. Camden and Amboy Railroad Company, 1 Baldwin, 226, is an authority to that effect; but the doctrine is a virtual surrender of the protection afforded by the constitution, and is contrary to the decisions in this and other States. Perry v. Wilson, 7 Mass. R. 395; Stevens v. Middlesex Canal, 12 Mass. R. 468; Callender v. Marsh, 1 Pick. 430; 2 Kent, (3d ed.) 339; Gardner v. Newburg, 2 Johns. Ch. R. 168; Eakin v. Raub, 12 Serg. & Rawle, 372; Bloodgood v. Mohawk &c. Railroad, 18 Wendell, 17.

5. The legislature have by express terms, or by necessary implication, prohibited this location of the railroad. The 15th section of the charter denies the corporation "authority to erect a bridge *over the waters* of Charles River, connected with the city of Boston"; and in the additional act of March 22d, 1832, (St. 1832, c. 153, § 1,) authority is given to erect a bridge across the waters of the Charles River, but only between the main dam and Canal Bridge. Before the construction of this dam the waters which flowed over the basins were the waters of Charles River, and they continue to be such, notwithstanding the dam. They remain navigable to a certain extent, and are still the public property so far as regards sailing on them and fishing in them; and the only change made is a partial obstruction of the communication between this and the other portion of the river.

6. Our last point is, that the location so injurious to the plaintiffs, was made, not from motives of public policy, but by reason of a pecuniary consideration paid to the defendants by the South Cove

Corporation, and is therefore void. Commonwealth v. Sawin, 2 Pick. 547; Commonwealth v. Cambridge, 7 Mass. R. 158. It is said that the charter of the South Cove Corporation contemplates that the road should pass through the basins and terminate on the cove; but it is not to be inferred that the legislature, or the plaintiffs, supposed that this would be done without obtaining a lawful right, either by contract or otherwise, to pass in this direction.

Aylwin, for the defendants.

The contract between the Commonwealth and the Boston and Roxbury Mill Corporation creates no franchise as to the water power itself. A franchise is a public liberty or right, granted to a private person for public purposes. Finch's Law, 114; 2 Bl. Comm. 37. The Act of 1814 establishes the Boston and Roxbury Mill Corporation, authorizes the building of dams, the inclosing of tide waters, and the taking of toll. These may be franchises. The power to drive mills by the water thus penned in was *property*. The right of *using the water* was authorized *to be sold*. It was an *easement over land;* and the language in 16 Pick. 572, does not fairly warrant any other construction. The right to *dispose* of the water, although derived directly from the Commonwealth, altered not the nature of the property. All *lands* are thus held. No one pretends that a grant of land by the Commonwealth will create a franchise; and much less will an ownership in the waters flowing over it, or the right to use or sell it. The mill corporation had no right to sell its franchises, nor the water power company to buy them; so that the plaintiffs are not the assignees, in this respect, of the mill corporation. Franchises are not essential to a corporation. The King v. City of London, Skinner, 310.

By these acts, which are called a contract, the Commonwealth has not imposed on itself any restraint against resuming the water power, or the franchise, if it is one, for public uses. The subject-matter is but *property*, and like all other property is held liable to appropriation for such purposes. There is nothing to preclude the appropriation of a franchise, if necessary, to public use, an indemnity being made to the owner. Providence Bank v. Billings, 4 Peters, 562; 2 Kent, (3d ed.) 338, 340; Beekman v. Saratoga Railroad, 3 Paige, 72; Charles River Bridge v. Warren Bridge, 7 Pick. 459, 500, 522, 530, 531; Dartmouth College v. Woodward, 4 Wheaton, 689; Piscataqua Bridge v. New Hampshire Bridge, 7 N. Hamp. R. 67, 69; Charles River Bridge v. Warren Bridge, 11 Peters, 546, 547, 580, 582, 646; Dyer v. Tuscaloosa Bridge, 2 Porter, (Alabama,) 304; Anc. Charters, &c. 127; Prov. St. 5 Will. & Mary, c. 10; Plymouth

Colony Laws, 269; Lindsay v. Commissioners, 2 Bay, 38; Stough-ton v. Baker, 4 Mass. R. 522; Cottril v. Myrick, 3 Fairfield, 231; Vinton v. Welch, 9 Pick. 92.

The defendants contend, that every power and immunity to accomplish the end proposed, was granted to the railroad corporation, as well in regard to the location, as in regard to the property to be taken. The only restriction is, that a bridge shall not be erected over the waters of Charles River connected with the city of Boston, nor any obstruction be placed in those waters. And the defendants deny that the waters of the basins are the waters of Charles River. St. 1831, c. 72, § 1, 7, 15; St. 1832, c. 152; St. 1833, c. 91, and c. 187; St. 1834, c. 137.

They further contend, that the legislature must have had in view the route across the basins, and if not directly, certainly by implication, sanctioned this route. See St. 1827, c. 116; Report of J. F. Baldwin, to the Board of Internal Improvements, p. 21, 61, where there is an express proposal to bring the Boston and Providence Railroad across one of the basins; St. 1833, c. 17, § 6, (establishing the South Cove Corporation,) passed in January, 1833, previously to the actual location, which was in May, 1833; Resolves of 1829, p. 99.

The question of expediency as to an appropriation of property generally, for the railroad, is decided by the legislature, whose decision is final. St. 1831, c. 72; Commonwealth v. Breed, 4 Pick. 463; Spring v. Russell, 7 Greenleaf, 272; Wellington, Petitioner, 16 Pick. 101. The particular location is left to the railroad corporation; and the right of appropriation, by inevitable conclusion, extends to these basins. Rogers v. Bradshaw, 20 Johns. R. 740.

There is nothing in the nature of the act to be performed, which should restrain the legislature from delegating the power to fix on the location of a railroad. It has been the usage of this Commonwealth and of other States to delegate the power in similar cases; sometimes to the party interested, and sometimes to public boards or tribunals. 1 Special Laws, 309, 329, 357, 382, 466, 502; 2 Special Laws, 93; St. 1804, c. 125; St. 1822, c. 27; St. 1822, c. 57; St. 1827, c. 127; St. 1825, c. 183; Commonwealth v. Charlestown, 1 Pick. 185; Wellington, Petitioner, 16 Pick. 101'; Farmers' Turnp. Co. v. Coventry, 10 Johns. R. 400; Beekman v. Saratoga Railroad, 3 Paige, 74; Mohawk Bridge Co. v. Utica Railroad, 6 Paige, 561; Boston v. Schaffer, 9 Pick. 418. And the power to locate the railroad was a fit subject of delegation, because scientific and peculiar knowledge was required for the purpose, and it was for the interest of the corporation to select the best route.

Whether this is held to be a franchise, the enjoyment of which is interrupted, or mere property, the railroad corporation were authorized to interfere with it, because compensation was provided. In the 1st section of their charter (St. 1831, c. 72) the defendants are author. ized to lay out their road five rods wide, and for the purpose of cuttings, embankments, and procuring stone and gravel, to take as much more land as may be necessary, &c., "provided, however, that *all* damages that may be occasioned to any *person* or *corporation*, by the taking of such land or materials, &c., shall be paid for," &c. In the 7th section it is enacted, that the defendants shall be holden "to pay all damages that may arise to any person or persons, corporation or corporations, by taking their land for said railroad, when it cannot be obtained by voluntary agreement, to be estimated and recovered in the manner provided by law for the recovery of damages happening by the laying out of highways." The 8th section manifests the intent of the legislature by " damages occasioned," &c., for it provides, that " when the *lands* or *other property* or *estate* of any feme covert, infant, or person *non compos mentis*, shall be necessary for the construction of said railroad, the husband, &c., may release all damages for any *lands* or *estates* taken and appropriated as aforesaid. And to remove all doubts, the Act of 1833, c. 91, provides that in case the defendants shall not be able to obtain " the *land* or *other property* which they may take, &c., by voluntary agreement, &c., the said corporation, as well as the said owner or owners, may apply to the county commissioners to estimate the damages occasioned by taking the same." See, also, St. 1833, c. 187.

And there was a suitable tribunal to award the compensation, namely, that which was intrusted with the laying out of highways. In Boston, the mayor and aldermen are invested with this authority; and when the legislature, in St. 1831, c. 72, speak of application to the county commissioners, they must be understood to include the mayor and aldermen of Boston, who have the same powers as county commissioners. The St. 1834, c. 137, is confirmatory of this view. And if it be necessary, in order to uphold the validity of the act, the court are warranted by authority in adjudging, that a subsequent provision for indemnity (as in this statute of 1834) is equivalent to a contemporaneous one, when property is appropriated to public use. Rogers *v.* Bradshaw, 20 Johns. R. 745; Eakin *v.* Raub, 12 Serg. & Rawle, 366, 372; Bloodgood *v.* Mohawk, &c. Railroad, 14 Wendell, 52; Canal Appraisers *v.* The People, 17 Wendell, 572. At the time when the road was actually located, the St. 1833, c. 91, was in force, giving indemnity for " property " to be taken.

F. Dexter, on the same side:
The plaintiffs deny the right of the defendants to lay out and con-

struct the railroad over the basins, first, because the legislature had no power to authorize it to be done. In support of this position, it is said, that by the common law a franchise cannot be granted at variance with one previously existing; and further, that the State granted its eminent domain to the plaintiffs, and this grant is a contract which, under the Constitution of the United States, is not to be violated by another grant of eminent domain. ' But there is a fallacy in supposing it a grant of eminent domain. That cannot be be granted. It is inalienable, because it is an essential right of sovereignty. The legislature have merely exercised the right of eminent domain, through the agency of the plaintiffs and of the defendants. In the case of the Chesapeake and Ohio Canal against the Baltimore and Ohio Railroad, relied on by the plaintiffs, there were two acts of incorporation, the first authorizing the construction of a canal, the second of a railroad. The route of the canal was confined to the valley of the Potomac River; that of the railroad was not so restricted; but there was one place by the river where the canal *must* pass, and where it would be convenient for the railroad to pass, but both could not be accommodated; and the question was, which corporation was entitled to the preference. Neither of them had made its location there, but each claimed the right, and when the railroad corporation was beginning to lay out its road there, the canal corporation applied for an injunction; and the court determined, that the company first incorporated had the prior right. The case has but little resemblance to the one now before the Court. The question there was, of the power of either corporation to acquire a franchise by condemning private land to a public use; of the right to exert unexecuted power; here, the power had been executed by the plaintiffs, and they had thereby acquired a qualified property in the land, and the question is, whether the railroad corporation may take this private property; there, the legislature could not have given the railroad corporation the power to locate in the particular place, inasmuch as it would violate a previous executory contract. The power to locate the canal was not a thing that could be taken; it was not property, but a right to acquire property. Authorities have been cited to show, that the same franchise cannot be twice granted; and it is supposed, from some old cases, that franchises are more sacred from the reach of sovereign power than other property; whereas, those cases could not have arisen, but for a mistaken notion that' they were less sacred. The granting of franchises being a branch of regal prerogative, the doubt was, whether the king could not resume a franchise, and the Court held that he could not, because it *was* private *property*. Kings never thought of granting the same land a second time.

Boston Water Power Co. *v.* Boston and Worcester Railroad Corporation.

But the plaintiffs' franchise is not granted to the railroad corpora. tion. This corporation is not to exercise the powers of the mill corporation. The land, in or over which the mill corporation hold a franchise, is taken by the defendants for another public use, by which the plaintiffs' franchise is extinguished *pro tanto*. But why might not the franchise be taken for a public use? The writers on law, municipal and general, hold, that all private property may be so taken; and is not a franchise private property? It has all the incidents of property. It descends to heirs, it may be sold, it may be taken on execution to pay debts. But if the question were uncertain at common law, it has been settled by this Court, in the case of the Charles River Bridge; where it was held by all the judges, except one, that the old ferry right had been taken by eminent domain; and see Dartmouth College *v.* Woodward, 4 Wheat. 518, and Piscataqua Bridge *v.* New Hampshire Bridge, 7 N. Hamp. R. 35.

But it is said, that this is property holden under a grant from the State, and to take it away impairs the contract of that grant. But this stands on the same ground as other kinds of property granted by the State. All lands are deemed to be holden by grant from the State, and yet the plaintiffs concede, that land may be taken for public use. They argue, however, that such an appropriation of land is essential to sovereignty, to the public safety, but that it is not so in respect to franchises. This proceeds on the same fallacy, that their franchise is taken; whereas it is only land covered by the franchise. Or if the franchise ceases *pro tanto*, it is taken, not in violation of a contract, but by the right of eminent domain. Cannot the State take the land in the plaintiffs' basins for defence against an enemy? And, if so, cannot they take it for a railroad? The doctrine set up by the defendants will apply equally to mill ponds created under the general law allowing a mill-owner to flow the lands of other persons. He has a franchise as much as the plaintiffs, and however insignificant his mill pond may be, no railroad or highway could be carried through it against his consent.

It is further objected, that this land has once been taken for public use, and cannot be taken again. There is a dictum to that effect in West Boston Bridge *v.* County Commissioners, 10 Pick. 272; but it was never delivered as the opinion of the Court; s. c. 13 Pick. 196; and besides, there the appropriation was for the same use, a turnpike road being converted into a county road; here it is for a different use. Possibly a turnpike road might be taken by the legislature for a free road, upon making compensation to the turnpike corporation; but this is immaterial to the present case. So far as con-

27 *

cerns the plaintiffs, the land is private property, and therefore liable to be taken; so far as concerns the public, the legislature have full power to change the public use.

That the right to take this property for public use may be delegated, cannot be made a serious question. When county commissioners have a delegated power of determining whether, and when, and where, roads shall be made, and of taking property to make them, cannot a special commission be appointed to execute a work of a like nature, the expediency of which has been declared by. the immediate act of the legislature? It is said, that the county commissioners are a permanent and general tribunal, acting on all cases; but that does not vary the power of appointment. Nor is it a valid objection, that the railroad corporation is interested; this does not touch the right, but only the expediency of selecting it as the agent.

But if the legislature had the power to authorize the railroad corporation to take this property, have they exercised the power? Have they granted the authority? *Primâ facie* they have, because they have granted to the corporation, "all the powers, privileges, and immunities necessary to carry into effect the purposes and objects of the act," viz., "to locate, construct, and finally complete a railroad in or near the city of Boston, and thence to Worcester, in such manner and form as they shall deem to be most expedient; and, for this purpose, to lay out their road five rods wide through the whole length, and take as much more land as may be necessary" for the construction and materials of the road. This gives power to the defendants to lay out the road over such land as they should deem to be most expedient; and they have deemed this the most expedient. . The burden is on the plaintiffs to show, that their property is not embraced by the general words in the charter of the railroad corporation. They say, that the power to take it must be granted in express terms, or by necessary implication. This we deny. In all cases of grant and other contracts, the intent is to govern. In the case of private contracts, the Court is confined to the writings of the parties. But in construing public grants, as well as statutes, the Court will look at all the facts and circumstances that may indicate the intent; at least, all facts of a public nature; and will adopt a liberal or a strict construction. Preston v. Bowden, 1 Wheaton, 115. The design of the legislature was to have the railroad built; but this could not be accomplished, if at least necessary implication is required to enable the corporation to proceed. The Court, then, must look at all the circumstances, and see how the work can be done, and at a reasonable expense. There are no words in the charters under which the plaintiffs hold, either expressly or by necessary implication, exempting this property from being taken; nor is there any thing in the nature of the property itself to have that effect. As a franchise, it has no such privilege; as such, it is but private property, and what presumption is there, that the legislature did not intend to take it, if they have the same right over it as over other property? It is urged, that it is holden under a grant from the legislature, and if the legislature can impair it, it is not to be presumed that they will do so. But this applies equally to all lands. It is further said, that it has been once appropriated to public use. This is a fair source of argument in construing a subsequent act, and is entitled to more or less weight, according to the nature of the case. The plaintiffs ask, if we could lay out the railroad over the land occupied by the State-house, the State-prison, arsenal, &c. Certainly not, without a clear manifestation of the public will. But then, it is asked, how can we make the distinction? There are two answers; first, the buildings enumerated by way of instance are for public use exclusively; whereas, these basins are only *quasi* of public use; but, secondly, a better answer is, the importance of the use is to be regarded. But who shall determine whether the legislature intended to sacrifice one public interest to another? We answer, this Court, as a court of chancery. If a railroad corporation, under general words of grant, should undertake to pull down the State-house, this Court would issue an injunction. The question must be settled in extreme cases, by the relative importance to the public, of the thing to be done and the thing to be sacrificed; but in cases of little importance to the public, general words of grant must be interpreted in their ordinary sense. These basins are simply a mill pond, and their importance to the public is incomparably less than that of the railroad. Had the plaintiffs been remonstrants before the legislature, it is not to be believed, that their mill pond would have been permitted to divert the railroad from the route which the defendants should deem most expedient. Further, the course of legislation on the subject of railroads, and the documents and plans before the legislature, together with the face of the country in the neighborhood of Boston, show that there was no design to give special protection to these basins. Among the documents was a report of the board of internal improvements, with a plan on which was marked a route for the Boston and Providence Railroad, over the plaintiffs' receiving basin, and the charter for that railroad, containing no prohibition to cross such a basin, was granted at the same time with the charter for the railroad to Worcester.

The act incorporating the South Cove Company is a confirmation of the location of the railroad across the basins.

As to the prohibition to cross Charles River, it is a question of intent. The waters of the basins were no longer known as Charles River, and had ceased to be navigable. And if the prohibition to cross Charles River was meant to apply to the basins, why were not similar words of prohibition inserted in the charter of the Boston and Providence Railroad Corporation?.

It is alleged that this route was selected, not for the public benefit, but for compensation in money and facilities offered by the South Cove Corporation. This offer was expressly authorized in the charter of that corporation, but the directors of the railroad, in their answer, which is responsive to the bill and not controlled by evidence, swear that they went to the South Cove, because that was the best route; though they were enabled to go there by the bonus. The pecuniary inducement, therefore, does not invalidate their proceedings. Parks v. Boston, 8 Pick. 218.

J. Mason, in reply.

The Boston and Roxbury Mill Corporation had the right to use these waters in the basins, flowing over the lands of the Commonwealth and of individuals, and the plaintiffs were authorized to purchase and did purchase the same right; and this right has been decided to be a franchise. Whether a part of the eminent domain shall be deemed to be vested in the grantee of a franchise, is not important; it is sufficient that the franchise is founded on a contract, the violation of which by a State legislature, is prohibited by the Constitution of the United States. To permit a State to violate a contract on the ground of necessity, and to be the judge of the necessity, would render the prohibition nugatory. The right of eminent domain does not constitute an exception. Charles River Bridge v. Warren Bridge, 7 Pick. 502; s. c. 11 Peters, 570. The doctrine that eminent domain cannot be surrendered, is applicable to the several United States. Various sovereign rights, for instance, those of coining money, making war, have been yielded by them to the federal government; and when they bind themselves not to violate a contract, they may as well do so in a question of eminent domain in other cases. Chesapeake &c. Canal v. Baltimore &c. Railroad, 4 Gill & Johns. 108, 109, 144, 147, 178, 183, 185, 187, 230, 236, 273. It is said that in the case cited, the canal had not been located, whereas the grant to the mill corporation has been executed by the erection of the dams. If this can make a difference, then so long as the corporation does nothing it is protected by the law, but the moment it puts its right in execution, it forfeits protection; and the defendants' argument is *felo de se*, for we say that we have not executed the authority conferred on us; so that by their reasoning we are to be protected. It is said that to control the eminent domain will lead to disastrous consequences; if so, the Constitution may be altered.

But if the legislature have this transcendant power of eminent domain, they have no right to delegate it to a private individual or corporation. It belongs to the State, and is only intrusted to the legislature. The right to exercise it may be vested in public officers, as courts, &c., but here it is placed in the hands of an interested corporation, subject to no control by this Court, or even by the legislature, except by creating a new corporation to destroy the property of the railroad corporation. And it is said that this course is expedient, because the legislature have not the peculiar science and skill requisite for laying out a railroad; but may they not employ engineers and other persons competent to give them information and assistance? The legislature now, before they grant authority to construct a railroad, require the route to be specifically described. It is urged, that the usage is to delegate powers like those in question; we deny that there is any usage to delegate to private individuals or corporations powers so extensive as those claimed by the railroad corporation, and if there were, it could not avail. There is but little analogy between the case of taking land for a road, and the present case. If the railroad corporation is not confined to the taking of land, it may take a franchise or personal property.

Supposing that the legislature could grant the power to cross these basins, the plaintiffs insist that they have not done it. The legislature must in some manner describe the property to be taken, so as to show distinctly what is granted. The nature of the power, it being a transcendental power of the sovereign, forbids a loose implication of such a grant. The citizen is entitled to be protected against the exercise of so dangerous a power except by the legislature. Further, a grant by the government is to be construed strictly against the grantee; and the fact that it is founded on a valuable consideration, is not important in this respect. The defendants' charter authorizes them to take " land," but a franchise is not included in that term, nor in the broader expression " real estate," used in the charter of the Warren Bridge Corporation. 7 Pick. 344. It must appear with certainty that the legislature intended to destroy the previous franchise granted by themselves for the public benefit; and they would not allow it to be done without giving notice to the plaintiffs. The proviso, that compensation shall be made for all damages occasioned by the taking of land or materials, is not an extension of the grant but a limitation of it. The obvious intention is to compensate the owner of the land; whereas the defendants say that a corporation whose land and materials are not taken, is to have damages. In the 8th section of the railroad, charter *property* means~ *land.* In this section it is enacted, that when " the lands or other property or estate " of any feme covert, &c., shall be necessary for the construction of the road, the husband, &c., " may release all damages for any lands or estates taken and appropriated as aforesaid." The object was merely to enable some one to give a release of damages for persons under certain disabilities; and in the clause respecting the release the word *property* is dropped. In the additional act (St. 1833, c. 91, § 2,) in which the word *property* is used, the object was to enable the railroad corporation to apply to the county commissioners to assess the damages; previously the remedy lay in favor of the land-owner alone. The general statute of 1833, c. 187, does not aid the defendants, for it provides for compensation only " for lands or other property " taken by any railroad corporation " as allowed by their charter." If such a corporation may take other property than land, where is the limit? Why may they not take any personal property; for instance, a cargo of railroad iron imported by any individual?

The defendants urge, that the reports and plans before the legislature, and the charter of the South Cove Corporation, prove that the route over the basins was authorized. But they show that there were other routes that might have been taken; and besides, the legislature might well have supposed that the railroad corporation would purchase the right of crossing the basins. It is said that a plan exhibited a route for the Providence Railroad over one of the basins, and that this plan was published by order of the legislature; but it does not follow that the Providence Railroad Corporation was authorized by the legislature to take that route; nor would such authority to that corporation imply a like authority to the defendants; the implication would be the other way. The defendants say that this is a court of chancery; that it is not bound by the strict rules of law; and that it is to compare the value of the water power with that of the railroad, and decide in favor of the franchise which is the most valuable. If therefore the railroad is to extend from Boston to Albany, the legislature intended that it shall cross the basins; but if it is to terminate five miles from Boston, then the intention of the legislature is that it shall not cross them. The Court will not adopt this principle of construction.

It is impossible to include the plaintiffs' franchise under the terms *land and materials;* consequently no provision is made for compensating them.

SHAW, C. J., delivered the opinion of the Court. Several very important questions have been submitted to the Court in the present case, some of which, for reasons which will sufficiently appear, it is not now necessary to decide. An àbstract of the bill and a general review of the case, and of the question arising under it, will appear by reference to the report of a former decision, in the same case, upon the preliminary question of jurisdiction. *Ante* p. 266. The case then came before the Court on a general demurrer, in which all the facts alleged by the plaintiffs were admitted; and the question was, whether if the plaintiffs held and enjoyed all the rights set forth in their bill, and if without legal authority they had been infringed by the defendants, in the manner therein set forth, the plaintiffs were entitled to relief in a court of equity; and the Court held that they were. The question now arising is a very different one, and depends mainly upon the construction and legal effect of the several legislative acts under which the parties respectively claim. For the purpose of this hearing it is admitted, by the defendants, that the piers, embankments, and bridges erected by them in the construction of the Boston and Worcester Railroad in and over the full and receiving basins claimed by the plaintiffs, do, to a certain extent, diminish the volume of water which those basins would otherwise contain, and do therefore to some extent impair and diminish the water power to be derived therefrom. But they insist that this is *damnum absque abjurid;* that they are legally justified in so laying out the railroad over the basins; that the damage thereby suffered by the plaintiffs is not in consequence of a tort done by the defendants, to be deemed in law or equity a nuisance, or abated as such, but an act done by rightful authority, for which the remedy is by a compensation in damages, to be obtained in the manner provided by law. This, at present, constitutes the question between the parties. This is a question involving public and private interests of very great magnitude, and requiring the most mature consideration. In deciding it, the Court have the satisfaction of feeling that they have derived great benefit from a full, able, and ingenious argument, which seems quite to have exhausted the subject.

The first question which we propose to consider is, whether the legislature had the legal and constitutional authority to grant to the corporation created for the purpose of establishing a railroad from Boston to Worcester, the power to lay their road over and across the basins of the plaintiffs, on paying them the damage sustained thereby, and to keep up and maintain the same.

It is contended on the part of the plaintiffs, and this constitutes one of the main grounds of their complaint, that the legislature had no such authority, because they hold a franchise in and over all the lands, flats, and waters included in their full and receiving basins, obtained by a grant from the Commonwealth for a valuable consideration, and that the authority contended for by the defendants would constitute an interference with an encroachment upon their franchise, amounting in substance and effect, to revocation or destruction of the franchise, and a withdrawal of the beneficial uses of the grant. In order to judge of this, it is necessary to consider the nature and origin of the plaintiffs' rights as claimed and set forth by them, and the manner in which they are affected by the acts of the defendants, supposing them warranted by the act of the legislature.

We do not now stop to inquire into the objections taken by the defendants, that the plaintiffs have not complied with the conditions of the grants made to them, by the act incorporating the Boston and Roxbury Mill Corporation, and the several subsequent acts; that is a subject of separate and distinct consideration. Supposing them to have complied with those conditions, what are the rights claimed by them? The plaintiffs were authorized to inclose and pen up a portion of the navigable waters adjoining Boston, so as to prevent the ebb and flow of the tide therein, and to discontinue any further use thereof by the public for purposes of navigation, to make use of part of the public domain, being all that part of the land covered by water laying below low-water mark, or more than 100 rods from high-water mark, and to acquire by purchase or by appraisement, without the consent of the owners, that part of the soil belonging to individuals, and to have the perpetual use thereof for mill purposes, and to make a highway on their dams and take toll thereon. Other rights, no doubt, were incident, but this is a summary of their important rights and privileges.

The effect of the authority granted to the railroad corporation to lay their road over these basins, was to some extent to diminish their surface, and reduce their value. But the Court are of opinion, that this could in no proper legal sense be considered as annulling or destroying their franchise. They could both stand together. The substance of the plaintiffs' franchise was to be a corporation, to establish a highway and take toll, to establish mills, and to make use of land for mill ponds derived partly from the public and partly from individuals, either by purchase or by taking it, for public use, at an appraisement, by authority of the legislature. So far as this gave them a right to the use of the land, it constituted an interest and qualified property in the land, not larger or more ample, or of any different nature, from a grant of land in fee, and did not necessarily withdraw it from a liability to which all the lands of the Commonwealth are subject, to be taken for public use, at an equivalent, when in the opinion of the legislature, the public exigency, or as it is expressed in case of highways, when public convenience and necessity may require it. The plaintiffs still retain their franchise, they still retain all their rights derived from the legislative grants, and the only effect of the subsequent acts, is to appropriate to another and distinct public use, a portion of the land over which their franchise was to be used. We cannot perceive how it differs from the case of a turnpike or canal. Suppose a broad canal extends across a large part of the State. The proprietors have a franchise similar to that of the plaintiffs, to use the soil in which the bed of the canal is formed, and it is, in the same manner, derived by a grant from the legislature. It is a franchise. But if afterwards it becomes necessary to lay a turnpike, or a public highway across it, would this be a disturbance or revocation of the franchise and inconsistent with the power of the legislature in exercising the right of eminent domain, for the public benefit? It might occasion some damage; but that would be a damage to property, and, pursuant to the bill of rights, must be compensated for by a fair equivalent. It may be said, that the way might be carried high over the canal, and so not obstruct it. But suppose a railroad, a new erection, not contemplated when the canal was granted, and from the nature of which, it must be kept on a level, so as to subject the canal proprietors to considerable expense and trouble; whatever other objections might be made to it, it seems to us, that it could not be considered as a revocation, still less an annihilation of the franchise of the proprietors.

If it is suggested, that under this claim of power, the legislature might authorize a new turnpike, canal, or railroad on the same line with a former one to its whole extent, we think the proper answer is, that such a measure would be substantially and in fact, under whatever color or pretence, taking the franchise from one company and giving it to another, in derogation of the first grant, not warranted by the right of eminent domain, and incompatible with the nature of legislative power. In that case the object would be to provide for the public the same public easement, which is already provided for, and secured to the public, by the prior grant, and for which there could be no public exigency. Such a case therefore cannot be presumed.

If the whole of a franchise should become necessary for the public use, I am not prepared to say, that the right of eminent domain, in an extreme case, would not extend to and authorize the legislature to take it, on payment of a full equivalent. I am not aware that it stands upon a higher or more sacred ground, than the right to personal or real property. Suppose, for instance, that a bridge had been early granted over navigable waters, say in this harbor, at the place where East Boston ferry now is, and the extension of our foreign commerce, and the exigencies of the United States in maintaining a

navy for the defence of the county, should render it manifestly necessary to remove such a bridge; I cannot say that it would not be in
the power of the legislature to do it, paying an equivalent.

Or suppose, as it has sometimes been suggested, that these dams
of the plaintiffs, by checking the tide waters flowing through the
channels below Charles River bridge, and through the harbor of Boston, should have so far altered the regimen of the stream, as gradu-
ally to fill up the main channel of the harbor and render it unfit for
large ships; suppose it were demonstrated, to the entire satisfaction
of all, that this was the cause, that the harbor would become unfit
for a naval station, or for commerce, by means of which most extensive damage would ensue to the city, to the Commonwealth, and to
the eastern States, (for I mean to put a strong case for illustration,)
would it not be competent for the legislature to require the dams to
be removed, the basins again laid open to the flux and reflux of the
tide? I am not prepared to say that it would not, on payment of an
equivalent. But it is not necessary to the decision of this cause, to
consider such a case, because, as before said, the act of the defendants does not, in any legal sense, annul or destroy the franchise of
the plaintiffs.

Nor, in the opinion of the Court, is this exercise of power by the
legislature, a law impairing the obligation of contracts, within the
meaning of the Constitution of the United States. A grant of land
is held to be a contract within the meaning of this provision; and
such grant cannot be revoked by a State legislature. This was held
in regard to the revocation of grants of land by the State of Georgia.
Fletcher v. Peck, 6 Cranch, 87. And yet there can be no doubt, that
land granted by the government, as well as any other land, may be
taken by the legislature in the exercise of the right of eminent domain, on payment of an equivalent. Such an appropriation therefore
is not a violation of the contract by which property, or rights in the
nature of property, and which may be compensated for in damages,
are granted by the government to individuals.

The rights, by which individuals owning mills are enabled to flow
lands of proprietors of meadows, is essentially of the same character
with that of the plaintiffs, and the main difference is, that the former
are obtained by the operation of a general law, and the latter by a
special act. But in the former case, the mill-owners obtain an easement or franchise, not a property in the soil, and that, without and
against the consent of the owners, upon high considerations of public
expediency and necessity. But it seems to us, that it cannot be successfully maintained, that a railroad, canal, or turnpike, could not be
laid over such a pond, because it would diminish the capacity of the

pond, and proportionably lessen the mill power. Forward v. Hampshire and Hampden Canal Co. 22 Pick. 462.

It is difficult, perhaps impossible, to lay down any general rule, that would precisely define the power of the government, in the exercise of the acknowledged right of eminent domain. It must be large and liberal so as to meet the public exigencies; and it must be so limited and restrained, as to secure effectually the rights of the citizen. It must depend in some measure upon the nature of the exigencies as they arise, and the circumstances of particular cases. In the present case, the Court are all of opinion, that the rights of' the plaintiffs, in the land of the full and receiving basins, are not of such a character as to exclude the authority of the legislature, from taking a small portion of it, for laying out a railroad, it being for another and distinct public use, not interfering with the franchise of the plaintiffs, in any other way than by occupying such portion of this land.

But it is contended that the act in question is not valid, inasmuch as it does not provide a compensation for the damage done to the plaintiffs' franchise. We are however of opinion, that this objection is founded upon the assumption already considered, viz., that the taking of a portion of the land over which the franchise extends is a taking of their franchise. The act does not take away the plaintiffs' franchise, but provides for taking part of the land, in which the plaintiffs have a qualified right of property. This is provided for in the first section of the act of incorporation, which directs that all damage occasioned to any person or corporation, by the taking of such land or materials, that is, land five rods wide, for the purposes aforesaid, shall be paid for, by the said corporation, in the manner thereinafter provided.

It has been held, that these provisions for taking land, and providing for an indemnity, are remedial and to be construed liberally and beneficially, and will therefore extend to leaseholds, easements, and other interests in land, as well as to land held by complainants in fee. Ellis v. Welch, 6 Mass. R. 246; Parks v. Boston, 15 Pick. 203.

Another ground much relied upon to show that the act is unconstitutional and invalid, is, that the act does not of itself appropriate the specific land taken, to public use, but delegates to the corporation the power of thus taking private property for public use, and therefore, the appropriation, or the right of eminent domain, is not exercised by the competent and proper authority, and that such power cannot be delegated.

This power is certainly one of a high and extraordinary character, and ought to be exercised with great caution and deliberation. This objection deserves and has received great consideration. On the

whole, the Court are of opinion, that the act is not open to this objection. Taking the whole acts of incorporation together, we are of
opinion that it sufficiently declares the public necessity and convenience of a railroad, fixes the *termini*, viz., in or near the city of Boston and thence to any part of Worcester in the county of Worcester,
in such manner and form as the corporation shall think most expedient.
Nothing therefore is delegated to the corporation, but the power of
directing the intermediate course between the *termini*. The question
of necessity for public use is passed upon and decided by the legislature. Whether the road goes over the lands of one or another
private individual, does not affect that question. So far as the objection is, that the power is delegated to the corporation instead of
being exercised by county commissioners or any other public body,
it is rather a question of propriety and fitness, than one of power.
In the present case we think that the interests of the corporation and
those of the public, were so nearly coincident, it being plainly for the
advantage of both that the shortest, safest, and cheapest route should
be chosen, that the power might be safely intrusted to a corporation
thus constituted. This mode of exercising the right of eminent domain, is warranted by numerous precedents, both in our own Commonwealth and in most of the other States of the Union.

We are then brought to another and very important inquiry, which
is this; supposing the legislature has a full and constitutional authority to pass an act, empowering the defendants to lay out their railroad
over the land used by the plaintiffs, whether they have in fact granted
any such power. This must depend upon the construction of the
act of incorporation, applied to the subject-matter, both of the contemplated railroad, and the existing works of the plaintiffs. The
latter contend that their works were contemplated to be works of
public utility, and upon that ground they were authorized to take
part of the public domain, and under the authority of the legislature,
to take the property of individuals, which would have been inadmissible on any other ground. Boston and Roxbury Mill Dam Corp. *v.*
Newman, 12 Pick. 467. They therefore insist, that as the lands had
been already appropriated to public use, by the grant to the plaintiffs,
it could not again be appropriated to the defendants by a subsequent
act. So far as this affects the power of the legislature, it has already
been considered. It was another and distinct public use, growing up
after the former appropriation, and which might be reached, without
defeating or essentially impairing the public use, to which it had
been already applied.

It is therefore a question bearing upon the presumed intent of the
legislature. It may be fairly argued, that though there is no limita-

tion of the power of the corporation in terms, still if the legislature had already appropriated a portion of the land lying between the *termini*, to another important public use, and especially if the construction contended for would wholly, or in a great degree, defeat such other important public use, it is not to be presumed that the legislature meant thus to extend the power, and so a limitation might be ingrafted, by necessary and reasonable implication, upon the generality of the act.

The terms of the act (St. 1831, c. 72) are certainly broad enough to include the power to take this land and pass over the full and empty basins of the plaintiffs. The first section authorizes the corporation to locate, construct, and finally complete a railroad, in or near the city of Boston and thence to any part of Worcester. The third section authorizes the president and directors for the time being, by themselves or their agents, to exercise all the powers granted to the corporation for the purpose of locating, constructing, and completing the railroad. The location is to be filed with the county commissioners. The president and directors of this corporation, therefore, are authorized to locate the railroad, between the *termini*, that is, to determine in what particular direction it should pass between the *termini*. To this extent they were to exercise their own judgment. And the Court are of opinion, that there is nothing in the nature of the plaintiffs' public works, or in the public use to which they were applied, and the extent to which that use would be impaired or diminished, by the taking of such part of the land as might be necessary for the location of this railroad, from which the power of locating the railroad over it, may be presumed to have been restrained by the legislature. Both uses may well stand together, with some interference of the later with the earlier, which may be compensated for by damages. In this respect, therefore, it differs from many of the cases put, where it is asked whether one canal, turnpike, or railroad, may be laid over the same line with a former one. Both cannot stand together, and one must supersede the other. And this shall not be construed to be the intent of the legislature, unless it appears by express words or necessary implication. In this respect, also, this case differs from the case in Gill and Johnson. There the canal and the railroad must necessarily occupy the same identical line, each for a public use; both could not stand together, and therefore it was decided, that a franchise already granted should not be considered as superseded and taken away by a subsequent legislative act, granting power in general terms.

So, if a power were given in general terms, to lay out a turnpike or railroad between *termini* definitely expressed, such general power ought not to be so construed as to take an arsenal, fort, state-house, or land already appropriated to a highly important public use, which would be defeated by such construction. It would be a question of legislative intent; and it could not be presumed, that the legislature intended that the power conferred by them should have such an effect, unless it were unequivocally expressed.

It was, however, contended, that the defendants were expressly restrained from building a bridge over the waters of Charles river, and although by a subsequent act they were authorized to build a bridge over Charles river, yet it was limited to be between the Western Avenue and Canal Bridge, and therefore, did not take away the first prohibition, so far as to build over the waters of Charles river, south of the Western Avenue, where they have in fact located the railroad. The words of this fifteenth section are, that nothing contained in this act shall be construed as giving the Boston and Worcester Railroad Corporation authority to erect a bridge over the waters of Charles river connected with the city of Boston. The natural and obvious meaning of this is, over Charles river, or across Charles river, that is, the bed or body of the river from one shore to the other, and not along the margin of the river. Any other construction would restrain them from building over a cove or creek adjoining to and connected with the river, which, to many purposes, may be considered the waters of Charles river; but such a restriction, we think, could not have been contemplated. This construction is strengthened by the consideration, that the subject of obstructing the navigation of Charles river, by bridges across the same, had been agitated before the legislature with great earnestness for several years before this act passed.

But there is another view of this subject, which seems quite decisive, which is this; whether or not the waters over which the railroad has been built, may have been considered the waters of Charles river, before the dams of the plaintiffs were erected, we think they had ceased to be so, and could not have been so considered and intended by the legislature, after they had been penned up and inclosed by these dams, and thus effectually separated from the river, which was done a long time before this act passed. We are, therefore, of opinion, that the prohibition to build a bridge over the waters of Charles river, as used in this act, did not prohibit the defendants from locating their road on these full and receiving basins, by means of a bridge or causeway, but was intended to apply to the waters of Charles river then open to navigation, and mainly to protect that navigation.

The Court are of opinion, upon the whole case, that the legislature had the constitutional power, to a limited extent, to exercise the right of eminent domain over the lands used by the complainants as their full and receiving basins, providing in the act suitable measures for making compensation to the complainants, if they sustained damage thereby; that the act did make such provision; that the power of the legislature was well executed, in declaring the general purpose and exigency of appropriating private property for public use, by establishing a railroad within certain *termini* expressed, and by granting to a corporation, established and constituted as the defendant corporation was, the power of determining the particular course and direction of the railroad between those *termini;* that the defendants were not restrained, by express words, or any necessary, just, or reasonable implication, from laying out their railroad as they have done, over the basins used by the complainants under their franchise, and therefore, that the averment of the complainants, that the railroad is laid over their basins without any just and lawful authority, and is consequently a nuisance, is not supported.

JOHN P. WEBBER *v.* THE EASTERN RAILROAD COMPANY.[1]

Essex Co., November Term, 1840.

Evidence of Damage to Land — Opinion of Witness — Presumption as to Boundary of Land upon Highway.

A witness, who had been for ten years secretary of an insurance company, and as such had been in the practice of examining buildings, with reference to insurance thereof, and who had also, as county commissioner, frequently estimated damages caused to estates by the laying out of highways and railroads, was held to have been rightly permitted, on a hearing before a jury impanelled to appraise damages sustained by a party by the laying out of a railroad over his land and near to his buildings, to give his opinion that the passage of locomotive engines, within one hundred feet of a building, would diminish the rent and increase the rate of insurance thereof against fire: *Held* also, that he was rightly permitted to testify that the directors of the insurance company, of which he was secretary, upon his consulting them as to an application for insurance on a building in the vicinity of the buildings of the party then before the jury, had declined to take the risk at any rate.

An estimate, not on oath, of damages that would be sustained by a party over whose land a railroad was afterwards laid out, made by a committee of a town, while a petition of the town for a change of the route of the railroad was before the legislature, and merely stating those damages as the least the party would take, is not admissible in evidence to a jury impanelled to appraise damages caused by laying out the railroad over the land, although such estimate was made at the request of an agent of the railroad company.

---

[1] 2 Metcalf's Reports, 147.

Webber *v.* The Eastern Railroad Company.

Where the sheriff instructed a jury, impanelled to appraise damages caused by the laying out of a railroad over a party's land, that by the legal construction of his title deed, which bounded his land on a way, he owned the land to the centre of the way, and was therefore entitled to damages for the value of the land over which the way passed; it was held that the instruction was so general and abstract, that no opinion could be expressed, as to its correctness, without much qualification.

.THIS was a proceeding upon a petition for a jury to assess the damages sustained by the petitioner by the laying out of the Eastern Railroad over his land. On the return of the verdict into the Court of Common Pleas, the respondents objected to the acceptance thereof, for the reasons hereinafter mentioned. The Court, however, accepted the verdict, and ordered it to be certified, with their adjudication thereon, to the county commissioners. The respondents thereupon alleged exceptions to the adjudication: *First,* because the sheriff, who presided at the hearing before the jury, admitted (the respondents objecting thereto) the testimony of John W. Proctor, Esq., that he had been for ten years secretary of an insurance company, and had been applied to for insurance on a house in the vicinity of the petitioner's land, over which the Eastern Railroad was laid, and that upon his consulting the directors of the insurance company, they declined taking the risk at any rate; and that in his opinion the passage of locomotive engines, within one hundred feet of a building, would increase the rate of insurance, and that the premium would be increased from one and a half to two per cent., and that the rents of buildings, so situated would be reduced from one fourth to one third. Said Proctor did not profess to be an expert, but testified that he had been county commissioner six or eight years, and had estimated damages for common roads and for railroads, and, as secretary of an insurance company, had examined and estimated the value of estates in every part of the county. *Secondly,* because the sheriff admitted in evidence (the respondents objecting) an estimate made at the request of an agent of the respondents, by a committee of the town of Beverly, (when that town petitioned the legislature to change the route of the Eastern Railroad,) of the damages that would be sustained by different proprietors of land, and among others by the petitioner. *Thirdly,* because the sheriff instructed the jury upon the point of the quantity of land taken, and as applicable to the title deed of the petitioner, which bounded him on a way, that the rule of law is, that a deed which so bounds a party, without any measurement of lines, carries him to the centre of the way, and that by the construction of the petitioner's deed of the land over which the railroad was laid out, he should be considered as the owner of the way upon which, by said deed, his land was bounded, and that he was entitled to recover damages for the value of the land over which said way passed.

This case was argued at a former term.

N. J. Lord, for the respondents.

Rantoul and *Ward*, for the petitioner.

SHAW, C. J.   This case comes before this Court by exceptions to the decision of the Court of Common Pleas, in accepting the verdict of a jury, allowing damages to the petitioner, occasioned by taking his land in Beverly, for the construction of the Eastern Railroad. The objection of the company to the verdict is founded on exceptions taken to the decision and directions of the sheriff, on the assessment of damages, which appear by a bill of exceptions allowed by the sheriff, and returned with the verdict.

1.   The respondents excepted to the testimony of John W. Proctor, called as a witness by the petitioner, on several grounds. One was, that he was called to give his opinion upon the question, whether the proximity of a railroad would be likely to increase the rate of premium of insurance against fire, when it did not appear that his acquaintance with the subject was such, as would warrant him to give his opinion in evidence.   It is true that in answer to a cross interrogatory, Mr. Proctor answered that he did not profess to be an expert.   But his statement of his experience and means of knowledge, in estimating the risks against fire, from his long having been secretary of a fire insurance office, and having been charged with the duty of examining buildings, and taking into consideration all circumstances bearing upon the risk and the rate of premium, rendered him, we think, quite competent to give his opinion as evidence to the jury upon that subject.

As to what other directors said, it would not be competent evidence, had the question been asked and objected to, and allowed by the sheriff; being merely hearsay. But if it came out unasked, as it apparently did, and no request was made to the sheriff to direct the jury to disregard it, this is no sufficient ground for a new trial. But taking the statement from the bill of exceptions, it appears to us that the testimony was to an act, rather than a declaration.   If an application was made in a case similar to that of the petitioner, and was in fact rejected, on account of the increased risk, that was an act and not a declaration, and was competent evidence to show that the proximity of a railroad to a building increases the fire risk.

2.   The second exception was, that the petitioner offered an estimate of damages by a committee of the town of Beverly, made at the request of the agent of the respondents, in which the damage to

the petitioner's estate, with a number of others, was set down, with a view to enable them to form a just comparison of the cost of the route first proposed, and of another proposed to be substituted; This estimate, though objected to by the company, was admitted.

This paper has been submitted to us with the exceptions. It purports to be the copy of an estimate, made by a committee of Beverly, of the damages to estates on the routes above and below Essex Bridge. It purports to be signed by Josiah Lovett, and to have been presented to Mr. Chase, one of the executive committee of the railroad company. On the route above the bridge, the item relied on is as follows. "John P. Webber & Son, lowest he will take $4,000." The Court are of opinion that this was not competent evidence, and ought not to have been admitted. It was not made in pursuance of any legal commission or authority, was not under oath, and bears no character of official authority. It is said to have been made at the request of the company; but that does not make it evidence against them. Besides, so far as it affects the estate now in question, it does not appear to express the judgment or opinion of the committee upon the actual value of the estate, or the damages which the railroad would occasion; but only the sum demanded by Mr. Webber, as the lowest he would take.

And we are of opinion that it was not merely irrelevant and immaterial, but was calculated to have an influence upon the minds of the jury. It does not appear upon what grounds this estimate was made. It does not purport to be an exact or just appraisement. It might be intended to induce the agents of the company or the legislature to adopt one route in preference to another, and may have been made by interested persons. In every view we have been able to take of it, it appears to us to be irrelevant and incompetent evidence, and therefore, upon this ground, that the verdict ought to be set aside, and a new trial granted.

3. It was also objected by the respondents, that the sheriff instructed the jury in reference to the quantity of land taken, and as applicable to the title deeds of the petitioner, that a deed bounding a grantee by a highway without any admeasurement of lines, carries him to the centre of the way. This direction is so general and abstract in its terms, that it is difficult to express an opinion on its correctness, without much qualification. It is undoubtedly true, that when a highway or town way is laid over the land of an individual, the public acquire a perpetual easement over the land, for all purposes to which a right of way is applicable, but the owner retains his fee in the soil under the way. He may, therefore, convey the adjoining land without the soil under the highway, or the soil under the

highway without the adjacent land, or both together. If the land under the way passes by a deed of the adjacent land, it passes as parcel, and not as appurtenant. It is a question of construction, therefore, in each particular case, and depends, as in all other cases, upon the intent of the parties, as expressed in the descriptive part of the deed, explained and illustrated by all the other parts of the conveyance, and by the localities and subject-matter to which it applies. In the present case, it does not appear, by the bill of exceptions, what was the particular description in the deed referred to, whether the way was a highway, town way, or private way; whether the grantor owned the soil under the highway, or how, or when, or in what mode, the way was laid out; all which circumstances might have more or less bearing upon the question of construction. It does not appear whether the way in question had been discontinued or not, before laying out the railroad; whether the railroad was laid over the way, so that one species of public easement was added to another, or superseded the other; which might be important circumstances, in considering the subject with a view to damages, as it was considered in the present case. We have thought it less important to give an opinion upon this abstract question stated in the exceptions, as the verdict must be set aside on the other ground; because, if the way had not been discontinued, if the owner of the land had ever been allowed damages for taking his land for a public easement, and the laying out of the railroad was merely superadding one public easement to another, or substituting one public easement for another, it would practically make very little difference in the assessment of damages. The right of the public to the easement being perpetual, and going to such use of the land, as supersedes the use of the owner to any beneficial or practical purpose, unless in the extraordinary case of a mine, or spring, or quarry under the way, the value of the dormant fee depending upon a very remote and improbable contingency, its value is too small to have much influence in the assessment of damages. Considering it thus unimportant, and depending upon many facts and circumstances not mentioned in the bill of exceptions, and supposing it quite probable that the question will not again arise, we have not thought it expedient to express any opinion upon this point.

Verdict set aside, and the result to be certified to the county commissioners, with directions to issue a new warrant, for the assessment of the petitioner's damages.

FRANCIS DODGE and another *v.* COUNTY COMMISSIONERS OF ESSEX.[1]

Essex Co., November Term, 1841.

Damages — Injury to Land not taken — Injuries to Property in constructing Road.

The damages occasioned by laying out and making a railroad, and which, by Rev. Sts. c. 39, § 56, county commissioners are bound to estimate, include injuries which are done, by a railroad corporation, to buildings near the line of the road, by means of blasting, in a proper manner, a ledge of rocks through which the railroad passes.

THIS petition for a mandamus was argued at the last November term, by *Rantoul* and *Ward*, for the petitioners, and by *Saltonstall* and *N. J. Lord*, for the respondents. The opinion of the Court, which was delivered at this term, shows all the facts of the case, and the grounds taken by the respective counsel.

SHAW, C. J. This is an application for a writ of mandamus to the commissioners, requiring them to assess damages for the petitioners against the Eastern Railroad Company. The facts, as set forth in the petition and admitted by the answer of the commissioners, are, that the plaintiffs are owners of a lot of land in Beverly with a house thereon, situated near the limits of the railroad, but not within them; that the railroad is near a ledge of rock; that the company, by the necessary operation of blasting said ledge of rock, for the purpose of grading their railroad, greatly damaged and nearly destroyed the petitioners' house.

This case presents the question, whether, under the provisions of the revised statutes respecting railroads, one can have compensation for damages, whose land has not been directly taken for the site of the railroad, nor for supplying materials for its construction.

It is not now necessarily a question, whether the property of an individual, thus necessarily and injuriously affected, and in effect withdrawn from the profitable use and beneficial control of the owner, is appropriated to public uses, within the provision of the 10th article of the declaration of rights. It was quite competent for the legislature, in providing for the prosecution of a great public work, to require compensation to be made to persons injuriously

---

[1] 3 Metcalf's Reports, 380.

affected by it, though not a case coming within the express requisitions of the bill of rights ; and the corporation, by accepting the act of incorporation, became bound by such provisions. It is a question, therefore, depending on the construction of the Rev. Sts. c. 39, which are referred to and made part of their act of incorporation.

It is contended, however, on the part of the' Railroad Company, that the remedy for a damage like that of the petitioners, where no land is taken or appropriated, is not to be sought by an application to the county commissioners, but by an action at common law. But it has been truly answered, on the part of the petitioners, that it is a reasonable and now well-settled principle, that when the legislature, under the right of eminent domain, and for the prosecution of works for public use, authorize an act or series of acts, the natural and necessary consequence of doing which will be damage to the property of another, and provide a mode for the assessment and payment of the damages occasioned by such work, the party authorized, acting within the scope of his authority, is not a wrongdoer; an action will not lie as for a tort ; and the remedy is by the statute, and not at common law. Stevens-v. Middlesex Canal, 12· Mass. 466 ; Stowell v. Flagg, 11 Mass. 364; Lebanon v. Olcott, 1 N. Hamp. 339; Calking v. Baldwin, 4 Wend. 667.

Still the question recurs, whether the statute does provide such remedy in the case stated. The provision is this : " Every railroad corporation shall be liable to pay all damages that shall be occasioned by laying out, and making and maintaining their road, or by taking any land or materials, as provided in the preceding section," &c. Rev. Sts. c. 39, § 56.

The Court are of opinion, that the provision is broad enough to embrace damage done to real estate, like that which the petitioners have sustained. · It is like the case of a house situated on the brink of a deep cutting, so as to become insecure, and so that it is necessary to remove it. It is a damage occasioned by the laying out and making of the road.

But it is contended that this is to be limited, by reference to §§ 54, 55, providing for the taking of lands for the line of the road, and also for materials, if without the limits of the road, by authority of the commissioners. But we can perceive no ground upon which the plain provision of § 56 is to be so limited. It undoubtedly provides for damages in those cases ; but it does not limit the provision to those cases.

But it is said that the damage done to the petitioners' house, not on the line of the railroad, was accidental and consequential, and not the necessary effect of making the railroad.

The statement made in the petition, and admitted in the answer, is, that the company located and constructed their railroad, through land next adjoining that of the petitioners; that they contracted with persons to blast a ledge of rocks in such adjoining land, and agreed to indemnify them against any damage arising therefrom; and that, in blasting said rocks, the house of the petitioners was necessarily destroyed.

An authority to construct any public work carries with it an authority to use the appropriate means. An authority to make a railroad is an authority to reduce the line of the road to a level, and for that purpose to make cuts, as well through ledges of rock as through banks of earth. In a remote and detached place, where due precautions can be taken to prevent danger to persons, blasting by gunpowder is a reasonable and appropriate mode of executing such a work; and, if due precautions are taken to prevent unnecessary damage, is a justifiable mode. It follows that the necessary damage occasioned thereby to a dwelling-house or other building, which cannot be removed out of the way of such danger, is one of the natural and unavoidable consequences of executing the work, and within the provisions of the statute.

Of course, this reasoning will not apply to damages occasioned by carelessness or negligence in executing such a work. Such careless or negligent act would be a tort, for which an action at law would lie against him who commits, or him who commands it. But where all due precautions are taken, and damage is still necessarily done to fixed property, it alike is within the letter and the equity of the statute, and the county commissioners have authority to assess the damages. This Court are therefore of opinion, that an alternative writ of mandamus be awarded to the county commissioners, to assess the petitioners' damages, or return their reasons for not doing so.

NICHOLAS FARWELL v. THE BOSTON AND WORCESTER RAILROAD
CORPORATION.[1]

Suffolk Co., March Term, 1842.

*Master and Servant — Liability of Master for an injury of one
Servant by another.*

Where a master uses due diligence in the selection of competent and trusty servants, and
furnishes them with suitable means to perform the service in which he employs them, he is
not answerable to one of them, for an injury received by him in consequence of the carelessness of another while both are engaged in the same service.

A railroad company employed A, who was careful and trusty in his general character, to
tend the switches on their road; and after he had been long in their service, they employed B to run the passenger train of cars on the road; B knowing the employment and
character of A. *Held*, that the company were not answerable to B for an injury received
by him, while running the cars, in consequence of the carelessness of A in the management
of the switches.

IN an action of trespass upon the case, the plaintiff alleged in his
declaration, that he agreed with the defendants to serve them in the
employment of an engineer in the management and care of their
engines and cars running on their railroad between Boston and Worcester, and entered on said employment, and continued to perform
his duties as engineer till October 30th, 1837, when the defendants,
at Newton, by their servants, so carelessly, negligently, and unskil-
fully managed and used, and put and placed the iron match rail,
called the short switch, across the rail or track of their said railroad,
that the engine and cars upon which the plaintiff was engaged and
employed in the discharge of his said duties of engineer, were
thrown from the track of said railroad, and the plaintiff, by means
thereof, was thrown with great violence upon the ground ; by means
of which one of the wheels of one of said cars passed over the right
hand of the plaintiff, crushing and destroying the same.

The case was submitted to the Court on the following facts agreed
by the parties : " The plaintiff was employed by the defendants, in
1835, as an engineer, and went at first with the merchandise cars,
and afterwards with the passenger cars, and so continued till October
30th, 1837, at the wages of two dollars per day; that being the
usual wages paid to engine-men, which are higher than the wages
paid to a machinist, in which capacity the plaintiff formerly was
employed.

[1] 4 Metcalf's Reports, 36.

" On the 30th of October, 1837, the plaintiff, then being in the employment of the defendants, as such engine-man, and running the passenger train, ran his engine off at a switch on the road, which had been left in a wrong condition, (as alleged by the plaintiff, and, for the purposes of this trial, admitted by the defendants,) by one Whitcomb, another servant of the defendants, who had been long in their employment, as a switch-man or tender, and had the care of switches on the road, and was a careful and trustworthy servant, in his general character, and as such servant was well known to the plaintiff. By which running off, the plaintiff sustained the injury complained of in his declaration.

" The said Farwell (the plaintiff) and Whitcomb were both appointed by the superintendent of the road, who was in the habit of passing over the same very frequently in the cars, and often rode on the engine.

" If the Court shall be of opinion that, as matter of law, the defendants are not liable to the plaintiff, he being a servant of the corporation, and in their employment, for the injury he may have received, from the negligence of said Whitcomb, another servant of the corporation, and in their employment, then the plaintiff shall become nonsuit; but if the Court shall be of opinion, as matter of law, that the defendants may be liable in this case, then the case shall be submitted to a jury upon the facts which may be proved in the case; the defendants alleging negligence on the part of the plaintiff."

C. G. Loring, for the plaintiff.

The defendants, having employed the plaintiff to do a specified duty on the road, were bound to keep the road in such a condition that he might do that duty with safety. If the plaintiff had been a stranger, the defendants would have been liable; and he contends that the case is not varied by the fact that both the plaintiff and Whitcomb were the servants of the defendants; because the plaintiff was not the servant of the defendants in the duty or service, the neglect of which occasioned the injury sustained by him. He was employed for a distinct and separate service, and had no joint agency or power with the other servants whose duty it was to keep the road in order; and could not be made responsible to the defendants for its not being kept in order. He could not, by any vigilance or any power that he could exercise, have prevented the accident. His duties and those of Whitcomb were as distinct and independent of each other, as if they had been servants of different masters.

The plaintiff does not put his case on the ground of the defendants' liability to passengers, nor upon the general principle which renders principals liable for the acts of their agents; but on the ground, that a master, by the nature of his contract with a servant, stipulates for the safety of the servant's employment so far as the master can regulate the matter.

The defence rests upon an alleged general rule, that a master is not liable to his servant for damage caused by the negligence of a fellow servant. But if that be sound, as a general rule, it does not apply here; for Whitcomb and the plaintiff, as has already been stated, were not fellow servants — that is, were not jointly employed for a common purpose.

The case of Priestley v. Fowler, 3 Mees. & Welsb. 1, on which the defendants will rely, was rightly decided. The case was clearly one of equal knowledge on the part of the two servants, and of voluntary exposure by the plaintiff to a known hazard not required by his duty; and both servants were jointly engaged in the same business when the accident happened to the plaintiff. But the reasoning and *dicta* of the Court went much beyond the case — in undertaking to lay down a general rule, as applying to all cases of damages sustained by a servant in the employment of his master, without discrimination as to the peculiar relations of the servant, and the causes of the injury received by him — and lead to unsound conclusions.

No general rule can be laid down, which will apply to all cases of a master's liability to a servant. But it is submitted that a master is liable to one servant for the negligence of another, when they are engaged in distinct employments, though he is not so liable, where two servants are engaged jointly in the same service; because, in the latter case, each servant has some supervision and control of every other. This principle may be illustrated by the relation which subsists between the owner of a ship and the master and crew. The owner contracts with them to navigate his ship, and of necessity he impliedly contracts that she is capable of navigation — seaworthy for the voyage. And if she prove otherwise, by reason of the carelessness of the builder or the shipwright employed to repair her, and the master and crew lose their wages, the owner must be liable and pay a full indemnity; and he has his remedy against the shipwright. See Eaken v. Thom, 5 Esp. R. 6. Abbott on Ship. (4th Amer. ed.) 457. In such case, the master and crew have no remedy against the shipwright by whose misconduct they suffer, because there is no privity of contract between him and them. But there is a privity of contract between them and the ship-owner, and this gives a perfect remedy, in the theory of the law. Many similar illustrations of the principle might be given. And unless the servant has a remedy against the master, in such cases, the great fundamental legal rule, that where there is a wrong there is a remedy, is violated or departed from.

In case of servants jointly employed in the same business, it may reasonably be inferred that they take the hazard of injuries from each other's negligence; because such hazard is naturally and necessarily incident to such employment; because they have, to a great extent the means of guarding against such injuries, by the exercise of mutual caution and prudence, while the master has no such means; and because, between persons employed in a joint service, there is a privity of contract, that renders them liable to each other for their carelessness or neglect in the discharge of such service.

It is a well-settled general rule, that a servant is not liable to third persons for his neglect of duty. Story on Agency, §§ 308, 309. If that principle applies to this case, so that the plaintiff has no remedy against Whitcomb, it would seem to be a sufficient reason for holding the defendants liable.

It is also a well-established rule, that if an agent, without his own default, has incurred loss or damage in transacting the business of the principal, he is entitled to full compensation. Story on Agency, § 339.

Fletcher and *Morey*, for the defendants.

The plaintiff must maintain his action, if at all, either on the rule of *respondeat superior*, as for a tort, or on an implied contract of indemnity. The early cases in which masters were held liable to a stranger in an action of tort, for the misconduct of their servants, were mostly those which respected the safety of passengers on highways, and were decided on grounds of policy. The doctrine of such liability was afterwards extended to cases that were deemed analogous. See 1 Bl. Com. 432, Christian's note. But no rule of policy requires that masters shall be liable to one servant for injuries received by him from a fellow servant. On the contrary, policy requires an entirely different rule, especially in the present case. The aim of all the statutes concerning railroads is to protect passengers; and if this action is maintained, it will establish a principle which will tend to diminish the caution of railroad servants, and thus increase the risk of passengers.

The defendants have been in no fault, in this case, either in the construction of their road, the use of defective engines, or the employment of careless or untrusty servants. So that the question is, whether they are liable to the plaintiff, on an implied contract of indemnity. The contract between the parties to this suit excludes the notion that the defendants are liable for the injury received by the plaintiff. He agreed to run an engine on their road, knowing the state of the road, and also knowing Whitcomb, his character, and the specific duty intrusted to him. The plaintiff, therefore, assumed the risks of the service which he undertook to perform; and one of those risks was his liability to injury from the carelessness of others who were employed by the defendants in the same service. As a consideration for the increased risk of this service, he received higher wages than when he was employed in a less hazardous business.

The defendants are doubtless bound, by an implied contract, to use all the ordinary precautions for the safety of passengers, and are liable for injuries which a passenger may receive in consequence of the negligence of their servants. But the plaintiff was not a passenger, and his counsel does not place his claim on that ground.

The only cases in which a servant has attempted to recover of a master for another servant's misconduct, are Priestley *v.* Fowler, 3 Mees. & Welsb. 1, and Murray *v.* South Carolina Railroad Company, 1 McMullan, 385; and in both those cases, it was held that the action could not be maintained. In those cases, it is true that both servants were on the same carriage when the accident happened by which one of them was injured. And the counsel for the present plaintiff has invented a rule of law, in order to escape from the pressure of those decisions. But admitting the distinction, and the rule which he advances to be sound, the case at bar is not thereby affected. The plaintiff and Whitcomb were not engaged in distinct and separate employments, but in the same service. They both were acting to the same end, although they had different parts to perform.

It will not be necessary for the Court to lay down a general rule, in order to decide this case for the defendants. Ordinary care is all that a master is bound to use in behalf of his servants; and the defendants have used such care. They used due diligence in selecting Whitcomb, who was careful and trustworthy. The case is analogous to that of a ship-owner, who is insured, and who has employed a competent master and crew. Though his ship is lost by the negligence of some of the crew, yet he does not thereby suffer the loss of his insurance. Walker *v.* Maitland, 5 Barn. & Ald. 174.

Loring, in reply.

In the case in 1 McMullan, 385, the plaintiff, as in the case in 3 Mees. & Welsb. 1, was jointly engaged in the same service with the other servant, whose negligence caused the injury. It therefore does not affect the principle on which the present plaintiff rests his cause.

⸱SHAW, C. J.   This is an action of new impression in our courts, and involves a principle of great importance. It presents a case, where two persons are in the service and employment of one company, whose business it is to construct and maintain a railroad, and to employ their trains of cars to carry persons and merchandise for hire. They are appointed and employed by the same company to perform separate duties and services, all tending to the accomplishment of one and the same purpose — that of the safe and rapid transmission of the trains; and they are paid for their respective services according to the nature of their respective duties, and the labor and skill required for their proper performance. The question is, whether for damages sustained by one of the persons so employed, by means of the carelessness and negligence of another, the party injured has a remedy against the common employer. It is an argument against such an action, though certainly not a decisive one, that no such action has before been maintained. ·

It is laid down by Blackstone, that if a servant, by his negligence, does any damage to a stranger, the master shall be answerable for his neglect. But the damage must be done while he is actually employed in the master's service; otherwise, the servant shall answer for his own misbehavior. 1 Bl. Com. 431. M'Manus v. Crickett, 1 East, 106. This rule is obviously founded on the great principle of social duty, that every man, in the management of his own affairs, whether by himself or by his agents or servants, shall so conduct them as not to injure another; and if he does not, and another thereby sustains damage, he shall answer for it. If done by a servant, in the course of his employment, and acting within the scope of his authority, it is considered, in contemplation of law, so far the act of the master, that the latter shall be answerable *civiliter*. But this presupposes that the parties stand to each other in the relation of strangers, between whom there is no privity; and the action, in such case, is an action sounding in tort. The form is trespass on the case, for the consequential damage. The maxim *respondeat superior* is adopted in that case, from general considerations of policy and security.

But this does not apply to the case of a servant bringing his action against his own employer to recover damages for an injury arising in the course of that employment, where all such risks and perils as the employer and the servant respectively intend to assume and bear may be regulated by the express or implied contract between them, and which in contemplation of law, must be presumed to be thus regulated.

The same view seems to have been taken by the learned counsel for the plaintiff in the argument; and it was conceded, that the claim could not be placed on the principle indicated by the maxim *respondeat superior*, which binds the master to indemnify a stranger for the damage caused by the careless, negligent, or unskilful act of his servant in the conduct of his affairs. The claim, therefore, is placed, and must be maintained, if maintained at all, on the ground of contract. As there is no express contract between the parties, applicable to this point, it is placed on the footing of an implied contract of indemnity, arising out of the relation of master and servant. It would be an implied promise, arising from the duty of the master to be responsible to each person employed by him, in the conduct of every branch of business, where two or more persons are employed, to pay for all damage occasioned by the negligence of every other person employed in the same service. If such a duty were established by law — like that of a common-carrier, to stand to all losses of goods not caused by the act of God or of a public enemy — or that of an innkeeper, to be responsible, in like manner, for the baggage of his guests; it would be a rule of frequent and familar occurrence, and its existence and application, with all its qualifications and restrictions, would be settled by judicial precedents. But we are of opinion that no such rule has been established, and the authorities, as far as they go, are opposed to the principle. Priestley v. Fowler, 3 Mees. & Welsb. 1; Murray v. South Carolina Railroad Company, 1 McMullan, 385.

The general rule, resulting from considerations as well of justice as of policy, is, that he who engages in the employment of another for the performance of specified duties and services, for compensation, takes upon himself the natural and ordinary risks and perils incident to the performance of such services, and, in legal presumption, the compensation is adjusted accordingly. And we are not aware of any principle which should except the perils arising from the carelessness and negligence of those who are in the same employment. These are perils which the servant is as likely to know, and against which he can as effectually guard, as the master. They are perils incident to the service, and which can be as distinctly foreseen and provided for in the rate of compensation as any others. To say that the master shall be responsible because the damage is caused by his agents, is assuming the very point which remains to be proved. They are his agents to some extent, and for some purposes; but whether he is responsible, in a particular case, for their negligence, is not decided by the single fact that they are, for some purposes, his agents. It seems to be now well settled, whatever might have been thought formerly, that underwriters cannot excuse themselves from payment of a loss by one of the perils insured against, on the ground that the loss was caused by the negligence or unskilfulness of the officers or crew of the vessel, in the performance of their various duties as navigators, although employed and paid by the owners, and in the navigation of the vessel, their agents. Copeland *v.* New England Marine Ins. Co. 2 Met. 440–443, and cases there cited. I am aware that the maritime law has its own rules and analogies, and that we cannot always safely rely upon them in applying them to other branches of law. But the rule in question seems to be a good authority for the point, that persons are not to be responsible, in all cases, for the negligence of those employed by them.

If we look from considerations of justice to those of policy they will strongly lead to the same conclusion. In considering the rights and obligations arising out of particular relations, it is competent for courts of justice to regard considerations of policy and general convenience, and to draw from them such rules as will, in their practical application, best promote the safety and security of all parties concerned. This is, in truth, the basis on which implied promises are raised, being duties legally inferred from a consideration of what is best adapted to promote the benefit of all persons concerned under given circumstances. To take the well-known and familiar cases already cited; a common-carrier, without regard to actual fault or neglect in himself or his servants, is made liable for all losses of goods confided to him for carriage, except those caused by the act of God or of a public enemy, because he can best guard them against all minor dangers, and because, in case of actual loss, it would be extremely difficult for the owner to adduce proof of embezzlement, or other actual fault or neglect on the part of the carrier, although it may have been the real cause of the loss. The risk is therefore thrown upon the carrier, and he receives, in the form of payment for the carriage, a premium for the risk which he thus assumes. So of an innkeeper; he can best secure the attendance of honest and faithful servants, and guard his house against thieves. Whereas, if he were responsible only upon proof of actual negligence, he might connive at the presence of dishonest inmates and retainers, and even participate in the embezzlement of the property of the guests, during the hours of their necessary sleep, and yet it would be difficult, and often impossible, to prove these facts.

The liability of passenger carriers is founded on similar considerations. They are held to the strictest responsibility for care, vigilance, and skill, on the part of themselves and all persons employed by them, and they are paid accordingly. The rule is founded on the expediency of throwing the risk upon those who can best guard against it. Story on Bailments, § 590, *et seq.*

We are of opinion that these considerations apply strongly to the case in question. Where several persons are employed in the conduct of one common enterprise or undertaking, and the safety of each depends much on the care and skill with which each other shall perform his appropriate duty, each is an observer of the conduct of the others, can give notice of any misconduct, incapacity, or neglect of duty, and leave the service, if the common employer will not take such precautions, and employ such agents as the safety of the whole party may require. By these means, the safety of each will be much more effectually secured, than could be done by a resort to the common employer for indemnity in case of loss by the negligence of each other. Regarding it in this light, it is the ordinary case of one sustaining an injury in the course of his own employment, in which he must bear the loss himself, or seek his remedy, if he have any, against the actual wrongdoer.[1]

In applying these principles to the present case, it appears that the plaintiff was employed by the defendants as an engineer, at the rate of wages usually paid in that employment, being a higher rate than the plaintiff had before received as a machinist. It was a voluntary undertaking on his part, with a full knowledge of the risks incident to the employment; and the loss was sustained by means of an ordinary casualty, caused by the negligence of another servant of the company. Under these circumstances, the loss must be deemed to be the result of a pure accident, like those to which all men, in all employments, and at all times, are more or less exposed; and like similar losses from accidental causes, it must rest where it first fell, unless the plaintiff has a remedy against the person actually in default; of which we give no opinion.

It was strongly pressed in the argument, that although this might be so, where two or more servants are employed in the same department of duty, where each can exert some influence over the conduct of the other, and thus to some extent provide for his own security; yet that it could not apply where two or more are employed in different departments of duty, at a distance from each other, and where one can in no degree control or influence the conduct of another. But we think this is founded upon a supposed distinction, on which it would be extremely difficult to establish a practical rule. When the object to be accomplished is one and the same, when the employers are the same, and the several persons employed derive their authority and their compensation from the same source, it would be extremely difficult to distinguish, what constitutes one department, and what a distinct department of duty. It

---

[1] See Winterbottom v. Wright, 10 Mees. & Welsb. 109; Milligan v. Wedge, 12 Adolph. & Ellis, 737.

would vary with the circumstances of every case. If it were made to depend upon the nearness or distance of the persons from each other, the question would immediately arise, how near or how distant must they be, to be in the same or different departments. In a blacksmith's shop, persons working in the same building, at different fires, may be quite independent of each other, though only a few feet distant. In a ropewalk, several may be at work on the same piece of cordage, at the same time many hundred feet distant from each other, and beyond the reach of sight and voice, and yet acting together.

Besides, it appears to us, that the argument rests upon an assumed principle of responsibility which does not exist. The master, in the case supposed, is not exempt from liability, because the servant has better means of providing for his safety, when he is employed in immediate connection with those from whose negligence he might suffer; but because the *implied contract* of the master does not extend to indemnify the servant against the negligence of any one but himself; and he is not liable in tort, as for the negligence of his servant, because the person suffering does not stand towards him in the relation of a stranger, but is one whose rights are regulated by contract express or implied. The exemption of the master, therefore, from liability for the negligence of a fellow servant, does not depend exclusively upon the consideration, that the servant has better means to provide for his own safety, but upon other grounds. Hence the separation of the employment into different departments cannot create that liability, when it does not arise from express or implied contract, or from a responsibility created by law to third persons, and strangers, for the negligence of a servant.

A case may be put for the purpose of illustrating this distinction. Suppose the road had been owned by one set of proprietors whose duty it was to keep it in repair and have it at all times ready and in fit condition for the running of engines and cars, taking a toll, and that the engines and cars were owned by another set of proprietors, paying toll to the proprietors of the road, and receiving compensation from passengers for their carriage; and suppose the engineer to suffer a loss from the negligence of the switch-tender. We are inclined to the opinion that the engineer might have a remedy against the railroad corporation; and if so, it must be on the ground, that, as between the engineer employed by the proprietors of the engines and cars, and the switch-tender employed by the corporation, the engineer would be a stranger, between whom and the corporation there could be no privity of contract; and not because the engineer would have no means of controlling the conduct of the switch-tender. The responsibility which one is under for the negligence of his servant, in the conduct of his business, towards third persons, is founded on another and distinct principle from that of implied contract, and stands on its own reasons of policy. The same reasons of policy, we think, limit this responsibility to the case of strangers, for whose security alone it is established. Like considerations of policy and general expediency forbid the extension of the principle, so far as to warrant a servant in maintaining an action against his employer for an indemnity which we think was not contemplated in the nature and terms of the employment, and which, if established, would not conduce to the general good.

In coming to the conclusion that the plaintiff, in the present case, is not entitled to recover, considering it as in some measure a nice question, we would add a caution against any hasty conclusion as to the application of this rule to a case not fully within the same principle. It may be varied and modified by circumstances not appearing in the present case, in which it appears, that no wilful wrong or actual negligence was imputed to the corporation, and where suitable means were furnished and suitable persons employed to accomplish the object in view. We are far from intending to say, that there are no implied warranties and undertakings arising out of the relation of master and servant. Whether, for instance, the employer would be responsible to an engineer for a loss arising from a defective or ill-constructed steam-engine : Whether this would depend upon an implied warranty of its goodness and sufficiency, or upon the fact of wilful misconduct, or gross negligence on the part of the employer, if a natural person, or of the superintendent or immediate representative and managing agent, in case of an incorporated company — are questions on which we give no opinion. In the present case, the claim of the plaintiff is not put on the ground that the defendants did not furnish a sufficient engine, a proper railroad track, a well-constructed switch, and a person of suitable skill and experience to attend it ; the gravamen of the complaint is, that that person was chargeable with negligence in not changing the switch, in the particular instance, by means of which the accident occurred, by which the plaintiff sustained a severe loss. It ought, perhaps, to be stated, in justice to the person to whom this negligence is imputed, that the fact is strenuously denied by the defendants, and has not been tried by the jury. By consent of the parties, this fact was assumed without trial, in order to take the opinion of the whole Court upon the question of law, whether, if such was the fact, the defendants under the circumstances, were liable. Upon this question, supposing the accident to have occurred, and the loss to have been caused, by the negligence

of the person employed to attend to and change the switch, in his
not doing so in the particular case, the Court are of opinion that it is
a loss for which the defendants are not liable, and that the action
cannot be maintained.

Plaintiff nonsuit.

INHABITANTS OF WORCESTER *v.* THE WESTERN RAILROAD CORPORA-
TION.[1]

Worcester Co., October Term, 1842.

Taxation — Exemption of Property held for Public Purposes.

The Western Railroad Corporation are not liable to be taxed for the land, not exceeding
five rods in width, over which they were authorized to lay out their road, nor for buildings
and structures thereon erected by them, if such buildings and structures are reasonably
incident to the support of the road or to its proper and convenient use for the carriage of
passengers and property — such as houses for the reception of passengers, engine houses,
car houses, and depots for the convenient reception, preservation, and delivery of merchan-
dize carried on the road.

SHAW, C. J.   In a petition to this Court for a writ of *certiorari* to
the county commissioners, the inhabitants of Worcester set forth,
that they are aggrieved by the doings of the commissioners, and pray
redress.   The petition states that the Western Railroad Corporation
have erected and are the owners of several valuable buildings, situated in the town of Worcester, to wit, a house for a passenger depot,
a freight house, a car house, and an engine house, and that said buildings stand partly within and partly without the line of the railroad
location; that in the year 1841, the corporation, being the owners and
occupants of the said buildings, the same were taxed, by the assessors of Worcester, their due proportion, with other real estate, to the
town and county taxes.   It appears that upon an application to the
county commissioners, they abated all that part of said tax, which
was assessed upon buildings lying within the limits of the location
of the road, and that they confirmed the tax upon the buildings or
such part of the buildings as lay without the limits of such location.
The complaint of the inhabitants of Worcester is, that no abatement

ought to have been made; that they have a right to tax said corporation for real estate, such as depots for passengers or merchandise, and buildings used as car and engine houses, although they lie, in whole or in part, within the limits of the location of the railroad, and although used for purposes incident to the business of the corporation, as carriers of passengers, and carriers of freight. Their claim is, that although the mere franchise or right of way, along the strip of land appropriated to the track of the railroad, may be exempted from taxation, yet that the real estate, consisting of buildings and other structures connected with it, is not entitled to the same exemption.

This is a question of great importance in its bearing upon the rights and interests of this class of corporations. To determine it properly, it becomes necessary to consider the nature and purposes of these corporations, the franchises granted to them, the duties required of them, and the objects they were intended to accomplish. These are to be sought in the particular act of incorporation, and in the general provisions of law applicable to them. By the act incorporating the Western Railroad Corporation, St. 1833, c. 116, § 1, the persons named, their associates, successors, and assigns, are made a corporation, to lay out and construct the railroad described; and for that purpose the corporation were authorized to lay out their road, not exceeding five rods wide, through the whole length, and for the purpose of cuttings, embankments, and procuring stone and gravel, to take as much more land as might be necessary for the proper construction and security of said road; with a proviso, stipulating for the payment of damages, for private property thus taken. By § 3, the president and directors, in behalf of the corporation, are authorized, not only to provide for locating, constructing, and completing said railroad, but for the transportation of persons, goods, and merchandise, &c.; to purchase and hold land, materials, engines, cars, and other necessary things, for the use of said road, and for the transportation of persons, goods, and merchandise. By § 4, a toll is granted, for the benefit of the corporation, upon all passengers and property of all descriptions, conveyed and transported on said road, with a qualified power, on the part of the legislature, to limit and regulate such tolls and profits. The act provides that the government of the Commonwealth may, after a certain time, and upon certain terms, purchase the railroad, and all the franchise, property, rights, and privileges of the corporation; that annual reports shall be made on oath, to the legislature, of all their doings, receipts, and expenditures; and that their books shall at all times be open to the inspection of any committee of the legislature appointed for that purpose. The general subject of railroads, as contained in the Rev. Sts. c. 39, §§ 45–86, embrace substantially the same provisions.

From this view of the various provisions of the law, by which the rights and duties of the Western Railroad Corporation are regulated, it is manifest that the establishment of that thoroughfare is regarded as a public work, established by public authority, intended for the public use and benefit, the use of which is secured to the whole community, and constitutes therefore, like a canal, turnpike, or highway, a public easement. The only principle, on which the legislature could have authorized the taking of private property for its construction, without the owner's consent, is, that it was for the public use. Such has been held to be the character of a turnpike corporation, although there the capital is advanced by the shareholders, and the income goes to their benefit. Commonwealth v. Wilkinson, 16 Pick. 175. It is true, that the real and personal property, necessary to the establishment and management of the railroad, is vested in the corporation; but it is in trust for the public. The company have not the general power of disposal, incident to the absolute right of property; they are obliged to use it in a particular manner, and for the accomplishment of a well-defined public object; they are required to render frequent accounts of their management of this property, to the agents of the public; and they are bound ultimately to surrender it to the public at a price and upon terms established.

Treating the railroad then as a public easement, the works erected by the corporation as public works intended for public use, we consider it well established that, to some extent at least, the works, necessarily incident to such public easement, are public works, and as such exempted from taxation. Such we believe has been the uniform practice in regard to bridges, turnpikes, and highways, and their incidents; and also in regard to other public buildings and structures of a like kind; as state-houses, forts and arsenals, court-houses, jails, churches, town-houses, school-houses; and generally to houses appropriated specially to public uses. Proprietors of Meeting-house in Lowell v. City of Lowell, 1 Met. 538.

The general principle is not denied in the present case, but the question is, as to the extent and the limits of this exemption from taxation. This limit, we think, is to be ascertained by considering the extent of the public easement intended to be acquired, secured, and maintained, and the franchise granted to the proprietors, to enable them to accomplish the proposed end.

By the act, the Western Railroad Corporation are not only to construct and maintain a road, on which carriages may run, but also to provide for the transportation of persons, goods, and merchandise, on such railroad. Such transportation of persons and goods is the object to be accomplished; and for this purpose they may hold land, materials, engines, cars, and other things. Articles so held are appropriated to public use, as incident and necessary to the object to be accomplished. But in regard to the quantity of land to be thus taken and held, the power is not unlimited, because its extent is regulated by the act of incorporation, by which the franchise is granted. The provision in the first section is this: " And for this purpose, the said corporation are authorized to lay out their road, not exceeding five rods wide, through the whole length, and for the purpose of cuttings, embankments, and procuring stone and gravel, may take as much more land as may be necessary for the proper construction and security of said road." To the extent of the five rods, it appears to us the legislature intended that the franchise of this corporation should extend, for any and all purposes incident to the object of its creation. It was contended in argument, that their franchise for public purposes extended only to the use of this strip of land as a way, and that if they had occasion for buildings and store-houses, as incident to their operations as carriers of persons and merchandise, they were to be regarded in their latter capacity, as carrying on a distinct business, for their own profit, and therefore that such buildings were not to come under the same franchise. But no such limitation is contained in the act of incorporation, and none such results from the nature of its provisions. The establishment of the rail track, and the maintenance of engines and cars, for the transportation of persons and goods, are all combined together, as one public object to be attained, and the privileges incident to the one are incident to the other. No doubt, in practice, the main use of the strip of land of five rods in width, in the greater part of its extent, will be for sustaining the track for the trains to pass over. But such restriction of its use is not found in the act, and therefore when the corporation have occasion to use any part of such strip of five rods for any of the purposes incident to their creation, it is within their franchise; and being used to promote the purposes contemplated by the act, it is exempted from taxation, as property appropriated to public use. This is the extent to which they are authorized to *take* land without the consent of the owner, and this therefore, we think, is the extent to which the law regards the land as appropriated to public use.

But in addition to the power of taking lands for the construction and use of a railroad, the corporation are vested with the power of purchasing lands. The main object of granting this authority, we think, was to enable the corporation to enter into agreements with private proprietors for such lands as they might want, to construct

30*

their road upon, so as not to be compelled to take it against the will of the owner, under the provisions of the act. But though this was the leading purpose, the authority was not limited to that. It was general in its terms, and authorized the corporation, by purchase, to acquire a title to land, beyond the limit of their location, which might be convenient, though not necessary to the accomplishment of their enterprise. But if the corporation have occasion thus to acquire lands by purchase, and erect buildings beyond their limit of five rods, (if not necessary, under another provision of the act, for obtaining materials for deep cuts or embankments requiring greater width,) such buildings or other real estate will not be considered as necessarily. incident to the railroad and its objects, and therefore will not be exempted from taxation.

So if any part of the lands, lying within the prescribed limit of five rods in width, should be used and appropriated to purposes not incident to the proper construction, maintenance, and management of the railroad, or to the use of it by the corporation, as carriers of passengers and goods, we are of opinion that the estate, thus used and appropriated, would be liable to taxation, like other real estate not exempted.

The Court are therefore of opinion, that this railroad corporation are not liable to taxation, for the land of the width of five rods, located for the road, nor for any buildings or structures erected thereon, so that they be reasonably incident to the support of the railroad, or to its proper and convenient use for the carriage of passengers and the transportation of commodities; and that this includes engine and car-houses, depots for the accommodation of passengers, and warehouses for the convenient reception, preservation, and delivery of merchandise, and all goods and articles carried on the road. From this view of the law, it follows that the decision of the county commissioners was right, and that the petition for a writ of *certiorari* must be dismissed.

Merrick, for the petitioners.

Washburn, for the respondents.[1]

---

[1] In Pennsylvania, railways and works of a public character have been exempted from taxation upon principles of public policy, as in Massachusetts. The earliest case in that State is The Schuylkill Bridge Company v. Frairley, 13 Sergeant & Rawle, 422. There was no express exemption from taxation either in the charter of the company or the general law of the State; but the Court considered the omission of bridges in the enumeration of the kinds of property subject to taxation as a sufficient

Inhabitants of Worcester *v.* The Western Railroad Corporation.

indication of the will of the legislature to relieve property of this nature from the burden of taxation. The case was affirmed in the Lehigh Coal and Navigation Company *v.* Northampton County, 8 Watts & Sergeant, 334, where it was held that the bed, berm-bank, and tow-path of a canal were not taxable as "land" under the statute, and that structures incident and necessary to the use of the canal were within the exemption, such as toll-houses and collector's offices. But in Railroad Company *v.* Berks County, 6 Barr, 70; s. c. *post*, the Court adopted a distinction similar to that adopted by the Supreme Court of Massachusetts in the foregoing case. Structures essential to the construction and use of the railroad were held not taxable, such as depots, engine houses, and buildings for the shelter and protection of cars; but buildings erected by the company for its own use and convenience, and for the purpose of increasing its business and profits, as machine shops, manufactories, workhouses, and yards, &c., for storing goods, were subject to taxation.

In Kentucky, on the contrary, a canal company was held liable to be taxed on all its property in the same manner as a private individual. The valuation was to be made of the lands of the company with all its improvements, including the canal itself and its appurtenances. The increased value given to the land by the construction of the canal, was to be included in the estimate. In other words, the company was to be taxed on the actual value of its property. Louisville and Portland Canal Co. *v.* Commonwealth, 7 B. Monroe, 160. So also in Rhode Island a railway company is liable to be taxed upon its rails, sleepers, &c., and its easement in the lands over which the road passes. 2 Rhode Island, 459; s. c. *post*.

So in Maryland a railway company was held liable to be taxed unless specially exempted by its charter. But the principle adopted for the valuation of the company's property, was to assess the buildings and the rails as of the value they bore irrespective of their being portions of the railway, and the land as land, and not as

of increased value by reason of its being used as a railway. Philadelphia, Wilmington, and Baltimore R. Co. *v.* Bayless, 2 Gill, 355; s. c. *post.*

In New York, under a statute requiring the real estate of a company to be assessed in the town or ward where it was situated, and its personal property in the town or ward where the company had its principal place of business or office, the Court held that the value of the real estate was to be ascertained by comparing the actual cost of the road in each town, with the value of the stock at the time of making the assessment; and the personal estate by deducting from the whole cost of the road the cost of the real estate including the railway itself. Mohawk and Hudson River R. Co. *v.* Clute, 4 Paige, 384; s. c. *post.*

It was held in Maine that a company could not be taxed for its real estate without an express direction of the legislature. The provision in the charter of the company that its capital stock should be held and considered as personal estate, was construed to change the legal nature of land, so that it could not be subjected to taxation except indirectly through the medium of the shareholders. Bangor and Piscataquis R. Co. 21 Maine, 533.

In England, a railway company is liable to be taxed or rated upon the annual value of the railway, that is to say, upon the sum which a tenant from year to year might be expected to pay for the railway by way of rent, assuming him to have the same power of using the railway, and the like privileges and advantages of the company. Regina *v.* London and South-Western Railway Company, 1 Adolphus & Ellis, N. S. 558; s. c. 2 English Railway Cases, 629.

This sum is to be ascertained by deducting from the gross receipts of the company. 1st. The interest of capital actually invested by the company in movable carrying stock. 2d. A per centage for the supposed tenant's profits. 3d. A per centage for the depreciation of the stock beyond the annual repairs, &c. 4th. A per centage for the annual costs of conducting the business, maintenance of the way, &c.

WILLIAM ASHBY and others *v.* THE EASTERN RAILROAD COMPANY.[1]

Essex Co., November Term, 1842.

*Damages — Injury to Wharf by Construction of Railroad in its
Front — Interest of Party in Land.*

A deed conveying a wharf, which extends from the upland below high-water mark, and
bounding on an arm of the sea in which the tide ebbs and flows, passes the flats as parcel,
and also as appurtenant to the wharf.

Where the proprietor of a wharf, which is bounded on an arm of the sea, claims the flats to
the channel, viz., to low-water mark, the burden of proof is on him to show that there was
an original natural channel, from which the sea did not ebb at low water, and that such
channel, or low-water mark, was so far below his wharf as to include the flats which he
claims.

Where the value of a wharf is impaired by the construction of a railroad across the flats
below it, the owner is entitled to recover of the proprietors of the railroad the damages
thus sustained by him.

A, the owner of a wharf, entered into a written agreement, not under seal, with B and C,
that certain machinery and fixtures should be erected on the wharf, at their common expense, and that the profits of the business to be carried on there should inure to their common benefit. A railroad was afterwards constructed across the flats below the wharf, and
A B and C joined in a petition for a jury to assess the damages thereby sustained by
them, and alleged in their petition that they were the owners of the wharf, &c. *Held*, that
if the jury believed, on all the evidence before them, that the petitioners had such an interest in the estate as entitled them to damages, and that they suffered damages jointly, then
they properly joined in the petition, and were entitled to recover.

THIS was a proceeding upon a petition to the county commissioners for a jury to assess damages, alleged to have been sustained by
the petitioners, by the laying out and construction of the Eastern

5th. A per centage for the renewal and
reproduction of the perishable portion of
the railway, such as rails, chairs, sleepers,
&c. Regina *v.* The Grand Junction Railway Co., 4 Adolphus & Ellis, N. S. 18 ;
s. c. 4 Eng. Railway Cases, 1 ; Regina *v.*
The Great Western Railway Co., 4 Eng.
Railway Cases, 26. A deduction is to be
made, although no money is actually expended or set apart for that purpose. Regina *v.* The London, Brighton, and South
Coast Railway Co., 3 English Law and Eq.
Rep. 329.

The increased value given to land and
buildings by their use and occupation for
the purposes of the railway, is a subject-
matter for taxation. Regina *v.* The London and South-Western Railway Co., 1
Adolphus & Ellis, N. S. 558.

Where a railway is situated in several
parishes, the company is to be taxed in
each parish upon the amount of the net
profits attributable to the portion of the
road within the respective parishes, and
not upon such proportion of the net profits of the road, as the number of miles of
road in the parish bears to the whole number of miles in the road. Regina *v.* The
London, Brighton, and South Coast Railroad Co., 3 English Law & Eq. Rep. 329.

[1] 5 Metcalf's Reports, 368.

Railroad over their land in Salem. The commissioners issued a warrant to the sheriff, requiring him to summon a jury to hear and determine the matter of the petitioners' complaint, and the sheriff performed the duty thus required of him. The jury gave a verdict for the petitioners, which was returned to the Court of Common Pleas, and was set aside by that court, upon exceptions taken by the respondents to the instructions given to the jury by the sheriff, at the hearing. The petitioners thereupon alleged exceptions to the decision of that court.

The facts of the case, and the instructions given to the jury, are stated in the opinion given by the chief justice.

Ward, for the petitioners.

N. J. Lord, for the respondents.

SHAW, C. J. Two exceptions were taken to the rulings of the sheriff, on the trial before the jury. The petitioners claimed damage, amongst other things, for certain flats, that is, land flowed by tide water, belonging to them and taken and traversed by the railroad. The petitioners claimed the flats in question, as parcel of or appurtenant to their estate situate in Salem on the westerly side of a cove, river, or arm of the sea, flowed by the tide, on which they had a wharf extending easterly below high-water mark. The railroad passed within about thirty or forty feet of the head of this wharf. The respondents contended, that the flats of the petitioners did not extend so far easterly as the line of the railroad, and that the railroad did not cover any part of the flats. This depended upon the construction of the deeds under which the petitioners claimed, and whether those deeds of the upland estate carried the right of flats, as parcel or appurtenant; and if so, what was the true line, by which that right of flats was bounded.

1. On the first point, the sheriff instructed the jury, " that by the construction of the petitioners' title deeds, they owned the flats to the channel, or low-water mark."

We are of opinion that this direction was right. By a regular succession of deeds, conveying the title, and extending back to 1805, the estate is described as a wharf bounding on South River. It appears that this wharf extended from the upland, below high-water mark, and that South River is an arm of the sea, in which the sea ebbs and flows. We are therefore of opinion, that the flats passed as a parcel, by force of the colony ordinance, and also as appurtenant to the wharf. Anc. Chart. 148; Doane *v.* Broad Street Association, 6 Mass. 332; Rust *v.* Boston Mill Corporation, 6 Pick. 158.

2. Upon the other point, the sheriff instructed the jury, " that if they were left in doubt, upon all the evidence, where the natural channel was, if there were such a channel, then the petitioners were entitled to go to the centre of the ancient river."

The Court are of opinion, that this direction was incorrect, and that the exception was well taken. If this tract of flats, called South River, had no channel running through it, that is, no depression, from which the tide did not ebb at low water, then it must have been a cove, and all the riparian proprietors on the cove would divide the flats amongst them, by lines drawn from their respective lands to the channel, running by the mouth of the cove, from which the tide flows into the cove, giving each a line on the channel, proportioned to his line on the cove. Rust v. Boston Mill Corporation, 6 Pick. 158. If there was an original natural channel, through the cove or river, formed by a stream of fresh water falling into it above, or otherwise, then it was a river or arm of the sea, through which the tide ebbed and flowed, and each riparian proprietor was entitled to the flats, to such channel or stream, if not exceeding one hundred rods.

In reference to the case of the fact being left in doubt by the evidence, the jury should have been instructed, that the burden of proof was upon the petitioners, to prove their title to the soil of the flats claimed, and for that purpose to prove that the original channel or line of low-water mark extended so far, as to include the soil, or some part thereof, over which the railroad was laid ; and that if they failed to establish their title by such proof their claim for damages on that ground could not be sustained.

The Court are therefore of opinion, that the decision of the Court of Common Pleas, declining to accept this verdict and render judgment upon it, was correct, and that this result be certified to the county commissioners, to the end that a warrant may duly issue for a new trial.

Another jury, summoned and impanelled by the sheriff, under a new warrant from the county commissioners, gave a verdict for the petitioners. The respondents filed exceptions to the instructions, given by the sheriff to this jury, but they were overruled by the Court of Common Pleas, and the verdict was accepted by that Court. The respondents brought the case again before this Court, on exceptions to the decision in the Court below. These exceptions (which fully appear in the opinion of the Court) were argued and overruled at the November term, 1843.

N. J. Lord, for the respondents.

Ward, for the petitioners.

SHAW, C. J. It appears by the bill of exceptions allowed by the sheriff, that at the trial before him, the evidence of legal title to the land, over which the railroad passes, was a deed showing the fee to be in William Ashby, one of the petitioners, alone. But it further appeared, that an agreement in writing, not under seal, had been entered into, between said William Ashby and two other petitioners, by which it was stipulated, that certain machinery and fixtures were to be erected on the premises, at their common expense, and that the profits of the business, to be carried on there, were to inure to their common benefit.

The respondents requested the sheriff to instruct the jury, that as the title to the estate appeared by the deeds to be in William Ashby alone, the three petitioners were not entitled, as owners, to recover in this process, and that the jury must find for the respondents. This instruction the sheriff declined giving; and he instructed the jury, " that if they believed, upon all the evidence, that the petitioners really owned the estate, and suffered the damage, if any, jointly, they were properly joined in this petition, and entitled to recover."

This direction, taken in connection with the subject-matter and the state of the question, was, we think, correct. The sheriff was not called on to give an opinion upon an abstract question of legal title, upon deeds. The question was, whether the petitioners had such interests in the estate, as would entitle them to recover for damage, done by the railroad, which impaired its value.

In Dodge v. County Commissioners of Essex, 3 Met. 380, it was held that parties interested in land, not taken for a railroad, but so near as necessarily to be damnified by it, are entitled to damages.

It is settled by a series of decisions, and now by statute, that to recover damage done to real estate by a highway or railroad, it is not necessary that the claimant should be tenant of the freehold, or legal owner of the estate. It is sufficient, that he has an interest, which will be impaired by the public work, so that he must sustain a loss by it. Rev. Sts. c. 24, §§ 31, 32. It is in this sense that the sheriff is to be understood in his instruction to the jury, to determine whether the petitioners were owners of the estate, and had suffered the damage, if any, jointly ; and so understood, it was correct. Notwithstanding, therefore, it appeared by the deed, that William Ashby was owner in fee of the estate, still if by force of the agreement entered into by him with the other petitioners, regarding it as a declaration of trust, or a demise, they became interested in the use and occupation of the estate, and in the machinery and fixtures set up and put in operation therein, then they were owners so far as to establish a claim for damages, if any had been sustained; and this was a proper question for the determination of the jury, upon the evidence.

If the petitioners were interested in one and the same estate, whether such interests were joint or several, it is within the spirit, if not within the express provision of the statute, that they should join in one petition for the assessment of damages. Rev. Sts. c. 24, § 48. This is manifestly for the benefit of the respondents, and is so regarded by the statute, which provides, that when the damages are several, the jury, after determining the whole damage, may apportion it amongst the respective parties who have sustained damage; or if any one has joined in such petition, whom they find to have sustained no damage, the jury may so report, and yet assess damages for the others. Rev. Sts. c. 24, § 50.

Judgment of the Court of Common Pleas, accepting the verdict, affirmed.

———◆———

IN THE MATTER OF THE WESTERN RAILROAD CORPORATION.[1]

Sinking Fund of Western Railroad — To be paid from Net Income — When insufficient no payment to be made in after years.

By St. 1838, c. 9, § 3, the annual payment which the Western Railroad Corporation is required to make, from its income, to the sinking fund, is to be made from its net income; that is, from the amount of money remaining to the corporation, on making up its annual account, after deducting from all its receipts the necessary expense of repairs and management, and also the amount of interest on the debt of the Commonwealth, which the corporation are bound to pay in behalf of the Commonwealth: And if such net income, in any year, is not sufficient for such payment, the corporation cannot be required to make up the deficiency from the income of succeeding years.

To the Honorable the House of Representatives of the Commonwealth of Massachusetts:

THE undersigned, Justices of the Supreme Judicial Court, have received a copy of the order of the Honorable House, requesting them to give their opinion on the following questions, in relation to the obligations imposed on the Western Railroad Corporation, by the

———

[1] 5 Metcalf's Reports, 596.

third section of the act passed on the 21st of February, 1838, entitled " An Act to aid the construction of the Western Railroad," viz : —

" 1st. Is the contribution of one per cent., which is to be paid to the sinking fund from the income of said corporation, payable from its gross or its net income?

" 2d. If the said contribution is payable from the net income of the corporation, and if, in any one year, the said net income should be insufficient for that purpose, can the corporation be required, in any event, to make up the deficiency from the income of succeeding years ? "

As the questions, on the face of them, seem to involve a controverted question of right between the Commonwealth and a private corporation, a question apparently and peculiarly fit to be decided in a regular course of judicial proceeding, we had doubts, at the first view of the subject, whether it was a case coming within the intent of the constitution, pursuant to which questions of law are to be proposed ; and whether it might not be expedient first to submit to the consideration of the Honorable House, whether it would be expedient to request an *ex parte* opinion in such a case.   Our doubt was this : As we have no means, in such case, of summoning the parties adversely interested before us, or of inquiring, in a judicial course of proceeding, into the facts upon which the controverted right depends, nor of hearing counsel to set forth and vindicate their respective views of the law, such an opinion, without notice to the parties, would be contrary to· the plain dictates of justice, if such an opinion could be considered as having the force of a judgment, binding on the rights of parties.   But as we understand that the session of the legislature is drawing to a close, and it might be inconvenient to the House to refer the matter back to them before acting upon it ;· and as an opinion upon an abstract question, without any investigation of facts, and without argument, must be taken as an opinion upon the precise question proposed, which cannot affect the rights of parties, should they hereafter be brought before the court in a regular course of judicial proceeding, we have thought it best, without further delay, to submit an opinion upon the questions proposed. We, therefore, ask leave to submit the following opinion of the subscribers, three of the Justices of the Judicial Court.   One of our number, Mr. Justice Wilde, having a small interest in the stock of the Western Railroad Corporation, asks leave, on that account, to decline the expression of any opinion on the subject.

The first question is, whether the contribution of one per cent., which is to be paid to the sinking fund from the income of the

Western Railroad Corporation, is payable from its gross or its net income?

This is proposed by the Honorable House as a question in relation to the obligations imposed on the Western Railroad Corporation, by the third section of the act passed on the 21st of February, 1838, entitled an act to aid the construction of the Western Railroad. St. 1838, c. 9, § 3.

We suppose the whole obligation of the corporation depends upon the provision referred to; and although there are some subsequent acts, making further loans of the Commonwealth's certificates of debt, of which, in like manner, the corporation are required to pay the interest annually, we have not specially referred to them, but confined ourselves to the obligation imposed by the provision specified in the question.

We are not quite certain that we understand precisely what is intended by the "gross income" of the corporation, and what by the "net income." But we suppose that in any mode of estimating the income of the corporation, the expenses of necessary repairs, and also of maintaining and employing engines and cars, for the carriage of passengers and freight, and all other necessary and incidental expenses of management, must be deducted from the actual receipts. Such balance only can justly be regarded as the income of the corporation.

In looking into the other parts of the act in question, we find it is provided, that the corporation, on receiving the certificates to be loaned to them, shall enter into an obligation, secured by a mortgage upon their whole property, stipulating, amongst other things, that they will pay the semiannual interest upon the Commonwealth's certificates of debt, and indemnify the Commonwealth from all such payments.

It is not to be presumed that it is contemplated by this act, that the corporation were to pay into the treasury of the Commonwealth a sum to be loaned and invested as a sinking fund, until the necessary duty — a duty due alike to the government and the holders of their securities — had first been performed, of paying the interest on those securities. But their whole stock and property being mortgaged to the Commonwealth, the only fund, out of which the corporation could pay the regularly accruing interest on the government securities, was the income from the use of the road. By force of the obligations which the corporation were bound to take on themselves, we are of opinion that the income of the road was specially pledged to the Commonwealth, and through them to the holders of their certificates of debt, to secure the payment of the semiannual interests thereon, before paying any thing into the treasury by way of sinking fund. It would have been manifestly worse than useless to require the corporation to pay a sum of money into the treasury, if it should thereby render them unable to pay the interest on the securities borrowed of the Commonwealth, by means of which the Commonwealth would be immediately liable for the same payment. We think, therefore, that the payment of such interest was a charge on the income, prior in its nature to any payment towards the sinking fund, and that the latter payment was to be made out of an income, diminished by the payment of such interest. And so, if subsequent loans of scrip were made to the corporation by the Commonwealth, under the like obligation, imposed on and assumed by the corporation, of paying the interest annually or semiannually, the payment of such interest would be a prior charge upon the fund, arising from the annual income of the road. By "net income," therefore, we understand the amount of money remaining to the corporation, on making up their annual account, after deducting from all receipts for passage and freight, and other revenue, if any, the necessary expenses of repairs and management, and also the amount of annual or semiannual interest on the debt of the Commonwealth, which the corporation are required by their obligation to the Commonwealth to pay in their behalf. Understanding the term "net income" in this sense, we are of opinion that the contribution of one per cent. towards the sinking fund, to be paid by the corporation to the treasurer, is to be paid out of their net, and not out of their gross income.

But the question may arise, — suppose the annual income, thus charged, should be insufficient to pay the contribution to the sinking fund, what is the consequence? We are of opinion that the corporation, in that event, are discharged of their obligation of paying it, in whole or in part, as the fund may wholly or partially fail. It is a well-settled rule of law, that an obligation to pay money out of a specified accruing fund is conditional; and if the expected fund does not arise, the obligation to pay becomes void. So, if an expected accruing fund is charged with the payment of several sums, in a certain order of priority, if the whole is absorbed in the payment of prior charges, the claims of subsequent parties must fail. The provision of the statute is, that after the said road shall be opened for use, a sum equal to one per cent. on the amount of scrip thus loaned, shall be annually set apart from the income of said road, and paid to said treasurer. If there be no such income, no such sum can be set apart, and the obligation to pay it, of course, does not arise.

In answer to the second question, we are of opinion, that if the net income of the corporation, in any one year, shall be insufficient to make the said contribution of one per cent. to the sinking fund, the corporation cannot be required to make up the deficiency from the income of succeeding years.

Strictly speaking, there can be no deficiency, for the making up of which the corporation are responsible. Their duty is to set apart, from the net annual income of each year, a sum of money, and to pay the same thus set apart. But if there be no income in any one year, from which it can be set apart, no duty arises, no debt is created, chargeable on the income of succeeding years. The whole duty of the corporation is performed.

But there is another consideration, leading to the same conclusion. The whole provision for a sinking fund, to be derived from the income of the road, is to take effect only when the road shall be opened for use. It supposes the case when the road has begun to accomplish the purpose for which it was established, and to yield a revenue, as well as to reimburse the loans made to raise the means for its construction, and to yield an income to stockholders, who have advanced their private capital for the same purpose. We think, therefore, the true policy and purpose of the provision was this ; that when the revenue from the road should be more than sufficient to pay the interest chargeable upon the loans made for its construction, then the one per cent. for the sinking fund should be set apart, and the balance, if any, paid in dividends to the stockholders ; and that the accounts of each year were to be settled and closed by the appropriation and distribution of the proceeds of such year.

In any point of view, therefore, in which we can consider the question, we are of opinion, that the contribution of one per cent., each and every year, to the sinking fund, is to be paid out of the net amount of the income of that year, if it be sufficient for the purpose, and not otherwise ; and that if the net income be insufficient, in any one year, to pay the contribution of that year, it does not constitute a deficiency chargeable upon the income of succeeding years.

LEMUEL SHAW,

CHARLES A. DEWEY,

SAMUEL HUBBARD.

Boston, March 13, 1844.

THE WESTERN RAILROAD CORPORATION v. ABEL BABCOCK.[1]

Hampden Co., September Term, 1843.

Contract — Specific Performance — Delivery of Deed to an Agent of a Corporation — Damages for Breach of Agreement to Convey Land.

It is a good defence to a bill in equity, praying for a specific performance of an agreement to convey land, that the defendant was led into a mistake, without any gross laches of his own, by an uncertainty or obscurity in the descriptive part of the agreement, so that the agreement applied to a different subject from that which he understood at the time; or that the bargain was hard, unequal, or oppressive, and would operate in a manner different from that which was in the contemplation of the parties when it was executed : But in such case the burden of proof is on the defendant to show such mistake on his part, or some misrepresentation on the part of the plaintiff.

Where a party agrees, for a certain consideration, to permit a railroad corporation to construct a road over his land, on any one of two or more routes, at their option, and to convey the land to the corporation, for certain sums, according to the route that shall be taken, after the road shall be definitively located, he cannot defend against a bill for specific performance of his agreement, by showing that he was induced to believe, either by his own notions or by the representations of third persons as to the preference of one route over another, that the corporation would select a route different from that which they finally adopted ; nor by showing that the corporation or its agents made representations as to the probability that one route would be adopted in preference to another, or as to the relative advantages of each route.

Where a party agrees under seal to permit a railroad corporation to construct a road over his land, and also agrees to convey his land to the corporation for a certain sum, after the road shall be definitively located, with a condition in the deed of conveyance that the deed shall be void when the road shall cease or be discontinued; specific performance of such agreement may be decreed, after the road is constructed over the land, although the corporation did not expressly bind itself to take or to pay for the land : And where, in such case, the corporation takes the land, constructs a road over it, and is, for three or four years, in actual possession and use of all the privileges which the performance of the party's agreement would give, and then files a bill against him for specific performance of his agreement, the bill will not be dismissed on the ground of unreasonable delay in filing it.

Where an agreement by deed is made with a corporation, and is delivered to an agent of the corporation, who was duly authorized to negotiate it, it is delivered to the corporation, and his acceptance thereof is the acceptance of the corporation.

In order to prevent a decree for specific performance of a contract, on the ground of inadequacy of consideration, the inadequacy must be so gross, and the proof of it so clear, as to lead to a reasonable conclusion of fraud or mistake.

Where a party who has agreed to convey land, for a certain sum, to a railroad corporation, for the site of a road, refuses to perform his agreement, and obtains an assessment, according to law, of his damages caused by the laying out of the road over his land, the measure of the damages to which he is liable for breach of his agreement, is the excess of the sum assessed at law over the sum for which he agreed to convey the land.

---

[1] 6 Metcalf's Reports, 346.

BILL in equity, filed on the 4th of May, 1842, praying for a decree for the specific performance of a contract.

The bill alleged that the defendant executed and delivered to the plaintiffs an instrument in writing, in the following words : " To all people to whom these presents shall come. Whereas the Western Railroad Corporation have caused surveys to be made, to ascertain the best route for the road authorized by their act of incorporation, and other routes are about to be surveyed, some of which pass, or may pass, over or through lands owned by me, or in which I have an interest; therefore know ye, that I, Abel Babcock, of Chester, in the county of Hampden, in consideration of one dollar paid to me, and for the further consideration hereinafter expressed, that said railroad be located through or over lands situated in Chester, on the west side of the west branch of Westfield River, on or near the locating line lately run by John Child, engineer of said corporation, do hereby for myself and my heirs, executors, administrators, and assigns, grant, assign, transfer, and convey to the said corporation, and for the use thereof, and their successors and assigns, full and free license and authority to locate, construct, repair, and forever maintain and use, the said railroad upon, through, and over my said lands, in such places and courses as the said corporation may judge necessary and convenient, and to take therefor my said lands, to the extent authorized by their charter, and within the following described limits : On the west side of said river, on or near the said western line run by said Child. And I do, for myself, my heirs, executors, administrators, and assigns, covenant and agree with the said corporation, that when said railroad is definitely located, I will, for the consideration hereinafter expressed, on demand, execute and deliver to said corporation, and their assigns, a deed of release and quitclaim of my said lands, taken as above specified, conditioned to be void, whenever said railroad shall cease and be discontinued; and will give such other assurances as may be necessary to carry into effect the object of these presents. Provided, however, that said corporation shall, when said railroad is definitely located, and my said lands taken therefor, pay me at the rate of fifty dollars an acre for all the land, which shall be taken for said road, now used as mowing, and fifty dollars an acre for the plough-land so taken as aforesaid, and eight dollars an acre for pasture-land so taken as aforesaid, and ten dollars an acre for wood-land so taken as aforesaid, and at the rate of one dollar for each rod in length through which said road shall run through my aforesaid lands, for the purpose of fencing the same, where a fence shall be absolutely necessary ; provided, however, that where no fencing is necessary, then the same shall not be accounted any thing in the computation for fencing; and where only one side of said road shall require fencing, one half the amount per rod of the aforesaid sum for fencing shall be computed. Reserving, however, a right to cross said railroad, to get to my other lands, in some reasonable place, doing as little damage to said road as may be; or, in case the said corporation shall choose to pay me four hundred and twenty dollars, as a gross amount of damages and fencing, I agree to release as aforesaid. In testimony whereof, I have hereunto set my hand and seal, this twentieth day of October, in the year of our Lord one thousand eight hundred and thirty six. Abel Babcock (seal)."

The bill then averred that the plaintiffs afterwards definitely located their road, according to the terms of their act of incorporation, and constructed the same over the defendant's lands, according to the terms specified in his contract above set forth, [describing the course, distance, &c., across said lands]; and that soon after said road had been definitely located, the plaintiffs demanded of the defendant that he should execute and deliver to them a deed of release and quitclaim of the lands, taken as above, conditioned as in the defendant's said contract was stipulated, and were ready, and offered, to pay the defendant, as a consideration therefor, at the rate and in the manner provided in said contract; and that the plaintiffs, on the 27th of April, 1842, tendered to the defendant $500, as and for the gross damages in said contract mentioned, and whatever interest might, under any circumstances, be due thereon, and demanded of him that he should execute and deliver to them a deed of release and quitclaim of said lands, taken by the plaintiffs, and at the same time tendered to him, for his signature and execution, the proper form of a deed; but that the defendants, at the several times above mentioned, refused to execute and deliver any deed of quitclaim of said lands, and had, at all times afterwards, so refused, although the plaintiffs had ever been, and still were, ready to pay to him the sum due to him by virtue of said contract.

The defendant, in his answer, admitted that he executed and delivered the contract set forth in the bill; but he averred that the same was not read by him, at the time of its execution, and that it was obtained from him either by fraud and misrepresentation, or mistake; that the said Child, mentioned in said contract as the plaintiffs' engineer, run and superintended the running of the lines across the defendant's lands; that one of said lines ran on the north side of said river, and near to the defendant's house; that another of said lines ran on the south side of said river, and crossed it near the head of an island therein, which belonged to the defendant, and was near to his saw-mill; that said last-mentioned line was run on the defendant's land about 160 rods; that at the time of the execution of said contract, the defendant was given to understand, and did understand, from the representations of Richard D. Morris, the agent of the plaintiffs, and who made the contract in their behalf, that the line last aforesaid had been adopted by the plaintiffs, and for which he wished to procure a release; and that as an inducement to the defendant to execute said contract, said Morris then and there represented that the plaintiffs would have to erect a bridge across said river, and that the defendant might use the same, in passing and repassing said river to and from his adjacent lands; and that it was in consequence of this inducement, and of the advantages so held out to him, and of these representations, that he executed the said contract.

The defendant further averred, that when said contract was executed, he was, and ever since has been, seised and possessed of two lots of land in Chester, lying upon a mountain, containing about 200 acres, covered with valuable timber, which can be obtained for profitable use only by running it down the mountain to a certain road of the defendant, which he constructed, at great expense, for the purpose of procuring said timber, and along which to draw it to his saw-mill, for use; that his saw-mill is adjacent to said lots, " and was valuable for the purpose of manufacturing timber:" That the plaintiffs located, constructed, and used their railroad, in the courses, &c., mentioned in their bill; but that such location and construction were made over and above the aforesaid road of the defendant, and along the northerly parts of said lots, in such a manner as to prevent him from getting down his timber from said lots, or getting it to his saw-mill, without very great and unwarrantable expense: That a part of said location and construction was made within the bed of said river, so as to obstruct the water, and endanger and render useless the defendant's saw-mill: That the damage, sustained by the defendant, in consequence of said location and construction, exceeds $2,500; and that, when said contract was executed, he had no knowledge that said Child had run any such locating line as that where said railroad is constructed, or any line near to the same, and that he now believes that no such line had then been run, or that any thing was said to him by said Morris, at the time of the execution of said contract, as to such line; that he did not understand the line, mentioned in said contract, to be the one now occupied by the plaintiffs; and that, if he had so understood it, he should not have executed said contract.

The defendant admitted that the plaintiffs made a tender to him, on the 27th of April, 1842, as alleged in the bill, and that he then refused to execute a deed of release; but he denied that the plaintiffs had, at any other time demanded any other deed, or that they ever made to him any other tender of payment of damages, or that he ever refused to execute any other deed.

The plaintiffs filed a general replication, and evidence was taken by both parties.

This case was argued at the last September term, principally upon the evidence. The defendant's counsel, however, contended, as matter of law, that specific performance should not be decreed, where the plaintiff has any adequate remedy : 2 Story on Eq. 23, 24 : That the plaintiffs, in this case, might apply to the county commissioners to assess the defendant's damages, and that they held the land by virtue of their act of incorporation and the laying out and construction of the railroad : That specific performance was not a matter of right in the party seeking it, but of discretion in the court, and should not be decreed where it is not strictly equitable, or where the bargain is hard, or made under a mistake, or where there has been a great change, after the contract was made, in the property which is the subject of the contract : 1 Sugd. Vend. (Amer. ed. of 1836,) 245 – 248; 2 Story on Eq. 47, 53, 79 – 81; Mechanics Bank of Alexandria v. Lynn, 1 Pet. 376 ; King v. Hamilton, 4 Pet. 328 ; Daniel v. Mitchell, 1 Story R. 172 ; Mortlock v. Buller, 10 Ves. 305 : And that there was such a want of mutuality in the contract set forth in the bill, as would induce the court to withhold the decree sought by the plaintiffs, even if there were no other objection to such a decree. 2 Pow. Con. 233, 234 ; 2 Story on Eq. 53.

R. A. Chapman, for the plaintiffs.

Wells and *W. G. Bates,* for the defendant.

The opinion of the court was made known at an adjourned term held in Hampden County, in January, 1843.

SHAW, C. J., This is a case in equity, in which the Western Railroad Corporation seek the specific performance of a contract made by them with the defendant, previously to the definitive location of their road, by which he stipulated to convey to them in fee, on certain conditions, as much of his land as would be necessary to their railroad, at rates therein specified. The bill sets forth the agreement by which he stipulated to receive compensation at certain specified rates per acre, for the different kinds of land which the railroad might traverse, and a provisional allowance for fencing. Proof was offered of the execution of the contract, as also of the final location of the road, passing, to a considerable extent, over the defendant's land, as also of the tender of the money, and demand of a deed conforming to the agreement.

The ground of defence is, that the defendant was deceived or mistaken, and led to execute an agreement different from that which he supposed he was executing; that he did not understand where the line was, as described in the agreement, but supposed the line contemplated to be adopted to be a different line from the one, over which the railroad was in fact located, and one, the adoption of which would have done him less damage.

This is mainly a question of fact upon the evidence, and has been so argued by the counsel and considered by the court.

The court, in the main, accede to the principles of law, stated by the defendant's counsel, as those upon which the defence is placed. In an application to a court of equity for a specific performance, a decree for such performance is not a matter of strict right, on proof of the agreement, but may be rebutted by showing that to require such an execution would be inequitable. A defendant, therefore, may not only show that the agreement is void, by proof of fraud or duress, which would avoid it at law; but he may also show that, without any gross laches of his own, he was led into a mistake, by any uncertainty or obscurity in the descriptive part of the agreement, by which he, in fact, mistook one line or one monument for another, though not misled by any misrepresentation of the other party, so that the agreement applied to a different subject from that which he understood at the time; or that the bargain was hard, unequal, and oppressive, and would operate in a manner different from that which was in the contemplation of the parties, when it was executed. In either of these cases, equity will refuse to interfere, and will leave the claimant to his remedy at law.

But, to establish either of these grounds of defence, the burden of proof is plainly on the defendant; and to bring his case within the former, he must show such mistake on his part, or some misrepresentation on that of the complainant, or his agent, seeking to enforce the performance of the contract. In doing this, it is not competent for the defendant merely to aver that he was under a mistake as to the description of the route, or other subject-matter of agreement, or, when the description was precise and clear, that he signed the agreement without reading or hearing it, where he had the means offered him of doing so. He must show an honest mistake not imputable to his own gross negligence.

One other consideration, which we think applicable to such a case, is this; that where a man has stipulated, for a certain consideration, to permit a company to construct a road over his land, by any one of two or more routes, at their option, it is not competent for him afterwards to resist the performance of his agreement, by showing that he was induced to believe, either by his own notions, or by the representation of others, as to the preference of one over the other, that a particular one was adopted, which he did not expect; nor would this result be affected, if the other party, or their agents, had made such representation, as to the probability of their adopting one route in preference to the other, or of the relative advantages of each. Having, by the terms of the contract, stipulated for the right to adopt either, and stipulated to pay a consideration for such right of choice, all representations respecting the probability of their adopting one rather than the other, must be considered as merged in the agreement; and if, in fact, the one route would cause more damage, and the land-owner intends to claim larger compensation in one case than in the other, the alternative must be stipulated for in the agreement itself.

One objection was taken to this agreement, not, we presume, to its legality, but to the fitness and propriety of enforcing its performance in equity; which is, that it was not mutual, because, although the defendant bound himself to convey his land at certain prices, the company did not bind themselves to pay him those prices.

In the first place, the contract, being under seal, and made upon a nominal pecuniary consideration, was binding in law, without other consideration. Again; it was conditional; it was the grant of a license to enter upon his land, and lay out their railroad over it, at their option. If they should not take his land, he would be entitled to no further compensation. But further; as this was a grant to them, on condition, of a license, with certain rights, interests, and easements in the land, there would be good ground to hold, that if they accepted and acted upon this grant, they were bound by the conditions, and that an action would lie for the money. As where a grant is made by deed poll, the grantee paying money, or performing any other condition, an acceptance of the grant binds the grantee to a performance of the condition, for which assumpsit will lie. Goodwin v. Gilbert, 9 Mass. 510.

But a more decisive, and perhaps more satisfactory answer is, that the direct stipulation of the defendant was to execute a qualified, defeasible conveyance of the land to the company, on certain payments being made. The payment was a condition precedent, and the company could obtain no benefit from the agreement, without first paying or tendering the stipulated rates of compensation. This was an ample security for the defendant, binding the company to a compliance with the agreement on their part, and renders the agreement reciprocal; and the condition subsequent, to be inserted in the deed to be made by him, rendering it void if the railroad over his land should be discontinued, was a sufficient guaranty that the grant would not continue when the land should cease to be appropriated to that public use.

That such an agreement, if fairly made, is a legal contract, and that it affords a proper ground for a decree for specific performance in equity, we can have no doubt.

In executing public works, where private property must be taken for public use, the cost of the work, as affected by the compensations thus to be paid, enters largely into the consideration, both of the legislature, and of those agents and commissioners, who may be intrusted with the consideration of the subject, in determining, first, whether the work shall be undertaken at all, and, if so, then what route shall be selected. Such a decision must be influenced mainly by a comparison of the expense with the utility of several proposed routes. If it is to pass over lands covered with dwelling-houses, or otherwise of great value and cost, it would be a strong inducement to the adoption of a less expensive route, or operate as a decisive objection to the enterprise. But the owners themselves know the value of the property, and the prices at which they are willing to part with it, for the accomplishment of the proposed object, taking into consideration the advantage, if any, which it may confer on their other property. A previous contract, stipulating provisionally for a grant of the land, or of a right of way over it, on certain specified terms, is well calculated to give authentic information, to prevent all mistakes and misunderstanding arising from mere verbal propositions and representations, and to secure the rights of all parties.

Taking such a contract, when fairly made, on good consideration, without fraud or duress, to be perfectly legal and equitable, a specific performance, by a decree in equity, is plainly the only *adequate remedy* that such a public corporation could have. The use of the land, when the location is fixed, is absolutely essential to their franchise, and a compensation in damages, in an action at law, would afford them no relief. Indeed, the right to the use of the land, for a public purpose, is secured by the constitution and the laws of the land, independently of any contract; and by their act of incorporation vested in the company, for the use of the public; and if a specific performance of the agreement, on the part of the land-owner, were not given in equity, and the result were that he should obtain his damages in the mode pointed out by the statute, if they should exceed the amount stipulated for in the agreement, the company, in an action at law, on the contract, would recover back the same amount, in damages. If, therefore, the agreement is a valid and equitable one, this remedy, by specific performance, ought to be allowed, to avoid circuity of action.

With these considerations in view, the court have considered the subject as one of fact upon the evidence. There is considerable conflict of evidence, especially as to what took place at the defendant's house, when the agreement was executed. Without stating the evidence at large, which is quite voluminous, the conclusions which we have come to, are these : That there was no fraud or false representation on the part of the company's agent; that the route, described in the agreement, was clearly and definitely stated as the west line, or Child's line, and was known to, or might easily have been known to, Babcock, the defendant, and was at least as well known to him as to the agent; that this was the line ultimately adopted by the company as the route of their road; that the agreement was read over to the defendant, before he executed it, with an honest purpose to enable him fully to understand it; that there was no mistake on the part of the defendant, as to the route expressed in the agreement ; and that, if he was induced, from any cause, to suppose that the company would not pursue the route they did, but adopt another, which he supposed would be more beneficial to them, and better for him, it is not a mistake into which he was led by the company's agent, nor one which affects this agreement.

And the result of the opinion of the court is, that the agreement is valid in law, that the defendant has shown no sufficient grounds to excuse him from a performance in a court of equity, and therefore that the complainants are entitled to a decree for such specific performance.

After the foregoing opinion was delivered, the counsel for the defendant moved for a rehearing. The motion was granted, and at the present term, another argument was addressed to the court, in behalf of the defendant.

Shaw, C. J. A rehearing of the cause has been had, before the full court, upon several grounds. 1. That the complainants are chargeable with laches in not having commenced their suit earlier.[1] Under the circumstances, we can see no ground for this objection. By the location, the complainants are and have been in the possession

---

[1] The defendant's counsel on this point, cited Watson v. Reid, 1 Russ. & Mylne, 236.

and actual use of all the privileges, which the performance of the defendant's agreement would give them, and all which they have occasion for; and all which they seek by this suit is a confirmation, by the deed stipulated for, of these privileges, as their right.

.2. That the company do not show that they accepted the defendant's contract, until this suit was commenced. We understand that Mr. Morris was the authorized agent of the company, and that the deed to them was made pursuant to the instructions given him for that purpose, and therefore the delivery of the defendant's deed to him was a delivery to the company, and his acceptance of the deed was an acceptance by the company. By such acceptance, the company were bound to the performance of the stipulations in it, on their part to be performed. The court are asked, by way of test, whether the defendant could have maintained an action against the company, as soon as they had located their road over his land, and taken possession of it, at the rates stipulated for in this contract. We think he could, and that this follows from the principle already stated, viz. that the grantee, in a deed poll, is bound, by its acceptance, to the performance of conditions stipulated to be performed on his part; and such obligation not arising from specialty on his part, assumpsit will lie to enforce it.

3. Another ground is inadequacy of consideration, because the damages are so much greater than were contemplated when the contract was made. Undoubtedly gross inadequacy of consideration is a good reason for not enforcing the specific performance of a contract. It is somewhat difficult to deal with this question of inadequacy of consideration, when the circumstances are so changed by the location of the railroad itself. At the present time the business of the vicinity may have greatly increased, and the value of all the lands adjacent or near to the railroad must be estimated as it is enhanced by the establishment of such a great public work and thoroughfare in its neighborhood; whereas, at the time this contract was made, it was valued as plough-land, mowing, pasture, and wood-land. It was at a time when the company had some latitude of choice, in determining where to build this great public work, and especially as to the precise route they would adopt. Besides, the defendant, when the route was uncertain and unsettled, might be induced, very justly and wisely, to offer his land at an under valuation, in respect to the enhanced value of the residue of his property, to be effected by the location of this road, in that direction. So far as this had any influence, if it had any, it was a consideration for the defendant's contract, in addition to the pecuniary compensation to be paid for the land, and renders it more difficult to draw any conclusion of inadequacy of consideration

from the stipulated rates of payment for the different kinds of land taken. Under these circumstances, we are of opinion, that to invalidate this contract, the inadequacy of consideration must be so gross, and the proof of it so great, as to lead to a reasonable conclusion of fraud or mistake; and we can perceive no such proof, nor any thing approaching to it.

4. Another ground relied on is, that, in the opinion formerly given, the court intimated that in case Babcock should receive a larger amount of compensation, by the award of commissioners, or the verdict of a jury, than he had stipulated by his contract to accept, the company, in an action at law on the contract, would have a right to recover back the difference; and this is supposed to be incorrect.

That proposition was not necessary to the decision of the cause, and it was put by way of illustration, in order to strengthen the conclusion that this was a fit case for a specific performance of the defendant's contract by a decree in equity, for this, among other considerations, that a suit at law would lead to the same result, by a circuity of action.

Our view was this: Supposing the defendant's contract to be a valid and legal one, subject to no legal or equitable objection, then he was bound by it to execute a deed to the company, on payment of the stipulated compensation for his land; and his refusal to do so on demand and tender, would be a breach. In a suit at law, on such breach shown, the plaintiffs would be entitled to recover such sum as would indemnify them for the actual and direct loss sustained by the non-performance of the contract. Such we understand to be the rule of law, in regard to damages. There may be a difficulty in fixing this by proof; but, when fixed, it is a rule of law as certain as the rule of damages on the non-payment of a note of hand. Such is the rule of damages on breach of a covenant of seisin or right to convey, when no estate passes; it is the sum actually paid, because that is the sum actually lost by the breach. Bickford v. Page, 2 Mass. 455; 4 Kent Com. (3d ed.) 474, 475. If the consideration actually paid cannot be ascertained, the damages shall be determined as nearly to it as the proof will admit. Smith v. Strong, 14 Pick. 128. Where a party stipulated to give his land for a public improvement, the value of the land was deducted from his other damages sustained, in an application for damages. Foster v. Boston, 22 Pick. 33. So in a covenant against encumbrances, the sum actually paid to remove the encumbrance is the measure of damages. Prescott v. Trueman, 4 Mass. 627; Brooks v. Moody, 20 Pick. 474. Indeed, the rule is too familiar to require many authorities to be cited in support of it.

Now, the view of the court was, that if the defendant here could proceed and obtain an award for damages larger than the sum which, by his contract, he had stipulated to take, then the loss sustained by the plaintiffs would be the difference between what they should thus be compelled to pay, under the award of commissioners, and the sum the land-owner had agreed to receive in full satisfaction. That sum would be the exact amount of their loss; and of course that sum would be the measure of their damages, in a suit for breach of this contract. It still appears to us that this is a correct view of the subject, and that, under the circumstances of this case, a decree for a specific performance will bring the parties to the same result, to which they would come by a circuity of action, if it were refused.

We are aware that this is not the result in ordinary cases, and depends upon the peculiar circumstances of this case. Ordinarily, when a decree for a specific performance of a contract to convey lands is refused by a court of equity, for any cause, the covenantor holds and retains the land, and the covenantee's only remedy at law is to recover a sum of money in damages. But, in the present case, the complainants have a right by law to take and hold the land for public use, to the same extent which they could do by force of the contract, and the landholder's only remedy would be to recover a sum of money as compensation for his land. When the sum, which he should thus recover by the award of commissioners, comes to be compared with the amount to be received by the contract, the difference is mere matter of computation; and if the owner of the land had gained any thing by the operation, it would be a gain in money, and a gain precisely commensurate with the company's loss. But, in either event, whether by the operation of law, or by force of a decree for a specific performance, the company holds the land.

Several other considerations were brought to the attention of the court, in behalf of the defendant, on the rehearing, which have been fully considered; but upon the best deliberation which they have been able to bestow upon a revision of the whole subject, they adhere to the opinion formerly expressed, that the plaintiffs are entitled to a decree for specific performance.

INHABITANTS OF CAMBRIDGE AND SOMERVILLE *v.* THE CHARLES-
TOWN BRANCH RAILROAD COMPANY.[1]

Middlesex Co., October Term, 1843.

Erection of Bridge over Highway — Mandamus.

A railroad corporation was authorized by a statute passed on the 17th of March, 1841, (St. 1841, c. 108,) to extend its road across H. street, which was the section of the Middlesex Turnpike: The same statute subjected the corporation to all the duties, liabilities, and provisions contained in the Rev. Sts. c. 39, and other statutes relating to railroad corporations, and also required that said extended railroad should cross H. street under the bridge: By a statute passed on the 13th of March, 1841, (St. 1841, c. 78,) the Middlesex Turnpike Corporation was dissolved, and the surrender of its charter accepted, to take effect on and after the 1st of June, 1841: In September, 1842, the county commissioners laid out and established H. street as a public highway, and ordered the towns of C. and S., in which that part thereof, over which the railroad had been extended, was situate, to erect a bridge over the track of the railroad across H. street. *Held,* that the railroad corporation was bound by St. 1841, c. 108, and Rev. Sts. c. 39, to erect and maintain said bridge, and that the towns of C. and S. were entitled to a writ of mandamus requiring the corporation so to do.

SHAW, C. J. This case comes before the court upon a petition of the inhabitants of Cambridge and Somerville, praying for a writ of mandamus to the Charlestown Branch Railroad Company, requiring them to erect a bridge over a certain highway, lying partly in one and partly in the other of those towns, and thereby save those towns from the expense of erecting such bridge.

It appears by the petition, that the highway in question was formerly a section of the turnpike road, called the Middlesex Turnpike; but that the portion of such turnpike lying in Cambridge, and in that part of Charlestown since incorporated into a new town by the name of Somerville, was called and known by the name of Hampshire street. This is admitted by the answer. The petition sets forth the grounds upon which the petitioning towns insist that it is the duty of the respondents to build this bridge. The respondents appeared and filed their answer, by which they admitted the facts as set forth, but denied their liability to build such bridge, and declared their intention not to do so, unless as a duty imposed on them by law. And the question is, whether they are under such legal obligation.

●

[1] 7 Metcalf's Reports, 70.

The Charlestown Branch Railroad Company were authorized, by St. 1841, c. 108, passed on the 17th of March, 1841, to extend their railroad, from its intersection with the Lowell road, north-westerly through Cambridge, crossing the road in question. By § 4, they were vested with all the powers and privileges, and made subject to all the duties, liabilities, and provisions contained in the 39th chapter of the revised statutes, and other statutes relating to railroad corporations.

At the same session of the legislature, and four days prior to the passage of the above act, an act was passed (St. 1841, c. 78) dissolving the Middlesex Turnpike Corporation, and accepting the surrender of their charter, (which was granted by St. 1805, c. 12,) to take effect on the 1st day of June following. By that act, it was provided, among other things, that said turnpike road, except so much as then already had been, or before said 1st of June should be, laid out and established as a town or county road, should be discontinued.

It further appears by the petition and answer, that the said section of the old Middlesex Turnpike was not laid out as a town or county road before the said 1st day of June, but that the same remained, in fact, an open way, and was used as a convenient private way, by all those proprietors owning lands adjacent to it, and, without restraint, by all other persons having occasion to use it; that in January, 1842, a petition was presented to the county commissioners for the county of Middlesex, praying that the same might be laid out as a public highway; and that such proceedings were had thereon, that at a session of said commissioners, held in September, 1842, the same was so laid out as a public highway, and the inhabitants of Somerville respectively, through which towns the same passed, were ordered to construct and complete the same, and to erect a bridge over the track of the Charlestown Branch Railroad, where such road crosses the same, of the length, dimensions, and construction in said order particularly set forth. It further appears, by the record of said commissioners, that this county road was laid out by the same lines, and of the same width, with that section of the old Middlesex Turnpike; that they awarded no damage to any person over whose lands the same passed, because, in their judgment, no person sustained any by the laying out of said road.

We are then to consider whether, under these circumstances, it was the duty of the respondents to erect, or be at the expense of erecting, this bridge, or whether that duty devolves upon the towns of Cambridge and Somerville.

The respondents, by accepting the franchise conferred on them by the act of the legislature, on certain conditions, became bound to the performance of all conditions and stipulations therein contained, on

SUPREME COURT OF MASSACHUSETTS.   379

Inhabitants of Cambridge and Somerville v. Charlestown Branch Railroad Co.

their part to be performed, to the same extent as if they were thereto bound by covenant. Among these duties are to be included those imposed by the general provisions respecting railroads embraced in the revised statutes. By the Rev. Sts. c. 39, §§ 66, 72, it is provided, that if any railroad shall be so laid out as to cross any turnpike road or other way, it shall be so made as not to obstruct such way; and the corporation shall maintain and keep in repair all bridges, with their abutments, which such corporation shall construct over or under any such way. Wherever, therefore, the rail track and the public way cannot cross each other on the same level, there must be a bridge, either for the way over the railroad track, or for that track over the way; and in either case, it is the duty of the corporation to build such bridge, because necessary to avoid obstructing the way, which they are bound not to do. And where, in the exercise of this duty, the railroad corporation build a bridge for the way, over the railroad, the statute makes it their duty to keep the same in repair.

Had the Middlesex Turnpike continued, or had the same been laid out as a town or county road, before the 1st of June, 1841, it is very clear that it would have been the duty of the corporation to construct and maintain the bridge in question without reference to the terms of the act by which this extension of their franchise was granted. But it ceased to be a public way legally established, though a public way *de facto*, from June, 1841, to September, 1842; and this circumstance gives rise to the question. The respondents contend, that the highway now existing, called Hampshire street, commenced in September, 1842, after their railroad was located and established, and therefore that it was the duty of those who were bound to construct the way and fit it for travel, to construct the bridge necessary for the travel to pass over their road. Were there no provisions in the legislative act, under which the corporation claim their franchise, bearing on this point, there would certainly be great weight in the argument of the respondents. We are then brought to the consideration of those provisions, and their legal effect upon the rights of the parties, taken, as they must be, with reference to the facts and circumstances as they then existed. It was competent for the legislature to grant the franchise upon any terms which might seem to them necessary and expedient for the public safety and convenience, or just and equitable in regard to individuals. They might require that bridges should be built over private as well as public ways, or even require that a bridge should be built where there was no way before, for the use of an individual proprietor, in order to connect one part of his farm with another, and thus diminish the damage occasioned by passing through his land. All such conditions, whatever may be the motive of the legislature in inserting them, become binding on the corporation by their acceptance of the franchise. In the act of 17th March, 1841, St. 1841, c. 108, § 1, in describing the extension, the right to which is granted to the corporation, it is put down as follows: "Thence to the intersection of Hampshire street with the Milk Row road; thence in Cambridge, crossing under said Hampshire street," &c. In a subsequent part of the act, § 5, it is provided that in crossing certain roads named, amongst others Hampshire street, "the said railroad shall pass under bridges. In crossing other roads or avenues, the said company shall, in the construction of the railroad, adopt such safeguards for the security of the public, as the county commissioners shall deem proper." Here is an express condition, that in crossing Hampshire street, the road now in question, the railroad shall pass under a bridge; and by the general railroad law, as before stated, when it is necessary that the railroad should pass under a bridge, it is the duty of the corporation to construct and maintain such bridge, and the abutments connected with it.

But it is contended, in behalf of the respondents, that although this provision was a requisition upon them, absolute in its terms, yet there was a condition, by necessary implication, that the way called Hampshire street should continue, without interruption, to be a public way, either as a turnpike road, or a county or town road; and as it had ceased to be either, at the time when their road was located and constructed, they were thereby exempted from this duty. But we are unable to perceive, in the circumstances of the case, any such implied exception. The act providing for the discontinuance of the Middlesex Turnpike had passed a few days previously. It was therefore known and understood by the legislature that, as a turnpike, it would cease to be a public highway on the 1st of June next ensuing. Yet no qualification was annexed to the duty imposed on the corporation to build a bridge over it. If any such exception had been intended, there seems to be no reason why it was not expressed. Besides; there seems to be no sufficient reason why the duty to build this bridge should be made to depend on its being continued a public way without interruption. The Middlesex Turnpike had been an open public highway thirty-five years. It may be presumed that buildings had been erected, and improvements made, by the adjacent proprietors of land, in reference to the use of the road as a way, public or private, and that it would be continued in some form; and if not laid out as a town or county road, that they would continue it for their own benefit. In that case, it was competent to the legislature to provide for the erection of a bridge over the railroad, in order to continue the use and enjoyment of such way to the proprietors; it would be an equitable interpretation in their behalf, which, it may be well presumed, was intended by the legislature. Or, as it had long been in use by the public, as a turnpike and highway, it might be presumed that it would soon be laid out, by the county or town authorities, as a public way; in which case, all the considerations of policy and equity, which would require the corporation to construct and maintain a bridge over an actually existing road, would apply to a road existing *de facto*, and contemplated to be legally established. In point of fact, soon after the discontinuance of this section of road as a turnpike, an application was made to the county commissioners to lay it out as a highway; and as speedily as it could be done according to the usual course of proceeding, where various corporations and persons are to have notice and be heard, the highway was established. In doing so, the commissioners seem to regard it rather as the restoration of a public easement in a new form, than as a wholly new proceeding. They lay it out according to the same lines exactly as the turnpike, and they award no damages to any of the proprietors. This may have been either because the proprietors had already been paid for a perpetual public easement in their land, and so not equitably entitled to damage; or because it was a benefit to them, exceeding the damage, in consequence of having their buildings and improvements adapted to its use. In either case, it must have been regarded, in substance, rather as a revival and continuance of an existing easement, than as the commencement of a new one, although the only form, in which the commissioners could act upon it, was by laying it out as a new public highway. These considerations strongly rebut the presumption of any implied exception to the obligation imposed on the corporation by the absolute requisition on them to build this bridge, and confirm the conclusion to be derived from the terms of the act, that the obligation to build this bridge was intended by the legislature to be an absolute, and not a conditional one.

But one argument has been urged by the respondents, which deserves consideration. It is said, that at the time when the railroad was located and constructed, the turnpike had been discontinued, the new road had not been laid out, and of course the land over which the way had passed, had become private property, and that the corporation could not enter upon it and erect a bridge and abutments, without committing a trespass. To this we think there are two answers. The first is, that, as it continued during the same time an open way *de facto*, used by the proprietors of the adjoining lands, and by others, and as it was apparently for the benefit of the proprietors, their consent was to be presumed until some dissent was shown; and as the respondents did not ask for a license to enter, or offer to enter and build the bridge, but on the contrary denied, and still deny, their obligation to do it, we think it is no excuse now to say, that if a license had been asked, it might have been refused, and they might have been regarded as trespassers. The other answer is, that although the law would not require the respondents to do an unlawful act, by trespassing on the land of private proprietors, yet that would only suspend, and not wholly take away, the obligation of the respondents to perform this duty. Suppose a railroad act had required the corporation to erect and maintain a bridge over their road, at a place designated, for the benefit of a particular proprietor, and his heirs and assigns, and the proprietor, in possession at the time of the location and construction of the road, should refuse the corporation his consent to their entering his land, to build the bridge; but afterwards the same estate should become the property of other owners, by descent or purchase. If such successors should tender the corporation a license, and request them to build the bridge, we are strongly inclined to the opinion, that the corporation would be bound to the performance of such duty; the obligation having been suspended, but not abrogated. But in this case no offer was made by the corporation, no license was refused by the proprietors, and it cannot be presumed that it would have been refused; because the act was for their benefit, and because, very shortly after the railroad was located, Hampshire street was laid out as a public way, and then there was nothing to hinder the corporation from entering and building the bridge. We are of opinion that they were not absolved from their legal obligation, although at the time of the location and construction of their railroad, the soil of Hampshire street was technically private property.

One other consideration may be briefly referred to, namely, that this duty of building the bridge was imposed by the county commissioners on the towns of Cambridge and Somerville, and therefore it belongs to them, and not to the respondents, to perform it. As between the commissioners and the towns, this was the only course which they could pursue; they having no authority to impose any obligations on the railroad corporation. But if the corporation were under a prior obligation to perform the same duty, and that, in effect, was an obligation to these towns, because it was to meet an expense which they would otherwise be obliged to meet, then these towns do perform their duty, by requiring it to be done by those who are bound to them by law to do it. It is as if they had taken a covenant or bond of indemnity from the respondents, that in case these towns should be required to build such bridge, the respondents would build it, and save the towns harmless.

SUPREME COURT OF MASSACHUSETTS. 383

Charlestown Branch Railroad Co. v. County Commissioners.

On the whole, the court are of opinion, that the railroad corporation were under a legal obligation to build the bridge in question over their road, and that the petitioning towns have such an interest in the performance of this duty, that they are proper parties to come into court, to obtain suitable process for requiring its performance ; and as there is no other suitable and adequate legal remedy for securing its performance, a writ of mandamus may be properly issued, directed to the respondent corporation, requiring them forthwith to erect and construct a bridge over their railroad, where it crosses Hampshire street, with suitable abutments and slopes, in general conformity to the orders and directions given by the county commissioners, in their decree laying out said public highway.

Writ of mandamus ordered.

Buttrick, for the petitioners.

J. Dana, for the respondents. ...

—————◆—————

THE CHARLESTOWN BRANCH RAILROAD COMPANY *v.* COUNTY COMMISSIONERS OF MIDDLESEX.[1]

Middlesex Co., October Term, 1843.

Time for taking Land — Filing Location — Damages — Construction of Contract.

The period of three years " from the time of taking " land for a railroad, within which, by Rev. Sts. c. 39, § 58, application must be made to county commissioners to estimate the damages for such taking, is to be computed from the filing of the location of the road, as required by § 75 of the same chapter.

A railroad corporation, after locating its road over a wharf, more than sixty feet, and filing the location with the county commissioners, agreed with the owners of the wharf to extend the road sixty feet on and over the same before a certain day, and the owners, in consideration thereof, agreed not to demand any damages for such extension : The road was made according to the location that was filed previously to such agreement. *Held,* that this was not an agreement of the corporation not to extend their road more than sixty feet over the wharf, and that the owners of the wharf were not thereby entitled to apply, after three years from the filing of the location, for an estimate of the damages caused by an extension of the road more than sixty feet over the wharf.

——————————————

[1] 7 Metcalf's Reports, 78.

PETITION for a writ of certiorari to bring up the record of the county commissioners concerning the allowance of damages to Mary Harris and another, owners of Harris's Wharf. The following facts appeared at the hearing : —

The petitioners were incorporated by an act passed on the 9th of April, 1836, (St. 1836, c. 187,) with authority to locate and construct a railroad on a line therein described ; and by the third section of said act, it was provided that if the location of said road should not be filed according to law, (that is, within one year,) or if said road should not be completed on or before the 1st of January, 1838, said act of incorporation should be void. By an act passed on the 27th of March, 1837, (St. 1837, c. 94,) the time limited in the former act, for the filing of the location of said road, was extended, so as to authorize the petitioners to file the same on or before the 1st of January, 1839, and the time for the completion of said road was extended to the 1st of January, 1840. By St. 1839, c. 126, the time for completing said road was extended to January 1st, 1841.

The petitioners filed with the county commissioners the last location of said road over and across Harris's Wharf, on the 20th of December, 1838, and began the making of the road over said wharf in May, 1840. Mary Harris and others, owners of said wharf, made a written application to said commissioners to estimate the damages caused by the taking of said wharf for said road ; which application was filed on the 29th of March, 1842. At the hearing of said application, the following agreement was read to the commissioners by the applicants' counsel :

" Memorandum of agreement made this 26th day of February, 1840, by and between the Charlestown Branch Railroad Company and Richard D. Harris, acting for himself and owners of Harris's Wharf.

" 1st. In consideration of the agreement herein contained, and to be kept and performed by the owners of said wharf, the said corporation promises and engages to extend its railroad across the dock between Gray's and said Harris's Wharf, and sixty feet over and on said Harris's Wharf estate, from the south-westerly line thereof, in the present direction of said railroad, to be located twenty-five feet wide, on or before the 1st day of June next.

" 2d. And in consideration of the above, the owners of said Harris's Wharf do hereby agree not to demand against said corporation any damage or compensation on account of its extending, locating, making, and maintaining its road as above described, and hereby release all such damages and demands, excepting however the claims that may be made by the occupants of said wharf for the expense of removing merchandise or other materials for or on account of said railroad company.

"3d. It is further understood and agreed, by and between the parties to this agreement, that the owners of said Harris's Wharf do not consent to have said Charlestown Branch Railroad extended, located, made, and maintained, on and over their said estate, more than sixty feet from the south-westerly line thereof, as aforesaid ; on the contrary, that they, the said owners, do object to any further extension of said railroad, on account of the injury which they allege said estate would suffer from such extension, and that said owners will claim all reasonable compensation for damage, that may be occasioned thereby.

"4th. It is also understood and agreed, by the parties aforesaid, that said owners of Harris's Wharf reserve to themselves the right to pass over and across said sixty feet of railroad, and all other rights not hereinbefore surrendered.

"Charlestown Branch Railroad Company,
by Charles Thompson, President.
"Richard D. Harris, for self and owners of
Harris's Wharf.'

The said applicants' counsel, at the same time, read to said commissioners a letter from the proprietors of said wharf to the agent of the said railroad company, dated May 13th, 1840, forbidding the company to extend their railroad across said wharf beyond the point mentioned in the foregoing agreement, and giving notice that they should claim full damages for all the injury which they might sustain from any act of the said company or its agents : Also a letter from said proprietors to the president of said company, dated June 26th, 1841, stating that the railroad was extended, about a year before, across said wharf, whereby the estate was much injured, and that said proprietors at that time made known to the agent of the company that they should demand remuneration for the land taken and the injury sustained ; wherefore they requested to know whether the president and directors "had fixed upon the amount to which they considered said proprietors entitled, or what course they purposed taking in relation to this claim." The answer of said president to this last letter, was also read to said commissioners. It was dated June 29th, 1841, and informed said proprietors that the directors of the railroad corporation had not taken any action upon the subject-matter of said proprietors' last letter.

The counsel for the railroad company moved the county commissioners to dismiss the application of the proprietors of said wharf for damages, because more than three years had elapsed, when said application was made, after the filing of the location of the railroad over said wharf, and the taking of said wharf and land by said company. The commissioners overruled this motion, and on the 1st Tuesday of September, 1842, awarded damages to the said Mary Harris and another, pursuant to their application.

J. Dana, for the petitioners.

By the Rev. Sts. c. 39, § 58, " no application to the commissioners, to estimate damages for land or property to be taken " for a railroad, " shall be sustained unless made within three years from the time of taking the same." The petitioners understand that the filing of the location is the taking meant by this 58th section. The filing of the location is notice to every person, over whose land the railroad passes, that his land is taken. On any other construction, parol evidence will always be required to show when the land was taken. As soon as the location is filed, either the corporation or the land-owner may apply to the commissioners to appraise damages. Harrington v. County Commissioners, 22 Pick. 263; Hallock v. County of Franklin, 2 Met. 558. By § 56, the corporation is liable to pay the damages caused by laying out and making the road. " Laying out " here means the same that is meant by " taking " in § 58. The decision in Heard v. Proprietors of Middlesex Canal, 5 Met. 81, is applicable to the case at bar.

Greenleaf and *Welch*, for the respondents.

As the private property in question has been taken for public uses, and the provisions of the Rev. Sts. c. 39, are remedial, the court will give them a liberal construction. The controversy is between the Commonwealth and the wharf-owners, and not between them and the railroad company ; and therefore, if those provisions are ambiguous, they are not to be construed *contra proferentem.*

The word " taking" is used differently in different sections of c. 39 of the Rev. Sts.; and therefore is not easily understood. By § 73, a railroad corporation may vary the location of its road, and file the location of the part of the road where the variations are made. Can a land-owner, in such case, have damages twice ?

The St. of 1836, c. 278, which prescribes the duty of county commissioners, when called upon to estimate damages sustained in cases like the present, speaks of " property taken or intended to be taken." This indicates that the filing of the location is the manifested intention to take, as distinguishable from the actual taking.

The case cited from 5 Met. 81, shows that the *completion* of the dam of the Middlesex Canal was the date from which the limitation of the time for applying for damages was to be computed. In the cases cited from 22 Pick. and 2 Met. it is true that the laying out of a road over land was held to entitle the land-owner to damages. But a "laying out" is perfectly intelligible; while a "taking" is not so.

Whatever may be the meaning of the word "taking," in the Rev. Sts. c. 39, § 58, the agreement of the parties, made on the 26th of February, 1840, was a waiver, by the petitioners, of the statute notice of their location. Prior to that agreement, no land was "intended to be taken" beyond sixty feet. See Fitch v. Stevens, 4 Met. 428; Stone v. City of Boston, 2 Met. 228. The petitioners do not complain that the damages awarded by the commissioners are excessive; and it is clear that the owners of the wharf are equitably entitled to receive them. And the court will not issue a writ of certiorari unless substantial injustice has been done. Hancock v. City of Boston, and Inhabitants of Whately v. County Commissioners, 1 Met. 123, 338; Gleason v. Sloper, 24 Pick. 181.

WILDE, J. This is a petition for a writ of certiorari to quash the proceedings of the county commissioners in awarding damages to Mary Harris and another, for their land, taken by the petitioners for their road, in pursuance of the Rev. Sts. c. 39. The error alleged is, that the application to the commissioners to estimate said damages was not made within three years after the land had been taken, as required by § 58. That section provides that "no application to the commissioners, to estimate damages for land or property hereafter to be taken, shall be sustained, unless made within three years from the time of taking the same," with an exception not applicable to the present case. The question is, whether the application was made within three years, as required by this provision; and this depends on the true meaning of the words "*taking the same.*" The respondents' counsel contend, that the lands were not taken until the petitioners entered thereon and commenced making their road. On the other hand, it is contended, in behalf of the petitioners, that the location of their road, and filing the same in the office of the county commissioners, was a *taking* within the true meaning of the statute.

The meaning of this section, without reference to other parts of the statute, is somewhat obscure; but with such reference, we think it sufficiently clear. By § 75, every railroad corporation is required, in all cases, to "file the location of their road, within one year, with the commissioners of each county, through boundaries of such portion thereof as lies within each county respectively." And by § 60, it is provided, that after any railroad corporation "shall, by virtue of their charter, have *taken* any lands or other property for the purpose of their railroad, the owner of any such land or other property may, at any time within three years from the time of taking the same, demand in writing of the treasurer or principal agent of the corporation, a plan, or description in writing, of the land or other property so taken; and said corporation, within thirty days from the time of such demand, shall deliver to him such description or plan; and all the rights of said corporation to enter upon or use said land or other property, except for making surveys, shall be suspended until they shall have so delivered such description or plan." By the taking of lands, as mentioned in this latter section, we think the filing of the location of the road, as required by § 75, was intended, and not the making of the road; for if the latter had been intended, no plan or description of the road would seem to be necessary or useful. The commencement of making the road would be a sufficient notice of its location. So the suspension of the rights of the corporation to enter upon or use said land, except for making surveys, implies, we think, that a plan or description of the road may be required before the road is made, or is begun to be made, although it cannot be required until after the land is taken. And a similar inference may be drawn from § 61, which requires the corporation to give security for damages and costs, if requested; and if not given, their rights to enter upon or use the land, except for making surveys, are to be suspended, as before mentioned. It is possible, though not probable, that surveys might be required after the railroad had been located, and the making of it had commenced; but it is not to be presumed that the legislature intended to provide for such a possibility. By § 56, the corporation are made " liable to pay all damages occasioned by *laying out* and making and maintaining their road." The words " laying out," in this section, and the words " *taken* " and " *taking*," in § 58, were intended, as it seems to us, to convey the same meaning. The remaining part of the section which makes a distinction between an intention to take lands or materials necessary for the purpose of making or securing a railroad, and the actual taking, does not apply to land over which the road is laid, and has but little, if any, bearing on the present question.

Taking into consideration these various provisions, we are of opinion, that the time of limitation of the application for the assessment of damages, by § 58, must be understood to have commenced on the petitioners' filing the location of their road with the county commissioners. This is equivalent to the laying out of highways and turnpike roads by the county commissioners. It was by that act that the corporation acquired a right of way over the land. They thereby took a title, and thus they took the land, according to the language of the statute.

It has, however, been ·argued, that by an agreement between the parties, the petitioners have varied, and thereby waived their location. But we cannot so construe the agreement. The petitioners agreed to extend their railroad sixty·feet on and over the Harris Wharf. · For this extension the owners of the wharf agreed to relinquish their claim for damages. But this does not imply an agreement, on the part of the petitioners, that they would not extend their railroad farther. And it was not so understood by the parties; for the owners of the wharf objected to any farther extension, and claimed the right to recover compensation for any damages they might sustain thereby. We are therefore of opinion, upon the whole matter, that the claim for damages was, before the application to the county commissioners, barred by the statute. The notice given to the petitioners, within the three years, that damages would be claimed is not material; and the claim for damages ought not to have been allowed by the county commissioners.

Petition granted.

COMMONWEALTH *v.* WILLIAM H. POWER AND OTHERS.[1]

Berkshire Co., September Term, 1844.

Regulations as to use of Road — Authority of Superintendents of Stations — Right to Exclude Persons when Violating Rules.

A railroad corporation has authority to make and carry into execution reasonable regulations for the conduct of all persons using the railroad or resorting to its depots, without prescribing such regulations by by-laws; and the superintendent of a railroad depot, appointed by the corporation, has the same authority, by delegation.

A superintendent of a railroad depot has authority to exclude therefrom persons who persist in violating the reasonable regulations prescribed for their conduct, and thereby annoy passengers or interrupt the officers and servants of the corporation in the discharge of their duties.

Where the entrance of innkeepers, or their servants, into a railroad depot, to solicit passengers to go to their inns, is an annoyance to passengers, or a hindrance and interruption to the railroad officers in the performance of their duties, the superintendent of the depot may make a regulation to prevent persons from going into the depot for such purpose; and if they, after notice of such regulation, attempt to violate it, and, after notice to leave the depot, refuse so to do, he and his assistants may forcibly remove them; using no more force than is necessary for that purpose.

---

[1] 7 Metcalf's Reports, 596.
33 *

If an innkeeper who has frequently entered a railroad depot, and annoyed passengers by soliciting them to go to his inn, receives notice from the superintendent of the depot that he must do so no more, and he nevertheless repeatedly enters the depot for the same purpose, and afterwards obtains a ticket for a passage in the cars, with the *bona fide* intention of entering the cars as a passenger, and goes into the depot on his way to the cars, and the superintendent, believing that he had entered the depot to solicit passengers, orders him to go out, and he does not exhibit his ticket, nor give notice of his real intention, but presses forward towards the cars, and the superintendent and his assistants thereupon forcibly remove him from the depot, using no more force than is necessary for that purpose, such removal is justifiable, and not an indictable assault and battery.

THIS was a complaint against the defendants, made to a justice of the peace, for an assault and battery upon Timothy Hall, on the 23d of March, 1844. The defendants appealed from the justice to the Court of Common Pleas. Trial before that court at the last June term. The judge before whom that trial was had made the following report thereof:

It appeared, that, at the time of the alleged assault, &c., the defendant Power was master of the depot of the Western Railroad, at Pittsfield, and that the other defendants were servants of the Western Railroad Corporation : That said Hall, having in his pocket a ticket for his passage in the railroad cars from Pittsfield to Richmond, and having a *bona fide* intention to go to Richmond, entered said depot about the time of the arrival of the cars for Richmond, and was proceeding to the platform, for the purpose of entering a car : That said ticket had been procured by another person, and that neither the defendants nor any other agent of the said corporation knew that Hall had it, or that he intended to go to Richmond.

Said Power alleged in his defence, that Hall was going to the platform to solicit passengers to go to his house, he being the keeper of a tavern near the depot; that said Power met Hall on his way to the platform, told him he must not go there, laid his hands upon and ordered him to leave the depot, without any previous inquiry as to his purposes; that Hall made no reply, but pressed forward and endeavored to reach the platform in spite of the efforts of said Power, who thereupon ordered the other defendants to put him out of the depot; and that they accordingly took him and forcibly put him out, not using any more violence than was necessary to accomplish that object.

It appeared in evidence, or was admitted on the part of the Commonwealth, that the innkeepers in the neighborhood of said depot had previously to this affair been in the habit of going, or sending their servants, to the platform, to solicit passengers, arriving in the cars, as customers to their several houses ; and that Hall had personally, and by his servants, participated in this practice; that this practice had become a great annoyance to passengers; that said Power, having been placed, by the railroad corporation, in charge of the depot, had addressed a circular letter to said innkeepers, about two weeks before the said assault, stating the facts, and requesting them to discontinue said practice, and giving them notice that they would thereafter be excluded from the platform; that all of them, except Hall, discontinued the practice, but that he continued to go to the platform and solicit passengers; that said Power had forbidden him, a day or two before the said assault, to enter the depot at all; that notwithstanding this, Hall had again forced his way to the platform, when the cars were in, against the remonstrances and efforts of said Power, who again told him that he must not come to the depot any more.

On this evidence, the defendants contended that they were justified in doing the acts complained of. The judge instructed the jury that the foregoing facts did not constitute a defence; and under said instruction, a verdict was returned against the defendants. But as the question of law in the case was, in the opinion of the judge, so doubtful as to require the decision of the Supreme Judicial Court, he made the foregoing report of the case, pursuant to the Rev. Sts. c. 138, § 12.

R. A. Chapman and *Colt*, for the defendants.

Every proprietor of lands or buildings has a right to the control of them, and may put out other persons, after ordering them to remove. Commonwealth v. Clark, 2 Met. 25. Common-carriers have the same right as others to the control of their premises. Though they cannot refuse to carry goods or passengers, without good cause, yet a passenger who is rejected, and *à fortiori* a person who does not claim the rights of a passenger, has not a right to remain on their premises against their will. Hall should have exhibited his ticket, or offered the fare, and claimed the rights of a passenger. See 2 Kent, Com. (3d ed.) 598; Bac. Ab. Carriers, B.; Inns and Innkeepers, C. 3; Spooner v. Baxter, 16 Pick. 411.

If Hall ever had any right to go to the platform, (which is denied,) he had forfeited that right by his previous conduct, and the defendants, as agents of the corporation, were well warranted in removing him, while they had a reasonable apprehension that he would cause disturbance and annoyance. Howell v. Jackson, 6 Car. & P. 723; Story on Bailm. § 476; Chit. Con. (5th Amer. ed.) 478; in Markham v. Brown, 8 N. Hamp. 523, it was held that the right of one to enter an inn, for the purpose of soliciting passengers for a stage coach, may be forfeited by his misconduct in disturbing the guests; and that an innkeeper may prohibit a stage agent from entering, until the ground of apprehension is removed. And in Jencks v. Coleman, 2 Sumner, 221, it was decided that proprietors of steamboats, though they are common carriers, may rightfully exclude persons from their boats, whose character, habits, or purposes interfere with the proprietors' interest; and all persons who refuse to obey the reasonable rules prescribed for the regulation of the boats.

Bishop, for the Commonwealth.

The law relied on for the defendants does not apply to the facts of this case. Exclusive right of possession of premises is necessary in order to justify a removal of others therefrom by force. One cotenant, who obtains possession of the whole, has no right forcibly to keep out another tenant. A railroad corporation is not, strictly speaking, a private corporation, like a steamboat or stage company, whose property is wholly their own. It is a public corporation, and takes private property for public use. It has not exclusive possession of the track, depots, &c., as against individuals and the public. The public have a right there, and going there is not a trespass. Therefore, if Hall was not a trespasser, the defendants had no right to expel him by force. Can an agent of a turnpike road forbid any person to travel on it; or can he seize a traveller who violates a by-law against passing over a bridge faster than on a walk, and turn him off by force?

The Rev. Sts. c. 44, §§ 1, 2, authorize corporations to establish by-laws, and prosecute for violations of them. But the railroad corporation has no by-law forbidding taverners and porters to crowd about the depots. A circular letter of the agent had been issued, without any authority from the corporation, and therefore was of no binding force.

But if Hall might rightfully have been excluded from the platform, by reason of his former conduct, yet he could not be legally excluded from the depot. He was seized before he reached the platform. One may stand on the line of his close, and prevent another's entry; but he cannot resist an approach towards it, by way of anticipating an injury. See Reynell v. Champernoon, Cro. Car. 228; Weaver v. Bush, 8 T. R. 81.

Further; Hall had a ticket, and a right to a passage, and a right to go through the depot to the platform, to claim a passage. He was not bound to give notice that he was a passenger; the defendants should have inquired of him what his purpose was, before laying hands on him.

Chapman, in reply.

The Rev. Sts. c. 44, § 2, give no authority to corporations to make by-laws with penalties, which shall affect *third persons*.

SHAW, C. J. This is a criminal prosecution instituted against Power and several of his assistants acting under his orders, charging an assault and battery upon the complainant, Timothy Hall. It comes before the court upon a report of the evidence. It appears that the learned judge did not give detailed instructions to the jury, upon the questions of law arising in the case; but the evidence being stated, the jury were directed that the facts stated did not constitute a defence; and a verdict, under that instruction, was rendered against the defendants. If it was competent for the jury, consistently with the rules of law, to render a verdict for the defendants upon this evidence, then the verdict should be set aside and a new trial granted. It becomes then necessary to inquire what the rules of law are, and how they apply to the evidence reported.

The Court are of opinion, that the railroad corporation, both as the owners and proprietors of the houses and buildings connected with the railroad, and as carriers of passengers, have authority to make reasonable and suitable regulations in regard to passengers intending to pass and repass on the road in the passenger cars, and in regard to all other persons making use of such houses and buildings. This authority is incident to such ownership of the real estate, and to their employment as passenger carriers; and all such regulations will be deemed reasonable, which are suitable to enable them to perform the duties they undertake, and to secure their own just rights in such employment; and also such as are necessary and proper to ensure the safety and promote the comfort of passengers. The reasonableness of such regulations must in some measure be judged of with reference to the particular depot at which they are adopted. Regulations may be proper and necessary at one of the termini of the road, where there is usually a great throng of passengers and other persons connected with the business of the road, which would not be required at a way station, where a few persons enter or leave the cars, and where they stop but a few moments.

And we are also of opinion, that the regulations, thus to be made and enforced, are not necessary to be made in the form of by-laws, to be carried into effect by penalties and prosecutions. Such by-laws are rather the regulations which a corporation have power to make in respect to the government of their own members, and of their corporate officers, or of municipal corporations, that exercise, to a limited extent, the powers of government. But the regulations in question are such as an individual, who should happen to be the sole owner of the depots and buildings, and of the railroad cars, would have power to make, in virtue of his ownership of the estate and of his employment as a carrier of passengers.

That a railroad corporation are to be deemed carriers of passengers, and are subject to the duties, and entitled to the privileges and powers incident to such employment, seems to be settled by various cases, in which suits have been sustained by and against them. They are in this respect on the footing of owners of steamboats. Both are modern modes of conveyance; but the rules of the common law are applicable to them, as they take the place of other modes of carrying passengers. Jencks *v.* Coleman, 2 Sumner, 221 ; Camden and Amboy Railroad Co. *v.* Burke, 13 Wend. 611; Pardee *v.* Drew, 25 Wend. 459 ; Pickford *v.* Grand Junction Railway Co. 8 Mees. & Welsb. 372. An owner of a steamboat or railroad, in this respect, is in a condition somewhat similar to that of an innkeeper, whose premises are open to all guests. Yet he is not only empowered, but he is bound, so to regulate his house, as well with regard to the peace and comfort of his guests, who there seek repose, as to the peace and quiet of the vicinity, as to repress and prohibit all disorderly conduct therein ; and of course he has a right, and is bound, to exclude from his premises all disorderly persons, and all persons not conforming to regulations ·necessary and proper to secure such quiet and good order. Markham *v.* Brown, 8 N. Hamp. 523.

We are also of opinion, that the power which the company thus have to regulate their several depots, they may delegate to suitable officers. Indeed, it· is the only mode in which a corporation can exercise their powers. And where they have appointed a superintendent with authority, by himself and his assistants, to have charge of the depot and manage its concerns, it is incident to his authority to exclude, or direct the exclusion of persons who persist in violating the reasonable regulations prescribed, and thereby interrupt the officers and servants of the company in the discharge of their respective duties, or among passengers.

If it be insisted, that by opening the doors of their depots, the company give an implied license to any and all persons to enter, it may be answered, that by thus opening their doors, they do *primâ facie*, give an implied license to all persons to enter, and no person is a trespasser by merely entering therein. But all such licenses are in their nature revocable; and if actually revoked, and due notice given to an individual or class of. individuals, and they still persist in entering, it is without a license, and the owner has a right to exclude them by force, if necessary, using no more force than is necessary for that purpose. Weaver v. Bush, 8 T. R. 78. Without such a power, the business could not be carried on; because the crowd of persons entering, without intending to take passage, might be so great as to exclude passengers.

In regard to the fact that Hall had a ticket at the time, and intended bonâ fide to go in the cars to Richmond, it appears to us that a fact within his own private knowledge, not communicated to the superintendent, when it was in his power to communicate it, cannot place the superintendent in the wrong, in a case where he would be otherwise justified. If Hall had repeatedly violated a reasonable regulation, in going upon the platform when expressly prohibited, and if the superintendent had reasonable ground to believe that he was repeating such violation, and he gave no notice that he then came there for another purpose, when it was in his power to do so, the superintendent and his assistants, acting on reasonable grounds of belief, must stand on the same ground of justification in this respect, as if Hall had no such purpose.

We are therefore of opinion, that, upon the evidence detailed in the judge's report, the jury should be instructed in a manner somewhat as follows: That if Power had been placed in charge of the depot by the corporation, as superintendent, he had all the authority of the corporation, both as owners and occupiers of real estate, and also as carriers of passengers, incident to the duty of control and management: That this power and authority of the corporation extended to the reasonable regulation of the conduct of all persons using the railroad, or having occasion to resort to the depots, for any purpose: That this power was properly to be executed by a superintendent, adapting his rules and regulations to the circumstances of the particular depot under his charge; and that it was not necessary that such regulations should be prescribed by by-laws of the corporation: That the opening of depots and platforms for the sale of tickets, for the assembling of persons going to take passage, or landing from the cars, amounts in law to a license to all persons, primâ facie, to enter the depot, and that such entry is not a trespass; but that it is a license conditional, subject to reasonable and useful regulations; and, on non-compliance with such regulations, the license is revocable, and may be revoked either as to an individual, or as to a class of individuals, by actual or constructive notice to that effect: That if the platform, as part of the depot, is appropriated to and connected with the entrance of passengers into the cars, and the exit of passengers from the cars, and for the accommodation of their baggage, and if the soliciting of passengers to take lodgings in particular public houses, by the keepers of them or their servants, is a purpose not directly connected with the carriage of passengers by the railroad, on their entrance into or exit from cars; that, if, when urged with earnestness and importunity, it is an annoyance of passengers, and interruption to their proper business of taking or leaving their seats in the cars, and procuring or directing the disposition of their baggage; or if the presence of such persons, for such a purpose, is a hindrance and interruption to the officers and servants of the corporation, in the performance of their respective and proper duties to the corporation, as passenger carriers; then the prohibition of such persons from entering upon the platform is a reasonable and proper regulation, and a person who, after actual or constructive notice of such regulation, violates or attempts to violate it, thereby loses his license to enter the depot; that such license as to him may be revoked; and if, upon notice to quit the depot, he refuses so to do, he may be removed therefrom by the superintendent and the persons employed by him; and if they use no more force than is necessary for that purpose, such use of force is not an assault and battery, but is justifiable: That as to the circumstances of the present case, if the superintendent had issued a circular, giving notice to all innkeepers and landlords, that he had prohibited them from entering the depot to solicit persons to go to their respective houses as guests, and if this notice came to Hall, and he afterwards, and after special notice to him personally, had attempted to violate this prohibition, and solicit passengers; and if, upon the particular occasion, he gave no notice of coming for any other purpose; and if the defendant Power met him on his way to the platform, told him he must not go there, laid his hands on him, and ordered him to leave the depot, without any inquiry as to the purposes of Hall, and Hall made no reply, but pressed forward and attempted to reach the platform, in spite of the efforts of Power; this was strong *primâ facie* evidence that he was going there with intent to solicit passengers, in violation of the notice and revocation of license; and that if he gave no notice of his intention to enter the car as a passenger, and of his right to do so; and if Power believed that his intention was to violate a subsisting reasonable regulation; then he and his assistants were justified in forcibly removing him from the depot: That if Hall gave no notice of his having a ticket, of his intention and purpose to enter the cars as a passenger, and of his right to do so, and that Power had no notice of it, then Hall could not justify his conduct, and make Power a wrongdoer, by proving the possession of such a ticket, or of his intent to go in the cars to Richmond, as a passenger; and that he was to be considered as standing on the same footing as if he had not possessed such ticket.

New trial granted.[1]

---

[1] The right of a railway company to make regulations to govern the conduct of

GIDEON STILES AND ANOTHER *v.* THE WESTERN RAILROAD COR-
PORATION.[1]

Hampshire Co., September Term, 1844.

*Dismissal of Contractor — Liability for Supplies previously fur-
nished — Declaration of Agent.*

The assistant engineer upon a railroad, having charge of the construction of a section of the
road, becoming dissatisfied with the contractor, dismissed him and assumed the work himself, agreeing with the workmen to see them paid. *Held,* that his subsequent declarations
could not be admitted to charge the company for supplies furnished to the contractors.

The declarations of an agent respecting a transaction, which are not made till after it is past,
are not admissible in evidence against his principal.

ASSUMPSIT to recover pay for a quantity of powder.
It appeared, from the report of the judge before whom the trial was

---

passengers and those who resort to the
stations of the company is recognized in
Hall *v.* Power, 12 Metcalf, 482 ; s. c. *post ;*
Cheney *v.* The Boston and Maine R. Co.
11 Metcalf, 121 ; s. c. *post;* Chillon *v.* The
London and Croydon R. Co. 5 Eng. Rail.
Ca. 4 ; The Eastern Counties Railway Co.
v. Broom, 2 Eng. Law and Eq. Rep. 406 ;
Roe *v.* The Birkenhead and Lancashire
R. Co. 7 Eng. Law and Eq. Rep. 546.

In Hall *v.* Power, 12 Metcalf, 482, s. c.
post, the court refused to sanction the proposition that the superintendent of a station had a right to order a person to leave
the station and not to come there any
more, and to remove him by force if he did
come, if in the judgment merely of the superintendent such person had violated the
regulations of the company. The court
held, that the superintendent might rightfully enforce such regulations by removing persons who actually violated them,
but that the power could not be irrespon-
sibly exercised, and that the superintendent became a trespasser if he removed a
person who had in fact committed no

breach of the regulations. But where the
superintendent exceeds his power, in such
cases, it seems that he alone is liable, and
that the company will not be held responsible unless it authorizes or commands the
acts complained of, or subsequently ratifies them. The Eastern Counties Railway
Co. *v.* Broom, 2 Eng. Law & Eq. Rep.
406 ; Roe *v.* The Birkenhead, &c. R. Co.
7 Eng. Law & Eq. Rep. 546. In the first
of these cases it was decided that the fact
that the solicitor of the company attended
at the examination, before the magistrate,
of an officer of the company charged with
an assault upon a passenger, was no evidence of a ratification by the company,
it not appearing that the facts were known
to the company.

And in the second case it was held that
no such ratification was to be inferred
from the fact that the secretary of the company, upon being applied to for compensation for a similar trespass, said that he
would make the necessary inquiry, and
afterwards said that it was a bad business.

[1] 8 Metcalf's Reports, 44.

had in the Court of Common Pleas, "that the construction of the
74th section of the Western Railroad was contracted for by Josiah
Baylies, who underlet the same to Stocking & Lord; and that Lord
was associated with Almon Lard, under the style of A. B. Lord &
Co., they having purchased of Stocking his interest in the contract;
that about the 1st of March, 1840, the workmen on said section
became dissatisfied and refused to work, because Lord & Co. did not
pay them; that Julius Adams, the assistant engineer, who had
charge of the section, agreed with the men to.continue their work,
and that the corporation (the defendants) would see them paid; and
that he dismissed Lard, and refused to permit him to remain about
the work; that the powder sued for was delivered and used on section 74, under a contract with Stocking & Lord, up to said 1st of
March; but that this contract was not for any particular quantity;
and that when said Adams became responsible to the workmen, he
assumed, in behalf of the defendants, to carry on the work and pay
all the expenses.

"The plaintiffs contended that the defendants were liable to them
for the powder furnished and used, after March 1st, 1840, on an
implied contract, although there was no evidence of any communication on the subject between the plaintiffs and any agents of the
defendants.

"To prove that the defendants, by the said Adams, had assumed
the work, and undertaken to pay all the expenses, the plaintiffs
offered Daniel Collins, Jr., as a witness; and he testified that he was
a merchant, and that, in the spring of 1840, he had difficulty in
getting his pay for goods sold to the workmen on said section; that
he went to said Adams, to ascertain the probability of getting pay,
and that Adams said to him that the men would now get their pay,
and that the corporation had assumed the work.

"The plaintiffs also introduced Nored Elder, as a witness; and he
testified that he had claims against A. B. Lord & Co., for provisions
delivered to their workmen; that he called on said Adams, about the
1st of April, 1840, to see about getting his pay; that Adams admitted
that the corporation had assumed the work, but remarked that they
did not feel obligated to pay any of the debts of Lord & Co., which
were contracted before the 1st of March, but that for any thing which
the hands wished to live upon, after that time, the corporation were
to pay."

The jury found a verdict for the plaintiffs, and the defendants
alleged exceptions to the admission of the foregoing testimony.

R. A. Chapman and *H. Morris*, for the defendants, cited Haven *v.*

Brown, 7 Greenl. 424; Thallhimer v. Brinckerhoff, 4 Wend. 394; Fairlie v. Hastings, 10 Ves. 126; 2 Stark. Ev. 43; Greenl. on Ev. § 113; Story on Agency, § 135.

W. G. Bates, for the plaintiffs, cited Angell & Ames on Corp. (2d ed.) 249; American Fur Co. v. U. States, 2 Pet. 358; Cobb v. Lunt, 4 Greenl. 503; Pool v. Bridges, 4 Pick. 378; Woods v. Clark and Haynes v. Rutter, 24 Pick. 35, 342; Story on Agency, 135–137, and notes.

WILDE, J. At the trial in the Court of Common Pleas, the declarations of the defendants' agent were admitted, to prove that they had employed the plaintiffs to supply the powder for which they demand compensation in this action; and it is very clear that such declarations are not admissible in evidence. The declarations of an agent are admissible only when made in regard to a transaction then depending. Such declarations are considered as part of the res gestæ, and so binding on the principal. When an agent is acting within the scope of his authority, his declarations accompanying his acts are admissible, as they may qualify his acts; but his declarations as to other matters and transactions are merely hearsay testimony. Such was the evidence admitted in the present case. It ought not to have been admitted, and the exceptions must therefore be sustained. Greenl. on Ev. § 113; Fairlie v. Hastings, 10 Ves. 126; Haven v. Brown, 7 Greenl. 424.

New trial granted.

ABEL BABCOCK v. THE WESTERN RAILROAD CORPORATION.[1]

Hampshire Co., September Term, 1845.

License to Construct Road over Land — Implied Rights thereunder — Right to Construct Culverts, Deepen Streams, &c.

A granted to the Western Railroad Corporation full and free license and authority to locate, construct, repair, and forever maintain and use a railroad, upon, through, and over his land, and to take his land therefor, to the extent authorized by their charter: The land was so situated that the embankment of the railroad would cause water to accumulate on

---

the upper side thereof, and it became necessary to provide for the passage of water to the lower side: The corporation therefore made culverts, in suitable places, and in a convenient manner; but the situation of the land was such that it was necessary to connect ditches with the culverts, and extend the ditches, beyond the line of the location of the railroad, into the land of A, in order to prevent the water from setting back so as materially to injure the railroad or damage the land of A. *Held*, that the corporation were authorized by said license so to make said culverts and ditches, under the rule of law, that a grant of a thing includes the means necessary to attain it. *Held also*, that the corporation were authorized, by said license, to deepen and widen in the land of A, beyond the line of the location of the railroad, the bed of a mountain stream, over which the railroad was laid out and constructed, to facilitate the discharge of the waters of the stream; such deepening and widening being necessary to secure the railroad from damage, or to prevent the land of A from being broken and washed away. *It seems*, also, that the corporation had authority to do the aforesaid acts, under their charter and the Rev. Sts. c, 39.

TRESPASS for breaking and entering the plaintiff's closes in Chester, lying on each side of the defendants' railroad, and there cutting ditches, &c.; and piling earth and stones on the plaintiff's soil adjacent · to the track of said road. Trial before the chief justice, who made the following report thereof:

After the plaintiff's evidence was introduced, the defendants gave evidence tending to show that the land was so situated that the embankment for the railroad would cause the water to increase on one side, and that culverts were laid under the road, in three places, to carry it off. The jury were instructed, that if the land was so situated that some expedient was necessary to provide for the passage of the water from the upper to the lower side, and these culverts were laid in suitable places, and in a convenient manner, the defendants had authority so to make them; and further, that if it was necessary to connect drains or ditches with these culverts, and if, by terminating them at the limits of the location of the railroad, the water would naturally dam up, or set back, so as materially to injure the railroad, or damage the land of the adjacent owner; and if it was necessary to extend such ditches beyond those limits, to avoid those consequences, the defendants were authorized so to extend them into the land of the adjacent proprietor.

There was evidence tending to show that the railroad crossed a mountain torrent, near its outlet into a river; that the water frequently rushed down this stream with great violence, and in great quantity; that the defendants had removed rocks, and deepened and widened the bed of the torrent, below the track of the railroad, to facilitate the discharge of the stream into the river. There was some conflict of evidence, on the question whether the bed of the torrent, thus deepened and widened, extended beyond the limits of the location of the railroad, into the plaintiff's land; but the evidence tended to show that it did. Whereupon the jury were instructed, that if it was necessary to widen and deepen the bed of this mountain stream, in order to facilitate the discharge of its waters into the river, and if this was necessary, to secure the railroad from damage or to prevent the land of the adjacent proprietor from being broken and washed away, then the defendants had authority so to deepen and widen the bed of the stream, beyond the limits of the location of the railroad. The jury were instructed that the defendants had this authority, either under their act of incorporation, (St. 1833, c. 116,) or under an agreement entered into between them and the plaintiff, which was given in evidence by the defendants, dated October 20th, 1836, and by which the plaintiff, for the consideration therein mentioned, under his hand and seal, did " grant, assign, transfer, and convey to said railroad corporation, and for the use thereof, and their successors and assigns, full and free license and authority to locate, construct, repair, and forever maintain and use the said railroad, upon, through, and over my said lands, in such places and courses as the said corporation may judge necessary and convenient, and to take therefor my lands, to the extent authorized by their charter," &c. (See ante, 366.)

The jury were further instructed, that the defendants had no right to enter upon the plaintiff's lands adjacent to the railroad, for the purpose of obtaining materials, or piling up and depositing waste earth or stones, without a license from the plaintiff.

To the foregoing instructions, except the last, the plaintiff excepted; and a verdict being returned for the defendants, the plaintiff moved that it should be set aside, and a new trial be granted. This motion was reserved for the consideration of the whole court.

G. W. Bates and Davis, for the plaintiff.

R. A. Chapman, for the defendants.

SHAW, C. J. Upon a review of the directions given to the jury, the court are of opinion that they were correct. They are founded on the obvious distinction between that which is necessarily incident to the prosecution of the work, and that which would only be convenient. Com. Dig. Grant, E. 11. Water can be drained off only in a particular direction, and by one method; that is, by making a drain from the place where it accumulates to a lower level. It is a general rule, we think, that a grant of power to accomplish any particular enterprise, and especially one of a public nature, carries with it, so far as the grantor's own power extends, an authority to do all that is necessary to accomplish the principal object. The court are

34 *

therefore strongly inclined to the opinion, that under the act of incorporation, passed March 15th, 1833, (St. 1833, c. 116,) and the general laws respecting the establishing of railroads, the corporation had the authority in question, independently of the plaintiff's deed. Rev. Sts. c. 39, §§ 45, 54, 56. Upon this principle, it has been decided that all persons — not merely those whose land is taken for laying the road, and for supplying materials, under §§ 54, 55, but by § 56, all persons who may sustain damage occasioned by laying out, making or maintaining their road — shall have a remedy against the corporation. Dodge v. County Commissioners, 3 Met. 380; s. c. *ante*, 336; Ashby v. Eastern Railroad, 5 Met. 371; s. c. *ante*, 356. The only ground on which such damages could be allowed is, that they are authorized, because they are the natural and necessary consequence of the acts authorized to be done. But this must be confined to that which is strictly necessary to accomplish the enterprise. When it is necessary to *take lands* of a greater width than five rods, for embankments, deep cuts, or the supply of materials, a license from the county commissioners is necessary. But such a taking ordinarily unfits the land for the uses of the owner, and is in its nature an appropriation; but we cannot consider the laying a drain through or under land, to draw off water, is such taking or appropriation, or requires such license.

But whatever might have been the rights of the corporation, by their act of incorporation and the laws limiting and defining the powers and duties of railroad companies, the court are of opinion, that the power exercised by the defendants was granted by the plaintiff's own deed. It is a well-known and reasonable rule, in construing a grant, that when any thing is granted, all the means to attain it, and all the fruits and effects of it, are granted also. *Cuicunque aliquid conceditur, conceditur etiam et id sine quo res ipsa non esse potuit.* By the grant of a ground is granted a way to it. Shep. Touch. 89. The plaintiff, by his deed executed before the acts done, and before the location of the road, granted to the corporation, their successors and assigns, full and free license and authority to locate, construct, repair, and forever maintain and use the said railroad, upon, through, and over his said lands, &c. If the laying of the drains or ditches in question, through the plaintiff's land, or the deepening of the bed of the mountain torrent, in his land, *extra viam*, beyond the limits of the five rods, was necessary to the construction, or to the maintenance of the railroad, the authority so to do was granted by this deed, and the direction to the jury, to that effect, was right.

Judgment on the verdict for the defendants.

EDMUND THOMAS *v.* THE BOSTON AND PROVIDENCE RAILROAD
CORPORATION.[1]

Norfolk Co., October Term, 1845.

*Duties of a Railroad Company as a Common-Carrier — Liability after
the Transportation of Goods is Ended while Deposited in Warehouse.*

Proprietors of a railroad, who transport goods over their road, and deposit them in their
warehouse without charge, until the owner or consignee has a reasonable time to take
them away, are not liable, as common-carriers, for the loss of the goods from the warehouse,
but are liable, as depositaries, only for want of ordinary care.

IN this action the defendants were charged, as common-carriers,
with the loss of a roll of leather.   At the trial in the Court of Common Pleas, before Wells, C. J., various points were ruled and various
exceptions alleged, which ultimately became immaterial.   The following is a report of all that is necessary to be here inserted :
It was proved or admitted that four rolls of leather, the property of
the plaintiff, were delivered to the defendants at Providence, to be
transported to Boston; that they were so transported, and were
deposited at the defendants' depot at Boston; that a teamster,
employed by the plaintiff, shortly after called at the depot, with a
bill of the freight receipted by the defendants, and inquired for the
leather; that it was pointed out to him by the defendants' agent,
Allen, who had charge of the depot; that the teamster then took
away two of the rolls, and soon after called again and inquired
for the other two; that he was directed where to look for them; and
that he found only one.
The defendants, to show that they were not liable for any loss
occurring while the goods were deposited at their depot, offered to
prove that they had, prior to this time, posted up notices containing
this expression: " merchandise, while in the company's store-houses,
is at the risk of the owners thereof;" and that these notices had been
so long posted up, and so extensively circulated, that the plaintiff
must be presumed to have known their contents ; and that the plaintiff, prior to the time of the loss, had frequently employed the defend-

ants to transport goods. for him. The judge ruled that the evidence was inadmissible.

The jury were instructed " to ascertain from all the evidence what was the contract between the parties, and if they were satisfied that it was the usage and practice of the defendants, not only to transport goods over the road, but also to deposit them in their warehouses, without charge, until the owner should have a reasonable time to remove them, and that they did provide warehouses or depots for the purpose of so storing the goods, this usage and conduct would be sufficient evidence for the jury to find that it was a part of the contract that the defendants should so store and keep the goods delivered to them for transportation; and that, if such was the contract, then their liability as common-carriers would continue while the goods were stored in the depot; but that in the present case, if the goods, after having been so stored, were actually delivered to the plaintiff or his agent, or if an arrangement was entered into between the parties, by themselves or their agents, by which the defendants agreed to part with the custody and control over the property, and the plaintiff agreed to assume the custody and control over it, although there was no actual delivery, or if the plaintiff or his agent so improperly conducted himself, either by language or acts, as to lead the defendants or their agents to believe (they acting with proper care-and discretion) that the plaintiff had undertaken to assume the control of the property, and had discharged the defendants from any further responsibility, and the defendants, in consequence, ceased to take any further charge or oversight of the property, the responsibility of the defendants would be thereby terminated: That the burden of proving these facts was upon the defendants."

A verdict was returned for the plaintiff, and the defendants alleged exceptions to the instructions given to the jury.

F. Hilliard, for the defendants.

The evidence of the posted notice should have been admitted. Whether it was sufficient to sustain the defence was a question for the jury, on all the facts proved. The cases of Dwight *v.* Brewster, 1 Pick. 50, and Phillips *v.* Earle, 8 Pick. 182, imply that a common-carrier's liability may be limited by notice. See also Boyce *v.* Anderson, 2 Pet. 155; Story on Bailm. § 554 *et seq.*; 2 Phil. Ev. 77; 2 Stark. Ev. 337; 2 Stephens, N. P. 970; Chit. Con. (5th Amer. ed.) 489; 2 Stephen's Com. 135; Down *v.* Fromont, 4 Campb. 40; Munn *v.* Baker, 2 Stark. R. 255.

After the leather was deposited in the defendants' depot they were liable, if at all, only as warehousemen, and for the omission of ordinary care. Garside *v.* Proprietors of Trent and Mersey Navigation, 4 T. R. 581; Young *v.* Smith, 3 Dana, 92; Rowe *v.* Pickford, 1 Moore, 526, and 8 Taunt. 83; Foster *v.* Frampton, 6 Barn. & Cres. 107; Allan *v.* Gripper, 2 Cromp. & Jerv. 218, and 2 Tyrw. 217.

D. A. Simmons and *Kingsbury,* for the plaintiff.

As the defendants cannot exempt themselves from responsibility by giving notice that they will not be liable, (Story on Con. § 468,) the evidence of such notice was rightly excluded. Cole *v.* Goodwin, 19 Wend. 251; Gould *v.* Hill, 2 Hill's (N. Y.) Rep. 623.

The defendants are liable as common-carriers, and not merely as warehousemen, until the goods are delivered to the owner, if he call for them within a reasonable time. 1 Bell's Com. 469; Streeter *v.* Horlock, 1 Bing. 34, and 7 Moore, 283; Golden *v.* Manning, 3 Wils. 429, and 2 W. Bl. 916; Forward *v.* Pittard, 1 T. R. 27; Ellis *v.* Turner, 8 T. R. 531; Matter of Webb, 8 Taunt. 443, and 2 Moore, 500; Davis *v.* Garrett, 6 Bing. 716; Hyde *v.* Proprietors of Trent and Mersey Navigation, 5 T. R. 389; Duff *v.* Budd, 3 Brod. & Bing. 177; Bodenham *v.* Bennet, 4 Price, 34; Birkett *v.* Willan, 2 Barn. & Ald. 356; Garnett *v.* Willan, 5 Barn. & Ald. 58; Storr *v.* Crowley, 1 M'Clel. & Y. 129; Stephenson *v.* Hart, 4 Bing. 476; Bourne *v.* Gatliff, 3 Man. & Grang. 690, and 4 Bing. N. R. 332.

The decision was made at October term, 1846.

HUBBARD, J. Sundry rulings were made during the progress of the trial, by the presiding judge, to which the defendant's counsel excepted, but which it is unnecessary now to consider.

The important question presented for the consideration of the court is, whether the defendants are common-carriers of the goods and merchandise intrusted to their care; and if they are, how long this relation continues. The charge on this part of the case was, that the jury, from all the evidence in the case, were to ascertain what was the contract between the parties; and if, from the evidence, they were satisfied that it was the usage and practice of the defendants, not only to transport goods over their road, but also to deposit them in their warehouses, without charge, until the owner of the goods should have reasonable time to remove them, and that they did provide warehouses or depots for the purpose of so storing the goods, then this usage and conduct would be sufficient evidence for the jury to find that it was a part of the contract that the defendants should so store and keep goods delivered to them for transportation; and that, if such was the contract, their liabilities as common-carriers would continue while the goods were so stored in the depot.

This is an important question to our community, from the magnitude and variety of the interests concerned in it.   The introduction
of railroads into the State has been followed by their construction
over the great lines of travel, of passengers and transportation of merchandise; and the proprietors of these novel and important modes of
travel and transportation, which have received so much public favor,
have become the carriers of great amounts of merchandise.   They
advertise for freight; they make known the terms of carriage; they
provide suitable vehicles, and select convenient places for receiving
and delivering goods ; and, as a legal consequence of such acts, they
have become common-carriers of merchandise, and are subject to the
provisions of the common law which are applicable to carriers.   By
the common law, carriers are, to a certain extent, the insurers of the
goods they carry, and are bound to deliver them agreeably to their
engagements, subject only to the exceptions which may prevent a
delivery, arising either from the act of God or from public enemies.
From the act of God : As where the loss is caused by lightning or
tempests; or on the water, where such exceptions are distinguished
as perils of the sea.   For a loss arising from such a cause they are
not held responsible ; because no vigilance can prevent nor foresight
guard against such liabilities, they being beyond human control; and
a guaranty against a loss from such a cause can only be provided for
by a special contract of indemnity, well known as the contract of
insurance.   And so of public enemies : The government itself is
called upon to protect its subjects from loss from such a hazard; as
private citizens have not the power to furnish the security and protection required.   But in all other cases the common-carrier is held
responsible, on the ground that he may guard against the accidents
and casualties to which the goods, in their transit, are exposed.   And
this law is enforced on principles of public policy, to prevent fraud
and collusion with thieves and robbers; the owner of the goods, not
being generally in a situation to oversee and protect his property,
having placed it in the possession and under the control of the carrier.
And the pay of carriers is graduated upon such liability.

But there is a material distinction between common-carriers and
other bailees of goods, as to the extent of their liability in the event
of loss of the goods, or damage happening to them.   The former are
liable, as before remarked, in all cases, with certain precise exceptions; while the latter are only liable for want of proper care and
reasonable diligence, according to the character of the bailment.
And the question in the present case is, whether the defendants are
liable as common-carriers, after the goods are safely stored in their
merchandise or warehouse depot.

The transportation of goods and the storage of goods are contracts of a different character; and though one person or company may render both services, yet the two contracts are not to be confounded or blended; because the legal liabilities attending the two are different. The proprietors of a railroad transport merchandise over their road, receiving it at one depot or place of deposit and delivering it at another, agreeably to the direction of the owner or consignor. But from the very nature and peculiar construction of the road, the proprietors cannot deliver merchandise at the warehouse of the owner, when situated off the line of the road as a common wagoner can do. To make such a delivery, a distinct species of transportation would be required, and would be the subject of a distinct contract. They can deliver it only at the terminus of the road, or at the given depot where goods can be safely unladed and put into a place of safety. After such delivery at a depot, the carriage is completed. But, owing to the great amount of goods transported and belonging to so many different persons, and in consequence of the different hours of arrival, by night as well as by day, it becomes equally convenient and necessary, both for the proprietors of the road and the owners of the goods, that they should be unladed and deposited in a safe place, protected from the weather and from exposure to thieves and pilferers. And where such suitable warehouses are provided, and the goods which are not called for on their arrival at the places of destination, are unladed and separated from the goods of other persons, and stored safely in such warehouses or depots, the duty of the proprietors as common-carriers is, in our judgment, terminated. They have done all they agreed to do; they have received the goods, have transported them safely to the place of delivery, and, the consignee not being present to receive them, have unladed them, and have put them in a safe and proper place for the consignee to take them away; and he can take them at any reasonable time. The liability of common-carriers being ended, the proprietors are, by force of law, depositaries of the goods, and are bound to reasonable diligence in the custody of them, and consequently are only liable to owners in case of a want of ordinary care.

In the case at bar, the goods were transported over the defendants' road, and were safely deposited in their merchandise depot, ready for delivery to the plaintiff, of which he had notice, and were in fact in part taken away by him; the residue, a portion of which was afterwards lost, being left there for his convenience. No agreement was made for the storage of the goods, and no further compensation paid therefor; the sum paid being the freight for carriage, which was payable if the goods had been delivered to the plaintiff immediately on the arrival of the cars, without any storage. Upon these facts, we are of opinion, for the reasons before stated, that the duty of the defendants, as common-carriers, had ceased on their safe deposit of the plaintiff's goods in the merchandise depot; and that they were then responsible only as depositaries without further charge, and consequently, unless guilty of negligence in the want of ordinary care in the custody of the goods, they are not liable to the plaintiff for the alleged loss of a part of the goods.

This view, which we have taken of the relation of the defendants to the plaintiff, as common-carriers in the transportation of his goods, and as the depositaries of them when stored in their warehouse, and the distinct liabilities arising out of these different relations, is fully justified by the decision of the Court of King's Bench, in the case of Garside v. Proprietors of Trent and Mersey Navigation, 4 T. R. 581. In that case, the defendants were common-carriers between Stourport and Manchester. The plaintiff's goods were taken at Stourport to be carried to Manchester, and from Manchester, by another carrier, to Stockport; and by agreement, they were to be kept in the defendants' warehouse, without charge, and to be kept till called for by the carrier for Stockport. A parcel of the plaintiff's goods, whilst thus stored, after being transported by the defendants from Stourport to Manchester for the plaintiff, were accidentally burnt with the warehouse, and the plaintiff brought his action to recover the value of them of the defendants, charging them as common-carriers. But the court were clearly of opinion that the duties of the defendants, as common-carriers, were ended on the storing of the goods, and that they then stood in the situation only of warehousemen, and were therefore not liable for the loss of the goods. Buller, J., remarked, that "the keeping of the goods in the warehouse is not for the convenience of the carrier, but of the owner of the goods; for when the voyage to Manchester is performed, it is the interest of the carrier to get rid of them directly: and it was only because there was no person ready at Manchester to receive these goods, that the defendants were obliged to keep them." And so in the case at bar, the plaintiff, who lived in a neighboring town, was not ready to receive all his goods, and they were left for his convenience, and not for any benefit to the defendants. See also Hyde v. Proprietors of Trent and Mersey Navigation, 5 T. R. 389; Matter of Webb, 8 Taunt. 443; Gibson v. Culver, 17 Wend. 305; 2 Kent. Com. (3d ed.) 600; Story on Bailm. §§ 446 – 450.

A great many cases have arisen, in which the question has been discussed whether the parties, who were attempted to be charged, were, under the particular circumstances proved, chargeable as common-carriers or not, and how far that liability might be limited or restrained by special contract or by public notice. But these cases do not, in our judgment, overrule or materially affect the decision in Garside v. Proprietors of Trent and Mersey Navigation, nor shake the principles upon which it rests. Neither do we intend to discuss the rights of passengers on railroads, in regard to their persons and luggage, nor the peculiar liabilities of the proprietors in regard to both. . We confine ourselves strictly to the case of merchandise deposited after it has been transported to its place of destination. The doctrine of the common law, as applied to common-carriers, is founded in practical wisdom and has long been consistently enforced ; and we are neither disposed to relax its requisitions nor give countenance to ingenious devices by which its provisions may be evaded. But, at the same time, we are equally indisposed to stretch it beyond its proper limits, or to apply it to cases which fall neither within its letter nor its spirit.

In the course of the trial, the defendants offered to prove that, prior to the transportation of the plaintiff's leather, they had posted up notices containing this provision, viz., " merchandise, while in the company's store-houses, is at the risk of the owners thereof;" and that from the length of time they had been posted, and the prior dealings of the plaintiff with them, he must be presumed to have had knowledge of the fact; but the evidence was not admitted.   We are not called upon, in this case, to decide as to the legal character of such notices ; a subject which has been fully considered in this country, as well as in England.   See Hollister v. Nowlen, 19 Wend. 234, and Cole v. Goodwin, 19 Wend. 251, and the long list of English authorities there cited, on page 269.

In the view of the law bearing upon this case, viz., that the defendants are not liable as common-carriers, the notice, we think, becomes unimportant, as it clearly would not screen the defendants from loss occasioned by their negligence or want of ordinary care ; and beyond that they are not chargeable.   Other questions which arose upon the trial it is not necessary to notice.

For the reasons stated, we think the learned judge erred in his instructions to the jury, that the liability of common-carriers continued to attach to the defendants while the goods were stored in their depot.   The verdict must therefore be set aside.   Upon the evidence, as reported, there appears little ground to charge the defendants with want of ordinary care in the custody of these goods; but that is a question to be settled on the further trial of the case.

New trial to be had in this court.[1]

---

[1] Two cases upon the liability of railway companies have been recently decided by the Supreme Court of Massachusetts, and will be reported in 1 Gray's

TIMOTHY HALL v. WILLIAM A. POWER AND OTHERS.[1]

Berkshire Co., September Term, 1847.

Authority of Superintendent of Depot — Right to Remove Persons by Force — Evidence in Justification.

The superintendent of a railroad depot has not a right to order a person to leave the depot, and not come there any more, and to remove him therefrom by force, if he does come, merely because such person, in the judgment of the superintendent, and without proof of the fact, had violated the regulations established by the railroad corporation, or had conducted himself offensively towards the superintendent.

In the trial of an action for an assault and battery, brought against the superintendent of a railroad depot, for expelling the plaintiff from the depot, for a supposed violation of one of the regulations established by the railroad corporation, the defendant cannot give in evidence former violations, by the plaintiff, of other regulations established by the corporation.

TRESPASS for an assault and battery. At the trial in the Court of Common Pleas, before Merrick, J., the plaintiff introduced evidence tending to prove that on the 22d of March, 1844, he sent his servant to the depot of the Western Railroad, at Pittsfield, to purchase a ticket for his passage in the cars from that place to Richmond, and that the servant procured the ticket by employing a third person to purchase it : That on the next day, the plaintiff, having the ticket in

Reports. In one case, Norway Plains Co. v. Boston and Maine Railroad, the company had transported the goods of the plaintiffs to Boston, where they arrived in the afternoon, and were unladen and deposited in the station, ready for delivery, but too late to be taken away and carried to their destination in the city on that day. The goods had been called for before they were unladen from the cars, by a truckman, who waited for them until he was satisfied that there would not be time to effect their removal that day. Before the next morning the goods were destroyed by fire. The court held, that after the goods reached their place of destination, and were ready for delivery to the owners, the company is no longer liable as a common-carrier, but merely as a bailee for hire, and that the company was not, therefore, liable, in this case, for the loss of the goods.

In the other case, Stevens v. Boston and Maine Railroad, the goods had arrived a day or two earlier at the same station, and were destroyed by the same fire. A teamster, employed by the owners, called for the goods the day previous to their destruction, and was told by an agent of the company that the goods had been sent away, although they were at that time laying in the building. For this mistake of their agent the company was held responsible.

[1] 12 Metcalf's Reports, 482.

his pocket, went to the depot, entered the room at the door where passengers usually enter to take the cars, and was proceeding through the room towards the stairs, which led to the platform where passengers entered the cars, when he was stopped by the defendant Power, but struggled to get by him, and was making his way to the stairs, when Power rang a bell: The plaintiff offered no evidence that any thing was said by either Power or Hall to the other: That the other defendants immediately appeared, and that Power ordered them to put the plaintiff out of the depot, which they did; the plaintiff at the same time resisting their efforts; and that this took place while the cars from the east were at the depot, and about to start for Richmond.

It was admitted that Power was superintendent at the depot, and that the other defendants were servants employed by the corporation, under him.

The plaintiff also gave evidence, that after he was expelled from the depot, and after the cars had left, he took his ticket from his pocket, and held it up, and requested those present to take notice that he had a ticket for Richmond; to which Power replied, that this was the first time he had shown his ticket.

The defendants then offered evidence, that for several months previously to this affair, a number of persons were in the habit of coming to the depot, at the time of the arrival and departure of the cars, for the purpose of soliciting customers for the several hotels in the neighborhood of the depot; and for the several carriages and lines of stages, which were accustomed to carry passengers to and from the depot: That the plaintiff kept a hotel near the depot, and that he and his servants were in the habit of coming, with others: That these persons were in the habit of crowding on the platform, to the great inconvenience and annoyance of passengers, and that frequent and great complaints were made by the passengers to the conductor of the train, and to Power, on this subject: That Power had frequently requested them to desist from the practice, but that his requests were disregarded, and the annoyance constantly grew worse: That about the 13th of March, 1844, he issued a circular, stating the facts, and requesting innkeepers and others to discontinue the practice, and giving them notice that they would thereafter be excluded from the platform; which circular was sent to the plaintiff, and was received and read by him: That all other persons, except the plaintiff, desisted from going to the platform, and remained outside of the depot: That the plaintiff denied the right of Power to restrain him from going to the platform as often as he pleased, and expressed a determination to disregard his request: That on several occasions he went to the platform, and that on Friday, and on Saturday morning, previously to the alleged assault, and while the trains were in, he forced his way down the stairs, against the efforts and remonstrances of Power; and that Power repeatedly ordered him not to come to the depot any more, on account of his conduct. Evidence was also offered, that at the time of the alleged assault, Power, before calling the other defendants to expel the plaintiff, and while he was going forward, told him not to go down stairs; to which the plaintiff made no reply, but pressed forward.

The defendants offered evidence to prove that the plaintiff had violated other regulations of the depot, by carrying baggage through the room appropriated to ladies, and in other particulars. This evidence was objected to by the plaintiff: and the defendants thereupon admitting, that at the time when Power expelled the plaintiff, he did not claim a right to expel him on account of the violation of any regulation besides that contained in the circular, and that they had no evidence to offer, in addition to that hereinbefore recited, tending to show that such expulsion was on account of the violation of any other regulation than that contained in said circular: the evidence was rejected by the court.

The cause was submitted to the jury, under instructions from the court as to the right of Power to remove the plaintiff from the depot by force, which were not objected to by defendants, except as follows, to wit: The defendants requested the court to instruct the jury, that Power had a right to order Hall to leave the depot, and not to come there any more, and to remove him therefrom by force, if he did come, if, in the judgment merely of said Power, the plaintiff had violated the regulations contained in said circular, or had conducted offensively towards said Power, although the fact that the plaintiff had violated such regulations, or had so conducted himself towards said Power, was not proved. But the court declined to give such instructions to the jury.

A verdict was returned for the plaintiff, and the defendants alleged exceptions.

R. A. Chapman, W. G. Bates, and *Colt,* for the defendant.

Bishop, for the plaintiff.

DEWEY, J. The great and leading principles, upon which a case like the present is to be tried before the jury, were, after much consideration, fully settled and announced in the case of Commonwealth *v.* Power, 7 Met. 596. The distinction between the right of the pub-

Hall *v.* Power.

lie generally to enter upon a railroad, or its depot, or any of its appendages, and that to enter upon a public highway, was there fully stated. The necessity and propriety of rules and restrictions as to the entering upon the grounds appropriated to a railroad, and that authority might be properly exercised by the superintendent and agents of the company, in enforcing such rules and regulations, having for their object the public convenience, and the quiet and safety of travellers, were fully recognized in the case above cited. Those doctrines we still adhere to. They were, as we suppose, fully stated to the jury, in the present case, by the presiding judge, as the rules of law governing this case, and to which the jury were to apply the evidence.

No exceptions were taken to the general course of the instructions as to the rules of law applicable to the case, or that those given did not comport with the opinion of this court in the case above alluded to. Two grounds of objection are taken; one arising upon the refusal of the presiding judge to give certain instructions asked for by the defendants' counsel; the other grounded upon the rejection of evidence offered by the defendants.

1. As to the instruction asked, which was to this effect, that the court instruct the jury " that Power had a right to order Hall to leave the depot, and not to come there any more, and to remove him therefrom by force, if he did come; if, in the judgment merely of said Power, the plaintiff had violated the regulations contained in the said circular, or had conducted offensively towards said Power, although the fact that the plaintiff had violated such regulations, or had so conducted himself towards said Power, was not proved."

This instruction, if adopted, would justify the defendant in removing a person who had in all respects conformed to the rules and regulations of the railroad company, and who had in fact demeaned himself with perfect propriety, if, in the judgment merely of the superintendent, he had violated any regulations of the company. This, we think, would be carrying the principle too far; quite beyond what the necessity of the case requires. With full power to make all necessary and suitable rules and regulations governing the conduct of all those who may enter, or attempt to enter, upon the railroad, at the depot for passengers, and with full power effectually to apply such rules and regulations, and remove every person who actually violates them, the company will possess all the authority that the exigency of the case will require. In the opinion of the court, this request for instructions was properly refused.

2. The remaining question is upon the exclusion of the evidence, offered by the defendants, to prove that the plaintiff had, on other

35 *

occasions, violated other regulations, and particularly that he had passed with baggage through the room appropriated to ladies. The evidence offered would seem to be irrelevant. Looking at the case presented on the bill of exceptions, the seizure of the plaintiff was to prevent his going upon the platform, and for violating that regulation, and not to prevent him from passing through the ladies' room with baggage, or because he was about to do so. The proposed evidence as to the plaintiff's carrying baggage, on former occasions, through the ladies' room, we think, was not material in its bearing upon the question submitted to the jury. This exception is therefore overruled.

Judgment on the verdict for the plaintiff.

LUKE HART AND OTHERS *v.* THE WESTERN RAILROAD CORPORATION.[1]

Hampshire Co., September Term, 1847.

Liability of Company for Fires — Proximate cause of Loss — Recovery by Insurance Company for Loss incurred.

A shop, adjoining a railroad track, was destroyed by fire communicated by a locomotive engine of a railroad corporation; and while the shop was burning, the wind wafted sparks from it, across a street, sixty feet, upon a house, and set it on fire, whereby it was injured. *Held,* that the owner of the house was entitled to recover of the railroad corporation the damages caused by the fire, under St. 1840, c. 85, § 1, which provides that when any injury is done to a building of any person " by fire communicated " by a locomotive engine of a railroad corporation, the said corporation shall be responsible, in damages, to the person so injured.

A's house, which was insured, was injured by a fire communicated by a locomotive engine of a railroad corporation, and the underwriters paid to A the amount of his loss, for which the railroad corporation was also by law responsible to him. *Held,* that such payment did not bar A's right to recover also of the railroad corporation, and that A, by receiving payment of the underwriters, became trustees for them, and, by necessary implication, made an equitable assignment to them of his right to recover of the railroad corporation; and that the underwriters on indemnifying A, might bring an action, in his name, for their own benefit, against the railroad corporation, and that A could not legally release such action.

THIS was an action of trespass upon the case, founded on St. 1840, c. 85, to recover the amount of a loss which the plaintiffs sustained by a fire alleged to have been communicated to their dwelling-

[1] 13 Metcalf's Reports, 99.

house by a locomotive engine of the defendants. The parties submitted the case to tĥe court, on the following agreed facts:

"On the 9th of July, 1845, a carpenter's shop, owned by William W. Boyington, adjoining the railroad track of the defendants, near their passenger depot in Springfield, was destroyed by fire communicated by the locomotive engine of the defendants. There was a high wind, which wafted sparks from this shop, while it was burning, over Lyman street, sixty feet, upon the dwelling-house of the plaintiffs, and set it on fire, whereby it was partially consumed.

"The plaintiffs were insured by the Springfield Mutual Fire Insurance Company, who requested the plaintiffs to commence a suit against the defendants, to compel payment by them of the plaintiffs' loss, and offered to indemnify the plaintiffs from costs, and to save them harmless, in reference to said suit. The plaintiffs refused to commence a suit, as requested, but demanded the amount of their loss of the said insurance company, who paid the same, first notifying to the defendants that they did not intend thereby to relinquish any claim which they might have against the defendants for the amount, in their own or in the plaintiffs' names. The insurance company, in the name of the plaintiffs, then brought this action to recover the amount paid by said company to the plaintiffs. After the action was commenced, and before the entry of the writ, the plaintiffs executed an instrument declaring that they had received payment of their loss, of the insurance company; that they had no claim against the defendants; that they (the plaintiffs) had not authorized the commencement of this action against the defendants, and did not wish to have it prosecuted; and fully releasing any claim which they might have against the defendants on account of said loss.

"At the May term of this court, in 1847, the case was opened to the jury, and the defendants presented the aforesaid release from the plaintiffs, and contended that the insurance company, in consequence of this release, could not maintain this action. The court ruled, that receiving payment of the loss by the plaintiffs, of the insurance company, constituted an equitable assignment, by the plaintiffs, to the company, of any claim they might have had. Whereupon the parties agreed to the facts before recited in relation to the origin of the fire.

"In case the court are of opinion, that receiving payment, by the plaintiffs, of the insurance company, amounted to an equitable assignment by them of any claim they might have had against the defendants; that the release referred to was in fraud of the insurance company; and that the defendants are liable for the loss, on the facts stated, the plaintiffs are to have judgment for the sum of

$623.65 damages, and interest on this sum, from the 14th of November, 1845. Otherwise the plaintiffs' are tŏ become nonsuit."

: *J. Willard* and *R. A. Chapman*, for the plaintiffs.

By St. 1840, c. 85, § 1, " when any injury is done to a building, or other property, of any person or corporation, by fire communicated by a locomotive engine of any railroad corporation, the said railroad corporation shall be held responsible, in damages, to the person or corporation so injured." And the question now is, whether underwriters, who have paid a loss caused by a fire so communicated, can come in, by subrogation, and recover of the railroad corporation, in the name of the assured, the amount of such loss. The following authorities show that they can. Tyler *v.* Ætna Fire Ins. Co. 12 Wend. 507, and 16 Wend. 397, *et seq.;* 1 Phil. Ins. (1st ed.) 464; 2 ib. 282; Godsall *v.* Boldero, 9 East, 72; New York Ins. Co. *v.* Roulet, 24 Wend. 505, 516; Richardson *v.* Washington Bank, 3 Met. 536; Carpenter *v.* Providence Washington Ins. Co. 16 Pet. 495; Bryant *v.* Dana, 3 Gilman, 349.

In such case, the nominal plaintiff cannot legally discharge the claim. Dunn *v.* Snell, 15 Mass. 481 ; Parker *v.* Grout, 11 Mass. 157, note ; Jones *v.* Witter, 13 Mass. 304.

Phelps, for the defendants.

· To constitute an equitable assignment, there must be some written agreement, or some order, showing a transfer for the benefit of the assignee. 2 Story on Eq. § 1047; Morton *v.* Naylor, 1 Hill (N. Y.) Rep. 583. In all the cases, in this Commonwealth, in which an assignment has been supported there has been some act of the assignor. See 15 Mass., 11 Mass., and 13 Mass., cited for the plaintiffs; Eastman *v.* Wright, 6 Pick. 316; Dennis *v.* Twitchell, 10 Met. 180. In the case at bar, the plaintiffs refused to assign their claim, and give a release to the defendants, on receiving payment of their loss.

It is said that the doctrine of subrogation does not rest on agreement, but on natural equity. Most of the cases in this Commonwealth are cases of sureties, where the equity is manifest. But the defendants are not sureties for the insurance company.

And what equity is there that the insurance company, which has received its premium for insurance should receive full indemnity from the defendants, who are involuntarily liable by a kind of penal statute ?

The defendants are liable for loss by fire, if at all, only by virtue of St. 1840, c. 85; and this statute is to be construed strictly, because it takes away from the defendants a common-law right. The fire, against which the plaintiffs were insured, was not "communicated by a locomotive engine" of the defendants to their building, but from the house which was set on fire by sparks from the engine. The proximate cause of the fire, and that cause only, should be regarded. Otherwise, the defendants might be made liable for the burning of a whole city.

The decision was made at September term, 1848.

SHAW, C. J. This is an action of first impression, and is, we believe, the first brought upon the St. of 1840, c. 85, involving the present question. The action is brought, in fact, by the Springfield Mutual Fire Insurance Company, for their own benefit, in the name of the present plaintiffs, under the circumstances mentioned in the agreed statement of facts, on which the case was submitted to our decision.

1. The first question in order, it appears to us, is, whether upon the facts stated, the defendants were liable to any body, and for any loss, by force of St. 1840, c. 85; the defendants insisting that the case is not within the statute. The statute provides, § 1, that "when any injury is done to a building or other property of any person or corporation, by fire communicated by a locomotive engine of any railroad corporation, the said railroad corporation shall be held responsible, in damages, to the person or corporation so injured."

It is contended that the plaintiffs' building was not burnt by fire communicated by a locomotive engine, within the meaning of the statute. And the case certainly presents a question of great importance, and of great difficulty. On the one hand, if the word "communicated" is used in the broad sense in which, without force or violence done to the language, it may be, to include all burnings, when a fire is communicated by the engine directly to one building, and thence by natural and ordinary means extending to others, without the intervention of any other means, the effect would be to charge the railroad company with damages to an unlimited amount, when a fire, thus originating in a village or city, has spread into a wide conflagration. The argument is earnestly urged, that the legislature could not have intended to impose a responsibility so serious and alarming; and it is insisted that the term "communicated" will bear, and ought to receive, a construction more limited, so as to restrain the operation of the statute to the case where the very particles of fire which fall upon, and kindle the flame in, the building burnt, must have emanated from the engine itself, without the intervention of any other object. If so restricted a sense as the latter had been intended by the legislature, it seems strange that they did not add some qualifying word, as "immediately" or "directly," to the word "communicated." Perhaps some light may be derived from a subsequent clause in the same section of the statute, which provides, that any railroad corporation shall have an insurable interest in the property for which it may be so held responsible, in damages, *along its route*, and may procure insurance *thereon* in its own behalf." These latter words, we think, describe buildings being near and adjacent to the route of the railroad, so as to be exposed to the danger of fire from engines, but without limiting or defining any distance. In this view of the statute, it seems difficult to lay down any general rule. From the language made use of, we cannot think it was intended to limit its operation to the very first building which might be touched with a spark or other fire from the engine, and not extend it to another building, contiguous though it may be, but belonging to another owner, which must necessarily burn with it.

In the present case, the fire was transmitted, by ordinary and natural means, from the shop first touched by sparks from the engine, to the plaintiffs' dwelling-house, immediately across a street not very wide. The building burnt was, then, near the route of the railway. Under these circumstances, the court are of opinion, that the plaintiffs' house was injured by fire communicated by the locomotive engine of the defendants, within the true meaning of this statute, and that they are thereby held responsible, in damages, to the plaintiffs, the persons injured.

2. The next question is, whether the insurance company having, pursuant to their contract of indemnity, paid the loss to the plaintiffs, are entitled to maintain this suit in the plaintiffs' name, but for their own benefit, to recover the damages to which the defendants are liable by the statute.

We consider this to be a statute purely remedial, and not penal. Railroad companies acquire large profits by their business. But their business is of such a nature as necessarily to expose the property of others to danger; and yet, on account of the great accommodation and advantage to the public, companies are authorized by law to maintain them, dangerous though they are, and so they cannot be regarded as a nuisance. The manifest intent and design of this statute, we think, and its legal effect, are, upon the considerations stated, to afford some indemnity against this risk to those who are exposed to it, and to throw the responsibility upon those who are thus authorized to use a somewhat dangerous apparatus, and who realize a profit from it. This indemnity, provided by law against a special risk, may be considered as a quality annexed to

the estate itself, and passing with it to any and all persons who may
stand in the relation of owners, however divided and disturbed such
ownership may be.   The effect of the statute is, to diminish the
specific risk to which such buildings may be exposed, from their
proximity to the railroad, and in this respect to put them upon an
equality with other risks.

Now, when the owner, who *primâ facie* stands to the whole risk,
and suffers the whole loss, has engaged another person to be at that
particular risk for him, in whole or in part, the owner and insurer are,
in respect to that ownership and the risk incident to it, in effect
one person, having together the beneficial right to an indemnity provided by law for those who sustained a loss by that particular cause.
If, therefore, the owner demands and receives payment of that very
loss from the insurer, as he may, by virtue of his contract, there is a
manifest equity in transferring the right to indemnity, which he
holds for the common benefit, to the assurer.   It is one and the same
loss, for which he has a claim of indemnity, and he can equitably
receive but one satisfaction.   So that, if the assured first applies to
the railroad company, and receives the damages provided, it diminishes his loss *pro tanto*, by a deduction from, and growing out of, a
legal provision attached to, and intrinsic in, the subject insured.   The
liability of the railroad company is, in legal effect, first and principal,
and that of the insurer secondary ; not in order of time, but in order
of ultimate liability.   The assured may first apply to whichever of
these parties he pleases ; to the railroad company, by his right at
law, or to the insurance company, in virtue of his contract.   But if
he first applies to the railroad company, who pay him, he thereby
diminishes his loss by the application of a sum arising out of the
subject of the insurance, to wit, the building insured, and his claim
is for the balance.   And it follows, as a necessary consequence, that
if he first applies to the insurer, and receives his whole loss, he holds
the claim against the railroad company in trust for the insurers.
Where such an equity exists, the party holding the legal right is con-
scientiously bound to make an assignment, in equity, to the person
entitled to the benefit; and if he fails to do so, the *cestui que trust*
may sue in the name of the trustee, and his equitable interest will
be protected.

But we think this position is exceedingly well sustained by authorities.   A case very much in point, in principle, is that of Mason *v.*
Sainsbury, first reported as a manuscript case, in Marshall on Insurance, (1st Amer. ed.) 691, and since in 3 Doug. 61.   It was an action
against the hundred, brought on the riot act, to recover damage sustained by the plaintiff in the riots of 1780.   The plaintiff had an

insurancé on which he had recovered, the insurance office having paid him without suit; and this action was brought in the name of the plaintiff, with his consent, for the benefit of the insurance company. It was decided by Lord Mansfield, and the whole court, that the plaintiffs were entitled to recover. Buller, J., said it was to be treated as an indemnity, in which the principle is, that the insurer and the insured are as one person, and the paying by the insurer, before or after, can make no difference. The same doctrine was fully recognized by the Court of King's Bench, in 1823, in the case of Clark v. The Hundred of Blything, 3 Dowl. & Ryl. 489, and 2 Barn. & Cres. 254. It goes upon the ground, that the hundred are liable at all events, and the private contract of insurance, dividing the risk, makes no difference in the owner's right to recover. It was likened by Lord Mansfield and Ashhurst, J., in 3 Doug. 61, to the case of abandonment in marine insurance, where the insurer is constantly put in the place of the insured.

A similar case afterwards came before the Court of Common Pleas, in 1838, and was very elaborately argued, and the principle above stated confirmed. Yates v. Whyte, 4 Bing. N. R. 272, and 5 Scott, 640. It was a case of collision at sea, in which the plaintiff claimed damages, sustained by reason of the defendant's vessel having run foul of his vessel, through the defendant's negligence. The plaintiff had recovered of the underwriters on his vessel a certain sum for the same loss, and the defendant contended that this sum should be deducted; but it was held that this was no answer, and that the sum thus paid by the insurers ought not to be deducted. This case was also distinguishable from the former in this respect; that, in this, the suit was not brought at the instance of the insurers. But the court clearly intimated, that the owners, having an absolute right, could recover their damages in that suit, and that if, under an indemnity against the same loss, he had already received payment, the money recovered in this suit would be held in trust for the insurers who had thus paid. It would be in the nature of salvage, received by the assured after payment of a total loss. This was distinctly held by Lord Hardwicke, in Randal v. Cockran, 1 Ves. sen. 98. Where owners of vessels, unjustly captured by the Spaniards, had received compensation from the underwriters, and afterwards, upon letters of marque and reprisal, granted by the government against the Spaniards, the owners received compensation, it was decided that the owners held the money, so received, in trust for the underwriters, in the nature of salvage. This was a case in chancery; but where the same principle can be carried into effect in the ordinary forms of proceeding, in a court of law, the same principle will be applied.   If the trust consists in an equitable liability to pay money, it will be recognized and enforced in a suit at law.

It is clear that the assured has a right to recover against the insurer, although he has a remedy, at the same time, against the party by law liable.   Thus, in Cullen v. Butler, 5 M. & S. 466, it is stated, by Lord Ellenborough, that it is no objection to the plaintiff's right to recover of the underwriter, that he may have a right also to recover against the person by whose immediate act the damage was occasioned.   This being true, and it being also true that a recovery against the underwriter is no bar to a suit by the assured against the party primarily liable, it follows, as a necessary consequence, that after a payment by the insurer, by compulsion of legal process or voluntarily, the assured becomes trustee for the insurer, and by necessary implication makes an equitable assignment to him of the right so to recover.   See opinion of Kent, C. J., in Gracie v. New York Ins. Co. 8 Johns. 245.

There is a more recent case bearing upon the question of the right of underwriters after payment of a loss to claim salvage obtained by the assured, the result of which may seem opposed to the above cases, because the underwriters did not recover back.   Brooks v. MacDonnell, 1 Y. & Coll. Exch. Rep. 500.   But it will appear, from that case, that the doctrine herein above stated was affirmed at the bar and by the court; and that the case was decided upon the ground that an abandonment had been refused, and a certain sum been paid, by agreement as a compromise of all claims on both sides.

In regard to the right of the insurance company to sue in the name of the assured, we think the cases fully affirm the position, that by accepting payment of the insurers, the assured do implicitly assign their right of indemnity from a party liable, to the assured.   It is in the nature of an equitable assignment, which authorizes the assignee to sue in the name of the assignor, for his own benefit; and this is a right which a court of law will support, and will restrain and prohibit the assignor from defeating it by a release.   The formal discharge, therefore, given by the nominal plaintiffs, is not a bar to the action.   See Payne v. Rogers, 1 Doug. 407; Whitehead v. Hughes, 2 Crompt. & Mees. 318; Phillips v. Clagett, 11 Mees. & Welsb. 84; Timan v. Leland, 6 Hill, 237; Browne on Actions, 105.

Judgment for the plaintiffs.

THE LEXINGTON AND WEST CAMBRIDGE RAILROAD COMPANY *v.*
WILLIAM CHANDLER.[1]

Middlesex Co., October Term, 1847.

*Closing Subscription Books for Stock — Fixing Amount of Capital
— Evidence that a Person is a Stockholder — Sale of Shares for
Non-Payment of Assessment — Notice of Sale to Stockholder.*

An act incorporating a railroad company provided that the capital stock should not exceed
two thousand shares; that no assessments should be laid on the shares to a greater
amount, in the whole, than one hundred dollars; that the number of shares should be
determined from time to time, by the directors; and that as soon as two hundred and fifty
shares should be subscribed, the company should proceed to construct and open the
road: C subscribed for five shares, and the directors, after more than two hundred and
fifty shares were subscribed, voted to close the subscription books of the capital stock, and
passed no other vote fixing the number of shares: C paid six assessments on his shares,
but neglected to pay the seventh, and the treasurer of the company, pursuant to the
Rev. Sts. c. 39, § 53, sold said shares at auction, for a sum insufficient to pay said assessment, and the company thereupon brought an action against C to recover the deficiency.
Held, that the vote of the directors to close the subscription books for shares, on a given
day, was in effect a vote fixing the number of shares at the number then subscribed for, as
ascertained by said books, and lawfully fixed the number for the time being; that C's
shares were legally liable to assessment; and that he was answerable for the deficiency
sued for.

When a defendant is sued as a stockholder in a railroad corporation for the sum remaining
due on an assessment upon his shares, after they are sold for non-payment of the assessment, it is competent and sufficient, for the purpose of showing him to be such stockholder, and liable for the assessment, to give evidence that he signed a subscription paper
for shares, before the corporation was organized; that he attended the meeting of the stockholders for the organization of the corporation, and that he wrote and distributed votes,
and himself voted, for directors.

A by-law of a railroad corporation provided, that in case of a sale of shares for non-payment
of assessments, the treasurer should give notice to the delinquent owner, when his residence was known, of the times and place of sale, by letter seasonably put into the mail.
Held, that this by-law was directory to the treasurer, and not a condition precedent; and
that a written notice of the time and place of sale, signed by the treasurer, and delivered
to the owner of the shares, or left at his dwelling-house, and received by him as soon as he
was entitled to receive it by mail, was sufficient.

SHAW, C. J. This is an action brought by the railroad company
to recover of the defendant the balance due on a seventh assessment
of ten dollars, on five shares of the capital stock of the company,
subscribed for by him. The action is founded on the provisions of

the Rev. Sts. c. 39, § 53, to recover the difference between the amount of the said assessment and the sum at which said five shares were sold; the same having been sold, by order of the directors, as delinquent shares.

The trial was had in the Court of Common Pleas, before the chief justice; and the case comes before us on exceptions to the rulings of the presiding judge. Upon one of those rulings the defendant obtained a verdict; and to that ruling the plaintiffs alleged exceptions. But in an earlier stage of the trial, the defendant had alleged exceptions to other rulings of the judge; and all the exceptions are now before us. Those of the plaintiffs, though last in the order of time, will be considered first.

The defendant objected to the right of the company to recover, because the directors had not, by a vote, pursuant to the plaintiffs' act of incorporation, (St. 1845, c. 186,) fixed the number of shares, of which the capital stock of the company should consist. The judge ruled that this objection was fatal; and it was upon this ruling that a verdict was found for the defendant.

The provision in § 3 of the act of incorporation is, that "the capital stock of said company shall not exceed two thousand shares, the number of which shall be determined from time to time, by the directors thereof, and no assessments shall be laid thereon of a greater amount, in the whole, than one hundred dollars on each share." It appears by the facts in the case, that the directors caused subscriptions for shares to be opened, and on the 7th of August, 1845, more than 250 shares being then subscribed, voted to close the subscription books of the capital stock; and no other vote was passed fixing the number of shares of which the capital should consist.

The ground upon which the defendant's argument rests is this; that until the whole number of shares is determined, no assessment can be laid on any of the shares subscribed for; that, in effect, the subscription is a provisional undertaking only, that the subscriber will pay such sum as his share bears to the whole number of shares; and if that number is not subscribed for, he may be liable for a larger proportion. Salem Mill Dam Corporation v. Ropes, 6 Pick. 23, and 9 Pick. 187; Central Turnpike Corporation v. Valentine, 10 Pick. 142; Proprietors of Newburyport Bridge v. Story, 6 Pick. 45, note. But we think the present is not within the principles of those cases. In each of them, the number of shares, of which the capital should consist, was fixed unalterably by the act of incorporation, and the proportionable liability of each share could not be fixed till the whole were taken up. But the act of incorporation of the present ·

plaintiffs is very different. Section 3 provides that the number shall not exceed two thousand, and that the liability of each shareholder shall not exceed one hundred dollars on each share. Section 4 provides that the company shall commence the construction of the road when two hundred and fifty shares are subscribed; and by § 3, the number of shares " shall be determined, *from time to time*, by the directors." Taking these provisions together, they constitute a system entirely different from those cited. The security of the subscriber is in the provision limiting the amount to which he may be assessed. The security for the enterprise is found in the provision authorizing the directors to enlarge and fix the number of shares, so as to furnish the capital required to complete the work, and expressly authorizing and requiring them to proceed when two hundred and fifty shares are subscribed. Of course, each subscriber, when he subscribes, knows that he will be liable to assessment, when this number is taken, and, by subscribing, assents to the terms.

The court are of opinion, that the vote of the directors, to close the books of subscription for shares, on a given day, there being then more than two hundred and fifty subscribed for, was in effect a vote fixing the number of shares at the number then actually subscribed for, as ascertained by the books, and that this lawfully fixed the number for the time being. From the nature of the case, the words " from time to time" authorized an enlargement, but could not authorize a reduction of the number. The number of shares being capable of being ascertained with certainty, the vote referring to them was sufficiently certain.[1]

It may be important, with a view to a new trial, to consider the exceptions taken by the defendant.

---

[1] The act of incorporation of the Norwich and Lowestaffe Navigation Company v. Theobald, provided that the whole of the prescribed capital should be subscribed before any of the powers and provisions of the company should be put in force. The defendant, in an action for calls, proved that the last signature to the stock subscription was affixed after the making of the call, though before the commencement of the suit, and the court held the action could not be maintained. 1 Moody & Malkin, 151.

In the case of the Waterford, &c., Railroad Co. v. Logan, 19 Law J. Rep. (N. S.) Q. B. 259, the court allowed the defendant to plead, that, at the time of making the calls, the required amount of capital had not been subscribed. The act of incorporation authorized the company to put in force the powers of the company for the construction of the road when a certain amount of capital had been subscribed. But in the subsequent case of The Waterford, &c., Railroad Co. v. Dalbiac, 4 Eng. Law and Eq. Rep. 155, the court held, that this did not restrain the company from making calls before the required amount of capital was subscribed, the object of the act being only to prevent the company from interfering with the property of others before a sufficient amount of capital was subscribed to insure the success of the enterprise.

1. Evidence was offered, tending to show that the defendant signed a subscription paper for five shares, before the organization of the company; that he was present at the meeting of the stockholders for the organization of the corporation, wrote and distributed votes, and voted for directors. The defendant objected to the subscription paper as evidence, on the ground that no valid or binding promise could be made to the corporation, before its organization: and that parol evidence was not sufficient to show that the defendant had made himself a subscriber to the corporation for any shares, or that he became a member of the corporation, by the transactions stated. This objection was overruled, and the subscription paper and acts of the defendant were admitted, as evidence of a ratification of his prior subscription.

We think this decision was correct. The action is not founded on a supposed common-law obligation, arising from a promise to take and pay for a number of shares named; but it is founded on a statute liability, created by the act of incorporation, binding upon all its members. The question is not, whether this subscription was a good promise at common law, made to a proper party, and on a good consideration; but whether he was a member of the corporation and a holder of five shares. And for this purpose the evidence was competent. He may be proved to be a member of the corporation, by being a petitioner for the act, or, being within the description of persons incorporated, by acting under it, and assisting to carry it into execution. Ellis v. Marshall, 2 Mass. 269. The subscription paper, though made before the organization of the corporation, was made after the act of incorporation was passed, and was *primâ facie* proof, competent and proper to go to the jury, both to prove the fact of his being a member of the corporation, and of the number of shares held by him, and, in the absence of any countervailing proof, decisive.

2. The other exception of the defendant is, that he was not notified of the intended sale of his shares, for the non-payment of assessments, by a letter sent to him by mail. This is founded on the sixth article in the by-laws of the corporation, which directs that "in case of sale, the treasurer shall notify the delinquent owner, when his residence is known, of the time and place of sale, by letter seasonably put into the mail; and his certificate that notice has been duly given shall be full evidence of the fact."

It appears, that a written notice, signed by the treasurer, was delivered to the defendant, or left at his dwelling-house, but that no notice of such sale was sent through the post-office. The court decided that the notice given was sufficient, provided that the jury were satisfied that it was in fact received by the defendant, as soon

36 *

as he was entitled to receive it by mail. We think this was right. The by-law intended to provide an easy, convenient, and, under ordinary circumstances, a certain mode of giving and proving notice ; but it was directory to the treasurer, and not a condition precedent. The by-law contains no negative words, and neither expressly, nor by implication, declares no other notice sufficient. The mode indicated by the by-law would be only constructive notice, and was not, we think, intended to take away the effect of actual personal notice.

It is sufficient thus to express an opinion upon the subject of the defendant's exceptions ; but the plaintiffs' exceptions being sustained, the verdict is set aside, and a new trial ordered in this court.

Nelson and *G. Farrar*, for the plaintiffs.

Buttrick, for the defendant.

———◆———

MARY WYMAN *v.* THE LEXINGTON AND WEST CAMBRIDGE RAILROAD COMPANY.[1]

Middlesex Co., October Term, 1847.

Assessments of Damages for Taking Land — Practice — Evidence of Value of Adjoining Land.

The provision in Rev. Sts. c. 24, § 19, that jurors for the assessment of damages caused by the laying out of a highway shall be taken from " the three nearest towns not interested," means the three towns nearest to the town in which the land lies, over which the highway is laid out : And by Rev. Sts. c. 39, § 57, this provision is extended to jurors for the assessment of damages caused by the laying out of a railroad.

Under Rev. Sts. c. 24, § 15, and c. 39, § 57, which direct that when two or more persons apply, at the same time, to the county commissioners, for a jury to assess damages caused by the laying out of a highway or a railroad, " the said commissioners shall cause all such applications to be considered and determined by the same jury," the most proper course for the commissioners is, to issue a single warrant to an officer, reciting all the cases that are to be heard by the jury : If separate warrants for each case be issued by the commissioners, yet if the officer summon a single jury, who hear and determine each case, their verdicts will not be set aside merely because several warrants were irregularly issued.

When several applications are made, at the same time, by owners of lands in different towns, for a jury to assess damages caused by the laying out of a highway or railroad, the jurors are to be taken from three towns nearest to the town in which the land of either of the applicants is situate : And when a single application, for such purpose, is made by one who owns land in different towns, the jurors are to be taken from three towns nearest to either of the towns in which his lands are situate : This is all that is practicable under Rev. Sts. c. 24, § 15, and c. 39, § 57.

———————————————————

[1] 13 Metcalf's Reports, 316.

Wyman v. Lexington and West Cambridge Railroad Co.

It is necessary that notice to jurors, who are drawn to assess damages caused by the laying out of a highway or railroad, should be served by a constable : Such notice may be served by the officer to whom the warrant for summoning a jury is directed.

On the hearing, before a jury summoned to assess damages caused to A by the laying out of a railroad over his land, he may give evidence of the price paid by the railroad company for the adjoining land of B purchased by them : But an owner of adjoining land cannot legally be permitted to state to the jury what, in his judgment, is the value of that land, though he be a farmer who has occasionally bought and sold land ; and if he be permitted to make such a statement, the verdict of the jury will be set aside, although they were instructed, that opinions, except of experts, were not evidence, and that the facts and reasons on which any opinion or judgment was formed, were the evidence on which they must form their opinion.

THIS was a proceeding upon a petition for a jury to assess damages sustained by the petitioner by the laying out of the respondents' railroad over her land in the town of West Cambridge. The petition was presented to the county commissioners in September, 1846, and they issued a warrant, directed " to any deputy sheriff of our county of Middlesex, Samuel Chandler, Esq., sheriff of said county, being interested;" to summon a jury, agreeably to law, to estimate the petitioner's damages. A deputy sheriff thereupon proceeded to execute the warrant, by causing jurors to be drawn by the proper authorities of Cambridge, Watertown, and Somerville, three towns nearest to West Cambridge, and by summoning said jurors to appear, &c.

When the jury convened, and before they were impanelled, the respondents objected, " that no jurors were taken from the town of West Cambridge, being the town in which the land of the petitioner is situate, and not being interested in the question : Also, that the jurors were summoned by the officer to whom the warrant was directed, and not by a constable : Also, that the jurors, in the cases of this petitioner and of George Pierce, were summoned under two warrants, both applications for a jury having been presented to the county commissioners, and passed upon, at the same time, for the assessment of damages occasioned by the laying out of the same railroad : Also, that the officer, with the two warrants, made but one requisition upon each of the towns for jurors." These objections were overruled, by the officer appointed to preside at the trial, and the jury was impanelled.

During the trial a witness for the petitioner was asked what was given, by the respondents, for land next adjoining the land of the petitioner. Another witness for the petitioner, a farmer who had occasionally bought and sold land, was asked what, in his judgment, was then the value of his own land next adjoining the land of the petitioner. Both of these questions were answered.

The jury were distinctly instructed by the presiding officer, and the rule was repeatedly stated, in their hearing, that opinions, except of experts, were not evidence: but that the facts and reasons, on which any opinion or judgment was founded, were the evidence on which the opinion of the jury must be formed.

Exceptions were duly taken to the proceedings aforesaid, and were allowed by the presiding officer.

The verdict of the jury was returned into the Court of Common Pleas, and was there ordered to be set aside. The petitioner appealed to this court.

Mellen and *G. Farrar* for the respondents.

1. A part of the jurors should have been taken from West Cam. bridge. By the Rev. Sts. c. 24, § 19, the officer who receives a war. rant for a jury to assess damages, caused by laying out a highway, is directed to "require of the selectmen of the three nearest towns, not interested in the question," to return jurors. And by Rev. Sts. c. 39, § 57, when application is made for a jury to assess damages caused by laying out a railroad, "the like proceedings shall be had thereon, as are provided in the twenty-fourth chapter, for the recovery of damages for laying out highways." What is meant by "the three nearest towns not interested?".

In St. 1801, c. 16, § 2, which provides for the speedy removal of nuisances, the jurors, who were to come before two justices of the peace, *quorum unus*, were directed to be drawn from the jury-box of "the three towns next adjoining to the town in which such nuisance may be." So in St. 1814, c. 173, jurors for assessing damages caused by flowing land by mill-dams were directed to be taken from "the three towns nearest to that in which the land injured is situated."

The change of language, in Rev. Sts. c. 24, § 19, above cited, is a change of the law. It was intended, by introducing language never before used on this subject, that jurors should be taken from the nearest point, if the town in which they live is not interested; both because they are better judges of the value of the land, and because less cost is thereby incurred. The words "towns not interested" mean not interested, as a body corporate, in the question to be tried, and not the interest of an individual member of the town, who may bring a question before the jury. And the interest of the town must be a legal interest. In the case at bar, the town of West Cambridge had no corporate or legal interest in the amount of the petitioner's damages.

2. The two applications of the present petitioner, and of Pierce, should have been treated, throughout, either as joint or several. The Rev. Sts. c. 24, § 15, require that both should "be considered and

determined by the same jury." But the officer treated the two cases, partly as joint, and partly as several. One requisition for jurors was made, in two cases, of owners of different lands, in which the two had no joint interest. As the cases now stand, there are two warrants and only one requisition; so that the record, in one or the other of them, must be incomplete. There should have been but one warrant, embracing both cases.

3. Notice to the jurors should have been served by a constable; the officer, to whom the warrant was directed, having no legal authority to summon them. Rev. Sts. c. 24, § 19; c. 95, §§ 15–17.

4. The price given by the respondents for land adjoining the petitioner's was not legal evidence for her. In the case of railroads there is not a free sale. The corporation offer more than the land is worth, in order to avoid adversary proceedings and the risk of the cost of a jury.

5. The farmer's judgment of the value of his own land, adjoining that of the petitioner was not admissible in evidence; and the effect of his testimony was not prevented by the remarks of the presiding officer concerning that species of evidence. 1 Greenl. on Ev. § 440; Needham v. Ide, 5 Pick. 510; Norman v. Wells, 17 Wend. 136; Gibson v. Williams, 4 Wend. 320; Dickinson v. Barber, 9 Mass. 225; Jameson v. Drinkald, 12 Moore, 148.

Buttrick, for the petitioner.

1. The jurors were taken from the right towns. The town nearest to the land in the town is not the town in which the land lies; so that if the intention of Rev. Sts. c. 24, § 19, was, that jurors should be taken from the nearest point, as the respondents contend, the language is not conformed to that intention. The manifest purpose of the revised statutes was, to put the cases of flowing lands, and laying out highways, turnpikes, and railroads, on the same ground. And this purpose cannot be effected in all cases, except by excluding the town in which the land is situate. For, in some questions of *ways*, the town where the land lies is interested, and in others it is not. If the respondents' objection prevails, it follows that jurors from other towns must come from the towns whose boundaries are nearest to the land over which the railroad passes. The word "adjoining" is not used in the statute; because there may not be three adjoining towns not interested. Therefore, the word "nearest" is used.

If West Cambridge could not be resorted to for jurors, in a highway case, then not in a railroad case; for Rev. Sts. c. 39, § 57, provide for "the like proceedings" in railroad cases, as in cases of highways. The revised statutes, throughout, recognize towns as parties

to highway cåses.   In Lanesborough v. County Commissiqners of
Berkshire, 22 Pick. 278, the court held that a town, in which a highway had been laid out by the commissioners, was a party that might
be aggrieved and appeal.   Before the revised statutes, towns paid
all damages in highway cases, and were therefore interested.   Yet in
flowing cases, and railroad cases, generally, towns are not interested.
The object of the statute, in putting all these cases on the same
ground, was, to exclude local interests and prejudices, and yet to
take the jurors from the vicinage.

2. It is objected that a single requisition of jurors, for two separate cases, was-made on two warrants.   In the first place, the court
cannot know, except from the venires issued by the officer, that two
cases were pending.   Is that judicial knowledge?   But secondly,
how is the provision of Rev. Sts. c. 24, § ·15, that all applications,
made to the county commissioners at the same time, shall " be
considered and determined by the same jury," to be carried into
effect?   Can two cases be consolidated by the officer, *nolens volens?*
We deny that this provision applies to railroads.   They go through.
many towns; so that the same jury cannot always decide two
cases that may be brought at the same time.   Two cases may be
brought at the same time, from different towns, so that the jurors
could not be brought from towns nearest to both.

3. The jurors were rightly summoned by the deputy sheriff to
whom the warrants were directed.   It is immaterial, however, whether they were rightly summoned, or summoned at all, as they were
regularly drawn, attended, were impanelled, and performed their
duty.   Patterson's case, 6 Mass. 486 ; Anon. 1 Pick. 196 ; The Rev.
Sts. c. 24, § 21, authorize the officer, who summons the jury, to
return a talisman, when there is not a full jury, by reason of
challenges or otherwise.   By § 28, the same officer is required
to give notice of the time and place of meeting to the presiding
officer, &c.; and by § 29, his fees for summoning jurors are prescribed.   These sections show that the officer, to whom the warrant
is directed, (who never is a constable,) may summon jurors.

4. The evidence of the price paid by the respondents for contiguous
land was properly received as a proof of a fact.   It was open to
the respondents to show, and for the jury to consider, whether the
price was an extorted or a fair one.

5. If the farmer's opinion of the value of his adjacent land was
improperly admitted in evidence, yet the remarks of the presiding
officer prevented its doing any harm.   Ellis v. Short, 21 Pick. 142.

DEWEY, J.   It has become necessary, in the decision of this and other cases before us, arising upon proceedings in relation to claims for damages for injuries sustained by the location of railroads, to decide as to the construction of the statute of the Commonwealth regulating the proceedings upon a petition for a jury to assess such damages. The right to a jury in such cases is given to either party who may be dissatisfied with the estimate made by the county commissioners, by the Rev. Sts. c. 39, § 57, wherein it is provided that, upon such petition being presented, " the like proceedings shall be had thereon as are provided in the twenty-fourth chapter, for the recovery of damages for laying out highways." This provision is to be kept in mind throughout this whole inquiry.

The Rev. Sts. c. 24, regulate the proceedings in such cases, upon a petition for a jury to assess damages occasioned by the location of a highway. Section 18 requires that the warrant, in such cases, " shall be directed to the sheriff of the county, or his deputy, who is disinterested, or to a coroner, requiring him to summon a jury of twelve men to hear and determine the matter of complaint." Section 19 enacts that " the officer who receives the warrant shall in writing require of the selectmen of the three nearest towns, not interested in the question, to return a number of jurors, not less than two nor more than six."

1. One point, arising upon § 19, is as to the true construction of the provision as to the towns from which the jurors are to be selected. Is the town, in which the land that is the subject of the claim for damages is situate, to be included as one of the three towns from which jurors are to be selected, or is it to be excluded ? The language of the statute is not definite or precise upon that point. It is a case where we are called upon to give a construction to general language of the legislature, and, as far as possible, we are to give effect to the legislative will. The earliest statute on this subject, that of 1786, c. 67, § 4, was very general, giving the party a right to a hearing before a jury " to be summoned by the sheriff or his deputy;" making no provision as to the towns from which they should be selected. The next statute in the order of time (St. 1802, c. 135, § 1,) provided that the jury in such cases should be drawn from " two or more disinterested towns in said county." This was followed by the St. 1827, c. 77, § 12, wherein it was provided that " such jury shall, in all cases, consist of twelve persons, and no more than three persons shall be taken from any one town," &c. To this have succeeded the Rev. Sts. c. 24, § 19, already cited.

The practical effect of the earliest statute was, to exclude the town where the land, which was the subject of inquiry, was situate; as such town was, under the earlier course of legislature, interested in the result, whether it was a question of the location of a road, or the assessment of damages. Hence such town would necessarily be excluded. But under more recent statutes, the damages awarded to the owners of lands are chargeable solely upon the county, and in the mere matter of such damages the town may have no pecuniary interest. We believe, however, that the practice has always been to exclude the town, in which the land is situate, from the list of towns from which a jury is to be summoned to assess damages to the landholder.

By the provisions of the revised statutes, not only the proceedings on the subject of damages, by reason of the location of railroads, is made to correspond with those of c. 24, in relation to highways, but similar provisions exist with regard to damages occasioned by the location of turnpike roads ; Rev. Sts. c. 39, § 3 ; and also in relation to damages occasioned by the erection of mills. Rev. Sts. c. 116, § 13. As to the latter subject, the St. of 1814, c. 173, which was in force at the time of the enactment of the revised statutes, very clearly excluded the town in which the land was situate, in the selection of towns from which a jury was to be summoned. That provision required the jury to be taken from " the three towns nearest to that in which the land injured is situated."

We now find, as already stated, these various cases of claims for damages, all regulated by one provision, that of Rev. Sts. c. 24. Considering the practice so long prevailing, the provisions actually existing at the time of enacting the revised statutes, excluding, by direct words, the town in which the land was situated, in the case of water-mills, and seeing no sufficient evidence of change of purpose, in this respect, in the revised statutes, and nothing in the language of the present existing laws, which requires a different construction, we are of opinion that " the three nearest towns " from which a jury is to be summoned, are the three towns nearest to that in which the land is situate, and exclusive of such town. A jury summoned in part from the town in which the land lies, that is the subject of damages, would therefore be irregularly summoned, and if seasonably objected to, their verdict would be set aside for that cause. [See note at the end of this case.]

2. The next question arising is as to the mode of proceeding where two or more persons apply at the same time for several damages for injury occasioned by the same highway or railroad. Shall the warrant for a jury, in such cases, be several or joint? Upon this point, the statute seems to be entirely explicit. By Rev. Sts. c. 24, § 15, " if two or more persons shall apply at the same time for joint or several damages, they may join in the same petition to the commissioners ; and if several applications shall be pending at

the same time before the commissioners for a jury to determine any matter relating to the laying out, alteration, or discontinuance of a highway, or the assessment of damages, the said commissioners shall cause all such applications to be considered and determined by the same jury." The proper course is, therefore, for the officer to summon but one jury for the various cases. Such warrant to the sheriff from the county commissioners should, more properly, be a single warrant, reciting all the cases to be heard by the jury. Separate warrants, however, embracing various cases of claims for damage caused by the location of the same railroad, acted upon by the officer, as a joint warrant, in all the subsequent proceedings, and heard by the same jury, would not be so far objectionable as to require us to set aside a verdict for that cause.

3. Upon the question of summoning the jury, where the lands of several petitioners for a jury are situate in different towns, or where the lands of a single petitioner are situate in different towns, the court are of opinion that the rule must be that of a selection of jurors from three towns nearest the town in which the land of either of the petitioners is situate, or, in case of a single petitioner, from three towns nearest to either of the towns in which his lands are situate, would be a sufficient compliance with the statute. This is all that is practicable; and the provision of § 15, above cited, requiring all petitions that are presented at the same time to be sent to the same jury, can only be carried into effect in this way.

4. As to the proper mode of giving notice to the jurors, after they have been drawn by the selectmen of the several towns, it has been contended that the only proper mode of notifying them is by a notice by a constable. This position is supposed to be warranted by the provisions of Rev. Sts. c. 24, § 19, requiring that "the jurors shall be drawn, summoned, and returned as in other cases." Taking this provision alone, and referring to c. 95, §§ 15 – 17, regulating the summoning of jurors for the regular terms of the higher courts, it would seem to provide for a notification to the jurors by a constable. No such provision existed in the earliest statutes on this subject, and the practice under them is understood to have been different. Looking at various other sections of c. 24 of the Rev. Sts., they are found strongly to indicate a different mode of proceeding. By § 18, the warrant is to issue to the sheriff, "requiring him to summon a jury." By § 28, "the officer, by whom any such jury shall be summoned, shall give seasonable notice of the time and place of their meeting to the person appointed to preside at the trial, and also to the person appointed as agent for the county," &c. By § 29, "the officer shall receive, for summoning the jurors, four cents a mile for all neces-

sary travel, and one dollar and fifty cents for each day that he shall attend upon them." The officer referred to in these sections is the sheriff or his deputy, and not a constable. See also § 21. In c. 95, on the other hand, the venires or requisition for jurors are to be served upon the selectmen by a constable, and all the proceedings are by a constable.

The court are of opinion that the law well authorizes the summoning of the jurors, in railroad cases, by the sheriff or his deputy; and that it is no objection to the regularity of the proceeding, that the jurors were not notified by a constable.

We do not mean to intimate that a notice to the jurors, by a constable, and an attendance by them in pursuance of such notice, all the proceedings being regular, would vitiate the verdict. However that may be, we are satisfied that a notification to the jurors, by the officer to whom the warrant is directed, is good and sufficient in law.

5. The further questions in this case arise upon the ruling of the presiding officer, upon the admission of evidence. In relation to the evidence which was admitted as to the price paid by the railroad corporation for the adjacent lot, we think it was competent. This was evidence of a fact, and not of an opinion. The price for which other adjacent lots had been actually sold was admissible, open, of course to any evidence explanatory of the circumstances attending such sale, and tending to show why the purchasers gave a price greater than the true value of the land. If it had been a price fixed by a jury, or in any way compulsorily paid by the party, the evidence of such payment would be inadmissible before the jury. Upon the principle on which we should admit evidence of other sales between other parties of adjacent lots, this evidence was admissible, and none the less so because the railroad corporation were themselves the purchasers.

6. The next objection taken is that to the competency of an inquiry put to a witness, of the following purport: "A witness who was a farmer, and had occasionally bought and sold land, was asked what, in his judgment, was the then value of his own land next adjoining the land of the petitioner." This evidence does not come from an expert, or one properly entitled to give an opinion as an expert. Whether the presiding officer did or did not so consider him, is not quite clear. As to the competency of evidence of mere opinions, although the law of this Commonwealth is very liberal, more so than in some of our sister States, yet opinions are not deemed competent evidence, except when given by experts, unless upon some controlling ground of necessity, resulting from the nature

of the inquiry. The evidence of opinion of the value of the property, that is the subject of the litigation, is of this character, and is admitted from the necessity of the case. Without it, you cannot, in many cases, bring before the jury such facts as will enable them to render a verdict for the proper damages for the value of the article which is the subject of damages. But such evidence of mere opinion as to the value of property is to be confined exclusively to the subject in reference to which damages are claimed. If you would aid the jury by reference to other articles, or property similarly situated, the evidence in reference to such other articles or other property must be that of facts, and not opinions. It is only by reference to facts that exist respecting the property, that a comparison is to be made that may aid the jury in estimating the value of the property in relation to which they are to assess damages. To allow any thing beyond this would be unnecessarily sanctioning the introduction of evidence of opinions of witnesses — evidence always somewhat objectionable in its character, and to be excluded as far as it is practicable. We think it was not competent for the party claiming damages to introduce the speculative opinion of the witness as to the value of adjacent land, and especially his opinion of the value of his own land, and, by the effect of such testimony, form a standard of comparison by which the jury might estimate the value of the land which was the subject of controversy. This testimony, in the opinion of the court, ought to have been excluded.

It was suggested, upon the argument, that the subsequent instructions of the presiding officer, as to the evidence of opinions, obviated the objection to the admission of this evidence. We are apprehensive that those remarks were not intended by him as excluding the evidence now under consideration. The jury were not instructed that the evidence was inadvertently admitted, but was now held incompetent, and to be rejected by them. This testimony having been improperly admitted, the verdict must, for this cause, be set aside, and the case sent to a new jury.[1]

---

[1] In the case of James Brown v. The Boston and Worcester Railroad Corporation, argued and decided at this term, said Brown had obtained a verdict for damages caused by the construction of the respondents' railroad in such a manner as to injure his land situate in the town of Framingham. The court set aside the verdict because a part of the jurors were taken from that town ; the respondents having objected to the competency of those jurors before the jury was impanelled.

G. Bemis, for the respondents.

Mellen, for the petitioner.

ABNER S. TAYLOR v. COUNTY COMMISSIONERS OF PLYMOUTH.[1]

Plymouth Co., October Term, 1847.

Assessment of Damages — Application for a Jury — Practice.

Under the Rev. Sts. c. 39, § 57, which provide that a party, who is dissatisfied with the estimate made by county commissioners, of the damages caused by taking land for a railroad,
"may apply for a jury to assess the damages, either at the same meeting at which such
estimate shall be completed and returned, or at the next regular meeting thereafter," if a
party applies for a jury, at the same meeting at which the estimate is completed and
recorded, and a jury is then ordered, and a warrant therefor issued, he cannot, by merely
omitting or refusing to proceed under that order and warrant, entitle himself to a jury on
applying therefor at the next regular meeting of the commissioners.

THIS was a petition for a mandamus, to be directed to the county
commissioners of Plymouth, commanding them to pass an order for
summoning a jury to estimate the damage done to the petitioner
by the Old Colony Railroad Corporation, by taking his land, and
constructing their road upon it. The petitioner alleged, in his petition, that said commissioners, on his application, assessed his damages, sustained by the construction of said railroad, at $300, and
caused their assessment and award to be recorded at their regular
meeting on the first Tuesday of August, 1846; that he immediately
made known to the commissioners, in writing, his dissatisfaction
with their assessment and award, and applied to them, in writing,
that his damages, so sustained, might be estimated and found by a
jury; and that the commissioners, at their regular meeting aforesaid,
passed an order that a jury be summoned for the purposes before
mentioned; "that it was not convenient, by reason of sickness and
affliction, to cause a jury to be summoned and to give their verdict,
within three months next after the time of passing said order, and a
jury was not summoned, and no verdict was agreed upon or rendered
by a jury, in the premises; whereupon the petitioner applied to said
commissioners, at their regular meeting at Plymouth, on the first
Tuesday of January, 1847, being the next regular meeting of said
commissioners, after the said award and assessment of damages was
made and recorded by them, as before mentioned, praying them that
said order for a jury might be renewed, or a new order passed for
summoning a jury in the premises, for the purposes mentioned in his

[1] 13 Metcalf's Reports, 449.

original application for a jury, as aforesaid;" that said commissioners caused notice of said last application to be given to said railroad corporation, and appointed a time for hearing the parties thereon, and after a full hearing thereon, of both parties, said commissioners refused to order a jury to be summoned upon said application, and ordered that the petitioner take nothing thereby.

The county commissioners filed an answer to said petition, averring that, at their meeting in August, 1846, they passed the order mentioned in said petition, and caused a warrant to be issued to the sheriff of Plymouth, directing him to summon and impanel a jury to assess the petitioner's damages in the premises, which warrant they then put into the hands of the petitioner, to be by him delivered to said sheriff: That the petitioner, at their next regular meeting in January, 1847, returned said warrant to them, with no return thereon by said sheriff, but with an indorsement thereon, in these words: " In consequence of sickness in my family, and other circumstances conspiring to prevent getting through with the jury trial, within the three months prescribed by law, I return the papers and warrant for a jury, into the clerk's office, unexecuted. Abner S. Taylor." That, at said last mentioned meeting of the commissioners, the petitioner also presented to them a petition for another order and warrant for a jury to assess his said damages ; but that they, believing that they had no authority to grant said last mentioned petition, ordered that it be refused, and that the petitioner take nothing thereby.

Coffin, for the petitioner.

T. H. Russell, for the respondents.

DEWEY, J. The right to a jury to assess the damages occasioned by the laying out of a railroad is given by Rev. Sts. c. 39, § 57. The application for such jury is to be made either at the same term at which the estimate of the county commissioners shall be completed and returned, or at their next regular meeting thereafter. The petitioner made his application for a jury, in due season, being at the term when the estimate of damages was returned by the commissioners, and a jury was then ordered, and a person appointed to preside at the hearing of the case before the jury. The warrant for such jury was duly made out and delivered to the petitioner, who wholly neglected to cause any further proceedings to be had thereon within three months from the date of the order for a jury. He now demands, as a matter of right, a second order for a jury. His second application, having been made at the next term after the estimate of damages by the county commissioners was returned, was in due time, as an original application, and, if not barred by his previous application and the order thereon, ought to be granted. The case, therefore, opens the inquiry as to the effect of the first order and warrant for a jury. The petitioner contends that no jury having in fact been called out in pursuance of it, it may be treated as a nullity, and his second application for a jury be considered as an original one. This view of the case does not seem to us to be a reasonable one. Some effect should be given to the first petition and the order thereon. The petitioner may select either of the periods named in the statute for filing his petition for a jury; but whenever filed, it requires action on the part of the county commissioners, and notice to the railroad corporation, and the corporation may appear and request the appointment of a presiding officer at the hearing before the jury, and such appointment may be made, and all the preliminary arrangements thus settled. The case having proceeded thus far, we do not think the petitioner, at whose request the jury has been ordered, can arbitrarily discontinue all further proceedings on such order, without affecting his right to make a new application for a jury.

Various cases may occur where the party would be entitled to a new jury. By force of the Rev. Sts. c. 24, § 35, it is so, when a jury, upon being called out, shall not agree on a verdict; and if, for any error, the proceedings are set aside upon a writ of *certiorari*, the party may have a new jury. To these cases may be added, generally, all others, where a verdict has failed to be returned, by some inevitable casualty, or the fault of some public officer charged with the execution of the process. If the person appointed to preside should, by reason of sickness or absence from the Commonwealth, or by declining to serve, thereby prevent the hearing before the jury, it might furnish a proper reason for a new warrant and order for a jury. Other cases might be mentioned, which might produce a like effect.

When such cases occur, a new petition is to be presented, setting forth the reasons for not proceeding on the original order, and praying for a new one. We understand, in the present case, that no sufficient reason was shown to exist for not executing the first order, and that it was neglected to be executed at the will of the petitioner, and for no good cause. The petitioner contends that he had the legal right, at his pleasure, to omit all further action on the first warrant, and demand, as of right, a second order for a jury. This, we think, he was not authorized to do. Having elected to take his order for a jury, at the meeting of the commissioners when they returned their estimate, he was bound to proceed thereon, unless he shows a good excuse therefor. The fact alleged as an excuse was of a character that was to be considered and adjudged upon, as to its existence, by the commissioners. We do not understand it to be suggested that there was any real incapacity of the party, disabling him from proceeding under the first warrant. We think the case not a proper one for a mandamus to the county commissioners.

Petition dismissed.

ROBERT PORTER *v.* COUNTY COMMISSIONERS OF NORFOLK.[1]

Norfolk Co., November Term, 1847.

Assessment of Damages — Filing Petition.

Though an original petition for a jury to assess damages caused by the taking of land for a railroad is not seasonably filed, if it be after the regular meeting of the county commissioners, next following that at which they completed and returned their estimate of such damages, yet if such petition be filed at the same meeting at which they complete and return such estimate, and they thereupon, without notice to the railroad corporation, pass an order and issue a warrant for the summoning of a jury, and the warrant is not served, they are authorized, and ought, upon motion of the land-owner, though the motion be not made until after their next regular meeting, to issue an order of notice to the railroad corporation to show cause why a jury should not be summoned on the original petition; the first order for a jury being void, for want of such notice, and the original petition being still pending.

PETITION for a writ of mandamus, commanding the county commissioners of Norfolk to pass an order for a jury to revise the estimate, made by said commissioners, of the damages caused to the petitioner by the taking of his land, &c., by the Stoughton Branch Railroad Company, or for such other relief to the petitioner as law and equity may require.

The facts set forth in the petition, and not denied, were these: On the 4th of July, 1844, before the adjournment of the regular meeting of the county commissioners, appointed to be held on the fourth Tuesday of June in that year, the Stoughton Railroad Company petitioned the said commissioners to estimate the damages caused to said Porter, (the petitioner,) by the location of their railroad. On

---

[1] 13 Metcalf's Reports, 479.

the 26th of December, 1844, said commissioners, at their regular meeting, awarded $1,000 to said Porter, and caused their estimate to be completed and returned. Said Porter, being dissatisfied therewith, immediately petitioned the said commissioners, in writing, for a jury. Whereupon they, at the same meeting, without any notice to said railroad company, ordered a jury; and on the 8th of January, 1845, their clerk, without any special application therefor, made out a warrant for a jury, and gave it to the sheriff, who, at the end of three months, returned it to the clerk's office unserved.

Both said petitions were continued, from term to term, to the June term of said Commissioners' Court, in 1845, at which last term, within six months from said commissioners' award aforesaid, but after an intervening regular term in April, 1845, said Porter filed a new petition, in writing, for a jury to estimate his damages. The petition was continued to September term, 1845, when said Porter, by his counsel, made a motion, in writing, to have an order of notice issue on his original petition for a jury, (which was filed on the 26th of December, 1844, then pending in said Commissioner's Court,) to said railroad corporation, to show cause why a warrant should not issue thereon; but said commissioners refused to issue any such notice. An order of notice was issued on said second petition, filed at June term, 1845, returnable on the 27th of October, 1845, at which time both parties appeared, and said commissioners refused to order a jury.

Wilkinson, for the petitioner.

The order passed in December, 1844, was of no validity, for want of notice to the railroad company. Central Turnpike, 7 Pick. 13; Hinckley, 15 Pick. 447; Brown v. City of Lowell, 8 Met. 172. And if the commissioners make an erroneous order on the petition, they should correct it. See Inhabitants of Mendon v. County of Worcester, 10 Pick. 235 ; Ex parte Weston, 11 Mass. 417.

By the Rev. Sts. c. 39, § 57, application for a jury to assess damages, in case of railroads, may be made at the same meeting at which the commissioners return their estimate, or at their next regular meeting. And by § 56, commissioners are to estimate damages "in the manner provided in the case of laying out highways." By Rev. Sts. c. 24, § 14, in case of highways, application for a jury to assess damages may be made at the meeting of the commissioners, at which the highway is laid out, or at their next regular meeting, or at any time not exceeding six months thereafter. The " six months," after the meeting succeeding that at which the commissioners' return of damages is made, (it is submitted,) is applicable to railroads, according to the provisions of c. 39. But if the court hold otherwise, yet the present petitioner is entitled to an order of notice on his first petition.

B. *Rand*, for the respondents.
The petitioner's remedy is lost by lapse of time. The "six months," in Rev. Sts. c. 24, § 14, were not extended to railroads, by c. 39; and an application for a jury, in case of railroads, can be made only at the commissioners' meeting at which the estimate of damages is returned, or at their next regular meeting.

DEWEY, J. The petition for a jury, filed with the county commissioners at their regular meeting in June, 1845, as an original petition, was not filed in due season; the Rev. Sts. c. 39, § 57, limiting the application to the meeting at which the estimate of damages by the commissioners shall be completed and returned, or at the next regular meeting thereafter.

It is contended that the application may be made within the period of six months, as in case of an application for a jury to assess damages in the location of a highway. But though the general course of proceedings is similar, in relation to a jury in the two cases, yet, upon this point, the cases differ, and a different statute provision exists. The only question, therefore, in the present case, arises upon the application for further proceedings upon the original petition filed at the proper term, and upon which a jury was ordered, but never called out by the petitioner. If such order had been a legal one, and a warrant had been duly issued thereon, and the petitioner, without any sufficient cause, had neglected to call out the jury, he would thereby be taken to have waived his right to a jury; as was held in Taylor v. County Commissioners of Plymouth, (*ante*, 436.)

Upon examining the records of the doings of the county commissioners, upon the original petition, it is quite apparent that no legal order was ever made, ordering a jury thereon. Such order could only be made after due notice to the corporation, or, what is equivalent, an appearance by them. Central Turnpike, 7 Pick. 13; Hinckley, 15 Pick. 447. The order being thus wholly illegal, no duty devolved upon the petitioner to call out the jury, in pursuance of such order; and he might properly treat it as a nullity. The proper order, upon the original petition, has not been made, viz., an order of notice upon the corporation to show cause why a jury should not be ordered upon the petition. That order it is yet competent for the county commissioners to make. The case is still

pending, and the subject of any proper order. If it has not been
duly brought forward upon the docket of that tribunal, it may be so
now. The petition is undisposed of, and the further proceedings
necessary to assess damages by a jury may yet be had thereon.

We think the proper order here will be, that an alternative mandamus issue to the County Commissioners of Norfolk, requiring them
to issue an order of notice to the Stoughton Branch Railroad Company to appear before them and show cause why a jury should not
be ordered upon the original petition of said Robert Porter, or that
said county commissioners show cause for not so doing.

———◆———

LOCKWOOD CAREY AND WIFE *v.* THE BERKSHIRE RAILROAD COM-
PANY.
OLIVER SKINNER *v.* THE HOUSATONIC RAILROAD CORPORATION.[1]

Berkshire Co., September Term, 1848.

*Action by Wife for Death of Husband — Action by a Father for Loss
of Child.*

An action on the case cannot be maintained by a widow, to recover damages for the loss of
her husband, or by a father for the loss of service of his child, in consequence of the death
of the husband or child, occasioned by the carelessness or fault of the agents or servants
of a railroad corporation.

THE first of the above named actions was originally commenced
by Eliza Ann Hewins, then the widow of Joseph H. Hewins, and is
now prosecuted in the joint names of herself and Lockwood Carey,
with whom she has since intermarried. It was an action on the
case, to recover damages for the loss of the life of the female plaintiff's late husband, in consequence of the negligence, carelessness,
and unskilfulness of the defendants' servants and agents.

On the trial, which took place in the Court of Common Pleas
before Wells, C. J., at the October term, 1845, the plaintiff (Eliza
Ann Hewins, then sole) offered to prove, among other things, that,
on the day of the alleged injury, Hewins was employed by an agent
of the defendants, with other laborers, to go on the defendants' road,

southerly of the station at West Stockbridge, as far as the north part of Great Barrington, to shovel snow from the track, in order that the trains might proceed; that he was employed as a day laborer, and to be paid by the day, and was not constantly employed by the company under any contract; that, on the day referred to, Hewins was engaged to clear snow from the track, until a car should be sent down to bring him and the other laborers back, and was directed to remain at work until he should be thus sent for; that this arrangement to bring back the laborers by the cars was made, in order that they might have a longer time to work; that, at evening, the cars were sent accordingly, and Hewins, and the other laborers, who were then at work several miles below, were taken on board the cars and brought back to the station at West Stockbridge; that, when the cars were approaching the station, and making arrangements to run into the place appropriated to them, they were, in consequence of the carelessness and inattention of the switch tender, directed towards and carried to the engine-house, the doors of which were closed; that the cars ran against the doors of the engine-house, stove them in pieces, and entered the house; that the engine was behind the cars, pushing or backing them up on the track and against the doors of the engine-house; that the cars were open or freight cars, and Hewins was sitting on the floor of one of them; that the engineer, seeing the danger, directed those in the cars to clear themselves therefrom; that Hewins, before he could thus clear himself, was thrown from the car in consequence of its striking the door of the engine-house; that, on being thrown off, he fell between the tender and the car, and was run over, and so severely injured and bruised, that he died of his wounds in eighteen or twenty hours afterwards; that Hewins's death was occasioned solely by the injuries so received; that he was the husband of the plaintiff, who was poor, and that, by his death, she was left to provide for herself and the support of three small children.

The judge being of opinion, that if the facts stated were proved, they would not entitle the plaintiff to recover, a verdict was thereupon rendered for the defendants, and the plaintiff filed exceptions.

H. W. Bishop, for the plaintiffs.

I. Sumner, for the defendants.

The second of the above named actions was also an action on the case, brought by the plaintiff for the loss of service of his son, aged about eleven years, who was killed by the cars of the defendants on the 24th day of February, 1847.

At the trial, which was in this court, before Dewey, J., the plaintiff proposed to prove, in order to entitle himself to a verdict, that the death of his son was caused by an accident which took place on the defendants' railroad, by reason of the carelessness or fault of the servants and agents of the defendants.

The case was taken from the jury, by consent, and reserved for the consideration of the whole court, upon the report of the judge.

J. Rockwell and *H. Wheeler*, for the plaintiff.

I. Sumner, for the defendants.

These cases were separately argued, but, presenting a single question only, for the consideration of the court, they were both embraced in the same opinion.

METCALF, J. These actions raise a new question in our jurisprudence. No case was cited, at the argument, in which a like action had been the subject of adjudication, or even of discussion. The case of Huggins *v.* Butcher, 1 Brownl. 205, and Yelv. 89, was referred to, where there is a *dictum* of Tanfield, J., in which Fenner and Yelverton, Js., are said to have concurred, that " if one beat the servant of J. S. so that he die of that beating, the master shall not have an action against the other, for the battery and loss of service, because the servant dying of the extremity of the beating, it is now become an offence against the crown, and turned into felony, and this hath drowned the particular offence, and prevails over the wrong done to the master, and his action by that is gone." This doctrine is also found in most of the digests and abridgments of the English law. But whatever may be the meaning or legal effect of the maxim, that a trespass is merged in a felony, it has no application to the cases now before us. In neither of them was the killing felonious, and there is, therefore, no felony, in which a private injury can merge.

If these actions, or either of them, can be maintained, it must be upon some established principle of the common law. And we might expect to find that principle applied in some adjudged case in the English books; as occasions for its application must have arisen in very many instances. At the least, we might expect to find the principles stated in some elementary treatise of approved authority. None such was cited by counsel; and we cannot find any. This is very strong evidence, though not conclusive, that such actions cannot be supported. But it is not necessary to rely entirely on this negative evidence. For we find it adjudged, in Baker *v.* Bolton and others, 1 Campb. 493, that the death of a human being is not the ground of an action for damages. In that case, the plaintiff brought an action against the proprietors of a stage-coach, which was overturned while he and his wife were travelling in it, whereby he was much bruised, and his wife so severely hurt, that she died about a month after. The declaration alleged, besides other special damage, that "by means of the premises, the plaintiff had wholly lost and been deprived of the comfort, fellowship, and assistance of his said wife, and had from thence hitherto suffered and undergone great grief, vexation, and anguish of mind." Lord Ellenborough held, that the jury could take into consideration only the bruises which the plaintiff had sustained, and the loss of his wife's society, and the distress of mind he had suffered on her account, from the time of the accident to the time of her death. And he announced the principle of his decision, in these words : " In a civil court, the death of a human being cannot be complained of as an injury." Such, then, we cannot doubt, is the doctrine of the common law; and it is decisive against the maintenance of these actions.

We are aware of the case of Ford *v.* Monroe, 20 Wend. 210, in which the plaintiff, in an action tried before, Cowen, J., recovered damages for the negligence of the defendant's servant, in driving a carriage over the plaintiff's son, ten years old, and thereby killing him. One ground of damage, alleged in the declaration, was the loss of the son's service for the period of eleven years ; and the jury were instructed, that the plaintiff was entitled to recover such a sum as the service of the son would have been worth, until he became twenty-one years of age. The case went before the whole court on a motion for a new trial; but no question was there raised, concerning the legal right of the plaintiff to recover damages caused by the killing of his son. For aught that appears in the report, that point was assumed, and passed *sub silentio,* both at the trial and in bank.

The English parliament, by a very recent statute, (9 and 10 Vict. c. 93,) have provided, that whenever the death of a person shall be caused by a wrongful act, neglect, or default, which would, if death had not ensued, have entitled the party injured to maintain an action to recover damages in respect thereof, the person who would have been liable, if death had not ensued, shall be liable to an action for damages, notwithstanding the death of the person injured shall have been caused under such circumstances as amount in law to felony ; such action to be brought within twelve calendar months after such death, by and in the name of the executor or administrator of the person deceased, and to be for the benefit of the wife, husband, parent, and child of the persons whose death shall have been so caused ; and in such action the jury may give such damages, as they may think proportioned to the injury, resulting from such death, to the parties respectively, for whose use such action shall be brought. And by our St. of 1840, c. 80, if the life of any passenger shall be lost by the negligence or carelessness of the proprietors of a railroad, steamboat, stage coach, &c., or of their servants or agents, such proprietors shall be liable to a fine, not exceeding five thousand dollars, nor less than five hundred dollars, to be recovered by indictment, to. the use of the executor or administrator of the deceased person, for the benefit of his widow and heirs.

These statutes are framed on different principles, and for different ends. The English statute gives damages, as such, and proportioned to the injury, to the husband or wife, parents, and children, of any person whose death is caused by the wrongful act, neglect, or default of another person ; adopting, to this extent, the principle on which it has been attempted to support the present actions. Our statute is confined to the death of passengers carried by certain enumerated modes of conveyance. A limited penalty is imposed, as a punishment of carelessness in common-carriers. And as this penalty is to be recovered by indictment, it is doubtless to be greater or smaller, within the prescribed maximum and minimum, according to the degree of blame which attaches to the defendants, and not according to the loss sustained by the widow and heirs of the deceased. The penalty, when thus recovered, is conferred on the widow and heirs, not as damages for their loss, but as a gratuity from the Commonwealth.

We believe that by the civil law, and by the law of France and of Scotland, these actions might be maintained. If such a law would be expedient for us, it is for the legislature to make it.

In the first of these actions, the exceptions are overruled; in the second, the plaintiff is to be nonsuit.[1]

---

[1] In the case of Armsworth v. The South-Eastern R. Co., 11 Jurist, 758, at Nisi Prius, which was an action under the English statute above referred to, Baron Parke instructed the jury that they were first " to determine, according to the ordinary rules of law, whether, if the deceased had been wounded by the accident, and were still living, he could recover compensation in the way of damages against the company for the wound given under the circumstances in evidence in the case." And if they were of opinion that the defendants under this rule were liable, "they must estimate the damages on the same principle as if only a wound had been inflicted."

In Blake v. The Midland R. Co., 10 English Law and Eq. Rep. 437, the question arose in the Queen's Bench, upon the construction of the statute " whether the jury in giving damages apportioned to the

Carey *v.* Berkshire Railroad Co.

injury resulting from the death of the deceased, to the parties for whose benefit the action is brought, are confined to injuries of which a pecuniary estimate may be made, or may add a *solatium* to those parties in respect of the mental suffering occasioned by such death."

The action was brought for the benefit of the widow of the deceased. It was proved that by his death she became entitled to a portion of his estate amounting to 7,000*l.*; that the deceased was in the enjoyment of a yearly income of 850*l.* which for their joint lives was estimated to amount to the sum of 13,188*l.*, leaving a difference of 6,188*l.* between the amount which she received from her husband's estate and the estimated value of his income. The learned judge, however, told the jury that the plaintiff would only have been entitled to be maintained out of her husband's income in her situation in life, and that they must, therefore, consider what portion of the 850*l.* she was entitled to. The judge also instructed the jury that it was for them to consider whether they would confine themselves to the pecuniary loss.

The jury having returned a verdict for 4,000*l.* a new trial was granted on the ground that the judge, at the trial, ought to have explicitly told the jury, that in assessing the damages they could not take into their consideration the mental sufferings of the plaintiff for the loss of her husband; and that as the damages certainly exceeded any loss sustained by her, admitting of a pecuniary estimate, they must be considered as excessive.

The law of Scotland, as to such cases, was fully considered, and the rule there adopted of giving a *solatium* for the mental sufferings of the parties, was held to be inapplicable to the English statute.

The impossibility of apportioning the damages among the parties entitled to receive them, if they were to be based upon the mental sufferings of the parties, was greatly relied upon by the court as indicating the intention of the legislature to confine the damages to the actual pecuniary loss of the sufferers.

The difficulties which surround this question are forcibly pointed out in an article in the London Jurist, vol. 18, part 2, p. 1, a part of which containing a notice of a case at Nisi Prius is here given. " On the 15th of December, 1852, the case of Groves *v.* The London and Brighton R. Co. was tried at Guildhall, in the Court of Common Pleas, before Jervis, C. J. That was an action brought by the executor of the deceased, for the benefit of four infant children. That the deceased had met with his death through the negligence of the defendants' servants was admitted, the only question being the amount of damages. In summing up, the learned chief justice referred to the case of Blake *v.* The London and Brighton R. Co., and told the jury that in assessing the damages they might take into consideration any injury resulting to the children from the loss of the care, protection, and assistance of their father. The jury gave 2,000*l.* Now, if the argument *ab inconvenienti* was permitted to prevail against the allowance of compensation for the mental anguish of the relatives, it ought not, we submit, to be without weight in considering the soundness of this direction. Juries have no small difficulties to contend with in assessing damages when they have before them evidence of the average profits, or the amount of the life income of the deceased; but these are but trifling to those in which they must become entangled in attempting a *pecuniary* estimate of the loss of the care, protection, and assistance of a father. In whatever light we look at the subject, either of money or morals, we become perplexed in the attempt to pursue it. It is conceived that in such cases evidence may be given of the character of the deceased, and in many cases, this would doubtless be of a most painful nature.

" Moreover, serious, practical difficulties would arise. Let us suppose, that, through the negligence of a pointsman — in the belief of his employers a trustworthy servant — an accident happens to a train containing the six following fathers: — An archbishop, a lord chancellor, an East

PITTSFIELD AND NORTH ADAMS RAILROAD CORPORATION, Petitioners, *v.* SARAH FOSTER.[1]

Berkshire Co., September Term, 1848.

*Assessment of Damages — Practice — Certificate of Proceedings by
Sheriff and Coroner.*

Where proceedings for the assessment, by a jury, of damages for land taken by a railroad
corporation, are conducted in part by a coroner, under the Rev. Sts. c. 24, § 23, and in
part by the sheriff, it is the duty of each of those officers to certify the proceedings
which take place before him ; and, in such a case, where the coroner presides, it is no
objection to the verdict, that the jury are not attended by a deputy sheriff.

IN this case, which was a proceeding under the authority of the
county commissioners for the county of Berkshire, for the assessment
by a jury of the damages sustained by the respondent, for land

---

India director, a lunatic, a wealthy but
immoral man, and one virtuous but a
bankrupt. It is needless to dilate on the
difficulties which juries would experience
if called upon to estimate the pecuniary
value of the parental care, protection, and
assistance of each of these."

The above case in the text would, we
conceive, have admitted of another defence, viz., that the accident which caused
the death of the plaintiff's husband was
occasioned by the negligence of a fellow
servant in the same general employment.
The English courts have admitted this
defence in actions under their statute,
though in the case above referred to,
of Armsworth v. The South-Eastern R.
Co., which was the first case which arose,
and which was the case of a servant of the
company killed by the negligence of a
fellow servant, the objection was not raised.
But the rule which Baron Parke laid
down in his charge to the jury, that the
action must be governed by the same principles as though the deceased party had
only been wounded, and had himself
brought the action to recover for his personal injuries, would open to the defendant in such a case, the defence that the
accident was caused by the negligence of a
fellow servant. Accordingly, in Hutchinson v. The York, Newcastle, &c., R. Co.
6 Eng. Rail. Ca. 580, the objection was
taken and held to be a valid defence. So,
also, in Wigmore v. Jay, Ibid. 589. And in
Thorogood v. Bryan, 8 Com. B. Rep. 115,
the court held it to be a good defence to
an action under the statute, against the
owners of a line of omnibuses, for running
against the plaintiff's husband, and killing
him, that the death of the deceased party
was caused by the negligence of the driver
of a rival coach in which the deceased
was a party. In short, it seems that any
defence is open to the company which
would have been available if the deceased
party had merely been wounded, and had
brought the action in his own name for the
personal injury.

[1] 1 Cushing's Reports, 480.

belonging to her which had been taken by the petitioners for the purposes of their road, it appeared, that the warrant was directed to the
sheriff of the county of Berkshire or his deputy, (the sheriff being
appointed therein to preside at the trial,) and was executed by the
sheriff, as to every thing required to be done under and by virtue of
the same, previous to the time appointed for the attendance of the
jurors; that the sheriff was unable to attend on that day from sickness or some other cause; and that the jury were impanelled, and all
the subsequent proceedings under the warrant conducted, by a coroner
of the county of Berkshire, by whom the execution of the warrant
was duly certified, and the same, together with the verdict of the
jury, returned to the Court of Common Pleas.

The petitioners objected to the receiving of the verdict, and moved
that it be set aside, on the ground, that the return was made by the
coroner, instead of the sheriff or his deputy, and that it did not appear,
that the jury was attended either by the sheriff or his deputy. The
court overruled the objections, and accepted the verdict; and the
petitioners filed exceptions.

H. W. Bishop, for the petitioners.

H. Byington, for the respondent.

DEWEY, J. The warrant for the county commissioners was directed
to the sheriff, and by him the jury were properly summoned. All the
proceedings previous to the time when the coroner was called upon
to act, by reason of the necessary absence of the sheriff, are properly
certified by the latter. The subsequent proceedings, which took
place before the coroner, so far as it is the duty of the presiding
officer to certify them, and the return on the warrant, are to be certified by the coroner.

It is no valid objection to a verdict of a jury, where the coroner
presides at the hearing by the jury, that the jury were not attended
by a deputy sheriff. We see no ground for objecting to the acceptance of this verdict.

Judgment of the Common Pleas affirmed.

THE CONNECTICUT RIVER RAILROAD COMPANY *v.* EBENEZER CLAPP.[1]

Hampshire Co., September Term, 1848.

Assessment of Damages — Uncertainty of Verdict — Interest — Costs — Practice, Right to Open and Close.

Where a jury, summoned to reassess damages for land taken for a railroad, rendered a verdict, in which they assessed the damages at a certain sum, " with interest thereon from the time when the said railroad company took possession of the land," it was held, that the verdict was void for uncertainty, and that the Court of Common Pleas had no authority to alter the same, or to supply any defect therein.

Qn the hearing before a jury summoned to reassess damages for taking land for a railroad, the party claiming damages has the right to open and close.

Where the Court of Common Pleas set aside a verdict of a jury, summoned to reassess damages for land taken for a railroad, they have no authority to award costs to the party objecting to the verdict.

THE county commissioners of Hampshire having estimated the damages of Ebenezer Clapp, of Hatfield, caused by the taking of his land for the location and construction of the road of the Connecticut River Railroad Company, the company, on the 2d of March, 1847, feeling aggrieved at the proceedings of the commissioners therein, requested them to cause a jury to be summoned for the purpose of reassessing the damages. A warrant was accordingly issued, in pursuance of which a jury was summoned and impanelled, who, on the 23d of June, 1847, after hearing the case and viewing the premises, rendered a verdict assessing the damages at " five hundred and seventy-five dollars, with interest thereon from the time when the said railroad company took possession of the land."

The verdict being returned into the Court of Common Pleas, at the October term, 1847, the petitioners moved that it be accepted for the sum of five hundred and seventy-five dollars.

The respondent moved that it be set aside : 1st, because it is in its terms uncertain and therefore insufficient ; 2d, because the officer presiding at the hearing before the jury ruled, that the petitioners had the right to open and close, and the hearing proceeded accordingly.

The Court of Common Pleas ordered the verdict to be set aside, for the reasons stated, and rendered judgment for costs in favor of the respondent against the petitioners; who, thereupon, appealed to this court.

C. P. Huntington, for the petitioners.

The statute of 1847, 259, which went into operation on the 24th of May, 1847, gives a right to lawful interest on the damages, as well as to costs.

1. The verdict is for five hundred and seventy-five dollars with interest thereon from the time when the petitioners took possession of the land. This is sufficiently certain in terms. Merrill *v.* Berkshire, 11 Pick. 269; Hodges *v.* Hodges, 5 Met. 205. The time of taking possession, from which the interest is to be computed, is the time of filing the location. Charlestown B. R. Co. *v.* County Commissioners, 7 Met. 78; s. c. *ante,* 383. And the interest may be computed accordingly. The location is to be filed with the commissioners, and the verdict is to be certified to them. They can compute the interest and render it certain. But if the verdict be defective in this respect, it may be remedied by rejecting a part of it. Lincoln *v.* Hapgood, 11 Mass. 358. Or the interest may be considered as a part of the damages. If the verdict be set aside for this cause, the case ought to be opened only as to the question of interest. A verdict may be void in part, and good in part. Winn *v.* Columbian Ins. Co., 12 Pick. 279; Boyd *v.* Brown, 17 Pick. 453; Robbins *v.* Townsend, 20 Pick. 345; Sprague *v.* Bailey, 19 Pick. 436, 442.

2. The petitioners, being the aggrieved party, were entitled to open and close. They have many affirmative facts to show, in the first instance; and the practice is, that they go forward. There is no reason why the same rule should not apply in this as in other cases. Ayer *v.* Austin, 6 Pick. 225.

C. Delano, for the respondent.

The statute of 1847 was enacted subsequently to the commencement of this proceeding and cannot affect it.

1. The verdict is so uncertain that it cannot be enforced without some further inquiry. It stands, in this respect, upon the footing of an award; and an award is void, if it require any further hearing. Billing on Awards, 130; Hewitt *v.* Hewitt, 1 Ad. & El. N. S. 110; Com. Dig. Arbit. E. 11; Lincoln *v.* Whittenton Mills, 12 Met. 31. The question, then, is whether this verdict involves any new inquiry. The interest is a part of the damages, and as it is to be assessed from a particular time, that time is a fact to be established like any other. The taking possession of the land is the time from which interest is to run. Does this mean the filing of the location, or the taking of actual possession? This question must be decided upon

by some competent tribunal; and thus some further inquiry is necessary to render the verdict certain.

2. It is important in cases of this kind, that the strict rules of practice should be observed. Who is the actor ? Who sets up the claim?
Is it the petitioners or the respondent ? Have the petitioners any
thing to answer, until something is made out on the other side?
Damages are not to be presumed in the outset. The rule is universal, that in inquiries as to damages, the actor goes forward. 1 Arch.
N. P. Int. 4, 5 ; 1 Greenl. Ev. §§ 75, 76, 77 ; Mercer v. Whall, 5 Ad:
& Ell. N. S. 447, where the rule is laid down by Lord Denman. The
form of the issue is not to be looked at so much as the substance.
The case is precisely analogous to an appeal. If there has been any
mistake in this point, the respondent is entitled to a new trial. Davis
v. Mason, 4 Pick. 156; Ayer v. Austin, 6 Pick. 225; Robinson v.
Hitchcock, 8 Met. 64.

Huntington, in reply.

It is said, that the statute of 1847 is not applicable to the case,
because it was not passed, until after these proceedings were commenced. The answer is, that the statute is remedial. But, in fact,
the present petition was commenced after the passing of the act.

As to the other point; — the respondent had had his damages
awarded and was satisfied. The petitioners undertook to show, that
the amount was excessive. To do this they must go forward. If
they had any thing to do, in the first instance, they were entitled to
open and close.

WILDE, J. This case comes before us on an appeal from the
judgment of the Court of Common Pleas. On the application of the
petitioners to the county commissioners, for a jury to reassess the
damages on the location and construction of a railroad over and
across the respondent's lands, a warrant was issued to summon a
jury for that purpose, who were duly summoned, as the law directs,
and who, after hearing the parties, returned their verdict to the
Court of Common Pleas, who, after hearing the parties, ordered and
decreed, in the premises, that the verdict of the jury should be set
aside, and that the respondent recover his costs of suit.

The Court of Common Pleas, as we understand, set aside the verdict for two reasons: 1st, because the verdict was uncertain, the
same being for a certain sum, with interest from the time when the
petitioners took possession of the respondent's land; 2d, because the
officer who presided at the hearing before the jury, erroneously ruled
that the petitioners had the right to open and close, and that the
hearing proceeded accordingly.

The counsel for the petitioners contends, that the verdict is sufficiently certain, as the Court of Common Pleas were authorized to compute the interest and add it to the sum assessed. But we think the court were not so authorized by the Rev. Sts. c. 24.·. By the thirtyfourth section, the court are authorized to receive the verdict, and adjudicate thereon, or to set it aside for good cause ; and by the thirtyseventh section, if the verdict be accepted and recorded by the court, it is to be conclusive on the parties to the proceedings; but the court are not authorized to alter the verdict, or to supply any defect therein, by any provision in the revised statutes. It is, however, argued, that this authority is given by the statute of 1847, c. 259, § 3, which provides that the county·commissioners may issue warrants of distress, to compel the payment of the damages assessed by the commissioners, or by the verdict of a jury, together with costs and lawful interest. But the power thus given by the statute is not sufficient to cure the defect in the verdict. If the Court of Common Pleas had rejected that part of the verdict relating to interest, and had so certified the verdict to the county commissioners, the commissioners would not be authorized to compute any interest before the return of the verdict, or before the time when the verdict was given ; whereas the jury intended that the interest should be computed from the time when the petitioners took possession of the respondent's land. We are of opinion, that the statute of 1847 cannot be so construed as to authorize the commissioners to compute interest, before the assessment of the damages, upon which the computation is to be made. Another decisive objection to such a computation of interest is, that the commissioners have no authority to ascertain the time when the petitioners took possession of the respondent's land. That was a fact for the jury to find.

As to the other ground of objection to the verdict, it seems to us quite clear, that the ruling of the presiding officer at the trial was erroneous. In cases where a reassessment of damages is to be made by a jury, after an assessment has been made by the commissioners, it is immaterial which party makes the application for such reassessment. The party claiming damages, the same being unliquidated, and to be settled by the jury, has the right of opening and closing the cause. 1 Greenl. Ev. §§ 76, 77 ; Mercer v. Whall, 5 Ad. & Ell. 447. In this case, the rule is, as we think, correctly laid down by Lord Denman, and is decisive as to the present case. " Wherever," he says, " from the state of the record at Nisi Prius, there is any thing to be proved by the plaintiff, whether as to the facts necessary for his obtaining a verdict, or as to the amount of damages, the plaintiff is entitled to begin." But where the *onus probandi* lies in the first instance on the defendant, he is entitled to begin. Wootton v. Barton, 1 Mood. & Rob. 518. So, in Davis v. Mason, 4 Pick. 156, it was decided, that where in trespass the defendant pleads soil and freehold in himself, without any other plea, and the issue is joined thereon, the right of opening and closing the argument before the jury belongs to the defendant. But it would have been otherwise, if the defendant had likewise pleaded the general issue. These latter cases obviously have no bearing on the present question. The only question for the jury in this case was a question of damages, which they were bound to assess without any regard to the previous assessment by the commissioners. There seems, therefore, no reason for allowing the petitioners to open and close. The result is, that the order of the Court of Common Pleas setting aside the verdict is affirmed, and the judgment for the respondent for costs is disaffirmed. The allowance of costs was premature; the court should have ordered a certificate of their adjudication to be transmitted to the county commissioners, in order that the petitioners might make application, if they should think fit, for a warrant to summon a new jury; as the law directs. Rev. Sts. c. 24, § 36.

Such a certificate of the adjudication of this court is to be transmitted to the county commissioners with the papers for further proceedings.

———◆———

JOSHUA MORSS v. THE BOSTON & MAINE RAILROAD.[1]

Essex Co., November Term, 1848.

Assessment of Damages — Obligation to Maintain Fences — Evidence.

Where county commissioners, in assessing damages for land taken for a railroad before the Act of 1841, c. 125, was passed, awarded a sum of money to be paid to the complainant, and also provided that the proprietors of the road should make and maintain certain fences for his benefit, and such complainant appealed from the award of the commissioners to a jury, who assessed damages in his favor, but made no order in their verdict as to the fences, it was held, that the proprietors of the road were under no legal obligation to make and maintain fences, agreeably to the award of the commissioners.

If, on a hearing before a jury for the assessment of damages for land taken for a railroad, it is agreed between the parties, that the proprietors of the road shall make and maintain fences against the owner of the land taken, along the line of the road, such agreement, if

———

[1] 2 Cushing's Reports, 536.

valid, can only be enforced against the proprietors of the road, in an action by the party with whom it is made, and not by any subsequent purchaser of the estate to which it relates. The fact, that the proprietors of a railroad have erected fences along the line of their road, against the land of a particular individual, is not of itself evidence of any obligation on the part of the proprietors to make or maintain fences for the benefit of such person.

THIS was an action on the case, to recover damages of the defendants, for an injury sustained by the plaintiff, by reason of the defendants' negligence in not making and maintaining a fence against the plaintiff's land, on the line of their railroad in Andover. The injury alleged was the loss of the plaintiff's cow, which was killed on the track of the defendants' road, by one of their locomotives.

It appeared, on the trial, which was before · Wells, C. J., in the Court of Common Pleas, that the cow escaped from the plaintiff's land, in consequence, as the plaintiff alleged, of a defect in certain fences which the defendants were bound to make and maintain, and got upon the track of the road, where she was struck by a locomotive and killed.   •

It was in evidence, on the part of the plaintiff, that, at the time of the location of the defendants' road, the plaintiff's land belonged to one Wardwell, who applied to the county commissioners to assess the damages to which he was entitled for the location; that the commissioners awarded him a sum in damages, and provided also in their award, that the defendants should make and maintain the fences ; and that an appeal was taken from this award to a jury, who assessed damages, but made no order in their verdict on the subject of the fences.

The plaintiff offered to prove, that, at the time of the hearing before the jury, it was understood and agreed by the petitioner and the defendants, both acting by their counsel, that the defendants should build and maintain the fences on both sides of their railroad, and that no damages were claimed or allowed by the jury to the petitioner for fences.

The plaintiff also offered to prove, that, in consequence of the agreement above mentioned, the defendants had made the fences along the line of their road, and that they fenced against the land of the plaintiff, along the line of the road, wholly on the one side and partly on the other, but that the fence was temporary on one side, and that at the part of the road where the alleged negligence existed, there was a high and steep embankment, which the defendants had not fenced at the time of the accident; that the defendants had at that time furnished materials for a fence to be built at the place in question, and had such materials on the ground, but no fence had been built; and that the defendants, by their agent, employed by their superintendent, who was authorized by a vote of the defendants to build the fences along the line of the road, both before and after the time of the accident, had promised and agreed to make the fence.

The court ruled, that a parol agreement to make the fences was inadmissible in evidence, and that the evidence offered as above was incompetent, and insufficient to charge the defendants with the duty of building or maintaining the fences.

The jury returned a verdict for the defendants, and the plaintiff alleged exceptions.

The case was submitted at a former term, without argument, by *N. J. Lord*, for the plaintiff, and *G. Minot*, for the defendants.

SHAW, C. J.[1]   The only question in the present case is, whether it was the duty of the defendants to make and maintain fences on the plaintiff's land, along the line of their railroad.   The action is on the case, for negligence, in not making and repairing such a fence; by means of which, as the plaintiff alleges, his cow escaped from his own land, and got upon the track of the railroad, and was killed by a locomotive engine.

It is not stated at what time this railroad was laid out, but we assume, that it was laid out prior to the year 1841.   By a statute passed in that year, (St. 1841, c. 125,) it was provided, that the county commissioners, in estimating damages for land taken for a railroad, might direct that fences and other structures should be built and maintained by the proprietors of the railroad, in relief of the owners of the land, and that such direction should not be altered or changed by the verdict of a jury.   But no such requisition, in terms, previously existed; and, assuming, as we do, that this road was laid out, and the damages assessed prior to the year 1841, the rights and duties of the parties must depend upon the preexisting provisions of the revised statutes.   If it was then competent for commissioners to direct fences, culverts, or bridges, to be made and maintained, it was in pursuance of their general authority to provide indemnity for the land-owner; and such fences and other structures might often afford a more adequate and permanent indemnity, than an award of damages in money.   But, as the law then stood, when an application for a jury was made and allowed, the whole question of damages was open for their consideration, and the order of the commissioners, directing the building of fences, as well as that for the payment of

---

[1] Wilde, J., did not sit in this cause.

money, was vacated and annulled; and not being reinstated by the
jury, the order remained void, and the necessary inference is, that the
whole damage was assessed in money. No duty, therefore, was
imposed upon the corporation by that proceeding, to build or repair
fences.

We are of opinion that the offer of parol evidence to prove that it
was understood and agreed, before the jury, that such fences should
be made, was rightly rejected. If such parol promise, made by persons authorized, and on good consideration, were available at all, it
could only be enforced in an action by the person to whom it was
made. But to allow it in this case, would be to give it the effect of
a covenant running with the land, to be enforced by any subsequent
owner.

The fact, that the corporation had placed fences on the plaintiff's
land, along the line of the track, affords no evidence of a duty, on
their part, in favor of the plaintiff, to make and maintain such fences;
the defendants may have done what they did for the better security
of their own trains, or for the safety of their conductors and passengers.

Exceptions overruled.

———◆———

GEORGE BRADLEY *v.* THE BOSTON AND MAINE RAILROAD.[1]

Essex Co., November Term, 1848.

*Negligence — Care in Running Engines — Observance of Statute
Regulations.*

The proprietors of railroads, when running their engines over crossings, are bound to exert
reasonable care and diligence, to prevent injury therefrom to travellers on the road crossed;
and whether such care and diligence have been employed in a particular case, is a question of fact, to be decided by the jury, upon all the circumstances.

A compliance with the provisions of the Rev. Sts. c. 39, §§ 78, 79, respecting the putting up
of notices at railroad crossings, and the ringing of a bell when engines are passing over
the same, will not exempt the proprietors of a railroad from their obligation to use reasonable care and diligence, in other respects, when running their engines over crossings, if the
circumstances of the case render the use of other precautions reasonable.

THIS was an action on the case, to recover damages of the defend-

———

[1] 2 Cushing's Reports, 539.

ants, for an injury sustained by the plaintiff, in consequence of collision, at a crossing, with a locomotive engine, driven by the servant
of the defendants.

At the trial, which was before Wells, C. J., in the Court of Common Pleas, it was in evidence, that the engine which occasioned the
damage had been recently repaired, and was being proved at the time
of the collision; that the regular train had passed the crossing just
before the collision took place; and that, from the formation of the
ground, and an interposing growth of wood, a bell, if rung according
to the provisions of the Rev. Sts. c. 39, § 78, could not be heard by a
person approaching the crossing by the road on which the plaintiff
came upon it.

The defendants contended that they were bound only to the exercise of ordinary care, and they offered to prove, that they used as
much care as those having charge of engines usually exercised in
passing railroad crossings; but the judge ruled, that such proof
would not of itself amount to a justification; and, in relation to
the care which the defendants were bound to exercise, instructed the
jury as follows:—

"That the defendants were bound to exercise reasonable care in
passing over crossings with their engines; that if railroads had
existed for so long a time that a practice or usage had prevailed,
settling what was proper and reasonable care to be observed at
crossings, the care ordinarily observed would be the test of reasonable
care; but, in consideration of the recent introduction of the use of
railroads, the proper course for the jury, in the present case, would be
to decide from their own judgment, whether, in view of all the circumstances of the case, and the explanatory evidence, a reasonable
care had been exercised by the defendants."

The testimony of persons experienced in the management of locomotive engines, giving their opinion as to whether the evidence
showed that reasonable care had been used in the present case, and
what was the proper method of managing engines at crossings, was
admitted without objection.

The defendants further contended, that if they had complied with
the provisions of the Rev. Sts. c. 39, § 78, in relation to notices, &c.,
they were not liable for any damage which might occur from
collisions at crossings, unless they were guilty of gross negligence. But the judge ruled, that a compliance with these regulations did not excuse the defendants from the use of the requisite
care, when circumstances rendered it reasonable for them to take
other precautions in order to prevent a collision.

The plaintiff contended, that the place where the collision occurred, from its dangerous situation, was an unsuitable one for proving an engine; and, as the bell could not be heard at that place, that the whistle should have been sounded; but the court left it to the jury to say, whether, in either of these particulars, the conduct of the defendants showed a want of reasonable care.

The jury returned a verdict for the plaintiff, and the defendants thereupon alleged exceptions to the several rulings and instructions above mentioned.

O. P. Lord, for the defendants.

N. J. Lord, for the plaintiff.

SHAW, C. J.[1] The nature of the plaintiff's injury does not appear by the bill of exceptions, but it is stated to have been caused by a collision with a locomotive engine in use under the care of a servant of the defendants.

The facts not being reported, we are only called upon to consider the rulings and directions of the court.

The defendants contended, that they were bound to exercise only ordinary care; and they offered to prove, that they had used as much care as those having charge of engines usually exercise, in passing railroad crossings.

But the court ruled that this proof (that is, proof of such care as those having charge of engines usually exercise) would not of itself amount to a justification, in relation to the care which the defendants were bound to exercise; but instructed the jury, that the defendants were bound to exercise reasonable care and diligence in passing over crossings with their engines; that if what was reasonable care at crossings had become established by usage, the care ordinarily observed would be the test of reasonable care; but, inasmuch as railroads were of recent introduction, and no such usage had become established, the jury would decide upon their own judgment, in view of all the circumstances, and the explanatory evidence in the case, whether the defendants had exercised reasonable care.

In the first place, the instruction prayed for, we think, in the terms in which it was expressed, could not properly be given. It assumed, that it was only the duty of the defendants to employ as much diligence as those having charge of engines usually exercised; not such diligence as engineers of ordinary skill and experience exerted.

---

[1] Wilde, J., did not sit in this cause.

But supposing the latter to be the rule intended by the prayer for instructions, it would not be correct. The true question is, whether the defendants used reasonable diligence, that is, the care and diligence which, taking into consideration all the circumstances of the case, the exigency required. It often happens, that the one of these propositions is equivalent to the other; as, where a practice has long existed, the course which has commonly been pursued by persons of ordinary skill and care will be usually the same as that which is reasonable, and will be the evidence and measure of what is reasonable. So, where horses, wheel carriages, boats, and vessels have been in use from time immemorial, what is commonly practised may be regarded as reasonable. But whether a party has been negligent or not, depends upon so many different circumstances, and the circumstances of each particular case may be so peculiar and unlike all other cases, that proof of usage would not apply. And so the judge directed, and, we think, rightly, that if railroads had existed so long, &c., usual care would be a proper test; but in consideration of the recent introduction of railroads, the question of proper care, &c., was for the jury to decide. This direction could not be considered as deciding upon a question of fact; it was reasoning from a fact, not contested, and assumed as one which was not questionable. It was a question depending on all the circumstances, regard being had to the relative positions of the roads, the intervening obstructions, the time of day or night, the weight and velocity of the engine; and what were reasonable and proper precautions, and the fact of negligence, were rightly left to the jury upon all the circumstances in proof. Wayde v. Carr, 2 Dow. & R. 255; Lynch v. Nurdin, 1 Ad. & Ell. N. S. 29.

It was further contended, that if the defendants had complied with the provisions of law, requiring a board to be placed at crossings, and a bell to be rung, (Rev. Sts. c. 39, §§ 78, 79,) they were not liable for any damage which might occur from collisions at crossings, unless they were guilty of gross negligence. But the court ruled otherwise, and directed that a compliance with these regulations would not exempt them from the obligation of using reasonable care in other respects, when the circumstances rendered it reasonable to use other precautions.

The statute makes certain positive regulations, and the defendants, at their peril, are bound to comply with them; but there are no negative words, and there is no implication that a compliance was to absolve them from any duty which they were under before; and, therefore, if other precautions were necessary, the defendants were still bound to take them.

In the case first above cited, it was held, that where the driver was on the wrong side of the road, if the circumstances were such as to justify it, the driver was not liable; and it was left to the jury, as a question of fact, upon all the circumstances, including that of being on the wrong side of the road, whether the defendant was chargeable with negligence.

So, whether, under the circumstances, if the bell of the locomotive could not be heard, it was the duty of the engineer to sound the whistle, we think it was rightly left to the jury whether reasonable precautions had been taken to give such notice as would prevent collision; the fitness of any particular expedient suggested depending upon the exigency of the case. Lack *v.* Seward, 4 C. & P. 106; Pluckwell *v.* Wilson, 5 C. & P. 375; Boss *v.* Litton, 5 C. & P. 407. And so, whether the place and the time and occasion were fit for trying a newly-repaired engine, was a question of fact rightly left to the jury.

The evidence is not reported, and we are not to presume that the jury found a verdict against the defendants, without proof of actual negligence and want of ordinary care, in the use of the road and of the engine. The defendants had a right to run their engines on the road at all times, for all suitable and proper purposes, using proper care not to interfere with the equal right of travellers to use the road crossed. On these grounds, the court are of opinion, that the directions of the judge at the trial were right, and that judgment be entered on the verdict.

Exceptions overruled.[1]

---

[1] The position here taken by the court, as to the observance of the requirements of a statute prescribing certain precautions against accidents, is sustained by the recent cases of The General Steam Navigation Co. *v.* Morrison, 20 Eng. Law and Eq. Rep. 267, and Morrison *v.* The General Steam Navigation Co., Ibid. 455; and also by Parker *v.* Adams, 12 Metcalf, 455.

In the latter case, which was one of a collision of carriages on the highway, it appeared that the defendant was on the wrong side of the road at the time of the accident. The defence was the negligence of the plaintiff himself. The plaintiff contended that he was entitled to maintain the action, notwithstanding his own negligence, by virtue of the provisions of the statute requiring parties to keep to the right of the highway, and making every person offending against the requirement liable for all damages sustained thereby. But the court held, that the common-law rule as to the duty of parties to exercise reasonable care to avoid an injury was not changed by the statute, and that a person whose own negligence had contributed to an injury, was no more entitled to recover for a violation of a statute, than for a violation of a common-law duty. In the case of The General Steam Navigation Co. *v.* Morrison, the declaration alleged a breach of the statute by the defendant in not exhibiting a light upon his vessel as required, whereby the plaintiff's vessel came

LUCY J. WALKER *v.* THE BOSTON AND MAINE RAILROAD.[1]

Middlesex Co., October Term, 1849.

Assessment of Damages — Objections to Proceedings of Jury — Qualifications of Jurors — Exceptions and Appeal — Warrant for a Jury — Setting Aside Verdict — Want of Notice — Rule of Damages in Respect to Flats Appurtenant to the Sea.

Objections to the proceedings before a sheriff's jury, impanelled to assess damages for land taken for a highway or railroad, — that the respondent had no notice of the application to the commissioners for a jury, — or that three disinterested commissioners were not present as required by the Rev. Sts. c. 14, § 27, — or that there were other cases of the same kind, which ought to have gone to the same jury, — cannot be taken advantage of on appeal, unless the grounds of such objections appear on the record; and it is not enough, that it does not appear, by the record, that the party had notice, — or that the business was determined by disinterested commissioners, or by consent, — or that there were other like cases which were put to the same jury.

If some of the jurors, summoned on a sheriff's jury, to assess damages for land taken for a railroad, are drawn from the town in which the land lies, this is an objection to those jurors only, and not to the others, and must be taken at the time the jury is impanelled; in which case, the sheriff may set aside the jurors so disqualified, and fill their places with others; but if the respondent proceed to trial, without taking the exception, it will be considered as waived, and cannot afterwards be taken on appeal to this court. (See Davidson *v.* Boston and Maine Railroad, *post.*)

Where flats appurtenant or incident to upland are taken for a railroad, the Commonwealth has no interest therein by way of easement, which requires the damages for taking the same to be assessed in the manner provided by the Rev. Sts. c. 24, §§ 48, 49, 50, where

---

into the defendant's vessel, and was injured. The court held, that this was insufficient, as the defendant might have, consistently with the allegations of the plaintiff, used abundance of other precautions, or the plaintiff himself might have been guilty of negligence. In the other case, which was a cross action by Morrison against the company, the court held, that no change had been made in the law by the Admiralty regulations in respect to the duties of parties in avoiding collisions, and that the common-law obligation to exercise reasonable care remained unaffected.

These cases are the converse of the above case in the text. In that the ob-

servance of the statute requirements was set up as a justification or excuse for not taking other precautions. In the other cases the neglect by the defendants to comply with the requirements was made the ground of liability, or was charged upon the plaintiffs as an excuse for the defendant's negligence. But the cases equally show that the common-law duties of parties as to the exercise of reasonable care in the avocations of life, to avoid injuring others, are not changed by statute regulations prescribing particular precautions. The case of Coe *v.* Platt, 18 Eng. Law and Eq. Rep. 505, appears also to sustain the same position.

[1] 3 Cushing's Reports, 1.

there are several parties having several estates or interests, at the same time, in the land taken.

If a party, aggrieved by the adjudication of the Court of Common Pleas, upon the acceptance or rejection of the verdict of a sheriff's jury, desire to bring his case before this court, upon questions of law, which do not appear in the warrant, the verdict, the sheriff's return, (including his instructions and directions to the jury,) or in the judgment of the court, this can only be done by a bill of exceptions; unless the court specify in their adjudication, as they may do, the grounds on which they accept or set aside the verdict; in which case, as well as in the former, the ground of the judgment becomes apparent on the record.

The provision of the Rev. Sts. c. 39, § 57, that a party dissatisfied with the estimate of damages made by county commissioners, for land taken for a railroad, may apply to the commissioners for a jury to assess the damages, either at the same meeting at which the estimate is completed and returned, or at the next regular meeting thereafter, limits the time within which the application must be made, but not the time within which it must be acted upon.

The warrant issued by county commissioners, on the application of an owner of land, for a jury to assess damages for land taken for a railroad, need not be in any particular form; but it should set forth, with sufficient certainty, the subject-matter into which the jury are to inquire, to wit, the land over which the railroad passes, — the petitioner's title to, or interest in it, — the location of the road, — and the incidental damages, if any, which the petitioner sustained, in addition to the value of the land taken; and this may be done either by reciting the substance of the petition in the warrant, or by annexing a copy of the petition thereto, and referring to the same in the warrant.

In adjudicating upon the verdict of a sheriff's jury the power of the Court of Common Pleas is not defined, but they are authorized to set the verdict aside for good cause; which may be either some irregularity or error apparent in the proceedings, as in the impanelling of the jury, or other conduct of the sheriff, or in his instructions and directions to the jury; or some fact affecting the purity, honesty, or impartiality of the verdict, such as tampering with jurors, or other misconduct of a party, or any irregularity or misconduct of the jurors, which fact may be brought to the knowledge of the court by evidence *aliunde;* but whether the Court of Common Pleas can set aside such a verdict, on the ground that the warrant issued improvidently, or without legal authority, or that the verdict is without or against evidence, or against the weight of evidence, has not been decided, and the court give no opinion.

If the Court of Common Pleas are called upon to set aside the verdict of a sheriff's jury on the ground that the respondent had not due notice of the application to the commissioners for the jury, the objection cannot be substantiated by showing that such notice does not appear by the warrant, the return, or the record of the commissioners; for it may, notwithstanding, be proved by evidence *aliunde,* that the respondent was summoned, or consented to take notice without summons, or, in fact, appeared before the commissioners.

The decisions of the Court of Common Pleas, upon questions of fact arising on the acceptance or rejection of the verdict of a sheriff's jury, are final, and cannot be reëxamined in this court on appeal; but the decisions of that court, upon questions of law arising on facts admitted or proved, may be revised in this court on appeal, provided the ground of the decision appear on the record, either as a part of the formal proceedings, or by a bill of exceptions, or otherwise.

The power of the Court of Common Pleas, in adjudicating upon the acceptance or rejection of the verdict of a sheriff's jury, is much more extensive than the power of this court, on an appeal from their adjudication; that court may set aside the verdict for any good cause; this court can only examine their judgment, to see if there is any error therein apparent on the record.

An appeal to this court, from a judgment of the Court of Common Pleas, accepting or rejecting the verdict of a sheriff's jury, for the assessment for damages for land taken for a railroad, is a summary proceeding, provided as a substitute for a writ of error in ordinary cases; and, upon such appeal, the adjudication of the Court of Common Pleas is to

be construed with the same liberality, as to defects of form and amendments, as is applicable to writs of error and proceedings on *certiorari*, and the case is to be considered in the
same manner, as if formally brought before the court by a writ of *certiorari*.

When an application is made to the county commissioners, for an assessment by a jury of
damages for land taken for a railroad, the party, against whom the application is made, is
entitled to notice thereof from the county commissioners; but in order that the objection of
a want of notice may be taken advantage of on an appeal, it must appear on the record,
that the party had not due notice of the pendency of the petition, before the warrant issued;
and it is not sufficient, that no averment appears on the record, that notice was given;
there being no occasion, in the proceedings before the commissioners, that the giving of
the notice should so appear.

Where a cove, inlet, or estuary, is so irregular and various in outline, and so traversed by
crooked and meandering creeks and channels, from which the sea does not ebb, that, in
dividing the flats therein among the conterminous proprietors, it is impossible to apply
any of the rules, which have been applied in other cases; the most that can be done is,
to take the colony ordinance of 1641, and apply it according to its true spirit, and, by
as near an approximation as practicable to the rules which have been judicially established to lay down such a line of division, as to give to each riparian proprietor his fair
and equal share.

A natural channel or creek, in which the sea ebbs and flows, and from which the tide does
not ebb, is a boundary to a claim of flats in that direction.

On the estuary of a river, or arm of the sea, through which there is a channel, the lines of
flats will ordinarily run towards such channel, and in the most direct course.

The purpose of the colony ordinance of 1641 was not so much to promote the erection of
wharves, and to facilitate navigation, as to declare the right of private owners in the soil of
the flats, between high and low water.

[The application of the rules, regulating the division of flats among conterminous proprietors, made in this case, can only be understood by a reference to the map.]

ON the 16th of March, 1844, the legislature of this Commonwealth established a corporation (St. 1844, c. 172,) by the name of
the Boston and Maine Railroad Extension Company, for the purpose of constructing a railroad beginning at a convenient point in
the Boston and Maine Railroad, near its junction with the Boston
and Lowell Railroad, and terminating in the public square at the
easterly end of Haverhill and Canal streets, in Boston. The route
prescribed in the act of incorporation, from the point where it was
directed to cross the Mystic River, by a bridge near Malden Bridge,
is thus described: " thence passing near the Mill Pond, at the outlet
of the Middlesex Canal, at least one fourth of a mile from the
M'Lean Asylum, by the way of Somerville or Charlestown, to a
point on the Charlestown Branch Railroad, near their engine-house in
Charlestown: *provided* it shall not cross the Charlestown Branch
Railroad, at any point east of the State Prison, without the assent
of the directors of the Charlestown Branch Railroad Corporation;
thence crossing Charles River by a bridge, above Warren Bridge, to
the city of Boston, between Haverhill street and Canal street; and
thence between said streets, to the public square, at the easterly end
of said streets." The corporation thus established was invested with

all the powers and privileges, and subjected to all the duties, liabilities, and restrictions, contained in the forty-fourth chapter of the revised statutes, relating to corporations, generally, and in that part of the thirty-ninth chapter, and the statutes subsequently passed, which relate to railroads. By an act passed on the 19th of March, 1845, (St. 1845, c. 159,) this corporation and the Boston and Maine Railroad were authorized to unite themselves in one corporation, to be called the Boston and Maine Railroad. The union took place accordingly, and the subsequent proceedings were in the name of the united corporation.

The company thus incorporated having laid out their road, and taken the land necessary therefor, the petitioner in the present case presented her petition to the county commissioners of Middlesex, at a special meeting of the board, on the 14th of November, 1844, for an appraisement of the damages, occasioned by the laying out and construction of the railroad of the respondents, over and across the flats appurtenant to the wharf estate owned by her. The commissioners, having first viewed the premises and heard the parties, at a meeting held on the first Tuesday of January, 1845, estimated and awarded the damages sustained by the petitioner, to be paid her by the company, at the sum of $800, with costs taxed at the sum of $45.87. The petitioner, being dissatisfied with this estimate, applied to the commissioners, at their next meeting, held by adjournment on the 25th of March, 1845, to have her damages estimated by a jury. The petition for a jury was continued, from time to time, until the 26th of March, 1846, when the prayer thereof was granted, and the clerk was directed forthwith to issue a warrant to the sheriff of the county, to summon a jury according to law, for the purposes mentioned in the petition.

The sheriff proceeded accordingly to summon and impanel a jury, who, on the 18th of July, having viewed the premises and heard the parties, rendered a verdict in favor of the petitioner, for her damages, estimated at the sum of $1,451.71. This verdict, being returned to the Court of Common Pleas, at the next September term thereof, was set aside, and the petitioner thereupon appealed to this court.

The objections, taken by the respondents to the proceedings before the commissioners and before the jury, upon which they relied as grounds for sustaining the Court of Common Pleas in setting aside the verdict, will be best understood by a reference to such of the papers and records in the cause, as were brought up to this court upon the appeal.

The first proceeding in the order of time, of which a record was produced in this court, was the petitioner's application to the county commissioners to have her damages assessed by a jury, which was as follows : —

" To the Hon. County Commissioners for the County of Middlesex, at their meeting to be held at Cambridge on the twenty-fifth day of March, 1845, by adjournment from the first Tuesday of January, 1845.

"The petition of Lucy J. Walker of Charlestown, in said county, respectfully represents : That at a special meeting of your Honors held at Charlestown, in said county, on the fourteenth of November last, she presented her petition for an appraisement of damages against the Boston and Maine Extension Railroad Company, occasioned by the laying out and constructing the railroad of said company over and across the flats appurtenant to the wharf estate owned by your petitioner, as set forth in her said petition, when and where your Honors, having viewed the premises, heard the respective parties. And at the meeting of your Honors, held at said Cambridge on the first Tuesday of January, 1845, you did estimate and award the damages sustained by your petitioner, to be paid her by said company, at the sum of eight hundred dollars, with costs taxed at the sum of forty-five dollars eighty-seven cents. That your petitioner is dissatisfied with said estimate, and wishes to have her said damages assessed by a jury. Wherefore she prays your Honors to issue your warrant for a jury to assess her said damages, agreeable to the statute in such cases made and provided."

The proceedings and order of the commissioners, upon this petition, appear by the following memorandum thereon, attested by the clerk : —

" MIDDLESEX, ss.　County Commissioners' meeting at Cambridge, January, 1846, and by adjournment at said Cambridge on the twenty-sixth day of March, 1846.

" This petition was presented to the county commissioners, at their January meeting last, and thence said petition hath been continued from time to time to this time. It is is now ordered, that the clerk forthwith issue a warrant, directed to the sheriff of said county of Middlesex, to summon a jury according to law in such case made and provided for the purpose in said petition mentioned."

The warrant, issued in pursuance of the foregoing order, under the seal of the commissioners, and attested by the clerk, was as follows : —

" To the Sheriff of our County of Middlesex.
" Greeting.

" Pursuant to the annexed order of the county commissioners, you are hereby required to summon a jury agreeably to the law in such case made and provided, to meet at some convenient time and place, and have them sworn, to consider and estimate the damages done to the petitioner named in said petition, by the laying out and constructing the railroad of said company, over and across the flats, appurtenant to the wharf estate, owned by said petitioner as aforesaid. All which being done within three months from the time of passing said order, you are to make return of this warrant, and of your doings herein under your hands, and also of the verdict of the jury under the hands and seals of the jurors, by whose oath the said damages shall be estimated, to the Court of Common Pleas, which shall be holden in said county, next after said verdict shall be agreed upon, that said court may adjudicate upon said verdict. And you are to notify the petitioner, and all others interested, of the time and place of your meeting for the purposes aforesaid. Given under the seal of said commissioners, at Cambridge, this fourteenth day of April, in the year of our Lord one thousand eight hundred and forty-six."

The sheriff returned the warrant, under his hand, with the following statement of his proceedings thereon :—

MIDDLESEX, ss. July 18th, 1846. Pursuant to the annexed warrant, I made application to the mayor and aldermen of the city of Cambridge, and the selectmen of the towns of Charlestown and Somerville, respectively, three nearest towns not interested in the question, requiring them to draw from the jury-box, of each of their respective towns, the names of good and lawful men to serve on the jury therein ordered, to wit, from the city of Cambridge four, from the town of Charlestown five, and from the town of Somerville three, and said mayor and aldermen, and said selectmen, made due return of said applications, as follows, to wit : Simon P. Clark, Edward Hyde, William P. Fiske, and Luther L. Parker, were returned from said city of Cambridge ; Samuel Lamson, Joseph W. Whitton, Thomas Dearing, Noah Butts, and Edward Hearsey, were returned from said town of Charlestown ; and Orr N. Town, John Runey, and Charles Adams, were returned from the said town of Somerville, as appears by the certificates of the mayor and aldermen of said city of Cambridge and said towns respectively. And I caused said persons so returned to serve as jurors, to be summoned to come before me on the 18th day of July instant, at nine o'clock in the forenoon, at the Neck Hotel, in Charlestown in said county.

And I gave seasonable notice to the parties of the time and place, when and where I should have said jury. And on the said eighteenth day of July instant, I proceeded to impanel said jurors, all of whom as above named being personally present, they were duly sworn, before me, to make a just and true appraisement of the damages sustained by the complainant in this case, and well and truly to try all such other matters as should lawfully be submitted to them under said complaint, and to give a true verdict therein according to law and the evidence given to them; and after said jurors had chosen Orr N. Town, foreman, by ballot, I conducted them to the premises, which they viewed ; after which, and after they had fully heard the parties, I caused them to be by themselves, when they agreed upon and sealed up their verdict, which is herewith returned into court."[1]

The jury returned the following verdict, under their hands and seals : —

MIDDLESEX, ss. June 18th, 1846. Verdict of the jury in the case of Lucy J. Walker, of Charlestown, petitioner, against the Boston and Maine Railroad Company.

" The jury impanelled by Samuel Chandler, sheriff of said county, to estimate and assess the damages sustained by the said Lucy J. Walker, occasioned by laying out and constructing the railroad of said company over and across her land and flats, as set

---

[1] The month seems to be mistaken in this return. By the verdict, it appears, that the proceedings before the jury took place on the 18th of June.

forth in her petition, having been first duly sworn, by Samuel Chandler, sheriff, and having chosen Orr S. Town foreman, by ballot, after viewing the premises, and fully hearing the evidence and the parties, do find, and our verdict is, that the said Lucy J. Walker recover, against the said Boston and Maine Railroad Company, the sum of fourteen hundred and fifty dollars and seventy-one cents, as her damages sustained as aforesaid. In witness, whereof, we have hereunto set our hands and seals, this eighteenth day of June, A. D. 1846."

The record of the Court of Common Pleas, a copy of which was in the case, contained a recapitulation of the proceedings already stated, and concludes as follows: —   -

"The parties appear, and being fully heard, and mature deliberation, by the court, being had in the premises, the court set aside the verdict aforesaid. From which order and decision of the court the said Lucy J. Walker appeals to the next supreme judicial court to be holden for this county.

The respondents objected, upon the foregoing proceedings: —
1. That they had no notice of the pendency of the petitioner's application for a jury.
2. That the petition for a jury was presented to the commissioners, at their meeting in April, 1845, and the warrant was ordered to be issued thereon in March, 1846; whereas, by the statute, the petition should have been presented and acted upon, at the same or the next succeeding meeting of the commissioners.
3. That it did not appear, when the matter of this petition was finally determined upon, that there were three disinterested commissioners present, or that the parties consented to the proceeding.
4. That some of the jurors were drawn from the town of Charlestown, in which the land taken by the respondents was situated, and which, therefore, was not an adjoining town.
5. That the jury were not directed to estimate the proprietary interest of the Commonwealth in the flats, and to deduct it from the whole value of the land.
6. That there were other cases of the same kind, which ought to have been put to the same jury.
The respondents also objected: —
-    7. That the direction of the sheriff, as to the mode of ascertaining the petitioner's interests in the flats, was erroneous.
The ground of this last objection appeared by the following certificate of the sheriff, as amended by the agreement of the parties: —
"It was proved, that the channel runs from Davidson's mill, so called, in the direction indicated upon the plan drawn by Charles Whitney, February 10th, 1846, passing the Boston and Maine Railroad and the Fitchburg Railroad, to the draw in Prison Point Bridge,

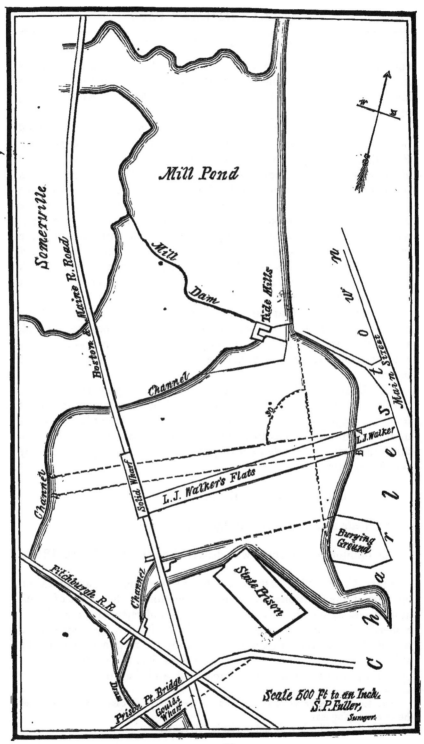

Mill Pond

Somerville.

Boston & Maine R. Road

Mill

Dam

Tide Mills

Channel

Main Street

Channel

Solid Wharf

L. J. Walker

L. J. Walker's Flats

Burying Ground

Charles River

State Prison

Fitchburg R.R.

Channel

Draw

Prison Pt. Bridge

Gould's Wharf

Scale 500 Ft. to an Inch.
S. P. Fuller,
Surveyor.

and that a channel also exists in front of the State Prison, as marked on the plan, from which the water does not recede at the lowest tides, between a point about opposite the north-west passage, or canal, into the prison grounds.

" The petitioner proved her title to the lot on the upland marked ' A B ' on the said plan, and the flats appurtenant, and called Stephen P. Fuller, surveyor, who testified to the correctness of the line of high-water mark, as shown on the plan, and that the lines from ' A B ' to ' C D ' were obtained by drawing a straight line across the mouth of the indentation, and giving to each abutter a width of flats upon said line, in proportion to the extent of his line upon high-water mark, as drawn upon said plan, and by the extension of those said lines, at right angles with said line drawn across as aforesaid towards low-water mark, one hundred rods, or to the channel, which results in giving the lot of each proprietor a portion of the flats of equal width throughout.

" It was agreed, that the plan, which was before the jury, of the channel of Miller's River, towards which the said lines are directed, and of the flats, and shore of the bay, between said river and Somerville and Charlestown, is correct, and to be considered a part of the record.

" At the request of the petitioner, I directed the jury, that, by law, the flats of the petitioner were ascertained by drawing straight lines from the opposite corners of her upland ' A B ' towards low-water mark, one hundred rods, to points marked on said plan, ' C D.' To this ruling, the respondents excepted, and at their request I hereby certify the same." [1]

S. Bartlett and *J. Dana*, for the petitioner.

R. Choate and *T. Farrar*, for the respondents.

The opinion of the court was delivered on the 26th March, 1849.

Shaw, C. J.[2]　This case comes before the court, by an appeal on the part of the petitioner from an adjudication of the Court of Common Pleas, by which that court set aside and rejected the verdict of a sheriff's jury, awarding damages to the petitioner, for lands alleged to belong to her and to have been taken by the respondents in laying out their railroad. The petitioner now asks that this verdict, returned by the jury in her favor, may be accepted, and that judgment may be

[1] The localities, referred to in this and the three following cases, are delineated on the accompanying map.
[2] Wilde J., and Fletcher, J., did not sit in this cause.

rendered thereon. To this the respondents object, and insist oh various grounds of exception, both to the petitioner's title, the instruc. tions of the sheriff, and to the correctness and regularity of the proceedings. The record before us does not show upon what grounds the Court of Common Pleas proceeded in disallowing this verdict; but if any of the exceptions and grounds of defence, taken by the respondents, are well founded, and it thus appears that the petitioner cannot recover, then the judgment is to be affirmed, and all further proceedings in the case terminated. We shall therefore proceed to consider these exceptions and grounds of defence, as they appear upon the record, and have been brought to our attention in the argument.

The first and material question, which lies at the foundation of this inquiry, is this; what questions are open, upon an appeal like the present, from an adjudication of the Court of Common Pleas, ordering the acceptance or rejection of the verdict of a sheriff's jury, returned into that court, pursuant to statute. The whole course and form of proceeding are comparatively new, and no very definite practice in relation thereto has yet been established.

It has been decided that an appeal lies, in a case like the present, by force of the Rev. Sts. c. 82, § 6, giving such appeal in any civil suit or proceeding whatever, from a judgment or decision founded on matter of law apparent on the record. Lanesborough v. Berkshire, 22 Pick. 278. But it is considered, that such an appeal must be strictly confined to the purpose for which it is allowed, namely, in order to afford a cheap, simple, and prompt mode of reëxamining a judgment in matter of law, which would be examinable and liable to be reversed or affirmed on writ of error. Ward v. American Bank, 7 Met. 486.

This rule is not confined to a writ of error in the strict technical sense in which that term is used; because such a writ of error lies only in cases of judgments rendered according to the course of the common law. But the appeal being given in matters of law, apparent on the face of the record, in every civil suit and proceeding, it must extend to judicial proceedings not according to the course of the common law, and where certiorari would be the proper mode of bringing the proceeding before this court, for reëxamination, in matter of law? Such was the case of Lanesborough v. Berkshire, first above cited.

But as such an appeal is, in effect, a summary proceeding, given as a substitute for a writ of error, it will be construed with the same liberality, to reach the merits and justice of the case, as that with which a writ of error is directed by the statute to be construed. The

Rev. Sts. c. 100, § 23, provide, that after judgment any defect or imperfection may be rectified or amended, either by the court in which
it is rendered, or by the court to which it shall be removed, if substantial justice requires it. And the next section provides, that no
judgment shall be reversed for any defect or imperfection in the
matter of form, which might by law have been amended.

The obvious purpose of these provisions is, to prevent the reversal
of judgments upon technical exceptions and matters of form, when
such reversal is not necessary to reach the substantial justice of the
case. The case of a *certiorari*, if not within the terms, is certainly
within the spirit and equity of the statute, and clearly within the
reason of the rule. And so it has been settled in a series of cases,
that a *certiorari*, which is an application addressed to the sound discretion of the court, will not be granted, when substantial justice has
been done; Rutland v. Worcester, 20 Pick. 71; or where a road has
been located and made, and much expense incurred; *Ex parte* Miller,
4 Mass. 565; Whateley v. Franklin, 1 Met. 336; or on account of
the shortness of notice to a town, where the town has appeared and
made no objection to the shortness of the notice; Commonwealth v.
Westborough, 3 Mass. 406; or where it does not appear on the
records of the proceedings, that a party has had notice, if it appear
aliunde that the parties substantively interested appeared, or much
time has elapsed. Hancock v. Boston, 1 Met. 122. And the court
are of opinion, that upon an appeal, by which a case is brought
before this court, to be reconsidered upon questions of law, and
where the court are to reëxamine it in a summary way, as would
be done more formally on *certiorari*, the court are to consider the case
in the same manner as if thus formally brought before them.

But in getting an adjudication reversed and annulled by *certiorari*,
the party moving has two processes to go through. As the issuing
of a writ of *certiorari* is not a matter of right, the party must first
apply to the court by petition, and set forth the grounds and merits
of his case; upon which, notice to show cause is given to the adverse
party, and on the hearing of the petition, the question is discussed
upon its merits, and the petition is granted or denied according to
the substantial justice of the case. If denied, the adjudication will
stand unreversed, although there may be grounds of legal exception.
It is granted only when, upon grounds of justice and law, the judgment is irregular and erroneous, and in the opinion of the court ought
to be annulled. Now when the popular and more summary process
of appeal is substituted for the more formal and cumbrous one of
certiorari, this court, as the revising tribunal, are called upon to exercise both branches of this jurisdiction, as well that which is exercised

upon the petition for a *certiorari*, as that which is exercised in reversing or affirming the judgment upon the return of that writ. With these preliminary views of the nature and scope of the inquiry before us, we will proceed to examine the alleged grounds of error apparent on this record.

1. The first exception is, that the respondents had no notice of the pendency of the petitioner's application for a jury, previously to the issuing of a warrant therefor by the commissioners.

There is no doubt, that in point of law, the corporation, against whom a warrant for a jury is prayed for, is entitled to notice from the county commissioners, in order that they may have an opportunity to adjust the damages by negotiation, or to agree upon a committee to assess them. Central Turnpike, Petitioners, 7 Pick. 13. That case was decided on a petition for a *certiorari*. But the question still recurs, how must the objection be made to appear, and how shall the party excepting take advantage of it? That he may petition for a *certiorari* to remove the adjudication, under which the warrant issued, as soon as he has notice of the fact, is one remedy; but it is insisted, that it is not an adequate one, and that it has not been allowed in this stage. Hinckley, Petitioner, 15 Pick. 447. In that case, the objection was sustained on an appeal, affirming an adjudication of the Court of Common Pleas to the same effect. But in that case, it is stated, that the verdict was rejected by the Court of Common Pleas, on the ground, that no notice was given by the commissioners, without stating how the fact appeared; it might have been by an agreed statement, or in the judgment itself, and, further, no exception was taken to its consideration.

In the more recent case of Brown v. Lowell, 8 Met. 172, before this court, on appeal from the Court of Common Pleas, affirming their judgment setting aside the verdict of a sheriff jury, although there was another reason for setting aside the verdict, yet it was also held to be erroneous, on the ground that the commissioners had given no notice of the pendency of a petition for a jury. No objection, however, was taken, that the point was not open upon the appeal: but, on the contrary, both parties desired the opinion of the court upon it.

But without questioning the authority of these cases, and without denying that the objection may have been rightly taken before the Court of Common Pleas, and in due form brought before this court, we think it nowhere appears on this record, that the respondents had not due notice of the pendency of the petition before the warrant issued.

In order to understand what questions this proceeding before the
40 *

Court of Common Pleas, and by appeal before this, presents, it becomes necessary to examine somewhat in detail the nature of these
proceedings, and the form and matter of the record to be examined.
We have already said, that this course of proceeding is anomalous,
and that it differs from the ancient course of proceeding, when these
matters were under the jurisdiction of the Court of Sessions, possess-
ing all the attributes, and proceeding with all the forms, of a strictly
judicial tribunal.

But the functions of the county commissioners are rather adminis-
trative than judicial, and up to a certain point, they act rather as
public agents and arbitrators than as judges. Still, the legislature
probably thought it necessary, in compliance with the injunctions of
the constitution, to give to those, whose property was taken for pub.
lic use, the privilege of a trial by jury.

Up to this point, the subject is left under the administration of the
commissioners; but, after the issuing of a warrant, and the matter
being thus put in train for the trial by jury, it seemed necessary that
provision should be made for the examination and allowance or dis-
allowance of the verdict; and as that might involve great questions
of public and private right, it was probably considered more conformable to the analogies of the law, and the general principles on which
justice is administered, to commit this function to a strictly judicial
tribunal. It is therefore provided, that the verdict may be returned
to the Court of Common Pleas, who shall receive the same, and adjudicate thereon, and may set the same aside, for good cause. Rev.
Sts. c. 24, § 34, reënacting, in this respect, St. 1827, c. 77, § 12.

From this view, it is manifest, that the time and mode in which
the matter is first brought under the cognizance of the Court of
Common Pleas, is the time when the verdict is first returned there
by the sheriff. Their record will then, after the usual caption, set
forth the warrant, the return of the sheriff, and the verdict of the
jury. And these, as far as we can perceive, are all that is before
them as matter of record; all the anterior proceedings have been conducted before the county commissioners.

We are not aware that there is any particular form in which a
warrant from the commissioners is framed, and it is probable that
different commissioners and clerks adopt different forms. Whatever
may be the form, we think it should set forth, with sufficient certainty, the subject-matter into which the jury, under the direction of
the presiding officer, are to inquire. It should describe the land over
which the road passes, the petitioner's title to, and interest in it, the
location of the road, and the incidental damages, if any, which the
petitioner has sustained, in addition to the value of the land taken.

This, we think, may be done, by reciting the substance of the petition in the warrant, or by annexing an authenticated copy of it, and referring to such copy in the warrant, by which it is effectually incorporated into, and made part of, the warrant. But such an annexation of a copy of the petition, with the orders of the commissioners, does not necessarily bring before the Court of Common Pleas the regularity of the anterior proceedings, as a matter of record; they are inserted *alio intuitu*, for the purpose of informing the sheriff and jury of the matter to be tried.

Then the question recurs, have the Court of Common Pleas no power to decide, in acting on the question of the acceptance of the verdict, that the warrant itself issued improvidently, or without legal authority? This certainly does not follow from the views we have taken. The powers given to the Court of Common Pleas, on the return of the verdict, are very large and indefinite; they are to adjudicate thereon, and may set the same aside for good cause. There is nothing to specify the nature of these causes. The impanelling of the jury by the sheriff, and all his other proceedings, will appear by his return, together with his rulings and decisions, which the law requires him to return; and all these are of course before the court for their consideration. There is no doubt, also, that whatever affects the purity, honesty, and impartiality of the verdict, such as tampering with the jurors, or other misconduct of a party, any irregularity or misconduct of juries, showing a good cause why the verdict should not be accepted, may be brought before the court by evidence *aliunde*, because such a cause vitiates the verdict, proves that it is not conformable to law and justice, and ought not to stand as the basis of a judgment.

Whether it would be competent for the court to set aside the verdict, as being without or against evidence, or against the weight of evidence, we believe, has not been decided, and we give no opinion. The language seems broad enough to include any and all causes, for which a court of law, in the exercise of its ordinary jurisdiction, may set aside the verdict of a jury, and order a new trial. Whether and to what extent, the generality of the language should be restrained by the subject-matter, and the implications arising from the objects and purposes of the statute, are questions to be considered as they arise.

But the power of the Court of Common Pleas over such a verdict is much larger than the power of this court on an appeal. The Court of Common Pleas may set aside the verdict for any good cause; we are merely to reexamine their judgment, in order to ascertain if there is any error therein apparent on the record. If, then, a party desires to bring his case before this court, upon questions of law, not appearing in the warrant, the verdict, the return of the officer, including his directions and instructions to the jury, and the adjudication of the Court of Common Pleas, it can only be done by a bill of exceptions filed and allowed in that court. We see not why that court may not specify in the adjudication the grounds on which they accept or disallow the verdict; and if such adjudication involve a question of law, it would then be apparent on the record. Otherwise, as already stated, it may be done by bill of exceptions. The language of the statute is very broad : " Any party aggrieved by any opinion, direction, or judgment of the Court of Common Pleas, in matter of law, in any civil action, suit, or proceeding whatever, whether it be according to the course of the common law or otherwise, may allege exceptions," &c. Rev. Sts. c. 82, § 12. Exceptions thus allowed and filed would become a part of the record, and come with it to this court. The questions presented in the case are then apparent on the record, and examined by this court on appeal.

Now, therefore, suppose that the cases cited, Hinckley, Petitioner, 15 Pick. 447, and Brown v. Lowell, 8 Met. 172, do fully warrant the proposition for which they were cited, to wit, that in adjudicating upon the verdict of a sheriff's jury, it is a good cause for setting it aside, that the respondents had no notice from the commissioners before the warrant issued, that principle cannot affect the present case. If the Court of Common Pleas were called upon to act on this ground, it would not be from any thing appearing in the warrant or return, but from facts brought to their notice by evidence *aliunde.* The fact, that no averment appears on the record that notice was given, could be of no avail, because there is no occasion why it should appear. Even if the record of the commissioners were produced, as such evidence of the fact, it would not be conclusive; because it might be shown, in answer to such objection, that in point of fact, the respondents were summoned, or consented to take notice, without summons, or in fact appeared before the commissioners. All this is matter of fact before the Court of Common Pleas, open to proof, by the commissioners' records, by testimony, and other competent evidence; and the conclusions of the Court of Common Pleas, upon all questions of fact, are decisive and final. Were it otherwise, an appeal to this court would bring before us all questions of fact, as well as of law, contrary to the plain intent of the statute. If there was no formal notice ordered or given, and no waiver, appearance in fact without notice, or other good excuse, as in the case of Hancock v. Boston, it was a pure question of fact. If upon any facts admitted or proved, the Court of Common Pleas decided, that decision could be corrected here only when apparent on the record, and could only appear on the record by a bill of exceptions taken there. We are therefore of opinion, that this first objection to the petitioner's verdict cannot prevail.

2. The next objection is, that the application for a jury was presented to the commissioners at their term held in April, 1845, and the warrant was issued at March term, 1846, whereas the respondents maintain, that the petition must be received and acted upon at the same or next succeeding meeting of the commissioners, and not afterwards. Rev. Sts. c. 24, § 14. The answer already given applies to this, that it does not appear on the record.

But the objection seems to call for some further remark; and it is obvious to us, that this provision limits the time within which the application must be made, and not that within which it must be decided upon. It would require express language to warrant a contrary conclusion, because much time may often necessarily elapse, for giving notices, hearing proofs, and for deliberation. But, further, the clause in question, " may be received and acted upon," is found in the chapter relating to highways, (Rev. Sts. c. 24,) and is not found in the chapter relating to railroads (Rev. Sts. c. 39). The latter merely provides, that either party dissatisfied, &c., may apply for a jury, at the same, or the next regular meeting, (extended to one year by the statute of 1847, c. 181,) omitting the words, " may be received and acted upon," upon which alone this objection arises, but proceeds to direct that the like proceedings shall be had thereon, as in the case of highways.

But as the preliminary proceedings, in regard to laying out, assessing damages, and making returns, are different in the two cases, the rules directing the mode of proceeding in the one can only be followed in the other so far as the same are applicable. In the case of highways, the commissioners assess damages, as of course, to all proprietors, whose lands are taken, and return the assessment, with their location, and thus fix the time within which application may be made for a jury. In the case of railroads, damages are assessed only on application to the commissioners, by one of the parties, within three years after the land is taken.

3. It is objected, that wherever there are opposing parties, no business can be finally determined by the commissioners, except by consent, unless there shall be three disinterested commissioners present. Rev. St. c. 14, § 27. It is a sufficient answer to this objection, that it does not appear, that there were not three disinterested commissioners present, or that the business was not done by consent. The presumption, conformably to the maxim *omnia rite acta*, is, that the proceedings were correct and conformable to law, unless the contrary is shown. Errors must be apparent, and not merely suggested.

4. The next objection, arising from the facts apparent upon the record, that is, from the return of the sheriff, is, that the law was not complied with, because some of the jurors were drawn from Charlestown, a town in which the land to be appraised lies. This would be a good exception, if seasonably taken before the sheriff and not waived. It has been held, under this provision, that the town in which the land lies is not a town next adjoining, within the provision of the statute. Wyman v. Lexington and W. Camb. R. Corp. *ante*, 436.

But this was an exception to the Charlestown jurors only; the other jurors were rightly drawn and summoned, and the exception should have been made at the time; and the respondents, by proceeding without exception, and taking their chance for a favorable verdict, are precluded from afterwards taking the exception. The fact must have been known to the respondents. It has been repeatedly held, that if there be an exception to a juror, and the party, knowing of such exception, proceeds to trial, it is inconsistent with good faith and fair dealing, for him afterwards to insist on such an objection. If he has any real objections to any juror, he must take his exceptions in due time and right order. Davis v. Allen, 11 Pick. 466; Simonds v. Parker, 1 Met. 508. And the same rule applies to referees and county commissioners. Fox v. Hazleton, 10 Pick. 275; Ipswich v. Essex, 10 Pick. 519. In the case cited of Wyman v. Lexington and W. Camb. Railroad Corp., the exception was taken before the sheriff, and insisted on, seasonably.

If the exception had been made at the time, it would have been competent for the sheriff to set aside the jurors who were thus disqualified, and to fill their places with others to whom there could be no exception. The court are of opinion, that by proceeding to trial without exception, this objection to the summoning and impanelling of the jury was waived, and now constitutes no good ground of objection to the verdict.

5. Another objection taken is, that the jury were not directed to value the proprietary interest of the Commonwealth, and deduct it from the aggregate. This is founded on the Rev. Sts. c. 24, §§ 48, 49, 50, which provide for the case where several parties have different estates or interests, at the same time, in any land or buildings, and direct that the jury shall first determine the damage done to the whole, as an entire estate, in fee-simple, and then apportion the amount amongst the several parties, having several and distinct interests therein.

This is a very wise and useful provision, and should be carried into effect, according to its true intent and spirit. It is one intended for the relief and benefit of those who are liable to pay damages. But we consider it, to say the least, very doubtful, whether the exception can be taken in this stage of the proceedings, if it was not taken at or before the trial. It was not for the sheriff, or for the jury, without any direction in the warrant, without notice from the respondents, that any body but the petitioner had an interest in the land to be appraised, to assume the existence of such an interest, and act upon the assumption.

But it is a more satisfactory answer, that we cannot perceive that the Commonwealth had any such interest in these flats. It is doubtful, on the terms of the statute, whether it extends to persons having a mere easement, for light, air, or way, or other easements of the like kind. The statute speaks of parties having several estates or interests, and obviously, as its primary object, looks to the case of estates for life or years, carved out of the fee, as in the case of Ellis v. Welch, 6 Mass. 246. It may extend, perhaps, to such easements as constitute a service and burden upon the estate, and thus constitute a part of its aggregate value, to be distributed; and it may possibly extend to other easements, of which we give no opinion. But, upon the grounds suggested, the Commonwealth had no easement in these flats. The colony ordinance gives to the riparian owner "propriety" to low-water mark. This has been construed to be property, ownership, a full title in fee to the soil. The provision, that the owner shall not by this liberty prevent access to other men's houses, is a reservation in favor of adjacent proprietors, the owners of such houses and lands, and reserves no easement for the Commonwealth.　•

6. One other exception of the like description remains to be considered, which is, that there was one or more other cases of the same kind, and that they all ought to have gone to the same jury. We are not aware, from any thing apparent upon the record, that any other case of the same kind was pending before the commissioners, at the same time, or if there was, that it did not go to the same jury. It has been decided, that they need not be included in one and the same warrant. Richardson v. Curtis, 2 Cush. 341.

7. The next and by far the most important question, in this case, turns upon the title of the petitioner, and the directions of the sheriff, in regard to the division of the flats adjoining the petitioner's wharf. The whole of the soil, for the taking of which the petitioner claimed damages, consisted of flats lying between high and low-water mark. Her title to land bordering on a cove, in which the sea ebbed and flowed, was proved or admitted; and there was no proof or suggestion, that by any conveyance, the flats, or the upland, had been alienated, disconnected from each other; so that the inquiry as to the

petitioner's title involved the difficult question, in what direction the flats of the petitioner were to run, and by what lines they were to be measured and limited. No general rule of division has been laid down, and perhaps, from the nature of the case, none can be laid down. Many coves, inlets, and estuaries of rivers, are so irregular and various in outline, and so traversed by crooked and meandering creeks and channels, from which the sea does not ebb, that it is utterly impossible to apply to them any of the rules which have been applied to other cases. Such, to a considerable degree, is the character of the cove in question, though far from being as irregular as many others. The most we can hope to do is, to take the colony ordinance of 1641, and to apply it according to its true spirit; and, by as near an approximation as practicable, to the rules which have been judicially established, to lay down such a line of division, as to give to each riparian proprietor his fair and equal share.

We are of opinion, that the rule of division, prescribed by the sheriff, was not the correct one. It appears, by the case, that the stream running from the tide mills, along through the westerly part of these flats, is a natural channel or creek, from out of which the tide does not ebb. It must therefore be a *terminus* to a claim of flats in that direction. Sparhawk *v.* Bullard, 1 Met. 95. The lines directed to be drawn by the sheriff appear to have been drawn from the side lines of the petitioner's upland, parallel to each other, towards the channel of Miller's River, without regard to this creek, running from the tide mills. But we think, that this creek not only must form a limit to the claim of flats, but must tend to give the direction in which they run. On the estuary of a river, or arm of the sea, through which there is a channel, the lines of flats will ordinarily run towards such channel, and in the most direct course. Ashby *v.* Eastern Railroad Co. *ante*, 356.

There is also a creek on the easterly side, extending up from Miller's River, along in front of the State Prison, to a point opposite the western entrance into the State Prison, from which the tide does not ebb, which tends to give a character to this cove.

There is also a spur or narrow tract of flats, extending up in a north-easterly direction, between the State Prison lands, and the Charlestown burying ground, from which the tide does ebb, but which hardly seems to be a part of the cove, but a strip of flats, detached from it. Considering the peculiar formation of this tract of flats, the court are of opinion, that a line extending up from the upper end of the creek, or what some of the witnesses call the rudiments of a creek, in front of the State Prison, nearly in a continued direction, in its present course, to the upland, should form the easterly *terminus* of the shore line of the cove. This line will strike the upland or high-water line, near the north-westerly corner of the buryingground, as laid down on the map. Thence follow the shore line, or line of high-water mark, northerly and westerly, to the tide mill dam, and this is to form the upland or shore line of the cove. To form the outer or low-water line, draw a line across the narrowed space between the two creeks, as the mouth of the cove. If the low-water line is shorter than the high-water line, take the whole length of the upland, and ascertain each owner's proportion, and give him the same proportion on the low-water line, and in the same order, and then let lines be drawn from each proprietor's line, at high water, to his corresponding points in the low-water line, and this will define the limits of the flats of each owner.

It was urged in the argument for the petitioner, that the direction of each riparian proprietor's flats was not to be governed by the nearest creek or channel from which the sea does not ebb, if not adapted to navigation; but rather to the nearest broad, open, navigable channel to the sea. This argument was founded upon the suggestions made in many of the cases, that the colony ordinance was intended to promote the erection of wharves, and to facilitate navigation. No purpose of this sort is expressed in the ordinance itself; but is rather a comment upon its general policy; and we think it is too loose and uncertain, to form the basis of a practical rule for a division of this species of property among conterminous proprietors. The views of such proprietors and of those who might be called upon to declare and determine their rights, would probably differ essentially as to what the conveniences of navigation, from particular ports to the open sea, would require. The purpose of the ordinance rather seems to have been, to declare the right of private owners in the soil of the flats, between high water and low water, leaving the owners, with their rights thus ascertained, to use or appropriate their property, or sell and dispose of it, in any way which they might deem most beneficial.

But, then, if the directions of the lines of the proprietors of uplands are to be governed by the nearest creek or channel, from which the tide does not ebb, and not by the nearest broad, navigable channel to the sea, it may be asked, why we have not run these lines more directly to the channel from the mills, and not to the narrowest space between the two creeks; the answer is, that the creek from the mills is not straight. After running some distance, in a direction nearly southerly, it makes a bend easterly, below the respondents' railroad, almost at right angles with its previous course, so that in effect the lines we adopt are lines running towards that creek. We have therefore thought it most consonant with the principles of division of flats heretofore adopted, to consider the narrowest space between the two creeks as the mouth of the cove to be divided.

If it be urged, that by taking the shortest line between the two creeks, as the mouth of the cove, the flats spread out much broader below, before the lines of the proprietors within the cove extend outward one hundred rods ; and if the lines of these proprietors are narrowed in the manner proposed, they would not get their share outside; we may answer, though it is perhaps not material to the present case, that we see no reason, why, upon the same principle of giving an equal division, these same proprietors should not widen and spread in proportion, below the mouth of the cove, to low-water mark, or one hundred rods. We say it will not affect the present case, because, from an inspection of the map, we suppose that at the place where the railroad crosses the flats, the line is as short as at any place between the two creeks.

This mode of ascertaining the extent of the petitioner's flats may be liable to objections; we know no mode of dividing these flats, which would be free from objection. Believing that the sheriff adopted a different rule, and gave a different direction upon this point, the court are of opinion, that for this cause, the judgment of the Court of Common Pleas, setting aside the verdict, must be affirmed, and the case remanded to the county commissioners, with directions to issue a new warrant.

THE COMMONWEALTH OF MASSACHUSETTS v. THE BOSTON AND MAINE RAILROAD.[1]

Middlesex Co., January Term, 1849.

Assessment of Damages — Practice — Construction of Act authorizing a Railway Company to pass over Land of the State — Proceedings in behalf of the State — Construction of Contract between a Railway Company and the State — Competency of Jurors — Evidence — Damages for Crossing Flats — Sheriff's Instructions to Jurors — Notice to the State — Interest upon Damages.

County commissioners having awarded damages for land taken for a railroad, and the respondents having had their estimate revised by a jury, who also awarded damages,

---

[1] 3 Cushing's Reports, 25.

Commonwealth v. The Boston and Maine Railroad.

and the verdict of the jury having been accepted by the Court of Common Pleas, it was held, on appeal to this court, that it was open to the respondents to insist that no damages could be legally assessed against them.

An act of the legislature, by which a railroad corporation was established in the usual manner, and with the ordinary powers and privileges of such corporations, authorized the corporation to locate their road, so that the same might pass over certain land, which belonged to and was held by the Commonwealth as a body politic for a particular purpose, but without any expression in the act of a design, on the part of the legislature, to aid the corporation in their undertaking : It was held, that it was not the intention of the legislature, by such act, to grant the land of the Commonwealth, or any easement therein, to the corporation, without compensation ; and that if such land of the Commonwealth were taken by the corporation for their road, the Commonwealth might institute proceedings, and prosecute a claim for damages, before the appropriate tribunal, in the same manner as an individual proprietor.

Where general rights are declared, or remedies given, by law, the Commonwealth is included therein, though not named.

The attorney of the Commonwealth for the county of Suffolk, after the act of 1843, c. 99, abolishing the office of attorney-general, and previous to that of 1849, c. 186, reëstablishing that office, was authorized by law, upon the requisition of the governor, to institute proceedings before the proper tribunal, for the recovery of damages sustained by the Commonwealth for land taken for a railroad, and to prosecute the same to their final termination ; and such attorney had a right, also, with the permission of the court or tribunal in which the proceedings were pending, and for sufficient cause, to avail himself of the aid of other suitable counsel, in conducting and managing the same, under his direction and control, and upon his responsibility.

An agreement having been made between the Commonwealth and the Charlestown Branch Railroad Company, providing, amongst other things, that upon certain terms and conditions therein mentioned, the Commonwealth would authorize such corporation to institute proceedings, in the name of the Commonwealth, against the Boston and Maine Railroad, for the purpose of recovering all claims which the Commonwealth might have against the latter, for laying out and constructing their road over land of the Commonwealth, the money receivable for such damages to be paid to the treasurer of the Commonwealth, and by him retained until the performance by the Charlestown Branch Railroad Company of the covenants contained in the said agreement, and on their part to be performed ; and the Commonwealth having given such authority, and proceedings having been instituted accordingly in the name of the Commonwealth, by the Charlestown Branch Railroad Company against the Boston and Maine Railroad, for the recovery of such damages : It was held, that the contract was not illegal ; that the case was one in which the Commonwealth was a party and interested ; and that the damages were not limited to the amount to which the Commonwealth was entitled at the time of the making of the agreement, but were recoverable as of the time of the filing of the location of the railroad.

The same persons being summoned as jurors, to assess the damages severally sustained by two railroad corporations, for the taking of their lands lying contiguous to each other, by a third railroad corporation, for the road of the latter, it was held to be no objection to the competency of one of the jurors to sit as such in the cause first tried, that he was a stockholder in the other corporation petitioning, whose cause was to be tried immediately afterwards.

On a claim for damages for land taken for a railroad, the claimant may prove, by the testimony of the engineer who made the preliminary surveys and plans for such road, that the same might have been located, pursuant to the charter, in various modes which would not have required the taking of the land of such claimant.

The owner of flats crossed by a railroad bridge having raised the flats around and under the bridge, within the location of the road, but without the consent of the proprietors thereof, is entitled to recover by way of damages, against such proprietors, for so much of the expense of such raising and filling up, as is necessary to enable him to enjoy his other

Commonwealth v. The Boston and Maine Railroad.

lands; provided such necessity was caused by the location and construction of the railroad.

Where the owner of flats crossed by and taken for a railroad had previously caused the same to be surrounded by a sea wall and filled up, it was held, that the expense of such filling up was proper evidence to be considered by the jury, in estimating the damages sustained by the owner for the land so taken.

On a trial before a sheriff's jury, summoned and impanelled to assess damages for land taken for a railroad, the sheriff cannot be called upon to instruct the jury, as to the weight, effect, or sufficiency of the evidence.

In proceedings where the Commonwealth is a party or interested, and no other special mode of summons is provided by law, notice to the governor, as the chief executive officer, would, it seems, be considered as sufficient.

Where the estimate of a petitioner's damages, occasioned by the construction of a railroad, as made by the county commissioners, is revised by a jury, on the application of the respondents, and the amount reduced; and the verdict of the jury, on an appeal from the adjudication of the Court of Common Pleas accepting the same, is established by this court; neither party is liable to the other for the costs of the proceedings before the sheriff and jury, but the petitioner is entitled to recover against the respondents the taxable costs of the appeal.

If, on an appeal to this court from an adjudication of the Court of Common Pleas, either accepting or setting aside (see Parker v. B. and M. Railroad, post,) the verdict of a sheriff's jury, the verdict of the jury is established, interest is to be computed on and added to the amount of the damages awarded by the jury, from the time when the verdict was returned into the Court of Common Pleas, to the time of its affirmation by this court.

The judgment of this court, confirming the proceedings of a sheriff's jury, on an appeal from the adjudication of the Court of Common Pleas, either accepting or setting aside the verdict, when the amount of the damages has been liquidated by computing and adding interest, and the costs have been taxed, is to be enforced by a certificate to the county commissioners, directing them to issue a warrant of distress for the amount so ascertained.

THE Commonwealth of Massachusetts, on the 13th of November, 1800, became the purchaser of a lot of land in Charlestown, by a deed thereof of that date from Archibald M'Neil, in pursuance of a resolve of the General Court, passed at the January session, 1800, for the purpose of obtaining a site for the erection of a State Prison.

By this deed, M'Neil granted, sold, and conveyed to the Commonwealth a piece of land, particularly described therein, containing four acres and a half and seven rods of upland, according to a plan thereof taken by Joseph Aiken, being the point of land purchased by the grantor of Mary Lynde, together with all the flats adjoining thereto, to which the grantor derived title by force of the deed from Mary Lynde to him, and also a free and uninterrupted right of an open way, for passing and repassing, in any manner, at any time, the full width of forty-five feet, in a direct course between M'Neil's mansion-house and his rope-walk, from the public street in Charlestown to the land and flats conveyed, with all other appurtenances to the premises belonging.

On the 9th of April, 1836, (by St. 1836, c. 187,) the Charlestown Branch Railroad Company was incorporated, with authority to construct a railway from Swett's Wharf, in Charlestown, to a point on the Boston and Lowell Railroad, near the " one mile post," so called, according to the location specified in the act; one point in the direction of the road was "a point near the southerly corner of the land or wharf of the State Prison;" from whence the road was to be laid north-westerly by a straight line across the bay to the land of the M'Lean Asylum, and thence by a curve to its terminus in the Boston and Lowell Railroad.

By the act of incorporation, authority was given to the governor, with the advice and consent of the council, to sell, exchange, or otherwise dispose of to tHe corporation, such part of the land and flats owned by the Commonwealth, on the south-easterly and north-westerly sides of Austin street and the Prison Point Bridge, in Charlestown, and lying without the walls and fences of the State Prison, in such manner, and upon such terms, as they might deem for the interest of the Commonwealth; and also to make such arrangements with the corporation, concerning the building of their road, and the filling up of the flats in and upon the land of the Commonwealth, as should be considered just and expedient. The same section also provided, that the road should not be made until the governor, with the advice and consent of the council, should have approved of the location and proposed mode of building that part of the road, which might be constructed over the land and flats of the Commonwealth near the State Prison.

The time limited in the act of incorporation for filing the location and completing the road, namely, the 1st of January, 1837, was subsequently extended by the act of March 25th, 1837, (St. 1837, c. 94,) to the 1st of January, 1839, for filing the location, and for completing the road until the 1st of January, 1840; and the road was laid out and completed accordingly. By a subsequent statute passed March . 17th, 1841, (St. 1841, c. 108,) the corporation were authorized to extend their road from its terminus in the Boston and Lowell Railroad in a westerly direction.

By an act passed on the 3d of March, 1842, (St. 1842, c. 84,) to establish the Fitchburg Railroad Company, that corporation were authorized to lay out and construct a railroad from a point on the Charlestown Branch Railroad to Fitchburg, and to make arrangements with the latter corporation, either by a purchase or lease of their road, for the use of the same, from the point thereon where the Fitchburg Railroad commenced to its termination in Charlestown. By a subsequent act, passed on the 7th of February, 1846, (St. 1846, c. 21,) the Fitchburg Railroad Company succeeded to the corporate powers, privileges, and duties of the Charlestown Branch Railroad

41*

Company, (the corporate existence of the latter being continued for three years longer for certain purposes,) and the road of the latter became a part of the Fitchburg Railroad.

On the 16th of March, 1844, by an act then passed, (St. 1844, c. 172,) a corporation was established by the name of the Boston and Maine Railroad Extension Company, (subsequently united with the Boston and Maine Railroad, under the latter name,) for the purpose of constructing a railroad from a point in the Boston and Maine Railroad, in Wilmington, near its junction with the Boston and Lowell Railroad, to the public square at the easterly end of Haverhill and Canal streets, in Boston. A part of the route designated in the act was as follows: " crossing Mystic River by a bridge near Malden Bridge; thence passing near the Mill Pond at the outlet of the Middlesex Canal, at least one fourth of a mile from the M'Lean Asylum, by the way of Somerville or Charlestown, to a point on the Charlestown Branch Railroad, near their engine-house, in Charlestown ; provided it shall not cross the Charlestown Branch Railroad, at any point east of the State Prison, without the assent of the directors of the Charlestown Branch Railroad Corporation ; thence crossing Charles River by a bridge, above Warren Bridge, to the city of Boston, between Haverhill street and Canal street ; and thence between said streets to the public square, at the easterly end of said streets."

In the month of May following their act of incorporation, the Boston and Maine Railroad Extension Company laid out and commenced the construction of their road. The route located, so far as it is material to be here stated, was from a point on the Back Bay, about three eighths of a mile east of the M'Lean Asylum, in Somerville, in a straight line south thirty and a half degrees east across the Back Bay, the Charlestown Branch Railroad, the Prison Point Bridge, and Charles River, to the city of Boston. In thus laying out their road, the corporation crossed over the flats belonging to the Commonwealth, adjoining the grounds occupied by the State Prison, and appropriated to their own use about fifty thousand feet of land. The location was filed with the county commissioners of Middlesex, on the 12th of February, 1845.[1]

.. In pursuance of the provisions of the seventh section of the act incorporating the Charlestown Branch Railroad Company, an agreement was entered into by indenture, on the 15th of October, 1844, between the Commonwealth, of the first part, and the Charlestown Branch Railroad Company, of the second part, relative to a sale by

---

[1] The principal localities referred to in this case may be seen on the map inserted at age 469.

the Commonwealth, of a portion of the flats, belonging to the latter, near the State Prison.

The indenture first recites, that the Commonwealth are the owners of two certain tracts of land and flats situate in Charlestown, on the south-easterly and north-westerly sides of Austin street and the Prison Point Bridge, and lying without the walls and fences of the State Prison, (which tracts are particularly described in the indenture, by reference to a plan drawn by S. M. Felton and George A. Parker, dated October 4th, 1844,) and that the Charlestown Branch Railroad Company purpose to inclose the said flats by a sea wall, and to fill up the same on reasonable terms of agreement with the Commonwealth.

It is then agreed and covenanted on the part of the corporation, amongst other things, that they shall construct, on a suitable and safe foundation, a good, permanent, and substantial sea wall, round the flats contained in the two tracts described in the recital, by an exterior line designated on the plan, the same to be built and raised above the highest tides; that they shall also fill up the flats inclosed within the sea wall of suitable materials, and make the same solid land; that, when the filling up shall have been completed, they will construct a good and sufficient board or stockade fence between the Boston and Maine Railroad and the Charlestown Branch Railroad, on the one side, and the second described tract of land or flats, on the other side; that they will construct the whole of the sea wall, and fill up the flats contained in the second described tract, and construct the fence, in a faithful and substantial manner, and complete the whole work in eighteen months from the date of the indenture, at their sole risk and expense, and without any charge to the Commonwealth.

It is then agreed and covenanted, on the part of the Commonwealth, that, whenever within the period of eighteen months and a day from the date of the indenture, the corporation shall have constructed the whole of the sea wall, and completed the filling up of the second described parcel of land and flats, and shall have built the fence, and shall have done the work in a thorough and proper manner, to the satisfaction of James F. Baldwin, Esq., the Commonwealth shall then convey to the corporation, their successors and assigns, by a good and sufficient deed of quitclaim, all the right, title, and interest of the Commonwealth in and to the first described tract of land and flats, subject, however, to the rights of the proprietors of the two railroads, respectively, and of the Prison Point Bridge.[1] ·

---

1 A deed was made and executed accordingly, by the governor, on the 2d of October, 1846.

The indenture contained, also, with other stipulations and agreements on both sides, not material to the present case, the following
clause: —

" And said party of the first part hereby authorize said party of
the second part to institute proceedings, in the name of said party of
the first part, for the purpose of recovering all claims which said
party of the first part may have against said Boston and Maine
Railroad Extension Company for damages for taking for their railroad a part of said flats embraced in said first described tract of land
and flats, which proceedings shall be instituted and carried on at the
sole risk and expense of said party of the second part; and when the
amount of said damages shall be ascertained by the decision of the
commissioners, or the verdict of a jury, or in any other manner agreed
upon by both parties hereto, the said amount shall be paid to the
State treasurer, and he shall keep the same as a separate fund, and
when said party of the second part shall have performed their cove..
nants, herein contained, the said treasurer shall pay over said fund to
said party of the second part, for their sole use and benefit."

In December, 1845, the Charlestown Branch Railroad Company,
by their president, addressed a petition to the governor, representing
that they had nearly fulfilled, on their part, the agreement made
between them and the Commonwealth on the 15th of October, 1844,
and were nearly ready to receive the deed stipulated to be given them
in that agreement; but, before receiving the same, the corporation
were desirous of instituting proceedings immediately, in the name of
the Commonwealth, but at their own expense, against the Boston
and Maine Railroad, (with which the Boston and Maine Railroad
Extension Company had then been united,) " for the purpose of
recovering all claims," which the Commonwealth might have against
that company, for damages occasioned by the taking for their railroad a part of the flats mentioned in the agreement between the
petitioners and the Commonwealth, according to the provisions of
the same.   The petitioners therefore prayed that the governor would
forthwith direct the Commonwealth's attorney for the county of Suffolk to appear in the cause, and institute proceedings therein on
behalf of the Commonwealth.

This petition was referred to a committee of the council, who
reported thereon, that, in their opinion, the petitioners could only
proceed in a legal manner in the prosecution of their claims against
the Boston and Maine Railroad, after the governor should have
authorized the district attorney to institute proceedings in the name
of the Commonwealth; and the committee therefore recommended
that the governor be advised to refer the petition to the district

attorney for the county of Suffolk, and if, in his opinion, it was a proper case for the use of the name of the Commonwealth, in ascertaining the rights of the parties under the contract, that the attorney be authorized and directed, at the expense and risk of the petitioners, to cause such proceedings to be instituted, as should lead to a decision of the rights of the parties either by arbitration or by the courts of law.

This report being accepted and the governor advised accordingly, on the 24th of December, 1845, a letter of that date was thereupon addressed by Governor Briggs to Samuel D. Parker, Esq., Commonwealth's Attorney for the County of Suffolk, inclosing copies of the petition of the Charlestown Branch Railroad Company, and of the proceedings of the council thereon, and directing the attorney, if, on examination, he should be of opinion that proceedings ought to be instituted in the name of the Commonwealth, for the benefit of the petitioners, to give such direction to the president of the company, as the case might require, taking care that the Commonwealth should be saved harmless from any cost.

In pursuance of these directions, the Commonwealth's Attorney for the County of Suffolk, on the 2d of January, 1846, presented a petition in the name and on behalf of the Commonwealth to the County Commissioners of Middlesex, setting forth the interest of the Commonwealth in the land and flats already alluded to; that the proprietors of the Boston and Maine Railroad had located their road across the same, in such a manner as disadvantageously to separate the premises, and greatly to impair and injure the value of the residue; and praying the commissioners, after due notice: to the Boston and Maine Railroad, to view the premises and estimate the damages sustained by the petitioners by reason of the taking and appropriation of the same.

Upon this petition, due notice having first been given to the Boston and Maine Railroad, the commissioners had a meeting, at the Mansion House, in Charlestown, on the 21st of May, 1846, when and where the corporation appeared by their counsel, and James Dana and George W. Warren, Esqs., appeared for the Commonwealth. The meeting was adjourned to the 25th instant, when the corporation appeared as before, and the Commonwealth by Samuel D. Parker, Esq., Attorney of the Commonwealth for the County of Suffolk, at whose request Messrs. Dana and Warren were permitted by the sheriff, in his stead, to represent the Commonwealth. The commissioners, having viewed the premises and heard the parties, estimated the damages sustained by the Commonwealth, by the location and construction of the respondents' railroad, as alleged in the petition, at the sum of thirty thousand and five dollars, and ordered the respondents to pay that sum to the Commonwealth, with costs to be taxed by the commissioners.

The respondents, being dissatisfied with this estimate of damages, presented their petition to the county commissioners at the same session, praying that a jury might be summoned to determine the matter, and, if they should see cause, to assess damages for the claim of the Commonwealth as set forth in their petition. On this petition, the commissioners passed an order, dated July 3d, 1846, that the clerk issue a warrant directed to the sheriff of the county, to summon a jury for the purpose mentioned in the petition, at such time as the petitioners might call for it. The petitioners made their request to the clerk, on the 3d of October, 1846, and the clerk thereupon issued the warrant for a jury in the usual form.

At the meeting of the commissioners in September, 1846, it was agreed by the parties, that the verdicts in the case of the Commonwealth against these respondents, and in the case of James Gould and the Fitchburg Railroad Company, against the same respondents, pending at the same time, might be returned, whenever prepared; as of the September term of the Court of Common Pleas, then in session, and the suits carried up on exceptions to this court, so as to be heard as of the October term, 1846; that no objections should be made on account of the jury's not having been summoned within three months from July 3d, the date of the order, or on account of the date of the verdict being after the sitting of the court; and that the jury should be called out in or before the first week in November. This agreement was signed by the counsel and filed with the commissioners.

The sheriff proceeded to the execution of the warrant, and made application to the selectmen of Charlestown and Somerville, and to the mayor and aldermen of Cambridge, " the three nearest towns not interested in the question," (as stated in the sheriff's return,) to draw and return jurors, namely, Charlestown, five, Somerville, four, and Cambridge, five, for the purpose of estimating the petitioner's damages. Jurors being returned accordingly, the sheriff summoned them to attend him at the Mansion House, in Charlestown, on the 2d of November, 1846, and also gave notice to the parties of the time and place of their meeting, for the purpose expressed in the warrant.

The jurors attended at the time and place appointed, and one of them being excused, at his own request, and for reasons offered by him, the names of the others were arranged in alphabetical order, and the first twelve were called and sworn to make a just and true ap-

Commonwealth v. The Boston and Maine Railroad.

praisement of the damages sustained by the petitioners, and well and truly to try all such other matters as should lawfully be submitted to them under the complaint, and to give a true verdict therein according to law and the evidence given them.

The jury, having chosen a foreman, by ballot, were first taken to view the premises; and the sheriff then adjourned to the town hall, in Charlestown, for the purpose of hearing the parties and their evidence. The hearing occupied the second, third, and fourth days of November; and when the parties had been fully heard, the jury agreed upon their verdict, which was sealed up and returned with the warrant and the sheriff's proceedings under it to the Court of Common Pleas. The jury estimated the petitioner's damages, at the sum of twenty-nine thousand seven hundred dollars, and returned a verdict accordingly, which being accepted by the Court of Common Pleas, the respondents thereupon appealed to this court.

In the course of the proceedings before the jury, certain rulings were made and instructions given by the sheriff, which being objected to by the respondents, a statement thereof and of the evidence relating to the same was made by the sheriff in his return. These rulings and instructions, which were the subjects of inquiry in this court, were as follows : —

1. At the time appointed for impanelling the jury, Sidney Bartlett, James Dana, and George W. Warren, Esqs., appeared, as they stated, at the request of Samuel D. Parker, Commonwealth's Attorney for the County of Suffolk, to prosecute the claim of the Commonwealth before the jury. The respondents denied the right of these gentlemen so to appear, and they thereupon produced and exhibited to the sheriff the letter of the governor, already stated, with the copies inclosed addressed to the attorney for Suffolk, directing him to institute proceedings; and Mr. Parker, being present, produced and exhibited a letter from himself to Messrs. Bartlett, Warren, and Dana, in which he stated that his engagements in the Municipal Court, in Boston, were such, that he found it impossible to attend before the sheriff and jury, in the case of the Commonwealth against the Boston and Maine Railroad, and authorizing and requesting them to appear and act in his behalf in conducting the same. The sheriff thereupon ruled, that Messrs. Bartlett, Warren, and Dana were duly authorized to appear and prosecute the petition, as counsel for the Commonwealth.

2. Before the jury were impanelled, the respondents desired that the persons summoned and in attendance as jurors should be asked if they were any of them stockholders in the Fitchburg or Charlestown Branch Railroads. The question being put, John Fosdick,

returned as a juror from Charlestown, answered that he owned stock in the Fitchburg Railroad. The respondents thereupon objected to the competency of Fosdick to serve as a juror, on the ground, that the case of the petition of the Fitchburg Railroad Corporation, for the recovery of damages, against the same respondents, was to be tried immediately after this; that the two cases related to adjoining pieces of flats; that the persons summoned as jurors were the same in both cases; that a verdict fixing the value of the land in the first case would have an important influence upon the estimation of damages in the second; and that it was for the interest of the juror, as a stockholder in the Fitchburg Railroad, to have the land of the Charlestown Branch Railroad Company appraised at a high rate. The sheriff ruled, that it was proper, on the motion of either party, to put to any of the jurors summoned the questions prescribed by the Rev. Sts. c. 95, § 27. The counsel for the petitioners then moved, that these questions should be put to Fosdick; and having been so put and answered in the negative, under oath, the sheriff ruled that the juror was competent, and he was accordingly sworn and sat on the trial.

3. In the course of the trial, the petitioners offered the testimony of Samuel M. Felton, an engineer, who was employed to make the preliminary surveys and plans for the extension of the Boston and Maine Railroad, in order to show that the road might have been located, pursuant to the charter, in various modes which would not have crossed any of the lands of the Commonwealth. The respondents objected to the testimony, except as to the fact that the witness was employed to make the surveys. But the sheriff ruled otherwise, and admitted the evidence.

The witness then testified, that he was employed by the persons, who were afterwards incorporated as the Boston and Maine Railroad Extension Company, to make the preliminary surveys, which were presented to the legislature with their petition for a charter; that his plans showed two routes, one coming east of the prison, and the other west of the prison, and entering upon the long bridge of the Charlestown Branch Railroad; that neither of these routes touched the State Prison property of the Commonwealth, as shown on his plans; that he had since examined the premises, and ascertained that his western route could have been so modified as to keep a quarter of a mile distant from the buildings of the M'Lean Asylum, and not touch the flats of the State Prison; that the present line of the Boston and Maine Railroad is not a quarter of a mile distant from the lands of the M'Lean Asylum; that the original location of the Charlestown Branch Railroad through these flats was forty feet wide, which is wide enough for more than three railroad tracks; and that the present route of the Boston and Maine Railroad is a better line, as a railroad line, without regard to expense.

4. It having been shown in evidence, on the part of the petitioners, that the Charlestown Branch Railroad Company, subsequent to the 15th of October, 1844, had raised the flats under and around the respondents' bridge, passing over the premises and within their location, without proving any consent therefor, the respondents requested the sheriff to instruct the jury, that the petitioners were not entitled to recover the cost of such filling up.

The sheriff declined to give the instruction prayed for, but instructed the jury, that the petitioners were entitled to such sum for raising the flats under and around the respondents' bridge, passing over the premises and within the location of the respondent's road, as the jury should find was incurred from necessity, in order to enable the Commonwealth to enjoy their other lands; provided the jury should believe that such necessity was created by reason of the location and construction of the respondents' road.

5. In reference to the filling up of the flats, by the Charlestown Branch Railroad Corporation, in execution of the agreement entered into between them and the Commonwealth, on the 15th of October, 1844, some of the principal terms of which have been already stated, the petitioners called as a witness George A. Parker, who testified, that he had been engaged as a railroad engineer and surveyor for eleven years; that he superintended the filling up of the flats by the Charlestown Branch Railroad Company, the average cost of which, including the sea wall, superintendence, &c., was twenty cents a superficial foot; that the bridge of the respondents over the prison flats was built in October, 1844, on spruce piles, which were raised three and a half feet above high-water; that the other bridges of the respondents, which were built over the channels and tide-waters, were built upon oak piles; that from the different manner of building their bridge over the prison flats, and from their locating their road through the flats, five rods wide, he inferred that the bridge over these flats was a temporary structure, and that the respondents contemplated filling up these flats.

The same witness, being called by the respondents, testified, that the cost to the Charlestown Branch Railroad Company, of filling up that portion of the State Prison flats retained by the Commonwealth, including their portion of the exterior wall, was but sixteen and a half cents a superficial foot; and that the whole expense of fulfilling their contract with the Commonwealth, so far as respected the portion of flats retained by the Commonwealth, was $12,742.12.

The respondents thereupon requested the sheriff to instruct the jury, that the agreement of October 15th, 1844, between the Commonwealth and the Charlestown Branch Railroad Company, and the testimony of Parker as to the cost of the work of making the land for the Commonwealth, afforded a measure of the value of the land taken, and of the damages done to the residue, and also a measure of the damages sustained by the acts of the respondents, which the jury were bound to apply accordingly in their assessment of the damages. The sheriff declined so to instruct the jury, but instructed them, that the contract and testimony above stated afforded proper evidence of the damages sustained by the acts of the respondents, which the jury were to consider and weigh.

6. In order to prove their title to the premises in question, under the deed of M'Neil, already stated, which was in evidence, the petitioners introduced, amongst others, three witnesses : —

George Farrar, who testified that certain plans and explanations, which, were put into the case as those referred to in M'Neil's deed, were exact copies of the plans and explanations, which he found in the office of the secretary of the Commonwealth, filed with the deed of M'Neil; — Alexander Wadsworth, who testified that the plan put into the case as his plan was made by him from an actual survey, and that the lines of high and low-water and of the channels were accurately described thereon; — and Nathaniel Austin, who testified that he recollected the premises upon which the State Prison was built since the year 1783; that the same were well known to him as a place called Lynde's Point; that the copy of the plan exhibited by Farrar was a correct view of the point when he first knew it; and that the channel and low-water mark were correctly described on Wadsworth's plan.

The respondents requested the sheriff to instruct the jury, that this evidence was not sufficient to prove the title of the petitioners to the flats in question, because the petitioners had not shown that the flats were appurtenant to the upland described in M'Neil's deed to the Commonwealth. The sheriff declined to instruct the jury as thus requested.

7. The respondents requested the sheriff to instruct the jury, that the Charlestown Branch Railroad Company, prosecuting this claim for damages against the respondents, under the agreement of October 15th, 1844, could recover no damages beyond what the Commonwealth were entitled to at that time. The sheriff declined to give such instruction, but instructed them, that the petitioners were entitled to recover damages as of the time of the filing of the location of the respondents' railroad.

8. After the evidence had been given on both sides, the respondents requested the sheriff to rule and instruct the jury thereon, that. the Commonwealth could not be a party complainant under the Rev. Sts. c. 39; that the Commonwealth had no right to claim the damages set forth in their petition, in this or in any other form; and that the petition was presented by and for the benefit of the Charlestown Branch Railroad Company, under an illegal contract. .But the sheriff declined to give the instructions so requested.

B. R. Curtis and *T. Farrar*, for the respondents.

S. Bartlett and *G. W. Warren*, for the petitioners.

The opinion of the court was delivered on the 26th of March, 1849.

SHAW, C. J.[1] This case- comes before us by way of appeal from an adjudication of the Court of Common Pleas, accepting and affirming the verdict of a sheriff's jury, awarding damages to the Commonwealth, for land taken by the respondents for the construction of their railroad.

In regard to what questions are open upon such an appeal, we refer to the cases of Walker and the Fitchburg Railroad Company against these respondents, which have been argued at the present sittings, and in which opinions are given at the same time with this.

Upon the great question argued in this case, namely,.whether the Commonwealth can claim any damages against the respondents, under their act of incorporation, it was contended by the petitioners, that the question was not open upon this appeal, and that upon the petition of the respondents for a jury to assess the damages, it was too late for them to insist, that no damages could be assessed. But whether the Commonwealth can claim damages or not, it appears to us, is a question of law. If no damage can be claimed, this is a good reason why the Court of Common Pleas should have set aside a verdict assessing damages; and if they have accepted a verdict,.which ought to have been rejected, such acceptance is an error in a matter of law apparent upon the record, and, of course, open for revision here on appeal. .

The Boston and Maine Railroad Extension Company, which has since become merged in the Boston and Maine Railroad, the present respondents, was incorporated by an act passed on the 16th March,

---

[1] Wilde, J., and Fletcher, J., did not sit in this cause.

1844, (St. 1844, c. 172,) with authority to construct and complete a railroad, not definitely located by the act, but with liberty to locate the same within certain limits so described, that it might pass over a part of the flats belonging to the land owned by the Commonwealth, on which the State Prison stands, or it might be located within the same limits, without crossing any of the land or flats constituting the State Prison lot. The route commenced at a point on the Boston and Maine Railroad in Wilmington, fifteen or sixteen miles from Boston, and terminated within the city of Boston, crossing Mystic and Charles Rivers. The track of this road must necessarily cross the track of the Charlestown Branch Railroad Company; and it was provided in the act, that it should not cross that road at any point east of the State Prison, without the assent of the directors of the Charlestown Branch Railroad Company. The Boston and Maine Railroad Extension Company, in addition to the above and a few other special provisions, not material to this inquiry, are invested with all the powers and privileges, and made subject to all the duties, restrictions, and liabilities, set forth in the forty-fourth chapter of the revised statutes, and in that part of the thirty-ninth chapter, and the statutes subsequently passed, which relate to railroads.

It is now insisted, on the part of the respondents, that this being the grant of a franchise, with power to take land, it is of necessity a grant for public use, for otherwise it would not justify the taking of private property; that if it is for the public use, the presumption of law is, that the Commonwealth intended to grant whatever was necessary to make it useful; and if the grant was in terms to lay out the road over any portion of the soil of the Commonwealth, or of a power to locate it in such manner that it would pass over any soil of the Commonwealth, and it has been so located, it was in either case a grant of such land to a public use, for which the Commonwealth can claim no compensation.

In considering this question, our first remark is, that the inquiry is limited to lands of the Commonwealth acquired by purchase, not for a highway or other public easement, but to be held by the Commonwealth, as a body politic, for a particular purpose, and to be used as land, as for a public prison; that it is also limited to upland, and such flats as the colony ordinance annexes to the soil of private owners of land bordering on creeks or coves in which the tide ebbs and flows; and that this is wholly independent of the question as to the right and power of the Commonwealth, in its sovereign capacity, over soil under navigable waters, or over flats beyond one hundred rods from any upland. The inquiry relates solely to the property of the Commonwealth which it holds in fee, in its capacity as a body politic.

It appears to us, that the question is purely a question of intention, to be derived from the act of the Commonwealth, as applied to
the subject-matter, and expounded in conformity with the established
rules of construction. It is very clear, that the Commonwealth, by
an act of legislation, in express terms, may grant its lands, or any
qualified interest or easement in land. It is equally clear, that the
Commonwealth may grant a franchise, including a power to lay out
a way over its lands, upon such terms as the legislature may prescribe, among which may be a condition, that the grantees shall pay
a reasonable compensation for any land of the Commonwealth which
may be taken; and the corporation thus created, by accepting the
act, will bind itself to a performance of the condition.

Upon a careful examination of the act of incorporation, in the present case, the court are of opinion, that it was not the intention of the
legislature to grant the land of the Commonwealth, or an easement
therein, to this corporation, without compensation. The act is in the
common form, and the substance of the franchise is: to be a corporation; to take land; and to take toll. We think, that if the legislature had intended to aid the enterprise by an appropriation of money,
land, or other means, — such aid being unusual, — the purpose to do
so would be in the same way expressed. Instead of this, the grant of
the franchise is made to the corporation, subject to the duties and
liabilities set forth in the thirty-ninth chapter of the revised statutes.
One of the liabilities expressed in that chapter, § 56, is this: " Every
railroad corporation shall be liable to pay all damages that shall be
occasioned by laying out and making and maintaining their road, or
by taking any land or materials;" and the section then provides
modes in which such damages shall be estimated, assessed, and
paid. This is very explicit: " all damages occasioned by laying
out, &c."

It was argued, that this was intended to apply to the case of private persons, whose property should be taken under the authority of
the State, in virtue of its sovereign power, and in the exercise of its
right of eminent domain. No doubt this would be its operation, in
a vast majority of cases; but the language is broad enough to extend
to the land of the Commonwealth, and therefore, as a general rule,
intending it to include all land taken; and it would be competent
for the legislature, under special circumstances, and when it is intended to aid such an enterprise, by the grant of public land, to
express it in terms in the act, leaving the general rule to operate
when no such purpose is intended by the government.

An argument in support of the view, that the section alluded to
was only intended to apply to the case of private persons, was drawn.

42 *

from the language of the highway act, Rev. Sts. c. 24, § 11, which provides an indemnity for damages sustained by any *persons* in their property.

To this several answers may be given: In the first place, the lay-ing out of a public highway is the obtaining of a pure public ease-ment, where there is no reimbursement by tolls, or other benefits; whereas a railroad, like a turnpike, is obtained upon another princi-ple; and although the public accommodation is the ultimate object, the whole expense in the first instance is advanced by individuals, as a joint-stock company, to be afterwards reimbursed by a toll. If, therefore, the right to damages, on laying out an open, public high-way, were limited to private persons, it would not necessarily follow, that the same reason should extend to railroads.

But, secondly, it is not clear that the indemnity is limited to per-sons; for by the Rev. Sts. c. 2, § 6, clause 13, the word "person" may extend and be applied to bodies politic and corporate, as well as to individuals. And the preamble of the constitution sets forth that instrument, as the mode of forming the inhabitants of the Com-monwealth into a body politic. But without placing much reliance upon considerations of so technical a character, we think that where general rights are declared, and remedies given, they include the Commonwealth, though not named. If a new mode were provided by law, for securing or recovering a debt, for getting possession of real estate, or the like, the Commonwealth would have the benefit of such new mode when applicable, though expressed in general terms. But, if there be any difference in the terms used between the case of common highways, and the case of railroads, then it is to be presumed that such a difference was intended by the legislature; and the larger terms, in respect to railroads, "all damages occasioned," &c., must be held to apply to the present case.

But it was urged, that it could not be presumed that the legis-lature intended to exact money in any form for property taken for a public easement; because the public, whose property it is, would obtain their equivalent in the enjoyment of the easement. An answer to this has been suggested above; but perhaps it re-quires to be somewhat more fully considered. The public accom-modation is the ultimate object of the enterprise, and warrants the interposition of the sovereign power of the government to procure it, and to prescribe the necessary means of obtaining it, to the extent of taking individual property, at an appraisement, subject to be revised by a jury. But the government may adopt whatever means they think expedient for obtaining such public accommodation. They may do it by a tax or charge on towns or counties, or by direct appropriations from the public treasury, or by grants of land, either of that over which a way is to be built, or of other lands owned by the Commonwealth. The latter was a very common expedient, when the State was the owner of large tracts of unsettled land. Or the State may grant the franchise, and authorize individuals to raise a fund, and make all the required outlays, in the first instance, to be reimbursed by tolls or fares to be levied upon the transit of passengers or merchandise.

The latter, it is believed, has been the plan in regard to every railroad, thus far established in this Commonwealth. The whole plan and scheme of the enterprise is, that the entire outlay and all the disbursements, including the value of land necessarily taken, shall be advanced in the first instance by the corporation; and the tolls, fares, and freights to be levied on transportation are to be so adjusted, that the aggregate shall pay all expenses and afford a fair income to the proprietors upon their entire investment. It is to make the travel accommodated pay the whole expense of the accommodation. Why, then, although the use is a public one, shall it be presumed, that the Commonwealth intended to give land, in a particular case, any more than it shall be presumed, that they intended to give money from the treasury?

This claim cannot be considered an equitable one by the corporation upon the Commonwealth, if they have consented to receive their reimbursements in another form, namely, from tolls, freights, and fares; and the corporation can judge before they embark in the enterprise, whether this source is adequate, and they are under no obligation to undertake it. They have a chance of making large profits; and they run the risk of sustaining loss; but if a loss occurs, the Commonwealth are not liable.

The same general view, we think, is an answer to another argument of the respondents, that the railroad corporation are constituted agents for the public in laying out the road, and that if the land of the Commonwealth is taken by them for that purpose, it is taken by their own agents. This is partly true, but the conclusion drawn from it does not follow. The corporation are agents for the public, and invested with power, within certain limits, to exercise the right of eminent domain; and to fix within certain limits the precise location of the road, and thereby to designate the specific land to be taken; but they are not the agents of the public, invested with authority to bind them by any contract, or to appropriate public land, money, or other property to the promotion of the enterprise.

The next material question is, whether the Commonwealth is rightly represented in these proceedings, before the sheriff's jury, and whether these proceedings were rightly conducted in this respect, there, and before the Court of Common Pleas, and in this court.

The proceedings now under consideration commenced with the petition of these respondents to the commissioners, praying that a warrant might be granted to the sheriff, to summon a jury to revise the damages assessed against them by the commissioners. It is to be presumed, that the commissioners gave notice of this petition, in some form, to the Commonwealth, before ordering a warrant. The warrant then issued, directed to the sheriff, in the usual form, commanding him to summon a jury, to meet, &c., and if they see cause, to consider and estimate the damage done to the Commonwealth, by the erection and construction of their railroad over and across the land of the Commonwealth. And the sheriff was thereby ordered to give notice of the time and place of meeting for the purposes aforesaid to the petitioners and all others interested. The return of the sheriff states, that he gave seasonable notice to the parties; as the parties were the respondents on the one side, and the Commonwealth on the other, it results that the Commonwealth were summoned, and it is not objected that they were not duly summoned. When no other special mode of summons is provided by law, notice to the governor, as the chief executive officer, would probably be considered good notice.

It then appears, by a statement accompanying the sheriff's return, and as a part of it, that at the time appointed for impanelling the jury, Messrs. Bartlett, Dana, and Warren appeared in behalf of the Commonwealth, and their right to do so being denied by the respondents, proof was offered of a letter addressed by his excellency, the Governor, to Samuel D. Parker, Esq., Commonwealth's Attorney for the County of Suffolk, dated December 24th, 1845; and Mr. Parker, being himself present, filed a letter under his hand, addressed to Messrs. Bartlett, Warren, and Dana, requesting them, on account of his engagements elsewhere, to appear for the Commonwealth and act in his behalf in conducting the cause before the sheriff. The sheriff decided, that the Commonwealth was rightly represented, to which decision exception was taken.

Upon this point, two questions arise: first, whether Mr. Parker himself was duly authorized to appear and represent the Commonwealth; and, second, whether he could lawfully substitute and authorize other duly qualified counsellors at law to act in his behalf, in the case of his necessary absence. As to the authenticity of the act, by which this substitution was made, no question can arise, because Mr. Parker appeared in person, to answer to the summons, and by a paper under his hand, addressed to Mr. Bartlett and others, requested them to appear in his behalf; and by presenting this paper to the sheriff, to be put on file, gave him notice of this substitution, with the exigency which occasioned it; and made an implied request to the sheriff that the counsel substituted might be, so received.

1. As to the first inquiry. There was not at that time, nor has there been since,[1] any attorney-general, or recognized general law officer of the Commonwealth. That office was abolished in 1843, by an act to be more particularly examined presently. By the Rev. Sts. c. 13, §§ 28, 34, and following sections, the duty of representing the Commonwealth was distributed amongst the several prosecuting officers, namely, the attorney-general, the district attorneys, and the Commonwealth's attorney for the county of Suffolk. By § 29, the attorney-general was required to appear for the Commonwealth in the Supreme Judicial Court, when holden as a full court, in all cases of prosecution for crimes punishable with death; and by § 30, he was required, when called upon by the governor, or either branch of the legislature, to appear for the Commonwealth, in any court or tribunal, in any other causes, criminal or civil, in which the Commonwealth might be a party or be interested. By §§ 37, 38, the attorney for Suffolk and the district attorney are required, within their respective districts, to appear for the Commonwealth in the Supreme Judicial Court, the Court of Common Pleas, and the Municipal Court of the city of Boston, in all cases, criminal or civil, in which the Commonwealth might be a party or interested, with other duties not material here to be enumerated.

Such was the state of the law, when the office of attorney-general was abolished by the statute of 1843, c. 99. By § 2, the attorney for the county of Suffolk, and the several district attorneys, within their respective districts, were required to appear for the Commonwealth, in all prosecutions for crimes punishable with death. This, together with their existing powers, conferred by the revised statutes, constituted a sufficient provision for the appearance of the Commonwealth in all cases civil and criminal, before the Supreme Judicial Court, the Court of Common Pleas, and Municipal Court. By the former law, they were required to perform all the duties in these courts, in their respective districts, which the attorney-general was authorized to perform, and which were not required to be done by him personally. But the attorney-general was, by the same act, required to appear personally before the full court, in all capital cases, and in law argu-

---

[1] The opinion was delivered before the passing of the act 1849, c. 186, by which the office of attorney-general was reëstablished.

ments, and also when required by the governor or either branch of the legislature, to appear for the Commonwealth in any court or tribunal, in any other causes, 'criminal' or civil, in which the Commonwealth might be a party or interested. When the office of attorney-general was abolished by the statute of 1843, c. 99, the execution of these powers was provided for by the third section in the following manner: " The Commonwealth's attorney for the county of Suffolk shall also, when required by the governor, or either branch of the legislature, appear in all causes, in which the Commonwealth shall be a party, or be interested, and shall, when required, give his opinion upon questions of law submitted to him by the legislature, or the governor and council."

This provision was obviously designed to provide for the exercise of those powers of the abolished office of attorney-general, which were not clearly provided for by the previous laws vesting power in the district attorneys, and the additional power given to those officers and to the attorney for Suffolk, in a previous section ($ 2) of the aet.

The words are broad and unlimited; " in all causes " when required by the governor. It is argued, that this language must be taken with some limitation, arising from other provisions giving powers to the district attorneys; otherwise there would be a clashing of authorities.

This may be answered, first, by the obvious suggestion, that the governor is not likely to make such requisition, when the case is already sufficiently provided for by the local officer; unless in some extraordinary emergency, when the local officer is disqualified by interest, sickness, or otherwise.

But, secondly, this is a ministerial authority, and should it be vested in two different persons, it is but a concurrent authority, like that given by the revised statutes to the attorney-general, and the district attorneys, to be exercised by either in the absence of the other, or by both together if present.

And, thirdly, in the present case, we are of opinion, that there was no such conflict, and that the district attorney for the district, including the county of Middlesex, had no authority ex officio to appear and represent the Commonwealth. The district attorneys were required ex officio, within their respective districts, to appear for the Commonwealth in the Supreme Judicial Court, Court of Common Pleas, and Municipal Court, in all cases civil or criminal. This case, when before the commissioners, or the sheriff's jury, was not within this description; and, of course, the authority to conduct it was not with the district attorney. But the attorney-general, when required by the governor, was required to appear before any court or tribunal; a description including a case like the present. This last power was a power vested, upon a like requisition, in the attorney for the county of Suffolk, and was not extended to the district attorneys.

The court are therefore of opinion, that upon the requisition of his excellency, the Governor, Samuel D. Parker, Esq. had authority to appear for the Commonwealth. The letter of the governor, dated December 24th, 1845, was an authority to institute proceedings, and such authority extends to the prosecution of such proceedings to their termination; and when the object is to recover damages for land taken, it not only includes the proceedings in the first instance before commissioners, but the subsequent proceedings before the sheriff's jury, to obtain a verdict, and before the Court of Common Pleas to obtain an affirmance of such verdict. The intimation to the attorney, Mr. Parker, to take care that the Commonwealth is saved harmless, is a caution and direction for his government, but not a condition precedent to the vesting of the authority.

2. Supposing the Commonwealth rightly before the sheriff, by their attorney, Mr. Parker, we can have no doubt, that with the permission of the court, — in this case, of the sheriff, — he had a right to avail himself of the aid and assistance of other counsel, in the conduct of the cause; many cases must occur in the course of practice, when such a public officer, charged with numerous and exacting duties, may require the aid of other suitable counsel, although the responsibility, for the proper management and conduct of the cause, devolves on him. We are, therefore, of opinion, that the decision of the sheriff, in ruling that Messrs. Bartlett, Warren, and Dana were duly authorized to appear as counsel for the Commonwealth, was right.

It should have been stated, in its proper place, that, in opposition to the appearance for the Commonwealth, the respondents insisted, that the present was not a case in which the Commonwealth were a party, or interested, because, from other facts of the case, it appeared, that the suit was prosecuted at the instance and for the benefit of the Charlestown Branch Railroad Company. But we think the Commonwealth were both a party and even interested. They were a party, because they claimed damages in their own legal right, and when damages were allowed them by the commissioners, they were summoned in, on the application of the respondents, to answer to their appeal for a jury. And although they might claim to recover for the use and benefit of another party, the claim of such other party was like that of the assignee of a chose in action, who could not claim in his own name. But the Commonwealth are also interested. The amount, when recovered, is, by the terms of the assignment, to be placed in the treasury of the Commonwealth, and it is only upon compliance with certain terms, that it is to be paid out to the Charlestown Branch Railroad Company. This, therefore, is no answer to the claim of the Commonwealth to appear and prosecute for their damages.

·Several other questions were raised on the report, which we shall pass over summarily.

1. It was objected that the contract between the Commonwealth and the Charlestown Branch Railroad Company was an illegal contract, and gave no right or title to that company.

We cannot perceive upon what ground the respondents can raise that question. In this respect, the rights of the Commonwealth and of that company constitute but one claim against the respondents, and, if as against them the Commonwealth have a right to recover the claim, it seems immaterial to them, whether these damages rest in the Commonwealth's treasury, for their own benefit, or go to the Charlestown Branch Railroad Company, in satisfaction of services done by them on a contract between them and the Commonwealth.

2. Another ground of exception was, that Fosdick was held competent to sit as a juror, although interested in the event of a succeeding case. We think that was no sufficient ground for the exclusion of the juror.

3. The admission of the testimony of Felton. The most that can be made of this exception is, that the testimony was immaterial. But we are of opinion, that it was competent. It bore upon the question of localities, and might have a just influence in giving effect to the construction of the alleged grant; especially if there were any latent ambiguities, in the terms of the grant, which became apparent upon applying it to the local objects mentioned in the description.

4. Raising the flats under and around the respondent's bridge. The respondents requested the sheriff to instruct the jury, that as this was not done at their request, the Commonwealth could not recover the cost of such filling up. The sheriff declined so to instruct, but gave the instruction, that the petitioners were entitled to such sum, for raising the flats, under and around the respondents' bridge, and within the location of the railroad, as the jury should find necessarily incurred in order to enable the Commonwealth to enjoy their other lands, if the jury should believe that such necessity was created by reason of the location and construction of the railroad.

This instruction was correct. The claim was not to be allowed, because it conferred an incidental benefit on the respondents by filling up a tract of flats for their bridge, which the respondents might otherwise have themselves been at the expense of filling; but because it was a convenient and economical mode, on the part of the Commonwealth, of securing their own flats for use and enjoyment, instead of building two long sea walls; the expense thus incurred being like that of fencing and the repairing of other damage incidental to the taking of land. If this filling up saved the necessity of sea walls, along the line of the railroad, which would otherwise have been necessary, it was no objection to adopting such expedient, if not more expensive than sea walls, that it conferred a benefit on the respondents. Some mode of securing their own grounds was a necessary incidental expense, and as such allowable.

5. The testimony of George A. Parker. The rule, laid down by the sheriff, was accurately and carefully stated.

6. It was objected, that the Charlestown Branch Railroad Company could recover no damage under the contract of October 15th, 1844. The sheriff's instructions, upon this point, were correct.

7. Exception was taken, that the evidence offered by the petitioners, in relation to their title to the flats, was not sufficient to maintain their title thereto, because they had not shown that the flats in question were appurtenant to the upland described in M'Neil's deed to the Commonwealth, and the respondents requested the sheriff so to instruct the jury, which he declined.

The deed of M'Neil, conveying the land and flats appurtenant, was in evidence; and the possession of the upland, by the Commonwealth, was proved by Austin and Wadsworth, and also the localities and admeasurements, upon this point of title to the flats.

But the true answer to this objection is, that the question was purely one of fact for the jury, upon the evidence; that the sheriff could not be called upon to instruct the jury in regard to the weight, effect, or sufficiency of the evidence; and that no question of law arises thereon, which is open on this appeal.

When the above opinion had been pronounced, the petitioners moved for an allowance of interest on the amount of the damages awarded by the jury, and also for costs.

S. Bartlett, for the petitioners.

B. R. Curtis, for the respondents.

The opinion of the court was subsequently delivered.

SHAW, C. J. An opinion having been expressed in favor of the petitioners, affirming a judgment of the Court of Common Pleas, accepting a verdict, in their behalf, for damages for taking land, an application is now made by them for an allowance of costs, and also for interest on the verdict.

1. As to costs : the claim, as we understand it, is for the costs and expenses of the jury, and for the sheriff's costs, incurred after the estimate of damages made by the commissioners, together with the costs of the Court of Common Pleas, to which court the verdict was returned. We understand the facts to be, that it was conceded on the part of the petitioners, that the amount of the damages awarded by the county commissioners was somewhat larger than the amount awarded by the verdict of the jury ; that is, that the verdict of the jury reduced the amount of the commissioners' estimate to some extent.

The provision of the Rev. Sts. c. 39, § 62, which is the only direct provision on the subject in the railroad act, does not seem to reach the case. After having provided, in § 57, that either party, dissatisfied with the estimate of the commissioners, may apply to the commissioners to order a jury, the statute proceeds in this section to direct, that the railroad company may tender the amount of the damage as estimated, and if the owner shall refuse to accept it, with costs to be taxed to that time, and shall apply to a jury, &c., he shall pay all costs, unless he shall increase the damages ; and if the corporation shall apply, &c., of course, not having made a tender, because they are dissatisfied, and the ground of their complaint is, that the damages are too high, and if, on a final hearing, they shall not obtain a reduction of the damages, they shall pay all costs.

The provisions in the statute respecting common highways throw no light on the subject, because the course of proceeding is altogether different. There the petitioners for a road, in the outset, enter into an obligation to pay all costs, &c. Besides, the application for a jury can only be made by the land-owner, and cannot be made by the county. Baker v. Thayer, 3 Met. 312. Nor does the question depend upon the general statute, respecting the prevailing party, in actions at law. Hampshire and Hampden Canal Co. v. Ashley, 15 Pick. 496.

We are then brought back to the provisions of c. 39, § 62. Up to the time of the completion of the commissioners' estimate, the landowner, by implication, is entitled to his costs if he accepts such estimate ; because it is provided that the amount of the estimated damages may be tendered, and if the land-owner declines accepting such amount with costs, he proceeds at the peril of paying costs, if he does not increase the amount.

The statute then provides, that if the railroad company apply for a jury, and fail to reduce the damages, they shall pay all the costs. This is a clear implication, that if they do succeed in reducing the damages, they are not to pay costs. But this is the extent of such implication, and it does not follow, in such case, that the railroad company are to recover costs against the petitioners, and there is no express provision to that effect. We are, therefore, of opinion, that in a case like the present, neither of the parties is liable to the other for the costs of proceeding before the sheriff and jury; not the respondents, because they have succeeded in reducing the damages, and, therefore, by the necessary implication of the statute, are exempt from costs; nor the petitioners, because the statute charges them with costs, where they have refused a tender of the damages estimated by the commissioners, and have failed to increase the damages by a verdict of the jury. This rule, however, does not apply to the costs of the appeal from the judgment of the Court of Common Pleas, accepting the verdict of the jury, to this court. That appeal was taken by the railroad company, and the judgment of the Court of Common Pleas has been affirmed; and therefore we think that the petitioners are entitled to their taxable costs of the appeal, to wit, the travel, attendance, copies, entry in this court, and other taxable costs of the appeal. These costs are to be taxed here, and included in the certificate to the commissioners.

2. In making up the judgment in this court, we are of opinion, that interest ought to be allowed to the present time, from the time that the verdict was returned to the Court of Common Pleas. The amount then became liquidated, and in the nature of a judgment. The case of writs of error is very analogous. Rev. Sts. c. 112, § 14. The statute gives interest at six per cent, and allows a greater rate in certain cases. Whenever a case is detained in court for advisement, it has been the practice to allow interest on the verdict. Interest is allowed in debt on judgment as damages. And by a recent statute, interest is taxable on executions.

But we think this point is settled by Rev. Sts. c. 82, §§ 15 and 10. In the case of an appeal, if the defendant fails to enter his appeal, the court may, on complaint, affirm the former judgment, or render such judgment as law and justice shall require. We believe it has.been the practice, under this authority, to allow interest as an incident. So by § 14, the court may render a similar judgment, on complaint, when an acceptant fails to enter his exceptions. Then comes § 15, which, we think, applies to both cases, and vests the court with the fullest authority to make such order as the Court of Common Pleas should have done and render such judgment, &c.

We consider it the plain dictate of justice, when money is due on

The Fitchburg Railroad Co. v. The Boston and Maine Railroad.

a judgment, or on a verdict in the nature, of a judgment, and payment is prevented by the necessary time taken for reëxamining the
case, if it result in confirming the former judgment, and showing that
the party was then entitled to his money, that interest should be
allowed as a just compensation for the delay.

3. In regard to the mode of executing the judgment, the authorities
not having been collated, we were inclined to suppose, that an execution or warrant of distress from this court, under its general authority
to award all process necessary to carry its judgment into effect, would
be the proper mode.

But we think it is expressly provided for, by a recent statute, that
of 1847, c. 259, § 3, which directs that the mode shall be by a warrant
of distress, to be issued by the county commissioners. When, therefore, the amount of damages is liquidated by computing and adding
the interest, and the costs are taxed, a certificate will be awarded to
the county commissioners, directing them to issue a warrant of distress for the amount.

THE FITCHBURG RAILROAD COMPANY v. THE BOSTON AND MAINE
RAILROAD.[1]

Middlesex Co., January Term, 1849.

*Assessment of Damages — Setting aside Verdict of Jury — Remedy
for Irregular Proceedings by Certiorari — Practice in Assessing
Damages — Number of Jurors to be Summoned — Damages to
Wharves and Sea Walls.*

The authority of the Court of Common Pleas, to set aside the verdict of a sheriff's jury, for
good cause, is only to be exercised for some cause affecting the legality, justice, or merits
of the case.

If an adjudication of the Court of Common Pleas, setting aside the verdict of a sheriff's jury,
is founded upon any cause contained in the warrant, return, or verdict, such cause is
matter of law apparent upon the record, and will come before this court on appeal; if the
adjudication is founded on a cause shown *aliunde*, — under which designation, the record
of the anterior proceedings before the commissioners is to be included, if such record is
adduced for the purpose of showing any fact affecting the merits of the case, — such
cause is matter of fact, upon which the decision of the Court of Common Pleas is con-

[1] 3 Cushing's Reports, 58.

clusive ; and if either party objects in this court to any decision or adjudication of the Court of Common Pleas, in matter of law, the ground of such objection must be specially stated in the decision or adjudication itself, or in a bill of exceptions filed and allowed in that court.

If the proceedings of county commissioners, in estimating damages for land taken for a railroad, are irregular, the remedy is to be sought by an application to this court for a *certiorari*, and not by an application to the commissioners for a jury to revise the damages. If the latter course be taken, it is an admission that the previous proceedings are regular, and a waiver of exceptions thereto.

When application is made to county commissioners, for the assessment of damages for land, &c., taken for a railroad, and it is brought to the knowledge of the commissioners, before a warrant is issued for a jury, that there are other parties interested who have made no application, and such parties are thereupon summoned in, their damages are first to be assessed by the commissioners, before the case is sent to a jury.

Where the estimate made by county commissioners of the damages sustained by a tenant for years, in consequence of the location and construction of a railroad over his estate, is revised by a jury, on the petition of such tenant, and the verdict of the jury is set aside by the Court of Common Pleas, and the case remanded to the county commissioners ; it seems, that it is competent to the commissioners on the motion of the petitioner, to dismiss the petition for a jury, and to bring forward the original petition, and to summon in the reversioner to become a party thereto, and thereupon to proceed to estimate the whole damages, and to apportion the same between the parties interested. If such proceeding be objectionable, it can only be excepted to by the lessee, and not by the proprietors of the railroad.

On an appeal to this court, from an adjudication of the Court of Common Pleas, accepting the verdict of a sheriff's jury, assessing damages for land taken for a railroad, it being objected by the respondent, that the Board of County Commissioners, when making an estimate of the damages, in the first instance, was not duly constituted; and the ground of this objection appearing only on the record of the proceedings before the commissioners, a copy of which was among the papers in the case ; it was held, that this objection was not open upon the appeal, and that if well founded originally, the respondents had waived it by proceeding before the commissioners.

In executing the warrant for a sheriff's jury, it seems that the officer is not restricted by the Rev. Sts. c. 24, § 18, to summoning only twelve persons to constitute the jury, but that he is thereby directed to summon a jury to consist of twelve men; for which purpose, and in order to insure the attendance of twelve, it is not irregular to summon fourteen.

The line of the harbor of Boston, as established by the act of 1840, c. 35, at a particular part thereof on the Charlestown side, was fixed at a point described as fifteen feet distant from the south corner of Gould's Wharf, and three hundred and twelve feet distant from a sea wall from which Gould's Wharf projected; and the south corner of Gould's Wharf was found by measurement to be three hundred and two feet distant from the sea wall; it was held, on a trial before a sheriff's jury, that the sheriff was not bound to instruct them, either that there was such an ambiguity in respect to that part of the line, that it could not be determined upon the evidence, where the line was, or that the true line was ten and not fifteen feet from the south corner of Gould's Wharf; but that the question was one of fact, to be left to the jury upon the evidence.

The Charlestown Wharf Company were authorized by the act of 1841, c. 35, to extend and maintain their several wharves, lying between Gray's Wharf and the Prison Point Bridge, into the channel, as far as the line established by the act of 1840, c. 35, for the harbor of Boston, with the right and privilege to lay vessels at the sides and ends of such wharves, and to receive wharfage and dockage therefor : At the time of the passing of this act, the Charlestown Wharf Company were the proprietors of several wharves within the limits mentioned in the act, and, for a considerable distance between Warren Bridge and Prison Point Bridge, of a sea wall built below high-water mark, and filled up behind to high-water mark, and used for the purpose of landing lumber and other things upon,

43 *

with pier or pile wharves about eighty feet in width, projecting therefrom towards the channel: It was held, that the sea wall, being an artificial structure, adapted to the purposes for which it was used, was a wharf within the meaning of the act, and that the proprietors were thereby authorized to extend the same along their whole front to the line of the harbor.

Where the proprietor of a wharf in the harbor of Boston was authorized by an act of the legislature to extend the same into the channel to the line of the harbor; and, before any extension thereof, in pursuance of such act, the legislature incorporated a railroad company, with authority to locate and construct a railroad across and over the flats between such wharf and the line of the harbor; it was held, that the act authorizing such extension operated as a grant to the proprietor of the wharf, and was not a mere license revocable at the pleasure of the legislature, and revoked by the act incorporating the railroad company.

An act of the legislature having authorized a railroad corporation to make certain erections for their road between the channels of Charles and Miller's Rivers, in a manner particularly specified in the act; and such erections having been made accordingly, in the manner specified, whereby the course of the currents of these rivers was changed, and directed towards and upon certain wharves and flats, rendering additional sea wall and filling necessary to secure the same; it was held, that the damage thereby occasioned to the proprietor was *damnum absque injuria*, for which he was not entitled to recover against the railroad corporation.

On a proceeding before a sheriff's jury, instituted by the Fitchburg Railroad Company for the recovery of damages occasioned by the laying out and construction of the Boston and Maine Railroad over the land, wharves, and flats of the former, the respondents introduced a letter signed by the president of the petitioners, and addressed to the president of the respondents, dated the 10th of August, 1844, in the following terms: "The committee of the directors of the F. R. Co. have considered your application for a part of the flats of this company in C. for your corporation, and have come to the conclusion, that they are not prepared to dispose of any of said flats, or at this time to name any price for what the law allows you to take for your road, but that you can go on, and lay the sea wall as you propose, and fill up a sufficient width for the track, and settle all damages with Mr. James Gould, at your expense; and the whole matter shall be settled on equitable terms hereafter." P. S. "It is understood that the wall and filling up is to be considered as above. And it was in evidence, that the respondents had subsequently built a road and wall, as alluded to in the letter; it was held, that such letter and subsequent proceeding did not prove any contract or agreement between the parties, relative to the subject thereof.

A sheriff's jury, in making up their verdict, may, if they think proper, consider each item or charge of damage separately, and state in their verdict what items they allow, and the amounts thereof, severally, and what they reject; and where the verdict is returned in this form, any item of damage, which, in point of law, is objectionable, may be remitted or deducted, without setting aside the verdict.

The Fitchburg Railroad Company having claimed damages of the Boston and Maine Railroad, for land and wharves and certain flats, (over which they were authorized to extend their wharves,) taken by the latter for their road; and the sheriff's jury, by whom the damages were estimated, having returned a verdict assessing the greater part thereof "for the land over which the said company had a right to build a pier wharf," between the sea wall and the line of the harbor, "and for the injury to other land on which the said F. R. Co. had a right to build a pier wharf," and it was objected, that the verdict was erroneous, in giving the damages only for land over which the petitioners had a right to build a pier wharf: It was held, that though there might be some inaccuracy in the terms of the verdict, there was nothing to warrant the conclusion, that it did not include land owned by the petitioners and taken by the respondents.

JAMES GOULD, on the 15th of October, 1844, presented his petition, dated the 12th, to the County Commissioners of Middlesex, requesting them to view certain leasehold premises in his occupation, and estimate the damages sustained by him, in consequence of the location and construction of the Boston and Maine Railroad over and across the same.

The petitioner represented that he was the lessee, for the term of seven years, commencing on the 1st of April, 1839, of a certain wharf situated in Charlestown, being the wharf next south-easterly of Prison Point Bridge, (as described in the petition,) with the right and privilege to lay vessels upon and over a strip of flats thirty feet wide, adjoining each side and the end of said wharf, and the right to pass and repass to and from the demised premises with boats and vessels; that he had used the same for the purposes of a lumber wharf, and had also erected thereon a limekiln and other buildings where he carried on the manufacture of lime; and that the Boston and Maine Railroad Extension Company had located their railroad over and across the south-westerly part of the premises, and had taken and intended to take a strip of the same, five rods in width, passing directly through the limekiln and other buildings, by means whereof his wharf and premises had been rendered of little value for the purposes of a wood and lumber wharf, and of no value for the manufacture of lime.[1]

On this petition, the commissioners appointed a meeting at the Middlesex House in Charlestown, on the 15th day of November, then next, for the purpose of hearing the parties in relation to the prayer of the petition, and ordered notice to be given thereof to the Boston and Maine Railroad Extension Company.

The commissioners met accordingly; and the parties being present, the petitioner was allowed by the respondents to amend his petition, by adding to the description of the premises alleged therein to be injured, that he was also the lessee of a certain tract of land and flats (describing the same) next south-westerly of the Prison Point Bridge in Charlestown. This amendment was filed by agreement, and was to be considered as inserted in the petition.

The commissioners then proceeded to view the premises, and to hear the parties, and, having heard them, estimated the damages of the petitioner at $2,500, to be paid to him by the respondents, with costs, and continued the petition to their next meeting. At the next meeting, held on the first Tuesday of January, 1845, the petitioner, being dissatisfied with the commissioners' estimate, applied to them to issue a warrant for a jury to assess his damages. The commis-

---

[1] The localities, referred to in this case, will be found delineated on the map, inserted at page 469.

sioners granted the request, and a warrant was issued, and duly executed and returned by the sheriff, with a verdict of the jury esti-mating the petitioner's damages at the sum of $3,391.79, which was presented to the Court of Common Pleas, at the September term, 1845, for acceptance. The respondents objected to the verdict, for several reasons, and, amongst others, because no notice was given to the proprietors of the estates leased to the petitioner, pursuant to the provisions of the statute; and, therefore, that a judgment entered on the verdict would be no bar to further litigation, in which the value of the same property would again come in question; and because the verdict did not conform to the provisions of the Rev. Sts. c. 24, § 50, which require, in case any party interested in the estate has sustained damage, that the verdict shall find and set forth the total amount of damages sustained by the entire estate, and shall then apportion the same among the parties interested. The Court; of Common Pleas, after hearing the parties on the respondents' objec-tions, ordered the verdict to be set aside and the case to be remanded to the commissioners.

The proceedings of the Court of Common Pleas, in setting aside the verdict, being certified to the county commissioners, at their meeting on the first Tuesday of January, 1846, they, thereupon, at the request of the petitioner, ordered his petition for a jury to be dismissed, and his original petition, for an appraisement of damages against the Boston and Maine Railroad Extension Company, to be brought forward and reinstated on their docket. They then passed an order, in the following terms : " It having been certified, &c.; and now at this meeting the petitioner having requested the commissioners to estimate his damages as stated in his first petition; and it appear-ing from the same, and being proved by other evidence, that the peti-tioner is only entitled to an estate for years in the premises described in the petition, and that the reversion in fee of a part of the premises belongs to the Fitchburg Railroad Company, and of the other part to the Commonwealth of Massachusetts : It is ordered, that the peti-tioner give the Fitchburg Railroad Company, and the Commonwealth, notice of the pendency of his petition, by serving the clerk of the Fitchburg Railroad Company, and also the secretary of the Com-monwealth, with an attested copy of the petition and this order thereon, thirty days at least before the meeting of the commissioners, to be holden by adjournment from this meeting, &c., on the fourth Tuesday of March next, that such parties may then and there appear, if they see cause, and become parties to the proceedings under the petition."

At the adjourned meeting of the commissioners, on the fourth

Tuesday of March, 1846, the Commonwealth and the Fitchburg Railroad Company, having been duly notified according to the order of the commissioners, appeared and became parties to the proceeding in the matter of Gould's petition, the former by James Dana and George W. Warren, and the latter by E. R. Hoar, their attorney; and the commissioners thereupon appointed a meeting to be held on the 25th day of May, then next, for the purpose of viewing the premises, and hearing the parties, and directed notice thereof to be given to all persons and corporations interested, by serving the clerk of the Boston and Maine Railroad with a copy of Gould's petition and of the commissioners' order thereon, fourteen days before the time appointed for the meeting.

The commissioners met, according to their appointment, on the 25th of May, 1846, for the purposes above stated. At this meeting, two only of the commissioners attended; the third being absent, and his place supplied by one of the special commissioners. The return of the proceedings stated, that Charles Tower, Esq., one of the special commissioners, was present and acted instead of Ebenezer Barker, Esq., " one of the said county commissioners, who declined to sit on account of circumstances existing between him and the parties, which, in his judgment, rendered it improper that he should do so." The commonwealth appeared by Samuel D. Parker, Esq., " attorney therefor 'within and for the county of Suffolk, authorized and instructed thereunto, by its governor, under a resolve of the legislature thereof; " and the other parties by their respective attorneys.

The Fitchburg Railroad Company then filed with the commissioners a written statement of their claim for damages against the Boston and Maine Railroad, (with which the Boston and Maine Railroad Extension Company had then been united and merged,) embracing not only the property described in Gould's petition, but also other property which they alleged had been injured by the location of the respondents' road. This statement was filed by consent, and under an agreement signed by the parties, and filed with the commissioners, that, as it was desirable that the whole claim of the Fitchburg Railroad Company for damages against the respondents should be determined and adjusted at the same time, the respondents should take no exception to the claim, for the reason that it had reference to other property than that included and described in Gould's petition ; but that the commissioners, and a jury, should one be summoned in the case, might adjudge all damages specified in the claim, to which the company were legally entitled under the proceeding upon Gould's petition, and under the claim then filed, in the same manner, and to the same extent as if the claim of the company thereto were set forth in a separate petition regularly before the commissioners or a jury.

The petitioner Gould filed a statement with the commissioners, at the same meeting, withdrawing that portion of his claim for damages, which was set forth in the amendment to his original petition for the reason, that the premises therein described were the property of the Commonwealth, and comprised all the property described in his petition, in which the Commonwealth had any interest. Gould, at the same time, waived all claim for damages against the respondents, on account of his having been the lessee of the premises described in the amendment, and requested the commissioners to award him no damages therefor.

The attorney for the Commonwealth also filed a paper with the commissioners, consenting, on behalf of the Commonwealth, to Gould's withdrawal of his claim for damages as the lessee of the Commonwealth, and (without intending thereby to waive the Commonwealth's claim for damages under a distinct petition then pending before the commissioners) withdrawing the Commonwealth's appearance, or right to appear, in the proceedings on Gould's petition.

By the arrangement thus made among the parties, and carried into effect with the sanction of the commissioners, the case presented a claim of damages by the Fitchburg Railroad Company for land taken by the respondents, and a claim of damages by Gould, for an injury occasioned thereby to his leasehold estate in a part of the same premises.

The Fitchburg Railroad Company, in the statement of their claim filed as above mentioned, represented, that since the 16th of March, 1844, they had been, and then were, seised in fee of a certain parcel of land, wharves, and flats, in Charlestown, bounded southeasterly by Warren Avenue and Warren Bridge; southerly and south-westerly on Charles and Miller's rivers, by the line known as the "commissioners' line;" northerly by land and flats belonging to the Commonwealth of Massachusetts; and westerly and north-westerly by Front street, in Charlestown; with a right to lay vessels at the ends of all wharves built, or which might be built, on the premises, and the right to pass and repass to and from the same with boats and vessels: — that the respondents had laid out their railroad across the south-westerly part of the premises, five rods wide, and had taken for that purpose a portion of the petitioners' land, wharves, and flats, containing twenty-six thousand four hundred square feet; that four thousand five hundred and eleven square feet of the land so taken constituted a part of a wharf described in Gould's petition as taken by the respondents, and when taken was held by

Gould, with a right in the flats and docks adjoining, as stated in his petition, under a lease which expired on the first of April, 1846 :— that by the taking of their land, another part of the premises first mentioned, namely, a piece bounded on the north-west by land. of the Commonwealth, north-easterly by land taken by the respondents, and south-westerly by the commissioner's line, containing about seventeen thousand five hundred and thirty-six square feet, was much injured and reduced in value, and separated from all approach from the other land of the petitioners :— that by the taking of their land as aforesaid, and by the construction of the respondents' road, all the remainder of the premises first described were injured and lessened in value by being divided thereby in an inconvenient form, and by being cut off from all free and convenient approach by water, as they had before enjoyed; that by the construction of the railroad, and the building of the draw therein nearest the first described premises, the action of the current of Miller's River, and the tides therein, had been altered, so as to injure and endanger the washing away of the first described premises, and to render insecure any sea wall erected or to be erected thereon :— that by an act passed on the 25th of March, 1845, (St. 1845, c. 224,) the respondents were authorized to build a sea wall, and inclose and make solid the flats between Miller's River and Charles River, for the purposes of their road, to the extent therein limited, and were required to open and maintain a new and sufficient channel, for the waters and tides of Miller's River, westerly of the inclosure; and that by the erection and inclosure, and by the opening and maintaining of the new channel, the property first described of the petitioners was endangered and diminished in value, and the channels and approaches by water thereto were liable and likely to be filled up, obstructed, and destroyed.

The commissioners, after viewing the premises and hearing the parties, estimated Gould's damages at the sum of two thousand five hundred dollars, and the damages of the Fitchburg Railroad Company at the sum of forty-six thousand four hundred and forty-four dollars; which sums they ordered the respondents to pay to the petitioners, respectively, with costs to be taxed by the commissioners. The commissioners stated, in their return, that no damages were assessed by them for the Commonwealth, the claim therefor having been withdrawn; and that in estimating the damages, they had conformed to and observed the agreements of the parties. The return was dated on the first of June, 1846.

The respondents, being dissatisfied with the estimate of the commissioners, presented their petition for a jury, on the 2d of July, 1846. They alleged therein that all the anterior proceedings, (which they recapitulated and the record of which they prayed might be considered as part of their petition,) and the last-mentioned estimate of damages and order thereon, were irregular, oppressive, and illegal; that they were aggrieved and dissatisfied with the same; and that for want of a more direct remedy they applied for a jury to be awarded for the purposes and agreeably to the provisions of the statutes for such case made and provided.

The commissioners thereupon ordered the clerk to issue a warrant, directed to the sheriff, for the purposes mentioned in the respondent's petition, at such time as they should call for it; and the same was called for by them and issued accordingly, in the usual form, on the 3d of October, 1846. The parties had previously entered into the agreement, stated on page 490, in the case of the Commonwealth against these respondents, for proceedings in the execution of the warrant, after the expiration of the time limited therein, and returning the verdicts, when prepared, as of the September term of the Court of Common Pleas.

The sheriff proceeded to execute the warrant, and caused fourteen persons, namely, five from Charlestown, four from Somerville, and five from Cambridge, those being the "three nearest towns not interested in the question," to be drawn and returned as jurors, who were duly summoned and attended before the sheriff, at the Mansion House, in Charlestown, on the 2d of November, 1846, for the purposes mentioned in the warrant. Twelve of the persons so returned were then impanelled, with the consent of the parties, under a warrant directed to the sheriff for the assessment of damages in the case of the Commonwealth against these respondents. The jury so impanelled were occupied with that case until the fifth of November, when two of the five returned from Charlestown, being stockholders in the Fitchburg Railroad Company, were set aside by the sheriff, as interested, and the remaining twelve were impanelled and sworn, and proceeded to the trial of this cause, and after viewing the premises and hearing the parties agreed upon a verdict. The sheriff returned the verdict, together with a certificate of such of his rulings and instructions to the jury as the parties requested him to certify, and a statement of certain documentary and other evidence, which he was requested by the respondents to make a part of his return, to the Court of Common Pleas, by whom the verdict was accepted. The respondents then appealed to this court.

The jury, by their verdict, assessed the whole damages sustained by both the petitioners, Gould and the Fitchburg Railroad Company, at the sum of forty-three thousand four hundred and sixty-four dollars and ten cents, which they apportioned between them, in proportion to their several interests, and the damages respectively sustained by them.

The award of damages in favor of Gould, and the exceptions taken by the respondents to the rulings and instructions of the sheriff to the jury in his case, became immaterial, in consequence of a settlement between him and the respondents, which took place after the appeal and before the hearing in this court.

The verdict, so far as it relates to the claim of the Fitchburg Railroad Company, was as follows : —

"And to the said Fitchburg Railroad Company, the sum of forty thousand four hundred and fifty-one dollars and ninety-eight cents ; from which sum the jury deduct a claim of the said Boston and Maine Railroad Company, amounting to seventeen hundred and seventy-five dollars and ninety-eight cents, by agreement of parties; leaving a balance to the said Fitchburg Railroad Company, of thirty-eight thousand six hundred and seventy-six dollars, for their damages as aforesaid. Of which the sum of thirty-eight thousand one hundred and seventy-six dollars, together with one thousand seven hundred and seventy-five dollars ninety-eight cents, the amount of claim deducted as aforesaid, is for the land over which the said company had a right to build a pier wharf, which was taken by the said Boston and Maine Railroad, between the sea wall and the commissioners' line, and for the injury to other land on which the said Fitchburg Railroad Company had a right to build a pier wharf. And the sum of five hundred dollars is for the injury done to the land of the said Fitchburg Railroad Company, by the diversion of the current caused by the bridge, pier, and draw of the said Boston and Maine Railroad."

The questions, upon which the cause was argued in this court, arose upon sundry objections taken by the respondents to the anterior proceedings, as hereinbefore set forth, and to the form of the verdict, as above stated, and upon the rulings and instructions of the sheriff to the jury, as certified by him.

The respondents contended, that it was open to them to object to the anterior proceedings, on the ground, among others, that all those proceedings appeared on the record of the adjudication of the Court of Common Pleas, from which the respondents appealed. The record of that court, a copy of which was in the case, contained a recital of the petition of the respondents for a jury, in which all the anterior proceedings were summarily set forth, with a prayer that the record thereof, in full, might be considered as a part of the petition; also a statement of the verdict as rendered by the jury ; and, lastly, a statement of the acceptance of the verdict by the Court of Common Pleas, and the appeal therefrom by the respondents.

The respondents objected: 1st. That the proceedings of the commissioners, on Gould's petition, were irregular; 2d. That the board, when assessing the damages, was not properly constituted; 3d. That five of the jurors summoned were taken from Charlestown; 4th. That fourteen jurors, instead of twelve, were summoned; 5th. That the case did not go to the same jury with that of the Commonwealth, pending at the same time, against the same respondents; and, 6th. That the verdict was erroneous in awarding the principal part of the damages for the land over which the petitioners had a right to build a pier wharf.

The rulings and instructions of the jury, which were objected to, were as follows: —

1. The legislature, by an act, "concerning the harbor of Boston," passed on the 17th of March, 1840, (St. 1840, c. 35,) established certain lines therein described as the lines of the harbor of Boston, beyond which no wharf or pier should ever thereafter be extended into and over the tide waters of the Commonwealth. The fourth section established the lines on the Charlestown side of the harbor, commencing at the south-west corner of the most westerly navy yard wharf, and thence extending westerly to a point in the Prison Point Bridge. This line, so far as it is material to be here stated, commenced at "the south-east corner of the wharf belonging to the Charlestown Land and Wharf Company, nearly opposite a passage-way; thence north-westerly, about nine hundred and twenty feet, to a point in range with the east side of Fifth street, being two hundred and eighty-four feet westerly from the sea wall, measured on a line in range with said east side of Fifth street; thence, north-westerly about five hundred and ninety feet, to a point fifteen feet from the south corner of wharf B, occupied by Charles Gould, as a lime wharf, which point is three hundred and twelve feet from the sea wall of the Charlestown Land and Wharf Company; thence, north-westerly, about four hundred feet to Prison Point Bridge, at a point which is eighty-six feet easterly from the east side of the draw in said bridge, and three hundred and twenty-three feet south-westerly from the sea wall, measuring along the south-easterly side of said Prison Point Bridge." [1] The sixth section of the act provided, that no wharf or pier, then erected, on the inner side of the line, should be extended further towards the same, than such wharf or pier then stood, or might have been lawfully enlarged or extended, before the

---

[1] The names both of Gould and the Wharf Company are here incorrectly given. The corporate name of the latter is the "Charlestown Wharf Company."

passing of the act, without leave being first obtained from the legislature.

At the time this act was passed, the premises in question were the property of the Charlestown Wharf Company; a portion thereof being then under a lease to Gould, and occupied by him, as set forth in his petition. By an act passed on the 27th of February, 1841, (St. 1841, c. 35,) the company, their successors and assigns, were authorized, under certain limitations, to extend and maintain their several wharves, amongst others, those lying between Warren Bridge and Prison Point Bridge, into the channel, as far as the line established by the act above mentioned, with the right and privilege to lay vessels at the sides and ends of said respective wharves, (so much of the same as might be constructed in the channel to be built on piles,) and receive wharfage and dockage therefor. In the year 1843, before the incorporation of the Boston and Maine Railroad Extension Company, the Fitchburg Railroad Company became the owners of the premises described in their petition, by a purchase and assignment thereof, with all the rights belonging to the grantors, under the acts above mentioned, from the Charlestown Wharf Company.

The railroad of the respondents having been laid out in part over the flats, upon and over which the petitioners were authorized by the last-mentioned act to extend their wharves, to the line of the harbor, or "commissioners' line," as it was called, and the petitioners claiming damages for the flats so taken, it became important to ascertain the extent of their right thereto under the statute, and for that purpose to determine the course and position of the line of the harbor, relatively to the petitioners' other estate.

The petitioners contended, that the line run at the distance of fifteen feet from the south corner of Gould's wharf, as stated in the act, and as laid down on the plans exhibited by them to the jury. The respondents introduced evidence, that the south corner of Gould's wharf was three hundred and two feet distant from the sea wall, which would make the line contended for by the petitioners three hundred and seventeen feet from the sea wall, and thereupon insisted either that the line was at that part of it incapable of determination, or that it was five feet nearer the shore than it was alleged to be by the petitioners. This discrepancy was the subject of the first exception, which was thus certified by the sheriff: —

"In the course of the trial, it having been proved, that the south-east corner of Gould's wharf was three hundred and two feet from the old sea wall of the Charlestown Wharf Company, mentioned in the statute of 1840, c. 35, § 4, and that the commissioners' line laid down on the plans, and claimed by the petitioners, was fifteen feet in advance of said corner; the. respondents requested me to rule, that there is such an ambiguity in respect to that part of the commissioners' line, that it cannot now be determined, upon the present state of the evidence, where the line is, or secondly, that the true line is five feet nearer the shore, and I refused so to rule."

2. It appearing in evidence, that the sea wall of the Charlestown Wharf Company, between Warren Bridge and Prison Point Bridge, was built at different distances, below high-water mark, and above low-water mark, and was filled up behind and used for landing lumber, and other things thereon, and that the pier or pile wharves, projecting therefrom towards the channel, were about eighty feet wide; the respondents requested the sheriff to instruct the jury, that by the act of 1841, c. 35, the wharf company and their successors and assigns were not authorized to advance the sea wall, but only the projecting wharves, by a pier wharf, to the commissioners' line ; and, also, that the act, as a license to the company, was revocable by the legislature, before the company had acted under it, and was in fact revoked, as to that part of the flats taken by the respondents, by their act of incorporation.

The petitioners requested the sheriff to instruct the jury, that if they were satisfied of the existence of a wharf or wharves extending from the land of the Commonwealth towards Warren Bridge, as far as the lands extended for which damages were claimed, and between Warren Bridge and Prison Point Bridge, prior to and at the time of the passing of the act of 1841, c. 35, that the Charlestown Wharf Company were empowered by that act to build a pier wharf to the harbor line, as far as such wharf or wharves extended.

The respondents objected to the proposed instruction, on the ground, among others, that it did not discriminate, as the act of 1840, c. 35, referred to in the act of 1841, c. 35, did, between the wharves and sea wall then existing, and requested the sheriff to instruct the jury, that the right granted to the Charlestown Wharf Company by the last-named statute, to extend their wharves on piles to the commissioners' line, embraced only the wharf then existing, in distinction from the sea wall mentioned in the former statute, and did not extend to the sea wall, so as to authorize pile wharves to be built into the channel in front of it, on which there was then no projecting wharf.

The sheriff thereupon gave the instructions requested by the petitioners, and declined giving those requested by the respondents, with reference to the extent of the authority granted by the act of 1841, c. 35.

3. The petitioners having introduced evidence tending to show,

that the draw and piers of the respondent's bridge were so near the petitioners' premises, and had such an effect upon the currents, as to cause damage to the petitioners, the respondents requested the sheriff to instruct the jury, that if the draw and pier were constructed in conformity with the requisitions of the act of 1845, c. 224, (see page 515,) the petitioners were not entitled to recover any damages arising incidentally therefrom.

The sheriff did, thereupon, so instruct the jury, but at the same time, further instructed them, that if the draw and piers of the respondents' railroad were constructed according to the act, yet if the natural channel of the river, and the course of the currents, were thereby directed and turned upon the wharves and flats of the petitioners, washing away the soil, or endangering the wharves or sea wall, or making additional piling or ballasting necessary for their security, the erection of such draw and piers was a just ground for damages.

4. The respondents gave in evidence a letter addressed by the president of the Fitchburg Railroad Company to the president of the Boston and Maine Railroad, dated the 10th of August, 1844, in the following terms : " The committee of the directors of the Fitchburg Railroad Company have considered your application for a part of the flats of this company in Charlestown, for your corporation, and have come to the conclusion that they are not prepared to dispose of any of said flats, or at this time to name a price for what the law allows you to take for your road, but that you can go on, and lay the sea wall as you propose, and fill up a sufficient width for your track, and settle all damages with Mr. James Gould at your expense ; and the whole matter shall be settled on equitable terms hereafter." A postscript was added : " It is understood that the wall and filling up is to be considered as above."

The respondents thereupon requested the sheriff to instruct the jury, that this letter, in connection with the evidence of the subsequent building of the road and sea wall therein referred to, proved such an agreement or contract between the parties relating to the subject-matter in dispute, as to bar the petitioners from proceeding in this form for the recovery of damages.

The petitioners objected to this proposed instruction, on the ground, among others, that there was no proof of the terms of the application to which the letter purported to be an answer, or of any reply being made thereto; that the letter did not contain or prove any contract; nor was there any proof that the writer was authorized to make any contract on the subject.

The sheriff declined to instruct the jury as requested.

The petitioners having stated their claims for damages in separate

44 *

charges or items, for the purpose of having the questions of law severally arising on each distinctly presented, requested the sheriff to
instruct the jury, that if they should see fit, they could find the items
separately. The sheriff thereupon instructed the jury, that they
were first to find the total amount of the damages sustained by the
two claimants, Gould and the Fitchburg Railroad Company, and
then apportion the same between them, in proportion to their several
interests and the damages respectively sustained by them; and that
the jury would then be at liberty, if they should see fit, to state in
their verdict the items of damages, with the amounts, as they should
find them, against each.

B. R. Curtis and *T. Farrar*, for the respondents.

R. Choate and *E. R. Hoar*, for the petitioners.

Shaw, C. J.[1] The proceedings in this case came before the court
by way of appeal from a decision of the Court of Common Pleas,
accepting the verdict given by a sheriff's jury for damages against
the respondents for land taken for their railroad. This verdict was
given in favor of James Gould, and of the Fitchburg Railroad Company, who were the petitioners for damages against the respondents.
Since the cause was brought into this court, the claim of Gould has
been settled, and the proceedings, so far as he is concerned, are terminated and discontinued; and they are now no longer to be brought
under consideration, except so far as it may be necessary to consider
them, in deciding upon the regularity or legality of the proceedings
in relation to the other petitioners, the Fitchburg Railroad Company.
This case nominally comes before this Court of Appeal from the
Court of Common Pleas, upon matters of law apparent upon the
record; although it appears, in fact, that the judgment of that court
was not passed upon it; but that the hearing before the sheriff's
jury was had by consent, and the verdict made up, after that court
had adjourned, under an agreement of the parties to waive all exceptions to the irregularity of the course pursued; an irregularity much
more considerable than the most of those which have been urged on
our attention as sufficient to quash the proceedings.
1. In the first place, we have to remark, that the record of the
Court of Common Pleas, a copy of which is in the case, appears to
us to be entirely irregular. This is not, perhaps, a matter of sur-

---

[1] Wilde, J., and Fletcher, J., did not sit in this cause.

prise, when it is considered that the case was entered in the Court of Common Pleas after the court had adjourned, and when the clerk was left without form or precedent, and without the aid or direction of the court, to make up the record. This kind of proceeding is comparatively new, — founded on recent statutes, — so that there are no settled and established forms to guide the recording officer.

The court are of opinion, that the record is irregular in setting forth, as part of the record of the Court of Common Pleas, or the anterior proceedings of the county commissioners. For reasons set forth in the case of Walker *v.* Boston and Maine Railroad, (see ante, page 462,) we think that the proceedings in the Court of Common Pleas begin with the return of the sheriff of his warrant, and his doings under it as set forth in his return, including his decisions and instructions to the jury, and their verdict.

The mistake, on the part of the clerk, is a natural one; he is the recording officer of both courts, the county commissioners, and the Court of Common Pleas, and has the record of both tribunals officially before him, and in the absence of any particular directions from the court, he might naturally suppose, that it would be convenient to have a full and entire statement of the proceedings of both in his record of the action of the Court of Common Pleas, in affirming or setting aside the verdict.

If this were merely an irregularity in point of form, it would be of little importance. A more exact and better form might be adopted hereafter, and no great inconvenience would follow. But the respondents in this case have assumed, that all the doings of the county commissioners, from the first application of a tenant for years, for the assessment of his several damages, to the summoning in of the other parties, the assessment of the damages of those parties, even irregularities as to times of adjournment, and other supposed errors and mistakes of the minutest character, down to the return of the verdict to the Court of Common Pleas, are open on this record; and if any irregularity can be shown, it is a case for setting aside the entire proceedings.

But if parties were confined to taking their exceptions in proper time and due order before the commissioners and before the Court of Common Pleas, instead of their being opened here, in the first instance, it might appear, that acts which now seem to have been irregular passed by consent, or that exceptions were waived; or the objections may be of such a nature that if they had been taken seasonably, the supposed errors might have been corrected. It is a most important principle, in the administration of justice, that, in order to insure regularity and give litigant parties every advantage to which they are entitled, objections to irregularities will be received and sustained, if seasonably made; yet if the party entitled to take such objections passes them by, and proceeds to the further consideration of the case, he $s_h a_{ll}$ be deemed thereby to have waived them; otherwise, a party, knowing of defects of form and technical exceptions not affecting the substantial merits of the case, may lie by and take his chance for a favorable judgment, with a purpose and a power of defeating the judgment, should it be against him.

From this view, it is obvious, that if all the doings of the commissioners, of the sheriff and jury, and of the Court of Common Pleas, were opened before us on this appeal, great injustice might be done, either on the one hand by overlooking manifest errors and encouraging a laxity of practice, or on the other by setting aside judgments; upon nice objections in law not affecting their substantial merits. This would be contrary to the policy of the law, which, whilst it inculcates a strict and careful practice in all proceedings affecting the rights of parties, will not suffer judgments to be reversed for any defects or imperfections in matter of form, though found in the record. Rev. Sts. c. 100, §§ 23, 24. So, as to proceedings before the commissioners, they can only be reversed by a writ of *certiorari*, issued upon a petition, upon which the merits are fully investigated, on broad and equitable principles ; and no such writ will be granted, if substantial justice is done, or if the judgment has been carried into execution, in whole or in part, so that quashing it would lead to injurious consequences.

And so, we think, that where it is provided, that when the verdict of a sheriff's jury is brought before the Court of Common Pleas, they may set the same aside for good cause, it must be for some cause affecting the legality, the justice, and the merits of the case. If such adjudication is founded on matter presented by the warrant, return, and verdict, it is matter of law apparent on the record, and will be brought before this court for revision by an appeal; but if it is cause shown by evidence *aliunde*, including in this designation the record of the commissioners, if adduced for the purpose of showing any fact affecting the merits, it is matter of fact, on which the decision of the Court of Common Pleas is conclusive. If either party has matter of exception to any decision or adjudication of the Court of Common Pleas in matter of law, it must be either especially stated in the decision or adjudication itself, or in a bill of exceptions filed and allowed by that court.

1. The first object taken to this verdict is, that the proceedings upon the petition of James Gould were irregular. We are of opinion, that this objection is not open; that it is not apparent upon any part of this record; and, for the reasons already given, that it is not before this court. But as the objection was much relied upon, and

was urged upon the consideration of the court, it may be proper to consider whether it would avail the respondents, if more distinctly presented on the record.

The proceedings, which we are now revising, commenced with the petition of the respondents, of the 2d of July, 1846, to the commissioners, setting forth the anterior proceedings, and praying for a jury to revise the appraisement of damages made by the commissioners. In this petition, they set forth, that Gould made application to the commissioners to assess his damages; that they made an assessment; that Gould expressed his dissatisfaction and prayed for a jury; that a warrant for a jury was issued accordingly; that a verdict in his favor was returned; and that this verdict was set aside by the Court of Common Pleas, and the fact certified back to the commissioners. It appears, that this verdict was objected to by the respondents, on the ground, amongst other things, that Gould was a tenant for years of the property alleged to be damnified, and that the Commonwealth and the Fitchburg Railroad Company, respectively, were the owners of the reversions, in different parts thereof, and ought to have been made parties. The petition then further sets forth, that the commissioners ordered notice to be given to the Commonwealth and to the Fitchburg Railroad Company, who appeared; that Gould's petition for a jury was set aside or dismissed; that his first petition for an allowance of damages was brought forward; that the commissioners then estimated damages for Gould, for that part of the estate which he held as a tenant for years of the Fitchburg Railroad Company, and also damages for the Fitchburg Railroad Company for the injury to their reversionary interest; the application of Gould for damages for that part of the estate which he held of the Commonwealth being withdrawn. Upon this appraisement of damages, in behalf of Gould and of the Fitchburg Railroad Company, these respondents filed their protest, stating that this last estimate of damages and order for payment thereof were irregular, oppressive, and illegal, and that they were aggrieved and dissatisfied with the same, and that for want of a more direct remedy, they applied for a jury, agreeably to the statute for such case made and provided.

Several remarks arise upon this petition. By setting forth these proceedings, knowing of the irregularities, if there were any, and presenting a petition for a jury, in the nature of an appeal to another tribunal, without taking any exception, the respondents admitted the regularity of the proceedings and waived any exceptions to them. If they intended to except to the proceedings, in that stage, the remedy was by an application for a *certiorari* to set them aside.

But were these proceedings irregular? The ground now insisted upon in argument is, that when the verdict on Gould's claim alone' was set aside, and the case sent back to the commissioners, they had no authority to dismiss Gould's petition for a jury, and to go back to his application for damages, and summon in the Commonwealth' and the Fitchburg Railroad Company, to be heard in that stage of the proceedings. If a new order for a Jury had been made without summoning in these reversioners, the verdict would have been liable to the same objection as before, on exceptions taken by the respondents, and upon which, as it is stated in argument, and may have been so in fact, the verdict was set aside. But it is said, that these reversioners could not be summoned in to have their damages estimated by the commissioners; and that they could only go directly to the jury, in the first instance. This is alleged to be an express duty' enjoined on the commissioners by statute.

If this is so, it is contrary to the general policy of the statutes, which regard the assessment of damages, in the first instance, as made by the commissioners; and, by which, it is only when one or the other party is dissatisfied with the estimate, that the more cumbrous and expensive remedy in the nature of an appeal to a jury is provided. This point, therefore, requires examination. This statute relating to railroads (Rev. Sts. c. 39, § 56) provides, that railroad corporations shall be liable to pay all damages occasioned by the laying out, &c., of their roads, and that such damages shall be estimated by the commissioners, in the manner provided in the case of laying out highways. The next section (§ 57) provides, that if either party dissatisfied with the estimate of the commissioners may apply for a jury, at that or the next regular meeting, and the like proceedings shall be had thereon, as are provided in the case of laying out highways. The fifty-eighth section limits the time for making application to the commissioners, with some exceptions, to three years. These are the leading provisions in the railroad act, in regard to the liability for damages and their assessment and recovery; the mode of proceeding is referred entirely to the statute relating to highways. Now when it is said in the statute that "like proceedings" shall be had," it must mean similar proceedings where the cases are alike.

The respondents, recurring to the highway act, Rev. Sts. c. 24, rely upon §§ 48, 49, 50, 51, which provide, that where several parties' have distinct estates and interests in the land taken, as where there is a tenant for life or years, with remainders and reversions, the damages shall be appraised as of the entire estate; and also that when one of such parties shall apply for a jury, all the others may become parties, and for that purpose may be summoned before the commissioners. These sections then direct that the whole matter shall be determined by one verdict, appraising the whole damages, and apportioning them among the several parties according to their respective estates and interests, and that the verdict shall be binding and conclusive upon all who are parties or have notice; making no provision for a previous appraisement of damages by the commissioners, in behalf of those who are thus summoned in.

But, before applying these provisions, relating to damages for land taken for highways, literally and strictly to the case of persons entitled to damages under the railroad act, it is necessary to consider the difference between the two classes of cases, and especially the difference in the manner of commencing proceedings for the recovery of damages.

By the highway act, Rev. Sts. c. 24, § 11, it is made the duty of the county commissioners, in the first instance, and without any application therefor, in laying out a highway, if any person has sustained damage, to estimate such damage and return it with their location. The twelfth section directs, that such damages shall be estimated severally, and apportioned among the persons having different interests, and requires the commissioners to make return of such apportionment. The thirteenth section provides for a jury, in behalf of any person aggrieved by the doings of the commissioners, in the estimation of his damages. The provisions before cited provide what shall be done in regard to several parties having different interests when it comes before the jury.

Here, then, it is to be considered, that before proceeding to lay out and locate a highway, the commissioners are to give notice to all persons interested of the time and place, amongst other things, to make their claims for damages, to be returned with the location. This extends to all persons whose lands are traversed by the highway or otherwise damnified, whether general owners, or having particular estates and limited interests therein. It follows, therefore, that every person's claim for damages has been passed upon by the commissioners, and allowed or disallowed, on the return of the location; and when a jury is prayed for, no further estimate by the commissioners remains to be made for any party; and when application for a jury is made by a tenant, nothing more remains to be done, than to summon in the other parties to go before the jury.

But the course of proceeding is quite different in the case of railroads. The location is not made by the county commissioners, but by the corporation; and, therefore, no return of damages is made with the location. The statute (Rev. Sts. c. 39, § 55) contemplates, that the railroad corporation may purchase any land necessary for making of their road; and it is only in the event of their not being able to obtain it by agreement with the owner, that the damages are to be estimated and determined by the county commissioners.

Then as to the mode of obtaining an estimate of damages under the highway act, no application of the owner to the commissioners in the first instance is necessary. By the railroad act, (Rev: Sts. c. 39, § 56,) application must be made to the commissioners by the corporation or by the owner, and by § 58, such application may be made at any time within three years from the time of taking the land. So, in the application for a jury; in the case of a highway, it must be made at the meeting at which the location is returned, or the next succeeding meeting. But by the railroad act, (§ 57,) it must be made at the meeting at which the estimate of damages by the commissioners is completed and returned, or at the next regular meeting. So it follows, that whilst an application for a jury, in the case of highways, must necessarily be made within a few months after the location of the highway, it may be postponed for several years, in the case of railroads; though, in both cases, it is made promptly after the estimate of damages is made by the commissioners. It is in the nature of an appeal from their decision.

We have already suggested, that the whole scope of these acts implies and assumes, that the action of the jury is regarded as a revision of the estimate of damages by the commissioners. The Rev. Sts. c. 39, § 62, provide, that the corporation may tender the amount awarded by the commissioners, and if the owner afterwards proceeds to call a jury, it shall be at the peril of costs.

It therefore appears to us, that the difference between the two classes of cases warrants and requires some difference of proceeding, under the direction that "like proceedings" shall be had; and, therefore, that when parties, whose damages have not been estimated, are summoned in, their damages are first to be estimated by the commissioners, before the case is sent to a jury. This course seems obvious, and to arise by necessary implication, when the existence of such distinct interests is made known to the commissioners, before any warrant for a jury issues.

But it is contended, that when a warrant had once issued, on the application of Gould, although the verdict was set aside, and the case sent back to the commissioners, they were not at liberty to discharge the order for a jury made on his application, and to go back to his original application to assess damages. If it was within their jurisdiction first to estimate the damages for the Fitchburg Railroad Company, as reversioners, they must discharge the prior estimate made by them, in order to comply with the positive injunction of law, to appraise the estate as a whole and apportion the damages. Perhaps, by this mode, Gould's proportion might have varied from the original estimate, as made independently. If they had authority to do the thing, as no mode of proceeding is directed, we do not see why the form adopted was not a suitable and convenient one, to discharge the former order for a jury on his separate claim, and proceed to consider the claims of the parties as on the original petition.

But without deciding this point absolutely, we are of opinion, that the respondents could not object to it. If any body could object to it, it was Gould. The provision, that where there are leases and other distinct rights and interests in an estate, the whole shall be appraised and apportioned, is a rule manifestly prescribed for the security and benefit of those who are liable to pay damages. Without it, they would be deprived of the benefit of the mathematical rule, that all the parts are equal to the whole. Where there are several terms, longer or shorter, partial and derivative interests, if each were severally appraised by different juries, there would be danger that the aggregate of the parts would exceed the whole, to the injury of the respondents. Whether, therefore, Gould could or could not have objected to the course adopted by the commissioners, the respondents could make no such objection; and, as against them, there was no error in this respect, which they can set up against the claim of the Fitchburg Railroad Company who were thus summoned in.

2. It is objected, that the board of county commissioners was not duly and legally constituted. For reasons given in the case of Walker against these respondents, (see page 477,) this exception is not now open. If the board was not regularly constituted, the respondents, by proceeding, waived the objection. Ipswich v. Essex, 10 Pick. 519.

3. An objection was taken, that the jurors were not rightly summoned, there being five from Charlestown. This was an exception to the jurors from Charlestown; had it been made at the time, others might have been summoned.

4. Another objection to the jury was, that the sheriff summoned fourteen jurors, whereas the law requires him to summon a jury of twelve men. The provision of the statute (Rev. Sts. c. 24, § 18) seems to us no absolute restriction to his summoning only twelve jurors, but a direction to summon a jury to consist of twelve. The term jury does not necessarily imply twelve men. There are statutes, as in the cases of coroners' inquests, and some others, which provide for a jury to consist of less than twelve persons. Some regard is to be had to the usages of courts, and we believe it is common in all courts, in order to insure the attendance of twelve qualified jurors, to summon a few over the number, to provide for sickness, absence, and

other contingencies. But if it was an irregularity, it was waived by the proceeding.

5. A further objection was, that this cause did not go to the same jury with a previous one against the same respondents, because one of the jurors, who sat in the former, being interested in this, was set aside and another substituted. It would be difficult to say, that this was not the same jury; but the objection is not apparent on the record, and not open on this appeal.

II. Several questions were raised and discussed, respecting the correctness of the directions and instructions of the sheriff to the jury. All those which relate to Gould's claim are passed over and are not now in question; the proceedings of the several claimants being in their nature several. The Fitchburg Railroad Company were rightly before the court, after they were summoned in by the commissioners, and brought before the jury by the petition of the respondents.

1. The first direction, which was excepted to, turned upon the question, what was the true course and place of the commissioners' line of the harbor of Boston; to which, under certain limitations, the petitioners, as the assignees of the Charlestown Wharf Company, were authorized to extend their line. The statute of 1840, c. 35, establishing the line of the harbor of Boston, fixes it at the place in question at a point fifteen feet from the south corner of Gould's wharf, and three hundred and twelve feet from the wall of the Charlestown Wharf Company. In the bill of exceptions certified by the sheriff, this exception is thus stated: "It having been proved, that the south-east corner of Gould's Wharf was three hundred and two feet from the old sea wall, mentioned in the act of 1840, c. 35, § 4, and that the commissioners' line, as laid down on the plan and claimed by the petitioners, was fifteen feet in advance of said corner; the sheriff was thereupon requested by the respondents to rule, that there is such an ambiguity in respect to that part of the commissioners' line, that it cannot now be determined where the line is; or, secondly, that the true line is five feet nearer the shore." The sheriff refused so to rule, and the respondents excepted.

The court are of opinion, that this decision was right. The question was purely a question of fact upon the evidence. One point mentioned in the statute was the south corner of Gould's Wharf, and the line was fixed at fifteen feet distant. The other point was the sea wall, three hundred and twelve feet distant. The former was the first named and the nearest; the latter, the monument, was the most permanent. But the statute does not fix the point in the sea wall, from which the three hundred and twelve feet were to be measured, and the distance might be so measured as to satisfy both descriptions. But if that could not be done, one must yield. And further, if there was any ambiguity, it was a latent ambiguity, which arose from applying the terms of the statute to the local objects, and was therefore a question of fact for the jury.

2. The second exception turns upon the question, What were the rights of the petitioners, as the successors and assignees of the Charlestown Wharf Company, to extend their wharves beyond the line of low-water mark to the commissioners' line, by force of the statute of 1841, c. 35 ? This act authorized the proprietors both above and below Charles River Bridge, and between Warren Bridge and Prison Point Bridge, to extend their wharves into the channel to the commissioner's line, with the privilege to lay vessels at the sides and ends of their respective wharves, to be built on piles so far as they should be extended into the channel. There was evidence tending to show that the sea wall of the petitioners, between Warren Bridge and Prison Point Bridge, was built at different distances below high-water mark, and above low-water mark, filled up behind or towards the shore to high-water mark, and used for landing lumber and other things, and that there were pier or pile wharves about eighty feet wide projecting therefrom towards the channel.

The sheriff was requested to instruct the jury that the act of 1841, c. 35, did not authorize the sea wall to be advanced by a pier wharf to the commissioners' line, but only, the projecting wharves ; and secondly, that as a license it was revocable by the legislature, before it was executed at the part taken by the respondents. These instructions the sheriff declined to give. Both parties also requested instructions as to the right of the petitioners to extend out their whole wharf along the entire extent of the sea wall, upon which the sheriff gave the instructions requested by the petitioner, and declined giving those requested by the respondents. To this the latter excepted. The court are of opinion that the instructions given were right ; that the statute of 1841 operated as a grant to the Charlestown Wharf Company, and not as a mere revocable license, and was not affected by the act incorporating the respondents.

On the other point, the court are of opinion, that the sea wall built below high-water mark, and filled up back to high-water mark, and used to land lumber and other things upon, being an artificial structure adapted to such a purpose, was a wharf, and that the sheriff rightly instructed the jury, that under the act in question, the grantees, for themselves and their successors, were authorized to extend such wharf, along their whole front, to the commissioners' harbor line. It is to be considered, that without such grant, the owners would have had a right to fill up and cover their entire front to low-water mark.

But it is said, that the statute distinguishes between the sea wall and the wharves, and, therefore, that the same thing could not be meant by both these terms. The statute applies to a long line from the navy yard to the State Prison, some part of which had no sea wall or wharf in front of it. And further, it is said, that upon this construction, it would have been superfluous to authorize owners to lay vessels at the sides and ends of their wharves. But there was a good reason why this privilege should be granted, because, although the proprietors would have a right to carry out their whole front to the line, they might not do so, and probably would not, because it would be more useful to leave slips for the access of vessels, and to afford berths for vessels. Should they adopt that mode of improvement, and extend such wharves to the harbor line, and into the channel, with slips between them, the waters at the ends and sides of such wharf, so far as they projected beyond low-water mark, would be public water, and such a grant of a privilege to use them and to receive wharfage and dockage therefor might be thought necessary.

3. The next instruction asked for was relative to a claim made by the petitioners, for damages occasioned by the construction of the draw and piers, erected in the channel by the respondents, so near the petitioners' land, as to cause increased expense. There seems to be some contradiction in the instructions said to be given, and perhaps there may be some mistake in the statement. But we are satisfied, that the instructions authorized the jury to give damages for loss occasioned to the petitioners by the erection of a draw and piers, made by the respondents according to an act of the legislature, in the channel of Charles River, by which the course of the currents was changed, and additional sea wall and piling made necessary to secure the petitioners' land. This direction, we think, was incorrect. It is incident to the power of the legislature to regulate a navigable stream, so as best to promote the public convenience ; and, if in doing so, some damage is done to riparian proprietors, and some increased expense is thrown upon them, it is *damnum absque injuria.* But as this item was separately estimated in the verdict at the sum of five hundred dollars, it can be deducted, without the necessity of setting aside the verdict.

4. The respondents requested the sheriff to instruct the jury, that the letter from Jacob Forster, President of the Fitchburg Railroad Company, to Thomas West, President of the Boston and Maine Railroad, dated August 10th, 1844, with the evidence of the subse-

quent building of the road and wall, proved such an agreement or contract, relating to the subject-matter, as to bar the present claim; which instruction the sheriff refused to give.

This was, in our opinion, correct. The evidence shows no elements of a contract, but rather the offer of a contract declined. There is no price stipulated, no terms, no consideration. As a license, it added nothing to that which the company had before; and it probably referred to the equitable terms of settlement provided for by law, if not otherwise adjusted by negotiation.

5. The petitioners requested the sheriff to instruct the jury, that if they should see fit, they could find the items, or separate claims for damages separately. The sheriff did accordingly instruct them, that finding the entire damages and apportioning them as between landlord and tenant, they would then be at liberty, if they should see fit, to state in their verdict the items of damages, with the amounts, as they should find, against each. To these instructions the respondents excepted. We can perceive no tenable ground for this exception. As a general rule a jury is not bound to give a special verdict; but where there is an assessment of damages, founded upon distinct and separate grounds, it is a very convenient practice, and may often save a further trial, and subserve the purposes of justice, to state what items they allow and what they reject; and we can see no objection to it.

6. The last exception is to the form of the verdict, which is said to be erroneous, in giving the bulk of the damages for the land over which the petitioners had a right to build a pier wharf. Probably there is an inaccuracy in the terms of the verdict; perhaps some words were left out in copying, or otherwise. But it was merely an inaccuracy in words; a few words added would make it read, land " owned as well as" "land over which," &c. We see nothing to warrant the conclusion, that it did not include land owned by the petitioners and taken by the respondents. But take the language literally; "it is for the land over which the company have a right to build a pier wharf." This description embraces land above low-water mark, owned by the company, over which they had a right to build a pier wharf, or any other structure, as well as land below low-water mark, over which they were authorized to build a pier wharf by the special act of the legislature. This objection therefore affords no ground for setting aside the verdict.

The petitioners having moved for interest on the verdict, and for costs, the opinion of the court was subsequently stated.

SHAW, C. J. 1. Interest is to be computed on the verdict, after deducting $500 therefrom, according to the opinion heretofore given, to be computed from the time of the appeal taken in the Court of Common Pleas to the time of making up the judgment in this court.
2. The case having been brought before a jury by the petition of the respondents, and the estimate of damages made by the commissioners having been reduced by the verdict of the jury, no costs of the warrant and jury are to be taxed against either party; not in favor of the petitioners against the respondents, because they have reduced the damages; nor in favor of the respondents against the petitioners, because they did not tender the amount estimated by the commissioners, but, on the contrary, claimed a jury to reduce it. The taxable costs of the appeal are to be taxed for the petitioners here, and to be included in the certificate.
3. A certificate is to be issued to the commissioners, as in the preceding case.

———◆———

HAMILTON DAVIDSON AND OTHERS *v.* THE BOSTON AND MAINE RAILROAD.[1]

Middlesex Co., January Term, 1849.

Assessment of Damages — Joinder of Parties — Warrant — Interest in Flats covered by Tide Water — When Land is Taken.

The grantor of a tide mill and mill pond, who had reserved the right of boating and rafting through the pond, and of using the same as a depot for lumber, it seems, has no such proprietary interest in the premises, by virtue of such reservation, as to entitle him to become, or to render it necessary that he should be made, a party to a proceeding under Rev. Sts. c. 24, §§ 48, 49, 50, for the recovery of damages occasioned by the laying out and construction of a railroad through the granted premises.

Where an application is made and pending before county commissioners, for an estimation and adjudication of the petitioner's damages, occasioned by the construction of a railroad, it is competent for the respondents, if there are other persons interested who have not joined in the application, to cause such persons to be summoned and made parties, before a warrant for a jury is issued; and if the respondents neglect to do so, they cannot object before the jury, or afterwards, that such persons were not previously made parties.

Where the damages, occasioned by the construction of a railroad, are estimated by county

———

[1] 8 Cushing's Reports, 91.

commissioners, and both parties are dissatisfied with the estimate and apply to the commissioners for a warrant for a jury to revise the damages, it is only necessary that one warrant should be issued; but if separate warrants are issued on both petitions, the sheriff should execute and return them as one.

Where the petitioners before a sheriff's jury, impanelled for the purpose of estimating the damages occasioned by the construction of a railroad, rested their claim therefor on the ground, that a creek crossed by the railroad was a part of a tide mill pond belonging to the petitioners, and introduced in evidence the deed under which they held the premises, together with a plan and survey thereof, the correctness of which was testified to by the surveyor by whom they were made, it was held, that whether the creek in question was a part of the mill pond or not, was a question of fact for the jury, depending upon the description contained in the deed, and the bounds and monuments found upon the ground, answering to such description, and to which the description applied.

A sheriff's jury are not bound to find and return by their verdict, as an abstract proposition, what right, title, or interest, a party before them has in land, which he claims in virtue of a deed in evidence; nor are they bound to find a special verdict, upon the whole or any particular part of the case before them, though they may do so, if they think proper.

The owner in fee of a tide mill and mill pond having leased the same for years, and the proprietors of a railroad having constructed their road over a portion of the pond, the owner and lessee joined in a proceeding for the recovery of damages therefor, and introduced the lease of the premises in evidence; it was held, that the respondents were entitled, with a view to the assessment of damages, to have the jury instructed by the sheriff, as matter of law, whether the lease conveyed an interest in the soil covered with tide water, or only a right to use the water for a special purpose, as an easement, in connection with the other estate demised.

The owner of a tide mill, who is also the riparian proprietor of flats, from which the tide wholly ebbs, between his mill and navigable water has no right, either as against conterminous proprietors or the public, to have his flats kept open and unobstructed, for the free flow and reflow of the tide water, for the use of his mills or for navigation. The adjoining proprietors may build solid structures to the extent of one hundred rods, and thereby obstruct the flow and reflow of the tide, provided they do not wholly cut off the access of other proprietors to their houses and lands, and if the mill-owner, or other proprietors, suffer damages therefrom, it is *damnum absque injuria*. The public have a right to regulate the use of navigable waters; and the erection of a bridge, with or without a draw, by the authority of the legislature, is the regulation of a public right, and not the deprivation of a private right, which can be a ground for damages, or the taking of private property for a public use, which will entitle the owner to compensation.

When the location of a railroad is filed, the land over which it passes may then be *primâ facie* considered as taken; and the persons who are owners at that time may claim and recover damages therefor. If any person, when a claim for damages is made, claims damages for the taking of the same land, on the ground of an earlier title, the respondents must allege and prove such title in bar of the previous claim.

The owner of a right of flowage, which is injuriously affected by the construction of a railroad, is entitled to damages therefor.

THE proprietors of the Middlesex Canal, a corporation legally established in this Commonwealth, being the owners in fee of the tide mill and mill pond, and of the adjoining flats lying southerly of the same as delineated on the map inserted at page 469, leased the mill and mill pond to Hamilton Davidson, on the 1st of July, 1839, by an indenture of that date, for the term of fifteen years from the first day of May then next. Davidson, afterwards, and before the location of the road of the Boston and Maine Extension Railroad Company, as hereinafter mentioned, assigned the lease to John Wesson and John Gary, as tenants in common; and, on the 29th of August, 1844, the lessors conveyed their whole estate above mentioned, namely, the mill, mill pond, and flats, subject to the lease to Davidson, (which they assigned to the grantee,) by their deed of that date, to Rhodes G. Lockwood, who subsequently conveyed certain undivided interests therein to Hamilton Davidson and John Nesmith, as tenants in common with him.

The Boston and Maine Railroad Extension company, (afterwards merged in the Boston and Maine Railroad,) having laid out and constructed their road near and upon the premises, in such a manner as to effect the same injuriously, in the opinion of the owners and lessees, they presented their petition to the county commissioners, at the meeting of the board in June, 1846, praying an estimate and assessment of the damages, severally sustained by them, Davidson, Lockwood, and Nesmith, as owners in fee, and Wesson and Gary, as lessees for years, in consequence of such location and construction.[1]

The commissioners proceeded upon this petition and estimated the damages of the owners in fee at $1,866.66, and of the lessees for years at $333.33, and ordered the aggregate amount, with $44.20, costs, to be paid by the railroad corporation to the petitioners. Both parties were dissatisfied with the estimate, and applied to the commissioners for a jury to revise the damages. The commissioners ordered warrants to issue upon both applications, and they were issued accordingly, bearing date respectively the 28th of May, and the 5th of June, 1847.

The sheriff proceeded to execute these warrants, treating them both as one, and returned the same, with the verdict of the jury, to the Court of Common Pleas, at the December term thereof, 1847. Four of the jurors, as appeared by the return, were drawn and summoned from the city of Charlestown, in which the premises alleged to be injured were situated.

The verdict of the jury was, " that the said Hamilton Davidson, Rhodes G. Lockwood, and John Nesmith, John Wesson, and John Gary, recover against the Boston and Maine Railroad the sum of $2,690.96; and they apportion the said total amount of damages among the several petitioners, in proportion to their several interests,

---

[1] The location of the road, so far as it affected the estate or interest of the petitioners, is seen on the map. The railroad, where it crosses the creek, which makes a part of or runs into the mill pond, is constructed with a culvert for the passage of the water. Where it crosses the flats lying southerly and easterly of the mill pond, it is a solid structure.

and to the damages sustained by them, respectively, as follows, to wit, to the said Hamilton Davidson the sum of $448.49, to the said Rhodes G. Lockwood the sum of $448.49, to the said John Nesmith the sum of $896.99, and to the said John Wesson and John Gary the sum of $896.99."

The Court of Common Pleas accepted the verdict, and the respondents thereupon appealed to this court. The cause was argued here upon the rulings and instructions of the sheriff, at the trial, as certified by him at the request of the parties.

In the deed of the proprietors of the Middlesex Canal to Lockwood, under and with whom the petitioners Davidson and Nesmith claimed, the mill is conveyed by metes and bounds, with all [the rights, ways, easements, privileges, and appurtenances to the same belonging, and all the wheels, &c., together with a right of way particularly described; the mill pond is conveyed under the description of "all their right, title, interest, and estate, in and to the mill pond, and the land and flats covered with water, lying northerly and northwesterly of the aforedescribed premises, bounded," &c., &c., "with the dam aforesaid and all the waters of the said pond and of the creeks and streams entering the same, and all rights of flowage, and all other rights, easements, privileges, and appurtenances thereto belonging;" and the flats therein conveyed are described as "all right, title, interest, and estate of the said proprietors in and to the flats and land covered with water," lying southerly of the mill dam aforesaid, extending to a line specified, and westerly "to the easterly corner of the southerly end of the stone abutment of the railroad bridge of the Boston and Maine Extension Railroad."

In this deed the grantors reserved, among other things, the right to use the mill pond, for the purpose of passing and repassing through the same, with boats, rafts, and all things required to be floated on the waters of the canal, and for the purpose of a depot for lumber, timber, and other articles, to be placed and kept there at the convenience and pleasure of the grantors; the right to use the waters of the mill pond for lockage as they might require; and the right to draw off the water whenever it might be necessary for the purpose of repairing the locks, &c.

The lease contained, in terms, a demise of the mills, mill site, dams, wharves, sheds, houses, and water privileges, but nothing including the soil of the pond.

The petitioners set forth in their petition to the county commissioners, that Davidson, Lockwood, and Nesmith, were the owners in fee, as tenants in common, and that Wesson and Gary were the lessees for years, as tenants in common, of the mill and mill pond, described as in the deed of the same above mentioned, and " also of all the flats to both of the above described premises appurtenant and belonging :" and the petitioners averred, that as such owners and lessees, they occupied and possessed a mill standing on the premises, from which they had hitherto derived great emolument and advantage; that the Boston and Maine Railroad had located and constructed their road upon, over, and through the premises, and thereby taken a large amount of land and flats belonging to the petitioners, and greatly injured the premises adjoining; that, by the location and construction of the respondents' road across the mouth of the creek, at the head of which the petitioners' mill is situate, the respondents had greatly obstructed and impeded the flow of the tide water into the petitioners' mill dam; that by the location and construction of the railroad through the petitioners' mill dam, the respondents had greatly obstructed and prevented the tide-water, which overflowed the meadow and land above the pond, from flowing back into the pond; that, in consequence of these obstructions, the petitioners' mills could not be worked as effectually as before; and that the respondents, by the location and construction of their road, had greatly injured the premises of the petitioners for the purposes of a wharf.

The rulings and instructions complained of were as follows : —

1. The petitioners having introduced in evidence the deeds of the proprietors of the Middlesex Canal to Rhodes G. Lockwood, and of Lockwood to Davidson and Nesmith, and a plan and survey of the premises made by Charles Whitney, which he testified was correct, the respondents thereupon objected, that it appeared by the first named deed, that divers valuable rights and interests in the premises were reserved and retained by the grantors, which showed them to be still interested in the premises ; and, therefore, that no further proceedings could legally take place in the cause, until the grantors had been summoned in or made parties to the same. This objection was overruled by the sheriff, and the trial proceeded.

2. The respondents, premising that " the title shown by the petitioners, Lockwood, Nesmith, and Davidson, depending upon the deed above mentioned, and these petitioners claiming no interest in any land covered by the respondents' railroad, except across the creek near the culvert mentioned in their petition, the location of which appeared on the plan," requested the sheriff, secondly, to rule and direct the jury, that this evidence was insufficient to sustain the title of the petitioners to the land taken for the railroad or any interest therein, and also to direct the jury to find, and return in their verdict, whether or not these petitioners, on the evidence, had any, and what title or interest in such land, or in any and what part thereof.

The petitioners, thereupon, requested the sheriff to rule, that the deed from the proprietors of the Middlesex Canal to Lockwood did, by its terms, apply to the undisputed localities, and in legal construction, embrace and convey that portion of the pond or creek, which had been built upon and crossed by the respondents' road ; and, the effect and operation of the deed being thus decided, as a matter of law, that no question in regard to the same was to be submitted to the jury, nor were they to find any verdict, special or otherwise, in relation to the question of title.

The sheriff declined to instruct the jury, as requested by the respondents, or to rule, as requested by the petitioner; but, on the motion of the respondents, the petitioners objecting, he submitted to the jury, as a matter of fact, the question of the right and title of the petitioners to the premises described in the petition, to determine the same, upon the deed and other evidence, so far as respected the damages of the petitioners.

3. The petitioners having given in evidence a lease, dated July 1st, 1839, from the proprietors of the Middlesex Canal to Hamilton Davidson, with subsequent assignments thereof to two of the petitioners, together with evidence of the use and occupation of the waters of the whole pond and creek, as delineated on the plan, for carrying a mill, by the lessors and their grantors and lessees, for upwards of forty years prior to the filing of the location of the respondent's road, the respondents requested the sheriff, thirdly, to rule and instruct the jury, that the lease conveyed no right, title, or interest in the land covered by the respondents' railroad, or in any part thereof; and also to direct the jury to find, and return in their verdict, whether or not the petitioners, Wesson and Gary, had any and what right, title, or interest in such land, or in any and what part thereof. The sheriff refused to give this instruction, but did instruct the jury, that the lease, together with the evidence as to the mode and period of use and occupation of the waters of the pond, if the same were believed, did convey to the lessee, and those holding under him, the right to use and enjoy the waters of that part of the pond or creek, which was covered or crossed by the respondents' railroad.

4. The respondents presented a fourth prayer for instructions, to wit, that the petitioners had no right to have the flats, where the respondents' structure stands, remain open for the flow and reflow of the tide, or for the purpose of navigation to their wharf, otherwise than as they then were ; and also to direct the jury to find and return in their verdict, whether or not the petitioners, or any of them, had any and what right to have the said flats, or any and what part thereof, remain open for their use, for either of the purposes above mentioned.

The sheriff declined giving the instruction, as requested, but submitted to the jury, as a matter of fact, to be determined upon the evidence, so far as respected the damages of the petitioners,: the question of the right of the petitioners in and to the flats referred to, for the purposes mentioned ; and he further instructed them, in respect to the form of their verdict, that if they should be satisfied, that any of the petitioners were entitled to damages, they should first find and set forth in their verdict the total amount of the damages, and then apportion the same amongst the several parties, whom they should find to be entitled thereto, in proportion to their several interests, and the damages sustained by them respectively, and set forth such apportionment in their verdict; that if they should find any one or more of the petitioners not to have sustained any damage, they were to set forth that fact; and that they were not required by law to render a special verdict; but that they were at liberty to set forth the items upon which they should find damages, if they should see fit to do so.

5. The respondents submitted a fifth prayer for instructions, namely, that the owners of the land at the mouth of the creek, near the culvert and above, had a right to place any and what obstructions they pleased across the creek, and to dike out the tide waters or not at pleasure ; and also to direct the jury to find and return in their verdict, whether or not the petitioners had any and what right to have the creek remain open for the purposes of their mill pond and mill. The sheriff did not so instruct the jury, but instructed them, that if from the evidence they should believe, that the petitioners had not any right or title in and to the land referred to by the respondents in their prayer for instructions or to the use of the waters covering the same, then that the owner of such land had the right to place obstructions and do the other acts referred to by the respondents.

6. The respondents having introduced evidence, that they entered upon the premises described in the petition, and built the culvert before the middle of July, 1844, and that pile drivers were at work, under the direction of the respondents on each side of the outlet of the cove, on the 9th of the same July and afterwards; the respondents, thereupon, submitted their sixth prayer for instructions, namely, that the owners of the premises at the time the respondents took possession and built their road, were the parties entitled to institute this proceeding for damages, if any party were so entitled, and that their subsequent conveyance passed the premises subject to any encumbrance then acquired by the respondents by virtue of their charter; and, therefore, that none of the petitioners, but the tenants

for years, Wesson and Gary, had a right to prosecute this petition, even if the same were otherwise maintainable. The sheriff declined so to instruct the jury, but did instruct them that the parties who were owners and lessees, at the time the respondents filed the location of their road, namely, the 13th of February, 1845, had the right to present and maintain a petition, for the damages occasioned by the construction of the road to the premises owned or held by them, respectively, at the time of the filing of the location.

T. Farrar, (with whom was *R. Choate,*) for the respondents.

J. Dana, (with whom was *S. Bartlett,*) for the petitioners.

SHAW, C. J.[1] The petitioners, in this case, who are the owners and lessees of the canal tide mills, in Charlestown, demand damages for taking their land, as they allege, and for an injury to their mill privilege, occasioned by the laying out and construction of the railroad of the respondents. The case comes before this court by an appeal from an adjudication of the Court of Common Pleas, accepting the verdict of a sheriff's jury, by which damages were awarded to the petitioners, for alleged errors in matters of law apparent on the record and proceedings. We shall consider some of the more important questions raised by the exceptions and submitted to us in the argument.

The first objection, taken at the argument, is, that four of the jurors were summoned from Charlestown, in which the premises are located, and which is not an adjoining town.

This objection has been considered in the other cases against these respondents, and overruled, on the ground, that it was an exception to the jurors thus drawn; and that the respondents, if they were opposed to having them sit, should have excepted at the time. This rule is adopted in pursuance of a settled and salutary principle of law, that although a party shall have an opportunity to take advantage of any defect or irregularity, which he apprehends may be injurious to him, yet he must avail himself of it in due time and proper order, and having passed the proper stage, and taken his chance with the jury, as drawn, he shall be taken to have acquiesced and waived his exception. Merrill *v.* Berkshire, 11 Pick. 269; Simonds *v.* Parker, 1 Met. 508; Fox *v.* Hazelton, 10 Pick. 275; Hallock *v.* Franklin, 2 Met. 558.

---

[1] Wilde J., and Fletcher, J., did not sit in this cause.

Had the exception been then made before the sheriff, he might have sustained it, and either postponed the trial and summoned other jurors from another town; or, if the case was such that he could not lawfully proceed, he might have returned the warrant with the facts; and then the county commissioners might have issued a new warrant, as in case of death or insanity, or other casualty, which renders the execution of the warrant impracticable.

1. It was objected, at the trial, (and this was the subject of the first exception to the rulings of the sheriff,) that the proprietors of the Middlesex Canal were interested in the premises; they having, on a conveyance thereof, reserved certain easements therein, for rafting and boating through the mill pond, and laying logs and lumber therein. On referring to the deed in question, and to the proof of the localities, we are strongly inclined to the opinion, that the proprietors of the Middlesex Canal had no such proprietary interest in these premises, which would be injuriously affected by the location of the railroad, as would have given them any interest in the subject under the provisions of the Rev. Sts. c. 24, §§ 48, 49, 50. We are not prepared to say, that the legal distinction, between an estate and an easement in the premises taken, will always determine whether one has or has not a proprietary interest rendering it proper to make him a party or not with the owners, in a claim for damages. Possibly an easement for a mill privilege, for example, may be so large and valuable, as to render an interest therein much more important than that of a lessee for years or a reversioner. Yet there is one provision in the railroad act, which implies that a person having a private right of way may have a separate application for damages, by limiting the time within which such application shall be made. Rev. Sts. c. 39, § 71.

But the ground upon which we place the decision of this point is, that this is not an objection which the respondents can make before the sheriff's jury. The statute provision is designed for the security and benefit of respondents; that, in a proper case, they may have one entire appraisement of all damages done to any estate, and not stand in danger of being charged with more than one estimate, by being compelled to go to different juries upon distinct applications. And it is competent for the respondents, when called before the commissioners, if there are other persons having claims, to cause them to be summoned and made parties, before a warrant for a jury is ordered. This is the more important for the reasons stated in the case of the Fitchburg Railroad Company against these respondents, (see ante, p. 528,) because the damages of such persons are first to be assessed by the commissioners. If such persons, when duly summoned, do not come in and become parties, they are bound by the result. We are therefore of opinion, that the sheriff did right in overruling this objection. It appears by the record, that a jury was ordered to revise the damages awarded by the commissioners, as well on the motion and request of the respondents, as of the petitioners: it was clearly, therefore, the duty of the respondents to see that the proper parties were in, before they prayed for a warrant to the sheriff.

We may remark, in passing, that two warrants were issued in this case; a proceeding which was quite superfluous, although it was proper to recite in one warrant that it was made in pursuance of the request of both parties. It is like an appeal by both parties; when an appeal is allowed, the fact is stated in the record; but both need not be separately entered and prosecuted.

2. The deeds from the proprietors of the Middlesex Canal to Lockwood, and from Lockwood to Nesmith and Davidson, with the testimony of Whitney, and the plan and survey made by him, being introduced in evidence, each party requested the sheriff to instruct the jury, the one that the evidence did, and the other that it did not, make a complete title to the petitioners. But it appears to us, that the sheriff did right in not giving either instruction. It was a pure question of fact upon the evidence, whether the creek, over which the railroad was built, was a part of the pond; it depended upon the description contained in the deed, and the bounds and monuments found upon the ground, answering to such description, and to which the description applied. It was, therefore, rightly left to the jury.

The legal meaning, operation, and effect of a deed — the construction of a deed or other written instrument — is a question of law to be decided by the court. If it be uncertain what any particular clause or passage means, it is a patent ambiguity, and must be decided by the court, by the best means in their power, under the rules of exposition prescribed by good authority. But when the ambiguity arises from evidence *aliunde*, as whether a tract of water of a particular description is a creek or a pond, which depends upon width, shape, connection with other land or water, it is an ambiguity created by evidence *ab extra*; it is a latent ambiguity, and must be decided by the evidence. As already said, it is not for the court or presiding officer to direct a jury as to the weight or sufficiency of evidence. If either of the parties had desired the opinion of the sheriff, upon any question of the construction, meaning, or effect of the deed, it should have been specially presented and called for. We think the decision was right.

3. The next exception is stated thus: The petitioners Gary and Wesson claiming under the proprietors of the Middlesex Canal only, by the lease dated July 1st, 1839, without showing any title in the company, the respondents requested the sheriff to rule, that the lease conveyed no right, title, or interest in the land covered by the defendants' railroad, or any part thereof. The land thus covered, as appears by the evidence, and by the plan, is no part of the mill or land leased, but a part of the pond or creek, opening into the pond raised by the tide mill dam for holding in the tide water, for the purpose of driving the mills. The respondents requested the sheriff to rule and instruct the jury, that the lease conveyed no right, title, or interest in the land covered by the railroad, or any part thereof; that is, in the land covered by the creek or pond. They also requested the sheriff to instruct the jury to find, and return in their verdict, whether or not the lessees had any and what right, title, or interest in the said land, or any or what part thereof. This the sheriff declined, but instructed the jury that the lease and the evidence as to the mode and period of use and occupancy of the waters of the pond, if believed, did convey to the lessee, and those holding under him, the right to use and enjoy the waters of that part of the pond or creek covered or crossed by the railroad of the respondents.

This instruction was correct, so far as it went; but we think the entire prayer for instructions was such as the sheriff was not bound to give, because it required him to instruct the jury what right, title, or interest the tenants under this lease took in the land constituting the bottom of the pond or creek. We think the jury were not bound to return their finding upon that abstract proposition; or to find a special verdict upon the whole or any particular part of the case, though they might do so voluntarily.

But we are strongly inclined to the opinion, that the respondents were entitled to an opinion and direction, upon the construction of the lease, on this question, namely, whether, if the proprietors of the Middlesex Canal were the owners and in possession of the soil of the pond and creeks, as well as of the mills, mill site and dams, their lease operated as a demise of the soil of the pond, or only gave the lessees an easement therein for the use of the water connected with the mills. Considering that there may be a difference in assessing damages, between an interest in the soil covered with tide water and the right to use it for a special purpose, as an easement, in connection with other estate demised, we are of opinion, that if such a construction on a point of law had been specifically asked for, it would have been the duty of the sheriff, as presiding officer, to give it, and to give it as prayed for by the respondents. The lease contains

Davidson *v.* The Boston and Maine Railroad.

specifically a demise of the mills, mill site, wharves, sheds, dwelling-houses, &c., but nothing including the soil of the pond: the use of the pond, as a mere easement, would pass with the mills as incident; but a use would be sufficient to satisfy the implied grant under the term water privilege, and would not necessarily carry with it any greater interest in the soil of the pond.

A question might be made, whether the same rule does not apply to the deed of conveyance afterwards made by the proprietors of the Middlesex Canal to Lockwood, under which the title in fee is claimed. An interest in the land may be as effectually created by a lease as by a deed in fee; the former title being as perfect for the time as the latter in perpetuity. But there may be, and in this instance we think there is, a difference in the terms of the instrument. By the deed of conveyance, the proprietors of the Middlesex Canal conveyed to Lockwood, not only the mills, wharves, sheds, flats, &c., but also all the right, title, interest, and estate in and to the mill pond, and the land and flats covered with water, lying northerly and north-westerly of the aforedescribed premises, bounded as follows, &c., describing the pond by a very general description. Now, if the canal company owned the soil of the pond thus described, the deed was sufficient to pass it; and if the use of it for more than forty years to raise a head of tide water to drive the mills, without any adverse claim, was such *primâ facie* evidence of possession and title, as would be good until a better title was shown, and if the land over which the railroad passed should be found to lie within the limits of the pond, in contradistinction to the creeks running into it, the deed would be *primâ facie* evidence of title to the soil in those grantees, and entitle them to maintain a claim for damages against these respondents. But of this it is not necessary now to give a decided opinion.

4. The next exception is thus stated: The respondents requested the sheriff to instruct the jury, that the petitioners had no right to have the flats where the respondents' structure and railroad stands, (being the flats belonging to the petitioners, outside of their mill pond, to the south and east thereof, and between their mills and the channel from which the tide does not ebb,) remain open for the flow and reflow of the tide, or for the purposes of navigation to their wharf, otherwise than they then did; and also that the jury might find and return in their verdict, whether or not the petitioners, or any of them, had any and what right to have the flats, or any and what part of them, remain open for their use, for either of the purposes aforesaid. These instructions the sheriff declined to give, but did submit to the jury the right of the petitioners to the flats referred

46 *

to for the purposes mentioned, as a matter of fact upon the evidence, for them to determine the same so far as respects the damages of the petitioners. He also instructed them as to the form of the verdict.

This direction in regard to flats, we think, cannot be supported. The question was as to the right of riparian proprietors upon salt water, over an open tract of flats from which the tide wholly ebbs, and lying between upland territory and navigable water, kept open and unobstructed for the free flow and reflow of the tide water, for their mills or for navigation. This was a question of law, depending on the general laws of property, the colony ordinance in regard to flats, the usages of the country, and judicial decisions, and was proper to be decided as a question of law. And we are of opinion, as matter of law, that the petitioners had no right, as riparian proprietors, to have their flats kept open and unobstructed for the purposes stated, and that the jury should have been so instructed; also, that the petitioners, as tide mill-owners, had no right, either as against the public or as against conterminous and adjacent proprietors, to have their flats kept open, but only to the flow of water in the channel below low-water mark, and where the tide does not ebb. The adjoining proprietor, to the extent of one hundred rods, may build solid structures, and thus obstruct the flow and reflow of the tide, without objection, provided he does not wholly cut off his neighbor's access to his house or land; and if the mill-owner or conterminous proprietor suffers in consequence, it is *damnum absque injuria*. The public have a right to regulate the use of public navigable waters for purposes of passage; and the erection of a bridge with or without a draw, by the authority of the legislature, is the regulation of a public right, and not the deprivation of any private right, which can be a ground for damages. So far, therefore, as the railroad erected by authority of the legislature affected the right of the petitioners to pass or repass to and from their lands and wharves with vessels, it was a mere regulation of a public right, and not a taking of private property for a public use, and gave the petitioners no claim for damages.

5. The ground of the next exception was the refusal to grant the fifth prayer of the respondents for instruction to the jury. As we understand it, this was substantially a renewal of the third prayer in regard to title, and depended upon the question of fact; and the direction in effect was, that if the petitioners had either a title to the soil or a right of flowage at that place, which was injuriously affected by laying the railroad over it, it was a ground of damage. This appears to be unobjectionable.

6. The last exception was, that the petitioners were not owners of the land in question when the same was taken by the respondents. Whether the filing of a location is the only act of taking which fixes the right of private proprietors to claim damages, and the time from which the limitation runs, (Charlestown B. R. Co. v. Middlesex, 7 Met. 78; s. c. *ante*, 383,) is a question of difficulty. It would be difficult to say that one whose land has been appropriated and actually used could not apply for his damages. The corporation may never file their location. But supposing this to be so, the act of filing a location is a formal act of the assertion of a right, and it is notice to the public and to all parties interested.

It is a mere act of location, and the land may be considered *primâ facie* as taken, and the party then owner may claim accordingly, and may recover, unless another party claiming to be owner, and to have a right to damages on the ground of an earlier title, claims at the same time, and then the respondents must allege and prove such prior title in bar of the claim.

This seems to be just to the respondents, to save them from paying twice; but it prevents them from denying that their own authoritative act, intended as definitive, and to give notoriety, is not an act of taking, within the statute.

Verdict set aside, and cause remanded to the county commissioners to issue a new warrant to assess the petitioners' damages.

BENJAMIN PARKER v. THE BOSTON AND MAINE RAILROAD.[1]

Middlesex Co., January Term, 1849.

Assessment of Damages — What Injury is a ground for Damages — Practice — Railway Company estopped to deny that its Acts are legal.

If the owner of land, with buildings standing thereon, situated near the track of a railroad, but not crossed thereby, sustain any actual damage, capable of being pointed out, described, and appreciated in such estate, in consequence of and as incident to the construction of the railroad, he will be entitled to recover compensation therefor, against the proprietors of the railroad, in the mode provided by the Rev. Sts. c. 39, § 56.

---

[1] 3 Cushing's Reports, 107.

Parker v. The Boston and Maine Railroad.

If, in consequence of the excavation made for a railroad, the water of a well on an estate adjoining but not crossed by the railroad, is drawn off and the well thereby rendered dry and useless, the owner of such estate will be entitled to recover damages therefor, in the same manner as for land, &c., taken for the railroad.

The obstruction of a private way, in consequence of the construction of a railroad across the same, is a proper subject for damages, within the Rev. Sts. c. 39, § 56.

Where, in a petition for damages occasioned by the taking of land, &c., for the construction of a railroad, several distinct causes of damage are alleged, and a general verdict is returned, if one or more of such causes be not proper subjects of damage, it is not to be presumed, in the absence of any instruction by the sheriff relative to the same, that the jury gave any damages therefor.

A railroad corporation is estopped from denying, that a portion of the structure of their road, built at the same time with and as a part of it by their officers, engineers, and contractors, is authorized by their act of incorporation; and any person, entitled to recover for damages occasioned by such structure, has a right to assume, that in making the same the corporation acted in pursuance of their charter, and to have his equitable remedy for damages under the statute, (Rev. Sts. c. 39, § 56,) instead of treating the officers, engineers, and contractors of the corporation as trespassers.

A bridge, with lateral embankments, erected by a railroad corporation for the purpose of raising a highway and carrying it over their road, is as much a part of the structure authorized by their charter, as the railroad itself; and any person injured by the erection of such bridge and embankments, is entitled to recover his damages thereby occasioned, in the manner provided by the Rev. Sts. c. 39, § 56.

A claim for damages being made against a railroad corporation, on the ground of the erection by them of a bridge and embankments, as a part of the structure of their road, for the purpose of raising and carrying a highway over the same; and the respondents objecting, to the claim, that they had not taken the requisite preliminary steps, and consequently, were not authorized to erect the bridge and embankments; it was held, that the objection was one which the respondents had no right to make.

In order to authorize a railroad corporation under the provisions of the Rev. Sts. c. 39, §§ 67, 68, to raise or lower any way, it is not necessary that a previous agreement therefor should be made with the selectmen of the town, in which such way is situated, or that there should be a previous determination of the county commissioners, as to whether any and what alteration should be made. The railroad corporation are first to give notice to the selectmen of their intention to raise or lower the way in question: the selectmen are then within thirty days to notify the corporation of the alterations, if any, which they require; if the selectmen and the corporation shall not agree what alterations are necessary, application may be made by either to the county commissioners, to determine the same; and if selectmen give no notice to the corporation as to what alterations they require, the presumption is that they require none, but leave the whole matter to the corporation.

In order to entitle the abutters on a highway, which has been raised or lowered by a railroad corporation, under the provisions of the Rev. Sts. c. 39, §§ 67, 68, to recover the damages therefor, to which they may be entitled, if any, it is not necessary that the selectmen of the town should have either authorized or directed such alteration to be made.

The remedy for an injury occasioned by the alteration of the highway, for the purpose of raising or lowering the same, by a railroad corporation, is not by an action against the town under the Rev. Sts. c. 25, § 3, but by a proceeding against the corporation for damages, under the Rev. Sts. c. 39, § 56.

THIS was an appeal from an adjudication of Common Pleas, setting aside the verdict of a sheriff's jury upon the petition of Benjamin Parker against the Boston and Maine Railroad, for damages sustained by the petitioner, in consequence of the location and construction of the respondents' road.

The petitioner, on the 1st of November, 1845, presented his petition to the county commissioners of Middlesex, in which he represented and averred : —

That he was the owner of a certain lot of land, with the buildings
thereon standing, situated in Charlestown, and containing about two
acres, bounded south-westerly on Perkins street, south-easterly on
land of Richard Sullivan, north-easterly on the Winter Hill road,
and north-westerly on the boundary line of the town of Somerville,
and land of Lucinda A. Underwood and others : That the Boston
and Maine Railroad Extension Company had recently laid out,
located, and constructed their railroad near the south-easterly
boundary of the petitioner's land : That they had also constructed
a bridge over the Winter Hill road, where the railroad crosses it,
and within a few feet of the petitioner's land, where the same
bounds on the Winter Hill road, and had raised the bridge above the
former grade of the road, in order to allow the passage of locomotive
engines and cars under the same ; and, in order to allow the travel
on the Winter Hill road to pass over the bridge, had filled up the
road on either side of the bridge, and had raised the grade far above
the former level thereof, more especially on the north-westerly side of
the bridge ; and, in thus filling up and raising the grade of the road,
had made a high embankment in front of the petitioner's land, where
it bounds on the Winter Hill road : That by means of the filling up
and grading the road, and making the embankment as above stated,
the access to the petitioner's land from the road was greatly impaired, injured, and cut off: That, on the petitioner's premises above
described, and near his dwelling-house, there was a well, the water
of which had been drawn off, and which had become dry and useless,
in consequence of the depth of the excavation made by the company,
in constructing their railroad near the south-easterly boundary of the
petitioner's land : That the petitioner had always theretofore passed
and repassed to and from his premises over Perkins street, leading
from his estate to the Cambridge road, he having a right of way in
said street; that the company had located their road across Perkins
street, and, in constructing the same, had dug down, lowered, and
excavated that street, so that the passage over it had become difficult, dangerous, and unsafe: That, by means of all these acts and
doings of the railroad company, the petitioner's estate was greatly
injured and damaged, and the value thereof greatly diminished and
lessened, and the petitioner prevented from occupying, improving,
and enjoying his estate, as he previously might and was accustomed
to do : Wherefore the petitioner prayed the commissioners, after due
notice to the railroad company, to view the premises and estimate

the damages sustained by him by reason of the laying out, location, and maintaining of the railroad, and by reason of the acts and doings of the company in the premises.

On this petition, after notice to the respondents, the commissioners proceeded, on the 2d of December, 1845, to view the premises, and at their meeting in January following, made and returned an estimate of the damages sustained by the petitioner, who, being dissatisfied therewith, filed his petition for a jury at the same meeting. The commissioners ordered the petitioner to give the respondents notice of his application for a jury, and, on the 4th Tuesday of March following, notice having been given according to their order, the commissioners directed the clerk to issue a warrant for a jury. The respondents also being dissatisfied with the estimate, presented a petition for a jury, at the meeting in March, upon which the commissioners ordered a warrant to issue.

Pursuant to these orders, the clerk issued two warrants; one dated the 14th of April, and the other the 18th of June, 1846. In the first, which was issued upon the application of the petitioner, the sheriff was directed to summon a jury "to consider and estimate the damages done to the petitioner, named in said petition, by reason of the location of the Boston and Maine Railroad over his land aforesaid." In the other warrant, issued at the request of the respondents, the subject of the inquiry by the jury was described as "the damages done to Benjamin Parker, named in said petition, by the locating and constructing their said railroad, as in a former petition of the said Benjamin Parker is described."

The warrants were both executed at the same time, as one, on the 18th and 19th of June, 1846, and returned by the sheriff, together with the verdict of the jury, and a certificate of his rulings and instructions, to the Court of Common Pleas, to the next September term.

The verdict, by which the petitioner's damages were assessed at two hundred dollars, was set aside by the Court of Common Pleas, and the petitioner thereupon appealed to this court.

In the course of the trial, the sheriff was requested by the respondents to instruct the jury: 1st, That the building of the embankment on the Winter Hill road, as alleged in the petition, was not an injury to the land fronting on that road, occasioned by the laying out, making, or maintaining of the railroad; 2d, That the respondents had no authority, under their charter, to build the embankment in question, unless the same was required or assented to by the selectmen of Charlestown; and, it being admitted, that the selectmen had been duly notified by the respondents, and there being no evidence that they had either authorized or agreed to the building of the embankment, the respondents also requested the sheriff to instruct the jury, 3d, That if the selectmen neither authorized nor directed it to be built, the respondents were not liable for the damages thereby occasioned to the abutters on the Winter Hill road. But the sheriff declined giving the instructions as requested.

J. Dana, for the petitioner.

R. Choate and *T. Farrar* for the respondents.

SHAW, C. J.[1] It was admitted in the argument, that the respondents' railroad did not pass over any part of the petitioner's land, though the fact is incorrectly so stated in the warrant to the sheriff. Both parties applied to the commissioners for a jury to revise the assessment of damages, and upon these applications two distinct warrants were issued. The sheriff very properly consolidated the two, and returned them with a single verdict applicable to both. Perhaps it was proper for the clerk to issue two distinct warrants, in order that if one party should fail to take out his warrant and proceed upon it, the other party might nevertheless proceed upon his. On the warrant taken out by the respondents, the jury are to " estimate the damages done to Benjamin Parker, named in said petition," that is, the petition for a jury, " by the locating and constructing their said railroad, as in a former petition of the said Benjamin Parker is described." This reference, perhaps, to the original petition, is in terms sufficiently definite to make it part of the warrant, so far as to show what was the subject of the complaint and the nature of the damages sought to be recovered.

The petitioner sets forth, that he was the owner of certain land and buildings in Charlestown, bounding on one side on the Winter Hill road; that the Boston and Maine Railroad Extension Company (now the Boston and Maine Railroad) constructed their road near the boundary of his land, and built a bridge across the Winter Hill road, where it crosses the same, and raised the bridge above the former grade of the road, for the purpose of passing under the same, and filled up the road in order to pass over the bridge on either side, and raised the grade and made a high embankment in front of his land, by means whereof the petitioner's access to his land from the Winter Hill road was greatly impaired, injured, and cut off; that the respondents, in excavating for their road, dug so deep as to drain a well on

---

[1] Wilde, J., and Fletcher, J., did not sit in this cause.

the petitioner's premises, which has in consequence become dry and useless. The petitioner further avers, that he was previously accustomed to pass and repass over Perkins street, he having a right of way there; that the respondents located their road across that street, and in constructing the same, had dug down and excavated the street, so that the passage over it had been rendered difficult, dangerous, and unsafe. By means of all which acts, the petitioner alleges that his estate has been greatly injured, the value thereof diminished, and his enjoyment of the same impaired.

The sheriff was requested by the respondents to instruct the jury, that the building of an embankment on the Winter Hill road, as alleged in the petition, was not an injury to the land fronting on the road, occasioned by the laying out, making, or maintaining of the railroad. This instruction the sheriff declined to give. If the object of the instruction was to direct the jury that such embankment did no damage to the plaintiff's land, this was a pure question of fact, which they were summoned to try, and the sheriff was not called upon, nor was it within his proper province, to give such instruction.

But if it was intended to ask the sheriff to instruct the jury, that though such an embankment along the public highway leading to the bridge over the railroad did some damage, it was not a kind of damage for which the respondents were liable, as we suppose from the argument was intended, then such proposed instruction presents the main question in the present case. That question is, whether a party having land with buildings thereon, lying near the track of a railroad, but not crossed by it, can recover compensation for incidental damage caused to his land, by the construction of the railroad and the structures incidental to and connected with it.

The language of the general railroad act, Rev. Sts. c. 39, § 56, is very broad, declaring that "every railroad corporation shall be liable to pay all damages that shall be occasioned by laying out and making and maintaining their road, or by taking any land or materials, as provided in the preceding section."

This is a remedial provision, and to be construed liberally to advance the remedy. It is made in the spirit of the declaration of rights, giving compensation to persons sustaining damage for the public benefit. Whatever this provision, by its true construction, declares that the party damnified shall receive, the company, by accepting a railroad charter, bind themselves to pay.

The terms of the section must include damages which are caused by something else besides taking land and materials, because damages of that kind are distinguished from the former by the word " or." So the word " occasioned " points to any damage, which may be directly or indirectly caused by the railroad. We are of opinion, therefore, that a party who sustains an actual and real damage, capable of being pointed out, described, and appreciated, may sue a complaint for compensation for such damage; and we think that this point is settled by authority. Dodge v. Essex, 3 Met. 380; s. c. *ante*, 336; Ashby v. Eastern Railroad Company, 5 Met. 368; s. c. *ante*, 356. This question, we think, is not affected by the rule of law laid down in the case of Callender v. Marsh, 1 Pick. 418, that an abutter on a highway cannot obtain damages for raising or lowering the grade of the highway. That was founded on the ground, that the public had originally paid a full compensation for all damage to be done by them to the adjacent owners, by any reasonable or convenient mode of grading the way; and the rule has been altered by statute since. But were it otherwise, it would not have governed or affected this case. We think the language of this statute is broad enough to include all actual damages occasioned by laying out and fitting a railroad for use.

. And so in regard to the well. The claim for damages on this ground does not depend on the relative rights of owners of land, each of whom has a right to make a proper use of his own estate, and sinking a well upon it is such proper use; and if the water, by its natural current, flows from one to the other, and a loss ensues, it is *damnum absque injuria.* But the respondents did not own land; they only acquired a special right to and usufruct in it, upon the condition of paying all damages which might be thereby occasioned to others.

In regard to the allegations respecting Perkins street, it does not appear whether that street was a public or private way; and the sheriff was not asked to direct the attention of the jury to this distinction. If it was a private way, and the description in the petition would apply to either, the statute gives damages therefor, (Rev. Sts. c. 39, § 71,) by implication, by providing that the application for such damages shall be made within one year. It does not appear, that this application was not made within one year; but if it was not, the attention of the sheriff should have been drawn to it, and the respondents should have relied upon the limitation in the statute as a bar.[1]

---

[1] If the principle be admitted that a party, whose property is taken from him, or is injured under the authority of the government, can maintain no action at common law to recover damages or compensation for his loss, (see *ante*, page 166,

note,) it follows, necessarily, that the right to compensation must depend entirely upon the statute provisions in respect thereto.

In England, where there is no constitutional restriction upon the legislature

But if these grounds, or either of them, were not a proper subject of damage, we are not to presume, in the absence of any instruction, that the jury gave damages for them.

against taking private property for public uses, this principle holds true universally; and in this country it also holds true in all cases where the injury, done in the execution of statutory powers, does not amount to a taking of property within the meaning of the constitutional restrictions. Where property is taken in this country for public uses, the right is derived from the constitution and not from the statute.

The rights of the parties affected by such legislation being dependent entirely upon the statutes, it becomes important to ascertain what rules of construction are to be applied to such laws. It has been uniformly held, both in England and in this country, that such laws, being a direct interference with rights of property, are to receive a liberal construction in favor of the owner.

In Eton College, *ex parte*, 1 Eng. Law & Eq. Rep. 51, the Lord Chancellor laid down the principle, that where the general intent of the legislature is complete indemnification of the party whose land is taken, the court will so construe the language as to give effect to the general intent, and he therefore decreed that a railway company was liable to pay the costs of a reinvestment of money given as compensation for taking trust property. The rule had been laid down with great distinctness in the earlier cases of the Hungerford Market Company. The legislature, having impowered certain persons to purchase Hungerford Market, in order to enlarge and rebuild it, provided that if any person, tenant for years, from year to year, or at will, or occupier of any part thereof, should "sustain or be put to any loss, damage, or injury in respect of any interest whatever for good-will, improvements, tenants, fixtures, or otherwise, which they now enjoy by reason of the passing of this act" he should receive compensation. Several cases arose under this act, and the

principles then laid down have been followed in all the later English cases. In Ex parte Farlow the court held that a tenant from year to year, who had received notice to quit from the company, was entitled to compensation for the good-will of his premises, and the chance of a continuation of his occupancy, although he had no legal estate or interest which could be protected as against the landlord; the court decided that the statute contemplated complete indemnity to the parties who might be affected injuriously by the proceedings under the act; and the tenant was entitled to compensation, not only for such legal interests as might be protected at law, but for the feeble interest which he had in the chance or probability that the landlord would continue from year to year to renew the lease. 2 Barnewall & Adolphus, 341. This decision was subsequently affirmed in Rex v. The Hungerford Market Company, 1 Neville & Manning, 404. And in another case it was decided that a tenant whose lease had expired, was entitled to compensation for his chance of a renewal.

Relying upon these decisions, a tenant in the occupation of land which a railway company had purchased, and who had received of the company notice to quit at the expiration of his lease, applied for compensation in respect of his good-will, and the chance he would have had for a renewal had the property remained in the hands of his lessor. But the court held, that they must be governed, not by any general rules applicable to all cases where the same interests were involved, but by the construction of the act, under which the company was proceeding; and as the statute contained no terms comprehensive enough to cover this claim, as in the prior cases, those decisions could not be made precedents to govern the case under consideration. Rex v. The Liver-

Parker *v.* The Boston and Maine Railroad.

But it is insisted, that if either was wrong, the verdict must be set aside, as in cases of several counts in a declaration, where general

---

pool and Manchester R. Co. 6 Neville & Manning, 186.

These cases show, that while the courts give a liberal construction to statutes providing for compensation, the *right* to compensation is entirely dependent upon the statute provisions.

The Hungerford Market also gave rise to several other cases which served to elucidate this branch of the law. The company, in taking down a building, found it necessary to repair the party wall between themselves and the adjoining owner, and they accordingly took steps to remove the wall, under the general act regulating the rights and duties of adjoining owners. In doing so, injury was done to the adjoining owners, and they claimed compensation under the company's act. But the court held, that it was only for injuries which the company might do in the exercise of the powers conferred by its act; that it was liable to make compensation in the mode there pointed out. For all such injuries as the company might commit in the exercise of rights which it possessed in common with all private and natural persons, it was liable, like a natural person, to an action at law, but it could be proceeded against in the mode pointed out by the statute, only when it might plead the statute in justification of its acts. *Ex parte,* Yeates, 2 Neville & Manning, 340.

So where the company purchased a house, which it was not empowered to take compulsorily, under its act, and in pulling it down, injured the adjoining house, the court held, that compensation could not be claimed under the act, and that the injured party must resort to his action in the same manner as though the injury had been done by a private person. *Ex parte,* Eyre, 8 Neville & Manning, 622. But where a canal company, in executing its powers within the limits prescribed by the charter, injured property lying beyond the limits, it was held

that the owner was entitled to compensation. Rex *v.* The Nottingham Old Waterworks Co. 5 Neville & Manning, 498.

The expression " *injuriously affected* " is now employed in the English statutes to describe the injury for which the owner of land may claim compensation, and a liberal construction is given to the term, by the courts in favor of the land-owner. In Glover] *v.* The North Staffordshire R. Co. 5 Eng. Law & Eq. Rep. 385, the rule was laid down that where a railway company does that which would be an actionable injury to land unless done under the powers conferred by its charter, the owner is entitled to compensation.

In this case the railway crossed two private ways by which the plaintiff passed to and from his house. It does not appear that the roads were crossed upon the plaintiff's land, but a jury found that the crossing was an injury to the plaintiff's estate, and the court held that the company must make compensation.

The court had previously decided that where a railway company, in constructing its road, lowered the land in front of an estate in such a manner as to depreciate its value, it must make compensation for the injury. Regina *v.* The Eastern Counties R. Co. 2 Eng. Rail. Ca. 736.

In The London and North-Western R. Co. *v.* Bradley, 5 Eng. Law & Eq. Rep. 100, the Lord Chancellor clearly indicated his opinion that a company is bound to make compensation for injuries arising from the use of the road, as well as for injuries arising from its construction. Where, however, subsequent injury is sustained by a land-owner, which arises from an *improper* construction of the road, and not necessarily from the road itself, it seems that compensation cannot be claimed under the act, but the party must resort to an action at law. Lawrence *v.* The Great Northern R. Co. 4 Eng. Law & Eq. Rep. 265.

damages are assessed, and one count is bad, and it cannot be set right by the judge's minutes. But that is a rule strictly applicable to actions, and there is but a remote analogy between the cases to which it applies and the present case. This is a single claim for damages, with several specifications, and is much more like a common money count under which several promissory notes are given in evidence, and a general verdict rendered thereon. In such a case the judgment could not be arrested, by showing that some one of the notes so given in evidence was defective.

But the next general ground of exception is, that this bridge and embankment along the Winter Hill common road, and over the railroad, were made by the respondents, without authority derived from their act of incorporation ; that these acts were unauthorized ; and that, if the plaintiff has any remedy therefor against anybody, it is not by a claim for damages against the respondents.

If this bridge and embankment were made at the same time that the railroad was made by the. officers, engineers, and contractors of the respondents, we think they are estopped from denying that they acted by competent authority. This mode of proceeding indicated clearly enough that they professed to act under the authority of their acts of incorporation ; and we think that the individual proprietor had a right to assume that they so acted, and have his equitable remedy for damages, instead of treating the officers, engineers, and contractors of the company as trespassers.

But upon this point, it appears to the court, that the respondents acted in conformity with the provisions of their charter. Recurring to the railroad act, Rev. Sts. c. 39, it is provided in § 66, that if any railroad track shall be so laid out as to cross any turnpike road or other way, it shall be so made as not to obstruct such turnpike road or way. Then how, by whom, and in what manner, shall this adaptation to the old road be made ? Equity would answer, plainly enough, that it is not required to be made for the benefit of the turnpike company, or of the town ; it is an inconvenience to which they are subjected for the benefit and accommodation of the railroad, to which it is essential that it should be kept on a certain grade, whereas the grade of a turnpike or common road may be changed, though with some inconvenience. But the statute does not leave it to implication. The next section (§ 67) declares that every railroad corporation may raise or lower any turnpike or way for the purpose of having their railroad pass over or under the same ; the mode we shall refer to afterwards.

The statute, having thus declared that railroad corporations may raise or lower a highway, provides further (§ 72), that every railroad company shall maintain and keep in repair all bridges with their abutments, which such corporation shall construct over or under any turnpike road, canal, highway, or other way.   These provisions apply to the original laying out and construction of the railroad; and there are other provisions of the general act, and also of subsequent acts, as the act of 1842, c. 22, which apply to cases where, after the original laying out and construction of the railroad, alteration in ways becomes necessary.

All these provisions are parts of one act, to be taken and construed together as one system of rules; and hence it appears, that the raising of a common road, with an embankment of sufficient length on each side to form an easy slope to a high bridge, is a part of the franchise given by the charter, as much as the right to take private property or to pass over navigable waters.   These bridges, and the embankments extending laterally from, are as much a part of, the structure authorized by the charter, as the railroad itself.   This brings the case of one damnified by such structure within all the reasons and within all the provisions which give compensation for damages occasioned by the laying out, making, and maintaining of the railroad.

But the respondents further insist, that this bridge and these embankments were made without authority, because the respondents had not first agreed with the selectmen, or applied to the county commissioners to determine, what alterations were necessary.

This is an objection, we think, which the respondents have no right to make.   If they, as against third parties, were allowed to set up their own violations of the plain duties, which by their charter they have taken upon themselves to perform, and to rely upon such violations to defeat others of their rights, they would be taking advantage of their own wrong.   But for the railroad charter, and the authority vested in the company by it, this structure and embankment upon the common highway would be plainly a public nuisance, for which an indictment would lie.

But the sixty-eighth section, respecting the agreement of the parties, or, in case of their disagreement, the order of the county commissioners, is to be taken in connection with § 67, before cited.   This latter section declares the right of the company to raise the grade of the highway to the bridge; it is an absolute right, not depending upon the consent of selectmen or county commissioners; and the reference to these officers in § 68 does no more than prescribe the terms.   The sixty-seventh section provides, that before proceeding to make any alteration in a highway, the railroad company shall, in writing, notify the selectmen; and the selectmen, within thirty days, shall, in writing, notify the company of the alterations, if any, which they may require to have made. Then comes § 68, which provides that if the parties shall not agree what alterations are necessary, either party may apply to the county commissioners, who shall thereupon determine whether any and what alterations shall be made, and that their decision shall be final.

· It is contended, upon these provisions, that .alterations in a highway are unauthorized, unless there be an express agreement of the company and the selectmen, or an order of the county commissioners.

But we do not so understand this statute. The first act is to be done by the railroad company, who are to give notice in writing to the selectmen. It appears, in the present case, that this was done; and it does not appear that any answer in writing was given; or, if there was, it is in the hands of the respondents. But following the statutes, the next step is for the selectmen to give an answer in writing. Notice of what? their assent to, or, dissent from, the proposals of the railroad .company? Not at all; but notice of the alterations, if any, which they may require.

To this extent they have a right to prescribe. Can it be doubted, if the railroad corporation comply with such requisition, that they will thereby do their whole duty? Yet this will be no express agreement between the parties. It would be a requisition on the part of the party having power to prescribe, and obedience on the part of the party required to do something at his own expense for the public. It is only in case the parties shall not agree what alterations are necessary that either party may appeal to the county commissioners.

Supposing, then, that the notice of the railroad company to the selectmen, that they propose to alter the grade of the highway, is a condition precedent, the respondents have done their whole duty, in this respect, by giving the notice; unless the selectmen notify them what alterations they require, and the company fail to comply with their requisition, by altering the grade of the highway without making the required alterations, and without obtaining the order and decree of the commissioners. If the selectmen give no notice as to what alterations they require, the presumption is that they require none, but leave the whole matter to the company.

The third instruction to the jury, asked by the respondents, and refused by the sheriff, wa§, that if the selectmen neither authorized nor directed the making of the embankment, the railroad company were not liable for the damages to the abutters on the Winter Hill road.

The objection, founded on the refusal to give this instruction is substantially answered by the considerations already suggested. The bridge and embankments on the highway were not built by the direction or the authority of the selectmen; but by the company under the authority of the statute. Selectmen have no negative voice. They have a voice in directing the mode in which the.alterations shall be made, if they choose to raise it, in order that the accommodation of the public in highways, of which they are the guardians, may be insured; and this is the extent and limit of their power.

The last ground taken by the respondents which we shall notice is, that the plaintiff has no remedy against the respondents, but if he has any, it is against the town, under Rev. Sts. c. 25, § 6.

It appears to us, that this ground is wholly untenable. The section referred to provides for a very different case. It is to this effect: When any one, who is the owner of land adjoining a highway or townway, shall sustain damage by raising or lowering, or other act done for the purpose of repairing such way, the owner shall have compensation therefor, to be determined by the selectmen, with a right of appealing to a jury. This statute relates to entirely different subjects, namely, the laying out, altering, repairing, and improving townways and highways. It is with reference to altering the grade for the purpose of repairing such way.

But in the case of railroads, the corporation is declared to be liable; they have the power wholly independent of the authority of selectmen and county commissioners; they are in terms charged with the expense; they are to receive the benefit. The alteration, in the case before us, was not made for the purpose of repairing the Winter Hill road. By § 68, already cited, the selectmen had power to prescribe alterations, and, in case of a difference between them and the respondents relating thereto, to apply to the commissioners; and then it is provided, that if the railroad company unnecessarily neglect to make such alteration as the county commissioners direct, the selectmen shall have the same remedies as are prescribed for the recovery of damages caused by making such railroad.

Is not this a clear indication that the selectmen are to apply to the county commissioners, in the first instance, to assess their damages? The work is done by the company for their own benefit, and at their own expense; and we are of opinion, that whoever sustains an injury by it may obtain his damages in the mode prescribed for the recovery of damages for taking land or materials for a railroad.

The mode of recovering damages is clearly indicated by the fifty-sixth section. They are to be estimated by the commissioners, on application by either party, in the manner provided in the case of laying out highways; and, by § 57, either party may apply for a jury o assess the damages, and the same proceedings are to be had hereon as are prescribed in the twenty-fourth chapter, for recovering lamages for laying out highways. This, of course, must apply to ailroads, as nearly as practicable, but with such variations as the lifference of the two cases may require.

In a case like this, the town would in no event be responsible, nor vould the selectmen have any authority, and any application to hem must be fruitless.

There is no analogy between this case and the case of Currier v. Lowell, 16 Pick. 170, which was for the recovery of damages, sustained by the plaintiff, in consequence of an excavation made by the Boston and Lowell Railroad Company in a highway, for the safety nd sufficiency of which the town were still liable.

But the court are of opinion that the plaintiff is well entitled to recover; and supposing that the Court of Common Pleas decided otherwise upon matters of law apparent on the record, the adjudication of that court, setting aside this verdict, must be reversed, and the verdict accepted.

The petitioner having moved for interest on the verdict, and also or costs, the opinion of the court was subsequently stated by

SHAW, C. J. In this case, the respondents prayed for a warrant or a jury, and to some small extent reduced the amount awarded by he commissioners.

Interest is to be allowed on the verdict; and the taxable costs of he appeal, as in the case of the Fitchburg Railroad Company against these respondents; but no costs for the warrant and jury.

A certificate is to be sent to the county commissioners, certifying he judgment of this court, that the adjudication of the Court of Common Pleas setting aside the verdict returned in behalf of the petitioner be reversed, and judgment entered that the said verdict be accepted and affirmed, and that the county commissioners issue a warrant of distress to cause the same to be paid and satisfied.

THE BOSTON AND MAINE RAILROAD v. ARCHIBALD BABCOCK.[1]

Suffolk Co., March Term, 1849.

Construction of a Contract to Convey Land — Agreement as to Price of Land which a Company may take.

The defendant having entered into an agreement to sell the plaintiffs, a railroad corporation, " the land they take on the northerly side of the M. turnpike, adjoining T.'s land, at twenty cents per square foot, for each and every foot so taken by said company," and the plaintiffs having brought a bill in equity for a specific performance; it was held, that the agreement was not for a sale of the land generally, or of such part of it as the plaintiffs might elect, or of such as they should accept the offer of; but for the sale of such a part of the land described as the plaintiffs might take, in the exercise of the authority conferred on them by law to take land for their road.

If the terms of a contract are doubtful, a court of equity will not decree a specific performance.

THIS was a bill in equity for the specific performance of a contract, in which the plaintiffs alleged, that the defendant, on the 18th of July, 1844, was seised and was the owner of a certain piece of land in Somerville, particularly described in the bill, and, in consideration that the plaintiffs would purchase the same for their use as a corporation, signed a written paper, (which was made a part of the bill,) by which he agreed to convey to the plaintiffs the land above mentioned, for the sum of four thousand dollars, and also to sell to the plaintiffs the land they might take belonging to him on the northerly side of the Medford turnpike, adjoining Tenney's land, at twenty cents a square foot, for each and every foot taken; that, on the 1st of August, 1844, the agreement being then in full force, and unrescinded by the defendant, the plaintiffs elected to take of the defendant, under and on the terms mentioned in the same, a parcel of land belonging to the defendant, lying on the northerly side of the Medford turnpike, and adjoining Tenney's, and bounded and described as particularly set forth in the bill; that, on the same day, the plaintiffs notified the defendant of their election, and offered to pay him for a conveyance of the land, and did produce to him for that purpose and requested him to execute a conveyance of the same, and tendered him such a conveyance; that the defendant neglected to execute such conveyance, or to perform his contract, and had ever since neglected to perform the same; that the plaintiffs, in the confidence that the agreement with the defendant would be complied with by him in good faith, took for their corporate use the lot of land described in the bill, which they had elected to take, and located the track of their road on a part thereof, and that the remainder thereof was valuable to them; and that the defendant, afterwards, unmindful of his obligations under his contract with the plaintiffs, instituted proceedings before the county commissioners of Middlesex, for the recovery of his damages for the land so taken by the plaintiffs.

The prayer of the bill was, that the defendant might be enjoined from further prosecuting his claim for damages before the commissioners, and might be ordered to convey the land to the plaintiffs on the terms contained in the agreement between the parties.

The writing signed by the defendants, which was referred to in the bill, was as follows: —

" I hereby agree to sell and convey, by good and sufficient deed, the heater parcel of land bounded by Colonel Goodrich and others on the westerly side, northerly by the Medford turnpike, and southerly by the Winter Hill road, being the point of land between the turnpike and town road, containing one half acre and twenty-one poles, as per plan of Peter Tufts, Jr., with all the privileges and rights appertaining to said land, to the Boston and Maine Railroad Company, on the payment of four thousand dollars; and also agree to sell the said company the land they take on the northerly side of the Medford turnpike, adjoining Tenney's land, at twenty cents per square foot, for each and every foot so taken by said company."

The defendants demurred to the bill, assigning for cause: 1. That the writing referred to therein does not purport to contain any consideration, and none is alleged in the bill; 2. That it is not alleged in the bill, that the defendant, at the time of making the agreement, was the owner of the land, which was the subject of it; 3. That it is not alleged in the bill, that the land, of which a conveyance is sought, is the same, or a part of the same, mentioned in the agreement; 4. That the bill does not allege that the plaintiffs tendered the price of the land to the defendant.

J. Hall, for the defendant, referred to Allen *v.* Roberts, 2 Bibb, 98; German *v.* Machin, 6 Paige, 280; Boucher *v.* Van Buskirk, 2 A. K. Marsh. 346; Dwight *v.* Pomeroy, 17 Mass. 327; 1 Story, E. P. § 26; Wright *v.* Dame, 22 Pick. 55; Kendall *v.* Almy, 2 Sumner, 278; Carr *v.* Duval, 14 Pet. 77.

G. Minot, for the plaintiffs, referred to Boys *v.* Ayerst, Mad. & Geld. 316.

The Boston and Maine Railroad *v.* Babcock.

J. Dana replied.

FLETCHER, J.[1]   This is also a bill for the specific performance of a contract, which is annexed to and made a part of the bill. The court understand this contract to mean, that the defendant agreed to receive payment at the rate of twenty cents a square foot, for such portion of the land referred to, as the plaintiffs should take, in the exercise of the power given them in their charter, to take land for the purposes of their road. It seems impossible to put any other construction upon the terms of the contract. In the first part of the contract, the defendant agrees to sell the plaintiffs a certain piece of land, by metes and bounds, for a stipulated price. He then agrees to sell them "the land they take on the northerly side of the turnpike" at twenty cents a foot "for each and every foot so taken by said company." The agreement is not to sell the land generally, at so much a foot; nor to sell such land as the plaintiffs may elect to take; nor such land as they shall accept the offer of; but such land as they actually take, that is, such land as they had full power to take; and, for land so taken, they are to pay and the defendant to receive twenty cents a foot. By the terms of the contract, it is distinctly announced, that the act of taking is expected to be the separate, independent act of the plaintiffs. These terms clearly import the exercise of a power on their part; such a power as it was well known belonged to them, and which might be exercised to give effect to the agreement.

It was perfectly natural, that the corporation should wish to fix the amount, which they would be obliged to pay for land before taking it. The location of the road might be determined by the price to be paid for the land. The contract thus understood, therefore, was a perfectly natural and reasonable one, on the part of the plaintiffs, and such, it is believed, as is frequently made by railroad corporations. Before actually taking the land, as they had a right to do, they agreed upon the damages they would have to pay for it; and the quantity was, of course, by the terms of the contract, limited to the amount they might rightfully and properly take, under and by virtue of their charter.

Now, the bill, as framed, does not entitle the plaintiffs to enforce the performance of this contract. It does not appear, by the bill, that the corporation took any of the land referred to in the contract, under and by virtue of their charter, in the mode and with the formalities required by law. As it was in reference only to land which should

---

[1] Wilde, J., did not sit in this case.

be so taken, that the defendant stipulated, and it does not appear that any has been so taken, the plaintiffs can have no decree against the defendant.

But if the import and meaning of the contract were merely doubtful, it would not be in accordance with the principles of equity, to compel a specific performance. If contracts are not so certain in themselves, as to enable the court to arrive at the clear result of what is meant by all the terms contained in them, they will not be specifically enforced. It would be inequitable to carry a contract into effect, where the court are left in doubt as to the intention of the parties; for, in such case, the court might decree what the parties never intended or contemplated.

JEREMIAH HAYES v. THE WESTERN RAILROAD CORPORATION.[1]

Suffolk Co., March Term, 1849.

Master and Servant — Liability of Master to one Servant for Injuries occasioned by another Servant.

The proprietors of a railroad are not responsible to a brakeman in their employment, for an injury sustained by him in consequence of the neglect or fault of another brakeman engaged in the same service, even though the latter be at the same time the acting conductor of a train of freight cars.

If a brakeman, employed on a train of cars by the proprietors of a railroad, sustains an injury in consequence of the carelessness of another brakeman employed in the same service, and the injury would not have happened if the latter had performed his duty, it is immaterial, as respects the liability of the proprietors of the road, whether the train was short of hands or not.

THIS was an action on the case, for an injury sustained by the plaintiff, whilst in the employment of the defendants as a brakeman on a freight train between Worcester and Springfield. The case was tried before Wilde, J., and by him reported for the consideration of the whole court, as follows : —

The testimony of several witnesses tended to show, that on the night when the alleged injury occurred, there were about one hundred freight cars to go from Worcester to Springfield, the whole of which were under the charge of a conductor, who divided them into four trains, three being drawn by large engines, and one by a smaller

---

[1] 3 Cushing's Reports, 270.

engine. The conductor went on the first train. Each of the others was under the charge of a brakeman, acting as conductor and brakeman, as was usual in such cases.

The plaintiff was on the third train, which had from twenty-five to thirty cars. Three brakemen were provided by the company for this second train, but one of them did not take his place on the train that night when it left Worcester. It did not appear that any officer or agent of the company gave him leave of absence. The night was dark and stormy, and the track slippery. When the second train was about four miles out of Worcester, ascending a grade of thirty-five to fifty feet, six double cars in the rear broke loose, and, having no brakeman on them, ran down the grade, came in contact with the next train, where the plaintiff was, and inflicted on him the injury of which he complained.

There was evidence tending to show, that before the second train left Worcester, one of the brakemen spoke to the other, who was the acting conductor, and told him he wished to get on to the engine and warm his feet, and that the acting conductor told him he might do so, and he, the acting conductor, would take his place on the rear car. The evidence on both sides showed, that it was known to all engaged in this business of managing freight trains, that it was necessary to have a brakeman on the rear car; and there was evidence tending to show, that the defendants had given orders to their brakemen to that effect.

The evidence produced by both parties showed, that if a man had been stationed on the rear car, on this occasion, he could have stopped the cars, which were separated, and prevented the collision; but there was also evidence tending to prove, that two brakemen were not a sufficient number safely to manage a train of the size and weight of this one; and there was evidence to the contrary.

There was also evidence tending to show, that there were brakes on all the cars, and that the usual mode of conducting trains was to station the conductor and brakemen on the train, so that each would have an equal number of cars under his charge, each standing on the rear car of his charge.

The presiding judge ruled, that the defendants were not responsible to the plaintiff for any damage suffered by him in consequence of neglect of duty and breach of orders by the acting conductor of the second train; and that, as to the number of brakemen, the defendants would be responsible, if the number was not sufficient to insure safety, if the brakemen had all done their duty; but if they believed, that if the brakeman, whose duty it was to have been on the rear car, had been there doing his duty, the injury would not have

566

AMERICAN RAILWAY CASES.

Hayes v. The Western Railroad Corporation.

taken place, then it was immaterial whether the train was short of hands or not.

The jury returned a verdict for the defendants.

F. W. Sawyer, for the plaintiff.

B. R. Curtis, for the defendants.

FLETCHER, J. This is an action on the case, for an injury sustained by the plaintiff, at the time he was in the employment of the defendants, as a brakeman on a freight train between Worcester and Springfield, as stated in the report.

The case comes before the court upon exceptions taken by the plaintiff to the rulings of the judge who presided at the trial. It appeared from the evidence, that if a man had been stationed on the rear car of the second train, he would have been able to stop the cars which were separated, and thus have prevented the collision. There were on this train two brakemen. One of them, who would otherwise have been stationed on the rear car, went forward to warm himself, and the other agreed to take his place on the rear car, but neglected to do so, and by this neglect, the injury happened. This brakeman was also the acting conductor of the train for this particular occasion. He ought to have taken his station as brakeman on the rear car of the second train, as he agreed to do, and as he was required to do by the general orders of the defendants.

The judge ruled, that the defendants were not responsible to the plaintiff for any damage suffered by him in consequence of the neglect of duty and breach of orders by the acting conductor of the second train. To this ruling exception is taken.

This ruling is in accordance with the decision of this court in the case of Farwell v. Boston and Worcester Railroad Corporation, 4 Met. 49 ; s. c. *ante,* 339, in which it was settled, that a master is not answerable to one of his servants, for an injury received by him in consequence of the carelessness of another servant, while both are engaged in the same service. It is not necessary, on this occasion, to go into the reasoning by which the decision in that case was sustained. The case was thoroughly considered, and is believed to be fully sustained by reason and authority; and the court has no disposition to disturb the authority, or to depart from the decision of that case. The counsel for the plaintiff has endeavored to distinguish this case from the one referred to, and thus to withdraw the present case from the operation of that decision. He says, that in the case referred to, the party in fault, and the party injured, were of the same grade of employment, both being laborers; and that the case is therefore an authority only in reference to cases where the parties sustain the same relation to the corporation; but that when a laborer is injured by the neglect of an officer, the rule does not apply. The distinction for which he contends is, that though the company is not responsible to a laborer, for neglect of an ordinary laborer, yet they are answerable for the neglect of an officer, and that in the present case, the neglect was that of an officer.

It is not necessary to consider particularly the soundness of this argument, because, even if it were correct in principle, it fails entirely in matter of fact. It is distinctly set forth and settled by the report, that the party chargeable with neglect, and the party injured, were both brakemen of precisely the same grade. Although the brakeman in default was the acting conductor on this occasion, yet he was but à brakeman, charged with the duty of that class of laborers, and his neglect was in that character only, and not as a conductor. As between him and the other brakeman, it was a matter of indifference which took his station on the rear car: that was a matter of arrangement and concert between them; and this brakeman having engaged to take that station as such, and having neglected to do so, the default was the default of this brakeman; for which default, by the decision of this court in the case above cited, the defendants are not answerable to the plaintiff. The ruling in this particular was therefore clearly correct.

The second clause of the ruling was not objected to.

The last part of the ruling, as to the immateriality of the trains being short handed, is objected to as incorrect. But when it is established, that the injury complained of was occasioned by the neglect of the man on the train, and not by reason of the absence of the man, then surely the absence of the man becomes immaterial. The reasonings and calculations of the counsel; as to chances and probabilities, are skilful and ingenious, but chance and probability are too remote and contingent to be the basis of judicial decision in a case like this. The proximate cause is the object of inquiry, and when discovered, is to be regarded and relied on.

Then it was said, that whether material or not was to be left to the jury. But surely it was within the province and the duty of the court to instruct the jury, that a fault, if any, of the defendants, from which the plaintiff had not suffered, and of which he had no right to complain, was immaterial. Any fault of the defendants, not affecting the plaintiff, was certainly in legal contemplation immaterial in this case.   *Judgment on the verdict.*[1]

---

[1] The principle that, at common law, a ...which the latter may receive through the master is not liable to a servant for injuries   carelessness of a fellow servant, was first

laid down, in the English courts, in the case of Priestley v. Fowler, 3 Meeson & Welsby, 1, and has been since affirmed in the cases of Wigmore v. Jay, 5 Exchequer Rep. 334, and Hutchinson v. The York, Newcastle, &c. R. Co., 6 Eng. Rail. Ca. 580. In the latter case the court pointed out some limitations which would be made in the application of the principle. " A master," it was said, " is not exempt from responsibility to his servant for an injury occasioned to him by the act of another servant, where the servant injured was not, at the time of the injury, acting in the service of the master. In such case the servant injured is substantially a stranger, and entitled to all the privileges he would have had, if he had not been a servant." It was further said that the rule "must be taken with the qualification that the master has taken due care not to expose his servant to unreasonable risks. The servant, when he engages to run the risk of his service, including those arising from the negligence of fellow-servants, has a right to understand that the master has taken reasonable care to protect him from such risks by associating him only with persons of ordinary skill and care." This last limitation springs out of the principle, that, for an injury occasioned by his own negligence the master is liable to the servant. The declaration in this case charged the company with negligence jointly with its servants, and the plea denied the allegation of the company's negligence, and alleged that due and proper care had been exercised by the defendant in the selection of servants. This plea the court held to be proper and necessary to meet the allegation against the company of negligence.

But how far a master's duty to provide for the safety of a servant extends, has not been very clearly defined. The case of Seymour v. Maddox, 5 Eng. Law & Eq. 265, bears upon this point. The declaration alleged that the plaintiff was employed at the defendant's theatre, and that, through the floor of a stage over which the plaintiff was required to pass in the discharge of his duties, there was a

hole which it was the duty of the defendant to keep well fenced and lighted, but which he neglected to do, in consequence of which the plaintiff fell and was injured. The question before the court was, whether the relation of master and servant imposed upon the master the duty alleged in the declaration. The court held, that no such duty existed. " The servant is not," said Coleridge, J., in delivering his opinion, " bound to enter the master's service ; but if he does, and finds things in a certain state, he must take the consequence of any thing that may occur, owing to such state of things." See also Skip v. The Eastern Counties R. Co. 24 English Law & Eq. Rep. In this country the case of Priestley v. Fowler has been affirmed in several cases. Farwell v. The Boston and Worcester R. Co. 4 Metcalf, 49 ; s. c. ante, 339 ; Hayes v. The Western R. Co., supra ; Brown v. Maxwell, 6 Hill, 592 ; Coon v. The Syracuse and Utica R. Co., 6 Barbour, 231 ; affirmed on appeal, 3 Comstock, (see post, vol. 2) ; Murray v. The South Carolina R. Co., 1 McMullan, 385.

An attempt was made in Coon v. The Syracuse & Utica R. Co. to charge the company on the ground that the servant, through whose negligence the injury was caused, was of a higher grade than the plaintiff, the latter being, to some extent, under the control and direction of the former. But the court refused to make any distinction between this case and that where the servants held the same relative situation.

The plaintiff also contended that the negligence which caused the injury might be charged directly upon the company, and that it thus became liable for the injury, as its own act. The court, however, held, that the facts did not sustain this position. The question has not yet been decided whether a corporation can, under any circumstances, be directly charged with negligence. As a corporation, in general, acts only through its agents, there seems to be great difficulty in making it directly liable for negligence, unless it may be in cases where an order or direc-

Hayes *v.* The Western Railroad Corporation.

tion to do a negligent act, emanates directly from the company acting in its corporate capacity.

In the case of Scudder *v.* Woodbridge, 1 Kelly, 195, the Supreme Court of Georgia held, that, where a hired slave was killed by the negligence of other servants in the employment of the same person, the owner might recover the value of the slave from the party hiring him.

The Supreme Court of Ohio in the case of the Little Miami R. Co. *v.* Stevens, 20 Ohio, 415, (see *post*,) rejected the doctrine of Priestley *v.* Fowler, and held the company liable to a servant injured by the negligence of a fellow servant. This decision is clearly against the common law of England, and the judges were not unanimous in giving it.

The law of Scotland recognizes the liability of the master in such cases, and since the principle has gained a foot-hold in this country it may be proper to lay before the profession the reasoning upon which the doctrine is there sustained. We give, therefore, a report of a recent Scotch case, in which the difference between the law of that country, and of England is fully exhibited:

COURT OF SESSION.

DIXON *v.* RANKEN.

Saturday, January 31, 1852.

Master and Servant — Liability of Master.

A master will be held liable in damages for injuries done to a workman in his service, in the course of his employment, by a fellow-workman, also in the master's service.

THIS was an appeal from the Sheriff-Court of Glasgow. The action was brought by Mrs. Banken, the widow of a workman in Dixon's employment, against Dixon for damages, for the injury and loss sustained by her through the death of her husband, caused by the negligence of a fellow-workman, also in the employment of the defendant, in working a coal-pit of the defendant. The sheriff-substitute (Skene) found the defendant liable in damages, and to this judgment the sheriff (Alison) adhered.

Patton (with whom *Inglis*) for appellant, argued, that from the facts brought out in evidence the plaintiff had no claim for damages. But even supposing it proved that the death of her husband had been occasioned by the act of his fellow-workman, Dixon could not be held liable. Hutchison, 22d May, 1850, 19 L. J. Ex. 296; Wigmore, 22d May, 1850, 20 L. J.; Priestley *v.* Fowler, 3 M. & W. 1.

Pattison, for respondent. The liability of the master to his servant for injuries done by his fellow-servant, has never been disputed in Scotland, whatever may be the law in England. Sword *v.* Cameron and Gallatly, 13th Feb. 1839. There are not many cases which can be cited, just because the rule has never been disputed.

The LORD JUSTICE CLERK, after going over the evidence, which he held to establish that the injuries had been caused by the negligence of the fellow-workman, said, — It is said, entirely on the authority of certain decisions and opinions of the Courts of England, that the master is not responsible — as I understand in any circumstance — to those employed by him for any injuries caused by the carelessness, inattention, and unskilfulness of other servants in his employment. That there are many cases in which the master will not be liable for injuries done by his servants, whether to a third party or to another servant acting at the time in his master's service, is quite true; but such exceptions (for such they are in the law of Scotland) depend on the state of the facts and the nature of the misconduct in the particular case. These exceptions will cover some of the extreme cases put in the English opinions; while others of these cases seem to apply to the master's liability to third parties. I observe, so far as I can follow or understand the English cases, that the judges lay down the doctrine that by the law of the contract of service as fixed in England, the servant runs all risks arising from the misconduct and unskilfulness of other servants of the same master, for the dangers from such are risks incident to the labor he undertakes in that particular

48 *

service. If this is the law of England, then the decisions referred to follow necessarily. But this forms only another instance, from which it appears how widely different in essential principles are some of the most common contracts of the law of Scotland and England. The law of Scotland as to the contract of service in regard to such matters as are here raised is perfectly fixed. The master's primary obligation in every contract of service in which his workmen are employed in a hazardous and dangerous occupation, for his interest and profit, is to provide for and attend to the safety of the men. That is his first and leading obligation, paramount even to that of paying for their labor. This obligation includes the duty of furnishing good and sufficient machinery and apparatus, and of keeping the same in good condition — and the more rude and cheap the machinery, and the more liable on that account to cause injury, the greater his obligation to make up for its defects by the attention necessary to prevent such injury. In his obligation is equally included, as he cannot do every thing himself, the duty to have all acts by others whom he employs, done properly and carefully, in order to avoid risk. This obligation is not less than the obligation to provide for the safety of the lives of his servants by fit machinery. The other servants are employed by him to do acts which, of course, he cannot do himself, but they are acting for him, and instead of himself, as his hands. For their careful and cautious attention to duty, and for their want of vigilance, and for their neglect of precaution by which danger to life may be caused, he is just as much responsible as he would be for such misconduct on his own part, if he were actually working or present. And this particularly holds as to the person he intrusts with the direction and control over any of his workmen, and who represents him in such a matter. The servant, then, in the contract of service in Scotland, undertakes no risk from the dangers caused by other workmen from want of care, attention, prudence, and skill, which the atten-

tion and presence of the master, or others acting for him, might have prevented. His master is bound to protect him from such dangers. There have been many cases in Scotland, at all periods, and during the last fifty years, a very large number, which proceeded on this as a fixed principle of the law as to the contract of service. Of course there arise a number of cases in the varied trades of modern society, in which the acts of the servants may be of such a kind that, although not criminal, they yet do not involve the master in liability; and in such cases the law was clearly admitted on all hands, although its application was matter of nicety. The case of Sword is a case which eminently and very strongly brings out the doctrine of the law of Scotland. The injury there was caused by the culpable negligence or rashness of the other workmen employed by the tenant of the quarry, in precipitately firing off a blast, contrary to the plain precautions required for the safety of the men. The law, that the master is liable for injuries done by servants to one another was not disputed. The sole question was, in truth, whether the plaintiff was not to blame, and was not himself the sole cause of the injury he received. I refer to the full notes of Lord Cockburn, and to the detailed opinions of Lord Gillies, of the late Lord President and Lord M'Kenzie, to show how perfectly settled and rooted is the doctrine of the law of Scotland as to the contract of service as to this point. It is in vain to attempt to disturb it in this court; and having heard what is now advanced, I have only to say, that I shall not regard the point as again open for argument. But then it is quite within this doctrine, as settled in our law, to contend that the fault of the man himself occasioned the injury, or that the other workmen were versantes in illicito, or that he and they were misconducting themselves. No attention whatever can be paid to the plea in this case, that the workmen were told to hold on, and that they did not do so, and so violated the instructions given. The master is bound, in such a case, to have such

Hayes *v.* The Western Railroad Corporation.

control over the men as will insure that being done which their safety requires. Every kind of neglect and carelessness on the part of the workmen, is a violation of instructions, direct or implied; and, therefore, to admit this plea, would, in truth, be to protect the master in almost every case from the consequences of the negligence and recklessness of his workmen.

Lord MEDWIN gave no opinion on the point of law, as he held the facts in evidence did not establish the case of the plaintiff.

Lord COCKBURN concurred with the Lord Justice Clerk as to the effect of the evidence. The plea that the master is not liable rests solely on the authority of two or three very recent decisions of English courts. And these decisions certainly do seem to determine, that in England, where a person is injured by the culpable negligence of a servant, that servant's master *is* liable in reparation, provided the injured person was merely one of the public : but that he is *not* so responsible, if the person injured happened to be a fellow-workman of the delinquent servant. It is said, as an illustration of this, that if a coachman kills a stranger by improper driving, the employer of the coachman is liable ; but that he is not liable if the coachman only kills the footman. If this be the law of England, I speak of it with all due respect. But it most certainly is not the law of Scotland. I defy any industry to produce a single decision, or dictum, or institutional indication, or any trace of any authority to this effect, or of this tendency, from the whole range of our law. If such an idea exists in our system, it has as yet lurked undetected. It has never been directly condemned, because it has never been stated. The case of Sword gave the court a fair opportunity of applying the principle if it existed, — for there it was a workman who had been hurt by the negligence

of his fellow-workers, — but the employer was found liable. Many similar cases have occurred, and they have all been disposed of without the interference of this conception. The whole course of our practice has proceeded on the assumption that the liability of an employer did not cease, merely because, besides employing the wrongdoer, he also employed him to whom the wrong was done. I am clear for adhering to our own rule, and to our own legal and practical habits. The new rule seemed to be recommended to us not only on account of the respect due to the foreign tribunal — the weight of which we all acknowledge — but also on account of its own inherent justice. This last recommendation fails with me, because I think that the justice of the thing is exactly in the opposite direction. I have rarely come upon any principle that seems less reconcilable to legal reason. I can conceive some reasonings for exempting the employer from liability altogether, but not one for exempting him only when those who act for him injure one of themselves. It rather seems to me that these are the very persons who have the strongest claim upon him for reparation ; because they incur danger on his account, and certainly are not understood, by our law, to come under any engagement to take these risks on themselves.

Lord MURRAY. I do not pretend to know, and have not examined the law of England on the present question. But one point I hold to be clear by the law of Scotland, that a master who carries on a manufacture of any kind in which the lives of those in his employment are exposed to danger, is bound to have all his machinery, &c., in a most sufficient state. Here the evidence shows it was not, and I therefore cannot hesitate to hold the master liable.

The Court adhered.

THE INHABITANTS OF SPRINGFIELD v. THE CONNECTICUT RIVER
RAILROAD COMPANY.[1]

Hampden Co., September Term, 1849.

Location of Railway over Highways — Jurisdiction of County Commissioners.

Where a railroad corporation, under a general grant of power, lay out and construct their
road over and along a public highway, the town, within which such highway is situated,
may proceed in equity against the corporation in this court, under its general jurisdiction
in matters of nuisance, in order to ascertain whether such laying out and construction is or
is not within the power granted to the corporation; and it is immaterial, in this respect,
whether the way in question be a highway, properly so called, or a town way.

The fourth section of the Act of 1849, c. 222, which gives county commissioners jurisdiction
of all questions touching obstructions to highways by railroads, if it does not relate exclusively to the raising or lowering of such ways when crossed by a railroad, which the court
did not decide, has no effect to deprive this court of its jurisdiction of a case commenced
therein before the passing of the act.

Where a town was divided, and a part of it established as a new town, after the commencement of a suit in equity by such town against a railroad corporation, for a nuisance
to a public highway, which, upon the division, fell within the limits of the new town, and
the act for the division provided that such suit should be assumed, and might be prosecuted to final judgment by the new town, at their expense and for their benefit, but in the
name of the old town; it was held, that the division did not operate to vacate or otherwise
affect the suit.

An act of the legislature, which authorizes the construction of a railroad between certain *termini*, without prescribing its precise course and direction, does not *primâ facie* confer power
to lay out the road on and along an existing public highway; but it is competent to the
legislature to grant such authority, either by express words, or by necessary implication;
and such implication may result either from the language of the act, or from its being
shown, by an application of the act to the subject-matter, that the railroad cannot, by reasonable intendment, be laid in any other line.

THIS was a bill in equity, in which the plaintiffs set forth that so
much of Front street, in the village of Cabotville, in the town of
Springfield, as extended from the southerly end of Cabotville Bridge
westerly to the north end of Cabot street, was established by the
county commissioners, for the county of Hampden, as a highway, in
October, 1834; that so much of Front street as extended from the
north end of Cabot street, westerly to Dwight street, was laid out
by the selectmen, and accepted by the town of Springfield, and the
same established as a town way in April, 1841; that Front street, so
established as a county and town way, had ever since been and still

was used by the citizens of Springfield, and the public generally, as a highway, and that several streets, containing a large population and much travelled over, opened into Front street, and that the same was constantly passed and repassed by a great amount of travel, consisting of foot passengers, carriages, teams, &c. ; that that part of the Connecticut River Railroad Corporation, which was then known as the Northampton and Springfield Railroad Corporation, did, in the year 1845, illegally and without right, lay down and construct, through the entire length of Front street, a portion of their track, being a part of the branch extending from the main track to the villages of Cabotville and Chicopee Falls ; that the track through Front street had ever since been, and still was used by the defendants, and the defendants were daily running a great number of trains of cars, drawn by a locomotive engine at a great rate of speed, upon and over said track ; that the defendants, by so doing, rendered the travel through Front street unsafe and inconvenient, and greatly obstructed and encumbered the same, and constantly endangered the lives and property of all persons having a right and wishing to pass through said street, and that such illegal obstructions constituted a grievous and insufferable public nuisance ; that the defendants thereby rendered the plaintiffs constantly liable for double damages, for all injuries to persons and property caused by such obstructions, while the plaintiffs could only recover of the defendants the actual damage so caused; whenever the plaintiffs might be compelled to pay double damages ; that the plaintiffs had requested the defendants to remove their track, or to erect suitable barriers by the side of the same, and to give the plaintiffs sufficient indemnity against all damages caused to the plaintiffs by said track, and the use thereof ; and that the defendants entirely neglected and refused so to do. The plaintiffs, therefore, prayed that the defendants might be restrained by injunction from longer running their cars and locomotive engines upon and over their track through Front street.

The defendants, in their answer, admitted the use of Front street as a highway, and the laying out and construction of their branch track along said street; but alleged that it was mostly on the northerly side thereof, aside from the worked and travelled part, and that the same was daily used for running cars drawn by a locomotive engine at a moderate rate of speed ; and denied that they did the same illegally and without right ; or that they had thereby rendered the travel through Front street unsafe and inconvenient, and obstructed and encumbered said street, and endangered the lives and property of persons having a right and wishing to pass through said street ; or that they had thereby created a nuisance, or rendered the plaintiffs liable for double damages; but they admitted the request as to the removal of said track, and as to the barriers and indemnity: And they further alleged that, in the location and construction of said track, they had complied with the requisitions of St. 1845, c. 170, § 1; that it was necessary and expedient to adopt the location complained of, and there to construct and maintain their road; and that as to such location, construction, and maintaining, and the running of cars and engines, and all other matters complained of, they had acted under the authority granted to them by the legislature, and in conformity with the laws of the Commonwealth.

The plaintiffs filed a general replication.

The Act of 1848, c. 233, passed after the filing of the bill, in this case, but previous to the answer, to incorporate a part of the town of Springfield, including the highway in question, into a separate town, by the name of Chicopee, provided (§ 3) that "The suit in equity, now pending in favor of said town of Springfield, against the Connecticut River Railroad Company, shall be assumed, and may be prosecuted to final judgment by said town of Chicopee, in the name of said town of Springfield, at the expense and for the benefit of said town of Chicopee."

By the Act of 1845, c. 170, § 1, under which the defendants claimed authority to lay out and construct the railroad in question, in the manner complained of, they were authorized to construct and open for use a branch railroad, from the main track of their road, in the village of Cabotville, to and near the mills in said village, passing up the south bank of Chicopee River, near the same, and thence extending up said river into the Chicopee Falls village. The third section declares that, in such construction, the defendants may exercise all the powers and privileges, and shall be subject to all the duties, restrictions, and liabilities, set forth in the general laws relating to corporations.

G. Walker, for the plaintiffs.

The Act of 1845, c. 170, gives no express authority to the defendants to occupy a highway; nor do the circumstances imply any such authority. It does not appear that the road could not be constructed anywhere else. See Thacher *v.* Dartmouth Bridge Co. 18 Pick. 501; Boston Water Power Co. *v.* Boston & Worcester Railroad Corp. *ante,* p. 298; Commonwealth *v.* Coombs, 2 Mass. 489; Wales *v.* Stetson, 2 Mass. 143; Commonwealth *v.* Stevens, 10 Pick. 247; West Boston Bridge *v.* Middlesex, 10 Pick. 270; Wellington *v.* Middlesex, 16 Pick. 87, 89, 104; Kean *v.* Stetson, 5 Pick. 492; Commonwealth *v.* Charlestown, 1 Pick. 180; Arundel *v.* McCulloch, 10 Mass.

70.   The defendants have no such authority under the general laws of the State, in the absence of any specific authority. Boston Water Power Co. *v.* Boston & Worcester Railroad Corp. *ante*, p. 298; St. 1837, c. 185, §§ 4, 5.   The Act of 1846, c. 271, does not apply. The town is liable for double damages to a party injured. Currier *v.* Lowell, 16 Pick. 170.   But the corporation is only liable for single damages to the town.   Lowell *v.* Boston & Lowell Railroad Co. *ante*, p. 284.

C. P. Huntington, for the defendants.
The defendants were not only authorized, but required to build the road where it is located.   St. 1845, c. 170, § 1 ; Rev. Sts. c. 39, §§ 46, 47, 48.   To the point, that under a general power, highways may be obstructed, see Newburyport Turnpike Co. *v.* Eastern Railroad Co. *ante*, p. 294; Lowell *v.* Boston & Lowell Railroad Co. *ante*, p. 284; Wales *v.* Stetson, 2 Mass. 143; Boston Water Power Co. *v.* Boston & Worcester Railroad Corp. *ante*, p. 298; Commonwealth *v.* Worcester Turnpike Co. 3 Pick. 327; Coomes *v.* Burt, 22 Pick. 422; Roscoe, Cr. Ev. 516, 742; The King *v.* Pease, 4 B. & Ad. 30; The King *v.* Ouze Bank Commissioners, 3 A. & E. 544.
The Act of 1849, c. 222, § 4, has ousted the jurisdiction of this court, except as a court of appeal; and has a retroactive operation. Springfield *v.* Hampden, 6 Pick. 501.   And see St. 1849, c. 159; Bemis *v.* Upham, 13 Pick. 169.

R. A. Chapman, also for the defendants.
The bill states no case for an injunction; it alleges a public nuisance, which is no ground for maintaining this suit, without showing a special private injury.   Bigelow *v.* Hartford Bridge Co. 14 Conn. 565; 3 Dan. Ch. Pr. 1858; Rowe *v.* Granite Bridge Corp. 21 Pick. 344; Stetson *v.* Faxon, 19 Pick. 147, 154.   The liability to double damages is not a ground of such special injury, being too contingent. And the injury should be one which cannot be compensated in damages.   Dana *v.* Valentine, 5 Met. 8; Ingraham *v.* Dunnell, 5 Met. 118; Atkins *v.* Chilson, 7 Met. 398.
This proceeding is vacated by the passing of the act incorporating the town of Chicopee.   St. 1848, c. 233.

H. Morris replied.   By the third section of the act referred to, this suit is expressly saved.

SHAW, C. J.   This is a bill in equity, brought to enjoin the defendants from maintaining a railroad and running cars thereon, upon and over a public highway in Springfield, on the ground that such maintainance of the railroad is unauthorized, and constitutes a nuisance. It presents a very important question; one which, in the great multiplication of railroads, is likely to affect deeply the interests of many parts of the Commonwealth, and which has not yet been decided.

A preliminary objection was taken, that the inhabitants of a town, in their corporate capacity, have no such interest in the preservation and protection of the highways and town ways, within their limits, as will warrant them in applying to this court for the exercise of its jurisdiction, in case of nuisances, to restrain and prevent such nuisance. We have not examined the subject very thoroughly, but we are inclined to think that, as the town is responsible for the construction and amendment of highways and town ways, and for damages to travellers for losses occasioned by obstructions and defects, they have a right to invoke the equity power vested in this court in cases of nuisance, to determine whether such a use of the ways, as is claimed by the defendants in the present case, is or is not a justifiable act under the powers granted them.

It is further contended, that the original jurisdiction of this court, if it ever existed, is taken away by the Statute of 1849, c. 222, by which (§ 4) the original jurisdiction of all questions touching obstructions to turnpikes, highways, or town ways, caused by the construction or operation, of railroads, is vested in the county commissioners. This provision, taken in connection with the preceding section, we think relates to the raising or lowering of bridges, ways, or the like, when crossed by a railroad, so as to adapt them to each other, and to render such crossings safe; and does not vest in the commissioners the jurisdiction of deciding, whether the railroad is laid down or located in conformity with the grant of power given in the act of incorporation. But whether such be the true construction of the act or not, it would not affect this case, which was commenced long before that act passed; and the jurisdiction having once attached, it will not be held to be taken away by a subsequent act without express words, nor then, if vested rights would thereby be affected.

The fact, that since the suit was commenced the town of Springfield has been divided, and that the place where the nuisance is alleged to exist falls within the new town of Chicopee, has no effect to vacate the suit; because the act of incorporation contains a saving clause, which is sufficient to avoid any such effect.

We are then brought to the main question, namely, whether the defendants had authority, by the Act of 1845, c. 170, § 1, granting them the right to build this branch, to build it over and along a public way previously established. It is stated and admitted, that Front street, in Cabotville, is partly a highway, laid out and established by the county commissioners, and partly a town way, laid out by the selectmen, and the laying out ratified by the vote of the town. These two modes of establishing ways are both legal; and though one is called a highway, and the other a town way, yet, for most purposes, both are regarded as public ways, for obstructing which any party is liable to indictment, as for a nuisance, and for damage in consequence of any defect in which the town is liable to the sufferer. For all purposes of this inquiry, therefore, there is no distinction between them.

As the giving of authority to build and maintain a railroad is the grant of a right to take private property for a public use, and to deal with property appropriated to other public easements and uses, it is manifestly a high exercise of the sovereign right of eminent domain, and can only be effected by the clear and unequivocal authority of the legislature, who are constituted the judges of what the public good requires.

It is somewhat remarkable that, in a matter so deeply affecting private rights and interests, the precise location or line of railroad, on the ground, is not fixed by the act granting the power, nor is it provided that it shall be fixed by any board of public officers, who may be supposed to act impartially. In laying out highways, the precise course of location is fixed by the county commissioners, formerly the court of sessions, a public body of disinterested officers, supposed to act as impartial arbitrators between the public and individual proprietors.

But in railroads, the authority to the corporation is to locate, construct, and complete a railroad within certain *termini,* giving the general direction, but leaving the precise location to be determined, not by the county commissioners, but by the company. The corporation must file their location with the commissioners within one year, defining the courses, distances, and boundaries, but the commissioners have no power of prescribing or altering it. Rev. Sts. c. 37, § 75. So, after having made a location, the corporation may vary it, and take other lands within the limits prescribed by their act of incorporation, and file a location of such variations. Rev. Sts. c. 39, § 73. And, on the petition of any railroad corporation, the commissioners may authorize an original location, or an existing location to be altered, without the limits prescribed by the charter of such corporation. Rev. Sts. c. 39, § 74. Considering how large the powers are which are thus vested in railroad corporations, the court are of opinion that they ought to be construed with a good degree of strictness, and not enlarged by construction.

The authority, under which the defendants claim to have located and laid out the railroad in question, is found in the Act of 1845, c. 170, which was passed in addition to the Act of 1842, c. 41, by which this company was incorporated. The Act of 1845 provides, (§ 1,) that the company may construct and open for use a branch railroad from the main track of the road, in Cabotville, to and near the mills in said village, passing up the south bank of Chicopee River, near the same, and thence extending up said river to the Chicopee Falls village ; the location of that part of the branch now in question, from the main road to the mills in Cabotville, to be filed in one year from the passage of the act, and that to Chicopee Falls village in five years. The act further provides, (§ 3,) that said corporation, in the construction of their railroad and branch, shall have all the powers and privileges, and be subject to all the duties, restrictions, and liabilities set forth in the Rev. Sts. c. 44, and in that part of c. 39 which relates to railroads.

It is the common case of an act, authorizing the location and construction of a railroad between *termini*, one of which, the junction, as the *terminus a quo*, is fixed, and the other, the *terminus ad quem*, " to and near the mills in Cabotville ; " and the course or line is no more exactly designated than by the terms, " passing up the south bank of Chicopee River, and near the same," and thence extending up said river to Chicopee Falls village.' The beautiful and apparently accurate survey and plan of a part of Cabotville, and of the river, the streets, and the track of the railroad, exhibit all these localities to great advantage, and present the question at a single glance.

As no company or persons have authority to lay out a railroad, except so far as such power is conferred by the legislature, the court are of opinion that, by a grant of power by a legislative act, to lay out a railroad between certain *termini*, where the precise course and direction are not prescribed, but are left to the corporation to be located between the *termini*, no authority is given *prima facie* to lay such railroad on and along an existing public highway longitudinally, or, in other words, to take the road bed of such highway as the track of their railroad. The two uses are almost, if not wholly, inconsistent with each other; so that taking the highway for a railroad will nearly supersede the former use to which it had been legally appropriated. The whole course of legislation, on the subject of railroads, is opposed to such a construction. The crossing of public highways by railroads is obviously necessary, and of course warranted ; and numerous provisions are industriously made to regulate such crossings, by determining when they shall be on the same and when on different levels, in order to avoid collision; and when on the same level, what gates, fences, and barriers shall be made, and what guards shall be kept to insure safety. Had it been intended that railroad companies, under a general grant, should have power to lay a railroad over a highway longitudinally, which ordinarily is not necessary, we think that would have been done in express terms, accompanied with full legislative provisions for maintaining such barriers and modes of separation as would tend to make the use of the same road, for both modes of travel, consistent with the safety of travellers on both. The absence of any such provision affords a strong inference that, under general terms, it was not intended that such a power should be given.

But the court are of opinion, that it is competent for the legislature, under the right of eminent domain, to grant such an authority. The power of eminent domain is a high prerogative of sovereignty, founded upon public exigency, according to the maxim: *Salus reipublicæ lex suprema est,* to which all minor considerations must yield, and which can only be limited by such exigency. The grant of land for one public use must yield to that of another more urgent. Land appropriated to a public walk or training field may, in case of war, be required for a citadel, when it is the only ground which, in a military point of view, will command all the defences of a place, in case of hostile attack. Chesapeake & Ohio Canal Co. *v.* Baltimore & Ohio Railroad Co. 4 Gill & Johns. 1; Boston Water Power Co. *v.* Boston & Worcester Railroad Corp. *ante,* p. 298; Wellington *v.* Middlesex, 16 Pick. 87, 100.

But when it is the intention of the legislature to grant a power to take land already appropriated to another public use, such intention must be shown by express words, or by necessary implication. There may be such a necessary implication. Every grant of power is intended to be efficacious and beneficial, and to accomplish its declared object; and carries with it such incidental powers as are requisite to its exercise. If, then, the exercise of the power granted draws after it a necessary consequence, the law contemplates and sanctions that consequence. Take the familiar case of the Notch of the White Mountains, a very narrow gorge, which affords the only practicable passage for many miles through that mountain range. A turnpike road through it has already been granted. Suppose the gorge not wide enough to accommodate another road, but the legislature of New Hampshire, in order to accommodate a great line of public travel, should grant power to lay a railroad on that line; they would, by necessary implication, grant a power to take some portion of the road bed of the turnpike.

In the present 'case, it is manifest that there are no words in the Act of 1845 which give the defendants authority to locate and construct their railroad over Front street, where it was actually laid, or over any other highway in Cabotville; and if they had the power, it must be derived from necessary implication, though no such implication appears on the face of the act. If it exist, it must arise from the application of the act to the subject-matter, so that the railroad could not, by reasonable intendment, be laid in any other line. The grant of a right is, by reasonable construction, a grant of power to do all the acts reasonably necessary to its enjoyment. It is not an absolute or physical necessity, absolutely preventing its being laid elsewhere; but if, to the minds of reasonable men, conversant with the subject, another line could have been adopted between the *termini*, without taking the highway, reasonably sufficient to accommodate all the interests concerned, and to accomplish the objects for which the grant was made, then there was no such necessity as to warrant the presumption that the legislature intended to authorize the taking of the highway.

Whether the laying of this railroad, on and over Front street, was necessary, that is, reasonably necessary, as above explained, in order to accomplish the object contemplated by the legislature, depends upon the application of the act to the localities; and this warrants and requires evidence *aliunde* to establish the facts. It is a fit case, therefore, in our judgment, to be referred to three commissioners, of competent skill and experience in such subjects, to examine the whole subject, and to consider and report : —

Whether, under the grant of an authority to the defendants to construct and open for use a branch railroad, from the junction or main track of their road in the village of Cabotville, to and near the mills in said village, passing up the south bank of Chicopee River, near the same, and thence extending up said river into the Chicopee Falls village, it was, by fair and reasonable intendment, necessary to lay and construct the same upon and along Front street, or either of the public ways in Cabotville, or not; and, as incident to this inquiry, to consider whether, by such fair and reasonable intendment, the said railroad could or could not have been laid out and constructed, 1st. Between Front street and the canal; or, 2d. Over the canal; or, 3d. Between the canal and the mills; or, 4th. Between the mills and the bank of Chicopee River; considering, for this purpose, the street, the canals, the mills, the land, and the entire space between the street and Chicopee River, as they were in March, 1845, when the act was passed by the legislature :

Also, if they should be of opinion that it was necessary to lay the railroad over Front street, where it now is, whether any, and, if any, what further fences, gates, barriers, guards, or other precautions are required by the Act of 1846, c. 271, in order to render it safe and convenient for the general travel to pass through, over, and across that street.

. *Commissioners appointed accordingly.* ··

Enoch W. Lyman *v.* The Boston & Worcester Railroad Corporation.[1]

Middlesex Co., October Term, 1849.

Liability of Company for Fires.

The Statute of 1840, c. 85, making the proprietors of railroads responsible for injuries by fire, communicated from their locomotive engines, applies to railroads established before as well as since its passage; and extends as well to estates, a part of which is conveyed by the owner, as to those of which a part is taken by authority of law, for the purposes of a railroad.

This was an action on the case, on the Act of 1840, c. 85, § 1, to recover damages of the defendants, for an injury sustained by the plaintiff in the destruction of certain buildings on his land, in consequence of fire communicated thereto by a locomotive engine of the defendants, while passing on their road. The case was submitted upon an agreed statement of facts.

The buildings, for the destruction of which the action was brought, were burnt and destroyed at the time alleged in the declaration, by means of fire communicated from a locomotive engine of the defendants, while passing on their road. The plaintiff was insured against fire at the time of the accident, in the sum of $800 on the buildings destroyed, by the Middlesex Mutual Insurance Company, by a policy dated February 25th, 1842; which was subsequent to the opening of the whole of the defendant's road for travel.

The plaintiff demanded payment of his loss of the defendants; but the claim not being settled by them, or the amount agreed to, the plaintiff assigned the same to the insurance company; who thereupon paid him the sum of $800, and agreed to pay him such further sum as should be recovered of the defendants. This suit

---

was then commenced by the insurance company, and is now prose-cuted by them, in the name and by the authority of the plaintiff.

The land, on which that part of the defendants' road was laid, where the engine was passing when the fire was kindled, was conveyed to the defendants by William Jackson, February 15th, 1834, by a deed of warranty, in the common form, with an additional covenant, that the grantor would make and maintain all such walls and fences as might be necessary, on the boundary lines between the granted premises and his own land.

The land, upon which the buildings stood that were burnt, was adjoining the land conveyed by Jackson to the defendants, and a part of the same close, before such conveyance was made, and was conveyed by Jackson to the plaintiff, November 1st, 1837. The buildings destroyed stood upon the close before either of these conveyances was made; but large additions and improvements were put upon them, and the personal property destroyed with them was placed therein subsequently to the conveyances by Jackson.

E. R. Hoar, for the plaintiff.

G. Bemis, for the defendants.

1. The Act of 1840 does not apply to the defendants; they acting under their charter, granted before its passage. Burroughs v. Housatonic Railroad Co. 15 Conn. 124; s. c. *post*, vol. 2; Whiteman v. Wilmington & Susquehanna Railroad Co. 2 Harring. 514; s. c. *post*; People v. Platt, 17 Johns. 195; Crenshaw v. Slate River Co. 6 Rand. 245; Commonwealth v. Breed, 4 Pick. 460; Nichols v. Bertram, 3 Pick. 342; Derby Turnpike Co. v. Parks, 10 Conn. 522.

2. It does not apply in cases where the rights of the railroad company are obtained by contract with the owner; here the owner, in giving a deed of land for the purposes of a railroad, must have contemplated the risk of fire from engines running on the road. Webber v. Eastern Railroad Co. *ante*, p. 331; Brearley v. Delaware & Raritan Canal Co. 1 Spencer, 236; Lowell v. Locks and Canals, 7 Met. 1; Tucker v. Bass, 5 Mass. 164; Fuller v. Plymouth, 15 Pick. 81; Babcock v. Western Railroad Corp. *ante*, p. 399; Western Railroad Corp. v. Babcock, *ante*, p. 365 – 370; Foster v. Boston, 22 Pick. 33; Dodge v. Essex, *ante*, p. 336.

DEWEY, J.[1] The Statute of 1840, c. 85, imposes upon railroad

---

[1] Fletcher, J.; did not sit in this cause.

corporations a general liability for damages occasioned by fire communicated from their locomotive engines. It is contended, however, that the provisions of this statute do not apply to a case like the present, where the title of the plaintiff is derived from one who has himself, by his deed, granted the land embraced within the location of the railroad, and by the very terms of the grant has conveyed it for the purpose of being thus used for a railroad. The argument is, that the grantor having thus granted a certain definite parcel of land for the purpose of a railroad, out of a much larger parcel retained by him, the grant is subject to all the consequences necessarily attendant upon such a use of the same, and particularly such as would result from the running of engines, and the exposure of property in his adjacent land to such injury and loss as would naturally result therefrom; and that the railroad corporation, while in the exercise of their appropriate business, are only responsible for ordinary care and diligence in the manner of using their road.

It is not contended, that the statute was not intended to embrace the case of those whose land has been taken under the provisions of the charter of the railroad; but the argument assumes a distinction between those who convey the right to appropriate a portion of their land to the proprietors of a railroad, by deed, and those who do no other act than suffer their land to be taken by such proprietors, under their authority to enter upon and take land for the purposes of their road, paying therefor such damages as the county commissioners or a jury shall award.

We can perceive no sound distinction between the cases supposed. Each of these modes of acquiring the necessary real estate for the purpose of a railroad is authorized, both by the general laws and by the acts creating railroad corporations. In each, the land owner is supposed to receive full satisfaction for all the injuries necessarily resulting from the use of the same for a railroad. But with the use of locomotive engines, greater hazard to contiguous buildings and property, owned by the adjacent land owners, may arise, than was originally contemplated, or ought to be left to the ordinary common law remedies.

We consider this provision of the Statute of 1840, c. 85, as one of those general remedial acts passed for the more effectual protection of property, against the hazards to which it has become subject by the introduction of the locomotive engine. The right to use the parcel of land appropriated to a railroad does not deprive the legislature of the power to enact such regulations, and impose such liabilities for injuries suffered from the mode of using the road, as the occasion and circumstances may reasonably justify.

These provisions, in the act referred to, are of general import, and equally embrace the cases of those who have by deed granted to a railroad corporation the right to enter upon and use their land, or have given a title to the land itself included within the location, and those other persons whose land has been taken and held merely by the force of the location of the railroad under the charter authority. These principles, we think, are sufficient to decide the present case, and warrant us in ordering judgment for the plaintiff.

----◆----

GILES A. MEACHAM v. THE FITCHBURG RAILROAD COMPANY.[1]

Middlesex Co., October Term, 1849.

Sheriff's Jury — Towns not interested —, Parties to· an Assessment of Damages — Mortgagor and Mortgagee.

The " three nearest towns not interested," from which jurors are to be taken to estimate the damages caused by the laying out of a highway·or railroad, are the three towns nearest to and exclusive of the town in which the land lies, over which the highway or railroad is laid.

A sheriff's jury, to assess damages for land taken for a highway or railroad, may be summoned by the constables of the several towns from whence they are taken, or partly by such constables, and partly by the deputy sheriff by whom the warrant is executed.

The mortgagee of land taken for a railroad need not be made a party to proceedings by the mortgagor, for the assessment of damages, provided he gives his assent thereto by a writing filed in the case.

The want of proper parties to a proceeding before a sheriff's jury, for the assessment of damages for land taken for a highway or railroad, must be objected before the commissioners, upon the application for such jury.

In estimating the damages for land taken for a highway or railroad, any direct and peculiar benefit or increase of value accruing therefrom to land of the same owner, adjoining or connected with the land taken, and forming part of the same parcel or tract, is to be considered by the jury, and allowed by way of set-off; but not any general benefit or increase of value received by such land, in common with other lands in the neighborhood ; nor any benefit to other land of the same owner, though in the same town.

The time, at and from which the benefit accruing to the owner of land, taken for a highway or railroad, is to be estimated, in assessing his damages for such taking, is that of the actual location.

THIS was an appeal from a judgment of the Court of Common Pleas, accepting the verdict of a jury, summoned at the request of the petitioner, to revise the damages awarded to him by the county commissioners, by reason of the taking of his land in 'Watertown, in this county, by the respondents, for the construction of a branch railroad to that town.

The questions submitted to the court arose upon the proceedings at the trial before the jury, and are thus stated in the report thereof by Seth Ames, Esquire, the presiding officer.

Before proceeding with the trial, (the jurors summoned being in attendance at the time and place appointed,) it was moved by the respondents that the jury should not be empannelled, for the following reasons : —

1st. Because none of the jurors were drawn, summoned, or returned from the town of Watertown, in which the lands alleged to have been injured, by the laying out of the railroad of the respondents, are situated ; the town of Watertown having no interest in the question to be tried by the jury.

2d. Because certain of the jurors, namely, those from the city of Cambridge and from the town of Brighton, were summoned by constables of said city and town, respectively, and not by the deputy sheriff who executed the warrant.

3d. Because certain of the jurors, namely, those from the town of West Cambridge, were summoned by the deputy sheriff who executed the warrant, and others of them by constables of Cambridge and Brighton.

This motion was overruled, and the respondents excepted.

4th. The jury were thereupon empannelled and sworn, and the trial proceeded ; and it being made to appear that the lands described in the petition had been mortgaged as collateral security, for a debt to Luke Forbes and Samuel Stickney, and that neither of the mortgagees had been summoned in to become a party, and there being no evidence that the mortgage had been paid or released, the respondents objected to any further proceeding by the jury, to estimate the damages alleged to have been sustained in the real estate described in the petition.   But as the petitioner produced and filed in the case a written paper, signed by the mortgagees,[1] whereby they

---

[1] The following is a copy of this paper : —

" The undersigned, mortgagees of the land situated in Watertown, in the county of Middlesex, belonging to Giles A. Meacham, through which the Fitchburg Railroad Corporation have located and constructed their Watertown Branch Railroad, hereby signify their assent to the assessment and award of the damages done or caused to said land, by the jury who are summoned on the petition of said Meacham, to estimate said damages; and we do hereby waive all objection to the proceedings in said Meacham's

consented to the assessment and award of damages to the petitioner, and waived all objection to the proceedings in his behalf, the presiding officer overruled the objection, to which the respondents excepted.

5th. The respondents then proved that the petitioner, at the time of the laying out of the railroad, and ever since, was the owner of certain other lands and buildings in Watertown, near, but not adjoining the lands described in the petition; they then offered evidence for the purpose of showing that, since the laying out and construction of the railroad, and in consequence thereof, the lands and buildings of the petitioner, other than the lands described in the petition, and separate therefrom, as aforesaid, had increased in value to the petitioner. But the evidence so offered being objected to, the presiding officer decided that it was inadmissible; and to this decision the respondents excepted.

6th. Being requested by the parties to direct the jury, as to the rules of law by which they were to be governed in estimating the petitioner's damages, after receiving the testimony on both sides, the presiding officer instructed the jury, (among other things,) that if they were satisfied that the laying out and construction of the respondent's railroad had created or occasioned any benefit or advantage to the lands of the petitioner, described in his petition or immediately adjoining or connected therewith, rendering the part not actually occupied by the respondents, more convenient or useful to the petitioner, or giving it some peculiar increase of value in the market, as compared with other lands generally in the vicinity, it would be their duty to allow for such benefit or increase of value, by way of set-off, in favor of the respondents; but that, on the other hand, if the construction of the respondent's railroad, by increasing the convenience of Watertown generally, as a place of residence, and by its anticipated and probable effect or influence in increasing the population, business, and general prosperity of the place, had been the occasion of an increase in the saleable value of real estate generally near their depot, including the petitioners' said lands, and thereby occasioning a benefit or advantage to him in common with other real estate owners in the vicinity, this benefit would be too contingent, indirect, and remote, to be brought into consideration in this question of damages to a particular parcel of land. To these instructions the respondents excepted.

behalf, and to the assessment and award to him of the full amount of said damages. Dated at Watertown, this thirteenth day of August, in the year eighteen hundred and forty-seven."

7th. The presiding officer also instructed the jury that, for the purposes of this trial, the land might be considered as taken by the respondents, when their track was actually staked out, and its precise location thereby indicated; that any benefit to the petitioner's property, in order to be allowed to the respondents, by way of set-off, must be some increase upon the value which it had at the time of such taking, and not at any previous time; and that no allowance was to be made for any effect produced by the general expectation that there was to be such a railroad, or by the passage of its charter. And to this instruction also the respondents excepted.

E. R. Hoar, for the respondents.

E. Buttrick, (with whom was *J. J. Clarke*,) for the petitioner.

DEWEY, J. The first objection stated in the bill of exceptions, that none of the jurors were returned from the town of Watertown, was directly overruled in the case of Wyman *v.* Lexington and West Cambridge Railroad Co. *ante*, p. 426, and is not further urged. The next objection to the validity of these proceedings, the summoning of the jurors by a constable, is certainly one which is not free from difficulty. It was much considered by us in the case just alluded to. The jury, in that case, were summoned by the sheriff, or his deputy, and the question was as to the legality of such service. This opened the general question, and in the opinion given in that case, while we sustained the proceedings, we did not express any thing adverse to the right of summoning jurors by a constable, as in other cases. The various provisions of the revised statutes, on this subject, are to some extent apparently conflicting. By c. 39, § 57, the proceedings are to be the same as in the case of highways; and by c. 24, § 18, which provides for the summoning of jurors in cases of highways, it is enacted, that the jury shall be summoned by the sheriff, or his deputy; but in § 19 it is provided, that the jury shall be " drawn, summoned, and notified as in other cases." This latter section would embrace constables, as proper officers for summoning the jurors; that duty, in ordinary cases devolving upon them.

In the present case, it appears that the requisition was duly issued by the sheriff upon the selectmen of the various towns, requiring the drawing of the jurors; that the sheriff gave the proper order, as to the time of the assembling of the jury; and that all the error suggested upon the most strict construction of the statute was, that the jurors were notified by a constable of the time and place of the hearing. The jurors thus notified having actually attended, the objection, as will readily be seen, is a mere matter of form. Their proper selection being secured, and the time and place of their meeting being properly appointed, it would seem quite immaterial whether the jurors attended upon notice by a deputy sheriff or a constable, or even voluntarily, without any formal notice. It seems to us, therefore, that it is no valid objection to this verdict, that some of the jurors were notified by a constable. It is within the provisions of the nineteenth section of the twenty-fourth chapter, taking the same literally, although not probably the mode contemplated by the legislature. As heretofore stated, we held in the case of Wyman v. Lexington & West Cambridge Railroad Co. that the eighteenth section authorized the summoning of the jurors by the sheriff or his deputy; and we are of opinion that this is more obviously within the statute provisions. But the language of the nineteenth section goes somewhat further, and apparently authorizes the summoning of jurors in these cases by a constable. In view of these statute provisions, relating to the irregularity suggested, we do not feel authorized to set aside this verdict on the ground that the jurors were notified by a constable.

The next objection is virtually disposed of by the view which we have taken of the one preceding. It does not vary the result, that the jurors from two of the towns were notified by a constable, and the others by a deputy sheriff. The latter mode was clearly legal, and, to the extent it was adopted, does not vitiate the notice to the other jurors.

In reference to the fourth objection, as to an outstanding mortgage, the court are of opinion, that the petitioners having produced and filed a paper signed by the mortgagees, assenting to the assessment and award of damages to the petitioners, and waiving all objections to the proceedings, by reason of their holding such mortgage, this objection was removed.

As to the omission to summon the mortgagees, we think that the whole matter of new parties is more properly cognizable before the commissioners, upon a hearing before issuing a warrant for a jury. Upon the application for such jury, notice is given to the adverse party, who may appear and interpose all valid objections to the right of the petitioners to recover damages, or to have them assessed by a jury.

The most important and difficult question in the case is that which arises as to the ruling of the presiding officer, as to submitting to the jury, in reduction of damages, the fact that the petitioner was the owner of other lands and buildings in Watertown, near to, but not adjoining or parcel of the land described in the petition. This subject is confessedly one of difficulty. The general doctrine was very broadly advanced in Commonwealth v. Coombs, 2 Mass. 489, 492, that the benefit occasioned by laying out a highway to the other property of the party seeking to recover damages for his land actually taken, should be considered in reduction of the damages for the land taken. The Rev. Sts. c. 24, § 31, in like manner provide, generally, for an allowance by way of deduction for such advancement in value of other property.

That there must be some limitation of the proposition, that the respondents may show in reduction of damages any collateral benefit which the petitioner has received in his other property, seems quite obvious. The party, whose land has been taken for a railroad has a right, in common with his other fellow-citizens, to the benefit arising from the general rise of property in the vicinity, occasioned by the establishment of the railroad, and the facilities connected therewith.

It would operate with great inequality to hold, that where there are various individuals, each owning large trading or manufacturing establishments in the immediate vicinity of a railroad, but without being adjoining to or connected with the located limits of such railroad, one of whom is the owner of a parcel of land situate in another part of the town, over which the railroad is actually located, that, as to the latter, he is, by way of reduction of damages, for his land thus taken, to be charged for all the incidental benefits which he receives from the location of the railroad in the vicinity of his other land and establishment, while his neighbor, who is equally benefited, is exempt from any contribution to this object.

It is difficult to draw the line with precision, and, at the same time, to establish a rule which will do equal justice to all concerned. The rule which was taken at the hearing before the jury, we think, approximates as nearly to the standard as any that can be adopted. It embraces the land as to which damages are claimed, and any land of the petitioner adjoining or connected therewith, as one parcel or tract of land; and if, in any portion of such land, the location of the railroad has occasioned a rise in value, and the petitioner has received any peculiar benefit from the location of such road, it is the duty of the jury to make a deduction, by way of set-off, and a reduction of damages on account of such advancement in value of the remaining portion of the lot or parcel of land. Thus limited to the land adjacent to that taken for the railroad, or connected as one tract or parcel of land therewith, the rule will be found to be reasonable in itself, and of easy application. The great and leading principle, to authorize such reduction of damages, is the direct benefit, or increase of value to the remaining part of the tract or parcel of land, by reason of the railroad's passing through the lot or'tract, as to which. the damages are claimed. We approximate very nearly, in this way, to the rule of direct benefit, or actual increase of value, in the adjacent land, and exclude the more uncertain and fanciful estimation of anticpated advantages to other parcels, more or less remote, and which share only in the common benefit of the lands of the citizens generally.

The further instructions to the jury upon this point seem to have been entirely correct, and in accordance with the principle of the other ruling.. The respondents are not to have the benefit of any increase in value of the petitioner's adjacent land, so far as he has been benefited by the railroad, merely in common with all the citizens of the neighborhood or village, by the anticipated general rise of property, by reason of the railroad's passing through the town and in the vicinity of their lands. It is only the increased value of the land of the petitioner, arising from the location of the road over some part of it, which is to be taken into consideration. If such location over the land of the petitioner has raised the value of his adjacent lands, then a reduction or offset is to be allowed the respondents on that account.

It is the increase of value occasioned by the location, and of course has reference to the state of things existing at the time when the land is taken by the location. The presiding officer directed the jury to take the earliest period indicating such location, namely, "the staking out of the road." This being most favorable for the respondents, it is unnecessary to decide whether that period, or the subsequent one of the actual official return of the real location, would have been, strictly speaking, the more correct. The principle adopted was the right one, that the actual location of the road was the period of time in reference to which the increased value of the adjacent land was to be estimated, with a view to the set-off. Upon the whole matter, the court were of opinion that the verdict of the jury was properly accepted; and that the exceptions taken to the proceedings were rightly overruled by the Court of Common Pleas.

DANIEL MCELROY & WIFE v. THE NASHUA AND LOWELL RAIL-
ROAD CORPORATION.[1]

Middlesex Co., October Term, 1849.

*Negligence — Duty as to the safe carriage of Passengers — Liability
for Injuries occasioned by Servant of another Road.*

The proprietors of a railroad, as passenger-carriers, are bound to the most exact care and
diligence, not only in the management of their trains and cars, but also in the structure
and care of their track, and in all the subsidiary arrangements necessary to the safety of
passengers.

A railroad company are responsible for an injury sustained by a passenger in their cars, in
consequence of the careless management of a switch, by which another railroad connects
with and enters upon their road, although the switch is provided by the proprietors of the
other road, and attended by one of their servants, at their expense.

THIS was an action on the case, to recover damages of the defendants, for an injury alleged to have been sustained by the female
plaintiff, while riding as a passenger in the defendants' cars, from
Lowell to Nashville. The case was submitted to the court upon an
agreed statement of facts.

The defendants are common-carriers, carrying passengers for hire
between the above-mentioned places, and the female plaintiff had
taken her passage and paid the fare, from Lowell to Nashville, in the
evening train of the defendants.

By the thirteenth section of the act of incorporation, granted to the
defendants by the legislature of New Hampshire, power was reserved
to authorize any other railroad corporation to connect with, enter
upon, and use the Nashua and Lowell Railroad, at a point where
the Concord Railroad was afterwards made to enter upon the same,
and at the point where the alleged injury was incurred. After the
incorporation of the defendants, the legislature of New Hampshire
also incorporated the Concord Railroad Corporation, and granted
them the right to connect with, and enter upon and use, the Nashua
and Lowell Railroad, at the point where they did enter the same, and
where the accident happened.

The Concord Railroad Corporation, in accordance with the powers
thus granted, made a switch and connecting track in the defendants'
road, so as to pass to and from the same, and entered thereon and

placed a switchman there, to let the Concord cars pass on and off the
road. This switchman, at the time of the accident, and ever before,
was the servant of the Concord Railroad Corporation, and was in no
wise the servant of the defendants, or in any manner under their
authority or control. By an arrangement between the two corporations, the defendants hauled the cars of the Concord Railroad Corporation over their road to Lowell, after they had entered thereon,
and also hauled them back from Lowell to a point about a fourth of
a mile below the junction of the Concord railroad, and there detached
them and went on over the switch to the end of their road, leaving
the Concord train to follow by force of the momentum previously
given to them, but at so slow a speed, as to arrive at the switch, after
the defendants' train had passed, and then to be switched off by the
switchman upon the Concord railroad.

On the evening in question, the Concord train was detached as
usual, and the defendants' cars, in the rear one of which the female
plaintiff was, passed on, and the engine, tender, and forward car
passed over the switch in safety, but by the carelessness of the
switchman, the switch became changed, so that the defendants' baggage car, and the passenger car above mentioned, were turned off
upon the Concord railroad, and broken from the forward cars, and
thereby and thereon the injury was occasioned, for which this action
was brought.

The defendants were incorporated by the legislature of New
Hampshire, to build that part of their road which lies in that State,
and by the legislature of this Commonwealth, to build that portion
of their road which is in this State; and the two corporations were
afterwards united by acts of the legislatures of this Commonwealth
and New Hampshire. The point where the accident happened is in
New Hampshire.

The question of damages only was submitted to the jury, and a
verdict taken by consent of the plaintiff, upon the facts as above
stated, subject to the opinion of the whole court.

J. G. Abbott, for the plaintiff, cited Ingalls v. Bills, 9 Met. 1; Story,
Bailm. §§ 601, 602; Ang. Car. §§ 536, 537, 538; Stokes v. Salton-
stall, 13 Pet. 181; Bostwick v. Champion, 11 Wend. 571; Cole v.
Goodwin, 19 Wend. 251; Waland v. Elkins, 1 Stark. R. 272.

T. Wentworth, for the defendants, cited Ang. Car. §§ 521, 523;
Story, Bailm. §§ 590, 602; Bennett v. Dutton, 10 N. H. 481; Haw-
kins v. Hoffman, 6 Hill, 586; Boyce v. Anderson, 2 Pet. 150; Mc-
Kinney v. Neil, 1 McLean, 540.

SHAW, C. J.   The court are of opinion, upon the facts agreed, that the defendants are liable to the plaintiffs for the damage sustained by the wife, whilst travelling in their cars.   As passenger carriers, the defendants were bound to the most exact care and diligence, not only in the management of the trains and cars, but also in the structure and care of the track, and in all the subsidiary arrangements necessary to the safety of passengers.   The wife having contracted with the defendants and paid fare to them, the plaintiffs had a right to look to them, in the first instance, for the use of all necessary care and skill.   The switch in question, in the careless or negligent management of which the damage occurred, was a part of the defendants' road, over which they must necessarily carry all their passengers; and although provided for and attended by a servant of the Concord Railroad Corporation, and at their expense, yet it was still a part of the Nashua and Lowell Railroad, and it was within the scope of their duty to see that the switch was rightly constructed, attended, and managed, before they were justified in carrying passengers over it.   Had the action been, in form, on the implied contract of the defendants, in undertaking to carry a passenger, to have a safe road, and apply and use all necessary care and skill, the liability of the defendants might have been more clear and manifest; but the duty is the same, and in most cases of this kind of carelessness, negligence, or want of due skill, in the performance of duty undertaken to be done for hire and reward, it is at the election of the plaintiff to declare in assumpsit, and rely on the promise, or to declare in *tort*, and rest on the breach of duty.   Whether the plaintiffs might have maintained an action on the case against the Concord Railroad Corporation for the negligence of their servant, or whether the defendants may have a remedy over against the Concord Railroad Corporation, by the terms of the statute under which the latter were allowed to come on to the defendants' road, or by the terms of their contract, we give no opinion.   Waland *v.* Elkins, 1 Stark. R. 272.

Judgment on the verdict for the plaintiffs.[1]

---

[1] The Supreme Court of Massachusetts in the case of Ingalls *v.* Bills, 9 Metcalf 1, laid down the rule in general terms which in the above case is applied to railway companies, " that *carriers of passengers for hire*, are bound to use the utmost care and diligence in the providing of safe, sufficient, and suitable coaches, harnesses, horses, and coachmen, in order to prevent those injuries which human care and foresight can guard against."

In Christie *v.* Griggs, 2 Cambell, 79, it was held, that proof of the injury to the plaintiff threw upon the defendant the burden of showing that he had exercised all the care which he was bound to do.

In Stokes *v.* Salstonstall, 13 Peters 181, which was an action for injuries to a pas-

ANNA M. WHITE AND ANOTHER *v.* THE FITCHBURG RAILROAD
CORPORATION.[1]

Middlesex Co., October Term, 1849.

Evidence of Value of Land — Price paid for adjoining Land.

On the trial of a petition before a sheriff's jury, for an assessment of damages for land taken
for a railroad, evidence is not admissible to show the price paid by the respondents, for
land adjoining the land in question, under an award of arbitrators mutually agreed upon
to estimate the same.

THIS was a complaint against the respondents, for an assessment
of the damages for taking the petitioners' land, in the construction of
the Watertown Branch Railroad.

At the trial before a sheriff's jury, the petitioners offered to prove,

---

senger, occasioned by upsetting a stage
coach, the court laid down the rule as to
the burden of proof in the following language. "The facts that the carriage was
upset and the plaintiff's wife injured, are
primâ facie evidence that there was carelessness, or negligence, or want of skill on
the part of the driver, and throws upon the
defendant the burden of proving that the
accident was not occasioned by the driver's
fault. It being admitted that the carriage
was upset and the plaintiff's wife injured,
it is incumbent on the defendant to prove
that the driver was a person of competent
skill, of good habits, and in every respect
qualified and suitably prepared for the
business in which he was engaged; and
that he acted on this occasion with reasonable skill, and with the utmost prudence
and caution; and if the disaster in question was occasioned by the least negligence,
or want of skill, or prudence on his part,
then the defendant is liable in this action."
This rule, as to the burden of proof,
was applied to railway companies in Car-
pue *v.* The London and Brighton R. Co.

5 Q. B. 747. Lord Denman, C. J., in
that case charged the jury "that they
must be satisfied that the accident had
been brought about by the negligence of
the defendants in the course of carrying
the plaintiff upon the railway; and that it
having been shown that the exclusive
management, both of the machinery and
the railway, was in the hands of the defendants, it was presumable that the accident arose from their want of care, unless
they gave some explanation of the cause
by which it was produced; which explanation the plaintiff not having the means of
knowledge could not reasonably be expected to give."
In Skinner *v.* The London, Brighton,
&c. R. Co. 2 Eng. Law & Eq. Rep. 360,
the point came directly before the court
in banc upon a motion for a new trial on
the ground of misdirection in the judge at
nisi prius in charging the jury "that the
fact of the accident having occurred was
primâ facie evidence of negligence to fix
the defendants." The court held the
charge to be right.

that the respondents having laid out their railroad through land of
Levi Thaxter, which was adjoining the petitioners' land, Thaxter
made a deed thereof to the respondents, but not being able to agree
upon the price, the parties submitted the matter to the determination
of arbitrators, who awarded a certain sum to be paid for the land,
which was accordingly paid by the respondents.

The sheriff rejected the evidence, and at the request of the petitioners certified his ruling.

A. H. Nelson, for the petitioners, referred to **Wyman** *v.* **Lexington and W. Cambridge Railroad Co.**, *ante*, p. 436, in which it was
decided, that the price voluntarily paid by a railroad company
for land of another person adjoining the land taken, was admissible
in evidence, and the court said that, "if it had been a price fixed by a
jury, or in any way compulsorily paid by the party, the evidence of
such payment would be inadmissible;" and he argued that the
price paid under the award, could not be said to be " in any way
compulsorily paid."

The COURT, without calling upon *E. Buttrick*, for the respondents,
overruled the exception.

━━━━━━━━━

JOHN BOYNTON *v.* THE PETERBOROUGH AND SHIRLEY RAILROAD
COMPANY.[1]

Middlesex Co., October Term, 1849.

Land Damages — Heir entitled to and not Administrator.

Where the land of one deceased is taken for a railroad, the heir and not the administrator is
entitled to the damages for such taking, and to prosecute for the recovery thereof, although
the administrator has previously represented the estate to be insolvent, and afterwards
obtained a license to sell the intestate's real estate for the payment of debts.

THE petitioner in this case, as the administrator of the estate of
Oliver Page, having applied to the county commissioners for an estimate of the damages occasioned by the location of the Peterborough
and Shirley Railroad over the land of his intestate, and the same hav-

ing been estimated and awarded to him, the proprietors of the railroad applied to the commissioners to summon a jury to revise the
same. The commissioners accordingly ordered a jury to be summoned, and appointed Charles R. Train, Esq., to preside at the trial.
At the trial before the jury, it appeared, that Oliver Page died
on the 26th of November, 1846, seized of the land afterwards taken
by the respondents for their road; that Boynton, the petitioner, was
duly appointed administrator of Page's estate, and accepted that
trust; that, on the 12th of January, 1847, the administrator represented the estate insolvent to the judge of probate, who thereupon
appointed commissioners to examine the claims against the same;
and that the estate was, in fact, deeply insolvent; that the respondents filed the location of their road over the land in question, on the
22d of March, 1848; that, on the 11th of April, 1848, the petitioner
obtained a license from the judge of probate to sell the real estate
of his intestate for the payment of debts; and that Page left one
daughter his sole heir.

The respondents requested the presiding officer to instruct the jury,
that upon the facts proved, the petitioner had no such interest in the
land taken, as would by law entitle him to recover damages therefor;
but the presiding officer, for the purposes of the trial, instructed the
jury otherwise, and they returned a verdict accordingly for the petitioner. The respondents excepted to this instruction, and the presiding officer certified the same with the verdict. The Court of Common Pleas ordered the verdict to be set aside, and the petitioner
appealed to this court.

G. F. Farley and *F. A. Worcester*, for the respondents.

B. Russell (with whom was *J. P. Converse*), for the petitioner.

SHAW, C. J. This case certainly presents a question of some difficulty. Oliver Page died seised of real estate, leaving one daughter
his heir at law. His estate was represented insolvent, and it is conceded, proved to be insolvent; so that the whole of his property,
including the proceeds of all his real estate, to be sold by his administrator, under license, was insufficient to pay his debts. After the
death of the intestate, and before his administrator had obtained
license to sell the real estate, the respondents filed their location, by
which a part of said real estate was taken for the railroad. The question is, whether the heir or the administrator has the right to claim
and receive the damages for the land thus taken.

No act of legislation has provided for this case, and there is no judicial decision in point. The argument for the administrator carries with it a strong semblance of equity. The policy of the law certainly is, to make a deceased debtor's real estate liable for the payment of debts, and the heir takes his inheritance subject to that liability, so far as it is created by law. But the same law, which has declared this liability of real estate for the payment of debts, has prescribed the mode, and the only mode, in which it shall be carried into effect, and that is, by a sale under a license. The heir then takes the estate according to the well-known rule of inheritance, at the time of the decease of the ancestor, subject only to be divested by a sale, pursuant to law, conducted in the manner prescribed by statute. All the legal consequences of this relation are held to follow. The heir is the owner till he is divested; he has the exclusive possession and right of possession; he may take the rents and profits to his own use, and without account. The administrator has no interest or estate, and until a recent statute, not affecting the question, he had no right of entry or action in or to the estate, before license obtained. He had no claim to the rents and profits, and his sale, when made, took effect from the time it was made, and did not relate back to the decease of the ancestor. These are familiar principles, which do not need the citation of authorities for their support.

The right to damages for land taken for public use accrues, and takes effect, at the time of taking, though it may be ascertained and declared afterwards. That time, in the case of railroads, *primâ facie*, and in the absence of other proof, is the time of the filing of the location. See Charlestown Branch Railroad v. Middlesex, *ante*, p. 383, and Davidson v. Boston and Maine Railroad, *ante*, p. 534.

In the present case, the heir at law being seized and possessed of the estate taken, at the time of the taking, subject only to be defeated by a sale, not then made, or authorized and licensed by the competent authority to be made, the court are of opinion, that she was the owner within the meaning of Rev. Sts. c. 39, §§ 55, 56, and entitled to the damages, to be recovered of the respondents for such land; and of course that the administrator was not so entitled.

Judgment of the Court of Common Pleas rejecting the verdict for the administrator, affirmed.

THE PORTLAND, SACO, AND PORTSMOUTH RAILROAD COMPANY *v.* JOHN GRAHAM.[1]

Suffolk Co., March Term, 1846.

Assessments upon Shares of Stock — Proceedings to Enforce For-feiture.

When a statute prescribes the terms on which shares in the stock of a railroad company may be sold for the payment of assessments, and the shareholder be held to pay the balance if the shares are not sold for a sum sufficient to pay the assessments, those terms are condi-tions precedent, and, unless they are strictly complied with,.the sale is illegal and the share-holder not chargeable.

A statute, incorporating a railroad company, provided that if any subscriber or stockholder should neglect to pay any assessment on his shares, the directors might order the treasurer to sell the shares at public auction, after giving a certain notice, to the highest bidder, and that the same should be transferred to the purchaser, and that such delinquent, subscriber, or stockholder, should be held accountable to the company for the balance, if his shares .should sell for less than the assessments due thereon, with the interest and costs of sale: G., a subscriber, neglected to pay assessments, and his shares were advertised for sale, by an auctioneer, without any reference, in the advertisement, to the order of the treasurer, and were bid off, at public auction, by T., for a sum less than the amount of the assessments: T. did not pay for the shares; the sale at auction was abandoned; and the shares were sold to others, at private sale, for the sum bid therefor by T.: The company afterwards brought an action against G. to recover the balance due on the assessments. *Held,* that the action could not be maintained.

THIS case was argued at the last March term, on a report of the trial thereof before Wilde, J.   The facts, so far as they relate to the points decided, sufficiently appear in the opinion of the court.

C. G. Loring and *Dehon,* for the plaintiffs.

Fletcher and *Pope,* for the defendant.

SHAW, C. J.   Many very important questions in regard to the organization of the plaintiff railroad company, the regularity of the assessments, the sufficiency of the notices, and the like, have been raised and very ably argued, which we have not found it necessary, for the reasons which will be obvious, to decide.

The action is brought to recover assessments of $100 each, on one hundred shares of the stock of the company; whereupon it is alleged

---

[1] 11 Metcalf's Reports, 1.

that the defendant subscribed for the said hundred shares, and that twenty assessments of $5 were laid on each share, no part of which was paid by him. It further appears that the company did in fact sell the said hundred shares, as the shares of a delinquent stockholder, in the manner hereafter, for the sum of $70 each, making the sum of $7,000; so that the actual claim of the plaintiff is for $3,000, being the difference between the amount of assessments and the proceeds of the sale.

There are two sets of counts founded on two distinct aspects of the plaintiffs' claim. In the first place, they claim as upon an open, executory contract, founded on an alleged special promise and undertaking by the defendant, by a subscription to an engagement to take and pay the assessments upon the said hundred shares, and alleging the non-payment as a breach. Supposing this to be a valid promise to the corporation, and upon a good consideration, (all which is contested,) still it would be a mutual promise, by the defendant to take and pay for the shares, and by the company to transfer the shares to him on such payment. But as the company have sold the same identical hundred shares, as delinquent shares, and realized the sum of $7,000 upon them, they have regarded him as a proprietor, a delinquent proprietor, and transferred his shares to other persons; and they have thereby disabled themselves from transferring the same shares to him. They cannot comply with the terms on their part. It is therefore unnecessary to consider whether there was any such legal obligation, superadded to the statute liability imposed on stockholders, created by such special promise.

The other set of counts found the claim of the company on such statute liability. It is imposed by the statute of Maine (which is the act of incorporation of this company) and by the by-laws made in conformity with it. Sect. 3 of the statute empowers the president and directors to make equal assessments, from time to time, on all shares in said corporation, and directs that "the treasurer shall give notice of all such assessments; and in case any subscriber or stockholder shall neglect to pay any assessment on his share or shares, for the space of thirty days after such notice is given as shall be prescribed by the by-laws of said corporation, the directors may order the treasurer to sell such share or shares at public auction, after such notice as may be prescribed as aforesaid, to the highest bidder, and the same shall be transferred to the purchaser; and such delinquent subscriber or stockholder shall be held accountable to the corporation for the balance, if his share or shares shall sell for less than the assessments due thereon, with the interests and costs of sale, and he shall be entitled to the overplus if his share or shares should sell for more." The by-law, art. 16, does little more than confirm and enforce this power, and direct specifically the mode in which it shall be carried into effect.

The difference, in this case, between the amount of the assessments and the proceeds of the sale, was $3,000, with interest and costs; and the question is, whether, upon the facts, the plaintiffs have entitled themselves to recover upon this ground. To charge the defendant upon this statute liability, the terms of the statute must be strictly complied with. They are conditions precedent.

The court are of opinion that these conditions have not been complied with. 1st. Because notice of the sale of the shares was not given by the treasurer, pursuant to an order of the directors, as required by the statute. The notice, as published, was given by Mr. Degrand, the auctioneer. He states, in his testimony, that he was directed so to give notice, by the treasurer; but it does not so appear in the notice itself. On the contrary, it purports to be given by order of the directors, without any allusion to the order or authority of the treasurer. This might, perhaps, require some consideration if it stood alone. 2d. But we think a more decisive objection to the regularity and legality of the sale, as a sale, of delinquent shares, is, that they were not sold at auction. This, we think, appears, upon the evidence submitted to the court.

The shares were bid off by John Tibbetts. Whether he ever intended to be himself a purchaser, or whether he bid them off for the defendant, is perhaps left doubtful upon the evidence; but after the lapse of several days, he failed to make good his payment, according to his bid; and the corporation took no measures to enforce the performance of his contract, according to his bid, either by an action or by a resale of the shares on his account. The sale at auction was relinquished, the shares were subsequently sold in different parcels to other persons, at private sale, without any other reference to the sale at auction than that of taking the price bid by Tibbetts at the auction sale, as the rate at which they were sold at private sale. There is nothing indicating that these purchasers came in and took Tibbetts's bid, if that would have been admissible. There was no privity or communication between them and Tibbetts. On the contrary, after Tibbett's bid had been relinquished, the shares were sold by a distinct, original, private contract to other purchasers.

As the stockholder is only made liable, by the statute and by-law, for the difference between the amount of assessments and the proceeds of a regular sale of the shares at auction the defendant is not liable for the difference between such assessments and the proceeds of a private sale, and therefore the action cannot be maintained on this liability created by statute.

Plaintiffs nonsuit.

---◆---

IRA CHENEY *v.* THE BOSTON AND MAINE RAILROAD COMPANY.[1]

Suffolk Co., March Term, 1846.

Passengers — Right of Company to Regulate Fares — Rules as to a Passenger proceeding to the End of his Journey without Stopping.

By the rules of a railroad company, the purchasers of tickets for a passage on the road, from one place to another, were required to go through in the same train; and passengers who were to stop on the road, and afterwards finish their passage in another train, were required to pay more than when they were to go through in the same train : A, not knowing these rules, purchased a ticket for a passage from D to B, and entered the cars with an intention to stop at E, an intermediate place, and to go to B in the next train: When he took his ticket, he was informed of the rule that required him to go through in the same train, and a check was given him, on which were the words "good for this trip only:" The con-ductor of the cars then offered to give back to A the money which he had paid, deducting the amount of his passage from D to E, which A refused to accept, but demanded the ticket in exchange for the check: He stopped at E, went on to B on the same day, in the next train, and offered his check, which was refused, and he was obliged to pay the price charged for a passage from E to B, and afterwards brought an action against the com-pany for breach of contract, and for money had and received. *Held*, that the action could not be maintained.

ASSUMPSIT for money had and received, and for a breach of a con-tract by the defendants in not carrying the plaintiff, upon their road, from Durham (N. H.) to Boston. The case was submitted to the Court of Common Pleas, upon the following statement of facts :

" The plaintiff, in May, 1844, purchased tickets at the depot of the defendants' road, at Durham, for a passage for himself and his wife, from Durham to Boston, and paid for said tickets $1.87½ each. It was and is a rule of the defendants, that passengers purchasing tickets for a passage on said road, from one place to another, must go through in the same train of cars ; but the plaintiff did not know of this rule at the time of purchasing said tickets, and he got into the cars with the intention of stopping, with his wife, at Exeter, between

---●---

Durham and Boston, and about twelve miles from Durham, and of going on to Boston in the next train. The plaintiff was informed of the defendants' rule aforesaid when he came to take his tickets, and checks were given him in lieu of the tickets, upon which were the words 'good for this trip only.' The conductor offered him back the money which he had given for his tickets, deducting the amount of his fare from Durham to Exeter, which the plaintiff refused to accept, but demanded back his tickets in exchange for his checks. Twelve and a half cents less is charged by the defendants for each ticket from Durham to Boston, than for separate tickets from Durham to Exeter, and from Exeter to Boston. But this fact was not known by the plaintiff. The plaintiff and his wife stopped at Exeter, and went on to Boston on the same day, in the next train, and he offered his checks, which were refused, and he was obliged to pay $1.50 each for tickets from Exeter to Boston."

The parties agreed that if the plaintiff was entitled to recover, on these facts, judgment should be rendered for him for $20 damages and costs. The Court of Common Pleas rendered judgment for the plaintiff, from which the defendants appealed.

Putnam, for the plaintiff.

G. Minot, for the defendants.

DEWEY, J. This case involves no question of the general duty of railroad companies to carry passengers who offer themselves and are ready to pay the usual rate of fare. It is only a question whether one who purchases a ticket, entitling him, by the rules of the company regulating the tariff of fares, to a continuous passage through, and avails himself of the reduction in price allowed to such passengers, can insist upon being taken up as a way passenger, at such stations as he may elect to stop at, he having voluntarily abandoned the train that went through.

The question really is, what was the contract between the plaintiff and defendants. Now the case stated by the parties expressly finds that the price of tickets entitling the party to a passage in the cars from Durham to Boston, in one continuous passage, was $1.87½ for each, and for a passage from Durham to Exeter, and from Exeter to Boston, as separate trips, $2. Such was the regular and ordinary charge. It is true that the tickets themselves do not describe the passage to be one by the same train. Nor do they purport to entitle the holder to a conveyance by two separate trips, first, by taking the cars to Exeter, and thence by a subsequent train passing from Exeter to

Boston. They are silent as to the mode. It therefore was a contract to carry in the usual manner in which passengers are carried who have tickets of that kind.

It is said that the rules of the company were unknown to the plaintiff when he purchased the tickets, and therefore he ought not to be affected by them. This might very properly be insisted upon in his behalf, if it were attempted to charge him with any liability created by such rules; especially if it were attempted to enforce any claim for damages by reason of them.

The question, as to the right of the plaintiff to be transported as a passenger, does not depend upon his knowledge, at the time of the purchase of his ticket, of the difference of the price to be paid for a passage through the whole distance by one train, or that of a passage by different trains. The plaintiff might have inquired and informed himself as to that. If he, did not, he took the mode of conveyance, the price of the ticket, and the superscription thereon, secure to him under the rules and regulations of the company. It appears, however, that before reaching Exeter, the plaintiff was fully apprised of the different rates of fare, and the rules applicable to way passengers, and that the agent of the defendants, the conductor of the train, offered to refund to him the money that he had paid for his ticket, deducting the usual fare from Durham to Exeter, which the plaintiff refused to accept. In the opinion of the court, this was all that the defendants were required to do; and as the plaintiff declined this offer, and thereupon left the train, stopping at Exeter, he voluntarily relinquished his passage through by a continuous train, for which he held a ticket, and whatever loss he has sustained was occasioned by his own act, and occurred under such circumstances as preclude him from all claim for damages for any default in the company in the matter. Nor can he sustain any legal claim to recover back the sum paid for his first ticket, or any part thereof. The offer to that effect was refused by him.

Judgment for the defendants.

GIDEON STILES AND ANOTHER *v.* THE WESTERN RAILROAD COR-
PORATION.[1]

Hampden Co., September Term, 1846.

Evidence — Competency of Witnesses.

B contracted with a railroad corporation to construct a section of the road, and afterwards underlet the section to C, D, and E jointly, and not jointly and severally, and then C underlet it to D and E, who proceeded in the work for a short time, and then stopped: The corporation then assumed the work and finished it, and were sued by S for articles furnished, under a contract with C and D, for the completion of the work, and used by the corporation: S released B and C from all liability for the articles, and introduced the testimony of D in support of the claim. *Held,* that D was a competent witness.

Though a leading interrogatory to a deponent is objected to when it is filed, yet if the answer thereto shows that he was not led by it, or if the answer relate to matter proved *aliunde,* respecting which the party, who objects to the interrogatory, has given evidence, the interrogatory and answer may be read to the jury, on the return of the deposition.

ASSUMPSIT to recover pay for gunpowder, furnished by the plaintiffs, after March 1st, 1840, and used in the construction of a part of the defendant's railroad.

The new trial, which was ordered in this case, (*ante,* 397,) was held in the Court of Common Pleas, before Colby, J., when it appeared in evidence that a contract was made by the defendants and Josiah Baylies, for the construction by him of the 74th section of their road; that Baylies underlet this section to Stocking, Lord, and Lard, jointly, and not jointly and severally, and that Stocking underlet it to Lord and Lard, who went on with the work until near the 1st of March, 1840; that a difficulty then took place between Lord and Lard and their workmen, by reason of their neglect to pay the workmen's wages; in consequence of which the work was for a short time suspended. The plaintiffs offered evidence to prove, that while matters were in this state, the defendants, by Julius Adams, their authorized agent, entered upon, and assumed to finish, the work, and thereby became liable for the articles furnished by the plaintiffs; and this was the principal question submitted to the jury.

It appeared that the powder sued for was delivered by the plaintiffs, on a contract between them and Stocking and Lord, but that this contract was not for any particular quantity.

[1] 11 Metcalf's Reports, 376.

The plaintiffs offered the deposition of Lord, one of the above-mentioned firm of sub-contractors. The defendants objected to the deponent's competency, on the ground of interest; and they relied upon the contract entered into between him and the said firm, on the one part, and the said Baylies, on the other, which was substantially the same as the contract between Baylies and the defendants. The plaintiffs had released Baylies and Stocking from all liability to them on account of the claim in suit. The judge ruled that the deponent was a competent witness, and the deposition was read to the jury.

In the plaintiff's bill of particulars was a credit to the defendants of $200, dated June 12th, 1840; and the defendants introduced evidence tending to show that this sum was paid at that time by Lord and Lard. For the purpose of explaining this payment, the plaintiffs offered to read the ninth interrogatory and answer, in Lord's deposition, they not having been read in chief, with the rest of the deposition, but being put in, as above stated, by way of rebutter — the defendants insisting upon the objection offered to the interrogatory, when it was filed. But the judge ruled that it might be read, and it was read to the jury accordingly. The eighth interrogatory and answer were also objected to by the defendants, for the reasons stated in the deposition; but the judge admitted them, and they were read to the jury. (These interrogatories and answers are stated in the opinion of the court.)

The jury found a verdict for the plaintiffs; and to the several foregoing rulings of the judge the defendants alleged exceptions.

R. A. Chapman and *H. Morris*, for the defendants.

W. G. Bates, for the plaintiffs.

WILDE, J.[1] The question on the case reported is, whether Lord, whose deposition was admitted in evidence, was a competent witness. The objection is, that he was interested in the event of the suit. By the facts reported, it appears that the defendants contracted with Josiah Baylies for the construction of a section of their railroad, and that he underlet the same to a company consisting of the said Lord and one Stocking and one Lard; and that the same was underlet by said Stocking to the said Lord and Lard. It also appears that the plaintiffs had released Stocking and Baylies from all liability to them on account of their claim in this action. This release ope-

---

[1] Hubbard, J., did not sit in this case.

rates as a bar to any action that the plaintiffs might bring either against Baylies, or against Stocking and Lord. The release to Baylies alone would be sufficient to bar an action for damages against Stocking and Lord; for he could not suffer any by the non-fulfilment of their contract; and the release to Stocking operates as a release of Lord also ; their contract with Baylies being joint, and not joint and several. It is clear, therefore, that Lord would not be liable to the plaintiffs, if they had failed to recover in this suit. If, however, it were otherwise, Lord's interest would be the same ; for he would be liable to Baylies, and Baylies would be liable to the defendants, if the plaintiffs recover against them. In such case, his interest would be equal; but, having been released by the plaintiffs, his interest is in favor of the defendants; and on either ground he was a competent witness.

Some objections were made to the answers to two interrogatories put by the plaintiffs, on the ground that they were leading. But there does not appear to be any ground for either of the objections. The eighth interrogatory was, " did you, after the dismissal of your company as aforesaid, exercise the same care and superintendence over the work as before ? State particularly what you did," &c. The answer was, that he had exercised no superintendence over the work after that time. So that, if the question was a leading one, the witness was not led thereby ; and that is a sufficient answer to the objection. The 9th interrogatory was, "did you give to plaintiffs a note for $200 ? If so, explain by whom said note was paid, and how it was paid." The answer was, "on or about the 1st of April, 1840, I gave a note of $200 to Gideon Stiles, payable at the Hampden Bank in sixty days, which note was given for powder delivered to our firm by the plaintiffs, previous to February, 1840. The note was paid by Mr. Adams. He brought the note to me, and said the corporation would not accept it, and that I must give Mr. Stiles an order on him (Adams) for the $200. Mr. Adams took Mr. Stiles's order for $200, and gave me up the note." Now the existence of this note was proved *aliunde*, and the defendants had introduced evidence respecting it, and the purpose of reading the answer to this interrogatory was to explain the payment. The form of the question was wholly immaterial.

Exceptions overruled.

EDWIN DRAPER AND ANOTHER *v.* THE WORCESTER AND NORWICH
RAILROAD COMPANY.[1]

Worcester Co., September Term, 1846.

*Evidence of the Delivery of Goods — Competency of a Servant of a
Company.*

In an action upon the case against a railroad corporation, to recover damages for the non-delivery of goods intrusted to the defendants for transportation, and in an action of trover to recover the value of such goods, a servant of the defendants employed by them to load and unload cars, and deliver freight, at the depot where the goods arrived, is a competent witness for the defendants, to prove that all the goods were delivered, at such a depot, to the plaintiff or his agents.

THIS was an action upon the case, to recover damages for the non-delivery of 36 barrels of flour, part of a lot of 1135 barrels, delivered to the defendants at Norwich, to be transported, for the plaintiffs, to Worcester. The declaration also contained a count in trover.

At the trial in the Court of Common Pleas, before Merrick, J., the defendants admitted that they were common-carriers, and, as such, received said 1135 barrels of flour from the plaintiffs to be transported for them, as alleged in their declaration.

The plaintiffs introduced evidence tending to show that the defendants presented to them a bill for the freight of the whole quantity of 1135 barrels; that they paid the same; that a part of said flour arrived at the defendants' depot in Worcester, and was received by the plaintiffs; and that a part thereof had not been received by them.

The defendants' counsel, in opening their defence, stated that they insisted that the whole quantity of 1135 barrels of flour had been delivered, at their depot in Worcester, to the plaintiffs or their agents. The defendants then called George H. Haven as a witness, to prove their alleged defence. He was objected to by the plaintiffs on the ground of interest, and was examined by them on the *voir dire*. On this examination, he testified as follows: " I was in the employ of the defendants when this flour arrived. I was freight-house laborer to load and unload cars, and deliver freight. It was my duty to deliver freight which came there."

The plaintiffs insisted that said Haven's interest was proved, and denied his competency; but the court decided that his interest was not proved, and admitted him to testify. A verdict was returned for the defendants, and the plaintiffs alleged exceptions to the admission of Haven's testimony.

Bacon and *Hartshorn*, for the plaintiffs.
Haven was not a competent witness for the defendants. 1 Greenl. on Ev. §§ 390, 394, 395; 1 Stark. Ev. 188; Tylor *v.* Ulmer, 12 Mass. 163; Morish *v.* Foote, 8 Taunt. 454, and 2 Moore, 508. The exception, in cases of necessity, does not apply to this case; as it exists. only when the principal offers the agent to prove an act done within the scope of his authority. Agents never are admitted as witnesses to disprove their own negligence. 1 Greenl. on Ev. §§ 416, 417; Green *v.* New River Co. 4 T. R. 589; Fuller *v.* Wheelock, 10 Pick. 135; Noble *v.* Paddock, 19 Wend. 456; Dudley *v.* Bolles, 24 Wend. 465.

B. F. Thomas, for the defendants.
The case cited from 4 T. R. 589, and other cases like it, proceeded on the ground that the record or the evidence showed that the carelessness of the offered witness was the cause of action. In the present case, it does not appear that negligence, either of the defendants or their servants, is the ground of action. The defendants may be liable for theft, robbery, fire, &c., in which no servant of theirs was implicated. The record of this case could not be used against Haven; for it would not show any concern of his in the action or the result of it.
The exception, as to the admissibility of agents to testify in behalf of their principals, should be liberally applied to corporations, that must do all their business by agents. See 1 Greenl. on Ev. § 416; 1 Stark. Ev. 90, 100, 112, 113; Ross *v.* Rowe, cited in Roscoe on Ev· 85, and in 2 Stark. Ev. 754; Fisher *v.* Willard, 13 Mass. 379; Spencer *v.* Goulding, Peake's Cas. 129; Alexander *v.* Emerson, 2 Littell, 27.

SHAW, C. J. The defendants admit themselves to be common-carriers of merchandise, and the action is brought against them in that capacity. The only question brought up by the exceptions is, whether Haven, called as a witness by the defendants, and objected to by the plaintiffs, on account of interest, was competent or not.
In opening the defence, the counsel stated that the defendants expected to prove that the whole quantity of flour, forwarded by the

plaintiffs, had been delivered from their depot in Worcester. The witness, being examined on the *voir dire*, testified that he was in the employ of the defendants, when this flour arrived; that he was a freight-house laborer, to load and unload cars and deliver freight; that it was his duty to deliver freight which came there.

It is not easy, perhaps, to draw a precise line between the cases of servants called by their masters, where the matter drawn in question is the carelessness and negligence of the servant, and cases where servants and agents are called to testify to acts done in the usual course of their employment, and where their masters may gain or lose by their testimony. In the former, they are held to be incompetent; in the latter, they are competent. Perhaps the true distinction is this ; that where, by the pleadings and issue, or the actual state of the inquiry, the question is upon the liability of one to answer, in consequence of the negligence or carelessness of a particular servant, and where the servant may be liable over, in an action to the master, such servant shall be held incompetent for his employer, without a release ; because, in a suit over against the servant, the verdict and judgment, in the case in which he is offered, would be evidence for the employer against the servant, either as to the main fact, or as to the amount of damages sustained. But where the question is of a general nature, as in trover or case for the non-delivery of property, no such use could be made of the judgment, and the objection to the competency of the witness could not exist. It is difficult to perceive the interest which the witness has in the present suit, when we consider that such interest must be direct, and not contingent, possible, or uncertain, and that it must be an interest in the event of the suit, and not merely in the question or subject-matter. Bent v. Baker, 3 T. R. 27. The witness is not called to disprove his own negligence. Such fact is not directly or necessarily charged, or drawn in question. Green v. New River Co. 4 T. R. 590; Noble v. Paddock, 10 Wend. 457.

But the precise ground on which we decide that this witness was competent is, that the case is within that well-established exception to the general rule, which admits agents, factors, brokers, carriers, and subordinate agents and servants in all departments of business, to testify, as competent witnesses, to the receipt and payment of money, the delivery of goods, and all acts usually done by such classes of persons, within the scope of their ordinary occupation and employment. It is founded on those considerations of general expediency, growing out of the usual order and course of business ; and without such modification of the general rule, business would be greatly impeded. A different rule would operate as a great obstruction to the transactions of merchants, ship-owners, carriers, and other dealers; but it would nearly prevent the operations of corporate companies, who must act entirely through various classes of officers and agents. 1 Greenl. on Ev. §§ 416, 417.

The only case cited in the argument, which seems opposed to this view, is that of Fuller v. Wheelock, 10 Pick. 135. That case is very different from the present. There the witness was the authorized agent of the plaintiff to receive the money, and had given his receipt for it. Upon the evidence, therefore, he was immediately liable to the plaintiff, in an action for money had and received; and he was called, without a release, to testify to facts which would exonerate him from such action. Besides; he was not a general agent, called to testify to acts in the usual course of his employment, but was specially authorized, and for aught that appears to the contrary, by power of attorney, to do that particular act. That case is not an authority applicable to the present.

Exceptions overruled.

JOPEPH LEWIS *v.* THE WESTERN RAILROAD CORPORATION.[1]

Worcester Co., September Term, 1846.

Liability as Carriers — Delivery of Goods — When not Liable for Negligence of Servants.

If A, for whom goods are transported by a railroad company, authorizes B to receive the delivery thereof, and to do all acts incident to the delivery and transportation thereof to A and B, instead of receiving the goods at the usual place of delivery, requests the agent of the company to permit the car, which contains the goods, to be hauled to a near depot of another railroad company, and such agent assents thereto, and assists B in hauling the car to such depot, and B there requests and obtains leave of that company to use its machinery to remove the goods from the car; then the company that transported the goods is not answerable for the want of care or skill in the persons employed in so removing the goods from the car, nor for the want of strength in the machinery used for the removal of them, and cannot be charged with any loss that may happen in the course of such delivery to A.

THIS was an action to recover damages alleged to have been

---

[1] 11 Metcalf's Reports, 509.

caused by the defendants' negligence in the delivery of a block of marble.

At the trial in the Court of Common Pleas, before Merrick, J., it appeared that a block of marble, weighing about four tons, was brought from Pittsfield to Worcester, on the 28th of February, 1844, in one of the defendants' freight cars, and that the plaintiff paid the freight: That before the block arrived, one Lamb, a truckman, usually employed by the plaintiff to do his trucking, and who had been by him particularly requested to obtain and bring the block to him, had applied to the superintendent of the depot of the Boston and Worcester Railroad Corporation, at Worcester, for leave to use the derrick and machinery of that corporation in unlading the block from the car and placing it upon the truck, as there were no such derrick and machinery at the defendants' depot in Worcester: That upon the arrival of the block at the defendants' depot, Lamb went to the depot of the Boston and Worcester Railroad Corporation, with his truck, to receive and transport the block to the plaintiff; and that one M'Coy, (who was employed by the defendants, and whose business it was to deliver and receive freight,) assisted by said Lamb and his truck horse, drew the car, on which the block had been transported by the defendants, from the defendants' depot to the junction of the two railroads, and shifted the switch, and drew the block to the depot of the Boston and Worcester Railroad Corporation, and proceeded to remove the block from the car to the truck, by the aid of the aforesaid derrick and machinery; and that, while attempting to do this, the hook, which fastened the chain of the derrick around the block, gave way, and the block fell and was broken.

It further appeared that the defendants had never before brought any stone, of this size and description, over their road, to Worcester, and that neither they nor any of their agents had ever before undertaken to deliver articles of any kind at the depot of the Boston and Worcester Railroad Corporation, nor at any other place than their own depot, nor with any other machinery than their own; that M'Coy had never been authorized nor permitted to undertake to deliver articles at any other place; that his duties were to receive the articles which were to be sent from Worcester, and give written receipts therefor, and to deliver to owners or consignees articles brought to Worcester, according to the way-bills; and that, in these duties, he was subordinate to the station agent.

The plaintiff introduced evidence tending to show that the defendants had not the means or conveniences for delivering a stone of this size and description, at their depot. But the defendants also introduced evidence tending to show that this stone might have been safely and conveniently delivered on the platform of their depot.

The defendants contended that they were not liable in this action. But the judge ruled, that if M'Coy did not complete the delivery of the stone at the defendants' depot, and undertook to deliver it at the depot and with the machinery of the Boston and Worcester Railroad Corporation, and if, in the course of the delivery, the injury happened through his negligence in the mode of delivery; or through a defect in the machinery, which a proper vigilance would guard against, then the defendants were liable.

The jury returned a verdict for the plaintiff, and the defendants alleged exceptions to the judge's ruling.

Ashmun, for the defendants.

M'Coy's authority was special and limited. He was not, in any sense, a general agent of the defendants, with discretionary powers. And as he did not act within the scope of his authority, in attempting to deliver the block at the depot of another corporation, the defendants are not responsible in this action. Story on Agency, §§ 79, 80, 81, 94, 126, 131, 458, 459, 460; 2 Rol. Ab. 533; Lamb v. Palk, 9 Car. & P. 629; Thayer v. City of Boston, 19 Pick. 511; Williams v. Mitchell, and Foster v. Essex Bank, 17 Mass. 98, 479; Olive v. Eames, 2 Stark. R. 181. Besides, M'Coy's undertaking to deliver at another depot was at the request, or suggestion, or with the consent of Lamb, the plaintiff's agent. If this agent had not been instrumental in the removal of the block to another depot, or if M'Coy had taken it there upon his own suggestion alone, perhaps the plaintiff might have maintained an action for non-delivery by the defendants; but he could not, even on such a state of facts, maintain this action for carelessness in the delivery.

No question of fact, as to the extent of M'Coy's authority, was submitted to the jury. The evidence on that point was clear and uncontradicted. If the plaintiff had contended that this authority was larger than appears in the bill of exceptions, he should have put that question to the jury. Witte v. Hague, 2 Dowl. & Ryl. 33; Dyer v. Pearson, 3 Barn. & Cres. 38; Brady v. Giles, 1 M. & Rob. 494. But the judge, at the trial, ruled that if M'Coy *undertook* to deliver the block at the depot of the Boston and Worcester Railroad Corporation, and if the injury happened through his negligence in the mode of delivery, then the defendants were responsible. No such legal inference can be drawn from these facts.

The duty of common-carriers is to make a right delivery of goods, at the proper place of destination, according to the usage of trade, or the course of business. Story on Bailm. § 509, and cases there cited. A compliance with this duty would have been the unloading of the block at the defendants' depot, upon the ground, in a safe and con-

• venient place. It was no part of their duty to place it upon the plaintiff's truck. The plaintiff, for his convenience, chose another mode and another place of delivery; and he took the responsibility of the measure. The defendants knew nothing about the sufficiency or fitness of the machinery provided by another railroad corporation, and ought not to be held as insurers for it, in any respect; especially as it was the plaintiff who sought and obtained the leave to use it.

The defendants were not common-carriers of the block when it was injured. They were carriers between their depot in Pittsfield and their depot in Worcester, and not from their own depot to that of another corporation; and their responsibility terminated at their own depot. Ackley v. Kellogg, 8 Cow. 223.

However universal the custom may be for carriers to deliver goods to the owner, at the place of destination, still the parties may, by their contract, waive it; and if they do, the carrier is discharged. In the case at bar, the leave, asked and obtained by the plaintiff, to use the machinery of another corporation, and his drawing of the block to the depot of that corporation, were, in law, a waiver of the right to have the block delivered at the defendant's depot, and a discharge of their liability as carriers. Strong v. Natally, 1 New Rep. 16; Matter of Webb, 8 Taunt. 443; Story on Bailm. § 541.

Barton and *F. H. Dewey*, for the plaintiff.

The defendants are to be held responsible for the safe delivery of the block to the plaintiff, unless prevented by inevitable accident, by public enemies, or by his act. 1 U. S. Digest, Bailment, 157, 158; Story on Bailm. §§ 507 – 510; Dusar v. Murgatroyd, 1 Wash. C. C. 13; Eagle v. White, 6 Whart. 505. And the burden is on the defendants to exonerate themselves, by proof of one of these three grounds of excuse. Hastings v. Pepper, 11 Pick. 44; Craig v. Childress, Peck, 271; Story on Bailm. § 529.

The defendants' responsibility did not cease upon the safe arrival of the block at Worcester. They were bound to deliver it safely to the plaintiff. Story on Bailm. 538. The plaintiff might have waived his claim on the defendants for the safety of the block, after its arrival. But in order to constitute such waiver, he must have taken exclusive possession of it, or have terminated the custody of the defendants by an act or direction which did not flow from their duty. It is not till the transit is ended, and the delivery is either completed or waived, that a carrier's responsibility ceases. Story on Bailm. §§ 541, 542. In the case at bar, the plaintiff did not take exclusive possession of the block at the defendants' depot. It does not appear that he knew of its arrival until after it was broken. Nor did Lamb take

exclusive possession of it for the plaintiff. He merely assisted M'Coy*
to remove it to another depot. Besides, Lamb had no authority to
waive any of the plaintiff's rights. He was merely a special agent
to transport the block to the plaintiff. His being accustomed to do
the plaintiff's trucking did not make him a general agent. 2 Kent
Com. (3d ed.) 620, 621 ; Story on Bailm. §§ 126, 127, 459.

The defendants had not delivered the block to the plaintiff before
it was broken, according to the usual course of business. Dudley v.
Smith, 1 Campb. 167 ; Story on Bailm. §§ 538, 542. The only question then is, whether the acts of the plaintiff, or of Lamb, were such
as to discharge the defendants from their usual liability. The
defendants are responsible for the acts of their agents done within
the scope of the agent's authority. M'Coy was their agent to receive
freight and to deliver to owners or consignees articles brought to the
defendants' depot. From the nature of his duties, and from the
necessity of the case, he must have had some discretionary power.
Different articles must be delivered at different places and in different ways. A block of marble weighing four tons could not be properly unloaded upon the platform of the depot. A delivery there
would not be a discharge of the defendants' duty. Story on Bailm.
§ 509. It appears that no stone of this size had ever before been
brought to the depot. It was a new case; and it is a matter of
great uncertainty, at least, whether the stone could have been properly delivered at the defendants' depot. M'Coy must be considered
as acting within the scope of his employment, when he drew the
car, which contained the stone, to the other depot, for the purpose
of delivering it there. The defendants, in order to avoid their
liability for the acts of their general agent, should have given
notice that his authority was limited in the particular case. See
Story on Bailm. (3d ed.) §§ 507, 507 a. Hern v. Nichols, 1 Salk.
289; Gibson v. Colt, 7 Johns. 390; Munn v. Commission Co.
15 Johns. 54; Matthews v. West London Water Works Co.
3 Campb. 403; Howard v. Baillie, 2 H. B. 618; Dawson v. Law-
ley, 4 Esp. R. 65; Ellis v. Turner, 8 T. R. 531; Owings v. Hull,
9 Pet. 607; Damon v. Inhabitants of Granby, 2 Pick. 345 ; Jeffrey v.
Bigelow, 13 Wend. 518; De Mott v. Laraway, 14 Wend. 225;
Guerreiro v. Peile, 3 Barn. & Ald. 616; 3 Chit. Law of Com. &
Man. 198 – 202; Story on Agency, §§ 127, 131, 133.

DEWEY, J. The general principles of law, regulating the duty of
common-carriers in safely conveying and delivering property committed to their charge, required a delivery of this block of marble to
the plaintiff; and if there had been no peculiar circumstances in the

present case, affecting the mode and place of delivery; if the servant of the defendants had, of his own suggestion, undertaken to make such delivery at another place than their depot, and in the execution of such purpose had damaged the block; it may be that, for such misconduct of their servant, they would have been responsible, though he acted without particular orders, and in an unusual manner, in the discharge of the duties appertaining to his office.

The counsel on both sides have argued the case very much upon the point of the liability of the defendants for the acts of M'Coy, under the assumption that he was the director in moving the block from the depot of the defendants, and that it was carried for delivery to the other depot, for his convenience. But the leading error, as it seems to us, in presenting the case to the jury, was in disregarding the facts tending to show that the defendants were excused from all liability of safe transportation and delivery, after the block left their depot.

The duty of the defendants was to transport the article, and deliver it at their depot. But this duty may be modified as to the manner of its performance. The omission of the defendants to remove goods from the cars, and place them in the warehouse, or upon the platform, would not, in all cases, subject them to an action for non-delivery, or for negligence in the delivery. Suppose a bale of goods was transported by them, and, on its arrival at the depot, the owner should step into the car and ask for a delivery there, and thereupon the goods should be passed over to him, in the car. The delivery would be perfect; and if any casualty should subsequently occur, in taking out the bale, the loss would be his. The place and manner of delivery may always be varied with the assent of the owner of the property; and if he interferes to control or direct in the matter, he assumes the responsibility.

The real question in the case is this: Were the defendants discharged from further liability for the safe transportation and delivery of the block, after it left their depot? It seems to us that there was evidence tending to show this. Had the plaintiff been personally present at the depot, and done the same acts that Lamb did, we suppose no one would doubt that the defendants would have been discharged from all further liability, after the block left their depot. The whole then turns upon the extent of Lamb's agency, and the effect to be given to his acts, in reference to the delivery. As to this point, we think there was an omission, or want of precise direction, in the charge of the presiding judge.

The court are of opinion that the jury ought to have been instructed as to the effect of the acts of Lamb, as follows: 1st. That if Lamb was authorized and employed by the plaintiff to take and receive the delivery of the block, which, being of unusual size and weight, required peculiar care and attention to deliver ; and if he was the authorized agent of the plaintiff to do all acts incident to the delivery and transportation of the block ; and if Lamb, instead of receiving the block at the depot of the defendants, requested their agent for delivery to permit the car containing the block to be hauled to the Boston and Worcester Railroad derrick, and if Lamb requested the use of that derrick for the purpose of removing the block from the car to his truck ; then these acts, being incident to the delivery of the block, were acts within the authority conferred on Lamb by the plaintiff, and bind him in the same manner as if done by himself. 2d. That if Lamb requested M'Coy to deliver the block, or consent to the delivery thereof, in this mode, instead of delivering the same at the defendants' depot, and with the means there provided, then, from the time the car left the defendants' depot, and premises, and went to the derrick of the Boston and Worcester Railroad, the defendants ceased to be liable either for the care and skill of the persons employed, or for the strength and sufficiency of the machinery employed for the purpose ; and that the persons employed must be regarded as the agents of the plaintiff. 3d. That the general duty of the defendants as common-carriers, was to make a true delivery of goods at the usual place, which, in this case, was their own depot at Worcester ; but that it was competent for the plaintiff to assent to a delivery elsewhere ; that if the plaintiff desired such a special delivery, to which the agent of the defendants assented, then, from and after the time that the block had gone from the regular place of delivery, with respect to such special delivery the block might be regarded as constructively delivered, so that the defendants were exempted from the duty of making any other or different delivery.

New trial granted.

INDEX.

ACTION.   Page

Where damages have been assessed by the commissioners to a land-owner for injury done him by excavations in his land for the purposes of a railroad, an action on the case to recover further damages cannot be sustained against the railroad corporation. *Aldrich* v. *Cheshire Railroad Co.* 206

The plaintiff's buildings were supplied with water from a permanent spring. After an excavation had been made in his land for the purpose of a railroad, water appeared in the excavation, about fifteen feet below the surface of the ground, and the spring disappeared. Damages were assessed to him before the excavation was made. *Held,* that the injury to the spring must be presumed to have been considered by the commissioners, and that an action to recover damages therefor could not be sustained. *Ibid* 206

If, on a hearing before a jury for the assessment of damages for land taken for a railroad, it is agreed between the parties, that the proprietors of the road shall make and maintain fences against the owner of the land taken, along the line of the road, such agreement, if valid, can only be enforced against the proprietors of the road, in an action by the party with whom it was made, and not by any subsequent purchaser of the estate to which it relates. *Morss* v. *The Boston and Maine Railroad* ....:.................... 454

When a statute remedy is exclusive, and when concurrent with common-law remedy. 218

No action can be maintained at common law against a company for injuries arising from the exercise of the statute powers. .... 164 – 166, 337

Company becomes liable if its powers are exceeded. 165

Or are negligently exercised. 338

Principle denied in Georgia and New York. 166

To recover balance due after sale of shares for non-payment of assessments. 422

An action on the case cannot be maintained by a widow, to recover damages for the loss of her husband, or by a father for the loss of service of his child, in consequence of the death of the husband or child, occasioned by the carelessness or fault of the agents or servants of a railroad corporation. *Carey* v. *The Berkshire Railroad Co.* 442

The fourth section of the Act of 1849, c. 222, (of Massachusetts,) which gives county commissioners jurisdiction of all questions touching obstructions to highways by railroads, if it does not relate exclusively to the raising or lowering of such ways when crossed by a railroad, which the court did not decide, has no effect to deprive this court of its jurisdiction of a case commenced therein before the passing of the act. *Springfield* v. *The Connecticut River Railroad Co.* 572

ACTION (*Continued*).

Where a town was divided, and a part of it established as a new town, after the
commencement of a suit in equity by such town against a railroad corporation,
for a nuisance to a public highway, which, upon the division, fell within the
limits of the new town, and the act for the division provided that such suit
should be assumed, and might be prosecuted to final judgment by the new town,
at their expense and for their benefit, but in the name of the old town ; it was
held, that the division did not operate to vacate or otherwise affect the suit.
Ibid................   572

The remedy for an injury occasioned by the alteration of the highway for the purpose of raising or lowering the same, by a railroad corporation, is not by an
action against the town under the Rev. Sts. c. 25, § 3, (of Massachusetts,) but
by a proceeding against the corporation for damages, under the statute. *Parker*
v. *The Boston and Maine Railroad*....   547

An action may be maintained by a corporation upon a promissory note given to
the commissioners for receiving subscription for stock in payment of an instalment...... ....:........   226

Where a covenant purported to be made between two persons by name, of the
first part, and the corporate company, of the second part, and only one of the
persons of the first part signed the instrument, and the covenant ran between the
party of the first part and the party of the second part, it was proper for the
person who had signed on the first part to sue alone ; because the covenant
enured to the benefit of those who were parties to it. *Philadelphia, Wilmington,
&c. Railroad Co.* v. *Howard*...   70

A's house, which was insured, was injured by a fire communicated by a locomotive engine of a railroad corporation, and the underwriters paid to A the amount
of his loss, for which the railroad corporation was also by law responsible to
him. *Held,* that such payment did not bar A's right to recover also of the railroad corporation, and that A, by receiving payment of the underwriters, became
trustees for them, and as a necessary implication, made an equitable assignment
to them of his right to recover of the railroad corporation ; and that the underwriters, on indemnifying A, might bring an action in his name, for their own
benefit, against the railroad corporation, and that A could not legally release
such action. *Hart* v. *Western Railroad Co*....   414

The attorney of the Commonwealth for the county of Suffolk, after the Act of 1843,
c. 99, abolishing the office of attorney-general, and previous to that of 1849,
c. 186, reëstablishing that office, was authorized by law, upon the requisition of
the governor, to institute proceedings before the proper tribunal, for the recovery
of damages sustained by the Commonwealth for land taken for a railroad, and
to prosecute the same to their final termination; and such attorney had a right,
also, with the permission of the court or tribunal in which the proceedings were
pending, and for sufficient cause, to avail himself of the aid of other suitable
counsel, in conducting and managing the same, under his direction and control,
and upon his responsibility. *Commonwealth* v. *The Boston and Maine Railroad*..   482

Where a railroad passes over parts of two counties, the Railroad Corporation may
maintain an action of assumpsit in that county wherein they have an office which
is "made the depository of the books and records of the company by a vote of
the directors, and a place where a large share of the business is transacted,"
although the company may at the same time have another office in the other
county, where the residue of their business is transacted, and in which the treasurer and clerk reside. *Androscoggin and Kennebec Railroad Co.* v. *Stevens*.....   140

AMALGAMATION OF COMPANIES.
    SEE CONSOLIDATION OF COMPANIES.

APPEAL.
    An appeal to the Supreme Court of Massachusetts, from the Court of Com-

· APPEAL (*Continued*).

mon Pleas, accepting or rejecting the verdict of a sheriff's jury, for the assessment for damages for land taken for a railroad, is a summary proceeding, provided as a substitute for a writ of error in ordinary cases; and, upon such appeal, the adjudication of the Court of Common Pleas is to be construed with the same liberality, as to defects of form and amendments, as is applicable to writs of error and proceedings on *certiorari*, and the case is to be considered in the same manner, as if formally brought before the court by a writ of *certiorari*. *Walker* v. *The Boston and Maine Railroad* 462

On an appeal to this court, from an adjudication of the Court of Common Pleas, accepting the verdict of a sheriff's jury, assessing damages for land taken for a railroad, it being objected by the respondent, that the Board of County Commissioners, when making an estimate of the damages, in the first instance, was not duly constituted; and the ground of this objection appearing only on the record of the proceedings before the commissioners, a copy of which was among the papers in the case; it was held, that this objection was not open upon the appeal, and that if well-founded originally, the respondents had waived it by proceeding before the commissioners. *The Fitchburg Railroad Co.* v. *The Boston and Maine Railroad* 508

APPRAISEMENT OF DAMAGES.

On a claim for damages for land taken for a railroad, the claimant may prove, by the testimony of the engineer who made the preliminary surveys and plans for such. road, that the same might have been located, pursuant to the charter, in various modes which would not have required the taking of the land of such claimant. *Commonwealth* v. *The Boston and Maine Railroad* 482

The owner of flats crossed by a railroad bridge, having raised the flats around and under the bridge, within the location of the road, but without the consent of the proprietors thereof, is entitled to recover by way of damages, against such proprietors, for so much of the expense of such raising and filling up, as is necessary to enable him to enjoy his other lands; provided such necessity was caused by the location and construction of the railroad. *Ibid.* 482

Where the owner of flats crossed by and taken for a railroad had previously caused the same to be surrounded by a sea-wall and filled up, it was held, that the expense of such filling up was proper evidence to be considered by the jury, in estimating the damages sustained by the owner for the land so taken. *Ibid.*. 482

The commissioners need not be called upon to appraise damages for materials taken by the Vermont Central Railroad Co., without the limits of their survey, under their charter, for the construction of their road, until after the materials are ascertained. *Vermont Central Railroad Co.* v. *Baxter* 240

The commissioners have jurisdiction to determine the damages for acts of the corporation, where those acts are such as the corporation, by their engineers, agents, or workmen, may rightfully do, by virtue of their charter, and the parties cannot agree upon the amount of damages; and it makes no difference, in this respect, whether the corporation admit or deny their liability. *Ibid.*..... 240

The commissioners, who are called upon to assess damages in such case, may award costs to the land-owner. *Ibid.* 240

In the case of land taken for a railroad, if the county commissioners refuse to assess damages on the ground that the party applying for them does not own the land, he is entitled to have their judgment revised by a jury; and a mandamus will lie in his behalf, to compel them to grant a warrant for a jury. *Carpenter* v. *The County Commissioners of Bristol* 280

Where the sheriff instructed a jury, impanelled to appraise damages caused by the laying out of a railroad over a party's land, that by the legal construction of his title deed, which bounded his land on a way, he owned the land to the centre of the way, and was therefore entitled to damages for the value of the land over

620

INDEX.

APPRAISEMENT OF DAMAGES (*Continued*).

which the way passed; it was held that the instruction was so general and abstract, that no opinion could be expressed, as to its correctness, without much qualification. *Webber* v. *The Eastern Railroad Co* 331

The provision in Rev. Sts. (of Massachusetts) c. 24, § 19, that jurors for the assessment of damages caused by the laying out of a highway shall be taken from "the three nearest towns not interested," means the three towns nearest to the town in which the land lies, over which the highway is laid out: And by Rev. Sts. c. 39, § 57, this provision is extended to jurors for the assessment of damages caused by the laying out of a railroad. Under Rev. Sts. c. 24, § 15, and c. 39, § 57, which direct that when two or more persons apply, at the same time, to the county commissioners, for a jury to assess damages caused by the laying out of a highway or railroad, "the said commissioners shall cause all such applications to be considered and. determined by the same jury," the most proper course for the commissioners is, to issue a single warrant to an officer, reciting all the cases that are to be heard by the jury: If separate warrants for each case be issued by the commissioners, yet if the officer summon a single jury, who hear and determine each case, their verdicts will not be set aside merely because several warrants were irregularly issued. *Wyman* v. *Lexington and West Cambridge Railroad Co* 426

When several applications are made, at the same time, by owners of lands in different towns, for a jury to assess damages caused by the laying out of a highway or railroad, the jurors are to be taken from three towns nearest to the town in which the land of either of the applicants is situate: And when a single application, for such purpose, is made by one who owns land in different towns, the jurors are to be taken from three towns nearest to either of the towns in which his lands are situate: This is all that is practicable under Rev. Sts. c. 24, § 15, and c. 39, § 57. *Ibid*... 426

It is necessary that notice to jurors, who are drawn to assess damages caused by the laying out of a highway or railroad, should be served by a constable: Such notice may be served by the officer to whom the warrant for summoning a jury is directed. *Ibid*... 426

The "three nearest towns not interested," from which jurors are to be taken to estimate the damages caused by the laying out of a highway or railroad, are the three towns nearest to and exclusive of the town in which the land lies, over which the highway or railroad is laid. *Meacham* v. *The Fitchburg Railroad Co*. 584

A sheriff's jury, to assess damages for land taken for a highway or railroad, may be summoned by the constables of the several towns from whence they are taken, or partly by such constables, and partly by the deputy sheriff by whom the warrant is executed. *Ibid*... 584

The mortgagee of land taken for a railroad need not be made a party to proceedings by the mortgagor, for the assessment of damages, provided he gives his assent thereto by a writing filed in the case. *Ibid*.......................... 584

The want of proper parties to a proceeding before a sheriff's jury, for the assessment of damages for land taken for a highway or railroad, must be objected before the commissioners, upon the application of such jury. *Ibid*............. 584

In estimating the damages for land taken for a highway or railroad, any direct and peculiar benefit or increase of value accruing therefrom to land of the same owner, adjoining or connected with the land taken, and forming part of the same parcel or tract, is to be considered by the jury, and allowed by way of set-off; but not any general benefit or increase of value received by such land, in common with other lands in the neighborhood; nor any benefit to other land of the same owner, though in the same town. The time, at and from which the benefit accruing to the owner of land, taken for a highway or railroad, is to be estimated, in assessing his damages for such a taking, is that of the actual location. *Ibid*... 584

APPRAISEMENT OF DAMAGES (*Continued*).

Landowners not entitled to a jury in Vermont............................. 220

Objections to the proceedings before a sheriff's jury, impanelled to assess damages for land taken for a highway or railroad, — that the respondent had no notice of the application to the commissioners for a jury, — or that three disinterested commissioners were not present as required by the Rev. Sts. (of Massachusetts) c. 14, § 27, — or that there were other cases of the same kind, which ought to have gone to the same jury, — cannot be taken advantage of on appeal, unless the grounds of such objections appear on the record ; and it is not enough, that it does not appear, by the record, that the party had notice, — or that the business was determined by disinterested commissioners, or by consent, — or that there were other like cases which were put to the same jury. *Walker* v. *Boston and Maine Railroad*... 462

Though an original petition for a jury to assess damages caused by the taking of land for a railroad is not seasonably filed, if it be after the regular meeting of the county commissioners next following that at which they completed and returned their estimate of such damages, yet if such petition be filed at the same meeting at which they complete and return such estimate, and they thereupon, without notice to the railroad corporation, pass an order and issue a warrant for the summoning of a jury, and the warrant is not served, they are authorized, and ought, upon motion of the land-owner, though the motion be not made until after their next regular meeting, to issue an order of notice to the railroad corporation to show cause why a jury should not be summoned on the original petition ; the first order for a jury being void, for want of such notice, and the original petition being still pending. *Porter* v. *County Commissioners of Norfolk*.......... 439

Where proceedings for the assessment, by a jury, of damages for the land taken by a railroad corporation, are conducted in part by a coroner, under the Rev. Sts. (of Massachusetts) c. 24, § 23, and in part by the sheriff, it is the duty of each of those officers to certify the proceedings which take place before him ; and, in such a case, where the coroner presides, it is no objection to the verdict, that the jury are not attended by a deputy sheriff. *Pittsfield and North Adams Railroad Co.* v. *Foster*... 448

Under the Rev. Sts. (of Massachusetts) c. 39, § 57, which provide that a party, who is dissatisfied with the estimate made by county commissioners, of the damages caused by taking land for a railroad, " may apply for a jury to assess the damages, either at the same meeting at which such estimate shall be completed and returned, or at the next regular meeting thereafter," if a party applies for a jury, at the same meeting at which the estimate is completed and recorded, and a jury is then ordered, and a warrant therefor issued, he cannot, by merely omitting or refusing to proceed under that order and warrant, entitle himself to a jury on applying therefor at the next regular meeting of the commissioners. *Taylor* v. *County Commissioners of Plymouth*.............................. 436

Right of legislature to direct the re-hearing of a case........................ 43

The States have a right to direct the re-hearing of cases decided in their own courts. The only limit upon their power to pass retrospective laws is, that the Constitution of the United States forbids their passing *ex post facto* laws, which are retrospective penal laws. But a law merely divesting antecedent vested rights of property, where there is no contract, is not inconsistent with the Constitution of the United States. *Baltimore and Susquehanna Railroad Co.* v. *Nesbit*.. 39

See, also, COMPENSATION, and TAKING OF LAND.

ARBITRATION. .

It is not within the province of referees to award costs, unless so authorized by the submission. *Porter* v. *Buckfield Railroad Co*............................. 185

The part of an award by which costs are allowed without authority, may be set aside, without invalidating the residue of the award. *Ibid*................... 185

622

INDEX:

ARBITRATION (*Continued*).

The report of a case from *Nisi Prius* will be dismissed, though signed by the Judge, if it be found defective in any essential particulars. *Ibid* 185

See CONTRACT.

ASSESSMENT OF DAMAGES.

See APPRAISEMENT OF DAMAGES.

ASSUMPSIT.

Quære. Whether it can be maintained against a company to recover compensation for injuries resulting from the exercise of statute powers 171

Venue of action 140

BRIDGES.

Erection of, over highways 377

See HIGHWAYS.

BY-LAWS.

Power of the company to make 393

BAILMENT.

Railway companies are simple bailees of goods delivered to them for transportation, after they arrive at the place of destination and are placed in the company's warehouse 403

BOUNDARIES OF LAND.

Where, in Massachusetts, a cove, inlet, or estuary, is so irregular and various in outline, and so traversed by crooked and meandering creeks and channels, from which the sea does not ebb, that, in dividing the flats therein among the conterminous proprietors, it is impossible to apply any of the rules, which have been applied in other cases; the most that can be done is, to take the colony ordinance of 1641, and apply it according to its true spirit, and by as near an approximation as practicable to the rules which have been judicially established to lay down such a line of division, as to give to each riparian proprietor his fair and equal share. A natural channel or creek, in which the sea ebbs and flows, and from which the tide does not ebb, is a boundary to a claim of flats in that direction. On the estuary of a river, or arm of the sea, through which there is a channel, the lines of flats will ordinarily run towards such channel, and in the most direct course. The purpose of the colony ordinance of 1641 was not so much to promote the erection of wharves, and to facilitate navigation, as to declare the right of private owners in the soil of the flats, between high and low water. *Walker v. The Boston and Maine Railroad* 462

COMPENSATION.

If the owner of land, with buildings standing thereon, situate near the track of a railroad, but not crossed thereby, sustain any actual damage, capable of being pointed out, described, and appreciated in such estate, in consequence of and as incident to the construction of the railroad, he will be entitled to recover compensation therefor, against the proprietors of the railroad, in the mode provided by the statute. *Parker v. The Boston and Maine Railroad* 547

If, in consequence of the excavation made for a railroad, the water of a well on an estate adjoining but not crossed by the railroad, is drawn off and the well thereby rendered dry and useless, the owner of such estate will be entitled to recover damages therefor, in the same manner as for land, &c., taken for the railroad. *Ibid* 547

The obstruction of a private way, in consequence of the construction of a railroad across the same, is a proper subject for damages. *Ibid* 547

Where, in a petition for damages occasioned by the taking of land, &c., for the

COMPENSATION (*Continued*).

construction of a railroad, several distinct causes of damage are alleged, and a general verdict is returned, if one or more of such causes be not proper subjects of damage, it is not to be presumed, in the absence of any instruction by the sheriff relative to the same, that the jury gave any damages therefor. *Ibid* 547

A railroad corporation is estopped from denying, that a portion of the structure of their road, built at the same time with and as a part of it, by their officers, engineers, and contractors, is authorized by their act of incorporation ; and any person, entitled to recover for damages occasioned by such structure, has a right to assume, that in making the same the corporation acted in pursuance of their charter, and to have his equitable remedy for damages under the statute, instead of treating the officers, engineers, and contractors of the corporation as trespassers. *Ibid* 547

A bridge, with lateral embankments, erected by a railroad corporation for the purpose of raising a highway and carrying it over their road, is as much a part of the structure authorized by their charter, as the railroad itself; and any person injured by the erection of such bridge and embankments, is entitled to recover his damages thereby occasioned, in the manner provided by the statute. *Ibid* ... 547

A claim for damages being made against a railroad corporation, on the ground of the erection by them of a bridge and embankments, as a part of the structure of their road, for the purpose of raising and carrying a highway over the same ; and the respondents objecting to the claim, that they had not taken the requisite preliminary steps, and consequently were not authorized to erect the bridge and embankments ; it was held, that the objection was one which the respondents had no right to make. *Ibid* 547

In order to entitle the abutters on a highway, which has been raised or lowered by a railroad corporation, under the provisions of the statute to recover the damages therefor, to which they may be entitled, if any, it is not necessary that the selectmen of the town should have either authorized or directed such alteration to be made. *Ibid* 547

The damages occasioned by laying out and making a railroad, and which, by Rev. Sts. (of Massachusetts) c. 39, § 56, county commissioners are bound to estimate, include injuries which are done, by a railroad corporation, to buildings near the line of the road, by means of blasting, in a proper manner, a ledge of rocks through which the railroad passes. *Dodge* v. *The County Commissioners of Essex* 336

The charter of the Kennebec and Portland Railroad Company provides a remedy for the land-owner, to recover damage for the location and construction of the track across his land. *Mason* v. *Kennebec and Portland Railroad Co* 162

The remedy, thus provided, is exclusive of the remedy at common law. *Ibid* 162

In the estimate of that damage, is to be included the injury which may be done to the owner by the erection of an embankment upon the site of the road, whereby the communication is destroyed between the parts of the land which lie upon the opposite sides of the track. *Ibid* 162

Where the value of a wharf is impaired by the construction of a railroad across the flats below it, the owner is entitled to recover of the proprietors of the railroad the damages thus sustained by him. *Ashby* v. *Eastern Railroad Co* 356

A, the owner of a wharf, entered into a written agreement, not under seal, with B and C, that certain machinery and fixtures should be erected on the wharf, at their common expense, and that the profits of the business to be carried on there should inure to their common benefit. A railroad was afterwards constructed across the flats below the wharf, and A, B, and C joined in a petition for a jury to assess damages thereby sustained by them, and alleged in their petition that they were the owners of the wharf, &c. *Held,* that if the jury believed, on all the evidence before them, that the petitioners had such an interest in the estate as entitled them to damages, and that they suffered damages

COMPENSATION. (*Continued*).

jointly, then they properly joined in the petition, and were entitled to recover. *Ibid.*.. 356

The provisions of the charter of the Vermont Central Corporation, prescribing a mode for making compensation by appraisal, for injuries to land entered upon by them, may be fairly construed to apply to the property and interest of a turnpike corporation in the land embraced by their road, and in the road itself, as tangible property. *White River Turnpike Co.* v. *The Vermont Central Railroad Co.* 233

An act of the legislature having authorized a railroad corporation to make certain erections for their road between the channels of Charles and Miller's Rivers, in a manner particularly specified in the act ; and such erections having been made accordingly, in the manner specified, whereby the course of the currents of these rivers was changed, and directed towards and upon certain wharves and flats, rendering additional sea-wall and filling necessary to secure the same; it was held, that the damage thereby occasioned to the proprietor was *damnum absque injuria*, for which he was not entitled to recover against the railroad corporation. *The Fitchburg Railroad Co.* v. *The Boston and Maine Railroad*................ 508

The grantor of the tide mill and mill pond, who had reserved the right of boating and rafting through the pond, and of using the same as a depot for lumber, it seems, has no such proprietary interest in the premises, by virtue of such reservation, as to entitle him to become, or to render it necessary that he should be made, a party to a proceeding under Rev. Sts. c. 24, §§ 48, 49, 50, for the recovery of damages occasioned by the laying out and construction of a railroad through the granted premises. *Davidson* v. *The Boston and Maine Railroad*.... 534

The owner of a tide mill, who is also the riparian proprietor of flats, from which the tide wholly ebbs, between his mill and navigable water, has no right, either as against conterminous proprietors or the public, to have his flats kept open and unobstructed, for the free flow and reflow of the tide water, for the use of his mills or for navigation. The adjoining proprietors may build solid structures to the extent of one hundred rods, and thereby obstruct the flow and reflow of the tide, provided they do not wholly cut off the access of other proprietors to their houses and lands ; and if the mill-owner, or other proprietors, suffer damages therefrom, it is *damnum absque injuria*. The public have a right to regulate the use of navigable waters ; and the erection of a bridge, with or without a draw, by the authority of the legislature, is the regulation of a public right, and and not the deprivation of a private right, which can be a ground for damages, or the taking of private property for a public use, which will entitle the owner to compensation. *Ibid.*.. 534

When the location of a railroad is filed, the land over which it passes may then be *primâ facie* considered as taken; and the persons who are owners at that time may claim and recover damages therefor. If any person, when a claim for damages is made, claims damages for the taking of the same land, on the ground of an earlier title, the respondents must allege and prove such title in bar of the previous claim. *Ibid.*.. 534

The owner of a right of flowage, which is injuriously affected by the construction of a railroad, is entitled to damages therefor. *Ibid.*.................... 534

Where flats appurtenant or incident to upland are taken for a railroad, the Commonwealth has no interest therein by way of easement, which requires the damages for taking the same to be assessed in the manner provided by the Rev. Sts. c. 24, §§ 48, 49, 50, where there are several parties having several estates or interests, at the same time, in the land taken. *Walker* v. *The Boston and Maine Railroad.*... 462

An act of the legislature, by which a railroad corporation was established in the usual manner, and with the ordinary powers and privileges of such corporations, authorized the corporation to locate their road, so that the same might pass over certain land, which belonged to and was held by the Commonwealth as a body

COMPENSATION (*Continued*).

politic for a particular purpose, but without any expression in the act of a design, on the part of the legislature, to aid the corporation in their undertak. ing : It was held, that it was not the intention of the legislature, by such act, to grant the land of the Commonwealth, or any easement therein, to the corporation, without compensation; and that if such land of the Commonwealth were taken by the corporation for their road, the Commonwealth might institute proceedings, and prosecute a claim for damages, before the appropriate tribunal, in the same manner as an individual proprietor. *Commonwealth* v. *The Boston and Maine Railroad*... 482

The assessment of damages by commissioners is not a cumulative remedy, but is the substitution of one mode for another, and their decision is final upon the merits, subject only to the right of appeal. *Aldrich* v. *The Cheshire Railroad Co*.. 206

Where the land of one deceased is taken for a railroad, the heir and not the administrator is entitled to the damages for such taking, and to prosecute for the recovery thereof, although the administrator has previously represented the estate to be insolvent, and afterwards obtained a license to sell the intestate's real estate for the payment of debts. *Boyington* v. *Peterborough and Shirley Railroad Co*.. 595

Necessity for fences a ground of compensation............................. 213

See APPRAISEMENT OF DAMAGES.

COMPENSATION, DEPOSIT OF.

The Vermont Central Railroad Company took land in Burlington, under their charter, to which there were conflicting claims, and, upon petition to the chancellor, under the provisions of the statute of 1846, [Comp. St. 196,] were ordered to deposit in the Farmers' and Mechanics' Bank the amount of the land damages, as appraised by the commissioners, subject to the future order of the chancellor ; and, upon petition subsequently preferred by one who claimed to be entitled to the money so deposited, the chancellor, upon notice given to the company, no adverse claimants of the fund appearing, ordered the money so deposited to be paid to the petitioner. And it was held, that the statute contemplated, that the proceedings before the chancellor, in reference to the deposite of the money, should be summary and final ; and that, upon the petition being preferred by the claimant, the company had no interest in the question, and could not appeal from the order of the chancellor. *Haswell* v. *The Vermont Central Railroad Co*... 248

COMMON-CARRIERS.

Ground of their extreme liability... 346

The common-law liability of a carrier, may be restricted by a notice from him, brought home to the knowledge of the customer, as to the extent of the liability to be borne by the carrier. *Sager* v. *Portsmouth, &c., Railroad Co*............ 171

But no *notice* or *contract* can exonorate a common-carrier from liability for damage, occasioned by his *negligence* or *misconduct*. *Ibid*........................ 171

The want of suitable vehicles, in which to transport articles, is negligence on the part of a carrier. *Ibid*... 171

A common-carrier will be liable for damage to goods, resulting from disobedience of the directions given by the owner and assented to by the carrier, respecting the mode of conveyance. *Ibid*.. 171

If, with a *bailee* employed to carry goods for him, the owner stipulate to take upon himself the risk of "all damages *that may happen*" to the goods in the course of transportation, such stipulation will not exonerate the bailee from liability for damage to the goods, resulting from his *negligence* or *misconduct*. *Ibid*........ 171

COMMON-CARRIERS (*Continued*).

The damages, which, within the meaning of that stipulation, *might happen* to the goods, would not include such as resulted from *negligence* or *misconduct*. *Ibid*. . . 171

Such stipulation, however, would cast upon the owner, the burden of proving that the damage was *so* occasioned. *Ibid*. 171

Liability in carrying live stock. . . . . 171 – 181

In England, may exempt themselves from all liability in the transport of cattle by special agreement. 181

Not liable where there is not a complete delivery. 183

Railway company not bound to become carriers. 183

Proprietors of a railroad, who transport goods over their road, and deposit them in their warehouse without charge, until the owner or consignee has a reasonable time to take them away, are not liable, as common-carriers, for the loss of the goods from the warehouse, but are liable, as depositors, only for want of ordinary care. *Thomas* v. *Boston and Providence Railroad Co*. 403

If A, for whom goods are transported by a railroad company, authorizes B to receive the delivery thereof, and to do all acts incident to the delivery and transportation thereof to A and B, instead of receiving the goods at the usual place of delivery, requests the agent of the company to permit the car, which contains the goods, to be hauled to a near depot of another railroad company, and such agent assents thereto, and assists B in hauling the car to such depot, and B there requests and obtains leave of that company to use its machinery to remove the goods from the car; then the company that transported the goods is not answerable for the want of care or skill in the person employed in so removing the goods from the car, nor for the want of strength in the machinery used for the removal of them, and cannot be charged with any loss that may happen in the course of such delivery to A. *Lewis* v. *The Western Railroad Co*. 610

Railway companies are carriers of passengers. 394

As such have a right to make needful rules and regulations. 394

CONSIDERATION.

The interest a subscriber for stock acquires in the company is a sufficient consideration for a promissory note given for an instalment. 229

See CONTRACT.

CONSOLIDATION OF COMPANIES.

Agreement for creating the Philadelphia and Wilmington Railroad Company. . . . 27

How far the new company takes upon itself the contracts and duties of the old. . . 96

CONSTITUTIONAL LAW.

An action to recover damage for destroying the communication of a land-owner with different parts of his farm, either by taking the strip of land for the site of the road, or by the erection thereon of such an embankment, proceeds, not upon the ground that the land for the road was illegally taken, but upon the ground that the power, granted by the charter, had been transcended or abused. It therefore presents no basis for a decision as to the constitutionality of that power. *Mason* v. *Kennebec and Portland Railroad Co*. 162

CONSTRUCTION OF CONTRACTS.

See CONTRACTS.

CONSTRUCTION OF ROAD.

A granted to the Western Railroad Corporation full and free license and authority to locate, construct, repair, and forever maintain and use a railroad, upon, through, and over his land, and to take his land therefor, to the extent

CONSTRUCTION OF ROAD (*Continued*).

authorized by their charter: The land was so situated that the embankment of the railroad would cause water to accumulate on the upper side thereof, and it became necessary to provide for the passage of water to the lower side : The corporation, therefore, made culverts, in suitable places, and in a convenient manner; but the situation of the land was such that it was necessary to con- nect ditches with the culverts, and extend the ditches, beyond the line of the location of the railroad, into the land of A, in order to prevent the water from setting back so as materially to injure the railroad or damage the land of A. *Held*, that the corporation were authorized by said license so to make said culverts and ditches, under the rule of law that a grant of a thing in- cludes the means necessary to attain it. *Held, also*, that the corporation were authorized, by said license, to deepen and widen in the land of A, beyond the line of the location of the railroad, the bed of a mountain stream, over which the railroad was laid out, and constructed, to facilitate the discharge of the waters of the stream; such deepening and widening being necessary to secure the rail- road from damage, or to prevent the land of A from being broken and washed away. *It seems, also*, that the corporation had authority to do the aforesaid acts, under their charter and the Rev. Sts. c. 39. *Babcock* v. *The Western Rail- road Co*.. 399

CONSTRUCTION OF STATUTES.
A charter of a company a contract.. 20

How an act amalgamating two companies and providing that the new company shall have all the rights and privileges of the old one is to be construed....... 38

In what sense a charter is a contract..................................... 19

In what sense the word " forfeiture" is to be construed in a law, and how in a con- tract.. 19

Relating to the taxation of railways...................................... 37

Grant to public companies to be construed strictly........................ 58

This rule not to be applied till others fail............................... 63

Where general rights are declared, or remedies given, by law, the Commonwealth is included therein, though not named. *Commonwealth* v. *The Boston and Maine Railroad*.. 482

Courts cannot supply defects in a statute................................. 139

Implied right of locating a road... 238

As to the right to compensation.. 239

Company may take land without first making compensation................... 154

Whether such statute is constitutional, *quære*........................... 156

Meaning of the word " court"... 223

CONSTRUCTION OF TERMS.
Meaning of " gross negligence "... 177 – 182

Meaning of the word "between" in the location of a railway................. 63

How the term " forfeiture" in a contract differs in construction from the same term in a law... 19

CONTRACT.
In this particular case a covenant to finish the work by a certain day, on the one part, and a covenant to pay monthly on the other part, were distinct and inde- pendent covenants. And a right in the company to annul the contract at any time, did not include a right to forfeit the earnings of the other party, for work done prior to the time when the contract was annulled. *Philadelphia, Wilming- ton, &c., Railroad Co*. v. *Howard*.. 70

CONTRACT (*Continued*).

A covenant to do the work according to a certain schedule, which schedule mentioned that it was to be done according to the directions of the engineer, bound the company to pay for the work, which was executed according to such directions, although a profile was departed from which was made out before the contract was entered into. *Ibid* 70

So, also, where the contract was, to place the waste earth where ordered by the engineer, it was the duty of the engineer to provide a convenient place; and if he failed to do so, the other party was entitled to damages. *Ibid* 70

Where the contract authorized the company to retain fifteen per cent. of the earnings of the contractor, this was by way of indemnity, and not forfeiture; and they were bound to pay it over, unless the jury should be satisfied that the company had sustained an equivalent amount of damage by the default, negligence, or misconduct of the contractor. *Ibid* 70

Where, in the progress of the work, the contractor was stopped by an injunction issued by a court of chancery, he was not entitled to recover damages for the delay occasioned by it, unless the jury should find that the company did not use reasonable diligence to obtain a dissolution of the injunction. *Ibid* 70

If the company annulled the contract merely for the purpose of having the work done cheaper, or for the purpose of oppressing and injuring the contractor, he was entitled to recover damages for any loss of profit he might have sustained; and of the reasons which influenced the company, the jury were to be the judges. *Ibid* 70

The defendant having entered into an agreement to sell the plaintiffs, a railroad corporation, "the land they take on the northerly side of the M. turnpike, adjoining T's land, at twenty cents per square foot, for each and every foot so taken by said company," and the plaintiffs having brought a bill in equity for a specific performance; it was held, that the agreement was not for a sale of the land generally, or of such part of it as the plaintiffs might elect, or of such as they should accept the offer of; but for the sale of such a part of the land described as the plaintiffs might take, in the exercise of the authority conferred on them by law to take land for their road. *Boston and Maine Railroad* v. *Babcock* 561

An agreement having been made between the Commonwealth and the Charlestown Branch Railroad Company, providing, amongst other things, that upon certain terms and conditions therein mentioned, the Commonwealth would authorize such corporation to institute proceedings, in the name of the Commonwealth, against the Boston and Maine Railroad, for the purpose of recovering all claims which the Commonwealth might have against the latter, for laying out and constructing their road over land of the Commonwealth, the money receivable for such damages to be paid to the treasurer of the Commonwealth, and by him retained until the performance of the Charlestown Branch Railroad Company of the covenants contained in the said agreement, and on their part to be performed; and the Commonwealth having given such authority, and proceedings having been instituted accordingly in the name of the Commonwealth, by the Charlestown Branch Railroad Company against the Boston and Maine Railroad, for the recovery of such damages: It was held, that the contract was not illegal; that the case was one in which the Commonwealth was a party and interested; and that the damages were not limited to the amount to which the Commonwealth was entitled at the time of the making of the agreement, but were recoverable as of the time of the filing of the location of the railroad. *Commonwealth* v. *The Boston and Maine Railroad* 482

The defendants, a railroad corporation, agreed with the plaintiff, that they would pay him four shillings per rod for constructing the fence upon each side of their railroad through the land of the plaintiff, according to a specified plan. Subsequently the plaintiff having appealed from the decision of the commissioners assessing the land damages for the crossing of his land by the railroad, commis-

CONTRACT (*Continued*).

sioners were appointed by the county court, who, after appraising the damages to the land, reported, that an additional sum of one dollar per rod should be allowed to the plaintiff, for the purpose of building and keeping in repair such suitable fences on the line of the road over his land,. as he might elect, unless such fences were to be built and maintained by the defendants. Upon this re. port being returned, the plaintiff took judgment for the full amount of the appraisal, including the allowance for fences, and the amount of the judgment was paid by the defendants. *Held*, that the judgment upon the report must be regarded as a merger of the previous contract made by the parties for the construction of the fence. *Curtis* v. *Vermont Central Railroad Co* 258

And the plaintiff having proceeded, subsequent to the rendition of the judgment, and constructed the fence according to the contract, it was held, that, he was not entitled to recover of the defendants the difference between the contract price and the actual value of the fence to him for farming purposes, although he proved, that the fence so constructed by him under the contract was not such as he should have built for himself upon the line of the road through his farm, for his farming purposes, but that he would have built different fence, which would have been no more expensive, and would have been more durable and worth at least thirty cents a rod more than the fence constructed by him under the contract. *Ibid*. 258

The plaintiffs had contracted to build for the defendants certain sections of their railroad, at agreed prices. While the work was progressing, the defendants, with a view to some change in their location, desired a suspension of the work. Thereupon the contract was modified by the parties. For an agreed compensation, the work was to cease, till the further order of the defendants, and if the work should not be resumed within two years, the defendants were to pay the plaintiffs $750; if resumed within that time, the former contract was to apply to a residue part only of the said road sections ; and upon such resumption, the plaintiffs were, upon notice, to proceed with the work upon said residue sections, in the manner and at rates of price originally agreed. In the modified contract, a quantity of stones for the road, which the plaintiffs had procured, were purchased by the defendants, upon a stipulation that, if such resumption should take place, the stones should be repurchased by the plaintiffs. The location of the road having been altered, as to some of its sections, the defendants, within the two years, recommenced operating upon some of its unchanged parts. They gave notice to the plaintiffs of their intention, but employed another company to do the work. *Held*, that, as the work was resumed within the two years, the plaintiffs were not entitled to recover the $750. *Held*, also, that the plaintiffs were entitled to do the work, when resumed, and to recover damages for not being called upon and employed to do it. *Fowler* v. *Kennebec and Portland Railroad Co* 157

The construction of a contract by referees, appointed under a submission of common law to *settle the dispute in relation to that construction*, is not reëxaminable in this court. *Porter* v. *Buckfield Railroad Co* 185

Thus the plaintiffs contracted with the defendants to construct for them a railroad; the defendants reserved the right to alter the line or the gradients of the road, without the allowance of any extreme compensation, if the engineer should judge such alterations necessary or expedient; alterations were accordingly made, involving a large increase of expense, for that increase of expense the referees allowed compensation to the contractors ; *Held*, by the court, that the allowance of that compensation did not transcend the authority of the referees. *Ibid*. 185

Thus. again ; the defendants in the contract reserved the right to substitute *piling* instead of *embankment*, on a specified part of the road ; and the substitution was made, creating to the contractors an increased expense, for which the referees

53 *

CONTRACT (*Continued*).

allowed a compensation ; *Held*, that that allowance did not transcend the authority of the referees. *Ibid* 185

The submission stipulated, that the referees should take the contract, *as the basis of their action.* The contract required, that a fixed proportion of the cost of the road should be paid to the contractors, in the stock of the company. The referees, having ascertained the amount of that proportion, awarded that certificates for the same should be issued to the contractors ; *Held*, by the court, that this part of their award did not transcend their authority. *Ibid* 185

The certificates of the stock were demanded, but were not furnished. *Held*, the measure of damage is, not their *par value*, but their *marketable value*. *Ibid* 185

Where an agreement by deed is made with a corporation, and is delivered to an agent of the corporation, who was duly authorized to negotiate it, it is delivered to the corporation, and his acceptance thereof is the acceptance of the corporation. *The Western Railroad Co.* v. *Babcock* 365

In order to prevent a decree for specific performance of a contract, on the ground of inadequacy of consideration, the inadequacy must be so gross, and the proof of it so clear, as to lead to a reasonable conclusion of fraud or mistake. *Ibid* 365

Charter of a company a contract with the government 20

Law impairing the obligation of .... 56 – 326

Agreement to pay by instalments, how construed 101

Right of company to declare a contract at an end 103

Obliged to pay for labor already performed 104

Estimates of an engineer, when binding 104

Mutual and dependent covenants 102

Right of a contractor to extra pay for increased labor 105

When put an end to by a company reserved fund not wholly forfeited 104

When reserved fund is absolutely forfeited, with tools, &c 107

No obligation implied in a contract for service that the master shall indemnify a servant for injuries caused by a fellow servant 345

Whether there is any implied warranty in such case, *quære* 351

CORPORATION.

When it comes into existence so as to be capable of taking a promise 226

Is for some purposes treated as a citizen 143

COSTS.

There is no provision of law, by which the Atlantic and St. Lawrence Railroad Company, can be compelled, by an order of the County Commissioners, to pay for the " services of the commissioners and for their expenses," incurred while they were employed on petitions presented by the company to have the damages assessed, sustained by persons, by the location of that railroad over their lands. *Atlantic and St. Lawrence Railroad Co.* v. *The Cumberland County Commissioners* 133

Power of arbitrators to award costs 194

Where the Court of Common Pleas (in Massachusetts) set aside a verdict of a jury, summoned to reassess damages for land taken for a railroad, they have no authority to award costs to the party objecting to the verdict. *Connecticut River Railroad Co.* v. *Clapp* 450

Where the estimate of a petitioner's damages (in Massachusetts) occasioned by the construction of a railroad, as made by the county commissioners, is revised by

COSTS (*Continued*).

..a jury, on the application of the respondents, and the amount reduced; and the verdict of a jury, on an appeal from the adjudiction of the Court of Common Pleas accepting the same, is established by the Supreme Court of Massachusetts; neither party is liable to the other for the costs of the proceedings before the sheriff and jury, but the petitioner is entitled to recover against the respondents the taxable costs of the appeal. *Commonwealth* v. *Boston and Maine Railroad* 482

CROSSING HIGHWAYS.

See Highways.

CULVERTS.

Right to construct.. 399

DAMAGES.

Measure for breach of contract............................... : 194

Where a party who has agreed to convey land, for a certain sum, to a railroad corporation for the site of a road, refuses to perform his agreement, and obtains an assessment, according to law, of his damages caused by the laying out of the road over his land, the measure of the damages to which he is liable for breach of his agreement, is the excess of the sum assessed at law over the sum for which he agreed to convey the land. *The Western Railroad Co.* v. *Babcock*. 365

None can be recovered by a wife or father for the death of a husband or child.... 442

Principles on which damages are given for the death of a party under the English statutes... 446

No damages for personal suffering... 447

Payment of when road is not built... 47

Recovery back of money paid... 47

County Commissioners in Maine may estimate and award damages............. 138

May require security of company for payment............................. 138

What should be included in estimating.................................... 164

Right of a party to an appraisement by jury.............................. 220

DAMAGES FOR TAKING LAND.

See Compensation.

DEED.

A deed conveying a wharf, which extends from the upland below high-water mark, and bounding on an arm of the sea in which the tide ebbs and flows, passes the flats as parcel, and also as appurtenant to the wharf. *Ashby* v. *The Eastern Railroad Co.*.. 356

A deed, which is absolute in its terms, and without conditions or reservations, will have the effect to convey the land described in it, with all the privileges of drawing water from other portions of the grantor's land, which were then in use, as appurtenant to the land. And if water is conveyed in an aqueduct from a spring upon another portion of the grantor's land to the land conveyed, and there used at the time of the conveyance, any diversion of the water by the grantor, although upon that portion of his land not conveyed by the deed, will be a disturbance of the right of the grantee, for which an action may be sustained. The grantor cannot be allowed to say, in defence, that the grantee did not desire to use the water, or that he has suffered no detriment. *Vermont Central Railroad Co.* v. *Hills*... 262

The defendant was the owner and occupant of a messuage, to which water was conducted, for use, by an aqueduct, from a spring upon another portion of his land, and the Vermont Central Railroad Company having located their rail-

632   INDEX.

DEED (*Continued*).

road across the same, the commissioners were called upon to appraise the damages thereby occasioned by the defendant. At the hearing before the commissioners, the defendant stated, that he should use the water for the purpose of supplying a new house, which he contemplated erecting, and that the commissioners need not take the water into the account in assessing the damages. The president and engineer of the company were present, and heard this statement, and made no claim to the use of the water; and the water was not taken into consideration by the commissioners, in assessing the damages. The defendant received from the company the amount of damages assessed by the commissioners, and executed to the company an absolute deed of the premises, without condition or reservation. And it was held, that the right to use the water upon the premises passed by the deed. *Ibid* 262

EMINENT DOMAIN.

A franchise may be taken in the exercise of the power of 60

It is now settled law, that there is no implied contract by the State in a charter of a turnpike or other private corporation, that their property, or even their franchise, shall be exempt from the common liability of the property of individuals to be taken for the public use; that it may be taken, on proper compensation being made; that a railroad is an improved highway, and that property, taken for its use by authority of the legislature, is property taken for the public use, as much as if taken for any other highway; and that the legislature may delegate its power to a railroad corporation, to take private property for public use in the construction of their railroad, as well as to a turnpike corporation to take the like property for the public use in the construction of a turnpike road. *White River Turnpike Co. v. The Vermont Central Railroad Co.* 233

It is also settled, that where there has been a legislative grant to a private corporation to erect a bridge, a turnpike, or other public convenience, which is not in its terms exclusive, there is no constitutional obligation on the legislature, not to grant to a second corporation the right to erect another bridge, or turnpike, for a similar purpose, to be constructed so near the former, as greatly to impair, or even to destroy, the value of the former, — and this without making compensation to the first corporation for the consequential injury. *Ibid* 233

But so far as the real estate of such private corporation, or their interest in real estate, is concerned, they are entitled to the same constitutional protection that an individual would be. The property of either may be taken for public use by authority of the legislature, if compensation be made therefor, but not otherwise. *Ibid* 233

An act of the legislature, in the exercise of the right of eminent domain, appropriating to public use, on payment of a full equivalent, property or rights in the nature of property granted by the State to individuals, is not a law impairing the obligation of contracts, within the meaning of the Constitution of the United States. *Boston Water Power Co. v. Boston and Worcester Railroad Co.* 298

The act empowered the railroad corporation to locate and construct a railroad "in or near the city of Boston and thence to any part of the town of Worcester, in such manner and form as they should deem expedient." It was *held*, that the act sufficiently declared the public necessity and convenience of the railroad and fixed the general *termini*, and that the delegations to the corporation, of the power to fix the precise *termini* and the intermediate course between them, and thus to take private property for public use, did not render the act unconstitutional and invalid. *Ibid* 298

EVIDENCE.

When a defendant is sued as a stockholder in a railroad corporation for the sum remaining due on an assessment upon his shares, after they are sold for non-

EVIDENCE (*Continued*).

payment of the assessment, it is competent and sufficient, for the purpose of showing him to be such stockholder, and liable for the assessment, to give evidence that he signed a subscription paper for shares, before the corporation was organized ; that he attended the meeting of the stockholders for the organization of the corporation, and that he wrote and distributed votes, and himself voted, for directors. *Lexington and West Cambridge Railroad Co.* v. *Chandler*... 422

On the trial of a petition before a sheriff's jury, for an assessment of damages for land taken for a railroad, evidence is not admissible to show the price paid by the respondents, for land adjoining the land in question, under an award of arbitrators mutually agreed upon to estimate the same. *White* v. *The Fitchburg Railroad Co.*... 594

On the hearing, before a jury summoned to assess damages caused to A by the laying out of a railroad over his land, he may give evidence of the price paid by the railroad company for the adjoining land of B purchased by them : But an owner of adjoining land cannot legally be permitted to state to the jury what, in his judgment is the value of that land, though he be a farmer who has occasionally bought and sold land ; and if he be permitted to make such a statement, the verdict of the jury will be set aside, although they were instructed, that opinions, except of experts, were not evidence, and that the facts and reasons on which any opinion or judgment was formed, were the evidence on which they must form their opinion. *Wyman* v. *Lexington and West Cambridge Railroad Co.*... 426

A witness, who had been for ten years secretary of an insurance company, and as such had been in the practice of examining buildings, with reference to insurance thereof, and who had also, as county commissioner, frequently estimated damages caused to estates by the laying out of highways and railroads, was held to have been rightly permitted, on a hearing before a jury impanelled to appraise damages sustained by a party by the laying out of a railroad over his land and near to his buildings, to give his opinion that the passage of locomotive engines, within one hundred feet of a building, would diminish the rent and increase the rate of insurance thereof against fire : *Held*, also, that he was rightly permitted to testify that the directors of the insurance company, of which he was secretary, upon his consulting them as to an application for insurance on a building in the vicinity of the buildings of the party then before the jury, had declined to take the risk at any rate. *Webber* v. *The Eastern Railroad Co.*...... 331

An estimate, not on oath, of damages that would be sustained by a party over whose land a railroad was afterwards laid out, made by a committee of a town, while a petition of the town for a change of the route of the railroad was before the legislature, and merely stating those damages as the least the party would take, is not admissible in evidence to a jury impanelled to appraise damages caused by laying out the railroad over the land, although such estimate was made at the request of an agent of the railroad company. *Ibid.*......... 331

On a proceeding before a sheriff's jury, instituted by the Fitchburg Railroad Company for the recovery of damages occasioned by the laying out and construction of the Boston and Maine Railroad over the land, wharves, and flats of the former, the respondents introduced a letter signed by the president of the petitioners, and addressed to the president of the respondents, dated the 10th of August, 1844, in the following terms : " The committee of the directors of the F. R. Co. have considered your application for a part of the flats of this company in C. for your corporation, and have come to the conclusion, that they are not prepared to dispose of any of said flats, or at this time to name any price for what the law allows you to take for your road, but that you can go on, and lay the sea wall as you propose, and fill up a sufficient width for the track, and settle all damages with Mr. James Gould, at your expense ; and the whole matter shall be settled on equitable terms hereafter." P. S. " It is to be under-

EVIDENCE (*Continued*).
stood that the wall and filling up is to be considered as above. And it was in evidence, that the respondents had subsequently built a road and wall, as alluded to in the letter; it was held, that such letter and subsequent proceeding did not prove any contract or agreement between the parties, relative to the subject thereof. *The Fitchburg Railroad Co.* v. *The Boston and Maine Railroad*........ 508

The assistant engineer upon a railroad, having charge of the construction of a section of the road, becoming dissatisfied with the contractor, dismissed him and assumed the work himself, agreeing with the workmen to see them paid. *Held*, that his subsequent declarations could not be admitted to charge the company for supplies furnished to the contractors. The declarations of an agent respecting a transaction, which are not made till after it is past, are not admissible in evidence against his principal. *Stiles* v. *The Western Railroad Co*............ 397

B contracted with a railroad corporation to construct a section of the road, and afterwards underlet the section to C, D, and E jointly, and not jointly and severally, and then C underlet it to D and E, who proceeded in the work for a short time, and then stopped: The corporation then assumed the work and finished it, and were sued by S for articles furnished, under a contract with C and D, for the completion of the work, and used by the corporation: S released B and C from all liability for the articles, and introduced the testimony of D in support of the claim. *Held*, that D was a competent witness. *Stiles* v. *The Western Railroad Co*..... 604

Though a leading interrogatory to a deponent is objected to when it is filed, yet if the answer thereto shows that he was not led by it, or if the answer relate to matter proved *aliunde*, respecting which the party, who objects to the interrogatory, has given evidence, the interrogatory and answer may be read to the jury, on the return of the deposition. *Ibid*.............................. 604

Where the proprietor of a wharf, which is bounded on an arm of the sea, claims the flats to the channel, viz., to low-water mark, the burden of proof is on him to show that there was an original natural channel, from which the sea did not ebb at low water, and that such channel, or low-water mark, was so far below his wharf as to include the flats which he claims. *Ashby* v. *Eastern Railroad Co*.... 356

A deed, absolute in its terms, cannot be controlled by oral evidence of conversation between the parties, previous to its execution. *Vermont Central Railroad Co.* v. *Hills*.. 262

Where the question was, whether or not the paper declared upon bore the corporate seal of the defendants, (an incorporated company,) evidence was admissible to show that, in a former suit, the defendants had treated and relied upon the instrument as one bearing the corporate seal. And it was admissible, although the former suit was not between the same parties; and although the former suit was against one of three corporations, which had afterwards become merged into one, which one was the present defendant. The admission of the paper as evidence only left the question to the jury. The burden of proof still remained upon the plaintiff. *Philadelphia, Wilmington, &c. Railroad Co.* v. *Howard*...... 70

The evidence of the president of the company, to show that there was an understanding between himself and the plaintiff, that another person should also sign the paper before it became obligatory, was not admissible, because the understanding alluded to did not refer to the time when the corporate seal was affixed, but to some prior time. *Ibid*....... 70

In order to show that the paper in question bore the seal of the corporation, it was admissible to read in evidence the deposition of the deceased officer of the corporation, who had affixed the seal, and which deposition had been taken by the defendants in the former suit. *Ibid*.................................... 70

If the defendants had relied upon the paper in question to defeat the plaintiff in a

EVIDENCE (*Continued*).

former suit, they are estopped from denying its validity in this suit. It was not necessary to plead the estoppel, because the state of the pleadings would not have justified such a plea. *Ibid.* 70

Burden of proof in an action for negligence 593

In an action upon the case against a railroad corporation, to recover damages for the non-delivery of goods intrusted to the defendants for transportation, and in an action of trover to recover the value of such goods, a servant of the defendants employed by them to load and unload cars, and deliver freight, at the depot where the goods arrived, is a competent witness for the defendants, to prove that all the goods were delivered, at such a depot, to the plaintiff or his agents. *Draper v. The Worcester and Norwich Railroad Co* 607

It is not incumbent upon the plaintiff, in an action for negligence, to prove, in opening his case, the customary and usual conduct and practice in the management of locomotive engines and trains on railroads under similar circumstances; but if the defendants desire the benefit of the rules of engineering, under such circumstances, for their exculpation, they may show the custom, and if not unreasonable, — of which the jury must judge, — it will avail them. *Quimby v. The Vermont Central Railroad Co* 251

In the trial of an action for an assault and battery, brought against the superintendent of a railroad depot for expelling the plaintiff from the depot, for a supposed violation of one of the regulations established by the railroad corporation, the defendant cannot give in evidence former violations by the plaintiff of other regulations established by the corporation. *Hall v. Power* 410

Cattle going at large are to be presumed to be unlawfully so 144

In an action for negligence, the plaintiff must prove the negligence of the defendant and ordinary care on his own part 146

The fact, that the proprietors of a railroad have erected fences along their road, against the land of an individual is not evidence of an obligation on their part to do so. *Morss v. Boston and Maine Railroad* 454

EXPIRATION OF POWERS.

After the time has expired, within which a railroad company were, by their charter, to complete their road, they have no authority to take additional lands for the extension of their road, except by consent of the owner. *Peavey v. The Calais Railroad Co* 147

How the powers of a company may be determined 150

Effect of the expiration of the two limited for taking land upon the rights of the the company 150

Company may be compelled to take land although the time will expire before the proceedings are completed 150

Power to take land is exhausted by being once exercised 151

FENCES.

Company not bound to maintain against unclosed land 144

Not liable for injury to cattle straying upon road through want of such fence 144

Company not obliged to fence and provide cattle-guards in the streets of villages. 213

Company may be obliged to maintain fences although the statute does not in express terms require it 216

Where county commissioners, in assessing damages for land taken for a railroad before the Act of 1841, c. 125, was passed, awarded a sum of money to be paid to the complainant, and also provided that the proprietors of the road should make and maintain certain fences for his benefit, and such complainant appealed

FENCES (*Continued*).

from the award of the commissioners to a jury, who assessed damages in his favor, but made no order in their verdict as to the fences, it was held, that the proprietors of the road were under no legal obligation to make and maintain fences, agreeably to the award of the commissioners. *Morss* v. *The Boston and Maine Railroad*.. 454

The fact, that the proprietors of a railroad have erected fences along the line of their road, against the land of a particular individual, is not of itself evidence of any obligation on the part of the proprietors to make or maintain fences for the benefit of such person. *Ibid*... 454

By the Rev. Stat. (of New Hampshire) ch. 142, § 6, railroad corporations are not bound to make or keep fences, except against the land of persons adjoining the railroad, nor are they bound to keep cattle-guards. *Towns* v. *Cheshire Railroad Co*.. 210

At common law land-owner not compelled to fence...... 212

Where there are no statute regulations railway companies come under the rule of the common law.. 212

In New York, may be compelled to maintain half the fence.................... 213

At common law the owners of adjoining lands are under no obligations to maintain division fences. But by the statute of New Hampshire they are bound, if the lands are improved, to maintain the partition fence equally. *Dean* v. *The Sullivan Railroad Co*... 214

Railroad Companies, where they own their own track, are subject to the same liabilities as other owners. But where they do not own the track, and have merely a right of way, neither the companies or the land-owners are bound to fence the road. *Ibid*.. 214

But the statute of New Hampshire which provides, that, if a railroad company shall neglect to keep a suitable fence, the adjoining land-owner may, after notice to the company, make or repair the fence, and recover double the amount necessarily expended in so doing, imposes upon the company the duty to maintain fences in all cases, except where the land-owner has been paid for assuming it. And a party who has suffered special injury from the neglect of a company to maintain proper fences may recover damages for such injury in an action on the case. *Ibid*.. 214

The charter of the Vermont Central Railroad Company provides, that the company, upon complying with the conditions upon which they may take land for the use of their road, shall be " *seized and possessed of the land*." This does not make them owners of the fee, but gives them a right of way merely. Hence, although the charter makes no provision in reference to the obligation to maintain fences upon the line of the road, the general law of the State, in reference to the obligation of adjoining land-owners to maintain the division fences between them does not apply, but the obligation to maintain the fences rests primarily upon the company, and until they have either built the fences or paid the land-owner for doing it, a sufficient length of time to enable him to do it, the mere fact, that cattle get upon the road from the land adjoining is no ground for imputing negligence to the owners of the cattle. *Quimby* v. *The Vermont Central Railroad Co*.. 251

A land-owner may remove the fences of a railway company to cross road when company neglect to provide crossing..................................... 168

FIRES.

The Statute of 1840, c. 85, (of Massachusetts,) making the proprietors of railroads responsible for injuries by fire, communicated from their locomotive engines, applies to railroads established before as well as since its passage; and extends as well to estates, a part of which is conveyed by the owner, as to those

INDEX. 637

FIRES (*Continued*).

of which a part is taken by authority, of law, for the purposes of a railroad. *Lyman* v. *The Boston aud Worcester Railroad Co* 581

A shop, adjoining a railroad track, was destroyed by fire communicated by a locomotive engine of a railroad corporation; and while the shop was burning, the wind wafted sparks from it, across a street sixty feet, upon a house, and set it on fire, whereby it was injured. *Held*, that the owner of the house was entitled to recover of the railroad corporation the damages caused by the fire, under St. 1840, c. 85, § 1, which provides, that when any injury is done to a building of any person "by fire, communicated" by a locomotive engine of a railroad corporation, the said corporation shall be responsible in damages, to the person so injured. *Hart* v. *The Western Railroad Co* 414

FLATS.

Damages for when taken by railway company 356

FRANCHISE.

The legislature of Virginia incorporated the stockholders of the Richmond, Fredericksburg, and Potomac Railroad Company, and in the charter pledged itself not to allow any other railroad to be constructed between those places, or any portion of that distance; the probable effect would be to diminish the number of passengers travelling between the one city and the other upon the railroad authorized by that act, or to compel the said company, in order to retain such passengers, to reduce the passage-money. Afterwards the legislature incorporated the Louisa Railroad Company, whose road came from the West and struck the first-named Company's track nearly at right angles, at some distance from Richmond; and the legislature authorized the Louisa Railroad Company to cross the track of the other, and continue their road to Richmond. In this latter grant, the obligation of the contract with the first company is not impaired within the meaning of the Constitution of the United States. In the first charter, there was an implied reservation of the power to incorporate companies to transport other articles than passengers; and if the Louisa Railroad Company should infringe upon the rights of the Richmond Company, there would be a remedy at law, but the apprehension of it will not justify an injunction to prevent them from building their road. Nor is the obligation of the contract impaired by crossing the road. A franchise may be condemned in the same manner as individual property. *The Richmond, Fredericksburg, &c., Railroad Co.* v. *The Louisa Railroad Co* 48

Nature of the interest which a company has in its road 352

Has not the absolute property or power of disposal 352

The franchise of a corporation may be taken for public uses, like the property of individuals 237

Where there has been a legislative grant to a private corporation of a right to erect a work for public convenience, which is not in its terms exclusive, there is no constitutional obligation on the legislature not to make a similar grant to another corporation so near as to impair the value of the former 237

Interest of a company in the land of their road 256

The plaintiffs in a bill in equity praying for an injunction, allege that a corporation was authorized by its act of incorporation, to build a dam over an arm of the sea, (the shores of which were owned by individuals,) and from this main dam to certain upland above it to run a cross dam, so as to make on one side of the cross dam a full basin, and on the other an empty or receiving basin, and to cut raceways from the full basin to the receiving basin, and to use, sell, or lease the water power thus created; that the corporation erected the dams and created thereby a water power sufficient to turn twenty pairs of common millstones, and performed all the duties required of them by the legislature, and

VOL. I.— AM. R. CA.   54

FRANCHISE (*Continued*).

thereby ·became entitled to certain exclusive privileges; that the corporation, with the assent of the legislature, transferred all the water power and all their rights, privileges, and duties respecting the same, to the plaintiffs; that the plaintiffs thereby became entitled to the exclusive right and privilege of forever using the soil included within the limits of the full basin, for the purpose of flowing the same by the tide waters, and of keeping the soil included within the limits of the receiving basin uncovered by the tide waters, and of using it to receive and carry off the waters flowing from the full basin, and of holding and using all the water power which can be and is created by the dams, without any hinderance, obstruction, or diminution of the capacity of the basins, or of the right to cut raceways in the cross dam; and that the defendants, pretending to act under the authority of certain statutes, threaten to build a railroad through the basins and over the cross dam, and have actually commenced building the same by driving piles in both of the basins, and that the building of it will diminish the capacity of the basins and destroy two mill sites on the cross dam, whereby the water power will be diminished and the franchise of the plaintiffs. abridged. It was *held*, that the right of using the land of others in the basins, for the purpose of creating water power, was a franchise or easement; that such a franchise or easement in the basins was sufficiently set forth in the bill; that the acts of the defendants in filling up portions of the basins for the purpose of making a railroad, were, if illegal, a disturbance of the plaintiffs in the enjoyment of their franchise, for which the remedy at law would be an action on the case; that such an injury is, in strict legal consideration, a nuisance, and therefore is within St. 1827, c. 88, giving this Court jurisdiction in equity in cases of nuisance; that it did not appear on the face of the bill, that the plaintiffs had an adequate and complete remedy at law, and that the matter of complaint was a more fit subject for a bill in equity. *Boston Water Power Co.* v. *The Boston and Worcester Railroad Co*.............. 267

A corporation was empowered by its charter, to build a dam westerly from Boston to Brookline, over an arm of the sea, and from this main dam to run a cross dam southerly to the shore, so as to make on one side of the cross dam a full basin and on the other an empty or receiving basin, and to cut raceways from the full basin to the receiving basin, and to have the use of the land in the basins, derived partly from the Commonwealth and partly from individuals, either by purchase or by taking it for public use, at an appraisement; and to use, sell, or lease the water power thus created; and the corporation built the dams accordingly, and erected mills. It was *held*, that it was within the constitutional power of the legislature to authorize a railroad corporation to construct their road across the basins, making compensation to the water power corporation for the diminution and injury caused thereby to the water power. *Held* also, that the grant of this authority to the railroad corporation could not be considered as annulling or destroying the franchise of the water power corporation; and the right of the water power corporation to use the land constituted an interest and qualified property therein not larger nor of a different nature from that acquired by a grant of land in fee, and did not necessarily withdraw it from a liability to which all lands in the Commonwealth are subject, to be taken for public use. for an equivalent, when in the opinion of the legislature the public exigency requires it; and that the effect of the railroad act was merely to appropriate to another and distinct public use a portion of the land over which the franchise of the water power company was to be used. *Boston Water Power Co.* v. *Boston and Worcester Railroad Co*.. 298

If the whole of a franchise should become necessary for the public use, it *seems* that the right of eminent domain would authorize the legislature to take it, on payment of a full equivalent. *Ibid*.. 298

It was *held*, that the act authorizing the railroad is not liable to the objection that it does not provide for compensation for the damage done to the franchise of the

FRANCHISE (*Continued*).

water power corporation, for the franchise was not taken but only a portion of the land over which it extended, and for all damages occasioned by the taking of land the act makes provision. ' *Ibid* 298

FORFEITURE.

A clause of forfeiture in a law is to be construed differently from a similar clause in an engagement between individuals. A legislature can impose it as a punishment, but individuals can only make it a matter of contract. *Maryland* v. *The Baltimore and Ohio Railroad Co* 1

FORFEITURE OF CONTRACTS.

Right of a company to declare 104

In case of the company putting an end to a contract the contractor only forfeits as much of a reserved fund as will compensate the company for any damage arising from his delay 106

When a reserved fund is absolutely forfeited 106

When tools, materials, &c., may be forfeited 107

FORFEITURE OF STOCK.

When a statute prescribes the terms on which shares in the stock of a railroad company may be sold for the payment of assessments, and the shareholder be held to pay the balance if the shares are not sold for a sum sufficient to pay the assessments, those terms are conditions precedent, and, unless they are strictly complied with, the sale is illegal and the shareholder not chargeable. *Portland, Saco, &c., Railroad Co.* v. *Graham* 598

A statute, incorporating a railroad company, provided that if any subscriber or stockholder should neglect to pay any assessment on his shares, the directors might order the treasurer to sell the shares at public auction, after giving a certain notice, to the highest bidder, and that the same should be transferred to the purchaser, and that such delinquent subscriber, or stockholder, should be held accountable to the company for the balance, if his shares should sell for less than the assessments due thereon, with the interest and costs of sale : G., a subscriber, neglected to pay assessments, and his shares were advertised for sale, by an auctioneer, without any reference, in the advertisement, to the order of the treasurer, and were bid off, at public auction, by T., for a sum less than the amount of the assessments : T. did not pay for the shares ; the sale at auction was abandoned; and the shares were sold to others, at private sale, for the sum bid therefor by T. : The company afterwards brought an action against G., to recover the balance due on the assessments. *Held*, that the action could not be maintained. *Ibid* 598

GRANT.

The Charlestown Wharf Company were authorized by the Act of 1841, c. 35, to extend and maintain their several wharves, lying between Gray's Wharf and the Prison Point Bridge, into the channel, as far as the line established by the act of 1840, c. 35, for the harbor of Boston, with the right and privilege to lay vessels at the sides and ends of such wharves, and to receive wharfage and dockage therefor : At the time of the passing of this act, the Charlestown Wharf Company were the proprietors of several wharves within the limits mentioned in the act, and, for a considerable distance between Warren Bridge and Prison Point Bridge, of a sea-wall built below high-water mark, and filled up behind to high-water mark, and used for the purpose of landing lumber and other things upon, with pier or pile wharves about eighty feet in width, projecting therefrom towards the channel : It was held, that the sea-wall, being an artificial structure, adapted to the purposes for which it was used, was a wharf within the meaning of the act, and that the proprietors were thereby authorized to extend the same

GRANT (*Continued*).
along their whole front to the line of the harbor. *The Fitchburg Railroad Co.*
v. *The Boston and Maine Railroad.*... 508

Where the proprietor of a wharf in the harbor of Boston was authorized by an act
of the legislature to extend the same into the channel to the line of the harbor;
and, before any extension thereof, in pursuance of such act, the legislature incorporated a railroad company, with authority to locate and construct a railroad
across and over the flats between such wharf and the line of the harbor; it was
held, that the act authorizing such extension operated as a grant to the proprietor
of the wharf, and was not a mere license revocable at the pleasure of the legislature, and revoked by the act incorporating the railroad company. *Ibid.*...... 508

HIGHWAYS.
Obligation to erect bridges over.. . 377

Under Rev. St. (of Massachusetts) c. 39, § 67, providing that every railroad corporation may raise or lower any turnpike or way for the purpose of having their
railroad *pass over or under* the same," a railroad corporation may raise a turnpike road for the purpose of constructing the railroad across it *upon the same
level. Newburyport Turnpike Co.* v. *The Eastern Railroad Co.*............... 294

A railroad Corporation, in Massachusetts, was authorized by a statute passed on
the 17th of March, 1841, (St. 1841, c. 108,) to extend its road across H. street,
which was the section of the Middlesex Turnpike: The same statute subjected
the corporation to all the duties, liabilities, and provisions contained in the Rev.
Sts. c. 39, and other statutes relating to railroad corporations, and also required
that said extended railroad should cross H. street under the bridge: By a statute passed on the 13th of March, 1841, (St. 1841, c. 78,) the Middlesex Turnpike Corporation was dissolved, and the surrender of its charter accepted,
to take effect on and after the 1st of June, 1841: In September, 1842, the
county commissioners laid out and established H. street as a public highway, and ordered the towns of C. and S., in which that part thereof over
which the railroad had been extended was situate, to erect a bridge over the
track of the railroad across H. street. *Held,* that the railroad corporation was
bound by St. 1841, c. 108, and Rev. Sts. c. 39, to erect and maintain said
bridge, and that the towns of C. and S. were entitled to a writ of mandamus requiring the corporation so to do. *Inhabitants of Cambridge* v. *The Charlestown Branch Railroad Co.*... 377

In order to authorize a railroad corporation under the provisions of the Rev. St. (of
Massachusetts) c. 39, §§ 67, 68, to raise or lower any way, it is not necessary that
a previous agreement therefor should be made with the selectmen of the town, in
which such way is situated, or that there should be a previous determination of
the county commissioners, as to whether any and what alteration should be
made. The railroad corporation are first to give notice to the selectmen of
their intention to raise or lower the way in question: the selectmen are then
within thirty days to notify the corporation of the alterations, if any, which they
require; if the selectmen and the corporation shall not agree what alterations are
necessary, application may be made by either to the county commissioners, to
determine the same; and if selectmen give no notice to the corporation as to
what alterations they require, the presumption is that they require none, but
leave the whole matter to the corporation. *Parker* v. *The Boston and Maine Railroad.*.. 547

INCOME.
How gross income is distinguished from net income.......................... 362

INJUNCTION.
Granted to restrain company from illegal acts................................ 67

Upon a bill in equity, praying for an injunction and for relief, an Act of the Legis-

INJUNCTION (*Continued*).

lature ought not to be adjudged unconstitutional, on a mere preliminary hear. ing for the injunction, and before an examination into the general merits of the bill. Thus, upon such a bill, calling for an immediate injunction against a rail. road corporation, to stay their operations, under their charter, upon the plaintiff's land, upon the allegation that the powers, granted by the charter, were in viola. tion of the constitution, it was *held*, that, until the general merits of the bill should be examined, the injunction must be denied. *Deering* v. *The York and Cumberland Railroad Co* 152

INSURANCE.

See FIRES.

INTEREST.

If, on an appeal to the Supreme Court of Massachusetts from an adjudication of the Court of Common Pleas, either accepting or setting aside the verdict of a sheriff's jury, the verdict of the jury is established, interest is to be computed on and added to the amount of the damages awarded by the jury, from the time when the verdict was returned into the Court of Common Pleas, to the time of its affirmation by this court. *Commonwealth* v. *The Boston and Maine Railroad.* 482

JURY.

A party claiming damages of a railway company for land damages is entitled to have his right to damages tried by a jury.. 282

The provision in the charter of the Vermont Central Railroad Company, which authorizes a person, whose land has been taken for the use of the company, and who feels aggrieved by the appraisal of the damages by the commissioners appointed in pursuance of the charter, to appeal to the county court, and which provides that the decision of the county court shall be final in the matter, does not entitle the person thus appealing to have his damages assessed in the county court by a jury. The term "Court" may be construed to mean the *judges* of the court, or to include the *judges and jury*, according to the connection and the object of its use. Resort must be had for the purpose of determining the form of trial, where there is no express legislative provision, other than the use of the general term, to the nature of the question submitted to the court, and the mode, heretofore in use, of determining similar questions. *Gold* v. *The Vermont Central Railroad Co* 220

In cases analogous to those where land has been taken by a railroad corporation, pursuant to the provisions of their charter, it has never been the practice in this state; where the matter has been pending in the county court, to assess the damages by a jury, — but by commissioners, or perhaps by the judges of the court. *Ibid.* 220

The statute of November 2, 1846, which provides, that, when it becomes necessary to assess damages, *and no other provisions are made by law* for such assessment, the same shall be assessed by a jury upon the request of either party, does not entitle a person, whose land has been taken by the Vermont Central Railroad Company, and who has appealed from the appraisal of his damages by the commissioners appointed under the charter, to have his damages assessed by a jury in the county court; — since the general terms used in the charter of the company must be construed to have provided that the damages in such cases, should be assessed in the mode usual in this State in analogous cases, which is by the appointment of commissioners by the county court, or perhaps by the judges of the court, — but never by a jury. *Ibid* 220

How to be summoned.. 426

From what towns to be summoned.. 426

JURY (*Continued*).

Petitions for, in Massachusetts.. 436

When it should be filed.......................................,.................. 439

The warrant issued by county commissioners on the application of an owner of land, for a jury to assess damages for land taken for a railroad, need not be in any particular form; but it should set forth, with sufficient certainty, the subject-matter into which the jury are to inquire, to wit, the land over which the railroad passes, — the petitioner's title to, or interest in it, — the location of the road, — and the incidental damages, if any, which the petitioner sustained, in addition to the value of the land taken; and this may be done either by reciting the substance of the petition in the warrant, or by annexing a copy of the petition thereto, and referring to the same in the warrant. *Walker* v. *The Boston and Maine Railroad*... 462

The same persons being summoned as jurors, to assess the damages severally sustained by two railroad corporations, for the taking of their lands lying contiguous to each other, by a third railroad corporation, for the road of the latter, it was held to be no objection to the competency of one of the jurors to sit as such in the cause first tried, that he was a stockholder in the other corporation petitioning, whose cause was to be tried immediately afterwards. *Commonwealth* v. *The Boston and Maine Railroad*... 482

If some of the jurors, summoned on a sheriff's jury, to assess damages for land taken for a railroad, are drawn from the town in which the land lies, this is an objection to those jurors only, and not to the others, and must be taken at the time the jury is impanelled; in which case the sheriff may set aside the jurors so disqualified, and fill their places with others; but if the respondent proceed to trial, without taking the exception, it will be considered as waived, and cannot afterwards be taken on appeal to this court. *Walker* v. *The Boston and Maine Railroad*........\.. 462

In executing the warrant for a sheriff's jury, it seems that the officer is not restricted by the Rev. Sts. c. 24, § 18, to summoning only twelve persons to constitute the jury, but that he is thereby directed to summon a jury to consist of twelve men; for which purpose, and in order to insure the attendance of twelve, it is not irregular to summon fourteen. *The Fitchburg Railroad Co.* v. *The Boston and Maine Railroad*.............................. .,............................... 508

JURISDICTION.

In adjudicating upon the verdict of a sheriff's jury the power of the Court of Common Pleas is not defined, but they are authorized to set the verdict aside for good cause; which may be either some irregularity or error apparent in the proceedings, as in the impanelling of the jury, or other conduct of the sheriff, or in his instructions and directions to the jury; or some fact affecting the purity, honesty, or impartiality of the verdict, such as tampering with jurors, or other misconduct of a party, or any irregularity or misconduct of the jurors, which fact may be brought to the knowledge of the court by evidence *aliunde;* but whether the Court of Common Pleas can set aside a verdict, on the ground that the warrant issued improvidently, or without legal authority, or that the verdict is without or against evidence, or against the weight of evidence, has not been decided, and the court give no opinion. *Walker* v. *The Boston and Maine Railroad*........·... 462

If the Court of Common Pleas are called upon to set aside the verdict of a sheriff's jury, on the ground that the respondent had not due notice of the application to the commissioners for the jury, the objection cannot be substantiated by showing that such notice does not appear by the warrant, the return, or the record of the commissioners; for it may, notwithstanding, be proved by evidence *aliunde*, that the respondent was summoned, or consented to take notice without summons, or, in fact, appeared before the commissioners. *Ibid*..................... 462

INDEX. 643

JURISDICTION (*Continued*).

The decisions of the Court of Common Pleas, upon questions of fact arising on the acceptance or rejection of the verdict of a sheriff's jury, are final, and cannot be reëxamined in this court on appeal; but the decisions of that court, upon questions of law arising on facts admitted or proved, may be revised in this court on appeal, provided the ground of the decision appear on the record, either as a part of the formal proceedings, or by a bill of exceptions, or otherwise. *Ibid*.. 462

The power of the Court of Common Pleas, in adjudicating upon the acceptance or rejection of the verdict of a sheriff's jury, is much more extensive than the power of this court, on an appeal from their adjudication; that court may set aside the verdict for any good cause; this court can only examine their judgment, to see if there is any error therein apparent on the record. *Ibid*........ 462

LICENSE TO CONSTRUCT ROAD.
Implied rights under... 399

LOCATION OF ROAD.

Where a corporation was empowered by the legislature, in general terms, to locate and construct a railroad between certain *termini*, and between these *termini* lay an extensive tract of land already appropriated, under the authority of the legislature, to a distinct public use, namely, for mill ponds, by another corporation, and this tract might be crossed by the railroad, with some diminution, indeed, of the mill power, and which might be compensated in damages, but without essential injury, it was considered that there was nothing in the nature of such public use, and in the extent to which it would be impaired or diminished, from which the power of constructing the railroad over it might be presumed to have been restrained by the legislature. And it was *held*, that if the water in the basins above mentioned was once a part of the Charles River it ceased to be so after it was effectually separated by the dam and rendered unfit for the general purposes of navigation; and consequently, that a prohibition to the railroad corporation to build a bridge over the water of Charles River, connected with Boston, or to place any obstruction therein, was not intended to apply to the basins, but only to the waters of Charles River below the dam and open to navigation, and was designed mainly to protect this navigation. *Boston Water Power Co. v. The Boston and Worcester Railroad Co*... 298

Under a charter authorizing the construction of a railroad " to the place of shipping lumber," on a tide-water river, the right of location is not limited to the upland or to the shore, but the road may be extended across the flats and over tide-water, to a point, at which lumber may conveniently be shipped. *Peavey v. The Calais Railroad Co*... 147

Where a railroad corporation, under a general grant of power, lay out and construct their road over and along a public highway, the town, within which such highway is situated, may proceed in equity against the corporation in this court, under its general jurisdiction in matters of nuisance, in order to ascertain whether such laying out and construction is or is not within the power granted to the corporation; and it is immaterial, in this respect, whether the way in question be a highway, properly so called, or a town way. *Inhabitants of Springfield v. The Connecticut River Railroad Co*..................................... 572

An act of the legislature, which authorizes the construction of a railroad between certain *termini*, without prescribing its precise course and direction, does not *primâ facie* confer power to lay out the road on and along an existing public highway; but it is competent to the legislature to grant such authority, either by express words, or by necessary implication; and such implication may result either from the language of the act, or from its being shown, by an application of the act to the subject-matter, that the railroad cannot, by reasonable intendment, be laid in any other line. *Ibid*.................................... 572

LOCATION OF ROAD (*Continued*).
Although the charter of the Vermont Central Railroad Company does not in
terms empower the corporation to locate their road along the valley of White
River, yet it must be taken, in the absence of evidence to show that there was
any other practicable route to the proper point on the Connecticut River, designated in the charter, or that the route adopted was unsuitable, that the road was
properly located in the valley of White River. *White River Turnpike Co.* v. *The
Vermont Central Railroad Co...*   233

Under the tenth section of the statute incorporating the Vermont Central Railroad
Company, that corporation have power to enter upon and cross a turnpike road,
as well as any other highway, making compensation to the turnpike corporation
for the injury they should sustain ,. *Ibid.......................................*   233

See EXPIRATION OF POWERS.

MANDAMUS.
In the case of land taken for a railroad, if the county commissioners refuse to
assess damages, on the ground that the party applying for them does not own
the land, he is entitled to have their judgment reversed by a jury ; and a mandamus will lie on his behalf to compel them to grant a warrant for a jury. *Carpenter* v. *Commissioners of Bristol..*   280 ,

MASTER AND SERVANT
Liability of a master for the negligence of a servant...........................   284

Where a master uses due diligence in the selection of competent and trusty servants, and furnishes them with suitable means to perform the service in which
he employs them, he is not answerable to one of them, for an injury received by
him in consequence of the carelessness of another, while both are engaged in the
same service. *Farwell* v. *The Boston and Worcester Railroad Co..............*   339

, Rule the same though the servants are employed in different departments of duty.   347

A master is not liable to a servant for an injury which the latter receives from the
negligence of a fellow servant. *Hayes* v. *The Western Railroad Co...........*   564

Cases affirming this principle..   567

Law of Ohio and Scotland..   569

MATERIALS.
Right to take materials beyond the limits of the road...........................   245

NEGLIGENCE.
Liability of a company for an injury through negligence to a passenger does not
arise from contract, but from a social duty........................   126, 129

The proprietors of a railroad, as passenger-carriers, are bound to the most exact
care and diligence, not only in the management of their trains and cars, but
also in the structure and care of their track, and in all the subsidiary arrangements necessary to the safety of passengers. *McElroy* v. *The Nashua and
Lowell Railroad Co...*   591

A railroad company are responsible for an injury sustained by a passenger in
their cars, in consequence of the careless management of a switch, by which
another railroad connects with and enters upon their road, although the switch
is provided by the proprietors of the other road, and attended by one of their
servants, at their expense. *Ibid...*   591

Where a suit was brought against a railroad company, by a person who was injured by a collision, it was correct in the court to instruct the jury, that, if the
plaintiff was lawfully on the road, at the time of the collision, and the collision
and consequent injury to him were caused by the gross negligence of one of the

NEGLIGENCE (*Continued*).

servants of the defendants, then and there employed on the road, he was entitled to recover, notwithstanding the circumstances, that the plaintiff was a stockholder in the company, riding by invitation of the President, paying no fare, and not in the usual passenger cars. And also that the fact that the engineer having the control of the colliding locomotive, was forbidden to run on that track at the time, and had acted in disobedience of such orders, was no defence to the action. *Philadelphia and Reading Railroad Co.* v. *Derby*..................... 109

A master is liable for the tortious acts of his servant, when done in the course of his employment, although they may be done in disobedience of the master's orders. *Ibid*... 109

The proprietors of railroads, when running their engines over crossings, are bound to exert reasonable care and diligence, to prevent injury therefrom to travellers on the road crossed; and whether such care and diligence have been employed in a particular case, is a question of fact, to be decided by the jury, upon all the circumstances. A compliance with the provisions of the Rev. Sts. (of Massachusetts) c. 39, §§ 78, 79, respecting the putting up of notices at railroad crossings, and the ringing of a bell when engines are passing over the same, will not exempt the proprietors of a railroad from their obligation to use reasonable care and diligence, in other respects, when running their engines over crossings, if the circumstances of the case render the use of other precautions reasonable. *Bradley* v. *The Boston and Maine Railroad*............................... 457

A railroad corporation was authorized to construct its railroad across a highway, and in the progress of the work it became necessary from time to time to remove certain barriers, which were placed by the corporation across the highway for the protection of travellers, but were adopted by the town in which the highway was situated, and in consequence of the neglect of the workmen to replace the barriers, at night, a traveller, in 1832, sustained an injury, and subsequently, under St. 1786, c. 81, recovered double damages against the town. It was held, that the railroad corporation was bound to cause the barriers to be replaced at night, although its charter contained no express provision on this point; as otherwise an accident might have happened before the town had notice, actual or constructive, and no one would have been liable for the damages. *Held, also*, that the corporation was responsible for the negligence of such workmen, although they were employed by an individual, who had contracted to construct this portion of the railroad, for a stipulated sum, the work being done by the direction of the corporation. *Held*, also, that an action might be sustained against the corporation by the town for indemnity, the parties not being *in pari delicto*; but, that the town was only entitled to recover the single damages, as, beyond that extent, it had suffered from its own *constructive* negligence; and that the corporation was not liable for the costs and expenses of the action brought against the town by such traveller, it not appearing that such action was defended at the request of the corporation, or for its benefit. *Lowell* v. *The Boston and Lowell Railroad Co.* 284

The want of suitable vehicles to articles is negligence in a carrier.............. 171

Ground upon which a master is liable for the acts of his servant............... 344

The proprietors of a railroad are not responsible to a brakeman in their employment, for an injury sustained by him in consequence of the neglect or fault of another brakeman engaged in the same service, even though the latter be at the same time the acting conductor of a train of freight cars. *Hayes* v. *The Western Railroad Co*... 564

If a brakeman, employed on a train of cars by the proprietors of a railroad, sustains an injury in consequence of the carelessness of another brakeman employed in the same service, and the injury would not have happened if the latter had performed his duty, it is immaterial, as respects the liability of the proprietors of the road, whether the train was short of hands or not. *Ibid*........ 564

A railroad company employed A, who was careful and trusty in his general cha-

NEGLIGENCE (*Continued*).

racter, to tend the switches on their road ; and after he had been long in their service, they employed B to run the passenger train of cars on the road ; B knowing the employment and character of A. *Held*, that the company were not answerable to B for an injury received by him, while running the cars, in consequence of the carelessness of A in the management of the switches. *Farwell* v. *The Boston and Worcester Railroad Co* 399

And though the servants were employed at a distance from each other and in different departments of duty, no liability falls on the master 347

A company is not liable to a widow or father for the loss of the service of a husband or child, in consequence of the death of the husband of a child, occasioned by the carelessness or fault of the agents or servants of the company. *Carey* v. *The Berkshire Railroad Co* 442

Principles of the English statutes and decisions where death results 446

Company not liable where cattle are straying upon a highway 213

Or where it was the duty of the owner to maintain fences 213

A railroad company is not bound to maintain fences on the lines of their road, except when the same passes through inclosed or improved land. *Perkins* v. *The Eastern Railroad Co* 144

If an injury to another's cattle happen, (through want of such fences,) upon common and uninclosed land, it is not legally imputable to the negligence of the company. *Ibid* 144

Cattle are not to be presumed as lawfully going at large. There must be proof that the town gave permission. *Ibid* 144

The plaintiffs' mare escaped from their pasture into an adjoining highway, which was crossed by a railroad, in land not owned by the plaintiffs, and went thence upon the track at a place where it crossed the highway and where there was no cattle-guard or fence, and was killed by the engine: *Held*, that the corporation was not liable. *Towns* v. *The Cheshire Railroad Co* 210

The owner of cattle, which stray upon a railroad track by reason of the insufficiency of a fence, which the railroad company are under obligation to maintain, and who brings an action upon the case against the company for killing the cattle by means of a locomotive engine, is entitled to have the degree of care, which the company are bound to exercise, defined in a more strict manner, than by instructing the jury that the company are bound to the exercise of such care, as a man of ordinary prudence would use, who was the owner of both the railroad and the cattle; but if such instructions are given to the jury, the defendants cannot complain. *Quimby* v. *The Vermont Central Railroad Co* 251

What is the test of reasonable care 459

Compliance with statute regulations not sufficient to exempt a party from further care 461

Meaning of " gross negligence " 177–182

A company is liable for negligence in doing acts which are authorized by its charter 339

NOTICE.

Effect of upon the liability of common-carriers 171

Of intended sale of shares for non-payment of assessments 425

When an application is made to the county commissioners, for an assessment by a jury of damages for land taken for a railroad, the party, against whom the application is made, is entitled to notice thereof from the county commissioners ; but in order that the objection of a want of notice may be taken advantage of on an appeal, it must appear on the record, that the party had not due notice of the

NOTICE (*Continued*).

pendency of the petition, before the warrant issued; and it is not sufficient, that no averment appears on the record, that notice was given; there being no occasion, in the proceedings before the commissioners, that the giving of the notice should so appear.. *Walker* v. *The Boston and Maine Railroad* 462

In proceedings where the Commonwealth is a party or interested, and no other special mode of summons is provided by law, notice to the governor, as the chief executive officer, would, it seems, be considered as sufficient. *Commonwealth* v. *The Boston and Maine Railroad* 482

PASSENGERS.

May recover for injuries although riding gratuitously 109

PENALTY.

Right of a State to release a penalty imposed upon a company for non-performance of the provisions of its charter 17

PLACE OF BUSINESS.

Action may be maintained in 140

Is the residence of a company 142

Service of process may be made at 142

Foreign corporation must give security for costs though it may have place of business within the jurisdiction of the court 142

Brings a company within the jurisdiction of a court 144

PLEADING.

A statement in an answer explanatory of and showing the reason for another statement in the answer is not impertinent. *Tucker* v. *The Cheshire Railroad Co* 196

A bill prayed for an injunction against a railroad corporation, upon the ground that a certain railroad bridge which the respondents intended to build across the Connecticut River would injure the orator's bridge, which had been erected under a charter from the Legislature. The answer stated that the orator and his wife owned certain land adjacent to the bridge and held it and the franchise of the bridge by the same title. It was then stated that the assessment of damages to them was for injuries sustained by them as owners of the bridge and franchise, and also as owners of the land. *Held*, that the statement of the ownership of the land was not impertinent, because it explained the reason of the assessment. *Ibid.* 196

The court will not strike matter out of an answer as impertinent unless its irrelevancy be clearly shown. If the matter excepted to, be such as may require examination in some future stage of the case it will not be stricken out, but the benefit of the exception will be reserved to the orator upon the final hearing of the cause. *Ibid.* 196

A bill prayed that the respondents might be enjoined from erecting a railroad bridge across the Connecticut River upon the ground that it would injure the orator's bridge by infringing the vested rights conferred by his charter. The answer stated that railway communications were not discovered and brought into use until long after the date of the orator's charter. *Held* that this statement was not impertinent, because in order to determine the rights of the parties it might become necessary to inquire whether the orator's bridge were intended and calculated to answer the purposes of a railway bridge, and whether the latter were so different from the former that it could not be considered as violating the exclusive privileges conferred by the orator's charter. *Ibid* 196

The respondents are bound to deny or admit all the facts stated in the bill, with all their material circumstances, without special interrogatories for that purpose. *Ibid.* 196

PLEADING (*Continued*).

In order to sustain a demurrer for want of jurisdiction, pleaded to the whole of a bill in equity, it must appear that no substantial and essential part of the complaint is within the equity jurisdiction of the court. *Boston Water Power Co.* v. *The Boston and Worcester Railroad Co*... 267

To a bill in equity, in which it was alleged that the plaintiff was the owner of a water power, and that he had leased a part of it, and that the defendant had by a nuisance diminished the water power, the defendant demurred because the lessee was not made a party plaintiff; but as it did not appear on the face of the bill, that the interest of the lessee would be affected by the diminution of the water power, there being a surplus beyond the quantity leased, the demurrer was not sustained. *Ibid*... 267

POWER TO TAKE LAND.
See EXPIRATION OF POWERS.

PRACTICE.

On the hearing before a jury summoned to re-assess damages for taking land for a railroad, the party claiming damages has the right to open and close. *Connecticut River Railroad Co.* v. *Clapp*... 450

If a party, aggrieved by the adjudication of the Court of Common Pleas, upon the acceptance or rejection of the verdict of a sheriff's jury, desire to bring his case before this court, upon questions of law, which do not appear in the warrant, the verdict, the sheriff's return, (including his instructions and directions to the jury,) or in the judgment of the court, this can only be done by a bill of exceptions; unless the court specify in their adjudication, as they may do, the grounds on which they accept or set aside the verdict; in which case, as well as in the former, the ground of the judgment becomes apparent on the record. *Walker* v. *The Boston and Maine Railroad*... 462

The provision of the Rev. Sts. (of Massachusetts) c. 39, § 57, that a party dissatisfied with the estimate of damages made by county commissioners, for land taken for a railroad, may apply to the commissioners for a jury to assess the damages, either at the same meeting at which the estimate is completed and returned, or at the next regular meeting thereafter, limits the time within which the application must be made, but not the time within which it must be acted upon. *Ibid*... 462

On a trial before a sheriff's jury, summoned and impanelled to assess damages for land taken for a railroad, the sheriff cannot be called upon to instruct the jury, as to the weight, effect, or sufficiency of the evidence. *Commonwealth* v. *The Boston and Maine Railroad*... 482

The judgment of this court, confirming the proceedings of a sheriff's jury, on an appeal from the adjudication of the Court of Common Pleas, either accepting or setting aside the verdict, when the amount of the damages has been liquidated by computing and adding interest, and the costs have been taxed, is to be enforced by a certificate to the county commissioners, directing them to issue a warrant of distress for the amount so ascertained. *Ibid*... 482

County commissioners having awarded damages for land taken for a railroad, and the respondents having had their estimate revised by a jury, who also awarded damages, and the verdict of the jury having been accepted by the Court of Common Pleas, it was held, on appeal to this court, that it was open to the respondents to insist that no damages could be legally assessed against them. *Ibid*. 482

The authority of the Court of Common Pleas, to set aside the verdict of a sheriff's jury, for good cause, is only to be exercised for some cause affecting the legality, justice, or merits of the case. *Fitchburg Railroad Co.* v. *The Boston and Maine Railroad*... 508

PRACTICE (*Continued*).

If an adjudication of the Court of Common Pleas, setting aside the verdict of a sheriff's jury, is founded upon any cause contained in the warrant, return, or verdict, such cause is matter of law apparent upon the record, and will come before this court on appeal; if the adjudication is founded on a cause shown *aliunde*, — under which designation, the record of the anterior proceedings before the commissioners is to be included, if such record is adduced for the purpose of showing any fact affecting the merits of the case, — such cause is matter of fact, upon which the decision of the Court of Common Pleas is conclusive; and if either party objects in this court to any decision or adjudication of the Court of Common Pleas, in matter of law, the ground of such objection must be specially stated in the decision or adjudication itself, or in a bill of exceptions filed and allowed in that court. *Ibid.* 508

If the proceedings of county commissioners, in estimating damages for land taken for a railroad, are irregular, the remedy is to be sought by an application to this court for a *certiorari*, and not by an application to the commissioners for a jury to revise the damages. If the latter course be taken, it is an admission that the previous proceedings are regular, and u waiver of exceptions thereto. *Ibid.* 508

When application is made to county commissioners, for the assessment of damages for land, &c., taken for a railroad, and it is brought to the knowledge of the commissioners, before a warrant is issued for a jury, that there are other parties interested who have made no application, and such parties are thereupon summoned in, their damages are first to be assessed by the commissioners, before the case is sent to a jury. *Ibid.* 508

Where the estimate made by county commissioners of the damages sustained by a tenant for years in consequence of the location and construction of a railroad over his estate is revised by a jury, on the petition of such tenant, and the verdict of the jury is set aside by the Court of Common Pleas, and the case remanded to the county commissioners; it seems, that it is competent to the commissioners on the motion of the petitioner, to dismiss the petition for a jury, and to bring forward the original petition, and to summon in the reversioner to become a party thereto, and thereupon to proceed to estimate the whole damages, and to apportion the same between the parties interested. If such proceeding be objectionable, it can only be excepted to by the lessee, and not by the proprietors of the railroad. *Ibid.* 508

The line of the harbor of Boston, as established by the act of 1840, c. 35, at a particular part thereof on the Charlestown side, was fixed at a point described as fifteen feet distant from the south corner of Gould's Wharf, and three hundred and twelve feet distant from a sea-wall from which Gould's Wharf projected; and the south corner of Gould's Wharf was found by measurement to be three hundred and two feet distant from the sea-wall; it was held, on a trial before a sheriff's jury, that the sheriff was not bound to instruct them, either that there was such an ambiguity in respect to that part of the line, that it could not be determined upon the evidence, where the line was, or that the true line was ten and not fifteen feet from the south corner of Gould's Wharf; but that the question was one of fact, to be left to the jury upon the evidence. *Ibid.* 508

Where an application is made and pending before county commissioners, for an estimation and adjudication of the petitioner's damages, occasioned by the construction of a railroad, it is competent for the respondents, if there are other persons interested who have not joined in the application, to cause such persons to be summoned and made parties, before a warrant for a jury is issued; and if the respondents neglect to do so, they cannot object before the jury, or afterwards, that such persons were not previously made parties. *Davidson v. The Boston and Maine Railroad*. 534

PRACTICE (*Continued*).

Where the damages occasioned by the construction of a railroad, are estimated by county commissioners, and both parties are dissatisfied with the estimate and apply to the commissioners for a warrant for a jury to revise the damages, it is only necessary that one warrant should be issued; but if separate warrants are issued on both petitions, the sheriff should execute and return them as one. *Ibid* 534

Where the petitioners before a sheriff's jury, impanelled for the purpose of estimating the damages occasioned by the construction of a railroad, rested their claim therefor on the ground, that a creek crossed by the railroad was a part of a tide mill pond belonging to the petitioners, and introduced in evidence the deed under which they held the premises, together with a plan and survey thereof, the correctness of which was testified to by the surveyor by whom they were made, it was held, that whether the creek in question was a part of the mill pond or not, was a question of fact for the jury, depending upon the description contained in the deed, and the bounds and monuments found upon the ground, answering to such description, and to which the description applied. *Ibid.* 534

A sheriff's jury are not bound to find and return by their verdict, as an abstract proposition, what right, title, or interest, a party before them has in land, which he claims in virtue of a deed in evidence ; nor are they bound to find a special verdict, upon the whole or any particular part of the case before them, though they may do so, if they think proper. *Ibid* 534

The owner in fee of a tide mill and mill pond having leased the same for years, and the proprietors of a railroad having constructed their road over a portion of the pond, the owner and lessee joined in a proceeding for the recovery of damages therefor, and introduced the lease of the premises in evidence; it was held, that the respondents were entitled, with a view to the assessment of damages, to have the jury instructed by the sheriff, a matters of law, whether the lease conveyed an interest in the soil covered with tide water, or only a right to use the water for a special purpose, as an easement, in connection with the other estate demised. *Ibid.* 534

A sheriff's jury, in making up their verdict, may, if they think proper, consider each item or charge of damage separately, and state in their verdict what items they allow, and the amounts thereof, severally, and what they reject ; and where the verdict is returned in this form, any item of damage, which, in point of law, is objectionable, may be remitted or deducted, without setting aside the verdict. *The Fitchburg Railroad Co. v. The Boston and Maine Railroad.* 508

The Fitchburg Railroad Company having claimed damages of the Boston and Maine Railroad, for land and wharves and certain flats, (over which they were authorized to extend their wharves,) taken by the latter for their road ; and the sheriff's jury, by whom the damages were estimated, having returned a verdict assessing the greater part thereof " for the land over which the said company had a right to build a pier wharf," between the sea-wall and the line of the harbor, " and for the injury to other land on which the said F. R. Co. had a right to build a pier wharf," and it was objected, that the verdict was erroneous, in giving the damages only for land over which the petitioners had a right to build a pier wharf: It was held, that though there might be some inaccuracy in the terms of the verdict, there was nothing to warrant the conclusion, that it did not include land owned by the petitioners and taken by the respondents. *Ibid.* 508

PUBLIC COMPANIES.
Railway companies so treated 170

PUBLIC WORKS.
Railroads to be deemed public works. 352
A railway is a public highway. 295

REGULATIONS OF ROAD.

A railroad corporation has authority to make and carry into execution reasonable regulations for the conduct of all persons using the railroad or resorting to its depots, without prescribing such regulations by by-laws; and the superintendent of a railroad depot, appointed by the corporation, has the same authority, by delegation. *Commonwealth* v. *Power*....................................... 389

By the rules of a railroad company, the purchasers of tickets for a passage on the road, from one place to another, were required to go through in the same train; and passengers who were to stop on the road, and afterwards finish their passage in another train, were required to pay more than when they were to go through in the same train: A, not knowing these rules, purchased a ticket for a passage from D to B, and entered the cars with an intention to stop at E, an intermediate place, and to go to B in the next train: When he took his ticket, he was informed of the rule that required him to go through in the same train, and a check was given him, on which were the words " good for this trip only:" The conductor of the cars then offered to give back to A the money which he had paid, deducting the amount of his passage from D to E, which A refused to accept, but demanded the ticket in exchange for the check: He stopped at E, went on to B on the same day, in the next train, and offered his check, which was refused, and he was obliged to pay the price charged for a passage from E to B, and afterwards brought an action against the company for breach of contract, and for money had and received. *Held*, that the action could not be maintained. *Cheney* v. *The Boston and Maine Railroad*......................... 601

REMEDY.

For injuries done under the authority of a statute must be confined to the mode provided by statute... 164 – 166

RESIDENCE.

Of a company, at its place of business..................................... 142

SINKING FUND.

By St. 1838, (of Massachusetts) c. 9, § 3, the annual payment which the Western Railroad Corporation is required to make, from its income, to the sinking fund, is to be made from its net income; that is, from the amount of money remaining to the corporation, on making up its annual account, after deducting from all its receipts the necessary expense of repairs and management, and also the amount of interest on the debt of the Commonwealth, which the corporation are bound to pay in behalf of the Commonwealth: And if such net income, in any year, is not sufficient for such payment, the corporation cannot be required to make up the deficiency from the income of succeeding years. *Western Railroad Co.*.. 360

SPECIFIC PERFORMANCE.

It is a good defence to a bill in equity, praying for a specific performance of an agreement to convey land, that the defendant was led into a mistake, without any gross laches of his own, by an uncertainty or obscurity in the descriptive part of the agreement, so that the agreement applied to a different subject from that which he understood at the time; or that the bargain was hard, unequal, or oppressive, and would operate in a manner different from that which was in the contemplation of the parties when it was executed: But in such case the burden of proof is on the defendant to show such mistake on his part, or some misrepresentation on the part of the plaintiff. *The Western Railroad Co.* v. *Babcock*...... 365

Where a party agrees, for a certain consideration, to permit a railroad corporation to construct a road over his land, on any one of two or more routes, at their option, and to convey the land to the corporation, for certain sums, according to the route that shall be taken, after the road shall be definitely located, he can-

SPECIFIC PERFORMANCE (*Continued*).

not defend against a bill for specific performance of his agreement, by showing that he was induced to believe, either by his own notions or by the representations of third persons as to the preference of one route over another, that the corporation would select a route different from that which they finally adopted; nor by showing that the corporation or its agents made representations as to the probability that one route would be adopted in preference to another, or as to the relative advantages of each route. *Ibid.* 365

Where a party agrees under seal to permit a railroad corporation to construct a road over his land, and also agrees to convey his land to the corporation for a certain sum, after the road shall be definitively located, with a condition in the deed of conveyance that the deed shall be void when the road shall cease or be discontinued; specific performance of such agreement may be decreed, after the road is constructed over the land, although the corporation did not expressly bind itself to take or to pay for the land : And where, in such case, the corporation takes the land, constructs a road over it, and is, for three or four years, in actual possession and use of all the privileges which the performance of the party's agreement would give, and then files a bill against him for specific performance of his agreement, the bill will not be dismissed on the ground of unreasonable delay in filing it. *Ibid.* 365

If the terms of a contract are doubtful, a court of equity will not decree a specific performance. *Boston and Maine Railroad v. Babcock* 561

STOCK.

The State of Maryland, in 1836, passed a law directing a subscription of $3,000,-000 to be made to the capital stock of the Baltimore and Ohio Railroad Company, with the following proviso, " That if the said company shall not locate the said road in the manner provided for in this act, then, and in that case, they shall forfeit $1,000,000 to the State of Maryland for the use of Washington County. In March, 1841, the State passed another act repealing so much of the prior act as made it the duty of the company to construct the road by the route therein prescribed, remitting and releasing the penalty, and directing the discontinuance of any suit brought to recover the same. The proviso was a measure of State policy, which it had a right to change, if the policy was afterwards discovered to be erroneous, and neither the commissioners, nor the county, nor any one of its citizens acquired any separate or private interest under it, which could be maintained in a court of justice. It was a penalty, inflicted upon the company as a punishment for disobeying the law; and the assent of the company to it, as a supplemental charter, is not sufficient to deprive it of the character of a penalty. The provision in this case being a penalty imposed by law, the legislature had a right to remit it. *Maryland v. The Baltimore and Ohio Railroad Co.*   1

Act of company fixing number of shares..................................... 424

Subscription for by a State.. 1

STOCKHOLDER.

May recover damages for negligence of company............................ 109

SUBSCRIPTION FOR STOCK.

By section four of the statute incorporating the Vermont Central Railroad Company, certain persons named are constituted commissioners for receiving subscriptions to the capital stock of the company; and it was enacted as follows, — " And every person at the time of subscribing, shall pay to the commissioners five dollars on each share for which he may subscribe, and each subscriber shall be a member of said company; " and it was further enacted, that when one thousand shares should be subscribed, the commissioners might issue a notice for the stockholders to meet and elect directors. The defendant, after some

SUBSCRIPTION FOR STOCK (*Continued*).

other shares, but less than one thousand, had been subscribed for, subscribed for fifty shares, and, instead of paying to the commissioners, in money, five dollars upon each share at the time of subscribing, he gave them his promissory note for that amount, being two hundred and fifty dollars, which was made payable to "The Commissioners of the Vermont Central Railroad Company," on demand, for value received. This note was received from the commissioners by the corporation, upon its organization. And it was held, that the note was given upon sufficient consideration, and that it was a valid note in the hands of the corporation. And also, that an action might be sustained upon the note in the name of the corporation. *Vermont Central Railroad Co.* v. *Clayes* 226

And it was also held, that the provision in the charter, that each subscriber should be a member of the company, and the fact that others had subscribed for stock previous to the defendant's subscription, were sufficient to show, that the corporation was *in esse* at the time of making the note, and so capable of taking the promise, through their agents, the commissioners, notwithstanding their right to organize was made to depend upon certain conditions, which were not fully complied with until after the note was executed. *Ibid.* 226

An act incorporating a railroad company provided that the capital stock should not exceed two thousand shares; that no assessments should be laid on the shares, to a greater amount, in the whole, than one hundred dollars; that the number of shares should be determined from time to time, by the directors; and that as soon as two hundred and fifty shares should be subscribed, the company should proceed to construct and open the road : C subscribed for five shares, and the directors, after more than two hundred and fifty shares were subscribed, voted to close the subscription books of the capital stock, and passed no other vote fixing the number of shares : C paid six assessments on his shares, but neglected to pay the seventh, and the treasurer of the company, pursuant to the Rev. Sts. c. 39, § 53, sold said shares at auction, for a sum insufficient to pay said assessment, and the company thereupon brought an action against C to recover the deficiency. *Held*, that the vote of the directors to close the subscription books for shares, on a given day, was in effect a vote fixing the number of shares at the number then subscribed for, as ascertained by said books, and lawfully fixed the number for the time being: that C's shares were legally liable to assessment; and that he was answerable for the deficiency sued for. *Lexington and West Cambridge Railroad Co.* v. *Chandler* 422

A by-law of a railroad corporation provided, that in case of a sale of shares for non-payment of assessments, the treasurer should give notice to the delinquent owner, when his residence was known, of the times and place of sale, by letter seasonably put into the mail. *Held*, that this by-law was directory to the treasurer, and not a condition precedent; and that a written notice of the time and place of sale, signed by the treasurer, and delivered to the owner of the shares, or left at his dwelling-house, and received by him as soon as he was entitled to receive it by mail, was sufficient. *Ibid.* 422

SUPERINTENDENTS, AUTHORITY OF.

A superintendent of a railroad depot has authority to exclude therefrom persons who persist in violating the reasonable regulations prescribed for their conduct, and thereby annoy passengers or interrupt the officers and servants of the corporation in the discharge of their duties. *Commonwealth* v. *Power* 389

Where the entrance of innkeepers, or their servants, into a railroad depot, to solicit passengers to go to their inns, is an annoyance to passengers, or a hinderance and interruption to the railroad officers in the performance of their duties, the superintendent of the depot may make a regulation to prevent persons from going into the depot for such purpose; and if they, after notice of such regulation, attempt to violate it, and, after notice to leave the depot, refuse so to do,

654 INDEX.

SUPERINTENDENTS, AUTHORITY OF, (*Continued*).

he and his assistants may forcibly remove them; using no more force than is necessary for that purpose. *Ibid.* 389

The superintendent of a railroad depot has not a right to order a person to leave the depot and not come there any more, and to remove him therefrom by force, if he does come, merely because such person, in the judgment of the superintendent, and without proof of the fact, had violated the regulations established by the railroad corporation, or had conducted himself offensively towards the superintendent. *Hall* v. *Power* 410

TAKING LAND.

The State of Maryland granted a charter to a railroad company, in which provision was made for the condemnation of land to the following effect; namely, that a jury should be summoned to assess the damages, which award should be confirmed by the County Court, unless cause to the contrary was shown. The charter further provided, that the payment, or tender of payment, of such valuation should entitle the company to the estate as fully as if it had been conveyed. In 1836, there was an inquisition by a jury, condemning certain lands, which was ratified and confirmed by the County Court. In 1841, the legislature passed an act directing the County Court to set aside the inquisition and order a new one. On the 18th of April, 1844, the railroad company tendered the amount of the damages, with interest, to the owner of the land, which offer was refused; and on the 26th of April, 1844, the owner applied to the County Court to set aside the inquisition, and order a new one, which the court directed to be done. The law of 1841 was not a law impairing the obligation of a contract. It neither changed the contract between the company and the State, nor did it divest the company of a vested title to the land. The charter provided, that, upon tendering the damages to the owner, the title to the land should become vested in the company. There having been no such tender when the act of 1841 was passed, five years after the inquisition, that act only left the parties in the situation where the charter placed them, and no title was divested out of the company, because they had acquired none. *Baltimore and Susquehanna Railroad Co.* v. *Nesbit* 39

The Vermont Central Railroad Company, have power, under section sixteen of their charter, when necessary for the construction of their road, to take stone from land contiguous to the line of their survey, and to use land for the purpose of cutting and hewing stone thereon. *Vermont Central Railroad Co.* v. *Baxter* . . 240

The power of the corporation to take the land and other materials adjoining the line of the road, for the purpose of constructing their road, is conferred upon them by their charter, and is as necessary to exist in and be exercised by all the contractors on the road as by the corporation. This power, to be exercised within reasonable limits and in a proper manner, is necessarily delegated from the corporation to the contractor, and for this purpose the contractor is the agent of the corporation, and the corporation is liable to the land-owner, for the damages occasioned by the exercise of this power on the part of the contractor. And the liability of the corporation to the land-owner, in such case, is not affected by any stipulation in the agreement between the corporation and the contractor. *Ibid.* 240

The period of three years "from the time of taking" land for a railroad, within which, by Rev. Sts. c. 39, § 58, application must be made to county commissioners to estimate the damages for such taking, is to be computed from the filing of the location of the road, as required by § 75 of the same chapter. *Charlestown Branch Railroad Co.* v. *County Commissioners of Middlesex* 383

A railroad corporation, after locating its road over a wharf, more than sixty feet, and filing the location with the county commissioners, agreed with the owners of the wharf to extend the road sixty feet on and over the same before a certain

TAKING LAND (*Continued*).

day, and the owners, in consideration thereof, agreed not to demand any damages for such extension: The road was made according to the location that was filed previously to such agreement. *Held*, that this was not an agreement of the corporation not to extend their road more than sixty feet over the wharf, and that the owners of the wharf were not thereby entitled to apply, after three years from the filing of the location, for an estimate of the damages caused by an extension of the road more than sixty feet over the wharf. *Ibid*............... 383

When land vest in railway company.................................... 43

When a company becomes bound to take land........................... 47

Relation of the company to the land-owner in England................. 47

Specific performance of agreement.................................... 47

Railway company may purchase lands.................................. 353

Relation of the company to the land-owner........................... 168

TAXATION.

The Philadelphia, Wilmington, and Baltimore Railroad Company was formed by the union of several railroad companies, which had been previously chartered by Maryland, Delaware, and Pennsylvania, two of which were the Baltimore and Port Deposit Railroad Company, whose road extended from Baltimore to the Susquehanna, lying altogether on the west side of the river, and the Delaware and Maryland Railroad Company, whose road extended from the Delaware line to the Susquehanna, and lying on the east side of the river. The charter of the Baltimore and Port Deposit Railroad Company contained no exemption from taxation. · The charter of the Delaware and Maryland Railroad Company made the shares of stock therein personal estate, and exempted them from any tax, "except upon that portion of the permanent and fixed works which might be in the State of Maryland. *Held*, that under the Maryland Law of 1841, imposing a tax for State purposes upon the real and personal property in the State, that part of the road of the plaintiff which belonged originally to the Baltimore and Port Deposit Railroad Company, was liable to be assessed in the hands of the company with which it became consolidated, just as it would have been in the hands of the original company. Also, that there is no reason why the property of a corporation should be presumed to be exempted from its share of necessary public burdens, there being no express exemption. This court holds, as it has on several other occasions held, that the taxing power of the State should never be presumed to be relinquished, unless the intention is declared in clear and unambiguous terms. *Philadelphia and Wilmington Railroad Co.* v. *States of Maryland*... 21

Statutes imposing taxes... 31

The act incorporating the Bangor and Piscataquis Railroad Company, among other things, authorized them to "procure, purchase, and hold in fee simple, improve and use for all purposes of business, to be transacted on or by means of said railroad, lands, or other real estate, and to manage and dispose thereof, as they may see fit;" and provided, "that the capital stock of said company may consist of three hundred thousand dollars, and shall be divided into shares of one hundred dollars each *to be holden and considered as personal estate.*" *It was held*, that the real estate owned and used by the company, either as a railroad or as a depot, was not subject to taxation, otherwise than as personal estate, unless the legislature should specifically prescribe differently. *Bangor and Piscataquis Railroad Co.* v. *Harris*.. 131

The Western Railroad Corporation are not liable to be taxed for the land, not exceeding five rods in width, over which they were authorized to lay out their road, nor for buildings and structures thereon erected by them, if such buildings and structures are reasonably incident to the support of the road or to its proper

TAXATION (*Continued*).

and convenient use for the carriage of passengers and property — such as houses for the reception of passengers, engine houses, car houses, and depots for the convenient reception, preservation, and delivery of merchandise carried on the road. *Inhabitants of Worcester.* v. *The Western Railroad Co*................... 350

Exemption of public works from in Pennsylvania................................. 354

Taxation of such property in other States................................. 355

Principle on which railways are rated in England............................ 355

TRESPASS.

When the legislature has authorized an act, the necessary and natural consequence of which is injury to the property of another, and at the same time has prescribed the mode of compensation, he who does the act cannot be liable as a wrongdoer. *Aldrich* v. *Cheshire Railroad Co*... 206

A company cannot be held liable as a trespasser for acts authorized by its charter 337

Parties acting under the authority of a statute cannot be trespassers............ 167

If an innkeeper who has frequently entered a railroad depot, and annoyed passengers by soliciting them to go to his inn, receives notice from the superintendent of the depot that he must do so no more, and he nevertheless repeatedly enters the depot for the same purpose, and afterwards obtains a ticket for a passage in the cars, with the *bonâ fide* intention of entering the cars as a passenger, and goes into the depot on his way to the cars, and the superintendent, believing that he had entered the depot to solicit passengers, orders him to go out, and he does not exhibit his ticket, nor give notice of his real intention, but presses forward towards the cars, and the superintendant and his assistants' thereupon forcibly remove him from the depot, using no more force than is necessary for that purpose, such removal is justifiable, and not an indictable assault and battery. *Commonwealth* v. *Power*... 369

Company not liable as a trespasser for the trespass of an agent................. 397

See SUPERINTENDENTS, Authority of,

VERDICT.

Where a jury, summoned to reassess damages for land taken for a railroad, rendered a verdict, in which they assessed the damages at a certain sum, "with interest thereon from the time when the said railroad company took possession of the land," it was held, that the verdict was void for uncertainty, and that the Court of Common Pleas had no authority to alter the same, or to supply any defect therein. *Connecticut River Railroad Co.* v. *Clapp*..................... 450

WARRANT.

See JURY.